HUDSON TAYLOR
&
CHINA'S OPEN CENTURY

Book Six: Assault on the Nine

By the same author:

Hudson Taylor and China's Open Century
Book 1: Barbarians at the Gates
Book 2: Over the Treaty Wall
Book 3: If I had a Thousand Lives
Book 4: Survivors' Pact
Book 5: Refiner's Fire

HUDSON TAYLOR

&

CHINA'S OPEN CENTURY

BOOK SIX
Assault on the Nine

A J Broomhall

Hodder & Stoughton
and
THE OVERSEAS MISSIONARY FELLOWSHIP

British Library Cataloguing in Publication Data

Broomhall, A J
Hudson Taylor & China's open century.
Bk. 6: Assault on the nine
1. China. Christian missions. Taylor,
Hudson – Biographies
I. Title
266'.0092'4

ISBN 0 340 42629 2

 Printed in Great Britain for Hodder & Stoughton Limited, Mill Road, Dunton Green, Sevenoaks, Kent by Cox & Wyman Limited, Reading, Berks. Photoset by Rowland Phototypesetting Limited, Bury St Edmunds, Suffolk. Hodder & Stoughton Editorial Office: 47 Bedford Square, London WC1B 3DP.

FOREWORD TO THE SERIES

China appears to be re-opening its doors to the Western world. The future of Christianity in that vast country is known only to God. It is, however, important that we in the West should be alert to the present situation, and be enabled to see it in the perspective of the long history of missionary enterprise there. It is one of the merits of these six remarkable volumes that they provide us with just such a perspective.

These books are much more than just the story of the life and work of Hudson Taylor told in great detail. If they were that alone, they would be a worthwhile enterprise, for, as the *Preface* reminds us, he has been called by no less a Church historian than Professor K S Latourette 'one of the greatest missionaries of all time'. He was a man of total devotion to Christ and to the missionary cause, a man of ecumenical spirit, a man of originality in initiating new attitudes to mission, a doctor, a translator, an evangelist, an heroic figure of the Church.

The historian – whether his interests be primarily military, missionary, or social – will find much to interest him here. The heinous opium traffic which led to two wars with China is described. The relationship of 'the man in the field' to the society which sent him is set before us in all its complexity and (often) painfulness. And the story of Biblical translation and dissemination will be full of interest to those experts who work under the banner of the United Bible Societies and to that great fellowship of men and women who support them across the length and breadth of the world.

Dr Broomhall is to be congratulated on writing a major work which, while being of interest *primarily* to students of mission, deserves a far wider readership. We owe our thanks to Messrs Hodder and Stoughton for their boldness in printing so large a series of volumes in days when all publishers have financial problems. I believe that author and publisher will be rewarded, for we have here a fascinating galaxy of men and women who faced the challenge of the evangelisation of China with daring and devotion, and none more so than the central figure of that galaxy, Hudson Taylor himself. The secret of his perseverance, of his achievement, and of his significance in missionary history is to be found in some words which he wrote to his favourite sister, Amelia:

'If I had a thousand pounds, China should have it. If I had a thousand lives, China should have them. No! not *China*, but *Christ*. Can we do too much for Him?'

Sissinghurst, Kent — Donald Coggan

PREFACE

(See also the General Preface in Book One)

Anticipating the research to be done for this book, the Postscript of the previous book, *Refiner's Fire*, predicted a sweeping narrative of the final years of the saga. Far from it; what emerged from the archives has merited, in my judgment, retention of much that was to have been passed over. And Messrs Hodder and Stoughton have shown their usual magnanimity. The series is to end with a seventh volume. A digest of the seven must be someone else's work!

The preceding volumes have followed Hudson Taylor's development and early aims in going to China, his formative experiences and setbacks. They showed him as the reluctant founder of an organisation for which he planned no great expansion in size but only in achievement. Its few members, some of whom were of outstanding quality, a bare two dozen Westerners each with a Chinese colleague, were to invade the forbidden interior of China, carrying the gospel of Christ to the remotest provinces and to Manchuria, Mongolia and Tibet. But by 1874 his disappointment with so many of his early recruits, the repeated breakdown of his own health, and the testing of his own resolve and courage to extremes of endurance, brought him and his circle of intimate friends close to the end of hope.

Half-paralysed by an accident, and with his supporters' interest in the Mission and in China at its lowest ebb, Hudson Taylor could not escape the oppressing thought that *nine vast provinces with one hundred and fifty millions* of inhabitants had still to be reached with the gospel.[1] At the rate of progress being made by Protestant missions this could not be done in the lifetime of his generation. The coastal provinces of Zhili, Shandong and Jiangsu, Zhejiang, Fujian and Guangdong (map p 33), and three more through which the Yangzi River flowed – Anhui, Jiangxi and Hubei – had a nucleus of missionaries in them, mostly at the treaty ports. Beyond them the nine 'interior' provinces could only be reached with difficulty and danger from natural obstacles and hostile men: Henan, Shanxi, Shaanxi and Gansu in the north; Hunan and Guangxi south of the Yangzi; and Sichuan, Guizhou and Yunnan in the far west. Unlikely ever to return to China himself, he appealed from his bed for eighteen more men, two for each of the nine provinces, once again to leap 'over the treaty wall', defying the danger and resistance from the imperial Chinese government. No assault on mountain peaks has required more dedication or courage.

They began to come. And slowly his strength returned. Then, on February 21, 1875, as the new venture was beginning, Augustus Margary, a British consular interpreter, was murdered on the Burma border. Court intrigues and the dowager empress Ci Xi's seizure of power foiled attempts by the British minister at Peking, Thomas F Wade, to see justice done. Nothing could be less timely than for 'The Eighteen' to attempt to travel, let alone to live in deepest China.

At this point we take up the story. How in these circumstances, with more war clouds over China, could Hudson Taylor's goal be reached? That it was reached is common knowledge. How it was done takes us immediately into what may be judged the most historic eight or ten years of Hudson Taylor's life, and of the China Inland Mission. To Chauncey Goodrich, pioneer of the American Board, Hudson Taylor's success and influence on other missions lay in the magnitude of his vision. In retrospect Goodrich said, 'He extended this Mission till it has become a veritable octopus, stretching out its arms to the most remote borders of China . . .'[2]

Assault on the Nine builds on what is contained in Books 1 to 5. Descriptions of life and travelling conditions in China, of customs and beliefs, of dynastic rule and the place of mandarins and the literati in the life of the nation, and much else are again 'taken as read'. We stand back from the detail to see the ever widening picture, and find that even what looked like dry administrative routine is rich with human drama as the frontiers recede. Beginning in the spring of 1875 we find Hudson Taylor, aged forty-three, still dogged by ill-health but confident in his leadership of the young men and women who have caught his own spirit.

As before, my intention is to record events and statements rather than to 'write them up', showing the perspective of secular history and the relevance of contemporary personalities in government, Church and other missions. As the CIM expanded from scores to hundreds, the burden of administration increased, but what little I have included has been for the light it throws on the leading figures in the history. A confusing web of names and places may lose its complexity by reference to the Chronology and Tables

(Appendices 4, 5). Assessment and discussion are again reserved for the final volume.

One problem has defied solution after time-consuming research. The nineteenth-century convention of speaking and writing of people as Mr X or Miss Y without using their initials or 'given' name, was extended to Chinese colleagues. Tracing the achievements of these historic people is made doubly difficult because of surnames being restricted to the 'Old Hundred Names' and spelt with dialect variations. Chinese names, hard for the average reader to pronounce and remember, were simplified for home consumption, so that I have not succeeded in identifying the Chinese pioneers on whose companionship the Westerners' success depended. Historians of the Chinese Church are faced with a daunting problem which I regretfully do little to resolve. We wait expectantly for this gap in the literature of Christianity in China to be filled.

AJB

Note. Parentheses within quotations are used as follows: round brackets ( ) indicate original source material, including abbreviations and substitute Romanisation of Chinese words; square brackets [ ] indicate my own added comment or parentheses other than from original sources.

ACKNOWLEDGMENTS

The completion of this book has been delayed by factors beyond my control, but the patience and encouragement of readers waiting for it have already put me in their debt. Warm thanks also to David Wavre, Religious Books director of Hodder and Stoughton, for his understanding, and to all who have been inconvenienced by my reclusive existence for so long.

The chief sources have as before been fragile manuscripts and old books, too many to name. Of modern books John Pollock's *Moody without Sankey* and *The Cambridge Seven*, and Ralph Covell's *W.A.P. Martin* have helped me frequently. But Eugene Stock's expansive *History of the Church Missionary Society* (published 1899–1916), rippling with vitality and fact on many themes, continues to inspire.

Relatives of the 'Cambridge Seven' have kindly allowed some 'revelations'. I am particularly grateful to Sir Christopher Beauchamp, Bt, for facts about Sir Montagu's 'fortune'. To those of others about whom I have included less complimentary information in the interests of a full statement, I offer my apologies – my own family among them. When the earlier biographies were written, many contemporaries were still alive and only one-sided accounts were considered appropriate.

Once again, my deepest gratitude to Molly Robertson for more hundreds of pages of meticulous typing, to Val Connolly for all her artwork, and to my faithful advisers for reading it all in the rough and making perspicacious comments.

AJB

KEY TO ABBREVIATIONS

ABMU	= American Baptist Missionary Union
American Board (ABCFM)	= American Board of Commissioners for Foreign Missions
APM	= American Presbyterian Mission
Bible Societies	= American Bible Society, British and Foreign Bible Society (B&FBS), National Bible Society of Scotland (NBSS)
BMS	= Baptist Missionary Society
CIM	= China Inland Mission
CMS	= Church Missionary Society
HTCOC	= Hudson Taylor and China's Open Century
JHT	= James Hudson Taylor
LMS	= London Missionary Society
MMA	= Medical Missionary Association
MRCS	= Member of the Royal College of Surgeons
OMFA	= Overseas Missionary Fellowship Archives
P&O	= Peninsular and Oriental Steam Navigation Company
P&P	= Principles and Practice of the CIM
RGS	= Royal Geographical Society
RTS	= Religious Tract Society
SPCK	= Society for Promoting Christian Knowledge
SPG	= Society for the Propagation of the Gospel in Foreign Parts
SVM	= Student Volunteer Movement
SVMU	= Student Volunteer Missionary Union
The Mission	= China Inland Mission
WMMS	= Wesleyan Methodist Missionary Society
YMCA	= Young Men's Christian Association

GLOSSARY OF CHINESE TERMS

bianzi	= hair queue ('pigtail')
daotai	= Intendant of Circuit over 2 or 3 prefectures
fengshui	= 'wind and water', harmony of nature governing decisions
fu, zhou	= prefectures and cities
kang	= heated brick platform-bed
ketou	= ninefold bow and prostrations
laoban	= 'old plank', foreman, boss, boat captain
li	= Chinese mile, nominally one third of standard mile
likin	= Chinese tax on goods in transit
manzi	= barbarians, wild men
Nianfei	= rebels in north China
sanban	= 'three planks', skiff with oars or scull
Taiping	= rebellion in south China, 1850–64
Tong Wen Guan	= College of Arts and Languages
xian	= county town, district magistrate
yamen	= official residence of any mandarin
zanba (tsanpa)	= oatmeal or barley porridge
zhentai	= military governor
Zongli Yamen	= Chinese Ministry of Foreign Affairs

BOOK SIX: ASSAULT ON THE NINE

CONTENTS

MAPS AND DIAGRAMS

ILLUSTRATIONS

PART 1

OCTOPUS MISSION

1875–79

PROLOGUE

NO TIME TO 'TEMPT FATE'?

'The Margary affair' *February–November 1875*

The emperor was dead. An opium-smoker and good-for-nothing, Tong Zhi's passing was no great loss to the empire. But the manner of his dying mattered immeasurably. By her immediate actions his mother the Dowager Empress Ci Xi came under strong suspicion. On coming of age he had assumed power, ending her regency. With the help of Viceroy Li Hongzhang, and her staunch friend the imperial bannerman Yong Lu, a coup d'état had made her regent again, this time of her puppet, the infant Guang Xü emperor. When Tong Zhi's child widow Alude and unborn babe, the awaited true heir, also died mysteriously – by poisoning it was believed[1] – little doubt remained that Ci Xi was responsible. Such unscrupulous, cold-blooded scheming boded ill for court and nation.

When Augustus Margary, the young consular interpreter on Colonel Browne's expedition, and five of his Chinese companions were killed at Manyün (Manwyne) no one suggested that it had been at the instigation of the Peking Court.[2] On February 21 he left Manyün with some Chinese who had offered to show him the hot springs. They knocked him off his pony and speared him to death. His passport to take that route, to leave and re-enter China by the Burma border, had been issued in the summer of 1874 by the Zongli Yamen, the Peking Foreign Office (Book 5, p 431). Responsibility for the murder could never be firmly laid at the door of Zen Yüying, the acting-viceroy of Yunnan, nor of the mandarins of Manyün where he died. But the heads of the murdered men were exposed on the city ramparts like criminals, a tell-tale fact. Nor could Shan or Kachin tribesmen be confidently blamed for the attack, nor King Mindon of Upper Burma who resented and resisted British penetration through his territory, three hundred miles up the Irrawaddy River beyond his capital at Mandalay. Whether or not the blame could be laid where it belonged, Britain must be seen to obtain satisfaction or such acts would be repeated. T F Wade, the minister in Peking, heard on March 11 through the India Office that Margary had been killed on February 21, and at once formulated terms for reparation. He notified London that he had demanded a commission of enquiry, authority for a second expedition to replace the one attacked so treacherously, and 150,000 *taels* of silver to be deposited with him, Wade, pending conclusion of the matter. He did not add in his cable to London that at the same time he had revived old grievances regarding access to the emperor and tariff concessions and demanded that 'all claims arising out of the action of the (Yunnan) officials' were to be satisfied at once.[3]

The Zongli Yamen (Chinese Ministry for Foreign Affairs) accepted in principle Wade's first three demands, demurring only on secondary matters: but when by imperial decree Zen Yüying, as acting-viceroy, ultimately responsible for law and order in his province of Yunnan, was ordered to make the investigation, Wade insisted on someone of higher rank being appointed, and on a British officer being present. Unfortunately Wade's irascible temperament was unsuited to the judicious handling of such affairs, and plunged him into what Alicia Bewicke Little (in *Li Hung-Chang, His Life and Times*) called 'a cat's cradle of negotiations'. He had to consult London, but the telegraphic cable still ended at Shanghai, so he decided to go there to use it. The day after Alude's death on March 28, however, he issued an ultimatum – satisfaction by the 29th or he would withdraw his legation from Peking. His preparations to travel looked like a threat. The American envoy reported to his Secretary of State that Wade, with a full staff of secretaries and attendants, called at the Zongli Yamen where a 'rather stormy and electric' meeting took place.[4] To Wade's embarrassment his demands were accepted. Li Hanzhang, brother of Li Hongzhang and viceroy of Hunan and Hubei, was commissioned to conduct the enquiry, supervised by the Hon T G Grosvenor, Secretary of the British Legation, and two consular officials, E Colborne Baber and A Davenport, of whom we shall hear more. Even so, Wade left Peking (now Beijing) with several secretaries and their families, exciting rumours among the populace of impending hostilities. He stayed in Shanghai from April till July, with brief visits to Hankou and Fuzhou.

Arriving at Wuhan on July 7, Grosvenor reported to Wade that Li Hanzhang denied any knowledge of the attack on Colonel Browne's expedition, and was keeping him waiting. Wade then returned to the north and, fearing (it was said) that Grosvenor and his companion might be held as hostages, at an interview with Li Hongzhang in Tianjin extended his demands upon China. In Grand Secretary Li (p 67) he was faced by one of China's greatest statesmen of all time, who could in no circumstances appear to be ready to meet the demands of the foreigner. Thwarted, Wade stormed out of Tianjin on September 9 'with the most bellicose intentions', reaching Peking on the 14th. But as Henri Cordier, the French observer, said, Wade's warlike tone had little effect on the Chinese.[5] Yet again he presented an ultimatum. If he had struck his flag, the British merchant and missionary communities in Peking and Tianjin would have been left without protection throughout the winter, when the frozen approaches prevented naval intervention. His second departure, on October 11, therefore left the rest of the diplomatic corps strongly discontented, but on November 5 the imperial mission of enquiry with its British observers set out from Wuhan to ascend the Yangzi gorges to Chongqing.[6] From there they continued up the Yangzi to Yibin (Suifu) at the confluence of the Min River and the upper Yangzi, where they struck out over the mountains via Zhaotong into Yunnan, not reaching Kunming, the provincial capital, until March 6, 1876. So far so good. In November (1875) Thomas Francis Wade became Knight Commander of the Order of the Bath, a dignity probably calculated to help him in his difficult task.

Jackson's folly — *May–October 1875*

Brash and impetuous as ever, it was no time for Josiah Jackson, in southern Zhejiang, to come into conflict with the mandarins of Lishui (Chüchou) over premises he had rented there, but this he did. Throughout China rumours had spread and grown as news of Margary's death, of Wade being flouted, and of a new threat of war reached the people. A spate of anti-foreign, anti-Christian agitation in the Yangzi valley held the Catholics responsible for another wave of assaults on children, and for the surreptitious cutting off of people's *bianzi* (queues), the work of demons under the priests' control, with strong overtones recalling the Taiping rebellion. Hangzhou, Shaoxing and Ningbo, A E Moule reported, were disturbed by the same 'mysterious disappearance' of *bianzi*, 'snipped off by unseen shears'. But when the imperial edict ordering investigation into the murder of Margary set the tone, the provincial magistrates issued strong proclamations to rebuke and quiet the people.

After Jackson's rudeness to the magistrate, Consul Forrest sent a representative to restore peace and good relations at Lishui, and to find other accommodation for him. Wade referred the matter to London, and Lord Derby, Foreign Minister, replied understandingly,[7]

> Her Majesty's Government are fully sensible of the benefits which have been derived from the labours of the Missionaries of the Taylor Mission, and of the self-devotion and courage with which those labours have been pursued. At the same time, they cannot doubt that in this instance and on other occasions the Missionaries have shown an amount of indiscretion which must have created much ill will . . . I have accordingly to instruct you to inform the Taylor Mission that unless (Mr Jackson) and other members of the Mission exercise greater judgement for the future, Her Majesty's Government will find themselves reluctantly compelled to withdraw their passports.

For Jackson to play into Wade's hands at such a time of tension was lamentable. As soon as Hudson Taylor in London was informed, he dictated this memorandum to every member of the Mission:

> I understand (Lord Derby's letter) may mean not only the presumed offender's passport, but those of all members of the Mission. I cannot but think that His Lordship's judgement is based upon an incomplete acquaintance with the facts; but . . . I wish at once to impress upon you all most earnestly –
>
> First, the absolute necessity of desisting from making any representation, private, semi-official, or official, of any difficulties in the work to H M Consul or consular offices.
>
> Second, if possible to avoid personal (dealings) with Mandarins. (Communications with mandarins, if essential, must be in writing and worded very courteously, without demands or claims but as a favour. If refused), leave the matter entirely alone . . . Anything which may, fairly or unfairly, be termed indiscretion, may be taken as a reason for steps seriously embarrassing to the operations of the Mission, and which might place some, if they continue their work, in a position of antagonism to law and order.

Members must keep informed of the wider scene and behave appropriately. The danger of a national conflagration was never far away.

The Church in China[8] *1870–75*

A glance at the state of missions in general and the still struggling Chinese Church may help to show how the debilitated 'Taylor Mission' stood in the contemporary scene.

Roman Catholic societies were moving reinforcements into China in increasing strength and numbers, sisters as well as priests and male orders. In 1870 about 250 priests had been deployed throughout the empire. The Jesuits, concentrating on Jiangsu, Anhui and Zhili, had lost no time in following the victorious forces into territories taken from the Taipings. Immigrants from Hubei occupying land in Anhui left desolate after the Taiping slaughter included Catholic Christians who welcomed priests to live among them. Between then and 1878 a hundred new missionaries swelled the ranks of that society alone. Converts and adherents in Jiangsu and Anhui were reported in 1874–75 to number about eighty-nine thousand.

In contrast, for many years the provinces of Hunan, Hubei, Shaanxi, Shanxi and Shandong had been the sphere of the Franciscans, whose reception was very different. (See HTCOC Book 5 Appendix 3.) Baron von Richtofen, visiting hostile Hunan, received the impression that the most the missionaries could do, against bitter opposition, was pastoral care of descendants of 'old Christians' of the historic Church. While destruction of property continued, time-honoured tenacity kept the Christians together. In Jiangxi the Lazarists had about twelve thousand adherents in 1875 and ten years later the same number in Zhejiang. The far west was still the field of the Paris Mission (Société des Missions Étrangères de Paris) with extensive work in Sichuan, Guizhou and Yunnan supervised by five bishops and one hundred and fifty-seven priests in 1872, Chinese and foreign in roughly equal numbers. In Guiyang, the provincial capital, they had two cathedrals and nineteen European priests, as well as several minor establishments with their own clergy. Recovering from near-annihilation at the time of the Muslim rebellion, there were eight thousand Catholics in Yunnan. In Sichuan the adherents were ten times as numerous, and there were missions high in the Tibetan marches, even at Batang. In all of China the number of Catholics had risen from approximately 400,000 in 1870 to 500,000 by 1886, with 2,500 churches and chapels, 30 seminaries, 470 foreign priests and 280 Chinese priests.

By comparison the Protestant achievement looked puny.[9] Of the total of 436 missionaries in 1874, 210 were women in or near the treaty ports. By 1888 there were 489 men, 320 wives, 231 single women and 32,260 Chinese communicants, but the great majority were still in the coastal provinces. Protestant statistics were always confused by inconsistent reporting. Some societies included and others excluded missionary wives as working members. More significantly, the practice of recording baptisms and communicant members of the Churches but not all adherents, as the Catholics did, made true comparison impossible. Two (unnamed) veteran missionaries were still at work after thirty-eight years; twelve had survived twenty-eight years; and ten who arrived in 1854 (including Hudson Taylor, John Nevius and Griffith John) were still active after twenty-one years. In addition there were one hundred in Japan and twenty-five, all American, in Siam, as Thailand was still called. Having served since 1835, the American Baptist William Dean, DD, of Bangkok, was doyen of the missionary community in 'China' – everywhere east of Burma.[10]

Of the 'humble and despised' China Inland Mission (CIM), on January 1, 1875, twenty-one were in China and three on their way there, but as many as twelve were on leave in Britain after five or ten gruelling years in action. Even the editor of the *Chinese Recorder*, who should have been better informed, omitted the CIM from his statistical table and entered 'No report from CES' – the Chinese Evangelization Society which had ceased to exist in 1860. The largely unknown, 'eccentric' China Inland Mission had apparently lost its leader through ill-health and injury, had no adequate deputy leaders, and outside Zhejiang had been reduced by April to one recent arrival, F W Baller, the only one in the Yangzi region. Since February one single woman, Emmeline Turner, remained in China of all those who had so recently shocked staid treaty port society by going up-country in Chinese dress. The rest were out of sight and apparently out of mind. Sadly true was the fact that five of the *Lammermuir* party (named after the ship in which they sailed) had departed, four more and two of the children had died, and Jackson's days in the Mission were numbered.

Even the great Church Missionary Society had in 1872 reached its own 'low water mark' with a 'failing treasury' and 'scanty supply of men'. But by 1875 the tide had turned, candidates were multiplying, a decade of unprecedented advance had begun – in Africa and India, not China. Stirred by the death of David Livingstone on May 1, 1873, Church and State had responded. Together the *New York*

Herald and London *Daily Telegraph* sent H M Stanley on a second expedition into central Africa. His letter from Uganda in April 1875 led to the CMS Victoria Nyanza Mission, and by travelling down the Congo River in 1877 he opened the way for pioneering missions to enter in 1878 – led by the Livingstone Inland Mission, founded for the purpose by Grattan Guinness sending two of his Institute men, and followed by the Baptist Missionary Society (BMS).[11]

In China, Hudson Taylor's old friend John Shaw Burdon became Bishop of Victoria, Hong Kong, in March 1874, and in four years saw the Church in Fuzhou under J R Wolfe's supervision double its membership from eight hundred catechumens and communicants to more than sixteen hundred during a time of intense persecution. But few reinforcements came to strengthen the CMS in China, and expansion was restricted to adjacent areas. The same was true in general of other societies, some of which strongly discouraged their members from breaking out of the treaty ports as they longed to do. (See pp 91, 103, 212.)

Turn of the tide *1875*

In Britain a surprising transformation was taking place. From the lowest of low points in December, when Jennie Taylor had thought them 'unlikely to see China again' and Hudson Taylor with acute enteritis rewrote his will, when with the death of the intrepid Tsiu Kyuo-kwe the Chinese spearhead of advance into the interior had snapped off, and when the Mission appeared to be forgotten by all but an inner circle of faithful friends – a state of affairs described by Eugene Stock as 'pathetic in the extreme'[12] – the fortunes of the CIM changed dramatically.

The stricken man faced with the failure of his hopes was reading through the Bible systematically as usual. On November 29, 1874, he dated and marked Nahum 1.7, 'The LORD is good, a stronghold in the day of trouble; and He knoweth them that trust in Him.' In deep trouble himself, Hudson Taylor took courage. Then on December 6 he read Haggai, chapter 2, and heard God speaking to him. He marked (italics) verse after verse. Verse 4: 'Yet now be strong, O Zerubbabel, saith the LORD; and be strong, O Joshua . . . and be strong, all ye people . . . and work; for I am with you.' Verse 5: 'My spirit remaineth among you, fear ye not.' Verse 8: 'The silver is mine, and the gold is mine, saith the LORD of hosts.' Verse 15: 'And now, I *pray you, consider* from this day . . . from before a stone was laid . . . in the temple of the LORD.' Verse 18: 'Consider now . . . *From the day that the foundation of the* LORD'*s temple was laid*.' Verse 19: '. . . *from this day will I bless you*.' Verses 21–23: 'I will shake . . . I will overthrow . . . I will destroy the *strength* of the kingdoms of the heathen . . . for I have chosen thee.'

With prophetic insight he believed that the Holy Spirit was applying this passage to China and to himself. Did he see by faith the curbing of dynastic power and the promise of a harvest in China? 'Is the seed yet in the barn?' verse 19 asked. 'Yea, as yet the vine, and the fig tree, and the pomegranate, and the olive tree, hath not brought forth: *from this day I will bless you*' – with confident faith he underlined the words. Events proved him right. Five days later, on December 11, he marked Zechariah 2.8 with the date, 'He that toucheth you toucheth the apple of his eye.' Strength, 'gold', results and protection could be accepted as the Lord's provision if he forged ahead.

But not Hudson Taylor and the CIM alone. Standing back from the events in the foreground to get the perspective of a century on, it is clear that *this was the point at which the tide of all mission to China turned*. For by what now happened, the second of Hudson Taylor's aims, the invigoration of the Church in its duty to evangelise the world, began to be fulfilled. The story of Hudson Taylor's spiritual odyssey on the one hand, and of the Mission on the other, has often been told. But highlights such as the 'Cambridge Seven' have blinded us to this more significant event. Taking place in the shadows of personal weakness and public indifference, a movement began which quickly led to the gospel reaching the far corners of the Chinese empire. A demonstration of the fact of travel and residence in remote provinces being possible and safe threw open the gate for other missions. After a decade of proof to convince the Church, the headline event of seven 'sporting hearties' devoting their lives and wealth to the evangelisation of China gave impetus to the movement among the universities which sent thousands more into every continent and country. The dawn of 1875 brought in the age of Protestant missionary expansion, as significant as the advent of William Carey and Robert Morrison; it was the end of what had been, in Stephen Neill's words, 'a time of renewed awareness, and of small and tentative beginnings' in the eighteenth century.[13]

After private prayer for two full years, with only Frederick Baller, M Henry Taylor and A W Douthwaite to show for it, the publication of an 'Appeal for Prayer' for eighteen pioneers struck the strategic moment.[14] As a result of David Livingstone's death a tide was flowing in the Church again, so that 'by his death he effected more than he did by his life'. The theological colleges filled up and candidates of the main societies multiplied. D L Moody's first meetings and the 'holiness movement' associated with the presence in the country of another American, Pearsall Smith, and of Evan H Hopkins and others, led within a few months to Hudson Taylor receiving twenty applications for service in China.[15] Despite himself and to his surprise, the obscurity of the CIM was giving place to prominence. As when he launched the Mission in 1865 after painful years of testing and preparation, he found himself and the CIM the focus of growing popularity and influence.

THE NINE

Still working in bed but conscious of strength returning, getting up for one, then two, then three hours a day, he directed the attention of awakened Christians to 'the need and claims' of 'the nine provinces' of China still with no Protestant messengers of the gospel. With a variety of volunteer writers, John Stevenson, Henrietta Soltau or George King, a new arrival, sitting at his bedside at No 6 Pyrland Road, he achieved more than if he had been up and about.[16] A class of accepted candidates learned Chinese from him, and the advisory council for Mission affairs in Britain met frequently, also by his bedside. On January 25 they had been startled to be told that John Stevenson was about to sail to Burma in March, 'ere returning to Shaoxing' to pioneer the route into Yunnan which British arms had failed to open for commerce. 'China via Burmah' was a title in the last *Occasional Paper* to be published. Soon 'this mission to West China' was 'giving a wonderful impetus to interest in the whole Mission', and the announcement that Henry Soltau, honorary co-secretary of the CIM, was to leave his profession and go with him, fuelled the excitement (HTCOC Book 5, p 432).[17] After five months on his back, in April Hudson Taylor was on crutches going downstairs to work and up again at night, jubilant over the great developments in the making.

The quality of candidates acceptable to Hudson Taylor was made doubly clear. In the next few *years* only one stonemason, two carpenters and a housemaid measured up to his new criteria dictated by the sad events of the first ten years of the Mission. He now required an adequate basic education and standard of social behaviour, finding them among fewer artisans but more skilled craftsmen – a jeweller, an 'ornamental carver' and a dressmaker – more shop assistants, students, teachers, nurses and doctors, while he still referred others to the denominational societies and to his friend John Burdon in Hong Kong. By 1900 the one-time stonemason would be the most promising young director in the Mission.

'The Garibaldi spirit' of his reply to enquiries left no doubt that an easy life was the last thing they should expect (HTCOC Book 5, pp 434–5). 'Hard work, and little appreciation of it . . . to seal your testimony with your blood (and) . . . to take joyfully the spoiling of your goods' was for men and women 'who have this world under their feet', not those hoping 'to make the most of both worlds'. Nor was it rhetoric. Suffering and death were the price all too many had to pay. Not only that. With his council's approval he was requiring new missionaries to give two years to adaptation and language learning in China before marrying – in the spirit of Emily Blatchley who had heavily underlined part of Galatians 5.24 in her Bible, 'They that are Christ's have crucified the flesh *with the affections*'. Full-blooded dedication to their calling must be given, dedication like that of the priests of the Paris Mission whom he respected so highly, quoting T T Cooper's *Travels of a Pioneer of Commerce*.

> The young missionary, on entering China, strips himself of his nationality; he shaves his head, and adopts the Chinese costume, and conforms in all respects to the Chinese mode of life. His first two years are spent either at one of the principal mission stations, or at some outstation, in close attendance on an old and experienced Father, under whose care he systematically studies the language and manners of the people.[18]

The Brighton Convention *June 1875*

The 'holiness movement' was gaining momentum. Instead of only the Mildmay Conference, the summer of 1875 was to see three conferences for the strengthening of spiritual life, for all regardless of denomination who longed to live on a higher plane of obedience to the command of God, 'Be holy, for I the Lord your God am holy' (Leviticus 19.2). Christians aspiring to 'the higher Christian life' were flocking in hundreds and soon thousands, to hear Scripture expounded. Private conferences were being held at Broadlands (the future home of Lord Mount Temple and the Mountbattens), and later at Mildmay and Keswick.[19]

From May 31 to June 4, H W Webb-Peploe was to speak at a Brighton Convention on the theme '*As* ye have received Christ Jesus the Lord, *so* walk in Him', by faith. (The first Keswick Convention was to follow, June 28–July 2, after the Mildmay Conference of June 23–25, such was the spiritual hunger.) In April Lord Radstock had brought Pearsall Smith to meet Hudson Taylor. In the 'Keswick' community of old and young, he would be likely to find some responsive to the spiritual need of China and to the call of God. He decided to attend, using two sticks in place of crutches. It happened that the CIM 'year' was dated from the end of May, and his annual report was due. Hudson Taylor looked through his account books before going to Brighton, and found that since the formation of the Mission in 1865, donations totalling £52,000 had been received. Then he added up his May receipts to date. They came to only £68; 'nearly £235 less than our average expenditure in

China for three weeks'. At the daily half-hour of prayer for China in the Mission headquarters at No 6 Pyrland Road, he said to the household, 'Let us remind the Lord of it,' and prayed for that amount to be made up. In the evening the postman brought a letter containing a cheque for £235.7.9d to be entered anonymously as 'From the sale of plate' – to him another gesture of approval from God his Father of the course he was pursuing. Not surprisingly his address at the Convention was on 'Trusting God', that obvious but neglected right of all Christians. When later he wrote an article on the same theme, he ended it on the note, '"Trust in Him at all times", you will never have cause to regret it.' And after a few more weeks he coined the phrase 'Hold God's faithfulness' as an axiom or motto based on Mark 11.22, 'Have faith in God'.[20] To emphasise faith was to miss the point; simple trust in a faithful Father is everything. In this article he also used the words 'All God's giants have been weak men,' strength and self-confidence are all too often a handicap, whereas a sense of weakness and need will tap his limitless resources.

Returning from Brighton on June 4, Hudson Taylor found himself on the station platform with the Russian ex-Minister of Ways and Communications, Count Bobrinsky, who had been at the meetings. They should travel together, the count suggested. 'But I am travelling third class,' Hudson Taylor answered. 'My ticket admits of my doing the same,' the count replied. On the way he drew from his pocket-book a banknote for fifty pounds which he handed to Hudson Taylor as a donation. A foreigner's mistake, thought Hudson Taylor as he pointed it out (the equivalent of £1,599 or £2,000 today?). 'It was five pounds I meant to give, but God must have intended you to have fifty,' the count insisted.

Back at Pyrland Road, Hudson Taylor found the household had met together to pray about a remittance due to be sent to China. The funds in hand were forty-nine pounds eleven shillings short of what they ought if possible to send. He laid the count's banknote on the table before them.

Young men and women living in the climate of such happenings grew, as Jennie Faulding and Louise Desgraz had done, to rely on God whatever the circumstances, however far inland they might be. This was preferable to a fixed salary from 'the Mission' or any other source.

The tide was flowing; 'the Eighteen' were arriving; advance into 'the nine provinces' had begun; the means were coming in; and 'the Margary affair' was only one more hazard in the long adventure.

CHAPTER ONE

'NOT TO TRY BUT TO DO IT'
1875–77

Expand to consolidate! *Spring 1875*

On his feet again after months in bed, Hudson Taylor was surprising everyone by his energy and the fertility of his ideas. The 'forgotten' mission house in Pyrland Road was milling again with action. The young men and women who came and went recognised a leader in the semi-invalid who talked of such big things he wanted them to do. Some older ones had qualms. Over the years William Berger from time to time had found Hudson Taylor's pace breath-taking. He now cautioned that he should consolidate existing gains before advancing further.[1] It was the view commonly expressed by leaders of the great societies. So when he wrote to say it would be wise to call a meeting of the Mission's referees before becoming too deeply committed to occupying nine more provinces, and had expressed his opinion to some of the referees already, Hudson Taylor saw danger ahead. They were influential men who had agreed to commend the Mission when consulted by others, but were not an advisory council. Too easily progress could become bogged down in discussion with half-comprehending well-wishers who, once consulted, would need to be satisfied. In founding the Mission with Hudson Taylor in 1865, even William Berger had rejected the inclusion of a council who could repeat the blunders of the Chinese Evangelization Society (HTCOC Book 3, pp 237–8). The 'council of management' formed in 1872 to guide affairs in Britain when Mr Berger retired, was primarily to control the transmission of funds and the selection of reinforcements. They could gather round Hudson Taylor's bed informally. But in his state of health to have to defend his actions before an august body of referees, including titled gentlemen, was too much to face.

Instead, he wrote at length a respectful twelve-page document of policy and current practice involving a detailed report of progress to date, assuring them that consolidation of the gains already made was no less Mission policy than breaking new ground. 'The evangelization of China must be mainly effected by Christian (Chinese)', so constant teaching and training of them in the course of field work would be continued. The deliberate transfer of foreign missionaries from established churches would encourage congregations to conduct their own affairs. To demonstrate their progress, from time to time he published translations of sermons preached by men who had so recently been unenlightened pagans. Their grasp of truth and ability to expound it were apparent. Work built muscle, and learning in action was the best kind of school for Chinese and missionaries alike. Both were to advance together. The foreigners were to be the catalysts and examples, the scaffold, not the main frame of the Church. His aim was that they should be far outnumbered by Chinese working Christians. Some with families would have to be salaried or as colleagues have their expenses paid, but a greater and greater proportion would earn their own living or be supported by growing congregations. Mission statistics might well not include such men and women. But 'the conversion, instruction and qualifying of evangelists was a slow process'. Two guiding principles needed to be kept in mind. The older work needed time to develop, but to limit a mission to this was to run into soft sand. The sooner work began in every province the better, for great distances and marked dialect and cultural differences meant that each needed its unique methods.

Twenty-eight churches with more than a score of 'outstations' had already been formed under the leadership of seven ordained Chinese pastors, with thirty-three evangelists, twenty-seven colporteurs, six Scripture-readers or 'Bible-women' and two schoolmasters (cf Appendix 2). 'Upwards of fifty' places were occupied by resident Chinese and foreign church workers, and this consolidating work was itself expanding. The nine unevangelised provinces meanwhile cried out for attention. In the south and west were hill tribes for whom he 'yearned'. China was so vast; the task of reaching her myriads so appalling. 'We hope to do *more* and *not* less for the former work, *as well as* to attempt to carry the Gospel into the new regions.'

For supporters in general, Hudson Taylor published an article on the 'Plan of Operation of the CIM', taking its principles from the Acts of the Apostles.

> The early missionaries, appear to have scattered themselves. They visited important centres, usually in twos or threes; stayed there long enough to commence a work, and then trusted much to the keeping

> of God. (But) they had advantages . . . in the godly Jews and proselytes, already acquainted with the Old Testament scriptures . . . We may, therefore, anticipate the necessity of a somewhat prolonged residence in our districts, for the purpose of instructing in the word of God those who may be converted . . . Those who will be the Chinese workers of the future first need to be . . . given time to show what gifts they possess.[2]

His logic was convincing and satisfied his friends. Expansion and consolidation were to proceed hand in hand, the one nourishing the other.

There could be no thought of holding back. In fact the first pioneers of the unoccupied provinces were already in action. By then Henry Taylor had been travelling for two months in Henan with the LMS evangelist Zhang, becoming 'the first of the eighteen' to enter 'the first of the nine' provinces.[3] And Charles Judd had braved hostile Hunan province with his companions Yao Shangda and Zhang (Chang), only to be attacked and driven out. George King had reached China, hoping to pioneer the north-west. Others were either ready to go or in training – George Nicoll of Dundee, James Cameron, like the deceased George Duncan 'a six-foot Highlander', and George Clarke, an emigrant home from Canada.

'James Cameron was a tall, strong, manly yet gentle brother,' Grattan Guinness recorded, a shipwright building 'iron ships', 'who came to us in April 1874 from Jarrow on the Tyne. He was twenty-nine years of age, sensible, vigorous and trustworthy; slow but impressive and intensely earnest as a speaker, and blessed to many souls', a man with 'spiritual perception and a cultivated intelligence'. Cameron was to become known as the 'Livingstone of China'.

Back in 1866 when William Rudland was living with the incomplete *Lammermuir* party at Coborn Street, Bow, he had worked with Miss Annie Macpherson in her Shoreditch night-school for street arabs and factory hands. One day he had accosted a youth of fifteen in the street and urged him to attend the night school and Bible classes. The result was pandemonium. The spirited boy took every opportunity to disrupt the classes and incite the other boys, until given an ultimatum, his final chance to mend his ways. He submitted, and was helped to emigrate to Canada, where he worked on the transcontinental railways and as a lumberjack, earning enough to attend college in Canada and the USA during three deep winters. There a copy of *China: Its Spiritual Need and Claims* came into his hands and George Clarke returned to London, to Pyrland Road.[4] Hudson Taylor's advice to him when he sailed to China was, 'Travel, now the opportunity is given; even if you cannot say much, let the people see you; and sell what books you can . . . Do not tell me what you intend to do [lest his letters be intercepted], but tell me what you have done.' And, from long observation of thorny relationships between colleagues in China, 'I have made it a rule in my life that if a man cannot get on with me, I will do my best to get on with him.' These were not empty words: James Meadows could never forget his own journey home from China with Hudson Taylor in a French liner in 1871. Meadows had been put in a hot, stuffy cabin with a dozen strangers and found it and them intolerable. Hudson Taylor was in similar but better circumstances and had Meadows moved in with him, 'at the cost of much discomfort to himself for another five weeks on board. (I) felt inclined to be obstreperous . . . But he managed me so well, quieting and reconciling me to my surroundings, making me believe that he was even better off with my presence than without me.'[5]

Men of the best quality had enlisted. Large gifts had been donated by the dedicated Mrs Grace specifically for 'advance into *fresh* provinces' (Book 5, pp 394, 405). While prayer for the eighteen pioneers was being answered and funds provided, advance without delay must override all obstacles. A frank letter from another donor, Mrs Julia Rich of Sandringham House, Margate, revealed another hazard, the harm caused by falsehoods still in circulation.

> Dear Sir, . . . I hear from a friend who has been in China, that missionaries of your society are frequently reduced to such depths of poverty that they are induced to give up the work and take up with secular pursuits . . . and that even their children are sometimes so destitute that the heathen take pity on them . . .
>
> For this cause I have not continued my support of your Mission. Will you kindly . . . let me know if what I have stated is really the case.[6]

Hudson Taylor was grateful that she had written. It was easy for those who lived as Westerners in China to misjudge others who chose to live simply, close to the mass of Chinese. If they voiced their misgivings, as in the Lewis Nicol episode (Book 4, pp 264, 317), great damage could be done. There was no knowing how nany were alienated without saying why. So he replied, carefully xplaining the facts, here only summarised.

> Dear Madam, I am much obliged for your letter of inquiry . . . and shall be glad if you will kindly show your informant this letter, as he has been entirely misled. . . . I do not believe that any child or member of the family of anyone connected with our Mission has ever lacked food or raiment for a single hour, though in many cases the supply may not have come *before* it was needed.
>
> *No one* has been hindered in work by lack of funds; *no one* has ever suffered in health from this cause; *no one* has ever left the Mission on this ground, or has remained dissatisfied on this score, to my knowledge . . . One (who resigned) to support a widowed mother (and) one, a probationer, on being recalled to England . . . are the only members of the Mission who have engaged in any secular pursuits. . . . Seven persons have been removed by death. Four of them were consumptive when they went out, . . . three died of consumption . . . the other of smallpox. One died in China of child-birth, and the other two in England . . . To show you how we compare with others I will only refer to one Mission labouring in the same province as most of our missionaries. The aggregate strength of (that) Mission has been fifteen persons, of whom seven died and three resigned, and one returned . . .
>
> The effect of the trials of our faith [periods of stringency] on the Chinese we have found to be only beneficial . . . (they) have been stirred up themselves to give of their means to spread the Gospel instead of thinking the rich societies could do it all.[7]

Irs Rich renewed her support.

Two other incidents also encouraged Hudson Taylor to press on. 'irst, in May 1875 Edward Fishe and his wife (the Annie Bohannan /ho as the Taylor children's nurse had been through the Yangzhou iot) decided to return to China. 'I'm going whether you come or ot,' she declared to her vacillating husband. He became a daring ioneer. And then John McCarthy brought his ailing family home to ecuperate after eight and a half years in China, but was so intent on reaking new ground himself that after only three months in :ngland, spent energetically telling all he could about China, he /as away again.

'hat 'wonderful impetus' – Burma *April 1875–May 1876*

The 'Yunnan Outrage', 'respecting the attack on the Indian :xpedition to Western China and the Murder of Mr Margary' was common knowledge in Britain. The frustration of Her Majesty's Minister in China, in the heyday of Britain's imperial power and only fifteen years after Lord Elgin's capture of Peking (now Beijing), meant nothing to the news-reading public but a fresh resort to arms unless satisfaction was soon given. At the time, the geographical limitation of travel by Westerners into West China was considered to be Yichang, near the mouth of the Yangzi gorges. (This never applied to the Catholic priests who were escorted in secret by faithful converts or, when the international climate permitted, as dignitaries in style.) To go farther, up the rapids, was slow and dangerous. The alternative was to brave hostile Hunan to reach Guizhou, the sparsely populated austere mountainous scene of the long Miao rebellion.[8]

In 1868 a French expedition had left Saigon to explore the Mekong, and reached Kunming in Yunnan. T T Cooper had travelled from Wuhan as far as Batang only to be turned back, and the next year had tried again from Assam with the same result. Major (later Colonel) Sladen's expedition from Burma into Yunnan in 1868 had failed, as had Colonel Browne's in 1875 with the murder of Margary. So the departure of John Stevenson and Henry Soltau on April 6, 1875, to Burma, with the declared intention of entering Yunnan from Bhamo in the tracks of the two abortive government expeditions, could not fail to excite imagination.

While action to launch as many as eighteen young men into nine possibly resistant provinces at such a time struck some as irresponsible and others as daring faith to be encouraged, to Hudson Taylor both ventures – to Yunnan through Burma, and to the other provinces from the Yangzi – were reasonable. Strong expeditions like Colonel Browne's of one hundred and ninety-three men mostly armed and intent on promoting the hateful opium trade, could be expected to provoke opposition. Quiet friendliness, demonstrated by simple medical means, could pave the way for two Chinese-speaking preachers of 'virtue' to enter freely. At Bhamo they would be nine hundred miles from Rangoon but only one hundred from the Chinese border and in touch with caravans of Chinese traders. Half the population of Bhamo were Chinese, and five thousand more came over the border each year to trade. Two American Baptist missionaries to the Karen people of Burma had encountered some pack trains in the hills, each of several hundred animals driven by Roman Catholic muleteers who fell on their knees and kissed the missionaries' hands thinking they were priests.

As a gateway to China, Bhamo looked promising. As for the young 'eighteen', had not Hudson Taylor himself been demonstrating for over twenty years that foreigners were welcomed almost everywhere, as M Henry Taylor was finding in Henan? After all, for fifteen years it had been legal under the 'unequal treaties'.

Stevenson and Soltau arrived at Rangoon on May 14, 1875, to find Burma the scene of political unrest. At the time Lower Burma was governed from British India, but Upper Burma was still independent. In 1862 it had been open to commerce, including trade with China, but the British government still suspected King Mindon at Mandalay of having had a hand in thwarting Colonel Browne's expedition. Captain Cooke, the British Resident, had had to withdraw from Bhamo, and all merchants from Mandalay. Colonel Sladen was about to go by gunboat with a diplomatic representative and troops to confront King Mindon, so the Chief Commissioner could not allow Stevenson and Soltau to proceed up-country. Instead he advised them to call on the Yunnanese son of the late Muslim rebel 'king' of Dali, an exile in Rangoon. Both he and the Rangoon Chinese community received them warmly, provided them with Burmese and Mandarin language teachers, and introduced them to Chinese merchants from Mandalay and Bhamo. 'Natives from Yunnan have come down here to Rangoon *just* to meet us', Stevenson wrote.[10]

At last the opportunity came to visit Mandalay, and against the advice of many, because of the danger of war both in Burma and China, they left Rangoon on September 9 with a Burmese-speaking American missionary surnamed Rose. The journey from Rangoon to Bhamo by steam launch took twenty-five days, apart from interruptions, and by September 29 they could write that King Mindon had been 'both kind and cordial . . . (He) put no obstacle in the way' of their settling in Bhamo, and gave them a letter instructing the governor of Bhamo to provide a plot of land and facilities to buy building materials and hire workmen.

Word followed them from the Indian government forbidding their journey, but too late. They arrived at Bhamo on October 3, 1875. Professedly friendly, the governor secretly opposed them, and like Adoniram Judson they had to live and work in a *zayat*, a shed by the roadside, until the governor died a few months later. His successor then granted them the site they had chosen, near the city gate through which most Chinese went to and from Yunnan. Soon the confidence of the belligerent Kachin tribesmen was won by John

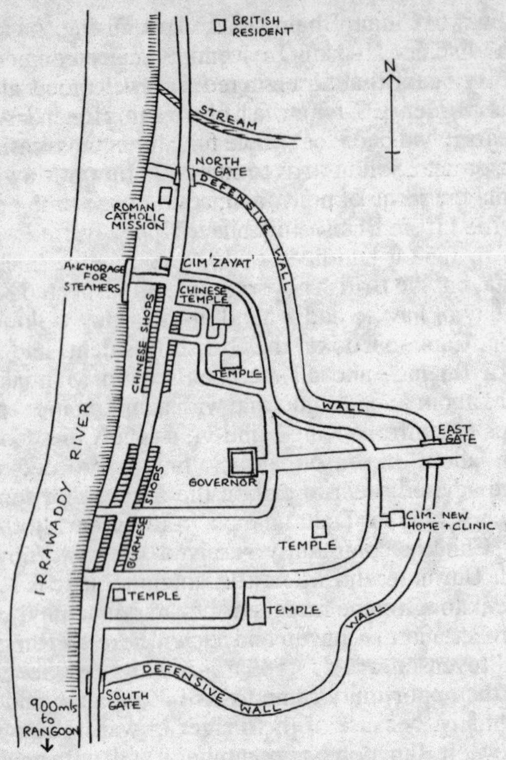

BHAMO: GATEWAY FROM THE WEST

Stevenson's attitude to them, and by Henry Soltau's amateur doctoring. Very unkempt, with menacingly long knives and spears, they even appeared attractive to Stevenson.

> Your letter about the Kak-hyens (Kachin) quite fired my soul [Hudson Taylor wrote in reply to a letter from Soltau]. Oh! I could not but exclaim that I might become a Kak-hyen to win them to Christ. They seem to me to be noble game – men whose changed lives will show what Christ *can* do, and I asked the Lord for thousands of them, for Christ.

His prayer was answered.

'The Chinese come by crowds,' Stevenson wrote, 'and they have taken the Scriptures into China.' But the British authorities sternly forbade him and Soltau to cross the border. They were still there, busy making friends, when Grosvenor's 'mission of enquiry' at last arrived, having witnessed a 'staged' investigation in Kunming of Margary's murder. But for British obstruction, Stevenson reported, entering China would be as simple for him as crossing into the next county at home. That day was to come. Bhamo was to play a part in the occupation of western Yunnan, and to remain an outpost of the CIM until 1915, the Mission's jubilee.

China's Millions — *June–July 1875*

In the last week of May 1875, after the Brighton Convention, Hudson Taylor made a crucial decision – to be unconventional again and to initiate an unusual means of informing people about China. Many had become interested and were wanting the facts. Some were critical and needed the facts. By no fault of their own, ignorance handicapped friend and critic alike. The secular press had attractive periodicals illustrated by steel-engravings – *The Illustrated London News*, *The Graphic* and others, the equivalent of today's 'glossy' magazines. No Christian publication had yet emulated them, though some leaflets were illustrated. To catch the eye, to honour the cause, to inform and to challenge was the need. It had to be. The result by today's standards is commonplace.

The *Occasional Paper* of the China Inland Mission was a simple pocket-sized pamphlet of ten to thirty pages. The last issue, in March 1875, had hinted at the hoped-for approach to the West China provinces of Guangxi, Guizhou and Sichuan through Burma and Yunnan, and another issue, No 40, was overdue. The 'wonderful impetus' already given by Stevenson's and Soltau's departure and first letters from Rangoon demanded this new 'leap forward'. But what should it be called? As ever, Jennie Taylor went straight to the point. The CIM existed for China's millions – the phrase Hudson Taylor had used again and again. 'China's Millions and our Work among them', she suggested, the title that held its own until the end of the year. After that *CHINA'S MILLIONS* was enough. For decades the phrase was to be echoed by thousands, falling naturally into Sarah Stock's hymn in 1898, 'China's millions join the strain, Waft it on to India's plain', and outlasting the 'open century'.

Work on it was immediately started, and within a month Volume 1 Number 1 was ready for the press. The magazine was ten inches by seven (later enlarged), a highly topical, eye-catching pace-setter.

VOLUME 1, NUMBER 1: THE LAUNCH OF *CHINA'S MILLIONS*

The front page carried an illuminated title surmounted by the Chinese characters for 'Ebenezer – Hitherto hath the Lord helped us', and 'Jehovah Jireh – the Lord will provide'. Beneath it came an engraving (by favour of *The Graphic*) of Shan people of the Burma-Yunnan border, and the opening words 'The province of Yun-nan is attracting much attention at this time, owing to the failure of the British exploratory expedition and the murder of the lamented Margary'. Facts about the Shan preceded an editorial. 'When periodicals are so numerous . . . why commence another? . . . Why is not a deeper interest felt in China by the people of England and . . . the Church? . . . They have never *seen* its glorious hills, its noble ruins . . . nor its crowded cities . . . its countless villages.' If they could, the wonders of China and the Chinese would speak for themselves. *China's Millions* would help to supply the need.

Immediately it plunged into a brief report from Henry Taylor about Henan, the first 'new' province to be entered. Then a Chinese Christian's account of how he had been so struck by John Stevenson's patient persuasion and the sight of foreigners frequently on their knees in prayer, that he asked Jesus to 'receive' him, and went on to become an evangelist.[11] Reports followed from different parts of China. Before extracts from Henry Soltau's letters from Burma, and a final full-page engraving of a scene on the porch of a Chinese roadside eating-house, came Hudson Taylor's main editorial under the title 'China for Christ', with the illuminated text, 'Whatsoever he saith unto you, do it!' He liked to emphasise his point.

> It was nine years on the 26th of May since the *Lammermuir* party sailed for China. . . . We have needed all the time since to gain

> experience, and to gather round us a staff of (Chinese) workers (to occupy) some fifty stations in five different provinces. . . . We believe that the time has come for *doing* more fully what He has commanded us; and by His grace we intend to do it. *Not to try*, for we see no Scriptural authority for trying. Try is a word constantly in the mouth of unbelievers, . . . far too often taken up by believers. In our experience, 'to try' has usually meant 'to fail'. (The Lord's) command is not 'Do your best,' but 'DO IT' . . . Do *the* thing commanded. . . . 'Whatsoever he saith unto you, *do it!*'

Here lay the secret of Hudson Taylor's own perseverance. It must also be true of the Mission.

The day G F Easton, an accepted candidate, ended his seven-year apprenticeship in south London, at last a master-printer, he walked all the way to Pyrland Road. Sharing his sense of achievement, Hudson Taylor asked him to see the first *China's Millions* through the press. Published in June 1875, the magazine has continued its unbroken existence to the present day, nearly one hundred and fifteen years later. With the extension of the Mission beyond China in 1951 it became the *East Asia Millions*. His candidates became salesmen. 'I sold the first six in a newspaper shop in Bow Road near Harley House,' George Clarke recalled. 'I pushed this new paper at Moody and Sankey meetings in London.'[12]

A man for the 'Millions' — *May 1875–76*

Before long Hudson Taylor himself would have to return to China. How to deal with candidates, *China's Millions* and the transmission of funds during his absence occupied his thoughts. Part-time honorary secretaries had found the work too demanding. But who could give his whole time to it? For years he had tried to persuade his sister Amelia and her husband Benjamin Broomhall to join him or another society in China. Amelia would gladly have gone, but Benjamin could not see it as the will of God for them and their growing family.[13] His partnership in the New Bond Street business was successful and he was giving his spare time to the early YMCA and as secretary to the Anti-Slavery Society. But while he made a comfortable home for his family, he lived often beyond his means, sometimes finding himself in extreme difficulty, for he was more generous than businesslike. In time the firm failed, the partnership broke up, to Hudson Taylor's relief, and Benjamin set up on his own in Surrey. There too, with his tenth child on the way, he failed to make ends meet and turned to Hudson Taylor for advice, as he had often done in the long years of their friendship.

In May 1875, therefore, probably on his way to the Brighton Convention, Hudson Taylor visited Benjamin and Amelia at Godalming. Once again he broached the subject of their devoting themselves exclusively to China where their hearts had been with him for more than twenty years. Aware of Benjamin's limitations, Hudson Taylor respected his abilities and had a place for him. His decision in the last week of May to launch *China's Millions* had confirmed in his own mind the proposition he now made. Would they join him at Pyrland Road for an experimental period, to help with the production and distribution of the magazine and to play host in their home to candidates who came for interviews and training? 'Mr T thought him the very man for the job', Louise Desgraz recalled. 'He would be a good judge of what was needed.'

With it he made a 'generous offer'. To avoid misunderstanding, as they were close relatives, he chose personally to provide them with a house and income.[14] Benjamin sold up and in July moved into No 5 Pyrland Road with the candidates. Amelia and her family of ten followed on August 24.

Hudson Taylor's home in No 6 had long since become too full, so rooms were taken next door in No 4 until vacant possession was obtained at the end of August, and a door opened between the two houses. His makeshift office was then exchanged for a more suitable room and things took on a settled appearance. As the Mission continued to grow, No 2 was acquired for Benjamin and family, and other houses for the Mission as the need arose.[15]

'Then Pyrland Road was only partially built . . . it was possible to jump out of the back windows and be almost in open country. . . .' Many a foolish escapade on the roof and races up and down the builders' ladders formed the memories of Benjamin's four boys and six girls, despite being under the teaching and firm hand of Miss Wilkin, their governess. In constant contact with the stream of Mission candidates, and under the influence of a crusading father and exceptionally prayerful mother, they could not but be caught up in the concern for China. Five of the ten became missionaries there, and one on the Mission staff in America.

Benjamin had at last found the niche in which his gifts were to be given full scope. He and Amelia came to be regarded as father and mother figures in the CIM, while Hudson Taylor filled the role of beloved leader and administrator.[16] But that lay ahead.

Still more of 'the Eighteen' *June–December 1875*

Cameron, Clarke and Nicoll were to sail on August 4, and in October Easton, the printer, and Elizabeth Judd's brother James F Broumton, a London business man, were to follow. To those who know the history of their great achievements, each of these names is its own monument.[17] C G Moore was another at Pyrland Road, a lecturer in theology retained on the home-staff to teach his fellow-candidates. In 1909 he recalled his first interview with Hudson Taylor, in the days when he was trying to do without the crutches.

> (His study) was largely occupied with packing cases and some rough bookshelves set along one of the walls. Near the window was a writing table littered with letters and papers. In front of the fireplace (unused) was a low, narrow, iron bed-stead neatly covered with a rug. (Nothing else was to be seen in the room that would not have been found in the most barely furnished office.) I hardly think there was a scrap of carpet on the floor, and certainly not a single piece of furniture that suggested the slightest regard for comfort or appearance. Mr Taylor . . . lay down on his iron bedstead and eagerly plunged into a conversation which was, for me, one of life's golden hours. Every idea I had hitherto cherished of a 'great man' was completely shattered – the high and imposing airs, and all the trappings were conspicuously absent; but Christ's ideal of greatness was there. . . . I strongly suspect that, by his unconscious influence, Mr Hudson Taylor did more than any other man of his day to compel Christian people to revise their ideas of 'greatness'.

Hudson Taylor spent long hours talking with the young men about how to cope with life in China, but still had his other work to do, with family life going on around them. George Clarke recalled, 'How well I remember Master Charlie (aged six and a half) putting most difficult questions to his father (and) occasionally Masters Howard and Herbert rolling (in a tussle) under the table.' The way he seemed to go on working day and night impressed James Broumton, as did Hudson Taylor's gratitude for comparatively small donations, and his thankfulness to God when he opened letters and found (them). He often prayed (at once) for God's blessing on the donors.

In early June, though still on crutches a year after his accident, Hudson Taylor visited Alexander Wylie (home from China with failing eyesight) and attended the stone-laying ceremony of Tom Barnardo's Ilford cottages. Then in July he took part in a succession of meetings to farewell Cameron, Clarke and Nicoll. In August he went to Guernsey for a holiday with his family, still working almost all of every day, and by September was 'in full harness' again.[18] But a visit to his parents in Sussex, with all the jolts of hansom cabs over cobblestones and trains starting and stopping, brought his pain back again for five days. At last by Christmas he could claim to be 'feeling (himself) again'. As he looked back over a year so remarkable, so filled with happenings undreamed of in the deep trough of December 1874, he wrote, 'We have had correspondence with more than sixty candidates . . . between 20 and 30 young (men) and 9 or 10 (women) have spent . . . from a few days to several months with us . . . in study and preparation for work in China. . . . We lack only four . . . to *fulfil* our petition for 18 this year'. The four were already in touch with him but not yet accepted. More than eighteen were to be chosen, though some did not sail for China until the new year.[19] During all this time in China the tension between Wade and the imperial negotiators was mounting.

The Eighteen in perspective *13th century–1877*

China had not always been anti-foreign. In the Yuan dynasty (1260–1368) Marco Polo had even been governor of Yangzhou, and many European merchants had lived and moved freely in the empire. Except during the anti-Christian phases (Book 1, ch 1) Nestorian and, later, Roman priests had been honoured and employed at the seats of government. Even during periods of persecution Catholic missionaries had travelled secretively in almost every province for seven centuries. In 1846 the Abbé Huc and Joseph Gabet had penetrated into Tibet before being deported.

Charles Gutzlaff, so fluent and adapted to Chinese ways that he passed as one of them, was the first Protestant to venture into several coastal provinces. And in 1815 Robert Morrison travelled overland from Peking to Canton in Lord Amhurst's cortège, as a guest of the emperor.[20] Robert Fortune the plant-hunter, W H Medhurst, Senior, and others had used disguise to probe the coastal hinterland at great personal risk. But in 1861, after the opium wars when recognition was granted under duress to the conquering nations, still tempting fate Captain Blakiston succeeded in reaching the Tibetan marches with a Lt Colonel Sarel. The future bishop S I J Schereschewsky of the American Episcopal Church travelled part of the way with them. Seven years later (1868) the Frenchman

Lieutenant Garnier of the Mekong expedition from Saigon, after failing to reach Dali from Kunming during the Muslim rebellion, withdrew northward to Dongchuan and outflanked the hostilities between Muslim rebels and government forces by an arduous detour across the Jin He, or River of Gold (see map p 123) via Huili to Dali and back.[21] Also in 1868 T T Cooper ventured through Sichuan as far as Batang and beyond Weixi, west of Lijiang, in the cause of discovery and commerce, only to be turned back.[22] Also in 1868 Major Sladen entered Yunnan from Burma and was forced to withdraw. Four years later, in 1872, Baron Ferdinand von Richtofen tried unsuccessfully to follow Marco Polo's route from Chengdu (his Sindafu) via the Jianchang (Chiench'ang) valley (his Caindu) and its chief city of Xichang (Ningyuan) and over the Jinsha Jiang (River of Golden Sand) to Kunming, Dali and Burma.

Colonel Henry Yule in his long introductory essay to Gill's two volume travelogue, *The River of Golden Sand*, takes pains to make it clear that all these remotest regions had long been 'habitually traversed' and some had been occupied for decades by devoted Catholic missionaries, with enforced interruptions. Where von Richtofen on his way to Xichang was attacked and forced back from the high Da Xiang Ling pass, south of Ya'an, Colborne Baber and (separately) George Nicoll of the CIM were to succeed. The letters of the Abbé Desgodins of Batang were published in 1872, showing him, like so many Catholic priests in faraway places, to be a traveller and observer of note.

Missionaries, often without knowing it, were to tread in the steps of secular travellers, but were more often to lead the way, criss-crossing territory later to become familiar to foreign railway engineers, merchants and employees of the Chinese Post and Salt Tax offices. They were a disappointment to the geographers, by failing to observe, measure or report on the terrain they traversed, and its products. Colonel Henry Yule wrote appreciatively of their spirit and their relationship with the Chinese, while deploring their neglect as explorers and prospectors. *People* were their overriding interest. To take the gospel to them mattered most. And anyway, few were trained in map-making or geology, although the use of a pedometer to count footsteps was a common practice among them. Their references to natural resources or other matters of interest to commerce or exploitation were few and far between. Travelling conditions were hard, whether their trail rose and fell thousands of feet or pressed endlessly on through dusty plains.

Josiah Cox's visit to Changsha in anti-foreign Hunan in 1864 had been made entirely by boat 'for the sake of his health',[23] and Paul Bagley entered Sichuan the following year (Book 4, p 102 and Personalia). While Cooper and Garnier were exploring the south-west in 1868, Griffith John and Alexander Wylie were braving hostile crowds in Chengdu and escaping with their lives, continuing northward to Hanzhong in Shaanxi and down the Han River back to Wuhan (map p 217). From Wuchang Cox's Wesleyan colleague W Scarborough visited the cities on the Han River as far as Laohekou (now Guanghua) in 1873, and made many shorter journeys, whereas Griffith John did not pursue his work in Hunan until the 1880s and '90s. His companion of 1868, Alexander Wylie, visited fifteen of China's eighteen provinces over the years, for the British and Foreign Bible Society. Alexander Williamson of the LMS, since 1863 with the National Bible Society of Scotland, also travelled extensively for a few years in the northern provinces before concentrating on the Presbyterian Church in Shandong. His colleague J McIntyre tried to reach Kaifeng in 1874 but was turned back at the Yellow River (Huang He) close to his goal, unlike another, Oxenham, who succeeded in 1868 in reaching Hankou from Peking (Beijing). Bible Society colporteurs, a sadly neglected corps of heroes in the published history of the Chinese Church, were constantly on the road, paying a high price in suffering (Book 4, p 321). But noteworthy because in strong contrast with the China Inland Mission, in reports of most societies published in the *Chinese Recorder* between 1875 and 1877 under the subtitle 'Itinerancy', is the recurring statement that little even of local travel had been or was being undertaken.

Hudson Taylor had appealed for volunteers to penetrate the nine remote provinces which few Westerners had dared to enter, where Catholic missionaries had previously only succeeded by being taken by loyal friends from one Christian home to another, and kept hidden out of sight. Since the treaties of 1858 and 1860 they had emerged under the French protectorate, bought or built imposing residences and asserted the treaty 'rights', assuming the titles and dignity of mandarins. None of these dubious advantages were available to the aspiring Protestant pioneer – no Christian homes or villages, no authority, few friends to guide or advise them. Knowledge, experience and tenuous footholds would have to be won by true trail-blazing.

The assault of 'the Eighteen' on the nine provinces unoccupied by

Protestant missionaries – for an assault it was, in terms of planning and intensity – had this marked characteristic, that it was deliberately to put down roots, to raise up Christian churches and so to achieve ambitious results, far removed from the haphazard wandering which appearances suggested. Echoing Charles Gutzlaff's policy of sending a mature Christian missionary to lead Chinese evangelists into every province, Hudson Taylor had declared his aim in 1873 to 'attain to one superintendent and two assistant foreign missionaries in a province, with qualified Christian helpers in each important city, and colporteurs in less important (ones, and) to commence a college for the more thorough training of our Chinese helpers.'[24] By January 1874 he was praying for fifty or a hundred additional Chinese evangelists (Book 5, pp 411–12) and his prayer for the eighteen missionary pioneers, begun in 1872, culminated during 1875 in the flood of applicants he was carefully sifting.[25]

First of the Nine[26] *1875*

The enterprise of the early pioneers is quickly appreciated by reference to a map (p 54). Conspicuously foreign, even in Chinese dress, they showed great courage, but not more than their Chinese companions needed, to be seen in their company. Before the advent of railways, Henan province, 450 miles from north to south and east to west, with an average population of 550 per square mile, depended for communication with other provinces on three rivers and the great imperial trunk road – an unpaved dirt track thronged with horse-drawn carts and mule litters, and loud with the shouts and curses of whip-cracking drivers. Within Henan, roads converged on Luoyang (previously Honanfu), described by von Richtofen as 'the Gate to the North-Western provinces and Central Asia'. There the trunk road began, to pass through Xi'an in Shaanxi, the ancient imperial capital, and over the mountains to Lanzhou in Gansu and on to Suzhou and Yümen, Jade Gate, 1,200 miles away.[27]

Extremes of temperature and an unreliable rainfall inescapably endured by the people, produced strong men inured to hardship, uncouth and easily angered, conservative and anti-foreign in some areas but intelligent, reliable, friendly and welcoming in other places.

On March 30, 1875, M Henry Taylor, after less than eighteen months of language study, wrote to Hudson Taylor 'As it is your wish that I should make Henan my future sphere, I turn my eyes towards its 25 millions with much desire.' He found a Christian named Zhang of whom he wrote as 'Chang, my brother' in the LMS church at Wuchang, and leaving Hankou with him on April 3 travelled overland, due north through Hubei (Griffith John's stamping ground) and deep through Henan. Selling copies of Scripture and preaching the gospel in the towns and cities as they went, they worked their way westwards from Runan (Runing) and Queshan (Choshan) as far west as Nanyang. Money and books exhausted, they then headed for home, to arrive at Hankou again fifty-six days later, on May 28. In the autumn after the great heat of summer, they returned, and for eighty-four days (October 24 to January 15, 1876) made a thorough tour of the province as far north as the Huang He, Yellow River.[28] At the prefectural city of Runan the chief innkeeper welcomed them as he had before, and when

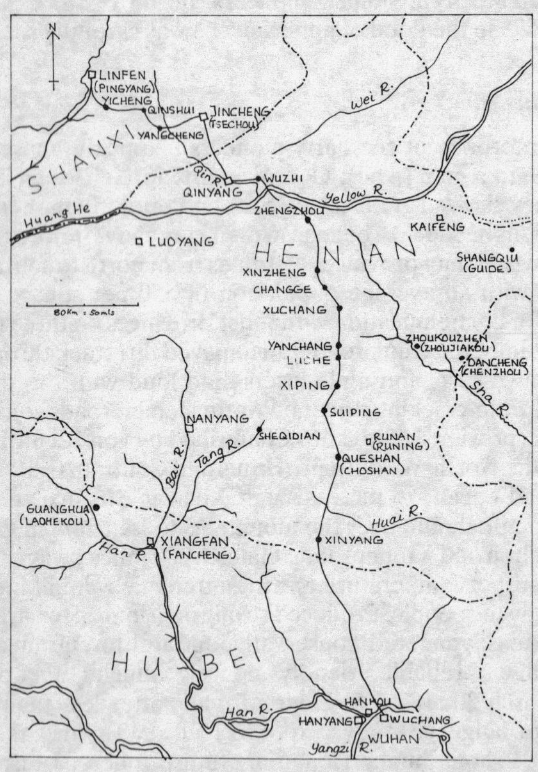

FIRST OF THE NINE: THROUGH HENAN TO SHANXI

incited to turn them out told the magistrate that he had read a Gospel and approved of it. Better still, they found four believers standing firm, the first-fruits of the Church of millions in Henan today. Fifty miles farther on they discovered a hundred Catholics at Zhoujiakou (now Zhoukouzhen) and at 'Cheng-chou', people who were 'proud, rude, callous and annoying to the last degree'. 'They trampled on our pearls and literally turned to rend us. We prayed for them and left.' They visited the cities of Kweiteh (now Shangqiu), Kaifeng and Luoyang, 150 miles apart, and were back in Wuhan on January 15, 1876.[29]

Hunan was the second of the unoccupied provinces to be entered (on June 10, 1875). Charles Judd, Yao Sifu the Hunanese Christian from Jiangxi and another named Zhang, probably Henry Taylor's companion, succeeded in renting premises but were driven out of Yueyang, the gateway to the province, at the mouth of the Dongting lakes.

In the early days of the Taiping rebellion with its quasi-Christian pretensions, Changsha the capital city of Hunan withstood a long siege in 1854 largely through the influence of the scholar-gentry. Ever since, the provincial governor's power had been less than that of the literati 'as four is to six', and opposition to foreigners and Christianity remained strong, whatever the attitude of the Peking government. Hunanese soldiers had formed the backbone of the imperial forces which overthrew the Taipings with Charles Gordon's inspiration in 1864, and Hunan's power in the empire continued to be immense.[30]

'Three parts upland and seven parts water', the province and most of its cities were served by waterways fed from the mountain ranges in the west and south. Changsha on the Xiang River dominated the east and south of Hunan, and Changde the western region, on the Yuan River from Guizhou province (map, p 94). The Yuan was therefore the natural route to Guiyang and Yunnan, taken by Augustus Margary on the way to Burma, and by the pioneers of the CIM in the period after the Chefoo Convention. Margary had had a taste of the prevailing xenophobia when on two occasions his boat was attacked and finally burned, even though he carried a Peking passport.

Later the same year Yao and Zhang returned to Yueyang, unmolested, but years were to pass before any foreigner could gain a true foothold. The conquest of Hunan is an epic story to which we shall return more than once.

CHAPTER TWO

'OUT OF THE LONG RUT AT LAST' 1875–77

The team complete *1875–76*

With the appeal for prayer published in January 1875 'that God will raise up this year eighteen suitable men', and the flood of men and women who besieged Hudson Taylor with correspondence and interviews, the end of the doldrums had been reached. From the ranks of the Mission itself six had volunteered and made an early start. John Stevenson had ten years' experience to his credit, and John McCarthy and Charles Judd more than eight. Frederick Baller and Henry Taylor had reached China together before the end of 1873, and Thomas Harvey in 1869, though he was at the time studying medicine and did not 'obtain his diploma' as a 'physician, surgeon and apothecary' until October 1875, or sail with his bride to Burma until February 1876.

To Henry Taylor had fallen the honour of leading the way, while Baller 'a most efficient missionary', waited on the Yangzi to receive the next reinforcements from home and initiate them into Chinese life. Henry Soltau from the office of Secretary in London sailed with Stevenson on April 6, 1875, hoping to make Bhamo a little more than a stepping stone to Yunnan. Young George King sailed alone on May 15 to reach Shanghai on July 14 after being shipwrecked. A week after he left London a strenuous round of farewell meetings began, to send off the 'three mighty men', James Cameron, George Nicoll and George Clarke. Fifteen hundred well-wishers thronged the Metropolitan Tabernacle to hear Spurgeon commission them before they left on August 4. Spurgeon gripped Nicoll's hand afterwards and said characteristically, 'May you grow a long "tail" and save many souls.'[1] Baller met them at Shanghai on September 26 and took them up the Yangzi. While Nicoll and Clarke joined the Judds at Wuhan, Cameron spent only three months at Jiujiang with a language teacher before being left alone at Anqing (scene of the 1869 riot) to sink or swim while he soaked up Chinese speech and ways. He learned fast and soon began travelling with a Chinese companion. More unknown young men and women whom Hudson

Taylor was training enter the story for the first time in 1876 and '77, soon to be bywords of brave exploration and evangelism. As if in reward for faithfulness in extreme testing, God was lavishing men and money on him for the fulfilment of his vision for China.

The day after Cameron's party sailed, G F Easton and James Broumton moved into their places at Pyrland Road, to follow in October. A month later J J Turner and Charles Budd travelled with John McCarthy to China. Even Benjamin Broomhall, father of ten, was considering whether to go with them. Hudson Taylor needed a mature man at the centre of things in China and thought his brother-in-law could do what was required. But he decided to stay. Joseph Adams had gone independently to Burma from Grattan Guinness's Institute, and in November joined Stevenson, Soltau and the Harveys at Bhamo as a member of the CIM. So within the year these sixteen men were at the scene of action, and five more were preparing to go after the New Year, Francis James, Edward Pearse and George Parker among them. With their departure Jennie wrote on February 29, 1876, 'This makes up the Eighteen'. In addition, but independently, a wealthy young Oxford graduate, Robert J Landale, went out with Hudson Taylor.[2]

For pioneering, men were wanted but women were not left out. On January 26, 1876, one of the most notable of early pioneers of either sex left with Francis James and Edward Pearse. Elizabeth Wilson, a niece of Hudson Taylor's old friend Miss Stacey, and already known to him for twenty-five years, was now 'a middle-aged lady of energy and means'. When Miss Stacey made a haven for the pale student recovering from 'dissection fever' in 1852 (Book 2, p 74) Elizabeth Wilson was there and impressed by his dedication. Caring for elderly parents had kept her from going to China sooner, but once free she delayed no longer. Hudson Taylor introduced her to the council on December 7, 1875, and, as intrepid as any of the men, she played a key role in the occupation of Shaanxi and then Gansu. Five young women followed later in the year to take their own place of honour in history only two years after reaching China.[3] 'Fresh lady candidates keep presenting themselves', Jennie told Louise Desgraz ambiguously; and soon afterwards added that Hudson was preparing to go back himself, to care personally for the growing numbers of novice missionaries in need of advice, and to see them into the kind of work most suited to each one.

In a review of the year's progress in *China's Millions* for December 1875 Hudson Taylor outlined his thinking about the designation of these pioneers, in a delicate pairing of personalities and denominational preferences.[4] But changing circumstances led, as he constantly found, to changes being made. What mattered was that the nine target provinces were constantly in view, for occupation as soon as possible, not as a distant goal. And not only the nine. Beyond lay 'Tibet, Kokonor, Turkestan and Sungaria' (map p 210). (The English and Canadian Presbyterians were already in Taiwan.) All this while the news from China was of the newly knighted minister Sir Thomas Francis Wade being thwarted, of war-clouds building up, and of Jackson's indiscretions threatening the denial of passports to the whole 'Taylor Mission'. Not only so, with growing military strength Japan was sending a naval expedition to Korea to obtain concessions by *force majeure*. The breakthrough by the eighteen was to be made while east Asia was as unstable as at any time.

Preparing to be away *1876*

Before he could leave London it remained for Hudson Taylor to provide for his own replacement as administrator in Britain. Since William Berger's resignation, part-time honorary secretaries had not succeeded in accomplishing as much as he had done with Mrs Berger's help. The Mission had grown larger. In January 1876 Richard Hill resigned, proposing George and Henry Soltau's younger brother William for appointment as a salaried full-time administrator. As long as Hudson Taylor was in the country he could manage while he trained William and devolved more work and responsibility on to Benjamin's shoulders. Even when in China he himself would continue to edit *China's Millions*, but its sub-editing and production would have to be done in London. On May 13 he suffered a bereavement as poignant as by the death of any close relative. Miss Stacey, who after his parents had been his closest friend and sympathiser and who had prayed unceasingly for him, died at her home in the village of Tottenham. His human foundations were shaken. For a week he was ill, grief-stricken, though her health had been failing for many weeks. He found it hard to address himself to his work and public engagements. One by one his props were being removed. Then he was himself again. He had to be. In a few days' time one of the big annual events of the Mission would be upon him.

At the tenth anniversary meeting in the great Mildmay Conference Hall on 'Lammermuir Day', May 26, 1876, (called 'the first of annual meetings') Hudson Taylor restated the 'aims and objects' of the Mission, making the emphasis that if the *practicability* of working in inland China were demonstrated, the Church of God as a whole in Europe and America would be encouraged to more adequate efforts.[5] The importance of this objective became increasingly apparent as the advance into the remote provinces took place. The casualties suffered by the Mission, he went on, far from being discouraging were a source of encouragement.

> It was anticipated, both by ourselves and others, that the hardships of pioneering would tell even more seriously in the way of sickness and death on our members, than on those of other Protestant Missions in China. (Instead) there has been *no* death or serious illness from *violence*; and the losses from the ordinary causes have been considerably below the average. . . . [Citing a review of the thirty years of CMS experience, a society enjoying public confidence,[6] he continued] 'Out of thirty-four ordained clergymen sent out only fifteen stayed more than four years . . . Of these fifteen, one is dead, one retired, two have been transferred to Japan, and eleven are still at work . . .' In the case of the American Baptist missionaries labouring in the same district as ourselves, out of . . . twenty-one persons, male and female, nine have been removed by death and six by retirement, during the last thirty years. In the ten years of the China Inland Mission (excluding those who have gone out within the last four years) of 39 persons of both sexes, 32 were able to stay more than four years, and 25 are still in connection with the Mission.

Then two unusual statements followed, the first illustrating the slow development of Mission practice in relation to naming specific financial needs, and the second demonstrating that there was no restraint on soliciting donations for other people's good causes. The fact that the Pyrland Road houses were up for sale was reported (p 48), with the comment:

> It would be a serious inconvenience were we obliged to relinquish them. . . . So we have prayerfully concluded to purchase them. . . . An immediate outlay of about £1000 is required . . . and we trust God will incline the hearts of His people to send special contributions for this, as a large saving to the Mission in rent will thus be effected.

At the time a home for missionaries' children was being opened at Coplow House, Tottenham, not by the Mission but as a private venture by Henrietta Soltau and a Miss Minchin, 'a lady of means', 'which will relieve us of much expense and responsibility'. They were open to receive contributions, and the Mission Council would be making grants to them from time to time.

In explanation, the occasion of these statements was exceptional, as the anniversary meeting was attended like a meeting of shareholders by the closest circle of supporters to whom reports were being made in confidence, as was not the case in meetings for the wider public elsewhere. Shortly afterwards, in June, he enclosed a lithographed letter in his own hand to the Mission's friends, with their copy of the *Millions*, saying, 'I feel that you and all who aid us by your prayers, your sympathy and your contributions are partners with us'. Asking them to promote the distribution of *China's Millions*, he mentioned that he had received several hundred pounds 'to cover the cost of publication . . . no small help now that requirements of the work exceed £150 a week', as was apparent from the Mission's annual statement of account. Nevertheless in later years, when this degree of reference to financial needs was criticised as being in breach of the 'no solicitation' principle, it gave place to the stricter interpretation which in contrast was called a 'conspiracy of silence'. It was difficult to steer between the shoals and to let integrity of motive govern the Mission's financial statements.

A highlight of the afternoon meeting was the moment when Hudson Taylor welcomed James Sadler of the LMS in Xiamen (Amoy) as a representative of the society which sent the first Protestant pioneers to China. Hudson Taylor also paid tribute to the Church Missionary Society, the Wesleyan Methodist and Presbyterian societies, and American and European missions. Taking the gospel to the vast empire of China was the task of the whole church and his habit of speaking of the CIM in relation to the rest was winning him their approval. Month by month he was conferring with the London Council about administration during his approaching absence. (We must touch on this because of what happened.) A year of 'temporary assistance' by Benjamin Broomhall had become a long-term appointment. The minutes of February 18, 1876, read that he was in future 'to be attached to the Mission in the same way as the missionaries' and, in August, 'would spend much of his time in holding meetings in the country on behalf of the Mission, together with such missionaries as may be at home'. Soon he was 'in Birmingham arranging for meetings' or 'at Bath conferring with ministers'. An administrative structure was taking shape which would remain intact for decades to come, expanded and adapted as necessary.

A statement of the 'Principles and Practice' of the Mission was drawn up, to be signed by each member as a proof of acceptance before going to China, as far as possible to ensure a partnership of like-minded people. All too soon the stark realities of a life too remote from their experience at the time of signing were to show some how superficially they had understood and weighed the cost of such discipleship, and the implications of trusting GOD, not Hudson Taylor, for their means of livelihood.

A week before he left the country on September 8, Hudson Taylor and the council went over the final arrangements for his absence. He intended to be away for only forty weeks, in order to devote time on his return to selecting yet more reinforcements. No new women candidates would be accepted or sent out meanwhile. He had prepared the contents of *China's Millions* for the rest of the year, and to protect Jennie from the criticisms borne by an editor, he restricted her share to sub-editing, with Benjamin selecting news items from recent correspondence. Her work was to be confidential and crucial. As when he was at home, she was also to open Mission letters and reply if she could, or to pass them on to Theodore Howard as council chairman, to William Soltau as cashier in charge of general office matters and of distribution of the *Millions*, and to Benjamin if they were concerned with public relations. No members of the council could spare time enough to represent Hudson Taylor in a major role as William Berger had done. Theodore Howard increased the part he played only after a few years. Benjamin and Amelia, young William Soltau and C G Moore were each as limited by inexperience of China as the other. So while Jennie could not be in charge, she had to be Emily Blatchley over again, the life and soul of the London headquarters while appearing not to be. At the same time she was mother of the six Taylor children, including her own two, no easy task while Herbert and Howard (fifteen and thirteen) were for ever 'sparring with each other'.

The Mission's accounts were available for inspection by donors, but the account books in which their names were recorded, Hudson Taylor declared, 'are to be considered sacredly private'. If they had survived, much enlightening information would be available to us, but the privacy has been perpetuated. Finally, Jennie, Benjamin and William Soltau would hold themselves ready to attend council meetings when invited to do so, but the responsibility for everything rested upon the honorary 'council of management' as before. It remained to be seen how this loose structure would work out in practice, the best that could be put together with available personnel.

Reconnoitring for bases *1875–76*

In China while T F Wade came and went, the young pioneers of the CIM were in action. In the last week of September 1875, when Stevenson and Soltau were in Mandalay to meet King Mindon, Cameron, Clarke and Nicoll were welcomed into the CIM's first transit home at Shanghai, 'opposite the old dock, in an old tumble-down Chinese shanty'.[7] They were put straight into Chinese clothes and the Chinese way of life, and sent six hundred miles up the Yangzi 'by an old junk of a steamer (with a) Chinese captain (taking) one week to Hankow' (Wuhan). This was the right start for them. Frederick Baller and his wife (Mary Bowyer) met the boat at Jiujiang and took James Cameron off for six months' intensive initiation into things Chinese (Baller's forte) there and at Nanjing. Nicoll and Clarke went on to join the Judds at Wuchang, to be trained by them, arriving in time to see Henry Taylor and the evangelist Zhang setting off on their second journey to Henan.

> Soon after arrival we went to the British consul (Challoner Alabaster) to register. He had received a letter from Sir Thomas Wade. [George Soltau in London had negotiated an agreement with the Foreign Office.] Read it slowly for us to copy. It said that if we eighteen men went into the interior we went on our own responsibility and could not look to the British government for protection.[8]

Stevenson and Soltau reached Bhamo at about the same time, October 3, a month before the Grosvenor Mission left Wuhan to see justice done over the Margary affair. And J J Turner and Charles Budd arrived at Shanghai with John McCarthy towards the end of 1875 to continue their training by him. Still 'the Eighteen' flowed in. Elizabeth Wilson with Francis James and Edward Pearse arrived on March 14, 1876, followed by George Parker and Horace Randle on May 20. While Wade had thundered in Peking and withdrew to Shanghai, and Lord Derby threatened to withhold the CIM's passports, the resurgent Mission, almost indifferent to their misgivings, was getting into place for its great push forward. In fact the first sorties were under way.

When Henry Taylor and Zhang arrived back at Wuhan in mid-January 1876 from their eighty-four day journey, George Clarke (after less than six months in China) was game to go with them on the next expedition. Incessant rain reduced the roads to quagmires and kept them waiting, but in mid-March they were away. Griffith John, who but for his mission's policy would himself have been a travelling pioneer, had to be content with giving them a send-off from his own home. Joined by the evangelist Yao Sifu[9] and taking barrow-loads of books and tracts, they followed the same route as before (map p 54), northwards through Hubei and into Henan, preaching at place after place as they went. At Runan (in Clarke's diary, Juning) 240 miles from Wuhan, the same friendly innkeeper received them, and they found that the two men, Mu and Wang, who had 'believed' on Henry Taylor's first visit, had been through bitter ostracism and rejection by their families, unshaken. As a result thirty of Mu's neighbours were interested in a religion that could make him so strong. On April 1 they baptised the two in a country stream, the first members of the Protestant Church in Henan which now numbers hundreds of thousands, even millions.[10] Henry Taylor succeeded in renting a house at the nearby county town of Queshan (Choshan), leaving Mr Mu in charge. So far everything was up to their expectations.

Travelling on, meeting Roman Catholics here and there and a man baptised elsewhere by the LMS, they came to Zhoujiakou (Chou-chia-kou, now Zhoukouzhen). There a minor military mandarin told them that when Henry Taylor was in Kaifeng in December 1875, the literati had bound themselves under an oath to kill him, and waited in groups of ten in the city streets for him to come selling books of the Bible and preaching. Enraged when they found he had moved on to Luoyang, they had torn down his landlord's inn sign and threatened to burn the inn to the ground.[11] Taylor, Yao and Clarke went on, through Guide (Kweiteh, now Shangqiu), but when their wheelbarrow men fell ill, and news arrived of 'disturbances' in Kaifeng against the Catholics, they returned by the way they had come. Yao joined Mu at Queshan, while Taylor and Clarke completed the journey to Wuhan. They had covered 800 miles in 80 days.

While they were away, John McCarthy took James Cameron to

visit the Anhui stations of Ningguo and Huizhou (Book 5, map p 38), leaving him for five months (April–August) with the Chinese Christians and no foreign companion. The experience was the making of him as a pioneer, fluent in the language, feeling at home living as a Chinese, and accustomed to travelling with little more than a bed-roll and a minimum of necessities.

The great heat of summer ruled out any major excursions, but in August when it eased a little three teams set out: Baller and Jiang Suoliang (Tsiang Soh-liang), the Zhenjiang pastor, took George King with them up the Han River; Henry Taylor set off on his fourth Henan journey, again with George Clarke; and Evangelist Zhang went with George Nicoll (joined later by James Cameron) overland through Shashi to Yichang on the Yangzi below the great gorges (map p 94). Yichang was to be their advanced base for penetration into Sichuan province, while whoever held the fort there would evangelise the surrounding Hubei countryside. Without difficulty they rented a house outside the south gate of the city and took possession. George Nicoll had been surprised to find on an evangelistic expedition with Charles Judd that they 'everywhere met with kindness, surpassing by far that shown to street preachers at home' in Britain. The people of Yichang were no less welcoming, although Yichang had been designated a treaty port.

Baller, Jiang Suoliang and King on reaching Fancheng (now Xiangfan) the starting point of two or three good routes to Xi'an, the capital of Shaanxi province, walked straight into trouble. All boats like theirs were being commandeered for troop movements, and they had to change their plans. To hire even a small boat in which to press on up the Han River rapids into Shaanxi they had to pay exorbitantly. They succeeded in entering this third of the nine provinces, but by the time they reached Xing'an (now Ankang) were running out of money and on September 26 had to turn back to Wuhan. The gospel had been preached without hindrance at every stopping place, and George King now knew the ropes for when he could try again. Yet they had only touched the fringe where eight Catholic priests were stationed permanently. By June 1882 when Baller had preached the gospel in thirteen different provinces, by nearly two thousand miles of foot-slogging without meeting a single Christian, his reward was to find fifty or sixty believers worshipping together at Fancheng – just six years after this river journey with George King.[12]

Records of Henry Taylor's and George Clarke's fourth foray into

Henan (map p 54) from August until October 25, 1876 are scrappy, and Clarke's diary seems not to have been preserved. A short report on December 12 in the *Shanghai Courier and China Gazette* applauded their 'pluck', but only two other references were published months later.[13] They spent six weeks in their rented house in Queshan before any trouble began. Suddenly an official arrived, had their servant beaten, took away their passport and drove them out. After they had left, a Chinese doctor friend was given 'fifty blows of the bamboo on the hand (and) the doorkeeper [probably the new Christian, Mu see p 63] received fifty blows on the mouth [with a leather strap, see Book 4, p 280]. A friend of Mr Liu [their local language teacher] was recognised on the street and received this brutal usage. All this is the work of a few of standing in the city. The mandarins dared not oppose them.' If such slight association with the foreigners endangered even educated local men, it was right to spare them by withdrawing, although no direct threat to Clarke and Taylor had been made. Renting premises too early had been a tactical mistake. They were seen off by the first official and some soldiers.

Back in Wuhan Henry Taylor wrote to Hudson Taylor for advice. By that time the Chefoo Convention had been signed and prospects were brighter. Good weather could last for another two months, but were there any reasons, Henry Taylor asked, why they should not return to Queshan so soon? Hudson Taylor's reply has not been kept, but on November 24 he told Charles Judd that he was keeping Taylor and Clarke with him at Zhenjiang. Henry Taylor had been shaken by his experience and needed the kind of encouragement Hudson Taylor could give.[14] In January he returned to Wuhan, ready to face Henan again, and bravely went on his fifth Henan journey without a missionary companion. George Clarke was taking Judd's place at Wuhan to free him for a major adventure through Hunan and into Guizhou, by a route which Clarke and others were to take after Judd returned.

Shirking nothing, these men were proving to be what their leader had hoped of them, determined 'not to try but to do it'.

The Chefoo Convention[15] *March–September 1876*

When the imperial mission of enquiry into the fate of Augustus Margary and his companions reached Kunming on March 6, 1876, the British observers became witnesses of a charade instead of an investigation. 'No witness of the murder was allowed to be produced.'[16] In a patently superficial trial, a subordinate officer and 'thirteen savages kidnapped to do duty as prisoners at the bar' stood accused of these murders. The two consular observers, E Colborne Baber and Arthur Davenport, reported afterwards that patently none understood the language of the indictment, 'nor did they look in the least like men who were pleading guilty to a capital charge'. It was the Tianjin massacre enquiry over again, pure farce. (Book 5, pp 267–8.) As they could obtain no true investigation, Grosvenor and his party left Kunming on March 25 and travelling via Dali and Tengchong reached Bhamo on May 21.

It was what the minister Sir Thomas Wade had expected. Refusing to accept the Kunming verdict, he demanded of Prince Kong the punishment of Zen Yüying (Tsen), the acting-governor of Yunnan who was ultimately responsible,[17] and returned to Tianjin (Tientsin) and Peking to press his point. There negotiations dragged on, with Li Hongzhang prepared to talk but the Zongli Yamen repudiating any concessions he might make, on the ground that Li had exceeded his brief. Wade finally struck his flag in June and for the third time withdrew to Shanghai for access to the international telegraphic cable.

From Shanghai he wrote to Lord Derby at the Foreign Office,

> It is currently reported, and generally believed, that the Grand Secretary Li Hung-chang[18] has received an imperial decree directing him to proceed to Chefoo [i.e. Yantai] to confer with me . . . with more than ordinary powers. (If negotiations should again be broken off) Her Majesty's Government could dictate terms.

Already in response to a request from Sir Thomas the Foreign Office had informed the Admiralty that a naval squadron was indispensable. Four ships had been ordered to Hong Kong in February and to 'Chinese waters' in March to reinforce his demands. As Hosea Ballou Morse observed, 'Sir T Wade's buoyant hopefulness was justified.' The Navy was eloquent when statesmanship failed.

When Wade struck his flag, Prince Kong asked Robert Hart whether this time the minister should be taken seriously, and enlisted Hart's help. Hart followed Wade to Shanghai, ostensibly to discuss commercial matters in his capacity of inspector-general of the Imperial Maritime Customs, but actually to bring him back to meet Li Hongzhang at Yantai. Wade agreed, and arrived at Yantai on August 10, where Li Hongzhang joined him a week later, delayed by desperate events at Tianjin. Afraid that Li would be taken hostage by the British, the merchants of Tianjin had tried to dissuade him, and his wife incited a popular rising to persuade him that if he went, the foreign community would be massacred. He was unmoved. A deputation of literati followed him to Yantai, only to return without seeing him, after being convinced by Gustav Detring, one of Hart's commissioners of customs, that this was truly a matter of peace or war, war which must also see retribution for the Tianjin massacre of 1870.[19]

Lord Macartney on his voyage up the coast to Tianjin in 1793 had weathered a storm in a tiny bay with islands at its mouth, that of Yantai. But the lee shore where he anchored was under a bluff, near the fishing village of Chefu. In accounts of the episode, 'Chefoo' became the name in common use, retained by Westerners as the port of Yantai grew and became popular as a health resort.

Six feet four inches in height, Li Hongzhang towered above his own countrymen and most Westerners, dominating them no less

LI HONGZHANG, VICEROY AND GRAND SECRETARY

with his large and 'brilliant' eyes. His appearance alone commanded respect but being equally astute in mind and wise in action, and a master of prevarication, he was a formidable opponent. Convinced of their integrity, he enlisted Hart, 'as calm as Wade was excitable', and Detring to advise him. As soon as he arrived Li recognised his advantage in the presence at Yantai of the diplomatic representatives of Russia, Germany, America, Spain, France and Austro-Hungary, all of whom had sensed crisis. Anxiously watching Wade's every move they were open to being played off against each other. For Wade had with him the admiral of the China station and another admiral in command of the 'Flying Squadron' poised at Dalian (Dairen, now Lüda) on the tip of Liaodong peninsula, just across the straits. No nation wished to be dragged into hostilities (map p 223).

It was Wade's conference, to wring 'satisfaction' of Britain's grievances from an adroitly evasive China, but such an unplanned confluence of observers could not but mean social exchanges between diplomats 'ashore and afloat'. Wise to the acute danger of war, Li Hongzhang seized the initiative, inviting the fifteen most influential individuals to a magnificent feast of alternating Chinese and European courses, and proposed a toast in Western style, that 'as "all within the four seas are brothers", the nations here represented may always dwell in peace and friendship . . . like brothers living together'. This conditioned Sir Thomas and his admirals to his mood as discussion ploughed heavily through the mire of ambiguous aims. But Wade 'was at his best at Chefoo'. After Li Hongzhang adopted Wade's own ploy of threatening to leave Yantai without an agreement, some order was eventually made of it. The 'Flying Squadron' came peacefully to lie 'in beautiful array in Chefoo harbour', and the 'Chefoo Convention' was signed on September 13, in three sections.

The first was a 'Settlement of the Yunnan case', providing for an imperial edict and proclamations in all provinces to ensure safe travel for foreigners throughout the empire if provided with a passport; for two years British officials were to visit Chinese cities at will, to see that proclamations were posted; trade between Burma and Yunnan, and a second expedition like Colonel Browne's were provided for, to be supervised by British officials stationed at Dali for five years; an indemnity of 200,000 taels was to be paid; and an imperial letter of regret was to be taken by a Chinese mission to London.

The second section on 'Official Relations' provided for the administration of justice at Chinese ports, and that China should treat foreign officials as Chinese representatives were treated abroad.

Under 'Trade', the third section, Yichang, Wuhu, Wenzhou and Beihai (Pakhoi) were to be opened as treaty ports; a consul was to reside at Chongqing; and six more 'ports of call' on the Yangzi were authorised. For good measure, a British mission was to be ensured safe passage through Tibet, from China to India. Wade feared that if British merchants were so 'enterprising' as to penetrate 1,500 miles up the Yangzi into Sichuan they would be massacred, so he accepted a ban on their residence in Chongqing, but no mention of missionaries was made.

Assessments of the value of the convention were as many as they were contradictory, both at the time and since. Wade succeeded in getting much of what he wanted, yet the *North China Herald* called it 'a mass of meaningless verbiage'. The merchants saw it as an ambiguous substitute for 'the clear and simple provisions of the treaty of Tientsin' (Tianjin) of 1858. The envoys of other nations saw no improvement on the negotiations they had disapproved of in Peking, and all the powers took advantage of China's concessions, while refusing to be bound by Wade's.[20] However, the missionary community hailed the news as being the answer to Valignano's cry 'Oh, Rock, Rock, when wilt thou open, Rock?' (Book 1, p 62) not foreseeing the accusation that those who acted on the convention were agents of the foreign powers.

Li Hongzhang had flatly refused to allow his colleague Zen Yüying, acting-governor of Yunnan, to be humiliated, and reported the convention to Peking in novel terms. British protests against punishment of the wrong people, he explained, were to be regarded less as concern for justice and past events than for security in the future. Those convicted by Chinese judicial process would not have been convicted by British law, so 'the memorialist (Li himself) would respectfully pray your gracious Majesties, as an exceptional instance of humanity . . . to deign to accord the request of the British Minister, and as an act of indulgence to consider the possibility of granting remission of their sentences.' Amnesty for all involved! A proclamation would prevent a repetition of the grievance. His ingenuity had secured a treaty which went little further than the Treaty of Tientsin while confusing its issues and at little cost to China. W A P Martin even called it 'a triumph for Li

Hung-chang'. Travel by foreigners in inland China had been legalised in 1858 and in 1876 was only made less hazardous. But this fact was of no small consequence to the travellers. When all was settled and the civilities followed, Li came aboard Admiral Ryder's flagship with a retinue of two hundred; 'his majestic height, his dignified bearing, his piercing eyes that seemed to see everything at once . . . made an ineffaceable impression'.

China ratified the convention immediately, on September 17, but the British government declined to do so. One clause left a loophole to restrict the import of opium. Nine years later, when further concessions were extorted from China on July 18, 1885, exempting opium from *likin* tax, Britain at last ratified the whole, on May 6, 1886. Guilt had been exposed. As Samuel Wells Williams maintained, the truth lay bare: the Bhamo route was wanted for opium, the insidious evil about which Henry Soltau had written and which Hudson Taylor published in *China's Millions* to throw light on the scandal of its growing grip on Burma as well as China.[21]

The imperial envoy appointed to London and Paris, Guo Songdao, arrived in London on January 21, 1877, and on February 8 in Sir Thomas Wade's presence presented his letters of credence and the one of regret (p 68). Wade had left China for good. Two years later Guo was replaced by 'Marquis' Zeng, the son of Zeng Guofan, but not before his own province of Hunan had vented its wrath on him by burning down his family home. For a time feeling against the convention was high. Zhang Zhitong (Chang Chih-t'ung), literary chancellor of Sichuan and one of China's most revered scholars, presented a memorial to the throne giving eight cogent reasons why China should go to war with Britain without delay. Too late, the die was cast.

'Not too soon and not too late' *September–October 1876*

The Kunming enquiry failed as James Cameron made his first journey in Anhui. Grosvenor, Baber and Davenport reached Bhamo a week after Joseph Adams and the Harveys arrived there on May 15, 1876. As it happened, the day after Sir Thomas Wade reached Yantai to confront Li Hongzhang, Hudson Taylor named the party of men and women with whom he himself would travel to China. Louise Desgraz and the five young women left on September 5 to join the French Mail at Marseilles, and William Rudland on a different ship. After another painful parting from Jennie and the children, Hudson Taylor followed on the 8th with Robert J Landale and W A Wills (who later joined the BMS). He intended to be back in Britain within a year. The fact of the Chefoo negotiations was known, but whether their outcome would be war or peace hung in the balance. The despatch of the Flying Squadron to China had looked ominous.

Eugene Stock, who on December 21, 1875, became editor of CMS publications and already respected Hudson Taylor, was to write admiringly of the formation of his team of pioneers during the eighteen months of political uncertainty, so that when agreement was reached they were almost all ready to enter their promised land, the unoccupied provinces.[22] R J Landale, 'a gentleman of means and education', was the son of a lawyer of the Supreme Court in Edinburgh, and a graduate of Oxford University who had become interested in China through a visit by C G Moore, the theologian candidate. Being able to pay all his own expenses and, apparently, on his father's advice going to see what he was embarking on before committing himself to membership of the CIM, Landale accompanied Hudson Taylor without obligation on either side, but with mutual appreciation and deepening confidence. Hunan, Guizhou and Guangxi were to be the scene of his daring travels.[23]

Seeming disaster marked the beginning of their journey. Hudson and Jennie had been up all night finishing essential work before he set off at 7.00 a.m. At the Gare du Nord, Paris, his most precious document box containing all the work he intended to do on the voyage was left behind. Sent on by the next French mail it reached him a month after he arrived in China, but by then his journey had been the enforced holiday he needed. He had time to write frequently to Jennie, using terms he had been unable to use while Maria's memory remained vivid. The Messageries Maritimes ship, third class, was luxury! Table-cloths and napkins! Linoleum on the cabin floors! How could anyone say it was not good enough? Had the Council understood about keeping funds flowing? 'Ask (them) to remit to China all they can spare.' The heat in the Red Sea, compounded by engine room heat and smells, seemed to emphasise the realisation that nothing ahead would be easy. '"Lo! I come to do Thy will, O God". This is our one duty, one privilege, is it not, darling – "to *do* Thy will" – you . . . in staying at home, I in leaving you.' 'Day by day, one hour at a time, let us do our Master's work.' In the South China Sea Hudson Taylor wrote that the women were to go to Yangzhou, but the publication of their movements must be avoided. Wade and the Foreign Office were still sensitive about the CIM. George Soltau had been negotiating with them since 'Jackson's matter' and 'by undertaking for all our missionaries that they should not appeal to our Consuls for help in any missionary difficulty. On this ground our passports are to be given to us as before. This does not preclude us from getting any help we can from the Mandarins.' He thought of first taking Louise and the girls to Hangzhou and from there to Yangzhou. A glimpse of the thriving indigenous church at Hangzhou would set a standard for them at the outset. The Shanghai newspapers published only the passenger lists of foreign river steamers, so leaving by canal boat or Chinese river boat would not be noticed. Nothing so leisurely awaited them. Not too soon and not too late, imperial proclamations in the farthest corners of the empire by guaranteeing protection invited entry. The day for which Robert Morrison and Samuel Dyer, Maria's father, had so longed at last had dawned – and the teams were ready to go, were well on their way. 'He who holds the Key of David, who opens and no man shuts . . . will open hearts as well as doors,' Hudson Taylor declared.[24]

Learning his limitations[25] *October–December 1876*

Letters waiting for Hudson Taylor at Hong Kong and again at Shanghai when he reached there on October 22, gave him the gist of the situation in China. 'In a word, I find matters better than I expected on the whole,' he told Jennie. For although Catherine (Duncan) Stronach's illness and Henry Taylor's dejection over his expulsion from Henan needed prompt action, good news outweighed the problems. 'An expedition to explore Tibet is to go next year. Yunnan *may* be opened within five years.' John McCarthy, writing from Zhenjiang to put him in the picture, went out of his way to compliment J J Turner on his attitude to the Chinese and growing grasp of the language. 'He is thoroughly at one with your views . . . Easton is fit and anxious to go forward. . . . If we can, we ought to go forward now.' (The phrase 'to go foward' was current for 'advance' and became a Mission cliché, still extant.) McCarthy himself would wait for Hudson Taylor but, he added, 'I am hoping that ere you arrive, there will be men on the way to the three northern provinces.' The imperial proclamations should already have been placarded in every city of the empire, and men should not delay in making the most of them. Easton and Parker were off to

Gansu, King and Budd to Shaanxi, and Turner and James to Shanxi with the good Nanjing teacher, 'Mr' Yao (i.e. Yao Xianseng), who had 'travelled widely in north China and lived long in Honan.' Nicoll had rented a house in Yichang, and Cameron was joining him from Anhui. A second letter on the heels of McCarthy's first reported the departure of the three teams each with two Chinese colleagues.

Frederick Baller was in Shanghai to meet the ship, and escorted Louise and the young women straight to Yangzhou, while Hudson Taylor and Landale, after two days of consular business obtaining passports, joined McCarthy, 'a great comfort', at Zhenjiang. Hardly had he arrived there than Hudson Taylor went down with 'enteritis', his 'thorn in the flesh', and was unfit to take normal food until mid-November or to leave Zhenjiang until a month later. Forced inactivity gave him the chance to think 'with mounting excitement' over the great things that were beginning to happen.

Ill or not, he had to take what came his way. So soon after her re-marriage in February to William Gavin Stronach of the British consular service, Catherine Duncan was dying in Zhenjiang.[26] Being a consul's wife had made her no less a missionary. As Hudson Taylor 'comforted her last hours', he told Jennie, she 'begged that (her daughter) Millie might be brought up with our children and I acceded to this – her dying request, uttered when the power of speech was almost gone.' He himself conducted the funeral, and her husband took Millie home. 'Make them welcome (even) if not convenient, for love of me, darling', he wrote. And six or seven-year-old Mary Jane Bowyer Duncan became one of the Taylor family for George Duncan's sake and for another reason: in April the consul's father, John Stronach of the LMS, the closest friend of Maria's father Samuel Dyer, had left China 'to return home for the first time since entering on mission work' thirty-eight years previously. Progress had appeared slow, but in his lifetime immense strides had been and were being made.[27]

Administrative problems that needed Hudson Taylor's attention were as varied as they were many. Word came that Fanny Jackson was having eclamptic convulsions as in previous pregnancies. There was nothing he could do to help. 'I cannot get about as I used to do,' he confessed to Rudland. But she survived again, for a few more years. Horace Randle, 'a very dear fellow' who had come to China with George Parker, was having epileptic fits. He had been so long without them that as a candidate it had not occurred to him to mention his past history. Yet he was to be an effective missionary for eighteen years before resigning in 1894.

Christian Chinese needing Christian wives, few of whom were available, looked as always to the mission schools for help. The right to arrange the marriages of pupils was by Chinese custom included in the contract which parents signed when leaving them in school until they reached a marriageable age. Only one, Shao Mianzi, was nearing that time. Sympathising with the Christian young men and widowers, Hudson Taylor took steps to enlarge the girls' schools under Louise Desgraz' control in Yangzhou and Zhenjiang. And when famine in the north led to hundreds of refugees flocking to the unaffected areas, he authorised the admission of two hundred more at Mission expense.

Josiah Jackson was keeping out of trouble, but problem missionaries occupied their director's thoughts: 'Those who cannot wait to get married' in spite of promising to give two uninterrupted years to gaining the language and experience first; or those who 'have forgotten that they undertook to wear Chinese clothes, and for whom everything and everyone is wrong.' C G Moore was rightly wrestling with his own hesitations and objections in London, before coming to China.

> You have referred to the individuality of your theological views . . . [Hudson Taylor wrote] but you know our platform and on the doctrines which we all need to hold . . . you have, I believe, no difficulty. Other points are of great importance, I admit, but we as a Mission do not attempt to limit ourselves to this or that view. Each member must be responsible to God for what he holds and in his own sphere of labour teaches. And even on the question of (Chinese) dress we only require a candidate to determine whether he will wear it or not, because harmonious action demands all working together to act alike (in any given area). [Moore should get ordained before leaving Britain but not discuss it with the Council 'as they are of diverse views on the subject'.] The native dress proves a real trial to some. . . . Are you prepared to bear it for Jesus' sake? The work we are attempting to do in the interior *cannot* be done without it.

He must also be willing to be isolated from fellow-Christians, and to have to change his location from time to time. Too many missionaries had settled down to static institutions.

To Edward Fishe, at last game not only to return to China but as a pioneer, 'The way to permanent residence in the interior may or may not *soon* open up. But itinerant work is *now* possible.' Would

Fishe join the Judds at Wuchang and alternate with Charles Judd in country travelling, going first to Guizhou? His answer to this fateful question was 'Yes', and he, Annie and the children sailed off to China. Another missionary, who made disparaging remarks about the Messageries Maritimes ships and himself chose to travel by a one-class ship in greater comfort though he had come from a 'working-class' background, roused Hudson Taylor's ire so that he exploded to Jennie, 'It makes me feel angry to hear such wicked and ungrateful remarks.' Henry Taylor, a casualty of heroic reconnoitring in the face of death-threats, still showed the stamina he looked for in everyone – that Hudson Taylor himself had shown from his earliest days in China. To give time and friendship to Henry Taylor was time well spent, while he himself was learning that he could not always be up at the front.

'Like a bombshell scattering us'[28] *October 1876–77*

With the arrival of Hudson Taylor in China an explosion of life and activity in the China Inland Mission took the foreign community by surprise. In the last three months of 1876 and through 1877, 'a most eventful year' because of so much happening at once, most of the eighteen pioneers travelled in most of the nine distant provinces and put down roots in some (Appendix 5). Within four months of the signing of the Chefoo Convention, six had been entered. In spite of writing 'I cannot run about as before', Hudson Taylor himself visited all but four of the Mission locations and outposts, scattered between Wenzhou in southern Zhejiang and Wuhan far up the Yangzi, before returning to Britain. With his recovery from enteritis, in mid-November, the box of documents left in Paris arrived, and from then on he was fully stretched. From time to time too many claims on his strength drew from him such groans as 'I have four times the work I can do'. Between him and John McCarthy was a secret of which even Jennie was in the dark – a scheme which might well have been banned or made too dangerous had it become known. The Convention had flung open the remotest regions of the empire, but for how long? A sense of urgency drove him to encourage more daring enterprises by his half-trained men than would otherwise have been thought wise. But McCarthy was a seasoned traveller in China.

For home consumption he sent a report of progress so far. His zest was apparent. Members of the CIM were on their way into six

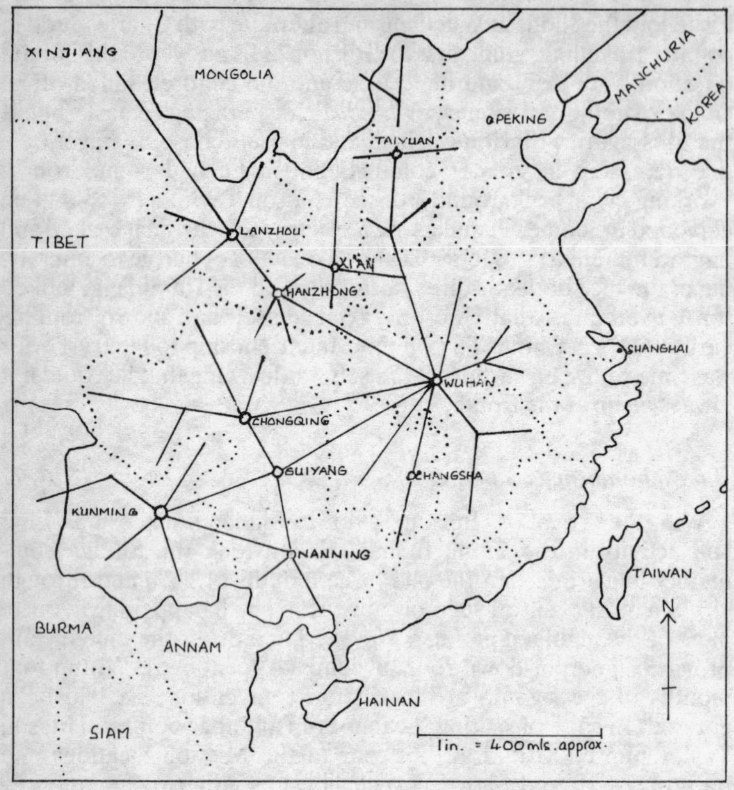

'LIKE A BOMBSHELL SCATTERING US'

'fresh' provinces. Only Guangxi had no one yet assigned to it, and Yunnan (see also maps, pp 123, 210) was barred to Stevenson and Soltau by the British government of India, not by China. An epidemic in Bhamo had carried off a Catholic priest and the hostile Burmese governor, but the latter's successor proved friendly, helped them to secure their building site and gave them a free hand to travel with friendly Kachin chiefs into the hills.[29] The British Resident could not deny them the right when they promised not to cross the frontier.

On November 3 Stevenson and Soltau set off. When John Stevenson had expressed an interest in the Kachins, someone in Rangoon had retorted, 'You should see what sharp spears and knives they carry'. But when they penetrated the jungle and for six weeks slept on earthen floors in the villages and met unfamiliar tribesmen without a qualm, they were not threatened but protected by those weapons. From near Matang they looked across the border into the plain of Longchuan and beyond to the mountains of Yunnan. 'The (Kachins) I look upon as our best allies,' Stevenson reported, and the Burmese governor 'said publicly that we were at perfect liberty to come and go from the hills as we please and when we please.' Yet, lest they hazard the hopes of the opium 'trade' from India, they were to be fettered by the British for four more years, until 1880. In Shanghai Hudson Taylor asked his friend Walter Medhurst, the consul-general, if he could obtain passports for Stevenson and Soltau such as McCarthy and some others had, valid for the eighteen provinces, so that they would be ready when the ban was lifted.[30] When the chargé d'affaires in Peking consulted India, they were thwarted once again. Yunnan in the far south-west and its twelve million inhabitants would have to wait.

Not so the north-west. The great provinces of Shaanxi and Gansu, with populations of about fifteen and sixteen millions, were accessible, after strenuous journeys across hot dusty plains and cold mountain ranges (map p 80). Shaanxi, the size 'of England and Wales combined, or the State of Nebraska', is broken by hills into three distinct regions. A high tableland in the north, around the city of Yan'an (Yenan) was inhabited by poor cave-dwelling immigrants from many provinces. In the central plain or valley of the great Wei River lies ancient Xi'an, intermittently the capital of China for a thousand years, home of the Nestorian tablet and, nearby, the vast tomb of Qin Shihuangdi (Ch'in Shih Huang Ti) with its army of terracotta figures, and a host of other historical treasures. In the north-eastern segment of the walled Ming city of Xi'an, 50,000 Manchus had their homes.

In the south of Shaanxi, beyond the Qinling (Ts'in-ling) 'mountains' (rising to 11,000 feet, but in reality a tangled, sparsely inhabited mass) are the Hanzhong plain and city, more akin to Sichuan than to the rest of Shaanxi. Access from the Yangzi valley was slow but comfortable, by boat up the Han River with rocky rapids the worst hazard. But to reach the Xi'an plain involved leaving the Han at Xiangfan (Fancheng) or Guanghua (Laohekou) after three weeks' travel from Wuhan, and striking overland east of the Qinling mountains on foot or mounted, for three more weeks of heat, dust and privation.

Gansu lay more weeks and mountain ranges away to the west and north-west. Long and narrow, this province stretched for nine hundred miles between Mongolia and Tibetan Qinghai, from the watered, mountainous south-east through Yümen (Jade Gate) to the deserts of Xinjiang, Chinese Turkestan. Lanzhou, the provincial capital, lay five hundred miles beyond Xi'an (map p 210). The four young men and their four Chinese companions who set out together by river junk from Wuhan on November 8, 1876, to make their first acquaintance with unknown territory, preaching and selling Christian books all along the way, would not return before the end of March. George King and Charles Budd with Zhenjiang Christians named only as Yao and Zhang were to travel widely in Shaanxi, while George F Easton and George Parker made for Lanzhou with Zhen, a Zhenjiang man, and the Yangzhou evangelist Zhang. King had only been up the river with Baller. All was new to the rest.[31]

Before they set out, Hudson Taylor had given Easton a piece of advice from his own experience. Learn to recognise official and merchant couriers on the boats and roads and see where they spend the nights. Such inns are dependable. Once, indeed, he himself had entered Hangzhou after the gates were closed at dusk, by hanging on to the rope thrown from the city wall to a courier (Book 4, p 391). Easton found that the couriers often had rented rooms for their own use in private homes, a useful tip for constant travellers.

Because these first evangelistic journeys are historic in the planting of the great Chinese Church, they deserve our close attention. Altogether they left the Han River above Laohekou at the end of February and hired baggage and riding mules for the mountain journey to Xi'an, preaching and selling books in every town and market they passed through. While the novice missionaries could do little themselves, they listened and learned all the time from the evangelists, and soon were carrying a full share of the work. 'The roads are shockingly bad; we have walked the whole distance, about 22 miles,' Easton wrote. In every place of any size in which they looked, the imperial edict about foreign travellers was in evidence. Here and there 'the officials issued it after our arrival, and were very polite to us.' Xi'an was reached on December 20, and only when their passports had been examined were the foreigners admitted to the city, to preach with good attention each day. There they parted, the Gansu team pressing on, to enter the province on December 28, and King, Budd and their companions setting out on a month of travelling and preaching on the Xi'an plain.

Two by two, always one Chinese with one Westerner, and a pack mule loaded with books, the pairs meeting occasionally at prearranged rendezvous, they covered the north-eastern region of Tongguan (map p 413), Chengcheng, Tongchuan and Sanyuan, returning to Xi'an on January 26. After a few days they tackled the cities west of the capital (map below), but found at the first (probably Xianyang) that 'some of the literary men had been pasting up printed placards well fitted to inflame the minds of the people against us and our work'. So they wisely withdrew and went to other cities, again separating in pairs to meet at Fengxiang, near Baoji. At

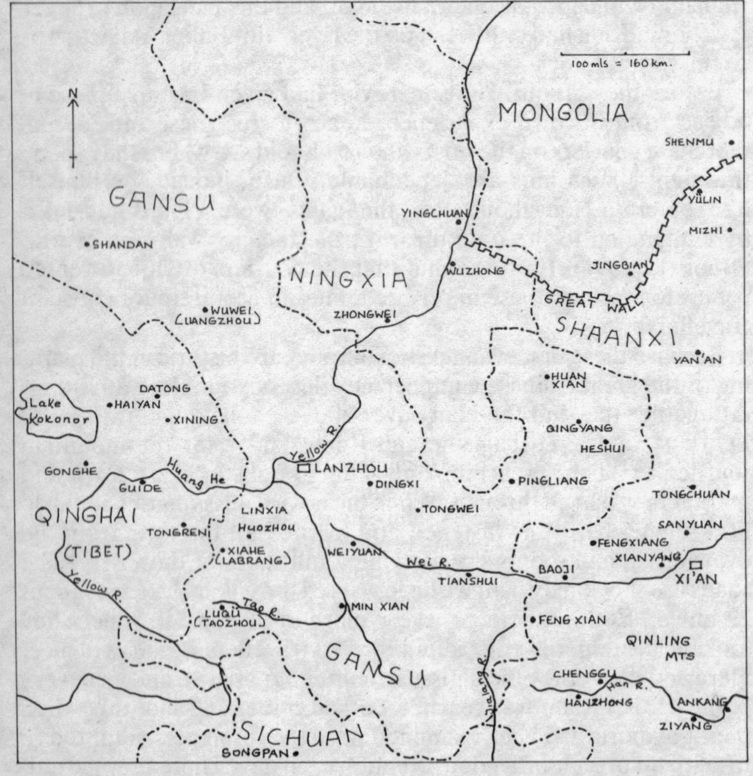

FIRST TO THE NORTH-WEST: SHAANXI AND GANSU

Qishan the 'people were kind and the authorities courteous, as we find them at most places'. In this way they worked until the end of February, when they made a quick journey back to Laohekou, reaching Wuhan on March 24 and Zhenjiang, to report to Hudson Taylor, on April 4, five months after setting out. No one was playing at it. This was evangelism on the grand scale, however fleeting the impact on any single community.

Entering Gansu for the first time on December 28 or 29 by the Pingliang road, Easton, Parker and their friends met with large audiences of well-behaved people to whom not only the gospel but the common terms for God and religious ideas seemed entirely new. But if the number of books they bought gave a clue they seemed interested.[32] Pingliang was almost equally populated by Muslims and men from Hunan, one-time soldiers, but again they gave good attention to the preaching. After three days they started for Lanzhou; on January 5, over the hills to Longde (now in Ningxia) and Huining, where they were almost mobbed for books; past an old bed of the Huang He (Yellow River) and ruins of the Great Wall, to enter Lanzhou on January 20, 1876. 'The very first and only Protestant missionaries who have ever visited the place – the capital of a vast and important province, and the highway [the Silk Road] to regions beyond – find *two* Roman Catholic places of worship with (at least) one resident priest', exclaimed Hudson Taylor when he read their report. If only the gospel of justification by faith in Christ and his finished work of atonement for sinners who believe was preached, unobscured by Roman accretions! What was wrong with the Church? Christians were asleep. The eighteen were a drop in the bucket.

> I could at once locate fourteen more brethren with great advantage and designate five more [he wrote to Jennie]; and six sisters could also have immediate and useful employment. May the Lord give us grace to be faithful, so that He can entrust us with these twenty-five workers, and with all the funds required for the whole work.[33]

Expansion of the Mission must be closely related to facilities for absorbing them, not abstractly visionary. Experienced colleagues to train them, and teams for them to join as novices, must be available. They were. Then more must come, and God who sent them would provide for their needs.

In Lanzhou the stock of books and cash in hand were running low. Easton and Parker could not stay more than a week, though well-received by the mixed population of migrants from several provinces, including many Peking merchants. They started homeward on the 27th, travelling through Weiyuan and some towns on market day, thronged with eight to ten thousand people, the ideal opportunity for preaching. That their stock of books was exhausted seemed tragic. On February 9 they reached Tianshui (Ts'in-chou), a city made up of six small townships unified by one main three-mile street. Then on through 'mountains very grand and majestic, and scenery really beautiful' to re-enter Shaanxi on February 22 and, with scarcely a diary comment, to brave the rapids on the upper Han River, past Hanzhong (map p 210), trans-shipping at Laohekou and Wuhan, to reach Zhenjiang and Hudson Taylor on April 9, one year since George Parker left Britain and eighteen months since Easton sailed!

Hudson Taylor himself, arriving at Shanghai in 1854 at the age of twenty-one, with no known friends in China, had begun his active work after a few months spent in learning Chinese, and had travelled often alone 'over the treaty wall'. Twenty-three years later he had confidence in his young men and trusted God to see them through these journeys, many hundreds of miles removed from each other and human aid.

The struggle for Henan[34] *January–May 1877*

Cheered by his weeks with Hudson Taylor, Henry Taylor returned to Wuhan, to wait for a Christian man named Dai, whom they had sent into Henan to assess the attitude of the literati at Queshan. He arrived on January 17 with a good report (which proved to be mistaken) and on the 27th Henry Taylor left without George Clarke (deputising at Wuchang for Charles Judd) but with a brave Christian named Chu as his companion. On arrival at Queshan they found the rented house occupied by a family installed by the literati, an ominous sign; all their possessions removed by the instigator of the opposition; and the magistrate unwilling to displease these opponents by helping the foreigner. 'All who have called on me have expressed surprise at seeing us back again, and consider us persons of great courage', Taylor wrote to Clarke. They told him about the beatings inflicted on his friends after he and Clarke left Queshan in October (p 65) and the ringleader came and offered to return his passport for a ransom of two hundred ounces of silver. 'Of course we refused.' Mr Hu, the Chinese doctor who had

had fifty blows on the hand, seemed unafraid to visit them. Although another riot was planned and the day fixed, it had not happened when Henry Taylor wrote to Hudson Taylor,

> I hold on my way only by the grace of God, and the belief that He has called me to open up Ho-nan to the Gospel. . . . One of the ring-leaders came in today and abused us . . . We hear this evening that they are determined to kill the foreigner, and that the emperor will promote them for so doing. 'Behold, Lord, their threatenings, and grant unto Thy servants that with all boldness they may speak Thy word.' . . . The young scholar [friend of their teacher] who received the fifty blows [on the mouth] last year is doing all he can to get us another house. [And four days later to Elizabeth Judd], All hope of success is gone. The whole city is in excitement. . . . Let Mr Taylor know . . . The rumours are of the worst kind. 'God is our refuge and strength . . .'

Yet Henry Taylor and Chu were still in Queshan six weeks later, had rented a different house and were about to move in when Taylor reported again:

> The opposition is very strong and the mandarin is one with the gentry . . . determined to drive us from the place . . . I sink beneath the burden. I almost despair of success . . . Still, I cannot dishonour my God . . . The literati hired a few hundred men who surrounded the house – created a disturbance and threatened the landlord's life; he came terror-stricken to us beseeching us to shield him.
>
> [While Henry Taylor was at the magistrate's *yamen* seeking justice] a messenger came with tidings that our house was surrounded by a mob and that my servant had been beaten very severely – which proved to be the case – so that we have no alternative but to leave . . . I would take a long (preaching) journey but I am too weak, being unstrung in body and mind.

Hudson Taylor had advised 'a conciliatory policy' in Henan: 'if they persecute you in one city, flee to another.' To withdraw might have been wiser than to make a brave trial of strength, but who is to criticise such tenacity? On May 12 Taylor and Chu arrived back at Wuhan, 'utterly sad', and inconsolable among all the comings and goings of the other teams. Hudson Taylor sent him as far as he could from the scene of his distress, to the peaceful, thriving church at Qü Xian on the Qiantang River in Zhejiang (map p 397). There he could see the second stage of 'occupation', a spontaneous Christian expansion into Jiangxi province led by an indefatigable Captain Yü.

Arthur Douthwaite would be the right man to deal gently with his broken spirit. Less than a year later Henry Taylor and George Clarke left Wuhan again (on Taylor's sixth attempt) with famine relief supplies for Henan, glad to have what Clarke called 'a glorious opportunity of exhibiting the *grace* of our Lord Jesus Christ.'

Long treks to Shanxi[35] *October 1876–January 1878*

At the time of Henry Taylor's first expulsion in October 1876, when the two teams were starting for Shaanxi and Gansu – just as Hudson Taylor arrived back in China – the first penetration by the CIM into Shanxi was also made. In 1869 one of Alexander Wylie's colporteurs named Wellman, and Alexander Williamson with Jonathan Lees of the LMS, had entered Shanxi selling for the Bible Societies, but until 1876 no mission had attempted to settle.

J J Turner, after ten months in China, and Francis James, after only seven months, left Zhenjiang on October 18 and Nanjing on the 23rd, on an epic first journey of 1,700 miles with 'the first-rate Nanjing teacher' Yao and a Chinese evangelist and 3,000 Gospels, 1,300 small books and many tracts.

Crossing the Yangzi at Nanjing they hired pack-mules and trekked mile upon mile through countryside and towns still ravaged by the Taiping rebellion of a decade earlier, but suffering again from drought and famine. Hundreds of destitute people were making their way southwards to find food. At Huaiyuan near Bengbu (map p 217) on October 29 they hired a boat, up the Guo River to Bo Xian, and there hired two carts to take them two hundred miles through Henan. They crossed the Yellow River near Kaifeng, 'a broad and rapid stream', wider than the Yangzi at Zhenjiang, by a large flat-bottomed ferry-boat, a barge carrying two carts, forty mules and horses, some cattle and sixty men, some with loads, rowed (probably) by a dozen standing oarsmen. At a busy town a few miles from the Shanxi border they engaged donkeys to climb the 'almost wall-like ascent' of the Taihang mountains to reach 'Tsechou', now called Jincheng, on the south-eastern uplands of Shanxi.

A mental picture of the province will colour the events we are coming to. Moated throughout its western flank and half its southern border by the south-flowing, silt-laden Yellow River, Shanxi is guarded on the east by the great rampart of the Taihang range. Only here and there could roads of any size break through these walls.

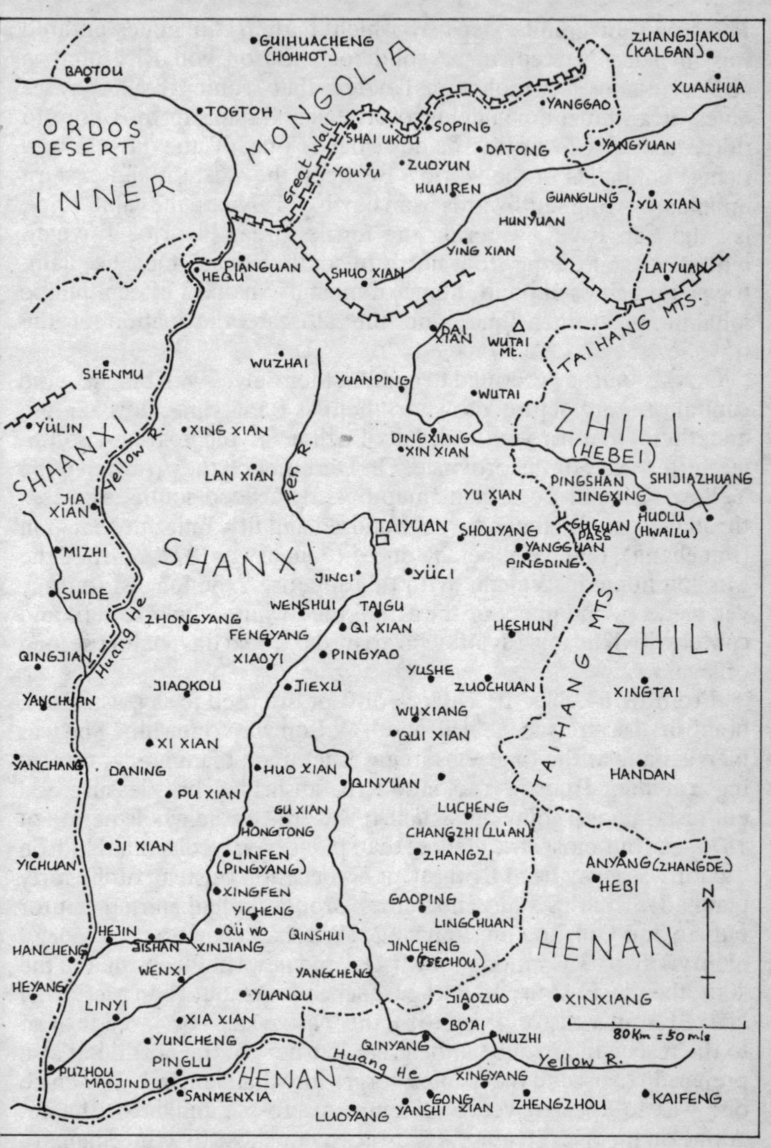

LONG TREKS TO SHANXI

The 'road' of granite steps by which Turner and James entered was in places carved in the solid rock. Baron von Richtofen, a geologist and geographer, estimated that 'some 13,500 square miles of anthracite coalfields with seams varying from twenty to thirty feet in thickness' made Shanxi 'one of the largest and richest coalfields in the world'. Between the western and eastern uplands, flowing southwards from north of Taiyuan, the capital city, lay the Fen River, watering the fertile Great Plain of Taiyuan, a hundred miles long from north to south. Throughout the plain, towns and cities abound, home of most of Shanxi's fifteen million inhabitants at that time, and the ultimate destination of the travellers.

On this journey they had to content themselves with reaching the capital of a prefecture known to them as P'ing-yang, now Linfen, and there to turn southward to Puzhou at the extreme south-western corner of the province. On December 8 they recrossed the Yellow River at Tongguan (map p 413), headed south-eastwards through western Henan for six hundred and fifty miles to Xiangfan (Fancheng), on December 28, and on January 8, 1877, reached the Mission home in Wuhan. With this appetiser, the longest journey yet made by members of the CIM, they wanted only to refit and confer with Hudson Taylor, who arrived the next day, before setting off again.[36]

'From 1876–1880 Mr. Taylor's advent, we used to say, was like a bombshell scattering us,' Elizabeth Wilson was to recall.[37] She was in Wuchang at the time, observing team upon team going, returning, catching Hudson Taylor's spirit, absorbing his pleasure and enthusiasm, and going out again. It was true of the whole period of 1876–80, but most strikingly of the sixty-seven weeks that Hudson Taylor was away from Britain on this occasion (instead of the forty planned). Charles Judd and James Broumton had started out for Hunan and Guizhou on January 2. (We shall come to their story.) Henry Taylor was waiting for Mr Dai and news of Queshan. On the 20th, the day Easton and Parker reached Lanzhou, John McCarthy arrived from a pastoral visit to all the Yangzi stations,[38] ready to go to the rescue of anyone on the great journeys to the north, but also preparing to ascend the Yangzi gorges into Sichuan and, though no one was to know it yet, to attempt to cross Yunnan to Bhamo. Alone on the river steamer, Hudson Taylor chose to write enigmatically even to Jennie, rather than risk letting the cat out of the bag,

> to request *very* especial prayer for him . . . as he may be in urgent need of it, and to continue *every day* till you hear further. If there be danger . . . McCarthy will be in it. . . . No less than six or seven of the unoccupied provinces are being simultaneously attempted, and there can be no such extensive evangelisation unattended with danger.

The risks had to be taken; the golden opportunity of a lifetime might not last; the literati might reject what Li Hongzhang had done, and repeat Henry Taylor's treatment everywhere.[39]

Hudson Taylor himself undertook to supervise the work in Anhui during McCarthy's absence, so they were conferring together late in the evenings. He was aware of these being momentous days and of being an instrument of God. 'He . . . is giving me very important work to do,' he told Jennie on the day McCarthy left. And in more than one letter he said that news of the old work and the new, of Christians standing firm and idolaters turning to Christ, made his heart 'sing for joy'. Longing to be with her again, he was convinced that he was still needed in China. The only hope of getting away seemed to be if Benjamin and Amelia would come to take his place as advisers to so many young men and women. Perhaps to telegraph for them would be more effective than writing! It was a passing whim, even a lapse of judgment which calm consideration led him to abandon.[40]

If the roads were not impassable through heavy snow and rains, except in Henan and Shanxi where the drought showed no sign of breaking, Turner and James would have got away already. But at last they did, on February 10. After they had gone Hudson Taylor revealed that for the third time since reaching Wuhan he was suffering gallstone colic. Three weeks earlier he had told Jennie, 'I am quite worn out . . . The pressure is too great, so many coming and going', with all that was involved of calculating and consulting, arranging with Chinese merchant firms for cash to be drawn in distant cities, waterproofing and roping baggage, bargaining with boatmen and paying wages. He found a regular despatch by courier every five days from Wuhan to Chongqing, and on to Guiyang and back. But did she know the hymn 'Jesus, I am resting, resting in the joy of what Thou art'? (except that he misquoted it). A new discovery, it had gripped his mind, echoing and re-echoing inescapably. So when the hubbub ended and he was quietly sailing down the Yangzi in a little houseboat again, he could say that the time in

Wuhan had 'greatly benefited' his health. McCarthy was heading for Sichuan, but in preparing material for the June *China's Millions* Hudson was taking excerpts from T T Cooper's *Travels of a Pioneer of Commerce*, to show 'what *Rome* is *doing* while we are *dreaming*'.

Turner and James had only been gone a few days, this time to settle in Shanxi permanently or for as long as possible, when their boat up the Han River struck a rock. Their books were ruined, their personal baggage damaged, and they were set on by pirates, but no lives were lost, so they went on. Hiring a large wheelbarrow to carry the remaining goods and each of them riding it by turns, they hoped to make a quick journey to Tongguan. But the barrow men cheated them repeatedly until they paid them off and hired a trundling ox-cart to pass through the central Henan plains. Crossing the Yellow River at Maojindu (between Sanmenxia and Pinglu) they travelled due north.

> The journey . . . has been nearly all through a famine-stricken district. . . . There has been no rain for two or three years. There is no grass. And the loose sandy soil is dried to powder, which drives about in clouds, . . . In some places many have already died of starvation. The beggars are dreadful. They go about in crowds, principally women and children. They surround the passer-by and kneel down and cry for a cash . . . These starving people cry in real earnest for a morsel of food . . . (or) holding out their basins in mute appeal.[41]

Only close to the rivers was any green vegetation to be seen.

'Passing through Pingyang and fifteen other cities', at last they reached Taiyuan on April 24 and made themselves known, received visitors, and on the 28th set out on an evangelistic itinerary in the great plain for two months. Twenty miles away they found the small town of Jinci with a spring of pure water, and made a good inn their base while they worked to acquire the Shanxi dialect. But towards mid-June their supply of cash was running low and it was time to lay in a new stock of books and Bibles. So, while Francis James moved into Taiyuan, J J Turner travelled by the main highway to Peking, and by ship from Tianjin to Shanghai. By then Hudson Taylor was visiting the southern region of Zhejiang and asked Turner to meet him in Wenzhou.[42]

Back in Taiyuan after an absence of two and a half months, first he and then James fell ill with typhoid fever. James hovered between life and death for several days, but by September 24 was

FULL STEAM AHEAD: A LONG-DISTANCE WHEELBARROW

strong enough to move to quiet Jinci to recuperate through October and into November. Then, returning to Taiyuan, James seemed well enough for the long journey first by cart to Xiangfan (Fancheng) on the Han River and on by boat to Wuhan. The famine had become so appalling that mobilising foreign aid had become their first priority. Passing through the worst areas would allow them to observe and describe conditions, and after raising funds to return with others to give what aid they could. So on November 28, 1877, they left Taiyuan – two days before Timothy Richard arrived on his first visit – and reached Wuhan on January 22, 1878, eleven months and nine days since leaving there. Both of them wrote gruesome accounts of the famine and Turner returned to Shanxi in March with companions and relief funds. James was still too weak.[43]

CHAPTER THREE

THE TENTACLES REACH OUT 1876–77

The lure of the west *December 1876–March 1877*

The lure of the west and south-west was as powerful as that of the north-west and north. Yueyang, gateway to the anti-foreign province of Hunan, had expelled Judd in 1875 (Book 5, p 434), and it seemed wise to occupy receptive provinces before challenging the chief source of inflammatory agitation so positively again. Its twenty-five millions must wait a little longer for the gospel. Judd's courage and experience were needed elsewhere for the present. But which provinces were receptive? Sichuan, the brimming rice bowl and market garden of West China with its twenty-seven millions of industrious people, drew like a magnet. Only loyalty to his mission board prevented Griffith John from adding Chongqing or Chengdu to Wuhan as his bases for intensive church planting. So he supported the CIM to the hilt. John McCarthy had an invitation from an influential, enlightened young man to visit his home at Guang'an deep in the heart of the province. He was ready to go. Beyond the well-watered plains (Sichuan means 'Four Rivers'), the mountains climbed westwards above ten thousand feet to the heights of Tibet and the 'Manzi', the 'wild', 'barbarian' tribes. South and south-westwards mountain ranges flowed in waves to join the plateau province of Yunnan ('South of the Clouds') where puffs of white cirrus hang motionless in the bluest of blue skies – as far as the Mekong and Salween chasms that moat the jungles of Burma. Throughout those ranges millions of 'minority people' of scores of different 'tribes' had their fortress homes, written off derisively as 'Lolos' by the dominant Han Chinese.[1] These were the 'barbarians' progressively forced back into the wilderness by the ever-expanding Han race.

Closer, between Hunan, Sichuan and Yunnan, the sparsely populated, unproductive turmoil of hills and valleys called Guizhou, held its own attractions. Scattered through the hills lived differing ethnic groups of Miao, the rebellious aborigines who had for decades been attacking the encroaching Han Chinese around them. Bordering Yunnan and Sichuan in the west lived about five million 'Lolos' – now called 'Yi', but who call themselves the Nosu – about equally divided between those who accepted Chinese domination and those who struggled to preserve their independence.

The great tableland of Yunnan and Guizhou, averaging five thousand feet above sea level, is tilted towards the east and south so that the main rivers flow out through Hunan to join the Yangzi, through Guangxi by the Red River to Canton, and through Indo–China. The direct route to Yunnan through Wuhan on the Yangzi was naturally up the Yuan River through Hunan and Guiyang, the capital city of Guizhou. Another major route was over the mountains from Chongqing in Sichuan. The perils of the brigand-infested overland routes and of the fierce Yangzi rapids left little to choose between them (map p 123).

Hudson Taylor had been corresponding with a unique figure in Guiyang, a Christian from Jersey named Mesny who had risen to an exalted rank in the imperial Chinese army, officially a mandarin like Charles Schmidt of Suzhou (Book 5, p 63).[2] Urging that missionaries be sent there, Mesny promised to assist them. Judd and James Broumton were to respond. (See on, p 97ff). In writing about this 'era of pioneers', K S Latourette described their exploits as 'biographical rather than institutional' – individual adventures rather than co-ordinated expeditions. Perhaps he was misled by secondary sources, for the fact that Hudson Taylor planned the nationwide strategy and worked out with each team their destination, approximate itineraries and practical details of stocks of scriptures, transport, funding and communication, is plainly evident in the manuscripts.[3]

Yichang: springboard for Sichuan[4] *August 1876–May 1877*

On August 28, 1876, George Nicoll left Wuhan by boat with evangelist Zhang, and a 'teacher', that is an educated Chinese with business ability sufficient to draw up contracts, to secure a foothold if they could at Yichang, as a base for entering Sichuan province. By the Chefoo Convention Yichang had been designated a treaty port, but no action had yet been taken and no merchants had moved there, though it was three hundred miles farther up the Yangzi from Wuhan, itself six hundred miles from Shanghai. Instead of following the Yangzi for 290 miles round two sides of a triangle, they took the short 150 mile route through the lakes to Shashi. There they made a portage to a larger junk on the Yangzi, and reached Yichang on September 16. An uncle of the teacher, acting as middleman, negotiated the rental of a house in the suburb outside the south gate of the city, and leaving the two Chinese in possession, Nicoll returned to Wuhan. 'May God allow us to keep this place in peace,' he wrote. 'The people do not want foreigners to come.'

James Cameron was to join him. Together with Jiang (Zhang) Suoliang, the Zhenjiang pastor, and two Wuhan Christians surnamed Zhang, they travelled to Shashi. This time they 'soon had a noisy crowd after (them), who were not sparing in missiles harder and more effective than foul names'. They reached Yichang on December 20, the day Easton and Parker arrived at Xi'an. As Chinese as they could be in dress and behaviour, the reception at Yichang was different. 'No one took notice of us in the streets.' Nicoll was to stay, 'to see how things would go,' while Cameron travelled in the surrounding country and up the Wushan rapids beyond Zhang his companion's home. In doing so he became the first member of the CIM to enter Sichuan.[5] Of Yichang he remarked, 'The evangelist says the (people) are well pleased to have the foreigners beside them,' a tribute to their adaptation to things

SHASHI: A BASE FOR HUNAN

Chinese. And on January 2, the day Judd and Broumton left Wuhan for Hunan and Guizhou, Nicoll wrote after walking through the city, 'I only heard the cry "foreign devil" once.' All went well, Cameron came and went, and Nicoll was left in peace to pass on the gospel to visitors and to share Jiang's preaching, so far as his grasp of the language allowed.

The Yichang 'settlement' riot — *March 1–5, 1877*

The time had come for John McCarthy to begin his secret journey with the evangelist Yang Cunling (Yang Ts'un-ling),[6] an ex-soldier, as his companion. Coming up the Yangzi from Zhenjiang in December 1876, they left Wuhan on February 2, 1877, 'in stormy, freezing

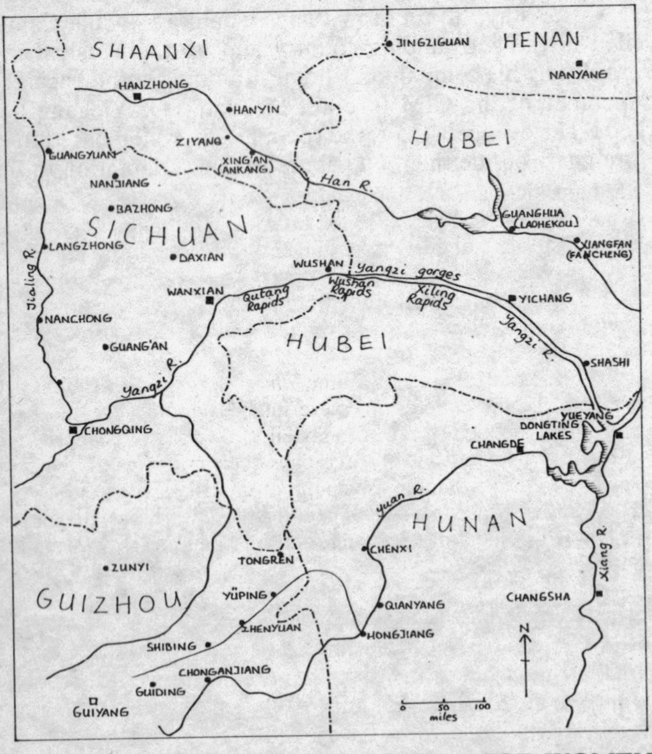

THREE RIVER ROUTES, 'SUITABLE FOR WOMEN'

weather' on snow and ice, and also taking the direct route to cut off the great bend of the Yangzi River, spent three or four days at Shashi preaching and selling books without opposition. People were friendly, but businessmen with whom they talked in those gregarious meeting places, the tea-shops, with one voice expressed their anxiety lest the development of Yichang as a port should spoil the trade of Shashi. Then moving on up the Yangzi they joined Cameron and Nicoll at Yichang on February 25.

Intending to stay only a few days while changing to a different type of boat for ascending the rapids, they walked through the city unmolested, arranged for money to be transmitted to Sichuan, and met only with friendliness. But Consul C King from Jiujiang, a vice-consul and three customs officials all in foreign clothes had arrived to survey and mark out a foreign settlement, and a violent protest was brewing. Already the customs men had been attacked. On March 22 the *North China Herald* reported,

> Some missionaries were also residing in the city . . . quietly going in and out among the people for some months. Everything seemed favourable to the consul's mission; but no sooner had negotiations been commenced . . . than the old hostility to every encroachment of the hated barbarian immediately manifested itself. The literati as usual were the instigators of the attack . . . Inflammatory placards were posted . . . reports were diligently circulated that the Foreign Powers intended to take forcible possession . . . ejecting the inhabitants, desecrating the ancestral graves, interfering with the (*fengshui*) of the city,[7] and bringing endless calamities upon the people.
>
> (The mandarins and even the *daotai* engaged in defining the territory for the concession) were insulted and maltreated by the mob. And the next step was to give notice to the missionaries, that unless they cleared out in three days their house would be pulled down, and they would be driven out at the risk of their lives. As the missionaries showed no sign of heeding these warnings, the mob was assembled by beating the gong, and an open attack was made on Saturday, March 3rd.[8]

On March 1 when the gongs had called the people to foregather at the bottom of the street, the landlady had discounted the warnings, John McCarthy noted in his diary. And as to move out would be interpreted as an admission of guilt, 'We decided to remain, come what might, to open the doors (to the public) as usual, and to tell all comers that we had nothing to do with the purchase of land, etc. We had a great rush of people apparently bent on mischief,' but calm and friendly conversation with the gift of pamphlets and the offer of books for sale convinced most that these foreigners were harmless. The prefect knew what was happening, for who could fail to hear the gongs and uproar, even before McCarthy asked him to intervene, but no one came to disperse the mob.

On March 2 more crowds assembled 'gathering in thousands at the sound of a gong' and a proclamation issued by the prefect and magistrate had no effect. McCarthy told their Christian companions they should leave while they could, for he, Cameron and Nicoll had decided to stay in the hope that doing so would win the approval of right-minded people. Not one would go; and Yang Cunling 'who was nearly killed at Fengyang Fu (on an earlier journey in North Anhui) was the most opposed of any to our moving away'. 'After a hearty prayer meeting we went to bed, commending ourselves to the care of our Heavenly Father.'

They were woken on the 3rd by the sound of the gong and 'we were told that they were coming to pull down the house'. The prefect's deputy came in his official sedan chair to remonstrate with a leading member of the literati, but the man's son turned the rabble on him. After breaking up the chair and giving the deputy a beating, they attacked the mission house, smashed down the frontage and swarmed in. To their surprise, calm, unarmed men met them and 'asked what it all meant'. 'Some were for seizing and beating us; some wished to take (our Chinese companions); but the majority, even in the midst of the uproar, shouted out that no one was to be hurt, and nothing of ours stolen . . . After they had demolished a good part of the place . . . the leaders managed to get them out.'

Very soon another 'surging, screaming mob' broke in, pillaging and destroying, until the magistrate arrived and with difficulty took control. Even so, 'there was yelling and roaring and knocking at the door. The old (mandarin) was green with fright.' Afraid that they would beat him as they had beaten the prefect's deputy, McCarthy agreed to leave the house in his care and move to a boat. The magistrate himself escorted them to the riverside and had them rowed to where the *daotai*'s gunboats were moored, sending their remaining possessions after them. McCarthy then went to see Consul King to report the facts, to explain that he had not called on him sooner simply to avoid any misunderstanding, and to insist that he did not want anyone punished on the Mission's account. At last on the 5th the viceroy, Li Hanzhang, arrived and peace was restored. 'A little Yangzhou riot' was Hudson Taylor's comment when he heard.

With so much happening in 1877 it may help us, in relating events to each other, if we glance ahead and later pick up these threads. Nicoll went down to Zhenjiang to report to Hudson Taylor, while McCarthy and Cameron stayed at Yichang in a house-boat provided (at a price) by the mandarins. On March 20 Cameron then accompanied McCarthy, his Sichuan friend Zhang, a teacher, and Yang Cunling up the Wushan gorges, as far as Wushan city in Sichuan. From there he returned to the boat at Yichang until allowed to reoccupy the house in the summer.

In his absence Charles Judd arrived on March 23 at Yichang, nearing the end of his own hazardous journey through Hunan to Guiyang and Chongqing and down the gorges; to his surprise the house was derelict and there was no sign of missionaries. He waited until the 29th before going on to Wuhan (map p 260) and on May 22 returned with Nicoll to make Yichang his own responsibility while Nicoll and Cameron continued their long-interrupted journey to occupy and evangelise the province of Sichuan.[9] Soon these early experiences were forgotten as attitudes changed and foreigners were accepted. Yet time and again, in place after place, the initial price of occupying key cities could be measured in alarms and violence. Yichang proved to be less useful as a supply base and staging post for Sichuan than had been expected, and the work there was transferred to the Presbyterian Church of Scotland.

Judd's long way to Chongqing[10] *January–March 1877*

Perhaps the most daring and dangerous journey was that taken by Charles Judd and James Broumton, through Hunan and the lawless border regions of Guizhou to Guiyang. Like all the other journeys it was to be evangelistic, which meant showing themselves openly and looking for audiences and customers for the books they had for sale. But the difference was that Judd was known and had been ejected from Yueyang, the gateway to Hunan; and on the route they planned to take, Augustus Margary (with passports from the Zongli Yamen in Peking), had been roughly handled at more than one place. He, according to Colonel Henry Yule, was 'the first Englishman to accomplish a feat that had been the object of so many ambitions'. So their journey was no light undertaking. Three Chinese companions were to work at Guiyang with Broumton, an evangelist named Chü, the colporteur Yao Shangda and a master-craftsman Sen Sifu.

Leaving Wuhan on January 2, in a small house-boat, they stopped to preach at most riverside towns and markets on the way up the Yangzi. At one place boats moored side by side stretched for a mile along the bank, showing how dense the population was, but they could not stay long to give them the gospel. At Yueyang a customs officer politely warned them not to go where there were no officials to protect them, and went into the city to tell the mandarins that they were coming.

It was eighteen months since Judd had been driven out (Book 5, p 434), but as they walked through the same city gate and into the streets, the cry was raised, 'Those foreign demons are come again. Kill them, beat them!' – 'but no one injured us'. Curses could not stop Judd. The Muslim petty officer in charge of a 'gunboat' (an armed junk with ten or twenty men) came aboard their boat saying he was under orders to escort them, and proved himself a true friend. This mandarin, named Ding Laoye had twenty small loaves of bread baked for them, and often helped foreign travellers on

YUEYANG: DOORSTEP OF HUNAN

subsequent occasions. 'We assured him that as we were not officials, but only private persons, we required no such honour.' He answered, 'The people are so fierce that (the mandarins) dare not put out' the imperial proclamation. Still the five missionaries were undeterred from preaching and selling scriptures; but as a precaution an escort of eight men stayed with them as far as the next city (maps pp 260, 267).

Their arrival at Changde at the westernmost end of the Dongting lakes on January 17 had the dramatic effect of bringing a succession of officials in full dress to call on them. 'Greater civility could not have been shown to us.' Yet something in the atmosphere decided them to move on early the next morning. No proclamations had been posted at Changde, or anywhere that they had touched at in Hunan; and it may safely be assumed that the ostentation of the visiting mandarins was directed not so much towards the foreigners as to the local literati and populace.

Tracking up rapids on the Yuan River for ten miles in unbroken succession, the safety of their boat dependent on the soundness of the plaited bamboo towing cable, they came to a narrow cleft with perpendicular rocks rising more than a hundred feet above the river. 'High up, perhaps 60 or 80 feet from the water . . . there lies a Chinese boat, fast in a cleft', probably deposited by an exceptional flash-flood, one of the hazards they faced.[11]

Augustus Margary had been protected with great difficulty from mob violence in the town of Pushi, near Chenxi, which Judd's party reached on January 27, but though they walked through the town more than once and preached at the city gate, no antagonism was shown. The fact that they were dressed not in outlandish costume but in civilised Chinese clothes could account for the difference. There they turned up a tributary to Mayang, negotiating rapids time and again. The boat was holed on a rock, but quickly repaired in the shallows, and on February 3 they crossed the border into Guizhou province – the day after McCarthy started for Sichuan, while Henry Taylor was heading for the fifth time for Queshan, and Easton and Parker were starting back from Lanzhou. At Tongren, Judd wrote, 'We heard some strange tales about the danger of our passing through Chenyuan' (four days further on). Margary's boat had been dragged ashore and burned at this city of Zhenyuan in 1875, but the phenomenon of five men handing out tracts along the mile-long main street created no disturbance. They had found that one of the boat's crew was a Christian from the LMS church in Wuhan, and the skipper was already interested in the gospel. On his own insistence the Christian boatman went all the way to Guiyang and back through Sichuan with Judd. (Now they were in the region of Alfred Bosshardt's and Arnolis Hayman's long captivity and privations at the hands of Mao's Fifth Army on the Long March of 1934–36.)

After Tongren the five had to climb on foot over the mountains, wearing local crampons, for the heavy night mists froze heavily on the rocks and trees, and when their feet could stand no more they hired mountain men with bamboo hammock chairs to carry them. The small city of Yüping had three times been burned down by rebellious Miao tribesmen and Shibing had been destroyed, but those Miao with whom the travellers had dealings were extremely hospitable. On and on they trudged through Chonganjiang and Guiding, until on February 19 they reached Guiyang, the provincial capital.

Thinking that to look at once for 'General' Mesny, the Jersey Christian married to a Chinese, might create difficulties for him, they planned to go to an inn, but Mesny was on the lookout for them.[12] The next day Broumton wrote,

> So here we are, ensconced in a beautiful house, where we are invited to remain as long as we please; our host offers us also a house that he owns in the city, or one in the country (thirty miles distant near a market town). He believes that the people there are ripe for the gospel.

In keeping with the Mission's strategy, they chose the city property on a hillock close to a busy thoroughfare, a site with tumbledown buildings on it. That mattered little. They moved into two habitable rooms, content to use an abundance of debris to create one tolerable house.

Mesny had told all his mandarin friends that the party were coming, so a stream of high-ranking visitors 'to whom he helps us to give the message of the Gospel' kept them busy. James Broumton had expressed the wish to live among the Chinese at Guiyang without a fellow-countryman, so that he might more quickly pick up the local dialect. He had his wish. He would be eight hundred miles from his nearest mission colleague, but for the present in Mesny he had an influential friend, and in his colleague Chü, the son of a prefect (so it appears), a useful mentor. John McCarthy was to visit him briefly at the end of May, just before Mesny left, but otherwise it was to be three months before the next travellers (Clarke, Fishe and Landale) joined him. After ten days as Mesny's guest Judd took his leave. To Hudson Taylor he explained,

> We passed through greater danger in Hunan than we were then aware of. There is a secret society in that province, headed by fifteen of the greatest men in China, formed for the purpose of (excluding) any foreigner . . . I have seen their private circular. I shall therefore, DV, return by way of Sichuan.[13]

Leaving on March 2 he and the Christian boatman reached Chongqing on the fourteenth (the first member of the Mission to arrive there) and at once hired a small boat to descend the gorges to Yichang. The providential presence of the boatman from the rapids of Hunan soon became apparent.[14] On March 17 they were overtaken by three armed men in another boat, one of whom drew his sword saying, 'You are a Romanist and we are determined to exterminate you.' Another boatload of a dozen men with swords and guns then arrived, arrested Judd and took him and his companion back upstream to the village where they had stopped to preach earlier in the day. 'One man with a drawn sword sat close by me (frequently feeling the edge of it), and several others in front each with his own weapon.' Judd's passport and a copy of the imperial edict issued by the governor of Sichuan were shown to the opium-smoking headman, but he said, 'I do not want these. Seize his boat.'

The boatman was told that they were to be held until dark and then killed and robbed, and after five hours of threatening flourishes of a sword or musket fire to alarm them, it looked as if 'there was little human hope of escape'. Judd then told his companion to slip away and get the magistrate in the nearest town to protect them. He was intercepted, but fearing that Judd had influential friends within call, their captors changed their tune and took them to another village. In a moment of confusion when another boat collided with theirs, Judd slipped the moorings and with only his boatman and one of the crew, rowed hard downstream in the dark for nearly twenty miles, fortunately free from rapids. Where passport and proclamation had failed, Judd concluded, God had delivered them from a very ugly situation. They went on down the Yangzi gorges and reached Yichang five days later, on March 23, to find the Mission house in ruins and no one there to greet him. Somewhere in the last Wushan gorge, they had passed McCarthy, Cameron and Yang Cunling, slowly working up against the current.

The whole journey from Wuhan to Guiyang and back again had

OARS OUT BETWEEN RAPIDS IN A YANGZI GORGE

taken three months, covering two thousand miles, and riverside piracy had posed a greater danger than the schemes of even Hunan's great men.[15] He arrived at Wuhan on March 29 at about the same time as Edward Fishe and his family, who were cheerfully on the way to join James Broumton at Guiyang, and only a few days after King and Budd (March 24) and before Easton and Parker (April 6) ended their own epic journeys.

A shaking of heads — *March–April 1877*

Hudson Taylor had been in Wuhan for five weeks, until all the teams of travellers had started out. Their dangerous mission weighed heavily on him, for he believed that missionary progress in China depended largely on its outcome. Already the 'strong base' or 'treaty port' policy of the mainly denominational societies had led to deeply entrenched institutional activity. Schools, hospitals and 'literature' production were proliferating. Failure to prove not only the accessibility of the whole empire, but that every part could be lived in safely, would confirm societies in the current philosophy of static mission being right, and extensive evangelism and church-planting being wrong. In his *History of the Church Missionary Society*, Eugene Stock wrote of this dichotomy,

> No forward movement can escape criticism. . . . Not a few CMS men agreed with the Presbyterian and other missionaries in the maritime provinces in shaking their heads over the CIM itineration. What good could such aimless wanderings effect? How could incessant journeyings over vast areas be called evangelisation? . . . The answer was that it was a good thing to familiarise the people with the fact that there were persons who affirmed that they had good tidings to proclaim. . . . The work, in fact, only proposed to be preparatory; and in that sense, after years showed that its success was unmistakable.[16]

Convinced of its rightness, Stock had touched on only one point to justify it. But there was also far more. Everywhere the travellers went preaching and 'gossiping the gospel', the seeds of the Church were sown. In some places small communities of Christians soon sprang up. In others fertile soil in the minds and hearts of men and women was made ready for the return of the sowers, who settled where they found a response. A decade later, seeing that it could be done, other missions followed suit and the Church in Europe and

America began to send reinforcements in their hundreds. This second of Hudson Taylor's declared objectives, awakening the Church, was as important as the first, direct evangelism.

Meanwhile criticism was strong, and Hudson Taylor feared that an attack might be made on the CIM at the approaching General Conference of Missions to be held in Shanghai. He decided that his best defence would be to disarm his critics face to face before rather than at the conference, and to lift the whole tone of discussion by emphasis on spiritual issues. In Hankou lived E Bryant of the LMS, who had expressed his views about Hudson Taylor and threatened 'to expose him' in the press. Late one evening Hudson Taylor (deliberately, his colleagues claimed) went to Bryant's house and said, 'I am in a difficulty, it is too late to cross the (Yangzi) tonight' (for the city gates of Wuchang would be closed before he could get in). 'Could you give me a bed?' 'Certainly, with pleasure', Bryant could not but reply, and until they retired to bed the two of them enjoyed an animated conversation, courteously steering clear of anything controversial. The next day, after his guest had gone, Bryant confessed that he was ashamed of himself, he 'did not know Mr Taylor was such a good man'.

A well-meaning but ill-informed article in the *Shanghai Courier and China Gazette* had given Hudson Taylor an opportunity to reply, filling in some facts which would surprise many readers. The journeys being made were, he wrote,

> working towards . . . more localised efforts than are now possible, (while) *besides this work*, we have fifty-two stations in five other provinces . . . being carried on by *resident* missionaries. . . . We aim at being an auxiliary agency (to the great Missionary Societies); and but for the work of our honoured predecessors and . . . fellow-labourers from Europe and America, the work we are doing would have been an impossibility.[17]

He reminded readers that colportage and itinerant preaching had played a leading part in the early stages of nearly all the established societies' work. This spadework done by Medhurst, Edkins, Burdon, Aitchison, Nevius, Griffith John and others was not to be forgotten by more recent arrivals. He continued,

> We propose to itinerate constantly *at first*, and subsequently to carry on localised work *only for a time* – till (self-supporting) native churches can be left to the ministrations of (Chinese pastors).

He then summarised the 'Plan of Operations of the China Inland Mission' published in 1875[18] and repeated,

> Again, in the new provinces, itinerant evangelism is the only work at present possible . . . and we shall not be slow to avail ourselves of opportunities (for settled work) when they do arise. The evangelisation of China must be mainly effected by native Christians. . . . We know, too, that many honoured missionaries now in the field would gladly leave their present posts, and go out into the regions beyond, if their various boards were convinced that it were possible and safe to send them. If our men succeed in locating themselves, they will surely be followed by more and abler workers.

David Hill and W Scarborough of the WMMS at Wuhan were in his mind, as well as Griffith John. And those who would be the Chinese evangelists of the future first needed to be converted and then instructed, trained and given time to show what gifts they possessed.

He had just three months for his diplomacy before the Shanghai conference, and planned to use the time purposefully to make the point that 'the head cannot say to the feet, I have no need of thee', and if the CIM were the feet 'shod with the preparation of the gospel of peace', they wished only to serve and encourage the head. Instead of travelling by steamer, he hired a little house-boat and, doing his routine correspondence, preparation of *China's Millions* and distribution of funds while he travelled from place to place, he systematically called on every missionary of his own and other missions as he was carried the five hundred miles down the Yangzi to Zhenjiang. To Jennie he had written on February 2 about the coming conference,

> Unless there is a great outpouring of God's Holy Spirit, very much harm may result – very much has already resulted from preliminary discussions about the term for God [the Term Question dividing translators (Book 1, p 309)]. In more than one station the missionaries cannot meet for prayer together through it. . . . Now *we* are not likely to pass without some blows if some have their wish. But God is an *almighty* Saviour and my hope is in *Him*.[19]

On his little boat he wrote again on February 16, explaining his journey. 'I do not want an explosion there against the CIM, and a warm feeling on the part of the (Hankou, Jiujiang, Nanjing, Suzhou, Hangzhou, Shaoxing), Shanghai and Ningbo missionaries may prevent it, if attempted by others.' After a weekend with the saintly Methodist David Hill at Wuxue (Wusueh) he was sure of a good beginning, and the next weekend calling on the American Episcopal Mission at Jiujiang forged new friendships. They did not know that he was sleeping in a garret at the CIM house, so open to the weather that one morning he swept up a heap of hailstones on his bedroom floor before beginning his day.

In an open letter published in the *Chinese Recorder*[20] he hailed the prospect of 'spiritual benefits from the gathering together of so many' men and women consecrated to the service of Christ and China. Undoubtedly the Shanghai conference would powerfully affect not only those present but those unable to attend, the Chinese Church and missionaries' home churches also. How important then that, as its conveners hoped, it should be 'signally blessed by the Holy Spirit', and what better than that delegates should come to Shanghai already 'filled with the Spirit'. For the CIM he arranged a preliminary conference at Wuhan, not for discussion but as spiritual preparation for the Shanghai conference and for the travellers, inviting members of the other missions to join in.

His calls at riverside towns and cities included those where Chinese Christians were the only missionaries, and one where the CIM missionary after a good start appeared to have lost momentum. The province of Jiangxi, he told Jennie, 'is stiff soil and none but *fully consecrated* men will do much there – *cross-loving* men are needed. Where are they to be found? . . . Oh! my darling, may God make you one (such) and me another.'[21] They had taken up the bitter cross of being separated for so long, but it was hard to carry. They were pining painfully as the weeks apart multiplied. Stay-at-homes would never succeed in buying up the unique opportunities of the present time.

For one month (March 17 to April 16) he worked at Zhenjiang, thinking constantly of the travellers. The arrival of George Nicoll straight from the Yichang riot, and of Henry Taylor's despairing notes from Queshan drove him to spend hours praying in his own room. In his reminiscences of this period, Nicoll said,

> Mr Taylor was a good deal troubled in spirit at the time. . . . When his day's work was done he would sit down with a little hand-organ and play and sing (the hymn) . . . 'Jesus, I am resting, resting in the joy of what Thou art', over and over again. One day a bundle of letters was brought to him. He stood against the desk to read them. Two were from foreign (missionaries) both telling of serious trouble impending, and two from Chinese, the same.

Hudson Taylor began to whistle the tune of 'Jesus, I am resting' and Nicoll asked 'How can you whistle, with such danger impending to the brethren?' 'Suppose,' he replied, 'I was to sit down here and burden my heart with all these things; that would not help them, and it would unfit me for the work I have to do. I have just to roll the burden on the Lord.'[22]

An unusual sequence of events was fresh in his thoughts, like a parable or sign from God. At Datong, on his way down the river, he found that a fire destroying a hundred homes had stopped at the Mission house, only burning one of its wooden pillars. At Zhenjiang a similar fire of houses 'all round us' had stopped after igniting only a window frame on the Mission premises. And at Yangzhou, flames had devoured a neighbouring temple but the premises between it and the Mission were spared – a dramatic deliverance, for 'several thousand pounds (weight) of gunpowder' were being stored there.

John Stevenson's wife and children were ill in Scotland, and he himself very run down, so early in April he lodged a protest to the Resident at Bhamo against the restrictions on his freedom of movement, and left Burma to return home for a year. Having in Stevenson a responsible senior member of the Mission in Britain made Hudson Taylor feel less torn between his responsibilities there and in China. He even told Jennie to train Charles Fishe in everything she was doing, so that if he sent for her there would be no delay. What should be done with their children does not appear in these letters. The pressure on him had eased a little.

In a Chinese river-steamer he returned to Wuhan, picking up members of the Mission at each port until on arrival there were seventeen crowded into the little Wuchang Mission house for the conference from April 23 to 26. McCarthy and Cameron were in Sichuan, but Nicoll and the Fishe family were there in Wuchang. Judd had arrived back from his long journey, and King and Budd from theirs. Easton and Parker had come in from Gansu on the eleventh, and George Clarke, Edward Fishe and Robert Landale were preparing to penetrate Hunan, Guizhou and Guangxi directly after the conference. It could not have been better timed.[23]

Sunday was spent in fasting and prayer.[24] From Monday to Thursday six LMS missionaries, six Wesleyans, W J Boone Jr of the American Episcopal Church and fourteen from the CIM met in the LMS chapel or at one of the missions. 'Waiting on God', with exposition of Scripture by Griffith John, Hudson Taylor, Boone and others took pride of place. Practical advice by Judd and Hudson

Taylor on upcountry travelling and living among the Chinese followed in the afternoons, each of the recent travellers giving accounts of their journeys. The veteran traveller, Griffith John, did not hide his delight. His message to the others he based on 'Tarry ye in Jerusalem until ye be endued with power from on high.' 'We have done very wrong in not waiting upon the Holy Spirit for power and guidance. We have been working like atheists, and I believe we have by this sinned awfully against the Holy Ghost.'[25]

Then on the final day all met for a united communion service. In Charles Judd's *Recollections* is this sentence, 'That time of waiting upon God for this Western movement (into the Western provinces) and the filling of the Spirit for the workers, was the time that Mr Griffith John got such wonderful help.' That (after Hudson Taylor) the most senior person present should be so benefited, capped everything. Representing the members of the other missions in gratitude for being invited, Griffith John said, 'I thank God for my brethren (the pioneers).' The conference was over, but the next day they met again, and on Sunday, April 29, three hundred or more Chinese Christians and twenty missionaries worshipped together. No one at Wuhan now thought of itineration as 'aimless wandering', or misunderstood what was being done. If the Shanghai conference could even approach this one in quality it would do far more than halt the 'shaking of heads'.

The Second General Missionary Conference[26] *May 10–24, 1877*

Seventy years had passed since Robert Morrison came to China, and thirty-four since the first inter-mission conference at Hong Kong which ended so tragically in the death directly afterwards of Morrison's son, John Robert, the chairman, and of Samuel Dyer, the conference secretary, Maria Taylor's father.[27] Since then missions to China had multiplied with little co-ordination, each going its own way, and strong influences were deflecting the emphasis from evangelism and establishing the Churches to a general 'Christianising' and 'enlightenment' or 'uplift' of the Chinese people. Whoever said, 'When the mind is at sea, a new word provides a raft,' expressed a truth.[28] A proposal in 1874 by the Presbyterian Synod of China, that all Protestant missions should meet at Shanghai, was welcomed as long overdue. But the tone of the conveners' general letter gave rise to misgivings. 'As China opens, our responsibilities increase' surprisingly continued, 'and as missionaries form perhaps the chief medium through which its (China's) people can receive Western truth and Western thought – and we thus in a large measure possess the power of influencing the future of this Empire – it seems incumbent upon us to adopt every available means to strengthen our position.' 'Christ crucified' was omitted in favour of the production of school books and 'scientific works', for 'such action would greatly aid the elevation of this people and promote the glory of God'. By the date agreed, disharmony over the Chinese term to be used for 'God', the old bone of contention, was threatening to make the conference as dangerous as it was necessary. In some quarters feelings were also running high over the CIM's independent policy of extensive evangelism. A fundamental dichotomy of aims and methods was threatening the unity of the missionary body.

The proponents of the new ideas were men of powerful intellect. Before long the CIM itself was to be penetrated and shaken by their arguments. In the view of those who shared Hudson Taylor's convictions, the differences had to be faced, but in the right spirit. Attendance at the conference was therefore representative of divergent views when it met in Shanghai from May 10 to 24, 1877. Such was the fear of serious classes of opinion that many stayed away, but several shipping companies reduced their fares for delegates, tempting some delegates to travel even a thousand miles. All told, about one hundred and forty men and women of eighteen missions, three Bible societies, several nationalities and uncounted denominations crammed the available accommodation in what was to become, in Hudson Taylor's words, 'the most important step China missions have yet taken'.[29] Subsequent issues of *China's Millions* devoted twenty-two pages to reporting the best of the proceedings, as well as complete tables of all missionaries by name, location and seniority. An impressive list of Sinologues (those versed in the Chinese classics) and translators with well-earned LLDs and DDs was matched by others later to be recognised by the universities; yet the names of unsung heroines of non-academic achievement, even a martyr, are there too – David Hill, Rudolf Lechler, R W Stewart, Hudson Taylor, M Henry Taylor, and others yet to make their mark. A high proportion had been in 'China' (including Siam) for twenty years or longer. As proceedings were to be in English, only one Chinese delegate was present, Dr V P Su Vong 'of the Arsenal' (Li Hongzhang's naval and military foundry at Nanjing). He 'urged . . . with great force in excellent English' a point made by Hudson Taylor, 'the paramount necessity' of a medical missionary 'not neglecting the spiritual aspect of his calling'. For the benefit of the Chinese Church in Shanghai, delegates also addressed audiences in their chapels, the variety of dialects represented making it simpler to speak in English and be interpreted.

Forty-five dissertations had been requested and were read, including one by Professor James Legge (*see* Personalia) on Confucianism. Unknown to him at Oxford, agreement had been reached to steer clear of contention over the 'Term Question' and his essay dealt strongly with the terms for 'God' used by the Sage. For a moment a flash of dissent threatened to inflame the conference, only to be 'hushed at once'. A widely representative committee was appointed to search for common ground, without success, and could only urge 'mutual forbearance'. Following each paper came general discussion, with each speaker restricted to five minutes, signalled by the chairman's bell. The result was 'terse, condensed, sharply defined, forcible and to the point, with little preface and no peroration but the *bell*'.[30]

The sessions, presided over by Carstairs Douglas LL D, of Amoy, covered a wide range of topics. The agenda reflecting the Biblical stance of the majority gave little scope to the advocates of 'the uplift of China by education'. In a 'masterly and powerful' keynote address, the veteran J V N Talmage DD, of Amoy, set the tone without platitudes on 'Preach the Gospel to every creature', followed by Griffith John on 'the Holy Spirit in relation to missionary work' and by the American Episcopal co-chairman R Nelson DD, on the necessity of 'Entire Consecration'. Alexander Williamson LL D of the National Bible Society of Scotland, one of the conveners, drew rounds of applause as he reviewed 'the Field of Labour in all its Magnitude', emphasising that preaching should hold priority over colportage; and discussion of James Legge's learned paper on Confucianism brought to their feet the men most fitted to comment – Alexander Wylie, Sinologue par excellence, on the effects of Confucian teaching on the moral character of the people; C W Mateer on its inculcation of atheism; Williamson on its excellence as a system of self-effort to rectify conduct, so far as it went, and Talmage on its deficiency in not recognising the fact of sin as man's chief failing. F F Gough drew attention to the effect of untruthfulness in Confucius' own teaching and practice on his followers; and Hudson Taylor and others warned against negative attacks on the error of a system, when positive presentation of Christian truth was Christ's commission.[31] Joseph Edkins DD, read a paper on Daoism and Buddhism, showing that, like aphorisms of Confucius, many quotations in each religion, familiar to Chinese audiences, were useful in presenting the gospel. M T Yates DD, contributed one on Ancestral Worship, 'the principal religion of the Chinese'. News arrived of a worsening famine in North China, but it made little immediate impact. Harrowing eye-witness accounts of famine conditions were needed to bring home to people's imaginations what was happening.

On May 12 the conference turned to 'the Matter and Manner' of preaching in China, introduced by a master of the art, William Muirhead, who advocated systematic, local itinerant preaching based on an established local church. The subject given to Hudson Taylor, 'Itineration, far and near, as an evangelising agency', had Wesleyan overtones, a good beginning.[32] But prejudice against the methods he advocated had been increasing. A 'new thing' like this raised conservative eyebrows. So Hudson Taylor explained what was being done, and why.

'Throughout he secured the deepest interest of his audience' as he spoke from 'long experience' of extensive evangelism, 'not as opposed to but as preparing the way for more settled labour'; an activity 'almost indispensable before the gospel would take root and flourish', but 'preliminary and preparatory' to concentrated localised evangelism. This approach he considered to be 'economical of time, and labour, and money to a high degree'. 'All education must be gradual; cramming . . . is not education.' It took time for the meaning of the gospel to dawn on many hearers. 'Time must be given it to strike its roots deep into the inner man.' 'It is my firm belief that during the ten or twenty years which generally elapse between the first visitation of a province and the larger ingatherings, *widespread* itineration would . . . gain much time – that whole prefectures, or even provinces, might *in that time* hear, and be mentally digesting, the elementary truths . . . As a preparatory work it succeeds.'

Dealing with practical issues, he strongly supported Alexander Williamson (who from 1863 to 69 had travelled widely through North China, Mongolia and Manchuria for the National Bible Society of Scotland and still represented it at Yantai) in stressing the priority of preaching the gospel, and the limitations of printed Scripture without explanation. What is more, itinerant evangelism was so demanding, so wearing, that robust young men were needed and should launch into it before an unfamiliar climate and conditions had affected their health. 'If the evangelists *walk* but a few miles a day, spending most of their time preaching, their expenses will be small (for) their comforts will be few . . . As to money, the carriage of silver is both cumbersome and dangerous, but the admirable system of banking that prevails all over China greatly lessens the difficulty. Sums of 100 taels and more can be remitted to any provincial capital of the empire by the ordinary banker's draft.' As for the importance of women missionaries, 'with prudence and care and *previous knowledge of the resources of a district* (a very important matter in some cases) I have found no insuperable difficulty even in overland journeys.'

The conference went on to consider medical missions, 'foot-binding' (the cruel custom of painfully deforming the feet of little girls 'to enhance their beauty'), and the work of women for the women of China. When it discussed education and the need for science and other Western knowledge to be taught by Christians before others used it as a weapon for destroying the Christian faith (which none challenged), harmony became threatened as much as by any topic after the 'Term Question'.[33] W A P Martin's and Young J Allen's papers by advocating secular literature and the teaching of Western science as more likely than religion to overthrow superstition, were voicing the views of a minority. As 'a product of his age, Martin identified his Christian faith with Western civilisation', not giving sufficient credence to the fact that Chinese reaction to the impact of 'Western influences' was still one of revulsion.[34] Yet Martin himself was theologically conservative and had no intention of forsaking orthodoxy. He only wished to modify the form of the message, not its content. But the form he proposed came close to obscuring if not changing the content, and was rejected by the conference after Griffith John and Hudson Taylor spoke for the majority.[35]

On another subject there was unity. 'What should be the relation of the Chinese churches to each other, and to the various foreign churches and societies by whom they have been gathered . . . without the surrender of any principles deemed true by any?' The absurd denominational connections of the Chinese Church with the divisions of the Church in Europe and America, Carstairs Douglas declared, were the only real obstacles. The constant danger existed of making 'a most injurious impression upon the government of China,' should Chinese Christians appear subservient in any way to an archbishop or assembly abroad. He could have been speaking in the twentieth century. Many agreed when John Nevius' colleague C W Mateer said 'Denominational feeling at home (in Europe and America) ought to be sacrificed for the sake of the unity of the Church (in China)'. Quoting Henry Venn, Frederick Gough added, 'the native churches will ultimately choose for themselves', for he could not see the denominations at home being willing to yield.[36] Diehard convention was to bind the Church in China until it needed the Communist revolution seventy years later to free them from Western prejudices.

In its appeal to mission boards, colleges and churches of the world to send reinforcements to China the conference, led by Hudson Taylor, declared that China, more extensive and greater in population than any other non-Christian nation, would become one of the great nations of the future. 'Though the oldest nation in the world (they) are as full of vigour and promise as ever. Intellectually they are fit for anything. . . . Their enterprise and perseverance are proverbial.' As great colonisers, emigrating in tens of thousands every year '(they will) ultimately become the dominant race in all these vast countries' of south-east Asia. Thirty-seven years past, it pointed out, there were only three Chinese Protestant Christians in all of China, but the conference knew of twelve or thirteen thousand in 1877. Then followed an historic statement from which flowed events affecting thousands of lives.

> We want China emancipated from the thraldom of sin *in this generation*. It is possible . . . The Church of God can do it, if she be only faithful to her great commission.

Twenty years later, when the Student Volunteer Missionary Union's first international conference adopted the watchword, 'The evangelisation of the world in this generation', Robert Wilder explained that its inspiration had come from that sentence in the Shanghai conference appeal. His father had used it and the Volunteers in America had adopted it in 1886.[37] At the 1877 Perth Conference in Scotland, Reginald Radcliffe cried out prophetically, 'Let us pray God to gift 2,500 women at a stroke, and 2,500 men at a stroke, and . . . to scatter them to the ends of the earth. . . . I implore you to obey the Lord Jesus: "Go ye therefore and teach all nations."' He lived to see the day.

During the conference when the qualifications needed by missionaries in China were being considered, its chairman, Carstairs

Douglas, a man of great intelligence, said, 'Some, alas, seem to be losing hope of getting duly qualified labourers (missionaries), and are asking for under-educated men to supply the urgent need. Let us beware of this fatal error. Let us not encourage the churches of Europe and America to *serve the Lord with that which costs them nothing*. Let us urge them to make sacrifices, to send their best students, their most gifted scholars.' Douglas had generalised, not stating clearly that intellectuals were needed if the attention of Chinese intellectuals was to be won. He appeared to have lost sight of the 'under-educated' giants, Morrison, Medhurst, Edkins, Wylie and others who had great achievements to their credit. Griffith John leapt to his feet in their defence, in defence of the CIM. He had not intended to speak, he said, but Dr Douglas' remarks drove him to do so. Years ago he used to think the same way, but his views had changed. China needed the very best, he agreed, but the best were not only those with the highest education.

> The best agents for this work . . . are men possessed of a strong physique, mental vigour, good sound common sense, a fair . . . education, a thorough knowledge of the Bible and above all consecration to God. . . . [Then he became specific, so recently had he personally been moved by such men.] It has been my privilege to come in close contact with not a few missionaries of the China Inland Mission. Though by no means an unqualified approver of all the modes of operation adopted by my friend Mr Hudson Taylor, [he still had strong reservations about the role of women] I cannot but feel that he has been wonderfully guided of God in the choice of his men. Some of them are well educated, having received college or university training; and by far the majority of those among them who have received only a fair English education, are men of real character and great worth. Some of them speak the language with as much correctness, fluency and fulness as any missionaries in China. . . . I have been struck by their simplicity of aim and preparedness to endure hardships in order to accomplish their missions. . . . I should rejoice to see hundreds and thousands of such men come out to China . . . (Many) appear to be as fit for (pastoral) work as the majority of their more highly educated brethren. . . . A man is not an *inferior* man because he has not had a college training; whilst a man may be a very inferior *missionary* in spite of the highest educational advantages . . . Let us encourage them and honour them, and never speak of them as offerings presented to the Lord of that which costs the Churches nothing.

Carstairs Douglas had spoken unguardedly, but the conference understood and forgave him. When in his closing, presidential address he said with a breaking voice that some present would not live to meet with the others again, there were those in his audience who realised that for a man of forty-seven to look twenty years older (his hair and long beard snowy white) could have only one meaning. Yet all were surprised when news came that six weeks after reaching Amoy he had died of cholera within a few hours of contracting it.[38]

The conference was over. Instead of ugly clashes, harmony had triumphed. The prospect of closer collaboration sent delegates back to work with their outlook changed. The 'feeling' towards the CIM had been 'very kind', Hudson Taylor told Jennie. Never again would those present make ill-informed criticisms of the Mission. But Elizabeth Wilson discovered, when he was 'almost distracted' by neuralgia from a decaying tooth, that throughout the conference he had again been sleeping on the 'malarial' ground floor, to leave room for someone else upstairs in the overcrowded CIM business premises.[39] When someone remonstrated with him that he was shortening his life by such acts of self-denial and overwork, Hudson Taylor replied, 'Does it not say in God's Word that we *ought* to lay down our lives for the brethren?'

A tour of the Zhejiang mission centres and a conference at Ningbo for Chinese and foreign Christians together still lay ahead before he could return to Britain.

An age of exploration *circa 1877*

It was the age of expansiveness, of the grand idea, of invention and discovery. The perspective of the China story needs a glimpse of the wider world. Disraeli, Earl of Beaconsfield, persuaded Queen Victoria to take the title 'Empress of India' and, opposed by many, proclaimed it on January 1, 1877. Britain annexed the Transvaal. Russia seized the island of Sakhalin from Japan, to protect the newly built port and naval base of Vladivostok, and declared war on Turkey. In the United States and Canada the Red Indians fought a losing battle against an irresistible tide of men, wagons and railroads pressing relentlessly westwards. The international scramble for colonies and spheres of influence lay ahead (1880–1900), but the mood was already there, waiting to respond to opportunity. Music-hall jingoism was expressing British conceit, while explosive Victorian energy needed only the incentives to launch new enterprises. Missionary attitudes of 'superiority' were the product of the age.

It was also the age of travel, exploration and missionary heroism. To get a balanced understanding of the scale of the CIM's journeys in China requires a glance at contemporary travel elsewhere in the world. David Livingstone had illuminated the vast continent of Africa by his discovery of the Zambesi River, the Victoria Falls and Lake Malawi (1849–59). His challenge to the university at Cambridge in 1857 gave rise to the Universities Mission, but his own return to Africa the same year was to endless difficulties and disappointments, not least Arab and Portuguese obstruction and use of the information he had provided to develop their slave trade. Back in London, he agreed to mount another expedition for the Royal Geographical Society, but only 'as a missionary' (1865), for he must preach Christ wherever he went. Anxiety for his safety prompted H M Stanley's search which found him on November 10, 1871, in his base at Ujiji – making *Stanley* 'the lion of the hour'.

Months again passed without word of Livingstone, so Lieutenant Verney Lovett Cameron, RN, was given command of another expedition penetrating in March 1873 from the east coast in search of him. In October Cameron met Livingstone's faithful bearers carrying his embalmed body to the coast, and went on to recover his papers and maps. Livingstone had died on his knees on May 1, 1873. During the next two years Cameron surveyed Lake Tanganyika (discovered by Speke in 1856), and followed its outlet to the Congo River. The hostility of tribal chiefs prevented his going down the Congo, so he made for the west coast, reaching Benguela on November 7, 1875, 'the first Englishman to walk right across Africa'.[40]

Belgium assumed sovereignty of the Congo Free State, and with great alacrity Henry Grattan Guinness founded the Livingstone Inland Mission on the same principles as the CIM. Men of Harley House, his Missionary Training Institute (James Cameron's fellow students), became the first missionaries to the Congo.[41]

'Victorian England reacted with its customary gigantic vigour'[42] to H M Stanley's challenge from Uganda published on November 15. A CMS team assembled under Lieutenant Shergold Smith (RN retired, a student at St John's Hall, Highbury) consisting of Alexander Mackay, an engineer; C T Wilson, a curate; T O'Neill, an architect; John Smith, a doctor; two mechanics, and a builder going at his own expense. Colonel J A Grant and Commander V L

Cameron advised them in their preparations, and by the end of May, 1876, they were at Zanzibar. Within three months the builder was dead. The two mechanics fell ill and returned home. On the doctor's insistence Mackay then followed to the coast but recovered, eventually to become the only one left in Africa. So began the saga of 'Mackay of the Great Lakes' and the Church of Uganda today.[43]

Nearer to China, John G Paton was living dangerously in the South Pacific, a life often threatened by violence and disease. John Coleridge Patteson was killed on Nukapu, one of the Melanesian islands in 1877. And after ten years in Polynesia James Chalmers and his wife arrived in New Guinea in 1877 to live among cannibals until clubbed to death by another tribe on January 2, 1901, with a fellow missionary and more than ten tribal Christians. By then the toll of CIM martyrs had reached fifty-nine.

In 1876 Ludwig Ingwer Nommensen of the Rhenish Mission paid his first visit to Lake Toba in the highlands of North Sumatra, homeland of the cannibal Bataks who had killed Samuel Munson and Henry Lyman of the American Board in 1834. There were fifty-two Batak Christians in all Sumatra. Nommensen 'claimed' the Batak for Christ and within the year 1876 the tally of Christians had risen to 2,056. By 1911 there were 103,505 and after the first world war nearly a million, when enumeration became increasingly of doubtful value. Today the CIM–OMF has members serving the Batak church.

None of this was melodrama but grim reality among primitives. In China it was a wholly different story. Travel was slow and often uncomfortable, but seldom were nights spent in the open. Sophisticated hostility was most to be feared, but where it was absent indifference or curiosity or frank friendliness met the traveller. Courage was still needed, for the unknown could as well be murderous antagonism as a welcome. The unpretentious simplicity of the missionaries' way of life was probably as good a passport or better than any ostentation.

Guizhou and Guangxi at a price[44] *May–November 1877*

The most ambitious journeys in China had begun before the Shanghai Conference. J J Turner and Francis James had reached Taiyuan in Shanxi on April 24, 1877 (p 84) and were 'itinerating' on the Taiyuan plain until their brush with death by typhoid before returning to Wuhan on January 22, 1878. Easton and Parker, King and Budd were back from Shaanxi and Gansu by April 6, but in each case said that neither could work again with the other. The fact that 'Satan (had) been active' troubled Hudson Taylor more by far than all the physical dangers and attrition suffered by his men. Defeat no less than success would be at a spiritual level, not physical. Henry Taylor had arrived 'utterly sad' from Henan on May 12, the day the new partnership of Easton and King left Wuhan together 'in good spirits' to return to Gansu, and Budd set off alone with a Chinese servant to Shaanxi. This time Budd went as far north as Yan'an, the cave-dwelling city which was to become the stronghold of Mao Zedong and the 8th Route Army before and during World War II. King and Easton reached Xi'an on June 20 and, re-entering Gansu, visited Pingliang and made Tianshui (Tsinchou to them) their headquarters (map p 80). But each of these long, taxing journeys was the second round.

The 'bombshell' that scattered one team after another from Wuhan, before and after the first conference there, sent Cameron and Nicoll on a daring exploration of the Tibetan marches (map p 123) and Marco Polo's Caindu, the Jianchang (Chien-ch'ang) valley beyond the mountain home of the 'independent' Nosu. It also sent George Clarke on a three-stage adventure, firstly through anti-foreign Hunan to Guiyang; then southward from there to survey the last of the nine unoccupied provinces, Guangxi; and finally back again through Sichuan. On this journey he was to conduct Edward Fishe and Robert Landale on their first pioneering venture with the occupation of Guangxi in view. His diary and report in the *Chinese Recorder*, worthy of the Proceedings of the Royal Geographical Society, tell the story.

On May 5, 1877, they sailed from Wuhan up the Yangzi in a small junk, stopping to preach at places on shore until they reached Yueyang on the 10th, the day the Shanghai Conference began and McCarthy started from Chongqing for Burma. Judd's return in March from his similar journey (pp 97–103) meant that they had benefited from his experience, and the friendly old Muslim mandarin, Ding Laoye, was ready to escort them from Yueyang across the Dongting Lakes. This time another Muslim, the chief military mandarin, also showed an interest in the gospel. Again they preached at towns and villages, except where the curious crowds became excited or the cry 'Kill the foreigner' was raised. 'What a field for Christ!' Clarke wrote. And when they met an old Christian from Wuchang who had heard Hudson Taylor and William Burns twenty years previously, and another man who had heard about Jesus in Shanghai, the way the gospel was penetrating China was brought home to them.

They reached Changde on May 21 and found they were expected. Not only so, officials and people in most places were civil and even friendly, and in most cities the imperial proclamation had been placarded since Judd passed through. High-ranking mandarins called and shook hands, leaving two soldiers to escort them, and when they moved on up the Yuan River, a highly-placed secretary and a gunboat went with them. 'We were escorted from city to city either by gunboats or soldiers till we arrived at Kweiyang (Guiyang).' Clarke felt like the Apostle Paul with the escort of horsemen he had not asked for. At Taoyuan, where Margary had been in trouble, a military mandarin in full dress with his official red umbrella came on board, and when they preached on shore the captain of another gunboat stood by them, helping to sell books. At place after place it was military men who showed the greatest interest and bought books.

On May 29 they were stoned at Chenxi by an excited mob, until a thunderstorm dispersed them, and their boatman pleaded with them not to go on through Zhenyuan in Guizhou where Margary's boat had been burned. But Judd had regretted travelling overland from Tongren, the alternative way, and the main river route with its rapids ought to be tested. 'We were determined to go, and promised to buy him a new boat should his own be burned on our account.' At Yüping, the first city inside Guizhou, the boatman became frantic and threatened to drown himself if they held him to his contract, so at last they relented and hired carriers for the last hundred and fifty or more miles. Zhenyuan apparently provided no excitements for there is no mention of it in Clarke's report.

They reached Guiyang and James Broumton on June 27, their fifty-third day since leaving Wuhan, a journey of 2,790 *li*. The Chinese mile is normally one third of a standard mile. 'We could obtain little information (about Guangxi) either as to route or people,' Clarke noted, 'excepting that they were hostile to foreigners, that the Roman Catholics had failed to obtain an entrance into the province, and that no books could be sold there.' Undaunted, after a week's rest he, Edward Fishe and the redoubtable Yao Sifu headed south for Guangxi province on July 4, through Duyün and desolate tribal country near the provincial border, over poor, muddy tracks with no bridges. 'We found that the *li* were very long, so I put on my pedometer to make a comparison', and used it for the rest of the journey. Very often what was called a *li* proved to be even longer than an English mile.

By common usage, the distances stated in *li* were estimates of difficulty rather than distance. A rough road was 'longer' than a paved one, and a steep descent 'longer' than a climb because harder on the legs. Clarke set his pedometer to read Chinese level *li* and recorded his readings in parallel with the alleged distances from place to place, thus: 78 57; 78 46; 88 75; 33 35; by no means neglecting matters of geographical interest. The object was to assess the feasibility of occupying the far western half of Guangxi province, leaving the east to missions based at Canton.

So they came out of the mountains and made for Qingyuan (now Yishan). 'We had to cross a river. I sent our party forward, and took a handful of books with which to keep the crowd back. After speaking a little I began to sell. The books were eagerly bought . . . the people crowded the boat. I had to sell, and soon they began to pull the books out of the boxes. We crossed the river and still they followed and bought. . . . We sold often at double or treble the Wuchang price. *The people would have books!* especially if illustrated . . . Hundreds of books were thus scattered.'

Later they crossed the Red River (map p 217) and after visiting Nanning, and a city near Pingxiang and the Tong king border, turned north-eastwards to Bose (Peh-seh) nowhere seeing signs of the imperial proclamation. Instead, doors were slammed in their faces and everyone seemed to have been warned by soldiers not to take 'the foreign devil' in. The harvest of hostilities at Canton, culminating in the capture of the viceroy and the occupation of his palace by British troops, in 1856–57, was still being reaped twenty years later.[45] Even Yao Sifu was more than a stranger among his own countrymen, who spoke a vastly different dialect. One day he tried to settle a quarrel between two coolies they had hired. Drawing a knife one cursed him saying, '"You are not in Hunan but Guangxi and I will kill you" – and made an attempt. He was quickly thrown down and seized by the throat and the knife was taken away. We were a little anxious about such a fellow.' The Canadian lumberjack had apparently not lost his grip (p 39). Western Guangxi was very barren and thinly populated. Finding their way from place to place with the greatest difficulty, at last they met a friendly prefect at Sicheng, who sent a guide for six days' travel to see them over high mountains, 'real lung testers', to Lo-huh (Luodian?), the nearest town in Guizhou. It was good to be among people again who could understand Mandarin Chinese.

Safely back at Guiyang on September 6, after two months on the road, Edward Fishe retired to bed, hoping that he and Clarke could return to his family at Wuhan by going through another part of Guangxi, down the West River to Canton. But for four days he had had a cold and from the 14th grew weaker. The trekking had been tough but not unusual, and in Clarke's words, Fishe was 'one who could bear much and seldom complains'. On the 16th he spoke of writing a report for the *Chinese Recorder*, but two days later he suddenly paused in his breathing and 'to our great surprise we watched him breathe his last.' The weak man of the early days had made good; the vacillator had been vindicated. His was the first death and the first grave in the nine provinces.[46] After the burial 'outside the East Gate', Landale stayed on with Broumton, and Clarke travelled back to Wuhan as Judd had done, via Chongqing, in itself a major achievement. Judd had described the journey, so Clarke confined himself to saying 'The part of (Sichuan) through which I passed is most densely populated.' This strongly indicated that instead of gliding down the Yangzi, he walked at least to Wanxian before shooting the great rapids. By comparison with his Guizhou and Guangxi travel, this phase of the journey was a holiday on granite-flagged trails, through luxuriant paddy fields, mulberry groves and orchards of fruit and oil-apple, with thronged tea-shops at frequent intervals and good inns. 'Not an hair of our head was hurt, nor any cash stolen by force (over) more than 10,000 *li*.'

But at Wuhan Annie (Bohannan) Fishe, widowed for the second time, was waiting to hear what had happened. George Clarke arrived on November 7, having travelled 3,000 miles in six months, making a total of roughly 5,000 miles through nine provinces since reaching China on September 26, 1875, little over two years before.[47]

CHAPTER FOUR

THE FARTHEST YET
1877

Baber, Mesny and Gill *January–November 1877*

When extracts from E Colborne Baber's account of his travels were read at the Royal Geographical Society in 1881, Sir Rutherford Alcock's successor as President, Lord Aberdare, called him 'one of the most distinguished' of cadets trained as foreign diplomats in China. He had been chosen to accompany the Hon T G Grosvenor as an interpreter 'because of his remarkable knowledge of the Chinese language', spoken and written, and had enhanced his reputation by writing a scintillating, witty account of their journey so full of useful facts that he was seen to be 'thoroughly imbued with the true genius of travel'.[1] Appointed after that expedition to be British Resident at Chongqing for the purpose of promoting trade, with the rank of consul, he penetrated the remotest regions to obtain information, and established the reputation on which he then became Chinese Secretary of Legation in Peking, charged with monitoring the *Peking Gazette* and handling all diplomatic documents in Chinese.

It happened that a freelance explorer, Lieutenant William J Gill, Royal Engineers, was in Peking to meet Sir Thomas Wade and to obtain passports and the impressive documents which would see him safely on his way to and if possible through Tibet and 'Chinese Turkestan' (Xinjiang, Sinkiang) to Kashgar. From there he hoped to cross Russia. A personal friend of Colborne Baber, and knowing 'not a dozen words' of Chinese, Gill jumped at an invitation to travel together from Shanghai to Chongqing, there to be equipped and sent on his way to Tibet or the far north-west. In Berlin he had discussed the journey with Baron von Richtofen, and in London with T T Cooper (Book 5, pp 25, 27) both of whom had made similar attempts on the Tibetan border with China. As a trained surveyor and geographer Gill's intention was to make detailed scientific observations, such as the Catholic travellers in most remote regions for all their skill had been unable to make or report in their *Annales de la Propagation de la Foi*.[2]

Baber and Gill left Shanghai on January 23, 1877, with their servants and literate staff, and reached Wuhan, 680 miles up the Yangzi, on the 30th. There they hired a junk and trackers, and arrived at Yichang on March 5, the day after the riot, to find Consul King, his vice-consul, the three European customs officials, a ship's captain, McCarthy, Cameron and Nicoll all licking their wounds (p 96). The consul in the company of the high ranking *daotai* had been 'mobbed and insulted' for marking out the projected foreign settlement, taking refuge in a temple from stoning and invective. On March 9 Baber and Gill went on, escorted up the gorges to Chongqing by a 'gunboat' in the form of an armed junk with 'trackers' to tow them against the current, and a detail of soldiers, to arrive on April 8.

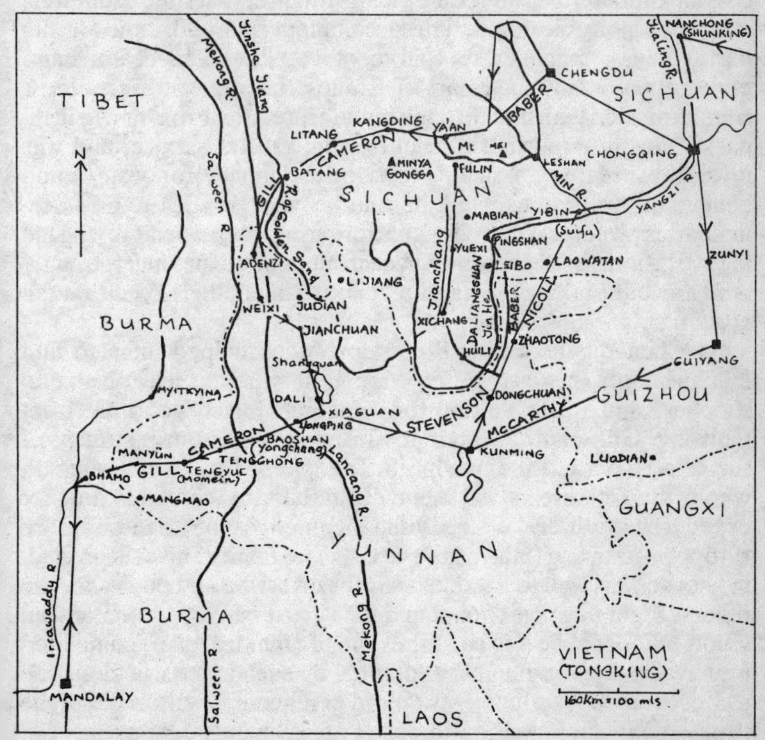

LURE OF THE WEST: LONG MILES IN THE MOUNTAINS

Colborne Baber made formal calls on the highest Chongqing mandarins the next day, and received their return calls with due ceremony, so that on the 11th he completed a contract for a furnished mansion worthy of his rank and nation. After nine weeks on their boat they moved in. Not more than a score or so of Westerners, apart as always from missionaries, had ever been to Chongqing, they noted, but Baber had passed through in December 1875 with Captain Grosvenor, and knew the ropes.[3]

Within two weeks Gill was ready to go on to Chengdu, the provincial capital, 'by myself' – meaning without Baber. Travelling in 'knickerbockers' with loads of personal baggage, including a hat box, guns and ammunition, and a large supply of silver distributed through the boxes, he rode in a sedan chair, attended by three coastal Chinese able to speak pidgin-English, a scribe, a quartermaster responsible for finding accommodation and food for the party, and a manager in charge of coolies, chair-bearers and muleteers. Finally, an escort of Chinese braves under an officer communicated with him through his interpreters. 'From first to last I passed for an important official on some secret service, and was invariably treated as such,' he rightly claimed, for who would believe the truthful explanation that he gave (at least to his intermediaries) when asked? The quartermaster rode ahead to engage the best rooms in the best inns at each night-stop, and meals by day. And any but ranking officials knelt and 'banged their heads' on the ground before addressing him.[4]

At Chengdu the senior Prefect or *daotai* helped them to find lodgings after they arrived on May 9, in which to leave his main supplies, and while waiting for 'General' Mesny to come from Guiyang, Gill set off again on the 18th to see the source streams of the Min River and the 'wild' Sifan people of Lifan and Songpan, whom the Chinese called '*Manzi*', 'barbarians'. For this rougher expedition of three hundred miles, going by Guanxian and back through Mianyang (map p 260) he took two ponies and a sedan chair for himself, as well as a sedan chair for his scribe and ponies for the others. Eight baggage coolies and the chair-bearers, grooms and an escort of four soldiers to clear the road of other travellers completed his cavalcade. But the guard supplied by each mandarin along the route, brought it up to twenty. Word of his coming ensured that the 'Chefoo Proclamation' had been posted where he would have it pointed out to him, even in the rooms assigned to him. By asking innumerable questions and making frequent use of his sextant and aneroid, he amassed a great deal of information, writing it up each evening. At Songpan on June 4 he climbed a hillside to see for himself a family of Sifan, and was back in Chengdu on the 20th to find that 'Mesny', as he called him, as a mark of social status, had arrived.

McCarthy springs his surprise[5] *March–August 1877*

After Colborne Baber and Gill had left Yichang following the riot, John McCarthy, the ex-soldier evangelist Yang Cunling and a 'teacher'[6] completed their own preparations and on March 20 started for Sichuan (map p 260). With them went Zhang the friend whose home he was to visit, and James Cameron for company through the first gorge and rapids. From Wushan Cameron returned to Yichang (p 94) and McCarthy completed the three hundred and fifty miles of gorges and rapids to Wanxian, without seeing Charles Judd after his escape.[7]

Leaving his teacher with the boat and baggage, and reducing their 'impedimenta' to what they themselves could carry if need be, McCarthy, Zhang and Yang Cunling struck out overland on foot. Passing through Liangshan and Dazhu, they stayed a week in Zhang's home, twenty-five miles from Guang'an. Zhang's father had been a mandarin at Peking (ie Beijing), and so warm was the welcome from family and friends that McCarthy could have stayed for months without exhausting the offers of hospitality made to him, he said. His relaxed friendliness drew the best out of people. No proclamations were seen in such out of the way places, but often he was greeted courteously as 'venerable foreigner', though he was in his prime at thirty-eight. A man from Guizhou made himself known as having met McCarthy in Hangzhou, and enquired after his children. Evidence was multiplying that foreigners *per se* were not the objects of hatred, and that simple knowledge of the gospel was being carried far and wide by Chinese travellers.

Turning northwards they visited Nanchong (Shunking) only six days' walk from Chengdu, and stayed with 'an expectant mandarin' for a few days. There they learned first-hand of the strong anti-Catholic feeling and persecution in the province since the previous year. Yet when he reached Chongqing, travelling down the Jialing River on a rice-boat, they found five newly arrived French priests. 'Persecutions *do not* prevent them from coming here, but rather seem to send them in greater numbers!' he wrote in his diary.

At Chongqing his secret plan entered its controversial phase. He was to walk from Chongqing to Burma and back (pp 123, 210). With some obliging consul's aid he had been issued with a passport valid for all eighteen provinces and without an expiry date. But at Chongqing he found Colborne Baber who had made the journey from Chongqing to Kunming and on to Bhamo with T G Grosvenor. If Lieutenant Gill had not come up the Yangzi with Baber on a private venture, and gone to Chengdu intending to court danger with 'General' Mesny in Tibet and Xinjiang, John McCarthy might well have been thwarted. As it was, he visited Baber several times, comparing notes, and as he raised no objections, went ahead with his own preparations. He rented premises for Cameron and Nicoll to use as a base, deposited in them whatever he could do without, and hired a carrier who knew the way the Grosvenor party had travelled from Yibin (Suifu, farther up the Yangzi) through the northern tongue of Yunnan province to the capital, Kunming.

This route would have taken him through remote territory around Zhaotong and close to the Jin He (River of Gold), the upper reaches of the Yangzi bordering the Daliangshan, home of the 'independent' Nosu people. But the carrier developed 'a bad leg', the teacher backed out and went home to Anqing, and Baber advised McCarthy not to linger in anti-Catholic Chongqing any longer than he must. So he and the faithful Yang Cunling left on May 10 to travel on foot through Guizhou instead. They soon fell in with the family of a mandarin and their retainers making the same journey; became their 'honorary medical adviser' and familiar friend, and 'had many opportunities of Christian conversation' with them.

'Wearing the Chinese costume, and having nothing strange or novel with me, we were enabled to move along without any difficulty, through the various towns and cities.' At several places the Société des Missions Étrangères de Paris had stations, for they had been in these south-western provinces for one hundred and twenty years already (Book 1, p 82). Indeed, 'all through those districts of (Sichuan) and (Guizhou) through which we passed, their followers must be reckoned by thousands . . . I met with mandarins and scholars who complained of the protectorate exercised over their converts.' In one town an old man showed him a book Charles Judd had given him, evidence that 'seed-sowing' paid off, even one at a time.

After crossing the border into Guizhou, 'the hills became steeper and steeper and the country more and more wild as we passed

ROADSIDE INNS AND FOODSTALLS

on. . . . All the way . . . our path was strewn with (wild) roses and blossoming plants, bird song and fragrance.' The Miao freedom fighters (in the neat modern phrase) had devastated such regions as had been occupied, and the surviving inhabitants had taken to growing opium poppies instead of food. One valley eight or nine miles long was entirely given up to opium and fully half the population were addicts. Guard-houses on the heights where a few soldiers watched for rebels or brigands, and 'a few wretched thatched huts, the only vestige that remained of a once flourishing town or village', proclaimed the misery of the province in strong contrast with Sichuan. There every available plot of soil was put to good use, and whitewashed lath and plaster cottages added beauty at every turn of the trail. On May 26 they toiled through 'a well-fortified and almost impregnable mountain pass' and below them in the plain could see Guiyang.

After living on his own as a Chinese since Judd left on March 2, James Broumton to his delight 'heard a knock on the gate, and looking out saw Mr McCarthy.' Mesny had invited Broumton over to his city home every Sunday evening for Christian fellowship and prayer together, but on May 28 he was to leave for Chengdu to escort Gill on his mapping adventure. He called to say goodbye and handed over a consignment of books and scripture which he had sent from Wuhan to distribute himself. Broumton confided to his diary that the parting was painful to him; Mesny had been a true friend.

McCarthy stayed two weeks to help Broumton, learning from Mesny and Guiyang Chinese about his own route ahead, and preaching the gospel systematically through the city. The Catholics were strong and numerous, with resident French priests, two cathedrals, and a chapel to the Virgin Mary. 'Being anxious to know personally what the feelings of the people were towards foreigners' in turbulent Yunnan, he decided to walk on following Margary's and (after Kunming) Grosvenor's route but, unlike them, with only Yang Cunling for company and two men to carry a share of Mesny's books. 'Being men of peace we carried no arms . . . but most of the travellers on the road were armed with swords, pistols or guns – firing them off occasionally.' Opium traders travelling 'in companies' or convoys of up to two thousand men presented 'a rather formidable appearance'. But, as McCarthy stated in his address at the Royal Geographical Society on April 28, 1879,

> Several years' experience has only confirmed my deep-rooted conviction that the truest protection for anyone travelling among strangers, is the knowledge on their part of the fact that he can do them no harm. The more he can make this apparent, the better it will be, not only for himself, but also for any that may follow after.

He had even contracted with his carriers that if they quarrelled with anyone on the way he would dismiss them, and had no trouble. He always looked for the same kind of accommodation in inns or private homes (or, on one occasion, an opium den) as a Chinese traveller would expect in the circumstances. At Kunming, which they reached on July 2, however, he was royally received by a fine old innkeeper with flowing white beard, and ended ten days of enjoyable conversation 'with mutual expressions of regret'.[8] But hostility to the French in Tongking across the southern border made it wise to lie low and refrain from 'doing anything . . . likely to cause excitement, and thus give trouble to the authorities'.

A French priest told him that 'it was well known that the former Governor had given instructions at first to have Mr Margary murdered on his journey to Bhamo, but that these instructions had been countermanded, and it was decided not to molest him unless he attempted to return.' A Manchu mandarin with whom McCarthy chatted at a stopping-place along the way 'was immensely pleased when he found that I always corrected the people who gave me official titles [such as the priests encouraged] assuring them that I was merely a teacher' – clearly evident anyway from the fact that he was not being carried in a sedan chair. 'We have always found that when we treated the Chinese in a kindly and gentlemanly way, as they ought to be treated, we received the same treatment in return.' Fluency in the language counted for much. And experience had taught him sound lessons. Engaging carriers by the month, and walking all the way eliminated the otherwise frequent source of trouble, hiring horses or men for shorter stages. 'I made it a rule, too, always to remain in the first lodging house we came to, irrespective of the comfort or discomfort of the place. By this means one was frequently able to wash and have dinner [hyperbole for rice or noodles and whatever went with it – as he was writing for the Bhamo resident, T T Cooper] before many knew we had arrived. Everywhere everyone was friendly' – except two other travellers, from Zhenjiang and Hankou, who were caustic until after a tiring trek McCarthy asked them to come and drink tea with him. 'We parted fast friends.'

Then on and on through July, leaving Xiaguan (near Dali) on August 1. Steep mountains, deep valleys, hot malarial chasms, a swaying chain-bridge over the Lancang (Mekong) River, and to their surprise they came to a city where almost pure Nanjing dialect was spoken and the inns were clean and spacious. Yongchang, as they called it (now Baoshan) had been peopled by immigrants from Nanjing, Yang Cunling's own city, and this was the dialect McCarthy had learned after leaving Hangzhou, so they were received almost as kinsmen.

Tramping on, they passed through an area where terrified people were camping in the hills to escape a plague – and on past hundreds of sealed coffins. By October a thousand had died.[9] Over the Salween by a double chain-bridge and two days of steep climbing brought them to Tengchong and then Tengyue (Momein), a walled city two miles square. Yang Cunling again found a descendant of Nanjing immigrants, who arranged safe conduct for them through the hills. So on August 17 they set out through wild, barren country, past Shan villages walled against marauding Kachins in the hills, fording mountain torrents up to the chin, and sometimes 'wading up to our knees for hours together (where) the only road was a water-course'. They mingled on market day with Shans, Kachins and Lisu tribes-people, and went on in a hollowed-out tree trunk to Manyün, the scene of Margary's murder with his companions and the display of their heads on the 'city' wall.

'Our arrival at Manyün excited a little comment, but as I at once put into circulation among the Chinese some literature which I had reserved for the purpose, and which showed satisfactorily the nature of my mission, the suspiciousness of the people seemed to pass away.' He lodged in an old widow's house, a devoted Buddhist loud in praise of the 'venerable' foreigner who had travelled so far to teach the people to be virtuous. From morning to night 'great numbers of people came to see and talk with the man who had walked across their great country'. And many who had been to Bhamo spoke appreciatively of the medical mission run there by McCarthy's friends. 'I had sent a card to the military mandarin in charge, excusing myself from calling on him on account of my travel-stained condition. He sent a most friendly reply, telling me to be sure and get a proper escort before crossing the hills, and sending kind messages to the members of the China Inland Mission in Bhamo, whose hospitality he had enjoyed when on his way down to Mandalay the year before.'

McCarthy had already arranged for a Kachin chief to see them safely over the border, and assured the mandarin that his practice was 'in everything possible to conform to the customs of the place' he happened to be in. Yang Cunling bought eggs from the mother of the man said to have killed 'poor Mr Margary', and when people raised the subject (never otherwise) McCarthy 'spoke of it as a thing that was long past, and said that a better understanding now existed between England and China, so that nothing of the kind could occur again'. Staying two nights in Kachin homes he found them 'extremely hospitable', for they had lost nothing by either Major Sladen's nor Colonel Browne's disciplined expeditions. Then in a small boat they completed the journey to Bhamo, on August 26.

Their daily walking distance of between 60 and 120 *li* (theoretically 20–40 miles, including some stretches by boat and sensible rest periods for one or two weeks where they could preach and sell Scripture) had taken them five months, covering a total distance of about 3,000 miles including detours.[10] In so doing he had become the first unofficial Westerner to cross China from east to west. Speaking at the Mission's annual meetings at Mildmay on May 27,

HIGHWAY TRAVELLERS; AND A WARNING TO ROBBERS

1878, John McCarthy paid tribute to Yang Cunling as an invaluable companion 'without whose assistance I should have been utterly unable to carry out this journey.' Unlike some situations in which novices with little of the language referred to the able Christians they travelled with as 'my native assistants', in McCarthy's case the ability and fluency were shared, while he took the risks and Yang Cunling met the objections of anyone biased against foreigners. 'It was not that we were able to *overcome* difficulties, arising from mandarins or officers trying to oppose our progress, but there was no difficulty in the way at all . . . It was in Burma that I found my first difficulty – not from the Chinese, not from the Shans, not from the Kah-chens, nor from the Burmans . . . but – from our own authorities.'

High praise from Alcock *March–August 1877*

Hudson Taylor's disappointment over John Stevenson and Henry Soltau being bottled up at Bhamo was for two reasons: their own promise not to cross through Kachin territory into Yunnan, and the knowledge that the British authorities would have closed Bhamo itself to them and therefore this route into China as soon as they went, promise or none. He himself had refused to give Rutherford Alcock any promise at Shanghai in the early days. On China's part the Chefoo Convention was being implemented. McCarthy said, 'In Yunnan . . . among the common people and the officials it is quite a recognised fact that foreigners have a right to go about in the country. And not merely . . . *a right to go* but it is *expected that they will go*. The only surprise that was ever expressed (in Yunnan) was that no (British) officials were yet appointed.'

The British government of India wanted the Burma route into China for opium, and because the Chefoo Convention left a loophole for a tax on the opium, Britain would not ratify it or let the route be used. Another death would complicate matters unduly. On March 27, 1877, Hudson Taylor warned Jennie in London that nothing about the ban on Stevenson and Soltau must be published, as no one in China must know about it. In fact, the less said the better about any adverse reception of CIM travellers anywhere. Even on July 26 he wrote in veiled terms lest his letter be intercepted in transit. 'The journeys are important and difficult and dangerous beyond the conception of most. One of our Irish friends is among the southern clouds, gone to visit a Scotchman' – that is, McCarthy is in Yunnan on the way to Stevenson. Stevenson had written saying that without question Bhamo would sooner or later be 'an important station for Yunnan'. The subject must be handled carefully.[11]

When John McCarthy arrived he was in no way bound to stay. If he had been hustled out immediately by Soltau and Adams, in the absence of Stevenson and Harvey, he could have continued the travels he intended, through the most southerly parts of Yunnan and up into Sichuan as far as Chengdu. Stevenson had gone home and the Harveys, shipwrecked on the way from Rangoon to Singapore, had only just exchanged their desert island for a ship to Calcutta.[12] But McCarthy was trapped. Two days after his arrival an official document was handed to him from T T Cooper, the political agent down the road. 'British Agency, Bhamo. 28 August 1877. No 71.' The viceroy wished no European British subject to cross the frontier, and the Burmese authorities had been asked to prevent missionaries and others from doing so. This notification, he said, was lest expensive preparations be wasted. Another, No 73, came hot on its heels as Cooper realised what might happen. (No 72 had presumably gone to his superiors.) He would be glad of McCarthy's assurance that he would not cross the frontier. It was given, and for good measure a full account of his journey, for which the viceroy himself sent his thanks.[13]

For six months John McCarthy waited in Bhamo hoping Lord Derby would relent and ratify the Convention. The agreeable placidity that made McCarthy a good missionary and a poor supervisor of others had once again limited his effectiveness. When Hudson Taylor referred in a letter to 'bungling at Bhamo' he probably had in mind this entanglement in the spider's web of officialdom. Writing to William Soltau in London, John McCarthy stated the belief which he later repeated to the Royal Geographical Society: the best way of opening up the route into China was not by armed expeditions but for small parties of unarmed Westerners to travel to and fro on peaceful missions. But if the Indian government were adamant, it was useless for him or Stevenson to knock their heads against a brick wall. 'If I had known as much when on the Kah-khyn (Kachin) hills as I learned on my arrival I would probably not have entered the lions' den . . . I had intended merely to call in to see our friends.' Too late. He gave up waiting and on April 25, 1878, he too arrived in England to be reunited with his family.

In the paper read at the Royal Geographical Society on April 28, 1879, he included observations of a geographical nature, but explained,

> My object in travelling in Western China was purely and simply a missionary one . . . while at the same time glad to obtain geographical and general information. The more frequently foreigners can travel among the people without exciting hostility, the sooner will the time come when, without let or hindrance, a more thorough and scientific knowledge of the country will be obtained . . . During the whole course of this journey I was not once called upon to produce my passport, nor had I once to appeal to any official for help or protection . . . Everywhere I received only civility and kindness. The journey . . . is but one of many which, within the last three years, have been taken by the members of the China Inland Mission . . . journeys which together represent more than 30,000 miles of travelling. . . . The spirit of the Chefoo Convention has been loyally carried out by the Chinese officials.[14]

The chairman and president, Sir Rutherford Alcock, declared the journey of more than 2,000 miles actually on foot 'infinitely more productive and fruitful than many' made recently, and attributed McCarthy's success to his wearing Chinese clothes and his fluency in the language. Present at the meeting was the Chinese ambassador Marquis Zeng, son of the late viceroy Zeng Guofan. Speaking through an intrepeter of China's long history and great future, he said that,

> The country possessed what would no doubt be a source of future power and wealth – ironstone and coal lying in close proximity over large areas. That had been the element of (Britain's) national development and power; but it was possessed in quadruple extent by China, where there were coalfields extending over thousands of square miles, and ironstone everywhere. With the help of European machinery and all the resources which European civilisation could give, China would develop her coal and iron industry.[15]

It was no secret. Anything missionaries might say in passing about China's natural resources could add little to the public knowledge of the facts proudly proclaimed by China's eminent envoy. Already Baron von Richtofen was writing his *China* (1877–81), full of geological data, and William Gill (promoted Captain) had reported on his explorations in the Royal Geographical Society's *Journal*. He was also completing his comprehensive two-volume narrative of his travels with 'Mesny' of Guiyang, prefaced with an eighty-page encyclopaedic introductory essay by the scholarly Colonel Henry Yule.

But we have looked ahead to 1879 and must return to two daring journeys, by Colborne Baber and by Mesny and Gill, and two more by Cameron and Nicoll, separately, to show in marked contrast how they went about it.

Gill's change of plan *July–November 1877*

With Lieutenant Gill's return to Chengdu and rendezvous with Mesny, an extraordinary companionship was formed. In his two fat volumes of travelogue Gill scarcely mentioned the companion on whom he was largely dependent. Mesny's imperial rank as a high mandarin exceeded even the *daotai* (prefects) of all the cities they passed through. This fourteen-stone warrior (90Kg) in a flowing scarlet warrior cloak, fluent in Chinese and thoroughly at home with the ruling class, commanded the respect of all they met. To anyone familiar with south-west China and this kind of territory, the voice of Mesny constantly supplying information and explanations can be heard in Gill's knowledgeable account of their experiences.

Yakub Beg, who in 1864 had defied Peking and set up his Muslim kingdom of Kashgaria for thirteen years, had at last met his match. Zuo Zongtang (Tsuo Tsung-t'ang), one of the greatest generals China has ever known, had advanced the whole length of the Great Silk Road and desert trail through Gansu and Xinjiang, taking Suzhou in Gansu in 1873, halting at Hami to grow grain for his troops in 1875, ending the Dungaria rebellion at Manaas in November 1876, and defeating Yakub Beg during the winter. The far north-west became almost depopulated, with only one in ten surviving. In May 1877 Yakub Beg died (in battle or by poison) and in the autumn Zuo Zongtang retook Kashgar and Yarkand. (But opportunist Russia had occupied Kuldja and the territory of Ili in 1871, and a new confrontation with China had begun. A part was to be restored in 1879 on payment of five million roubles by China, but a final settlement was not reached until 1881.)

Unfortunately for Lieutenant Gill, relations between Britain and Russia had also deteriorated since Russia declared war on Turkey in 1877, so his Xinjiang expedition had to be abandoned. Tibet was strongly resisting all attempts to penetrate her borders. His choice lay between giving up and returning to Britain from Shanghai, or making for Burma. For an expert geographer the Burma plan offered great possibilities. The route from Chongqing had been travelled and described already. Colborne Baber was about to attempt Marco Polo's route down the Jianchang (Chien-ch'ang) valley, through Xichang, from which von Richtofen had been repulsed at the outset of his last expedition (map p 123). But the Muslim rebellion in Yunnan had ended, and there was hope that where T T Cooper, after all the rigours of the Litang-Batang mountain journey, had been imprisoned and threatened with death at the hands of the outposts of Dali, it would now be possible to get through.

Gill and Mesny decided to take the high road to the Tibetan border and follow it southwards to Dali, there joining the Kunming to Burma road. Colborne Baber, who left Chongqing on July 8, could not have known of this change of plan. Nor could Cameron and Nicoll, about to set off on this identical journey.

So remote from each other are the two styles of travelling – the flamboyant cavalcade of great men with retainers, and the itinerant preacher with 'one man and a mule' – that both deserve attention. But while the geographers took every opportunity to keep detailed journals, the missionaries did their best on the way and at each night-halt to win a hearing for their message and to leave Christian booklets with literate listeners. Their diaries had to be written up by candle-light or a guttering wick in vegetable oil, before they turned in to sleep. The terrain and conditions were the same for mandarins and missionaries. Solitary Cameron would be the next to come this way.

Starting from Chengdu on July 10, with a large train of animals and men, and making good time through Ya'an and Qingqi (Ch'ing-ch'i), Gill reached Kangding on the 25th. A part-Chinese, part-Tibetan town at 8,850 feet, Kangding lay about 20 miles north of the dazzling peak of Minya Gongga, 24,900 feet, the gateway to the Litang road which went on to Batang almost on the border of Tibet proper. At once the prestige of Mesny and the kindness of the French bishop Monseigneur Chauveau ('Vicaire-Apostolique de Lassa', but calling himself a little more reticently 'Vicar of Tibet') brought them all the advice and assistance they needed. For the eighteen-day climb to Batang they would need to carry all the food their party could need, and have their own riding animals.

The prefect of Kangding presented General Mesny with a mountain pony strong enough to bear his weight up the mountains, always above 10,000 feet but often at 12,000 feet for long stretches, with passes at 14,500 feet before Litang at 13,280 feet and another at

16,570 feet, thirty miles before Batang. Gill bought two good ponies and retained his sedan-chair, hiring eight chair-bearers, four more ponies for his staff, and twenty-nine pack-animals for the provisions and his own baggage, not least an inflatable bath-tub of which he made good use, and his hat-box. An escort of soldiers made up the party that climbed steeply westwards to rest for two days at Litang, August 17–19, before braving the Batang road, infested with robbers. Suitably impressed and gratified by a box of cigars, the Litang mandarin sent bands of soldiers 'to scour the hills in all directions' and twelve Tibetan soldiers to swell the escort when they set out again on August 20. The long file of men and animals on the narrow rocky trail kept close together with guards in front, among them and bringing up the rear. *Mirabile dictu*, at every stopping place the 'Margary proclamation' was in evidence. The foreign notables would come to no harm.

Gill was enjoying himself, noting everything he saw and heard, and taking his barometric readings (for altitude) at frequent intervals, even ten or twelve times in a day as the track switch-backed over the wild plateau. Close to their trail the peak of Nenda rose to 20,500 feet like a canine tooth.[16] 'No words can describe the majestic grandeur of that mighty peak,' Gill wrote, 'whose giant mass of eternal snow and ice raises its glorious head seven thousand feet above the wondering traveller' – struggling along with bursting lungs even before the 16,750 foot pass, on jagged rocks so hard on feet and hooves that 'pony after pony succumbed and had to be replaced'. Fifty miles short of Batang the trail turned southwards and on August 25 they entered the 'town' of three hundred families but thirteen thousand lamas in the lamasery, to be welcomed with deep 'head-knocking' *ketous* from officials and soldiers, and by that 'gentleman of great intelligence' the Abbé Desgodins. Driven out of Bonga in 1865, when his premises were sacked, the Abbé had had to be content with Batang for the past twelve years, convinced that eventually he would get to Lhasa. The chief mandarin rose to the occasion, fêting the general and Gill as only the Chinese know how.[17]

According to reports, the approach of so large a party had alerted the Tibetans and 'thousands', probably hundreds, were watching the roads to intercept any attempt to cross the border. The track ran only a hundred miles from the Assam border, as Cooper had known when he attempted and failed to enter China from Assam in October 1869. Again the hills were scoured for potential attackers as the cavalcade started off on August 29 'with a small army of escorts', two hundred officers and men. Where the 'road' to Yunnan passed within five miles of Tibet, they saw a guard of three hundred Tibetans on a nearby hill-slope, and passed unchallenged. Now they were in the territory gashed in roughly parallel chasms by the great rivers of East Asia, the Jinsha Jiang or River of Golden Sand which, joined by the Yalong, a 'River of White Water', forms the Jin He, River of Gold, the Yangzi herself, as far as Yibin (Suifu) above Chongqing. 'The great plateau that extends over the whole of central Asia,' Gill explained, 'throws down a huge arm between (the River of Golden Sand) and the (Mekong)', its crest five or six thousand feet above the two rivers. Too often the excessively steep sides of the chasms defied any track to follow the rivers, so the Batang 'road' crossed the River of Golden Sand (200 yards wide even here) and followed the ridge from 15,788 feet to Adenzi (Atuntzu, now Deqen) at 11,000 feet.

In so wild a region the only shelter to be found was always of the crudest nature, its entrance 'deep in mud and slime of the blackest' where men and animals crowded into the stable-cum-living-room, and lit a log fire on the central hearth. A notched log gave access to a loft where cornstalks or barley straw might soften the rough rafters, and acrid smoke writhed weakly towards a roof vent and window space, open to wind and rain. So Adenzi with its few substantial buildings and first evidence of true Chinese influences felt like welcome civilisation again, shocked though Gill was to find that the immorality could be even grosser than at Batang.

T T Cooper had been told at Batang to follow the difficult Lancang River trail (the Mekong) to Weixi, fifty miles west of Lijiang, where unfriendly lamas and hostile officials would be sure to send him back, so his repulse and retreat to Batang came as no surprise to them. But Mesny and Gill by following the ridge above the Jinsha Jiang (River of Golden Sand), through Judian and then Jianchuan, had an easier journey, nonetheless involving steep descents of thousands of feet to cross tributaries only to climb as high again. It also gave them an acquaintance with the Lisu and Moso people and their hieroglyphs, leading them on September 27 to the Dali Lake and City. There they were fêted by civil and military officials for their exploits. Dali was the capital city of Western Yunnan, as it had been of the ancient Shan kingdom of Nan Zhao and more recently of the so-called Panthay Muslim kingdom. Francis Garnier had approached Dali in early 1868 after crossing over from Huili at the tip of the Daliangshan 'but had to leave in hot haste' when taken for an imperial spy.[18]

After that, the month-long trek to Bhamo held no surprises, never rising above 8,000 feet or dropping below 2,600 feet, to cross the Salween River. On October 7 (Gill recorded) they met a Christian Chinese whose companions, two carriers, were sick, and 'he was naturally very anxious about them, for if either should have died before they reached their homes, the foreigner, it would have been said, would have killed them', or at any rate have been held responsible. This timely reunion of Yang Cunling with General Mesny, to obtain medicine and give news of John McCarthy's safe arrival at Bhamo, Gill did not mention. Where to Yule's displeasure Cooper had disparaged Protestant missionaries, Gill had nothing to say. Colonel Yule himself referred readers to 'many interesting passages' in *China's Millions* adding 'but there is hardly any recognition of geography in it'.[19] But Gill wrote, 'Mr Margary seems to have left a deeply favourable impression wherever he went.' No other house in Manyün was worthy of a general and his foreign friend, so the magistrate gave up his own house to them before seeing them off with an escort of twenty soldiers. Gill rode with a gun-bearer at his stirrup and was fired on once, before the attackers saw the odds and decamped.

On November 1 they reached a tributary of the Irrawaddy where Cooper's boat was waiting with cigars and newspapers to welcome them. Six days in Bhamo as guests of the Resident must have included sociabilities with Henry Soltau and John McCarthy, whom he had met at Yichang after the riot (Stevenson having gone home), but after Gill's privations Cooper's hospitality filled his horizon. Certainly Mesny will have been a frequent guest at the Mission house in that little market town. On April 24, 1878, T T Cooper was assassinated by one of his own sepoy guards.

Gill's glittering technical report won him the Founder's Medal from the Royal Geographical Society and promotion to Captain, Royal Engineers. And Baron von Richtofen when he read it hailed Gill as 'an acute observer' of men and nature (on) 'one of the most successful and useful' journeys recently made.[20] His books remain, a fascinating description of 'the road over the high plateau', to which Yule added in his Foreword, 'More recently, some of the numerous agents of the society called the China Inland Mission have been active in the reconnaissance of these outlying regions.'

Colborne Baber and the Nosu *July–October 1877*

While Gill was visiting Songpan and Mesny was travelling from Guiyang to join him for his central Asian adventure, Colborne Baber in Chongqing was laying plans for his first exploratory investigation of the commercial potential of southern Sichuan. With his experience of Grosvenor's expedition (of 1875–76) behind him he knew what he wanted. For the journey from Kunming to Bhamo the provincial governor had provided an escort of nominally sixty men, but Grosvenor had also enlisted some Sichuan braves as a personal bodyguard. After the pack-train 'with our cumbrous *impedimenta* galling their reluctant backs (had gone ahead) our vanguard . . . of some ten tall fellows waving immense spear-topped banners, followed by as many . . . armed to the teeth' preceded the mounted diplomats 'attended closely at heel by followers' carrying their rifles and shotguns. Their servants, also mounted, brought up the rear with the sedan-chairs, medicine chest, more escorts and more carriers.

Thinking perhaps of John McCarthy, Cameron and Nicoll setting off on foot but still ignorant of how they fared, Baber wrote,

> No traveller in Western China who possesses any sense of self-respect should journey without a sedan-chair, not necessarily as a conveyance, but for the honour and glory of the thing. Unfurnished with this indispensable token of respectability, he is liable to be thrust aside on the highway, to be kept waiting at ferries, to be relegated to the worst inns' worst room, and generally to be treated with indignity. One may ride on pony-back, but a chair should be in attendance.[21]

Taking his place in a ferry queue was not for the high and mighty foreigner. And Baron von Richtofen's encounter on the pass above Qingqi near Ya'an had been partly due to having no sedan-chair, Baber claimed.

So Baber, armed and travelling 'alone', had fifteen coolies to carry the provisions of himself and his attendants when he left Chongqing on July 8. To his surprise, when he reached Chengdu on the twentieth, Gill and Mesny had left only ten days before, making not for Kashgar or Tibet but for Dali and Burma. They could have travelled together down Marco Polo's Caindu, the Jianchang (Chien-ch'ang) valley, he protested after being the first to make the journey. He visited Mount Emei (Omei), went on to Ya'an, crossed the Daxiangling pass, where von Richtofen, prospecting for minerals, had fallen foul of the garrison, and entered Qingqi, 'the smallest city in China', a walled market tightly closed in by steep mountain sides.

Crossing the Dadu River to Fulin, and on to Yuexi he came upon 'a glorious hill and valley region, inhabited by Chinese soldier-colonists, and those interesting mountaineers the Lolo people' – the Nosu. He was entranced. [The Chinese used 'Lolo' almost as they used 'Manzi' for a wide variety of minority peoples including Nosu, Shan, Sifan and smaller Tibeto-Burman groups between the Yangzi and Burma.] Baber expatiated on their appearance, the 'horn' into which their hair is gathered and bound above their foreheads, their capacious trousers and heavy tweed cloaks, and their women folk,

> joyous, timid, natural, open-aired, neatly dressed, barefooted, honest girls, devoid of all the prurient mock-modesty of (some women) . . . A sturdy Lolo lord of creation, six foot two high . . . went out and fetched two armfuls of them – about half a dozen (tall graceful creatures with faces much whiter than their brothers).

NOSU MAN AND GIRL
called Yi by the Chinese

But these were the Nosu on good terms with the Chinese surrounding their fastness; the Daliangshan, a territory the size of Wales.[22] The only way to meet the defiant 'independent' Nosu marauders in their own territory, those 'fiercely independent caterans . . . frequent in their raids on the Chinese' (Yule wrote) was by finding a feudal clan chief to guarantee the travellers' security, in exchange for appropriate gifts, bolts of cloth and cones of salt. Baber contented himself with following the borders, southwards to Xichang, eastwards to Huili, crossing the upper Yangzi where it is known as the Jin He, River of Gold or Golden River, and finally northwards along its precipitous eastern flank, to Yibin (Suifu), altogether three hundred miles. Of Xichang (at the time called Ningyuan) he recorded, 'A couple of months before our visit, a French missionary, the only European besides myself who has even entered the city was driven away by the staves and stones instigated by the Commandant.' But on the viceroy's orders the mandarins in every city posted the proclamation and welcomed Baber, so that it was widely reported that he was an envoy of the emperor to inspect the border regions.

At Huili his route had touched Garnier's and immediately diverged from it again. For on September 18 he crossed the Jin He (Golden River) at Qiaojia (Ch'iao-chia), a raging silt-laden torrent only five hundred feet in width, crushed between steep walls of rock. And instead of gaining the Dongchuan–Zhaotong–Yibin 'road', which he had taken with Grosvenor, he kept as close to the wild river as he could. To 'a Shanghai newspaper' he wrote,

> Thence through the wildest and poorest country imaginable, the great slave-hunting ground from which the Lolo carry off their Chinese bondsmen – a country of shepherds . . . lonely downs, great snowy mountains, silver mines. . . . No European has ever been in that region before myself, not even Jesuit surveyors; the course of the (Yangzi) as laid down in their maps, is a bold assumption, and altogether incorrect . . . It winds about among those grand gorges with the most haughty contempt for the Jesuits' maps.[23]

Baber's accurate sextant readings established the course of the Golden River fifty miles east of the position given previously. He meant 'no European geographer known to me', for later in his 'Travels and Researches' read at the Royal Geographical Society on June 13, 1881, he was to quote at length from the *Annales de la Propagation de la Foi*, 'luminous with ingenuous veracity' by a

French priest 'long resident in China', about how he was captured on January 2, 1860, by slave-raiding Nosu and held for forty-eight hours. The inhabitants of the Daliangshan had been driven across the Jin He, the north-flowing reach of the Yangzi, in the reign of Yongzheng (1723–36) and regarded these raids by up to three thousand fighters as collecting rent for their territory forcibly occupied by the Chinese.

When Lord Aberdare hailed Baber as 'fortunate enough' to have 'visited an entirely new country, and . . . come across a people of whose existence, race and character, hitherto nothing at all had been known' he was misinformed. To the people of China, the Catholic Church and readers of Marco Polo, much was already known. Even Sir Rutherford Alcock commented on Baber's 'discovery of what appeared to be a new language, and of a new people never before visited by any European'. The first entry into the Daliangshan was not in fact until considerably later, though Baber was told by a friendly Nosu shaman 'that under proper securities it may be travelled in safety'. As before, his genius for seeing, surveying and communicating his observations 'with extraordinary vivacity and force' was rightly praised. Of what he saw of the Daliangshan towards the end of his journey on the Zhaotong plateau he wrote,

> About twenty miles distant to the north-west, in a cloudy sky, rose a stupendous boss (which resembles a cap of liberty) the culminating point, and the terminal, of a snowy ridge some fifteen miles long . . . The summit falls to the (Yangzi) in a series of terraces . . . and abuts on the river with a precipice or precipices which must be 8,000 feet above its water. . . . I was standing too near those overwhelming heights and depths to be able to judge calmly of their proportions – physically too near the gorges, and mentally too close to the liberty-cap. . . . Later and maturer reflection has brought little result beyond a violent desire to go there again.

The name of that ridge is Taiyang Qiao – the 'Sun-bridge', because 'the setting sun traverses the crown of that portentous causeway'. And beyond it, to the north, the towering precipices of the Longtou Shan, the Dragon's Head, overhang the deep divide of the Meigu He, the River of the Beautiful Maiden.[24]

On October 18 he re-visited a prison in the little town of Pingshan, where he had been in January 1876 on the Grosvenor expedition, and found the same Nosu hostages as he had seen then. And from Yibin (Suifu) he returned to Chongqing by river boat.

Sichuan 'occupied' *May–October 1877*

At this point a glance back to May, after the Wuchang Conference, reminds us that Hudson Taylor's 'bombshell' had for the second time scattered available pioneers to the four winds. Charles Judd and George Nicoll rejoined James Cameron at Yichang (pp 94, 123), the springboard for Sichuan, where he had been living on a house-boat since seeing John McCarthy on his way up the Yangzi gorges, following the March 3 riot. At last he had regained possession of the damaged house, and this time his own travels were to expand dramatically while Judd stayed to develop the beginnings of the Yichang church. Chongqing was to be occupied, and the work in Sichuan to begin in earnest.[25]

With three Chinese Christians, Cameron and Nicoll travelled on a public goods-boat towed by 'trackers' up the awesome Yangzi gorges. 'Their stern and solemn grandeur baffles description,' Cameron wrote. 'I had passed through them several times previous to this, yet I could not leave the front of the boat, but had to sit (with Nicoll) drinking in the scene.' Against a swollen current it took them three weeks to reach Wanxian, so they finished the journey by land. As always, whether by boat or by foot it was, in the words of the conference agenda, 'itineration as an evangelistic agency'. 'Far and near', to fellow passengers and the inhabitants of hamlet, village, market, town and city they spoke about 'Christ Jesus crucified for sinners and raised to life again,' selling Gospels and explanatory books, always at risk 'of getting into trouble on account of recent disturbances with Roman Catholics'.

June and July they spent based at Chongqing at the house McCarthy had rented on his way to Bhamo, and they must have met Colborne Baber before he set out on July 8. He noted that missionaries of the CIM used it to rest in, coming and going in their work 'without the least trouble, as yet, of any kind,' – in the sense of meeting hostility.[26] Preparing to reconnoitre the fringes of Tibet, preaching the gospel as they went, they were ready to start when an unexpected visitor arrived. Charles Leaman, an American Presbyterian from Nanjing, had come with two Chinese Christians of Wesleyan background and 'a large supply of books', on his way to distribute them in Shaanxi and Gansu. On meeting Cameron and Nicoll, just back 'from an inland town', he changed his plan.

They left Chongqing together on August 14, working their way to Chengdu, four hundred miles in twenty-one days, never travelling on Sundays; and always drawing crowds of visitors, and selling all the books they could. Nine days in Chengdu they spent in the same way, while hiring pack-animals and laying in provisions for the arduous climb from Guanxian to Kangding, the shortest route to the gateway of Tibet. They set out on September 13 and reached the foothills on the 19th – the day following Edward Fishe's death at Guiyang. From the outset the animals were unequal to the rough going, and when they came to 'a suspension bridge made of bamboo ropes, 316 paces in length and 7 feet in breadth (with) 10 ropes underneath and five on each side [so Cameron wrote in his diary], we concluded to try the more southerly route . . . less difficult for mules.'

Day by day, in place after place, instead of recording geographical observations or the potential for trade, it was the people and how they listened to the gospel, or the Catholics and how they fared, who took pride of place in their journals. On September 27 they were told that Gill and Mesny had passed through two months before, and the next day they reached Ya'an. The danger of being prevented from going further by officials concerned for the safety of unarmed, unimpressive strangers, led them to 'work' there only until noon on the 29th before moving on. But the next day Nicoll was very ill with 'ague' and Leaman tired out. When the inns were full they were content to lie in rows with fellow-travellers on straw in a loft among the opium-smokers, and shared the common meals of peasant Chinese. It needed stamina. Cameron preached in a market-town until his voice gave way, and talked with men who followed him back to the inn. But with Nicoll sometimes too ill even to ride his pony, so that they could not travel, and the pack-mules often failing them, it was October 5 before they reached Qingqi (Ch'ing-ch'i) near the top of the mountain range only seventy miles beyond Ya'an. Qingqi proved to be not only the 'smallest city in China' but apparently the least interested in hearing what they had to say.

Here they faced reality. Their loads were too heavy for the animals to carry in such terrain, one older Christian companion was finding the going too much for his strength, and Nicoll's 'ague' showed no sign of improvement. They at least must return to Chongqing. Leaman offered to go with them. Showing that dogged perseverance which was to carry him on and on for six long years of pioneering, and to earn him the epithet 'the Livingstone of China', Cameron decided to go on without them.

Not one, but two of the most historic reconnaissances of mission history in China were about to begin. Cameron's has often been written about. But Nicoll's unplanned detour with Leaman has been overlooked because it did not receive the publicity given to Baber, to Gill or to Cameron. Their itinerary appears not to have been understood at first, for in the map of itineraries published in the *China's Millions* of 1878 it was misplaced. They followed the route almost unknown to Westerners and shunned by Chinese unless heading straight for Dali or Kunming, the route (as it turned out) that Baber had taken, encircling the Nosu homeland, the Daliangshan.

Cameron, 'one man and a mule'[27] *October 1877–January 1878*

The contrast between Gill's 'progress' and Cameron's humble 'itineration' could hardly have been greater, not that Cameron gave it a thought or knew any more of Gill than innkeepers may have told him along the way. Gill had been heading for Xinjiang when he left Chongqing. Just before Qingqi Cameron had met the *zhentai* (chen-t'ai) or military governor of Qianzhou on his way to Chengdu and had to make way for him and his cavalcade to pass – two hundred pack-animals of possessions, four sedan-chairs for his wives, son and himself, and 'many soldiers'. This was how the high and mighty did it, and he did not begrudge General Mesny or Gill their due.

After parting from the rest of his own party he wrote, 'I have a good mule, and also a good coolie as servant . . . My books and tracts, also a few more things, are in saddle bags carried by the mule I hope to ride. The bulk of my silver I carry on my person . . . and find it rather burdensome when I walk.' He rode for five miles and walked twenty when climbing, but on easy stretches rode more. Hoping to spend the Sunday resting, before arriving at Kangding (map p 123), he was asked to move out of his inn to make room for an official who was expected soon. As Baber said, 'You got pushed around unless you asserted your dignity.' But there were higher values than that. When he met the cavalcade of eighty men later that day, he was glad he had obliged. To be unimportant and free to pass the time of day with anyone without restraints, suited him well.

Now he was in semi-Tibetan country where the minority people (called 'Manzi' by the dominant Chinese) lived in Tibetan strong-houses. Vocabularies which he collected as he travelled (whereas

Gill had taken barometric readings) showed that these people were (with dialect differences) the same as those of Tibet proper, as the Abbé Desgodins was to confirm when he 'received (him) very kindly and courteously' at Batang (p 149) for that rare delight of 'strangers in a strange land', a meeting with a fellow-countryman or his equivalent.

On October 16 he left Kangding, having 'supplied the city well with tracts' and sold some books, to endure most primitive conditions at the night stops on the arduous way to Litang. Pages of his journal are filled with descriptions of the people, their houses, customs and language. Living at their level and eating their simple barley and oat *tsanba* made them friendly and communicative. In a *manzi* shack he took down a list of phrases.

> After I had written them down the host requested me to read them over, and was highly pleased with their correctness. . . . We were soon like old friends. . . . Supper being over . . . our sitting-room became the common bedroom. The females took one side of the room, while the master and his pet (son) shared the other side with us. . . . He told me if I ever passed again, to be sure and put up in his house.

People were the *raison d'être* of his being there, and their geographical environment incidental, revel in it though he did. After crossing the Yalong River at Hekou (the geographical fact failed to impress him),

> We had a huge snow-clad mountain to cross . . . It was bitterly cold, and the wind often seemed (to) enter our bones. Both of us have swollen and sore lips, and heavy colds with sore throats. [On the far side a friendly man hailed him from a hut and welcomed them to stay.] He brought each of us a large basin of soup with plenty of beef (and butter, milk and vegetables) in it (and) spent a good part of (Sunday) reading some books I gave him.

At one inhabited place the men looked so evil that Cameron and his man chose to pass on and take what they could find, rather than be robbed (at the least) or never be heard of again. There were nothing but shepherds' tents or watch-fires for mile upon mile as they climbed to 14,500 feet and descended in the dark, missing the 'halt' where they could sleep under cover. On and on they stumbled in good moonlight, until the dogs in another hamlet announced their arrival. But the people were afraid and would not open to them. At last one man relented and plied them with tea by a hot fire until they lay down to sleep. He told them they had come 170 *li* since the morning, but Cameron thought 150 *li* (fifty miles) nearer the mark. By 2.00 p.m. the next day, October 23, they were in Litang, at 13,280 feet 'one of the highest cities in the world', with its gilded lamasery roofs. They had done in six days what took Mesny and Gill a full ten (August 7–17) with their well-laden caravan.

Again James Cameron's lengthy and detailed observations on the place, the gilded lamasery, the lamas, the appearance and dress of the men and women, the Shaanxi origin of most of the one hundred Chinese in Litang were what ethnologists and missionaries looked for. As a geographer, Colonel Yule commented that Cameron's journal was 'that of a simple and zealous man (with) hardly any recognition of geography in it'. Zealous, certainly, for he yearned for Tibet to be open to the messengers of the cross, but not simple. Here at Litang after visiting the lamassery he wrote,

> Oh! When shall 'Christ and Him crucified' be preached to the multitudes who speak (Tibetan)? . . . My hope is in God – I know He will open it in His own time and way. He may not see fit to send me, but He will send his prepared ones; and when *His* time comes, they will have entrance.

The Abbé Desgodins of Batang had used very similar expressions of his own patient longings. But Cameron was also scientific, as his meticulous description of the decorations on a lamasery wall revealed.[28]

After Gill's account of preparations for the climb to 16,570 feet before Batang, and scouring the hills for bandits before the well-escorted party could set out, Cameron's quiet departure seemed to invite disaster. Too high a price was asked for any horse he approved of, and every animal offered to him had a serious defect. So with his one man and a mule he set off on foot. A friendly Shaanxi Chinese overtook him and welcomed them to his home on the first night, where a low *kang*, a platform of baked earth, served as a bed. With no fire and feeling ill, Cameron lay down 'with a burning skin, almost shivering with cold'. But the next night, after another day's march and with 'two calves for room-fellows', he slept well. At last, on October 29, he managed to buy a good horse, more cheaply than the bad ones in Litang and, still febrile, they climbed up and over a snow-clad pass with their faces and hands scorched by reflected sunlight and the biting wind. So painful were his eyes that he tried to walk with them shut. Untrained and probably unfamiliar with travel books about the dangers and difficulties of such conditions, his intelligence and indomitable spirit saw him through, enabling him to encourage his man and goad the mule over the worst stretches.

On October 31 they had to cross the highest point, sinking a foot deep into the snow, and when the sun was warm, splashing through rivulets on the trail. His own shoes became unwearable, and cheap straw sandals fell to pieces, yet they pressed on. The only alternative was to turn back. 'For more than sixty *li* (nominally 20 miles) we did not see a living soul, and then only one.' Missing the house they had been told of, as it was off the beaten track, they kept going, stopping only to feed the animals and fortify themselves with 'Zanba' (*tsanba*).

Long after dark they reached Batang and could find nowhere to sleep. 'They had no inns (of any kind). Strangers seek quarters in private houses . . . At last a woman took pity on us.' The dangerous journey of more than thirty miles, at risk from snowstorms, injuries and robbers, was over. 'Hitherto hath the Lord helped us', Cameron wrote – only to spend the night tormented by bed bugs, 'my old enemies'.

At first the officials feared that this brave or foolhardy young man was meaning to enter Tibet, only five miles away, and were 'much re-assured' to be told he had no such intention. Cameron's aim was to find the extent of Tibetan occupation of the heights above Yunnan. He called on the Abbé Desgodins and enjoyed a long talk with him in Chinese. 'This kind priest gave me much useful information . . . He advised me to call on the mandarin, so that if any disturbance took place he could not say he knew nothing about me.' Two mandarins also entertained him at length, asking what doctrine he taught, an opportunity Cameron welcomed, and promised an escort to see him over the stretch of road that ran close to hostile Tibetans. That afternoon they sent him a feast of ten dishes of 'meats'. He had nothing he could give them in return.

November 5 saw Cameron on his way to Adenzi (A-tun-tzu) with an alert escort of three and a young literate Tibetan he had engaged as a language informant. 'We passed the place where a man was killed by robbers only two days ago . . . They seemed to expect robbers, but we saw nothing and were not sorry.' 'In (Batang) my face and hands had time to heal, but yesterday evening and today have skinned my face again,' his diary for the 7th reads. Five official couriers joined them, making a party of eleven mounted men to pass the nearest point to Tibet, and they were told of a large body of Tibetans guarding the border. Looking out over Tibet itself, with Tibetan homes in view, Cameron sighed. When would Tibet open her frontier to the gospel? 'It will be open some day!'

Feeling unwell, he welcomed the kindness of 'Manzi' people in a well-cultivated valley, who pressed butter, nuts and curd and even a hen on them without haggling for payment. A few 'fathoms' of thread, 'and they went off well pleased . . . and we were very comfortable.' One of them had travelled with Mesny and Gill [Cameron's order of names] to Dali, taking a month to get back. The steep, broken, rocky tracks over the high ridges and deep chasms of the provincial border made progress slow and painful. So it was November 14 when they reached Adenzi in Yunnan. There he succumbed to high fever for two weeks and thought his end had come. What to do with his silver, the Mission's property, worried him as he lay helpless. 'See what a trouble it is to be rich!' he wrote when strong enough to continue his diary. Yet he cannot have had much silver left by this stage in his journey.[29]

On December 3 he thought he would recover if he had more exercise, and nearly changed his mind when on mounting the mule he all but fell off again. He had no strength to control it, and had to have it led, mile upon mile over the snowy mountains and across perilous rope bridges. One night he found himself in a Roman Catholic home, near where two foreign priests were living, and avoiding 'controversial matters' they talked about Jesus. But after travelling through the territory of two other ethnic minorities, the Moso and Minjia, he found himself in another Catholic home on the 8th – 'the kindest people I have met with on all my journey'.

An official from Adenzi on his way to Weixi caught them up when they were uncertain of the trail and guided them for a day or two, so on the 10th they found themselves among Chinese again, in Weixi where T T Cooper had been imprisoned by the Muslim rebels in 1868 and driven back to Batang. Mandarins and people were friendly to Cameron and sent escorts to see him safely through a lawless wilderness. 'What a field for a linguist,' he exclaimed when they met more and more aboriginal people. Like missionaries in a thousand situations he wished he could divide himself up between them. At Jianchuan he preached in Chinese to an attentive crowd, and on December 23 reached Dali, a fully Chinese city with a Catholic bishop in residence. At last he could go from teashop to teashop, sure of an audience and interesting conversations in each.

The rest of the way to Bhamo was plain sailing in comparison. From the time he left Dali on December 28, people he met remembered John McCarthy (1877), and in place after place gospel posters were still where he and his companions had pasted them up. Near Yongping, before crossing the Lancang (Mekong) River, a French priest told him that two other priests had gone towards Bhamo in 1876 and had never been heard of again. When Cameron reached Tengyue (Momein) on January 9 the inns were crowded with travellers waiting for the road ahead to be cleared of robbers. After a hot battle between the militia and a gang of them, fifteen men were brought in and beheaded. While he waited, one of John McCarthy's companions arrived. He had accompanied Yang Cunling from Bhamo to Kunming and was on his way back to Bhamo. Gill's story of the sick men he treated (p 139) was complete. They went on together.

With the road cleared of robbers, all Manyün's hostelries were full when they arrived, so McCarthy's man took them to a private home. The woman's son had been so ill in Bhamo that she had gone to him and was despairing of his life when Stevenson and Soltau had first arrived and cured him. At last, on January 18 a convoy of a hundred travellers, with Cameron's party among them, proceeded under an escort of Kachins into the mountains of the Burma border. A night in a Kachin chief's home and another bivouacking in the jungle, and they came to the Shan village of Manmo where Cameron waited for a week. No explanation is given, but a safe surmise is that McCarthy's man had told him of the Indian government's ban on re-entering China, so he sent ahead for advice. Should he retreat while he could? It was too late. T T Cooper, the Agent, heard of him and 'asked' him to come to Bhamo. He had no alternative if restrictions by the British were not to be extended.

When Hudson Taylor heard of the success of this and other journeys his admiration and gratitude were profound. He truly loved like sons these men who stopped at nothing for Christ's sake.

Nicoll 'in Baber's traces'[30] *October–November 1877*

George Nicoll's 'ague' left him after Cameron had started from Qingqi (p 145), and this altered the whole picture. Instead of heading back to Chongqing by the quickest route down the Min River from Leshan (Jiading), Charles Leaman and he could either work their way back through densely populated Sichuan, distributing the excess of books in their 'bulky baggage', or be enterprising and strike southwards, down the Jianchang valley – the way Colborne Baber had gone. They chose the second option.

Leaman's account of his travels and observations was published in the *Chinese Recorder* soon after his return to Nanjing. But its emphasis on the cultivated, populated part of Sichuan, barely outlining the southern route and referring only to the 'tribes' in general, shows where his interests lay. Nicoll on the other hand, although an academic and enthusiastic about the Nosu he met, seems to have left so little record of their journey that Hudson Taylor or whoever prepared the map for the 1879 bound volume of *China's Millions* may be forgiven for taking them by the direct route to Leshan and Chongqing. However, Leaman said enough to confirm the impression given by a letter from Nicoll to two trainees in Britain, Samuel R Clarke (unrelated to George) and J H Riley, who before long became quite as notable as pioneers, that he like Baber encircled the Daliangshan *except* for its northern end (map p 123). (He visited Leibo in 1880.)

Leaving Qingqi on October 10 they descended the Daxiangling from 9,360 feet, crossed the Dadu River and the Xiaoxiangling (9,700 feet) on the 23rd, in snow and ice, into the region of 'tame' and 'wild' Nosu, and three days later reached Xichang, 'a busy city and a fine rich valley'. 'We worked in this place with great satisfaction; the people were kind and did not molest us in any way,' Nicoll wrote. As for the Nosu they had encountered on the way, 'I felt quite at home with them, seeing so many things which reminded me of my native (Scotland)', not least '*oatmeal* cooked in the same way'. 'These Lolo [i.e. Nosu] women walk as erect as a soldier. . . . I longed to see someone among them with a heart burning with love for the Master. . . . I took a list of their words, so that I could test, as I went along, how far the language was the same; and I found that for over a hundred miles there was no difference . . . All the subject Lolos can speak Chinese.'[31] To the west of Xichang lay more unruly territory and the main body of Moso and Minjia people, extending right over the Yalong River and Jinsha Jiang (River of Golden Sand) to where Cameron had met them.

They went on a hundred miles to Huili, 'a larger and finer city,' and eastwards 'over a very difficult road' to cross the Golden River, the Yangzi, on November 15, 'a mighty river, two thousand miles from its mouth'. Unknown to them, James Cameron was lying alone and very ill at Adenzi as they climbed 'over very difficult hills' to Dongchuan on the ancient highway between Yunnan and Sichuan. If they had taken Baber's route down the west side of the Nosu territory, they deviated from it at this point and were too far east to see the Nosu he described, or the Sun-bridge and Dragon's Head. Shortly before Yibin they took to a boat and reached Chongqing on December 9, 1,600 miles and four months since setting out.

Charles Leaman was a townsman, not cut out for pioneering, so he had suffered from the discomforts of primitive conditions. He returned to Nanjing; and Nicoll compared notes with Baber, confirming that the Nosu language varied little from place to place along the borders. 'It was in his house that I saw the languages compared.'

As a missionary reconnaissance, with no wish to be the first Westerners to make it, this itinerary was a *tour de force* which with Baber's established the feasibility of living within reach of the Nosu, and of making contact with the 'independent' inhabitants of the Daliangshan. J H Riley was to attempt that, but never put down roots. The Paris Mission had tried and failed to settle in Xichang while the French Protectorate was so unpopular. One and another briefly entered the Daliangshan, from the east, the north and the west, for a few days at a time, and an armed French expedition was to cross over the independent territory in 1908, but not until after the second world war did missionaries travel and live in the heart of the Nosu homeland until compelled to leave under Mao's new regime at the dramatic end of the Open Century.

Director-at-large[32] *May–December 1877*

Throughout the Shanghai Conference in May, Hudson Taylor had been run off his feet. Constantly in demand for consultation and advice he had no rest, and racked by facial neuralgia from a decaying tooth, which sometimes drove him 'almost frantic', he was too busy to have it extracted. On May 24th the conference ended, in his view 'the most important step China Missions have yet taken', but he could see no hope of returning to London before August. The Zhejiang missionaries desperately needed a visit. One had become a shameless alcoholic, even attempting to lead a communion service when too intoxicated to stand. He must be replaced. 'Oh! may God make us a *holy* mission,' Hudson Taylor groaned, 'a united and loving mission, and then we shall be a *successful* mission.' Others were ill and disheartened. Wang Laedjün, as pastor and in effect bishop of an expanding network of churches, had come to consult him about his problems.

Preparation of 'copy' for *China's Millions* took high priority, for through it he reached not only a broad spectrum of interested Christians in Europe, Colonel Yule among them, but many in China too, consuls, merchants and members of other missions. He asked for a hundred copies of the bound volumes to distribute. Lord Radstock had written decrying so much news of travel and Chinese affairs, wanting in his spirituality more about people to pray for, news of baptisms and ordinations. To Hudson Taylor the pioneering was no less spiritual, as he looked ahead to the churches as yet unborn in each of the provinces being entered. Every issue had its spiritual highlight in his editorials in the series 'China for Christ' of the type Lord Radstock valued. Hudson Taylor was confident. 'It is impossible to meet everyone's view.' 'A paper just suiting Lord R would not please many. But much may be done to please him.' People must be informed. Factual knowledge made for understanding. If space allowed, he would multiply the articles on Chinese customs, beliefs, culture and history. Illustrations with explanations, of a Chinese wedding, a fortune teller, a gambling house, a street barber, monks, musicians, modes of travel and varieties of scenery made the *Millions* balanced and attractive. And Hudson Taylor worked all the harder to report evidence of the steady growth of the established congregations. The *Chinese Recorder* so recently supercilious about the CIM, was impressed by the bound volumes. '"China for Christ" is the motto of the untiring editor, and he makes his magazine impress this motto upon his readers by every page.' And later, 'We welcome this elegant periodical, brimful of interesting missionary news . . . The pictures are excellent.'

Achieving that result cost him distress as well as labour, and ceaseless difficulties for Jennie and those who helped her at home. To maintain the standard he did not stop at strong rebukes for them, if proof-reading lapsed or the spelling of Chinese words was inconsistent. Love-letters had to turn to painful business, even if it meant a string of strictures. 'Why do you not send me *proofs* of the *CM* early, instead of waiting till they are worked off?' She must remember that work on the forthcoming issues depended on what had gone into print, and mails were so slow to reach him. 'It is such a pity that the January picture was so badly printed and that you have not been more careful.' Again, 'I like the February *CM* very much and think you have done very well.' Another time a whole page of criticism of the printer's choice of type-face and other shortcomings showed her how fraught he was. She understood. 'I do like our absence from each other for Jesus' sake to cost us something, darling – to be a *real* sacrifice,' he said. 'I don't think a husband can love his wife *too* much, but he may be too much influenced by his love.' Their own love was disciplined. Jennie wrote, 'I do not want you to come, darling, before you have finished the work God has for you to do there,' and he agreed, but added, 'Almost sick at heart at our long absence – I hardly know how to finish my note.'

The unstable remaining missionaries of the *Lammermuir* era and their wives in Zhejiang needed more than a visit by Hudson Taylor. On June 8 he took Elizabeth Wilson with him, to stay at Wenzhou while he moved on. Older, mature and sensible, friendly and spiritual, she could restore hope where they were dejected and love where they were at loggerheads. She looked up to him for his unfailing attentiveness, saying 'I always had a sense of being sheltered as by a father, though he was five years younger than myself and generally far off.' They went by coastal steamer to Ningbo and visited all the other missions, in the spirit of the Shanghai conference. He proposed a Ningbo conference in Chinese for members of all the churches, and went on to Shaoxing. James Meadows had again reverted to foreign dress, choosing to be like other missions rather than like the Chinese to whom he was effectively devoting his life. His little daughter sat with her arm round Hudson Taylor's neck while he encouraged her parents. (In time she joined the Mission.)

The Hangzhou church had long since ceased to need foreign help except in teaching, and welcomed their friend as a father-in-God. He invited all members and their immediate families to a fellowship-meal and the Lord's Supper, and during the ten days he was there, June 16–27, he took part in the ordination of the evangelist Jiang Liang-yong (in dialect Tsiang Liang-yung; Book 5, pp 335–7) as assistant pastor of the Yühang congregation he had largely brought into being. They wanted to build a chapel. 'How about this suggestion?' asked Hudson Taylor: Now that they were strong enough, instead of accepting the help of Liang-yong at the expense of the Hangzhou Christians, how about working towards his full support themselves? They agreed. They would start by providing one fifth of his needs, adding one fifth for every additional ten members joining the church.

In Hangzhou itself, with this relief the congregation undertook the full support of Ren Ziqing (Nying Ts-kying, in local dialect), the schoolmaster–evangelist who had first been attracted to Christ by observing Jennie at Suzhou (Book 5, pp 233, 293). With Wang Laedjün away so much, visiting his daughter churches, Ren had been deputising for him. He was ordained assistant pastor, and in time became Laedjün's son-in-law and successor. The women of Hangzhou were still talking about Jennie, the 'Miss Happiness' who had become one of them from the day she first arrived. The greatest need in this work, Hudson Taylor told her, was more men and women missionaries (thirty more, he said when he passed through Singapore), especially women like her. Then back to Shaoxing, from June 27 to July 4, in temperatures of 90°–100° in the shade.

His pioneers were never far from his mind while he toured the consolidated results of earlier pioneering. Clarke, Fishe and Landale were arriving at Guiyang (June 28) and John McCarthy at Kunming. James Cameron and George Nicoll were travelling in Sichuan before their mountain journeys. Also to his joy, Samuel Dyer, Maria's brother, was taking over as China Agent of the British and Foreign Bible Society from Alexander Wylie, forced to retire with failing eyesight. In twenty years the distribution of the Bible Society's million Testaments had been completed by Wylie's great efforts. With greater freedom Samuel Dyer was to achieve even more than Wylie.

When Hudson Taylor and Elizabeth Wilson reached Sheng Xian for the weekend of July 7, they found signs of this still being perhaps 'the most successful of all our stations'. Not knowing that the Sunday service would be special in any way, Christians walked three, five and as far as fifteen miles to attend. When a man who had persecuted them was not deterred from heckling by Hudson Taylor's presence, they quietly continued the service, and afterwards he suggested to the *dibao*, the local police sergeant, that a word in the trouble-maker's ear might save them both from repercussions should the man go too far. These poor people excelled in hospitality when their visitors left: i.e. the Christians insisted on carrying them in mountain-chairs without payment. Throughout this southern tour from June 8 to the last week of September, the only nights not spent in Mission or Chinese Christians' homes were those on junks, along the coast or on the Qiantang River. 'The many new members in all these places was very cheering, and the evident (spiritual) growth observable in the older members impressed me.'

To Louise Desgraz he wrote, 'The work is *most* cheering – real and progressing. Many new Christians, getting no (material advantages) and hoping for none, on the contrary (are) suffering persecution . . . severely as I have seen.' Because she was being introspective again he had said in another note, 'The world is *unsatisfied*, too large a proportion of the Church is unsatisfied . . . all Christians should be *satisfied*, filled full and overflowing beyond self.' And from Saigon, on his way home in November, 'Forget there is such a person, good or bad, as Louise Desgraz; ignore *her* will and wishes . . .' She kept his letters. He was helping each of his growing mission family in the same way.

They travelled to Taizhou, Wenzhou, Lishui (Chüchou) and Jinhua – where they saw the original house from which James Williamson had been evicted in 1868 (Book 5, p 43), in use as a preaching hall by a nucleus of eight local Christians. 'We *shall* reap if we faint not!' he reminded Louise. Funds were not coming through to him for distribution, and on August 1 he told Jennie, 'I have only 2 cents in hand and all funds are dry,' except for some reserved for the Crombies' passages home. On September 11 and 12 his subdued excitement was evident as he named November 3 as a possible date for sailing at last (at his own expense), and that eight new Christians from Jiangxi province had come to Qu Xian to be baptised. Beginnings were slow, but altogether the CIM had baptised 755, of whom 75% were still in full standing.

Time was running out, and his hope of crossing Jiangxi again, to pack up at Zhenjiang, had to be abandoned. He travelled down the Qiantang River to Hangzhou and Ningbo and by steamer to Zhenjiang instead. On October 2 he left again with his baggage, depositing it in Shanghai and hurried back to Ningbo for the conference he had somehow convened, organised and now was to preside over. All meetings were entirely in Chinese, with Chinese and missionary speakers addressing Chinese delegates from the whole of Zhejiang in the church buildings of the CMS, three American Baptist and Presbyterian Churches, the United Methodist Free Church and the CIM, for eleven consecutive days.[33] He thought it 'excellent', immediately effective and a demonstration of how the Churches could work together and meet for the Lord's Supper without obtrusive differences. Then he returned to Shanghai and was waiting there when the Wusong railway fiasco reached its climax.[34]

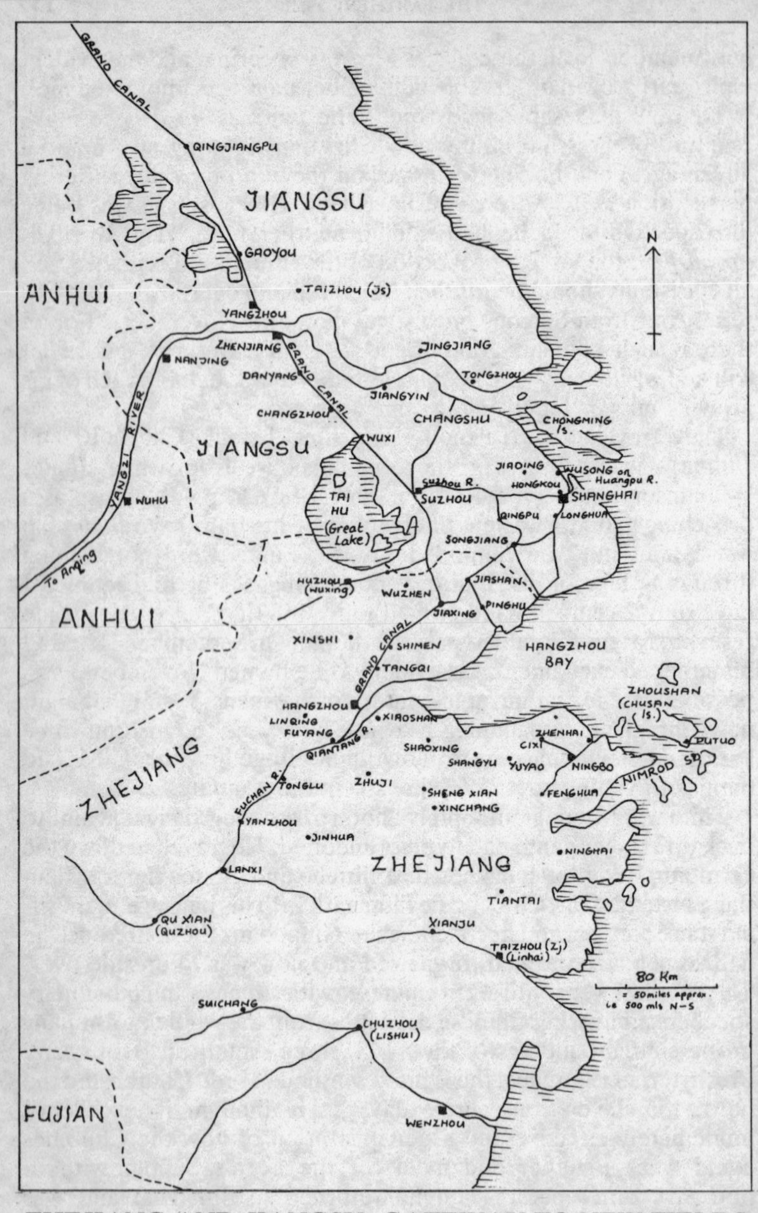

ZHEJIANG AND JIANGSU: GATEWAY TO NEW FIELDS

Meanwhile Cameron and Nicoll had set out for the borders of Tibet, George Clarke and Edward Fishe had gone into Guangxi, and Turner and James had been desperately ill in Shanxi. Since Turner came south to consult at Wenzhou, Hudson Taylor himself was 'very taken up' with the rapidly deteriorating famine situation in North China, and to leave China was as painful as it was necessary. But he was needed more in Britain than in China. King, Budd, Easton and Parker had sorted out their differences and were tackling the north-western provinces again. He wrote on October 26,

> 'Be faithful unto death and He will give you a crown of life.' Often read the 23rd Psalm and give your Amen to all its statements – *in faith* when you cannot do so *in feeling*. '*The Lord is* my Shepherd.' He *is*, He *is* . . . 'My cup runneth over.' *True*, *true*, for He says so . . . Never measure God's promises and statements by your feelings and attainments; accept *all* He says.
>
> Now, farewell, my dear brethren, beloved and prayed constantly for, my joy and crown! May God do for you all and *more than all* I would if I could for Jesus' sake!

It was only one of scores of such letters he was writing to his widely scattered foreign and Chinese family.

On October 17 he had just sent Jennie a telegram to say 'Coming', when word arrived that Edward Fishe had died. He postponed his sailing to the next French Mail, and sent for the grieving Annie and the children to join him and the Crombies. The Crombie children were so debilitated by chronic dysentery that he wondered whether they would reach Britain alive, for George and Anne were beyond caring properly for them. So he enlisted Emmeline Turner to join the party simply to look after the children.[35] On November 3 his close friend 'Mary Jones' of many memories since 1856 (Book 2, pp 346–8) died as 'Ann Maria, wife of Frederick Foster Gough, CMS'. The issue of *China's Millions* which reported the Ningbo conference, carried a meditation by Hudson Taylor on John 17.24: '*Father, I will* (*I long*) *that they also, whom thou hast given me, be with me where I am; that they may behold my glory*'. If we knew God better we would not be perplexed by his dealings with us. Edward Fishe had been about to take Annie and children deep into the interior, far from the Yangzi, the first wife and family to take such a plunge. Why did God take him? The *love* of Jesus is the answer. 'He does not rob one to enrich another, but does the *best* for all' – the best for the widow, for the orphan, for each of the bereaved, as for the one he takes to be with him in his glory – the best too for China and the Church. 'The happy death of Mrs Gough' was illuminated by the same light.

Travelling third class by the Messageries Maritimes, in Chinese clothes as far as Singapore for the sake of Chinese fellow-passengers, they sailed from Shanghai on November 9. Nothing would be gained, he told Jennie, by her meeting them in Paris. The Crombies' illness and the need to get to work in Britain as soon as possible would overshadow their reunion. His 'forty weeks' away had turned into more than fifteen months. By Aden he could not even face meeting her in public, it must be alone in their own home. But having 'God alone' for so long, without her as an added strength and joy, had been a wonderful experience. 'May the Lord Jesus not be *less* to you when I am with you again,' said his note from Naples. On December 20 he was with her and the children at last.

CHAPTER FIVE

FAMINE
1876–79

The 'Millions' in full use *1877–78*

The Britain to which Hudson Taylor returned on December 20, 1877, was a fast changing nation. Yet Britain was being outpaced by other nations. These were exciting times of accelerating invention and discovery, of science and industry. In the last thirty years of the century British steel production (at first the major world supply) was to rise to five million tons. But Germany was to increase hers to seven million and the United States to thirteen million, as world shipping and railways expanded. Lighting by electricity and incandescent bulbs was beginning to replace the hissing gas mantle. The microphone and telephone, the spreading telegraphic network, and at long last comprehensive sanitation through the Public Health Act began to transform living conditions in Britain. And worldwide travel and exploration by Christian missionaries exceeded that achieved by others.

Christmas allowed the Taylor family a brief holiday together after their long separation, a working holiday for Hudson Taylor himself. Herbert, nearing seventeen, and Howard, already fifteen, were no longer the sparring children they had been but thinking adolescents. Maria, nearly twelve, had Millie Duncan as a younger sister, with Charles Edward, nine, and Jennie's two toddlers, Ernest and Amy, for company. But the creaking state of the Mission's administration in Britain cried aloud for attention.

With the honorary office holders as before unable to spare enough time from their professions, and members of the Mission staff in London hobbled by their subsidiary status, Hudson Taylor had no choice but to step straight into work and responsibility. Reorganisation was urgent. The Mission's income had become chronically low and, as Jennie had warned him in a letter received at Aden, some members of the Council were asking for more than the role they had agreed to play in the Mission's affairs as a 'council of management' *in Britain*. Their claim was justified in that the selection of new members of the Mission was crucial, difficult and executive rather than advisory. Something so personal could not end with the individuals going abroad. But the principle of management of the Mission by participating leaders, rather than by boardroom directors, remained fundamental. For the moment action on that issue could be deferred, while he himself took the helm. To study the accounts and remit to China all he could send was his first aim.

Wherever he was, whatever his circumstances, creating an effective tool of each monthly issue of *China's Millions* continued to be an unrelenting priority. So easily could the magazine become a mere house-journal of news and anecdote. Every number must have a cutting edge, more than one, carrying its messages of many kinds deep into the awareness of readers. It must report to donors, inform and incite to action, if it was to justify so much thought and work. It was also the conductor's baton. Therefore each main theme must be chosen, and each leading article in the series 'China for Christ' must carry his insights to the Christian public. Christianity in Britain had become too comfortable and the Church turned in upon itself. 'Called to Suffer', the theme of one editorial, tried to restore right thinking. It was not only for the Mission's supporters, but intended for a far wider circulation, for Christian leaders, politicians and sister societies. It was as much his personal part in the evangelisation of China as almost any other role, whether directing the pioneers in their ventures or guiding the emerging churches in their development and witness.

So he crystallised his messages in his own mind and re-echoed them in a hundred and one different ways, never tiring of them himself or missing an opportunity to stress them. His skill as a communicator drew the comments of observers. 'Faith' he certainly mentioned as a Biblical subject, but as a by-product and not as often as has been supposed. *GOD's faithfulness* was his recurrent theme: God himself, by his very character unable to default on his sure promises. A Father God, faithful to his own children-by-adoption and bound to meet their needs of guidance, protection or material provision, whether personal or incurred in serving him. 'Trust HIM at all times; you will never have cause to regret it,' was the logical conclusion. 'Hold GOD's faithfulness' (p 36) expressed the essence of the Greek translated as 'Have faith in God', for the point was not a need to exert faith but God's reliability in response to any faith. 'All God's giants have been weak men,' Hudson Taylor pointed out in this same context, men like David, the secret of their greatness being dependence on GOD. 'Let us see that in theory we hold that God is faithful; that in daily life we *count* (we act) upon it.'[1]

Misconceptions of the aims and methods of the CIM led him also to reiterate year by year the core of his 'Plan of Operation'. Like the apostles, missionaries (Chinese and foreign together) would travel in small teams to strategic centres, stay there or return again for long enough to establish 'a work of God' and, trusting its continuation to the keeping of God, would move on to new regions. 'The necessity of a somewhat prolonged residence . . . for the purpose of instructing in the Word of God those who may be converted' was as much part of the plan as the itineration.

The emphasis on an indigenous Chinese Church, in *China's Millions* of 1875–76 and again after the Shanghai conference in 1877, reflected the importance Hudson Taylor attached to the establishment of self-governing, self-supporting churches.[2] 'We propose to itinerate constantly *at first*, and consequently to carry on localised work *only for a time* [the emphasis in his] – till native churches can be left to the ministrations of native labourers', with the help of visiting foreign teachers as long as it was needed and welcomed. Any perpetuation of Western denominational differences would be accidental, as individual missionaries left the mark of personal conviction on their teaching.

Apart from information about China and the progress of the CIM and other missions, all of which occupied many pages, one dominant topic claimed space at frequent intervals: opium. Henry Soltau wrote on the devastating effect of opium on the people of Burma, imposed on them by the British; Cardwell on the same effects in China.

> It is eating out the very vitals of the nation. It is the source of poverty, wretchedness, disease and misery, unparalleled in . . . any other country. It debases the debased to the very lowest depths of degradation. It closes the eye to all pity, and the heart to all shame and sympathy. See that poor wretch with the emaciated frame; he has parted with his land, his house, his furniture, his children's and his own clothing and bedding, and either sold his wife or hired her out for prostitution, and *all for opium*, to satisfy an insatiable appetite . . . until it has consumed his life.[3]

The leading article of the December issue of 1877 prepared as Hudson Taylor travelled in southern Zhejiang in September and October, bore the title 'Opium in China', followed by the words 'It

ANNUAL VOLUME OF *CHINA'S MILLIONS*
Red, black and gilt hardcover, fit for the Queen

is scarcely possible to think of England's responsibility in this matter without feelings of unspeakable humiliation and grief.' Travelling and settled missionaries alike wrote of vast numbers of people, even small children, smoking opium. Of nine viceroys all but three were said to be addicted. The resolution of the General Conference in Shanghai was then set out word for word, denouncing the trade, 'deeply injurious not only to China, but also to India, to Great Britain, and to the other countries engaged in it . . . It is a most formidable obstacle to the cause of Christianity' and should be 'speedily suppressed'. 'That which is morally wrong cannot be politically right.' The conference therefore urged that the (British) Indian Government cease to have anything to do with the production and sale of opium, and that attempts to obstruct the Chinese Government, in its lawful efforts to suppress the sale and use of opium, should be opposed. That obstruction currently sprang from the government in Britain itself.

He ran a series of engravings and woodcuts to illustrate the use and effects of opium-smoking. And another series of eight factual articles on the history of the opium traffic, 'dignified' since the opium wars and treaties by the word 'trade'.[4] He quoted Li Hongzhang, Guo Songdao, the ambassador to Britain and France, and other leading Chinese on the inevitability of a Chinese backlash against this British atrocity. Mr Gladstone too; and Sir Rutherford Alcock who cynically blamed the mandarins for being defeated and then signing treaties admitting the curse to China, 'a sign of weakness and . . . of want of courage'! By creating a nation of addicts Britain had driven China to grow her own opium where grain used to be harvested, and by impoverishing a teeming population had deprived her own merchants of an immense potential market for consumer goods.

Through 1878 and subsequently, this championing of the 'anti-opium' cause in *China's Millions* increased in crusading intensity, without diminishing the vigour with which the spiritual need of China and the main work of missions were presented.[5] Nor did such topics prevent the graphic portrayal of a yet more horrifying (only because more urgent) topic: famine.

The Great Famine *1876–77*

Natural disasters were almost commonplace in China. Devastating typhoons struck the southern maritime provinces, bringing floods in their wake. 'China's Sorrow', the Yellow River, from time to time broke her banks and inundated county upon county. Earthquakes, locusts, plague, pestilence and revolutions succeeded one another with frightening frequency. Lingering drought since 1874 had caused hardship for southern Shanxi and the remnants of a population reduced in numbers, health and livelihood by the Muslim rebellion in Shaanxi following the Taiping scourge. As far north as Linfen (Pingyang) in Shanxi the ruins left by the Taipings in 1853 were a grim reminder of bitter suffering at their hands. Evidence of great forests still remained on the Shanxi hills, stripped bare and eroded, so that from 1871 to 1875 vast areas of southern Zhili were inundated and scoured by floods which swept away the fertile topsoil. Hard on their heels in 1876 came drought and then famine lasting into 1880, extending to the border with Korea. Simultaneously the rains failed over the great area of eastern Shaanxi, most of Henan, southern Shanxi, and Shandong which at that time suffered most.[6]

South of the Yangzi, floods had played havoc with the harvests in central Hunan, Jiangxi and Zhejiang, but excessive rainfall in the southern coastal provinces of Fujian and Guangdong during the spring and summer of 1876 destroyed not only crops and homes but also thousands of people. 'As if this were not enough, a plague of locusts, devouring all they crossed, covered nearly the whole' of Jiangsu, inland Shandong and Zhili as far as north of Tianjin. Floods in five provinces, locusts in three and drought in nine during 1876 were succeeded in 1877 by drought and locusts again in much of the nine northern provinces. By then extreme distress due to the scarcity of food and its high prices had signalled the onset of what was believed to be the greatest famine the world had so far known.[7]

Timothy Richard (in 1874 the only one remaining of twelve members of the Baptist Missionary Society in Shandong) had moved from Yantai to Tsingchou (now Weifang) in 1875, and adopted Chinese clothes and a Chinese way of life. When famine set in he raised enough funds in Shanghai and other ports to begin distributing aid. The problem of orderly distribution to fighting mobs of starving people taxed his ingenuity. They went to all lengths, even of taking him prisoner with three cartloads of relief funds in coins. Then one day he read in 'the feeding of the five thousand', '*He made them sit down*.' In a flash he thought, 'A sitting crowd cannot crush.' Introduced with promises of orderly, fair distribution, the method succeeded. 'The *yamen* people were astonished.'[8] John Nevius joined him and the two of them distributed relief worth Mex. $200,000 in two months, in co-operation with the Chinese authorities (*see* Book 1, Appendix 7). But the fields were unsown and Timothy Richard forecast 'fearful disease and mortality' in the coming spring. Even during the winter of 1876–77 while relief was being administered in Shandong and Zhili, tens of thousands died.

When Hudson Taylor arrived at Wuhan on January 9, 1877, he found Henry Taylor back from his fourth expedition to Henan and first expulsion from Queshan. Joshua Turner and Francis James had arrived the previous day from their 1,700 mile journey through the parts of north Anhui, Henan and southern Shanxi devastated by the Taipings. They had met 'several hundred people, all miserably clad, and looking starved and wretched' heading southward from the spreading famine area. But they described the watered Shanxi valley around Linfen as 'well cultivated', in November 1876.

From then onwards, reports of distress multiplied rapidly. Henry Taylor set off again on January 26, and Turner and James on February 10, into the same regions, with the intention of settling 'permanently'. They walked into famine conditions. People were selling their possessions for cash with which to buy food at exorbitant prices. Then they sold their furniture, clothes, doors and window frames, roof tiles, the timber frames of their homes, and then their wives and children.

Hudson Taylor, preparing for the Wuchang and Shanghai conferences, visiting all the Yangzi Mission centres and coping with 'four times as much work' as he could handle, was thinking hard. What could he do for the destitute? In February he had told Louise Desgraz to expand her boarding schools at Zhenjiang and Yangzhou to take in more girls, the beginning of wider plans. As he travelled he wrote an editorial 'Letter from China' for the *Millions*, on 'Concern for the poor' and helpless. Psalm 41.1–3 had spoken to him.

> Do not let us spiritualise the text so as to lose its obvious meaning (of not merely sympathy but action). How much of the precious time and strength of our Lord was spent in conferring temporal blessings on the poor, the afflicted and the needy.[9]

Reaction against a 'social gospel' had not yet clouded the judgment of evangelical Christians. Action 'at the cost of personal self-denial' was the measure of true 'concern'. At his instigation the Wuchang and Ningbo conferences contributed relief funds. And in this spirit he and Jennie were soon to go 'beyond the call of duty'.

'Concern for the poor' *1877–78*

Hudson Taylor was in Shanghai, waiting for the newly widowed Annie Fishe and her children to join him and sail for home, when two letters came from Arnold Foster of the LMS. They had consulted together about the famine and Foster was raising relief funds in Yantai, Tianjin and Peking as William Muirhead was doing in Shanghai. Foster proposed going at once to the famine areas before returning with eye-witness accounts to arouse concern in Britain and the States. Henry Taylor and George Clarke were to take relief to Henan, and Turner and Francis James (recovering from typhoid fever) to distribute it in Shanxi. When food was available people were too poor to buy it, so even two teams of three men with cash to distribute could save thousands of lives.

The Chinese Government had granted 300,000 *taels* (£130,000), increased to 400,000 for its own relief measures, but they were 'utterly inadequate', 'a trifle . . . when we remember the corruption that exists among the officials and underlings who dole it out'.[10] Many altruistic mandarins were doing their best. Some gave even a year's salary to supplement their resources. Whatever was done, 'hundreds of thousands will be left to perish'. 'Considering the paucity of men who seem willing to join in the distribution', Foster wrote, he himself was torn between going to raise funds and staying to go inland with what there was. The Chinese authorities would provide armed escorts for anyone carrying silver into the famine areas. Hudson Taylor wrote, as he sailed on November 9, that he would launch an appeal as soon as he reached home.

Meanwhile the autumn crops had failed again over the whole of the famine area. R J Forrest, British consul and (by Muirhead's request) chairman of the newly formed Famine Relief Committee at Tianjin, was to write,

> In November 1877, the aspect of affairs was simply terrible . . . Tien-tsin was inundated with supplies from every available port. The Bund was piled mountain high with grain, the Government store-houses were full. (All possible means of transporting it were commandeered and) the water-courses were crowded with boats, the roads were blocked with carts.[11]

Disorganised relief measures were exacerbating the calamity.

A hundred thousand refugees had flocked into Tianjin, finding shelter in 'hovels made of mud and millet stalks', but typhus broke out and in the cold weather 400–600 died each night. A camp for destitute women, its only exit locked, was destroyed by fire in three hours with the loss of 2,700 women. Lumbering wagons, and barges on such waterways as still held water, were robbed of their grain on the way to Hwailu (now Huolu) and the Guguan Pass. Dried up canals did form roads for refugees and relief convoys, but the 4,000 foot escarpment into Shanxi all but defeated such attempts as were made to scale it by cart and mule litter. As Consul Forrest reported,

> The result was visible in the piles of grain in bags, the broken carts and the foundered mules which strewed the road leading up to the plateau.[12]
>
> [On the 130-mile mountain trail over the Guguan Pass] the most frightful disorder reigned supreme . . . filled with (an enormous traffic of) officials and traders all intent on getting their convoys over the pass. Fugitives, beggars and thieves absolutely swarmed . . .

A SPRINGLESS PEKING CART
larger for long distances, with more animals

> Camels, oxen, mules and donkeys . . . were killed by the desperate people for the sake of their flesh (while the grain they were meant to be carrying into Shanxi rotted and fed the rats of Tianjin). Night travelling was out of the question. The way was marked by the carcases or skeletons of men and beasts, and the wolves, dogs and foxes soon put an end to the sufferings of any (sick) wretch who lay down . . . in those terrible defiles . . . No idea of employing the starving people in making new or improving the old roads ever presented itself to the authorities. . . . Gangs of desperadoes in the hills (terrorised the travellers). . . . In the ruined houses the dead, the dying, and the living were found huddled together . . . and the domestic dogs, driven by hunger to feast on the corpses everywhere to be found, were eagerly caught and devoured . . . by the starving people. Women and girls were sold in troops to traffickers, who took the opportunity of making money in this abominable manner, and suicide was so common as hardly to excite attention.[13]

The natural southern route of access to Shanxi, from Tongguan in Shaanxi, across the Yellow River and into the central valley basin was undeveloped. The cart-tracks through billows and beds of dust could not sustain any bulk of traffic, even if supplies could pass through the equally terrible famine in Shaanxi. But streams of barely living refugees flowed southwards towards the well-watered Yangzi valley, littering the roadsides with corpses as they fell. Here too women and girls were being transported in exchange for cash or grain, their best hope being to become servant-chattels in southern homes. According to one report by Père de Marché in May 1877, based on a register kept in the *yamen*, 100,000 women and children had already been sold from the one county of Lingqiu in north Shanxi.[14] This was the route taken in December by Joshua Turner, carrying the emaciated Francis James in a litter to Wuhan, already crowded with refugees.

On November 11, 1877, the imperial *Peking Gazette* published a memorial to the throne in which the viceroy, Zeng Guochuan, brother of Zeng Guofan, said, 'There remains neither the bark of trees, nor the roots of wild herbs, to be eaten,' in southern Shanxi. Autumn sowing had been impossible. No less than three or four million people were starving, but by December the price of grain was still rising. Altogether, in the worst affected provinces, seventy-five million were in 'a state of fearful destitution', Sir Thomas Wade declared in a letter to *The Times*. 'The inhabitants of the United Kingdom and the United States combined hardly number seventy millions,' *The Times* commented.[15] As far away as Xi'an in

Shaanxi the price of bread was seventeen times its normal rate, but in Shanxi this was true of unmilled grain brought in by merchants and the government. Before the winter was out parents were eating their own children and neighbours were devouring those who died around them. The worst state of affairs had yet to be reached.

Britain was slow to react to appeals by the Lord Mayor of London, the Archbishop of Canterbury and the leading denominational missionary societies. Early in 1878 *The Christian* published a letter from Hudson Taylor which quickly led to donations being sent for famine relief, but because of the official action he kept his own appeals in a low key. The China Famine Relief Committee, formed in London in February with Arnold Foster as secretary, included Sir Rutherford Alcock, Sir Thomas Wade, Sir George Balfour, Sir Walter Medhurst, Robert Jardine, Professor James Legge and other men of influence. But as reports came from CIM missionaries, Hudson Taylor published them in *China's Millions* and the response grew steadily.[16] By July he could write for the September *Millions*,

> We took early occasion to draw attention to the great need, and in response were able to make our first remittance in September 1877. Since then we have received, including amounts given for orphanage (*sic*) £6000. This we have gladly remitted to China for distribution. The (Shanghai Famine) Relief Committee have received about £30,000. The (combined) Missionary Societies have also received about £5,000 more. [For a more realistic impression multiply by, say, fifty.]

He pointed out that some of his donors also contributed to the 'General Relief Fund'.

> Many will eagerly ask, What is the total amount? . . . Will it be believed that all that the people of England have given to lessen the sufferings of millions of people under a calamity such as the world has rarely if ever known, is only about £40,000! We think . . . of the more than £500,000 contributed for . . . the famine in India [Bengal in 1875 and southern India in 1876–77]. (Yet) we derive . . . a revenue averaging about £150,000 weekly from the sale of opium in China. (For the five months since the appeals were launched) the sale of opium in China for the same period in other (than) famine years would amount to about £3,300,000. In other words, our revenue from that which is ruining China, would exceed in two days all we have yet given to relieve the suffering Chinese . . . Why is this? . . . Because the actual state of things is not generally known.

He devoted fourteen pages of this issue of *China's Millions* to the famine, two to the opium scandal and only two to the Mission's normal work.

At first the provincial mandarins resisted offers of help. What base motives had the barbarians this time? It would be better for China to suffer alone than to play into their hands. But when the co-operation of the Relief Committee and distributors (all of them missionaries) was welcomed by no less than the Grand Secretary, Viceroy of Zhili and Guardian of the Throne, Li Hongzhang, together with Zeng Guochuan of Shanxi, officials loyal to them followed suit. Only in Henan did Henry Taylor and George Clarke receive a rebuff when the authorities at Kaifeng refused their funds and assistance, and in Shaanxi where F W Baller and J Markwick received the same treatment.[17]

The price of concern — *March–May 1878*

During the last week of March 1878 Hudson Taylor asked Jennie to pray about a new proposition. Only four months after arriving home to end the fifteen-month separation that had at times seemed intolerable, he knew they must part again. The plight of China, especially of her women and children, was preying on his mind. The 'very low' state of the Mission's funds had not changed. Donations were coming in for famine relief rather than for Mission purposes. Even so it was then that he authorised the missionaries in famine and refugee areas to take in two hundred destitute children, giving priority to orphans.[18] He told Louise Desgraz that he was praying for an increase of £5,000 in annual receipts and an additional £2,000 for outfits and passages for new missionaries.

Jennie expressed her confidence in God by saying, 'He wills that we should feel the need of asking, but He *cannot* fail us.' Then Hudson Taylor made his suggestion, that as he himself could not leave Britain yet, she should go, escorting a party of new members and supervising the orphanage scheme in China until he could come and join her. No time could be lost. If women and children were to be saved it must be at once. She was thirty-five and had two infants of barely three and two. The youngest could go with her.[19]

Two years later Jennie wrote to tell the seven children what happened. After praying about it for two weeks she decided on April 12 that she should go, and told her nursemaid, Jane, who offered to stay and work for Amelia if that would help. Amelia was away, but when she heard the news she said, 'If Jennie is called to China, I am called to care for her children', if Jane would stay to help. Apart from her own four boys and six girls, Amelia was running the Mission transit home and caring for candidates in training. To add Herbert and Howard, Maria and Milly Duncan, Charles Edward and Ernest would not make much difference. Before Jennie left, Amy her baby fell ill with whooping cough and had to be left behind too.

On April 16 Hudson Taylor told the council, and the next day Theodore Howard's mother, Hudson's old friend Mrs Robert Howard, called to say she thought it wrong for Jennie to leave her children and husband even for such a cause. As soon as she had gone Jennie went to her bedroom.

> I was feeling deeply how much it would cost me, so . . . I asked God to confirm me in going, (saying, '£50 just now would be worth more to me than a fortune at another time; it would be a guarantee of all other needs being met.') I felt like Gideon – that my strength in China would be, 'Have not I commanded thee?' and I wanted some fleeces to strengthen my own faith and as answer to those who would have me remain. . . . I did not doubt that God wanted me to go, but I felt sad . . . like Gideon . . . the least in his father's house . . . the most unlikely one . . .[20]

The 'fleeces' she put out were two prayers, one for enough money for necessities for the journey 'as we had none to spare', £4 would cover it, and one for a sizeable sum, £50 (at least £2,000 today) for herself and Hudson personally. She told no one, not even him, but at family prayers the next morning she told the children she wanted them to pray with her for two things which she would reveal when the answer was given, 'as His promise that He will bless those I leave behind more than if I stayed with them, and that He will stand by me and help me.' That afternoon a Mr Harris of Jersey, [the friend who had sent Hudson a pair of gloves with a half sovereign inside, in 1852 (Book 2, p 51)] called at Pyrland Road and asked, was she going? Yes, getting ready, she replied. He handed her a cheque for £10, the exact amount the Mission allowed for outfitting. 'I thanked God and watched eagerly for the £50 that I was expecting.'

On Monday, April 22, a letter came from Hudson's parents addressed to her and containing £50. She took it to show him, but as he had someone with him, left it without a word. When she returned he was considering how the Lord would have the money applied, and she said, 'Oh, that money's mine. I have a claim on it that you do not know of.' Then she told him the story of her 'fleeces'. Ten days later she left home, escorting a party of four young men and three women to China, and cheered by a gift the previous day of £1,000 (thought to be from John Challice) for setting up an orphanage.

Among those who saw them off at the station to join the French Mail at Marseilles was William Sharp, a solicitor who had recently joined the London Council. Hudson Taylor's parting exhortation to the new missionaries to make 'gentleness and faithfulness' the hallmark of their service among the Chinese had impressed him. But the Taylors' parting from each other drew from him the confession, 'I felt just as if I were parting with my own wife, and the thought was altogether more than I could bear . . . and yet I suppose that if God *called* us to part, He would enable us to do so with the same calmness that *you* enjoyed yesterday.' For decades to come he was to be an indefatigable servant of the China Inland Mission.[21]

When they had gone, Hudson Taylor wrote letters of welcome to China, with a good remittance to greet each of the new pioneers on reaching Shanghai. And to Jennie, saying that her mother was proud of her – a transformation from her earlier attitudes. For himself he wrote, 'I, darling, am *grateful* for the grace which has taken you from me . . .' He began to run a daily fever, 'anything but exhilarating', and confessed, 'I wandered sometimes from empty room to empty room like one who did not know what he wanted,' adding 'Milly clings a good deal.' His affinity for children had not left him, nor the motherless child's sense of loss. And later, 'I have more pleasure in *you*, in your absence, than your presence would afford; for it gives me more joy to see you enabled to put Jesus *first*, and find in *Him* your present gain . . .' But to ease his loneliness he asked Herbert, preparing to enter the London Hospital Medical College, to come and share his study and bedroom. Famine relief donations were coming in steadily, and gifts of plate and jewellery. In China's agony they were doing what they could.

The famine at its worst[22] *1878*

After the terrible winter of 1877–78 the hopes of all rested upon spring rains so that something, anything edible might come to life from the hard soil. Instead blue skies turned to brass as the season advanced. The *Peking Gazette* of March 15 carried a 'memorial' by the High Commissioner for Famine Relief, Yuan Baoheng, and by the governor of Henan. All the previously poor of the province, they testified, had disappeared – dead or dispersed to more fortunate provinces. In their place those who had been well-to-do or even wealthy were in the extremity of distress. Like the poor before them, those who could not move away (taking their valuables, only to be robbed on the roads) were resorting to cannibalism, even of their own kith and kin.[23] Consul R J Forrest also reported extensive cannibalism. But now it was no longer the dead and dying whose flesh was taken and skulls opened to extract the brains but, the *Peking Gazette* and *The Times* joined others in reporting, in some regions it had become unsafe to be alone, for some had taken to killing for food. Executions to deter villains had only limited success. Wolves which had become more and more dangerous in country places took to attacking men, women and children on city streets. Even after heavy showers in May, the first for three years, and more in July, the distress continued. Too weak to till and sow, many who had seed corn painfully hidden away dared not reveal it. What was sown had to be guarded until it could be harvested. The famine could only grow worse until October.

Hearing that conditions in Shanxi were worse than anywhere, Timothy Richard had left the famine relief in Shandong to his colleagues and travelled through stricken Zhili (Hebei) to Taiyuan, the Shanxi capital. The Peking and Tianjin Missions were supplementing Chinese government relief in their own province of Zhili. On November 30, 1877, when Richard reached Taiyuan with funds from the China Relief Committee and found that Turner and James had left only two days before, he consulted the mandarins, and following their advice began to organise relief work through the local officials of adjoining cities.[24] His courtesy and efficiency immediately impressed them and smoothed the way for all who joined him. He had made a study of etiquette and Confucian conduct.

Joshua Turner and Francis James reached Wuhan on January 22, 1878, from their interrupted 'permanent occupation' of Shanxi, and wrote poignant reports of travelling through 'ragged, homeless herds' of the starving, past corpse after corpse being devoured by dogs or birds. Their desperate appeals for help were among the first to be published. Lurid detail might move some donors who otherwise would read unmoved, as if it were a story.[25] James was too weak to return, but only eight days later, on January 30, Turner left him to regain his strength and, armed with funds contributed in Wuhan, started back to Shanxi. The overland route was too slow and dangerous. By river-steamer to Shanghai, from there by coaster to Tianjin, and inland through the Guguan Pass would take no longer. The Wesleyan Methodist missionary, David Hill, decided to go too, and joined him in Shanghai in mid-February. There a married man, Albert Whiting, an American Presbyterian from Nanjing visiting Shanghai, offered to accompany them, and they sailed together on March 9. Supplied by the Committee at Tianjin with 17,000 taels in silver (about £4,000–5,000) and given a military escort, they reached Taiyuan and joined Timothy Richard on April 2. Zeng Guochuan, the governor, and Commissioner Yuan immediately sent for them, treating them as honoured guests. To their proposal to go on at once to Linfen (Pingyang), where the famine was most grim, the governor 'objected in a polite way, but very decidedly'. The reason soon emerged. The extreme difficulty of bringing grain into the province, and the inadequacy of government funds with which to meet so vast a crisis, had made it impossible for Zeng and Yuan to provide for every district. Consul Forrest wrote,

> Any distribution made in the districts where the Chinese had started no relief would inevitably lead to an insurrection among the desperate inhabitants, who have hitherto been accustomed in times of distress to join their disaffected neighbours in (Henan) and (Shandong), and carry fire and sword from the Yellow River to the valleys of the Han and (Yangzi). A few foreigners giving help where the mandarins were doing nothing would have excited the people at once, and the pillage of one or two *yamens*, and the murder of a few (mandarins) would have been the signal for a general conflagration . . . It may be fairly stated that while the foreign relief at one time, but for extreme good sense, gave cause for much political uneasiness, it eventually, by the emulation which it excited, prevented an insurrection with which the Chinese government might have found it hard to deal.

By taking over where the governor had begun, they freed him to tackle a new area. He sent a representative with Timothy Richard and Whiting to one city, while another took David Hill and Turner to a second. Within a few days Albert Whiting was desperately ill, and died on April 25, 'carried off by (famine) fever', typhus.[26]

He was not the first or the last to make this sacrifice. Famine fever continued rife in Tianjin and Peking and throughout the famine area, taking the lives of three French Sisters of Charity and several priests; the Methodist W Nelthorpe J Hall on May 14, barely sparing his wife; Letitia Campbell of the American Episcopal Church on May 18; and John S Barradale of the LMS on May 25. His wife had succumbed to the fever in 1877.[27] 'Yuan Baoheng, the Famine Commissioner, followed next,' Consul Forrest added, 'and a large number of the assistants employed in distributing aid died, or were disabled by typhus . . . (Later) Mr Turner, of the China Inland Mission, and Mr Smith, of the American Board, survived fearful attacks.' But in Turner's case it was dysentery that nearly proved fatal.

Their sacrifice went far towards convincing the literati that not all barbarians were unscrupulous. Some were sincerely devoted to China's welfare. Grand Secretary Li Hongzhang on hearing of Hall's death said to his adviser, the customs commissioner G Detring, 'that there must be something in a faith which induced the foreign gentlemen to come to China and gratuitously risk their lives, and even forfeit them' for the Chinese.[28] One of the CIM famine relief workers, unnamed, wrote as this toll increased, 'It is probable that others of us will be called away. We must hold ourselves prepared, though of course we shall use every precaution against the fever. If I die . . . I wish to be buried here.' His colleagues used much the same words.

They quickly won confidence by systematic preparations that proved their integrity and the reliability of the people they dealt with.

> Our plan is to take the money in cash to the village temple, and then go round to the families on the list, with one of the head men, see the house, make some inquiries, compare their statements with the number of mouths entered on the list, then give them a ticket for money which they take immediately to the temple to be cashed. In some instances we strike off the name altogether. This plan is very laborious, but it brings us into contact with the people themselves, and prevents unfairness . . . We gave money to one village but the next day the headmen brought back the share of twenty people, saying they had (died) since the lists were made, only a few days ago.
>
> Today, one representative of each family from seven villages came by appointment to our temple. They gathered in the open space in front of the door and were admitted, two villages at a time, into the temple yard. Mr Richard distributed to one, and I (Turner) to the

> other. Each person came up to the table when his name was called, and received 800 cash (about three shillings) for each needy member of his family . . . In this way the wants of 1,400 or more persons and their families were supplied. In the evening it began to rain, and soon was pouring heavily. . . . Rain and money to buy seed came together.[29]

Jennie reached Shanghai on June 13 with her seven companions, where she handed them over to Baller, Judd and George Clarke. The women they took to the Mission language school at Yangzhou and the men to Anqing. Adam C Dorward was to become the intrepid pioneer of Hunan, J H Riley of western Sichuan, and Samuel R Clarke of the minority tribes of Guizhou. Fanny Rossier of Lac Leman, Switzerland, married George Clarke and went to Dali in Yunnan, weeks of travel beyond her pioneer 'sisters' by then in Chongqing and Guiyang.

July was the hottest time of year, and Wuhan proverbial as one of China's 'three furnaces'. Jennie's first job was to get the two hundred famine orphans into existing CIM premises, the CIM schools or into other care in the Yangzi valley region. She conferred with Louise Desgraz at Zhenjiang, went on to Anqing and back to Nanjing. Apart from one or two found here and there, the Yangzi valley turned out to be the wrong place for the purpose. Thousands of women and children were arriving from the north, to be quickly sold and carried off, out of reach. More significantly, the old rumours of exploitation of children by foreigners for sinister and immoral purposes (Book 5, pp 241–2) had not died out. It was unsafe to collect children except in the famine areas.[30] Then a letter reached her from Hudson Taylor, written on May 10 soon after she had left him. If orphanages should prove impracticable in the Yangzi region, he suggested, she should consider going to the heart of the famine, to Shanxi.

She had already written to Joshua Turner and Timothy Richard for advice. Was there scope for two or three women to help them? But at Nanjing she contracted cholera. It was widespread. William Rudland's second wife, a Brealey of Somerset, died of it on June 29, and Fanny Jackson on August 21, within twenty-four hours of her first symptoms. Chauncey Goodrich of Tianjin had married on May 30 and was widowed on September 3. But Jennie recovered quickly and was at Yangzhou when replies arrived from Shanxi. Typically she made little of her narrow escape. 'I spent some time in Nanking.'[31]

Consul Forrest reported on the actions of the Tianjin Relief Committee,

> In June, Mr Richard had begun to interest himself on behalf of some of the poorest orphans of (Taiyuan) and had fixed on a temple in which to locate them, when the Governor (Zeng) informed him that he (himself) would undertake such an institution in the city, and forwarded the rules under which he proposed to conduct it. [Very likely this too was to forestall accusations against the foreigner.] Mr Richard, thereupon, with the Governor's approval, commenced a systematic relief to the orphans, widows and aged, in some scores of the surrounding villages. In September, 1878, seven hundred and forty-four names were enrolled under the superintendency of Mr Turner, and on the 17th January, 1879, the numbers were: Orphans, 822; Aged and Widows, 334 – Total, 1156. Mr Hill, at Pingyang Fu, had adopted a similar plan with the approval of the officials.

It was August 8 when Jennie heard from Turner and Richard that her 'letter came to them as the answer to *many* prayers'. The opportunity in Shanxi was unique, they said.[32] On the ninth William Muirhead, as organising secretary of the China Famine Relief Fund, also wrote saying, 'Children could be obtained without prejudice to the missionary cause' in Shandong and Zhili – only eight years after the Tianjin massacre of orphanage nuns. 'The only *safe* way at present is to open an orphanage *in the famine district*.' By then Francis James was recuperating in Yantai and about to marry Marie Huberty, a Belgian who, like him, had joined the Mission in 1876. Jennie enlisted two more of their contemporaries, Celia Horne and Anna Crickmay, and with the ubiquitous Frederick Baller to escort them, sailed from Shanghai on September 21 to Tianjin.[33] They were waiting there for the honeymoon couple to join them when news came that Joshua Turner was alone and dangerously ill in Shanxi.

In May, David Hill and Turner had been permitted to start famine relief at Linfen (Pingyang) in the south of the province, with an official to vouch for them. And after bringing 51,890 taels of silver from Shanghai to the Committee in Tianjin, an American Presbyterian from Zhili named Jasper McIlvaine had begun distributing 3,000 taels of relief money at Tsechou (now Jincheng) also in the south of Shanxi. Between then and the end of September, Richard, Hill, Turner and McIlvaine had between them identified and provided 100,641 people with about 500 cash each, enough to keep them alive until such harvest as there might be. Then, as Timothy Richard wished to make a fleeting visit to Shandong to get married, Turner took his place for a few weeks, providing for the aged and orphans around Taiyuan. Two weeks later he became so ill with dysentery that by the time David Hill had come to the rescue on September 26 he was hovering between life and death. They needed help without delay.[34]

Baller and the three women set off as soon as the news reached them and, travelling by boat to Baoding, by cart to the foot of the pass and from there by mule-litter, arrived at Taiyuan on October 23. To their surprise the people of these disaster areas were friendly and open, unlike the reticent folk in the Yangzi valley. Francis James and his bride arrived a few days later and the Richards soon after them. Three more men for Shanxi, Parrott, Elliston and Drake, sailed on November 14.

THE COMMON MULE LITTER FOR THE MOUNTAINS
more stylish for mandarins

The prospect of 'any number' of children to care for, as Turner said, led Jennie to rent premises, set up an 'industrial school' for destitute women and begin taking in orphans. On November 22 Hudson Taylor wrote suggesting that she assess the prospects in Linfen also. By December both her refuge and Timothy Richard's school for destitute boys were daily being asked to take in more, but not to the extent expected. Deliberately, the governor's orphanage was admitting most.[35] All the same, with the 1,156 orphans and elderly in the missionaries' care one way or another, their hands were full. Shortly before Christmas two Yantai missionaries of the SPG, C P Scott and Albert Capel, joined David Hill at Linfen until May 1879, with 3,000 more taels, and Jennie deferred a move by the CIM in that direction. It later became the Mission's major sphere in Shanxi.

By February 1879 she herself had done what she came to do, and could leave the orphanage and 'industrial school' to Anna Crickmay and Celia Horne under Joshua Turner's care. (In 1881 he married Anna.) Jennie left Taiyuan on the 11th with Frederick Baller and was back in Shanghai on March 5, to meet Hudson Taylor and the reinforcements he was bringing.[36] Autumn rains had brought the prospect of food for all in 1879. But April and May were to see the highest death rate of the whole famine, from malnutrition, typhus, dysentery and, on top of it all, smallpox.

'A turning point' *1879*

The first rains in 1878 had held out some hope of an autumn harvest, but that still lay months ahead. The distress had become worse and worse until October, while speculators' mountains of grain rotted at Tianjin, waiting for the means of transport to improve. In northern Shanxi a third of the population died, according to Timothy Richard's careful estimate. Officials had no way of keeping accurate records. The village headman knew best. In southern Shanxi David Hill and Jasper McIlvaine estimated that three-quarters perished in each relief area. The Peking authorities placed the total of 5½ million in Shanxi, 2½ million in Zhili, one million in Henan and half a million in Shandong by the spring of 1879 when good harvests were expected. Nine and a half million died. To convey the government allocation of grain to Linfen in early 1879 would have cost 1½ million taels, before it could be distributed. By the sale of official titles and honours, 200,000 taels had been assigned for this.

A new horror then claimed more victims. Among those who had survived to enjoy eating again 'a pestilence of dysentery beat out typhus as soon as the harvest was gathered, and the stomachs of the people were inflamed by too great indulgence in unaccustomed foods.' Fields of millet stood unharvested, sagged and decayed. Their owners had died and others were too weak to do the work. Millions with no fields or income were dependent still on outside help. The London relief committees misunderstood news of the first rains and first harvest and closed their books in September 1878, even though in July the Shanghai committee had cabled, 'Available means exhausted. Appeal for prompt transfer of £5,000.' Recovery would depend on outside help for several more months.[37]

Although the aid to China amounted to about £50,000, 'a paltry sum' in the circumstances, of which £8,000 came through the CIM, £10,000 through other societies, and the rest through the London Committee, the initial response had not been sustained. In his preface to the 1878 bound volume of *China's Millions* (issued in 1879) Hudson Taylor said,

> Is it not humbling to think that the entire amount raised for the famine relief during 1878, though it has called forth (gratitude) from the most influential official in the empire (Li Hongzhang) and from the Chinese Ambassador in London (Guo Songdao), is actually exceeded by the amount we through our Indian government receive in three days from the sale of opium in China.

When Marquis Zeng succeeded Guo as ambassador in February 1879, he too expressed his gratitude and his wish to meet Hudson Taylor. In most of China a new attitude to missionaries was becoming apparent. They were being received 'kindly' and 'with respect'.[38] Consul Forrest testified of the relief workers,

> The officials treat the missionaries now with the most marked cordiality and assist them in every way in their power . . . That obdurate class 'the literati and gentry' are . . . confessing that their efforts for the relief of the suffering millions are not only an example to them but has really been the incentive which has produced Chinese action.
>
> H.E. the Grand Secretary and Viceroy, Li Hong-chang, did me the honour of dining with me yesterday, to celebrate Her Majesty's birthday . . . the first time a viceroy has accepted a consul's invitation to dine with him. He spoke most feelingly and thankfully of the (relief) efforts.[39]

F H Balfour, another British official, also wrote,

> The sight of so much self-sacrificing labour and Christ-like self-forgetfulness . . . has filled the (Chinese) with astonishment . . . Are these the foreigners we have heard so much about – the malignant, unscrupulous, deceitful foreigners?

To a very small extent the self-denial of the relief workers was atoning for the immense wrongs done to China. But, Hudson Taylor commented, the desperate spiritual state of the Chinese people was only beginning to dawn on the Western Church.

In gratitude China contributed in 1880 to the Irish Relief Fund. The days of uncomprehending prejudice and hostility were passing. Relatively progressive men like Li Hongzhang still had the diehards at Peking and the superstitious to contend with, but with American engineers and equipment the Kaiping mines had begun work in 1877, and the Shanghai Steam Navigation Company merged with the China Merchants Steam Navigation Company.[40] Dr Halliday Macartney, director of Li Hongzhang's arsenal at Nanjing, accompanied Guo Songdao to London and for thirty years, until December 1905, was 'the able, loyal and trusted adviser of each successive Chinese envoy' to London.[41]

On February 3, 1879, George Clarke, this time with A G Parrott as a companion, left Wuhan for Shanxi. They travelled via Queshan where a mandarin apologised for the treatment Henry Taylor and Clarke had previously received, and through Zhengzhou to Jincheng (Tsechou) in Shanxi.[42] Jasper McIlvaine had finished his work and gone, so they took responsibility for several villages which neither he nor the government had been able to help. Going from village to village and house to house, what moved them most deeply was 'the grief of the people that their *gods* had failed them' while strangers had kept them alive until things began to grow again. 'An old widow would walk several miles . . . merely to present us with a few vegetables as a token of her gratitude.' With returning hope also came revived hatreds; 'several attempts were made to get up a riot and expel us from the city'. So they moved on to Linfen, joining Turner and Elliston. By the summer little relief work remained for them to do, and they were free to spend their days preaching the gospel.

A journey of inspection was made in 1879 by W C Hillier of HBM consular service, Shanghai, on behalf of the China Famine Relief Committee with 2,000 taels to distribute to Shanxi.[43] Taking S B Drake, another of the newly arrived CIM men, for company, he left Wuhan on January 10. Southern Henan they found to be 'under cultivation as far as eye could see' but the people as 'contemptuous of the foreign devil' as in normal times – sure proof that Hillier was in foreign clothes. 'Mr Drake being in Chinese dress passed unnoticed.' But northern Henan showed all the physical signs of famine, in dismantled homes and government concentrations of refugees. At one city Hillier's appearance drew such unruly crowds that 'nothing but a small regiment of soldiers' could have controlled them. The magistrate was powerless. But all they wanted was to stare at him, for hours on end.

> Many towns and villages were almost empty . . . (we heard) nothing but the echo of our own footsteps as we hurried through . . . cities of the dead. We had the curiosity to enter into one of these houses, but the sight that awaited us there gave us both so terrible a shock that we went into no more . . . We gave up talking much about the things we had seen. The misery was too deep to be discussed. Only in some homes were the dead in coffins or bricked in by their families – to foil the certain alternative of being exhumed and eaten by starving neighbours.

At Linfen on February 18 they found Scott and Capel occupying a temple allocated to them by the authorities, and Richard and Turner living with David Hill in 'his own hired house'. Hillier and Drake handed over the funds to Hill and joined in their distribution. The thoroughness and wisdom of the way it was done drew praise from Hillier. Lest any headman should be accused of profiting from the distribution of funds, each was made a payment in full view of all, for the work they had put into drawing up lists and escorting the distributors from place to place.

Hillier left Linfen on February 25 and like Jennie took the road through 'the terrible (Guguan) Pass' to Tianjin. 'I met thousands of mules, donkeys, camels and men streaming through the Pass . . . all laden with grain . . . even little boys nine or ten years old being pressed into the work . . . Thousands of people are thus enabled to earn enough to support themselves.' In his report he dealt in gruesome detail with the deprivations by wolves and the lengths to which cannibalism had descended, before reviewing the measures needed to prevent a repetition of such a famine – reafforestation, road-making and eventually a railway even through those mountains. Nowhere in the records studied is there any mention of men being mobilised to widen the roads, improve the gradients and eliminate the bottle-necks while the famine lasted. R J Forrest also discussed the major measures needing to be undertaken by the Government. 'Venality and utter corruption' were the greatest problem, Hillier continued. In Shanxi 'even to myself, a "barbarian" in the genuine barbarian dress, perfect civility was shown in

DISEMBODIED SPIRITS

THE LIVE EAT THE DEAD

Woodcuts used to raise famine funds in provinces with plenty

and around Linfen, while to Messrs Richard, Hill and Scott [those fluent in Chinese] the respect was very marked.' (Not surprisingly a strong church resulted.)

From sixteen or seventeen times the previous market price, the value of grain had returned to five or six times the norm, and then to merely double the old price. The true famine was all but over, at a cost of not less then ten million lives, and probably thirteen million, with the expenditure of 125,487,858 taels by the Tianjin Famine Relief Committee alone.[44] But food was only one factor. Homes and livelihoods had still to be rebuilt. Even as far away as Gansu in 1880, George Easton found himself debarred from a house because in it were refugee women huddled together for warmth, through lack of clothing. He bought and distributed supplies of second-hand clothes.[45]

Other refugees had returned home hearing that harvests were being reaped, only to die because there was little to go round. The armchair critics could complain of *ad hoc* philanthropy being misplaced, money, labour and lives poured into a sieve, where prevention would have been better. But once the disaster had struck, it was cure, not prevention that was needed. The climate was beyond control, the destruction of forests had gone on for centuries, the venality of officials was beyond the influence of missionaries except in the long term, and *fengshui*, the barrier to the provision of road and rail,could only be circumvented by the Chinese themselves. Li Hongzhang did his conservative best, only to meet strong resistance. He yielded for the time being. Of about thirty missionaries who left their regular work to do famine relief, twelve were young men and women of the CIM.[46] Alexander Wylie of the LMS and Bible Society paid tribute to them at a meeting chaired by Lord Shaftesbury. 'Among the earliest volunteers were members of the China Inland Mission . . . There is one . . . fact of such a noble character that I think it ought to be held up to view, I mean the conduct of the heroic lady Mrs Taylor.' But leading the way and making so great a success of it were Timothy Richard of the BMS and David Hill of the WMMS. Joshua Turner had twice come close to death, and Francis James once. Only Albert Whiting of the American Presbyterian Mission gave his life in Shanxi, the other deaths being in Zhili. But following a severe illness while taking relief to Shaanxi, Markwick progressively lost his sight and had to leave China.

In 1880 the magistrate of Linfen Xian erected a six-foot stone tablet at the temple of the Linfen city god, giving what David Hill called 'the most accurate, vivid and concise' account of the famine he, Hill, had seen.[47] He told of a magistrate in Shandong who donated a whole year's salary, which prompted the leading literati of his city also to make large donations. Their 3,000 taels had been distributed unostentatiously in Linfen Xian. A glowing tribute to Hill, Turner and Richard (in that order) necessarily ended with the words, 'How profound then and how long-continued must have been the influence of the virtue and beneficence of his sacred Majesty the Emperor, that they should thus be moved by the call of Heaven.'

In his book *The British in the Far East*, the historian George Woodcock described Hudson Taylor's mission (as he called the CIM) as,

> a movement of dedicated men and women who would seek 'absolute simplicity in everything' . . . Sectarian disputes should be abandoned as unnecessary luxuries, an interdenominational movement, linked to no one Church, should be established, aimed at teaching uncontroversial Protestant Christianity . . . (with) a new type of missionary who would be willing to live and travel as an ordinary Chinese might do, and to look and speak like him, except that his speech would be of Christ. . . . From their initiative sprang a deeper involvement, among missionaries in general, in the massive social problems of China. In this respect the relief work undertaken by British mission workers during the great famines of 1876 to 1878 was a turning point . . . It is significant that Timothy Richard, the English Baptist who led the famine relief of 1876, should more than twenty years later have founded the Shansi Provincial University, one of the pioneer institutions of its kind in China.[48]

In 1880 a very highly qualified physician and surgeon, Harold Schofield, joined the CIM and began work at Taiyuan. The medical arm of the Mission had begun in earnest, to lead on to hospitals and leprosaria in several provinces, and many dispensaries.

The year apart — *May 1878–April 1879*

We return to Hudson Taylor. Reunion with his family for Christmas 1877 had been a necessary but secondary reason for his return home. The state of the Mission in Britain had compelled it. For lack of someone qualified to fill the role William Berger had played,

Hudson Taylor had had to rely on a make-shift staff of inexperienced men under the control of the 'council of management' (p 161). During his 'forty week' absence in China, Jennie in the wings as the experienced prompter had provided some stability, but management by part-timers, however devoted, had not been successful. Even the help of John McCarthy had failed to provide the needed coherence. When William Berger had been director, Hudson Taylor, although far away in China, had seldom felt so out of touch as Berger's successor had left him. With so much happening in China he was needed there above all. In as short a time as possible while in Britain he must reorganise. He must shed much of the routine burden of *China's Millions* as soon as he could find a reliable co-editor; and appoint an executive secretary empowered to get the administrative work done. He must also interview and send to China as many as he could of the twenty-four or more new missionaries he was praying for.

The number of constant friends of the Mission, committed to caring about China, praying and influencing others for the salvation of her dying millions, was still pathetically small. Spasmodic enthusiasm over pioneer journeys, famine or response to the gospel was not enough. So immense a cause needed commitment by many churches, personifying the Church at large, and by many more individuals with the devotion of his own parents and Amelia, of the Howards, Miss Stacey, Lord Radstock, the Beauchamps and others who never lost interest or stopped praying. This meant personally meeting as many as possible who showed initial concern, and addressing all the audiences he could. The knowledge that he was back in Britain led to more than enough opportunities of every kind.

After Jennie left Britain in May 1878 he gave himself increasingly to this work. He made a point of visiting each of his council members in his own home, to listen and to build on his dedication to the cause. He preached at churches of most denominations and at a succession of conferences. According to John Stevenson he always carried 'an 18-province revolver in his pocket', a folding map of China to help people grasp intelligently what was going on, the extent of the famine, and the significance of the great journeys being made. He had a copy of the map with the journeys marked on it bound into each annual volume of *China's Millions*, and at the twelfth anniversary meetings of the CIM he emphasised the importance of all the map demonstrated.

Factual reports of the Mission's progress took pride of place, but

Hudson Taylor's closing address went to the heart of the matter in two points he constantly made. Not surprisingly the first was 'the faithfulness of God', but the second stressed the moral and spiritual danger to young missionaries in a pagan environment, and therefore the need of unfailing prayer for them.[49] Expansion of the Mission's commitments had drawn questioning comments from some. So he reminded his audience that the successful adventure of invading and occupying the nine unevangelised provinces had been financed by funds donated specifically for that purpose, over and above the income for other purposes. But with the already increased liabilities, was the current move to send twenty or thirty *more* men and women prudent,

> with a current income not equal within a thousand or two thousand pounds to the expenses of the Mission? . . . Well, we have looked the thing in the face . . . and this is (our) conclusion: that with the current income of the Mission we have nothing to do, but with God we have everything to do; that *we* are not going to send out twenty or thirty missionaries, or one, but we are going to ask God to send (them); and if He sends (them) He is just as able to supply them as . . . those who went previously. [To the incredulous or cynical this may have sounded disingenuous, but of his translucent sincerity those who knew him were in no doubt. As for candid statements of the financial position, this was another annual business meeting of the equivalent of shareholders. Far more important were the purely spiritual issues.] If this is a real work for God it is a real conflict with Satan . . . with spiritual wickedness . . . We should not underrate the powers of darkness. . . . *This is the thing that causes me concern* . . . that God will *keep* our young (men and women) in spheres where they will be surrounded by such a mass of moral pollution . . . of scepticism and infidelity, as is enough to swamp them, to destroy their faith.[50]

He could have named colleagues he had in mind, and the influence of theologically unstable missionaries, but he spoke prophetically. In the next few years he was to grapple with case after case of defeat and defection.

No General Missionary Conference had been held since the first in Liverpool in 1860. (*See* HTCOC Book 3, p 479, note 22.) In confidence to Jennie, Hudson Taylor described the second, held at the Mildmay Conference Centre, October 22–25, 1878, as 'stiff, hard, cut and dried', neither well managed nor well attended and, in contrast with the inspiring Shanghai Conference of the previous year, sadly disappointing. But it had highlighted the unity of 'the field which is the world', as India, Africa and the islands of the seas as well as China had been represented. He had shared the platform at two meetings on China with his old friends Bishop John Burdon and Professor James Legge, and with Dr J L Maxwell of Taiwan, and reported them verbatim in the *Millions*. His own subject was 'The Progress and Success of Protestant Missions in China'. The annual Mildmay Conference and another in Glasgow claimed him for several addresses, but also to interview men and women wanting to go with him to China. In a stonemason[51] named William Cooper he was to see great hope for the future. The result of a year's work was that fourteen men and fourteen women left in 1878 and four more men in March 1879, followed by two in November.

Economic depression and political excitement over Russian expansionism from Turkey to Turkestan led potential donors to conserve their personal wealth, and missions suffered in consequence. Even when international pressure forced Russia to negotiate with China over Kuldja and Ili (pp 199f), the slow progress was paralleled by low giving and consequent perplexity for Mission leaders. At this time, however, new sources of income emerged. Lord Radstock, not a wealthy man, often sent donations to the Mission from wherever he might be in his travels as an evangelist on the Continent. During 1878 he was in Sweden, well received by the truly Christian queen, and largely responsible for a growing interest in missions to China. A donation came from Jonköping towards the orphanages, and in mid-January 1879 a gift of £200 to Hudson Taylor from Stockholm. Thomas Berger increased his contribution to £2,000 in the year. And the philanthropist Robert Arthington, to whom Hudson Taylor had appeared 'humble and very intelligent', arranged to meet him and offered £100 if the CIM were to devote a missionary to the tribal Miao of Guizhou, a plan already on foot.[52] Through Wylie's influence the Bible Society of Scotland offered £60 and the BFBS £100 towards the support of colporteurs working with CIM missionaries.

But as the year progressed there seemed to be no answer to the problem of administration in Britain after Hudson Taylor left again. George Soltau resigned and emigrated to Tasmania. Richard Hill proposed the appointment of William Soltau as a salaried secretary. The council minuted that in his representation of the CIM all over Britain, Benjamin Broomhall needed 'authentication' and in March resolved that he and William Soltau should be 'assistant secretaries'.[53] Still no solution to the major need could be found, that of the daily direction of the Mission in Britain. Hudson Taylor was praying for 'organising capacity' in himself, 'The Lord make me equal to increasing claims.'[54] In August he mentioned to Jennie that William Soltau's heart was not in his work, and that Benjamin although enthusiastic was 'never up to time and cannot economise. I do not now see a wise and prompt editor for *China's Millions*, (so) I must not leave till there is someone . . . who sees things from my standpoint, and on whom I can depend.' The need for administrators in China was as great, with the Mission growing so fast. Yet he himself at forty-six was senior to all other members with the exception of Elizabeth Wilson and Benjamin, and none yet showed the needed ability.

A return of 'ague' in June and July reduced Hudson Taylor to such poor health that the Beauchamps invited him to join them in the south of France and Switzerland. He had to take work with him, and for some days could not climb with the others, from pain in his side, but by early September was up on a glacier on three successive days, and walking seven or eight miles at a time, sometimes alone.[55] 'I am here for work – the work of getting well again,' he wrote. The effect of 'pure air from pure white peaks' was 'indescribable'. One day was doing him a month's good, the result of 'all this pleasure and all this kindness'. Then a day with William Berger in Paris 'to regain his full sympathy', and he was back at his desk and off again by the night train to the Dundee Conference, feeling 'wonderfully well'.

His eldest son, Herbert, was at medical college, and Howard, the second son, would soon be ready to join him although not yet seventeen. So Hudson Taylor arranged with the trustees of Maria's endowment of her children to advance the fees. That settled, he still had to arrange for the Mission before he could leave for China.

For lack of an obvious solution he appears to have aimed at a course of trial and error or a bold venture of faith, like walking on water. In September he deputed more work on the *Millions* to Benjamin, even to writing a major editorial, but someone to take over the chief responsibility was still 'a great unmet need' in December. He hoped to sail in February. January came and he told the council he must go. Invitations to speak at meetings in Holland crystallised his thoughts. He would go there on the way to Marseilles and the French mail boat to China. On February 4 the council minuted that Hudson Taylor would continue as editor, supplying John McCarthy with material and full instructions from China. But 'Mr Broomhall who will take the general direction of this and the rest of the home work' would supply items relating to 'home proceedings'. McCarthy was to take over 'meetings in the country', and Benjamin would deal with candidates until the council invited them to come into residence.

In view of what was to happen, a little more of this arrangement may be useful. The next day, February 5, another minute read,

> That Mr Broomhall be appointed the General Secretary of the Mission, with the distinct understanding on the part of Mr Taylor and the Council and himself, that he is considered responsible for the general superintendence and conduct of the home work of the Mission, Mr McCarthy and Mr (W) Soltau agreeing to act under his direction.[56]

Hudson Taylor told the council that he had asked Theodore Howard in the event of his (Hudson Taylor's) decease,

> to undertake, if only for a time, the position of Director of the Mission. . . . He hoped that ultimately there might be found in China . . . some one or more competent to direct the foreign work.

Again on February 10 they met to carry the arrangements further. Theodore Howard was appointed Director in Britain during Hudson Taylor's absence, with an emphasised reiteration of the principle 'that the *general* function of the council is to *advise* the Director or Directors for the time being'. This definition by the council itself answered those members who had wanted greater control, and went on to endorse the decision of February 5 by stressing that:

> (Mr Broomhall's) responsibility was not in any way diminished, nor the relationship of his fellow-workers to himself altered, but that in Mr Howard he would have one to whom he could refer in any circumstances requiring direction. . . . It was with this understanding . . . that (Mr Howard) had accepted the position of Director.

He could not take on more than that.[57] A 'president and premier' administration had been adopted, and after its teething troubles worked well enough for a while. No longer secretary to the Anti-Slavery Association Benjamin now concentrated his energies on China. The total membership of the Mission had been thirty-eight when he first joined the staff in 1875, and was sixty-nine in May 1879. When he retired in 1895 to devote his last sixteen years to the abolition of Britain's scandalous opium trade there were 630 members.[58] After praying for organising ability, Hudson Taylor had found his way through the impasse but, knowing Benjamin so well since boyhood together, he acted with no little courage. They had very much in common. Their openness to all denominations was a particular asset in a trans-denominational missionary society. Benjamin took the periodicals of each Church; and won the label of Baptist by presenting volumes of C H Spurgeon's sermons to outgoing missionaries, although he himself was both Anglican and Methodist in sympathy. He had found his niche and within five years was riding the crest of the Mission's heyday, a development impossible for anyone to foresee.

Benjamin's penchant for living to the limit of his means was closely linked with his breadth of interests and passion for reading. The floors and even staircases of his home groaned with the weight of books. Hudson Taylor understood. His own study walls were lined to the ceiling with bookshelves. Benjamin's Bond Street years and circle of friends and acquaintances probably accounted for the frock coat and silk 'topper' remembered by his family, for while he strongly believed in the power of a pen wielded in the silence of his study, he knew that in person he carried weight with all kinds of people.

Arrangements for Britain were only part of the picture. Sir Thomas Wade had returned to Peking and the CMS was feeling his prejudice again, following extremes of oppression in Fujian. After years of the church (doubling the number of Christians), the new theological college at Fuzhou was burned down on August 30, 1878. But reparations offered by the Chinese Government were diverted by the consul to the purchase of land for a race course, Eugene Stock recorded.[59] Hudson Taylor advised that CIM personnel should avoid passing through Tianjin lest word of their destinations inland should prompt Wade to restrict their movements. He planned that when the famine ended, stations should be opened in southern Shanxi from which to work in resistant Henan and Shaanxi. Later he wrote that Wade was not only taking strong action against the CMS but 'really against *all* missionary work (outside) foreign concessions'. Anti-French feeling and the war clouds of the Franco-Chinese hostilities in Indo-China in the 1880s were gathering. 'Things look dark for Missions in south China, and the same spirit and persecutions may spread northwards, but the LORD reigneth.'

The endless round of meetings continued, and the Mission's day of prayer was observed on December 31 at Pyrland Road. The varied nature of Hudson Taylor's life still had its medical episodes, even in Britain. An epidemic of 'spasmodic croup' was carrying off many small children in London, but under Hudson Taylor's treatment the Ballers' younger daughter was recovering. During the well-attended evening prayer meeting her nurse came to the door with the child in her arms, called Mrs Baller (Mary Bowyer) and showed her that the child was 'dead', blue and limp. They called Hudson Taylor. His first efforts to resuscitate her failed, but with mouth to mouth respiration for several minutes the child's colour changed and she began to breathe. Through the night she had occasional convulsions but survived unharmed – to become a member of the Mission in Hunan.[60]

A sidelight on the incident typified Hudson Taylor's attitude to prayer. When he was called to help, a woman in the meeting with strong faith-healing convictions appealed to him to pray for the child. 'Yes, pray,' he answered as he hurried out, 'while I work.' His son Howard's comment in later years when they had been close companions in many situations was, 'He prayed about things as if everything depended upon the praying . . . but he worked also, as if everything depended on his working.'[61]

Back to the fray *February–April 1879*

He crossed over to Holland on February 24, and spoke at four meetings at The Hague and Amsterdam, although 'almost too tired to think' from the pressure of last things to attend to before leaving London. To Benjamin, in charge without Hudson Taylor to consult, he wrote that he had been caught out, not knowing the language – a collection had been taken! Among many words of advice he said characteristically, 'I should not hesitate to shorten our (weekly) prayer meeting if ever it should seem to drag.'[62] Detailed instructions followed on how to cross Paris by cab, for the party of young men due to join him on the ship: J J Coulthard, William J Hunnex, Henry W Hunt, T W Pigott (paying his own way), William McCarthy and his wife. His hostess insisted until he agreed, on paying for a first class 'sleeper' to Marseilles. But this time through no fault of his own his medicine chest could not be found on the ship, with dire results. It had been crated for him, unlabelled as to contents. From Marseilles he paid a quick visit to William

Berger at Cannes, and to George Müller and C H Spurgeon at Mentone.

Describing him in his magazine *Sword and Trowel* Spurgeon said,

> Mr Taylor . . . is not in outward appearance an individual who would be selected among others as the leader of a gigantic enterprise; in fact, he is lame in gait, and little in stature; but . . . his spirit is quiet and meek, yet strong and intense; there is not an atom of self-assertion about him, but a firm confidence in God . . . His faith is that of a child-man . . . too certain of His presence and help to turn aside . . . (He has) about him a firmness which achieves its purposes without noise . . . He provokes no hostility, but . . . arouses hearty sympathy, though he is evidently independent of it, and would go on with his great work even if no one countenanced him in it. . . . The word China, China, China is now ringing in our ears in that, special, peculiar, musical, forcible, unique way in which Mr Taylor utters it . . . He did not deny the fact (that he was already growing a queue).[63]

He had been ill at Cannes and was worse by Naples, needing the missing medicines. They settled into a routine of Bible study, prayer and Chinese language lessons daily, and he formed a high opinion of all his party. At the end of the journey he described it as 'remarkably pleasant'. But by Singapore he was so ill with dysentery that they feared it might cost him his life to go on, but he went.[64] At Hong Kong he was well enough to take a wrangling *sanban* boatman ashore to see that his passenger knew not only the right fare but where it was placarded at the town hall for the boatmen's benefit.

A pile of letters awaited him, one telling him that Jennie was in Shanghai, and plunged him into the inevitable problems. E Tomalin, one of the December batch of reinforcements, had smallpox. He survived and married Louise Desgraz. George Nicoll offered to nurse him but had not been vaccinated. Francis James was talking of resigning over the financial policy. Jackson was in debt and being sued for medical fees which he refused to pay. Thomas Harvey's wife and newborn twins had died, and of three of Grattan Guinness's children taken ill, only Geraldine, aged sixteen, had survived. So it went on. But Jennie was her usual self, a worthy wife,

> I have been . . . thinking of them (the difficulties) with something of rejoicing. What a platform there will be for our God to work and triumph upon! And how clearly we shall see His hand! . . . In the Master's presence the servant's only responsibility, and his sweetest

> joy is to obey . . . Surely to need much grace, and therefore to have much put upon you, is not a thing to be troubled about. Don't you think that if we set ourselves not to allow any pressure to rob us of communion (with the Lord) we shall live lives of hourly triumph, the echo of which shall come back to us from all parts of the Mission? Our faith must gain the victory for our brethren and sisters.[65]

On April 22 they reached Shanghai, to be met by the faithful Thomas Weir and taken in his launch to the very door of the new CIM transit home, so small and cramped that Hudson Taylor began weighing up what kind of premises were really needed in Shanghai. It led in time to another of his major innovations. They spent the first day ashore in prayer with fasting, before tackling the problems. To Jennie he seemed very run down, though better than he had been. But his dysentery returned before he had even dealt with all the accumulated mail, and they were strongly advised by Dr Johnson of the LMS to go to Yantai to escape the approaching heat of summer. By then he was in a 'very low' state, and willing to be taken.

PART 2

FIRST-TIMERS

1879–83

CHAPTER SIX

CHEFOO AND CAMERON 1879–82

Bands on the Bund *1879–82*

Shanghai was no longer the settlement on a swamp of twenty-five years before, with ships' clinkers surfacing the paths. Metalled roads, rickshaws plying for hire, young bloods and sailors jostling through packed streets to the races, ladies taking the air on their menfolks' arms, watching the ships unloading in the muddy Huang-pu River, or listening in the comfort of their carriages to ships' bands on the Bund – all was as unlike the true China as could be. Shanghai was an entry port expanding constantly. The value of land and buildings in the American, British and French concessions alone, assessed in 1870 at 14 million taels had risen by 1905 to 220 million taels. Not only Shanghai but China and the nineteenth-century world were changing fast. Hudson Taylor himself was engineering one of the great transformations, the opening up of inland China. In Korea, Indo-China, Turkestan, as in Africa and elsewhere, the scramble for colonies and spheres of influence had begun. Before long the Western powers and Japan would be 'slicing the melon' of mainland China itself. Foreign issues played so large a part in the nation's affairs that all members of the Grand Council joined in deliberations of the Zongli Yamen, making it in effect a cabinet.[1] The old bone of contention between China and Japan, the suzerainty of the Ryukyu Islands, led both countries in 1879 to ask the advice of General Ulysses Grant, victor of the American Civil War and President, 1865–76. China conceded to Japan in 1881.

With the death of Yakub Beg and China's reoccupation of Kashgaria, the gentlemanly Chonghou of the Tianjin massacre events (Book 5, pp 240–43) was sent in 1879 to St Petersburg to settle the controversy over Ili. The sweeping concessions he made in his treaty so enraged the Peking court that on his return he was condemned to death by decapitation, although a Manchu imperial clansman.[2] The anti-foreign party at court had sensed fraternising with the barbarians in his actions. But the Western envoys resented what they saw as an attack on civilised diplomacy, and Russia confronted Zuo Zongtang's sixty thousand seasoned troops with ninety thousand of her own in the Kuldja-Ili area.

Through Robert Hart, China invited 'Chinese' Gordon to come and advise them. He had long interviews with the Grand Secretary, Li Hongzhang, his superior in the Taiping war, and in Peking, which led him to a startling conclusion.[3] He wrote to Dr Halliday Macartney,

> It struck me that the question is not between Russia and China; it is between the Manchus and the Chinese people; the former are on their trial before the people and they scarcely dare to give in to Russia. The Chinese people wish for war, in hopes of being rid of the Manchus.

In fact Gordon saw three factions, Li Hongzhang, the Imperial Court and the literati, to whom he was referring as 'the Chinese people'. Because in 1858 and 1860 the capital had been shown to be vulnerable, he advised,

> If you will make war, burn the suburbs of Peking, remove the archives and the emperor from Peking, put them in the centre of the country [as was to happen in 1900], and fight (a guerilla war) for five years. Russia will not be able to hurt you.
>
> If you want peace, then give up Ili.

He had clearly seen 'that if the emperor left Peking for the centre of China, there would be an end of the Manchu dynasty'.[4] Gordon was too blunt in speech for the Chinese, but did what he came to do and they took his advice. China chose peace, but with skilled diplomacy.

'In June 1880 the great queen of England addressed a personal appeal for clemency (towards Chonghou) to the great empress dowager' and, reading the hidden message in Gordon's advice, to mollify Russia, she extended a reprieve to him. Marquis Zeng then went to St Petersburg with Dr Halliday and concluded 'a bloodless diplomatic triumph' with the return of Ili and other retractions by Russia, for which he was loaded with honours.

Gordon had also pointed out the disadvantage to Peking of having no telegraphic link, even with Shanghai, and steps were quickly taken to rectify this. *Fengshui* had to oblige. In June 1881 the *Rocket of China*, a locomotive, made its first short journey. Modernisation had begun its cumbrous course – while Japan adopted every coveted skill and policy. Only four or five years earlier, Guo Songdao's companion envoy to Britain, Liu Daren, had reported to Peking: If railways were laid down in China, the large class engaged in the transport of men and goods – carters, boatmen, trackers and their likes – would find their occupation gone.[5] 'Japan has made her administrative system accord with that of European states; and she has copied Western dress, ceremony and customs. Accordingly Europeans despise the Japanese, as having sacrificed their own natural tastes and habits.' Farther afield, French encroachment in Indo-China heralded the bitter war with China of the 1880s, King Mindon of Upper Burma died and was succeeded by his cruel son Thebaw; General Roberts occupied Kabul; the Zulu war established Britain in yet another conquered territory; and from 1880 to 1885 the Irish question loomed large. While only the Franco-Chinese war was to threaten the CIM explicitly, Hudson Taylor was entering upon a period in some ways more painful than any yet endured. The capacity of the Church at home to lose interest was unchanged. The CMS in 1880 adopted an unprecedented 'Scheme of Retrenchment', to withdraw from Peking and parts of North India and drastically to reduce its men in training and sent overseas. The policy was reversed, but it illustrates the climate of support in Britain. As if tested to the hilt for four years and found reliable, Hudson Taylor was then to watch amazed as a golden era unfolded.

Chefoo – 'where the blue air sparkled' *1879*

The rocky northern coast of the Shandong peninsula is studded with little bays and coves, fringed with fine white sand. Stormy and cold in winter when the beaches were even stacked with ice floes driven ashore, Yantai was ideal as a holiday and health resort through most of the year. The bay, another lake of Galilee, is framed by hills and by The Bluff and islands shielding it from the open sea (p 67). The market town of Yantai and the anchorage for junks lay at one end of a long sandspit, and Chefu a fishing village at the Bluff end. Gutzlaff in his junk and Medhurst in the *Huron* would have called in at Yantai on their journeys, and the American Southern Baptists J L Holmes and his wife lived on a sailing-ship there in 1858. Across the harbour at Yantai lay a rocky point with perhaps a few fishermen's huts on it which, after the treaties of 1858 and 1860, became Settlement Point, the 'concession' occupied by a consul, foreign traders and missionaries. Holmes settled ashore;

Hudson Taylor's warm friend Joseph Edkins of LMS moved there with his bride from Shanghai; and, also in 1860, O Rao and Bonhoure of the Paris Evangelical Mission. Others followed: 1861 saw J L Nevius, the American Presbyterian, join Holmes; and two American Episcopalians, Parker and Smith; and two of Hudson Taylor's early protégés, Charles J Hall and R F Laughton of the BMS. Hall died of cholera, and Parker and Holmes were murdered before the year 1861 was out, but Dr McCartee of Ningbo came from 1862 to 1865, and one of the six unmarried missionary women in China, Miss C B Downing (also of the APM), in 1866. All of these built up their own work in Yantai and the provincial hinterland beyond. In 1863 more great names joined the list. Calvin W Mateer and Hunter Corbett joined Nevius, Corbett to stay on for most of his life.

So it continued. Alexander Williamson made 'Chefoo' his base for the National Bible Society of Scotland in 1863, and Charles Perry Scott for the SPG in 1874. More short-lived BMS missionaries and the indestructible Timothy Richard came and went. Augustus Margary and Challoner Alabaster of the British consular service enjoyed the very ecumenical Bible study sessions until posted elsewhere, Margary to die at Manyün. The Church of Scotland built a marble church; Nevius imported hundreds of saplings to improve the quality of Shandong's fruit orchards; the Chefoo Convention brought the Grand Secretary, Li Hongzhang, the envoys of Britain and several other states, and a fleet of warships in 1876. 'Chefoo' became known as 'the sanatorium of China', a popular naval resort for shore leave, to evade the diseases and heat of southern summers. Yantai was the port and Chinese city, but 'Chefoo' had come to mean a foreign settlement and all its affairs.[6]

Jennie had spent two days at Chefoo in the last week of October 1878, on her way to Shanxi, and had met a customs officer named Ballard and his wife, a missionary. Apart from that, when Dr Johnson urged them to go at once to Chefoo, she and Hudson were heading for the unknown, taking Coulthard and E Tomalin, a newcomer, with them as secretaries. The north was entirely new to Hudson Taylor and he was prostrate, able to take only milk. They ran into fog and made slow progress. Instead of two days they were likely to take four to cover the distance. The ship's supply of milk ran out and Jennie herself, seasick and not knowing what to do, watched him getting weaker. 'It was one of the saddest days I ever spent. Then at 9.00 p m I cried to God to undertake for us, to take away the fog, to teach me what nourishment to get for (him)'. Both of them believed that the Lord of heaven and earth who had calmed the storm, controlling wind and waves at a word, still could and often did intervene, in keeping with his command, 'Ask anything in my name'. She woke next morning to find the sun shining, and on going on deck met the 'second mate' who said the fog had lifted soon after 9.00 and they had had a clear night. They reached Chefoo late, but in daylight instead of darkness.

The ship stayed only long enough to disembark them into a *sanban* by which to reach the shore, and in it Hudson Taylor lay while Jennie and Coulthard went to consult Ballard. Chefoo had two 'hotels', too expensive for them, and private homes prepared to take lodgers. The Ballards would not hear of their going elsewhere, took them in and treated them as 'family' from May 8 until December 9 when Hudson Taylor, fully recovered, made an overland journey with Coulthard – right across Shandong and Jiangsu to Yangzhou and the Yangzi stations.

As his health steadily improved, he quickly saw that this was an exceptional place, of great potential for the Mission. Only a week after their arrival he was taken by boat across to the Bluff, to see if at that distance from the settlement young missionaries could learn the language among the Chinese of Chefu, or premises be rented for a convalescent home. Frederick Baller came up to Chefoo, and on June 24 they went across together and rented a house. Baller and Pigott moved in for four months.

Meanwhile progress was being made in another direction. John Nevius, a good friend since 1855, came to see Hudson Taylor and discussed with him the 'indigenous principles' he was developing in his Shandong work, later to be applied so successfully in Korea. And the British consul at Chefoo proved to be C T Gardner, of Zhenjiang and the second Yangzhou plot, of 1870. He had a vacant 'cottage' and Ballard a shack and unused warehouse, all of which Hudson Taylor rented. Much as the *Lammermuir* party had used William Gamble's old Chinese theatre in 1866, these makeshift quarters were roughly partitioned and adapted as the first foothold of the CIM.

Elizabeth (otherwise Jane) Judd had been so ill at Wuhan that only return to England held hope of her recovery. Hudson Taylor sent for Charles Judd to bring her and the children to the magic air of Chefoo, 'cool and bracing' instead of the 'stewing, damp heat (they were) accustomed to.' Charles was to be in charge at Chefoo

A CHEFOO COLOPHON
'where the blue air sparkles like champagne'

while Hudson Taylor ran the Mission. They arrived on June 28, 1879, when 'the furnace' of Wuhan was so extreme that Griffith John fainted at breakfast after one hot night. James Cameron, Frank Trench and others came to Chefoo for consultation and a rest, and the sixty-year-long history of 'Chefoo' as the Mission's life-saving health resort had begun. By August there were four at Chefu and seventeen in the Judds' bungalow and warehouse on Settlement Point.

Hudson Taylor was deeply immersed in work again, often late at night, so much that Jennie wrote, 'I am dreading the effect of over-work on (him).' He could not do things by halves. Difficulties of many kinds were crowding upon him. Members of the CIM were behaving irresponsibly. Some were being side-tracked by well-meaning missionaries of other persuasions. His old thorn in the flesh at Zhenjiang, Robert White, was at it again, denouncing 'organised' missions and unsettling them. And, to his great distress, Timothy Richard had been winning adherents to his own viewpoints in Shanxi.

So on July 30 Hudson Taylor sailed for Shanghai in a coastal steamer, to tackle the trouble on the Yangzi, and headed right into a typhoon.[7] Experienced as he was, this time he felt there was little hope as the ship was hurled about by wind and waves. '(At about one a m) I asked God to give me the lives of all on board, as He gave Paul.' He felt assured that his prayer was heard, removed his life-belt, turned his mattress over and slept on the drier side. The captain put the ship about and ran before the wind, the barometer began to rise 'soon after one a m' and they survived. Yantai was lashed by the typhoon, the sea wall and jetty partly washed away, small boats wrecked and the British and Chinese gunboats at full steam barely kept off the rocks. Jennie's letter called it 'awfully grand' and went on, 'I did rejoice . . . that you were in such *safe* keeping. I think some of our friends wondered that I was not more excited and anxious, but when our Father had you in the hollow of His hand, why should I fear? I only wished I were with you.' 'Don't work all night, or talk!' she told him, but knew it was hardly worth saying.

At Zhenjiang he found White very ill, 'a skeleton', and doctored him back to health. But C G Moore's young wife was also wasting away; in her case from 'hysteria' (anorexia nervosa). He sent them to Chefoo, where she hovered between life and death, nursed day and night by Jennie and others.[8] At Yangzhou he arranged for a new orphanage to be built, and wished he himself could stay and 'be a missionary again'. But after a month hard at work in the great heat he again became so 'dangerously ill', 'thin and weak' with dysentery, that he himself had to be taken down-river to Shanghai, and returned to Chefoo. He had been planning to travel with Coulthard and Jennie to Shanxi, and in Zhenjiang succeeded in obtaining eighteen-province travel passes. (Trench, Cameron and Pigott had each been given one, but few others were ever issued.)[9] Secretly he hoped to cross from Shanxi to Gansu and the south-west, even to Bhamo. But here he was, back at Yantai on September 12, recovering but too weak to contemplate another journey.

'Chefoo' – concept and tradition[10] *1879–1986*

Crowding under crude conditions in the warehouse might express the spirit of the CIM, to put values before comfort, but it could only be temporary. With so many missions working in or using Yantai as a base for evangelism there was no thought of the CIM adding to their number. But as a health-resort permanent premises were needed. And what better place could there be for a school for children of the Mission? Premises and sites in the Settlement were at a premium, and some missions had occupied Temple Hill overlooking the Chinese city. Beyond the sparse suburbs, fields stretched out towards the encircling hills for two or three miles eastwards above the long sandy beach and the mule road to Ninghai.

On September 19 Jennie's diary read, 'To Bay, for site.' A field of beans beside a gully with a freshwater stream looked ideal, two miles from the settlement and a few hundred yards from the sands. But how could they find the owner and enquire the price without giving him the whip hand in negotiations? At this point a farmer came up and said to Hudson Taylor and Judd, 'Do you want to buy land? Will you buy mine?' He owned the beanfield. It took little time to agree a fair price. It was theirs for ninety Mexican dollars (£18), and neighbouring owners were willing to sell too.

Hudson Taylor drew up plans for a house with five rooms upstairs, about five down and verandahs. They employed men to quarry stones from the gully, made their own bricks, sunbaked and fired, and bought the timber and fittings of a nearby wreck, *The Christian* – oak beams, Norwegian pine, and teak planking from another wreck for the floors. Cabin fittings provided doors, cupboards and 'a splendid sideboard', with locks and hinges and anything else they wanted at 'two dollars a hundredweight'. Glass for windows came from Shanghai. The completed house cost £562, less than Mex. $3,000, and the worst shortcoming was that the wooden plugs used to fill the ship's bolt-holes tended to come out. This house known as the 'Judds' house', or the first 'Sanitarium', served its purpose until 1915 when it was demolished to make way for a modern hospital. And the whole expanding complex played a vital role until taken by the Japanese in 1943.

Hudson Taylor took his share of supervision of the work and preaching to the workmen, the best change of occupation and exercise he could wish for. As Jennie noted on November 4, he was up at 2.30 a m to do Mission accounts before walking two miles from the Ballards to the site, a camp of matting shelters for masons, carpenters, brickmakers and missionary supervisors. Living and working with the Chinese, the language students were progressing 'famously'. Sundays on half-pay, with two gospel meetings for the men, led to conversions. One, Lao Chao, was head-servant of the Boys' School over forty years later.

Before the first house was ready, the foundations of a second sanatorium were laid, a convalescent home finished in December 1880, when the Taylors moved in. After that a school, intended for the Mission's children, and later a hospital, a dispensary and other facilities for Chinese were projected. As Dixon Hoste, of the 'Cambridge Seven' was to point out, Hudson Taylor was no mere ascetic, but a realist.[11] The first building was needed in a hurry, but the rest were built conventionally, in keeping with the standards of a treaty port, and planned for comfort and convenience.

THE PROJECTED ‘COLLEGIATE SCHOOL’, CHEFOO

On December 6, 1879, he told James Meadows that he proposed to open a boarding school, and within a year it materialised, on December 1, 1880. In W L Elliston he had the ideal schoolmaster.[12] The Judds' three sons became the first pupils, soon joined by others, until in mid-May 1881 there were sixteen. After many requests it was decided not to limit the school to children of the CIM, nor of other missions only. Eyes had been opened throughout the foreign community in China to the unique suitability of Yantai for this purpose. Consular and merchant families were also welcomed. When thirty had been enrolled and more were applying, Hudson Taylor bought land right down to the seashore. By September 1881 '50 or 60 scholars', boys and girls, some not resident, were in the school, and accommodation for one hundred and fifty boarders in a 'Protestant Collegiate School' was embarked upon. They were ready for thirty more by October, but Elliston was overworked and suitable teachers were not forthcoming from Britain as had been hoped. They did not need to be members of the Mission. The Taylors' eldest son, Herbert, had left medical school and was due in Shanghai on December 9. He joined the staff as Elliston's assistant. Miss C B Downing of the American Presbyterian Mission (p 202) took charge of the girls and, in a parallel venture, until she joined the CIM, an 'independent' lady, Mrs Sharland, ran a school for Eurasians in the port. By the end of August 1882 Hudson Taylor was planning a greatly enlarged school complex. The 'Chefoo School' had become popular and successful, and by 1883 fees were meeting all costs. During that year a small hospital, a dispensary and a chapel for the Chinese had also been added to the expanding facilities.

Even before the end of 1879 the *Chinese Recorder*[13] published a proposal by 'Sanitas' that by co-operative effort, costing up to 300 taels from each major society, a missionary sanatorium could be established at Yantai such as the CIM were erecting. 'Chefoo' had become far more than a misnomer for Yantai or only a summer resort. (Here we look far ahead.) As long as China's open century continued, no more vital element of the combined missionary venture existed. Chefoo was 'an important factor in (Western) life in China'. As Hudson Taylor told his parents in March 1880, once visit Chefoo and you will never be satisfied with England again! The schools acquired a reputation for good examination results in the College of Preceptors Examinations for some years, and then the Oxford Local Examinations. 'The best school east of Suez' gave the lives of thirty-four young men in the first world war; and among its alumni included the author Thornton Wilder and H R Luce, Editor of *The New York Times* and Editor-in-chief of *Life* and *Time* magazines. But 'Chefoo' was so much the personification of the Boys', Girls' and 'Preparatory' schools 'on the shores of an Eastern sea', from 1881 until 1943 (when they marched *en bloc* to internment in Japanese concentration camps) that 'daughter' schools at a score of other places in seven countries of East Asia have been and still are known by the same name. If the only way to give the gospel adequately to China was through men and women giving the best years of their lives, indeed a lifetime spent sacrificially, separations were inevitable if the children were to be properly educated. 'God will bless the chicks more through our sacrifice,' Jennie wrote to her mother. But schools on the field of action from then on meant shorter periods apart.

Constantly on the move *1876–83*

Ill-health had led to Hudson Taylor's recognition of 'Chefoo' as the God-given answer to one of the Mission's greatest needs. Recurring ill-health forced him time and again to retreat there from sorties, some adventurous, into the widely expanding field of the CIM. After being taken dangerously ill to Shanghai and shipped back to Yantai on September 10, 1879, he transferred his official business centre to Chefoo. There he had to stay, sometimes for months on end, often to his great distress for his influence was most felt through personal contacts. The rapid numerical growth of the Mission to more than seventy Europeans and well over one hundred Chinese in sixty-four locations, entailed incessant administrative correspondence and interviews, with the local building developments only as a welcome diversion. In his preface to the 1878 bound volume of *China's Millions*, after dealing with the great famine and iniquitous opium trade, he enlarged on the importance of Chinese missionaries.

> No greater blessing can be desired for China than that there may be raised up . . . a large number of men qualified to do the work of evangelists and pastors . . . The sooner a few converts can be gathered in each of the interior provinces, the sooner may we hope to have men in training for Christian work in widely distant parts of the empire.

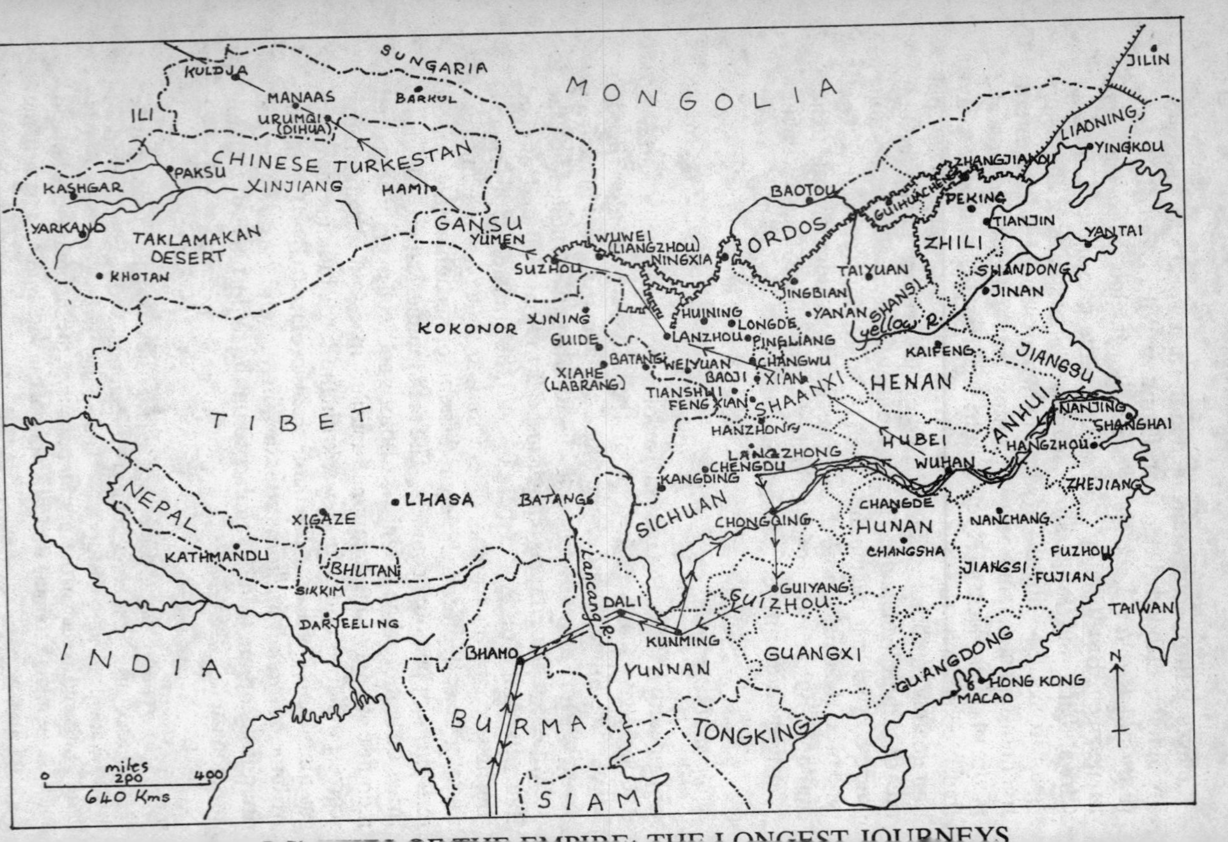

EMPIRE: THE LONGEST JOURNEYS

This led him on to 'the *accessibility* of the people'. Reviewing the journeys already made he concluded, 'These and other journeys (amount to) about 30,000 miles of travel' by about twenty pioneers in eighteen months. During the four years of his fifth period in China, this considerable achievement was to be repeated again and again as the foreign community in China watched it wide-eyed. Even to summarise the journals, reports, memoirs and biographies of the pioneers engaged in this great explosion of Mission energy (between 1876 and 1883) would take up many pages, but its importance justifies generous attention. By it Hudson Taylor and the CIM achieved the recognition denied them previously. But more, by such thorough penetration of the empire they were going far towards the fulfilment of the twin aims, 'to carry the good news of the love of God in Christ Jesus to the nation; and to awaken the Christian Church in other lands to China's claim upon it.' What might otherwise be incomprehensible is straightforward with the help of the maps and tables (Appendix 5).

Hudson Taylor himself made two trail-blazing journeys, and some of 'the Eighteen' were almost constantly on the move. James Cameron and a newcomer, Adam Dorward, men after his own heart, were inspired with the same refusal as he had shown at their age to allow hardship or hostility or disappointment to halt their preaching of the gospel. Some were always on the move within their own provinces. Some preached and sold gospels extensively as they reconnoitred for others to move into the places they identified as strategic. Together they 'made a definite mark in the history of missions in China.'[14] He himself held the reins, firmly, very firmly at times when discipline was needed, but very loosely in the case of men and women whom he could trust to plan and work and use scarce funds responsibly. To work out the broad plan with them gave him deep satisfaction. The sheer number of individually adventurous enterprises which he suggested and guided during this period is surprising, for all the activities of the sixty-four 'stations' were also under his personal supervision.

His own travels were as often 'trouble-shooting' as they were to meet, consult and re-inspire his team. In regional conferences such as neither he nor they could easily forget, he explained his strategy, listened carefully, and expounded from Scripture what God had been teaching him. 'Joe' Coulthard, his personal secretary wherever he went, said he 'seemed apparently to value anything one said.'[15] But these four years, exciting and successful in so many ways as he saw Christians multiplying in every province and missionaries taking root in most, demanded even more of Hudson Taylor (at 46–50 years of age) in personal trust in God and endurance of the Refiner's fire than he had needed at any time in the past. The Mission's lowest ebb had been reached in December 1874, but Hudson Taylor's personal low point came eight years later, in 1882.

Although most other societies chose to concentrate their work, notable exceptions existed. At the Annual Meeting of the CIM in London in May 1881, on his return from famine relief, David Hill said, 'I feel almost like a missionary of the China Inland Mission . . . almost one of them . . . I have been struck with . . . the adaptiveness (and) and aggressiveness of the China Inland Mission.' He felt shackled by 'the plant' of institutions, buildings, established by his own mission. One day he said to George Andrew, 'The policy of Mr Taylor is diffusion, while that of my Society is concentration . . . (My advice to you is) "Itinerate, itinerate",' urging him to read the memoirs of J J Weitbrecht, the great itinerant missionary of the early CMS in India, and the biography of William Burns.[16] The reward of his own brave expedition to Shanxi was the conversion of 'Pastor' Hsi. Virgil C Hart of the American Episcopal Church at Jiujiang travelled almost incessantly in his 'yacht' on the waterways of Jiangxi. Samuel Schereschewsky of the same Church was in Peking when he heard that a certain lady had arrived in Shanghai. He 'walked all the way' to propose to her. As Bishop from 1877 to 1883 his travels took him up and down the great Yangzi River. Alexander Williamson travelled far across Manchuria and north China for the NBS of Scotland. And Griffith John, after his tour in 1868 through Sichuan with Alexander Wylie, made frequent pastoral journeys from Wuhan into the hinterland of Hubei. In 1880 he ventured into anti-foreign Hunan, and again with John Archibald of the NBSS, in 1883 he was rioted out of Longyang.[17]

Apart from his own abortive journey in the typhoon from Yantai to Shanghai and then to Zhenjiang at the end of July 1879, Hudson Taylor and Coulthard, after only seven months in China, travelled overland for three hundred miles in twenty-four days (December 9 to January 2, 1880) by mule-litter through Shandong and Jiangsu from Yantai to Qingjiangpu (map p 158) and Yangzhou. No other Westerners had yet made this journey. His hope was to go overland from there to Shanxi as soon as some urgent work had been attended to. Jennie went by ship to join him at Zhenjiang for the purpose, for Tianjin was ice-bound at that time of year. But floods of correspondence, disciplinary problems and the need to spend from February 9 to March 24 at Wuhan despatching party after party of pioneers to the four winds kept him on a leash. This time 'the bombshell' broke through all precedents and previous restraints. Elizabeth Wilson herself, and other *women*, brides and single girls, were scattered to the far western provinces. The success of Jennie's Shanxi experiment with Celia Horne and Anna Crickmay had decided him on this even more daring innovation.

From then until mid-September he was constantly on the move, only in one place for a few days at a time (Appendix 5). Visits to each Yangzi River station in April and May, and a tour of southern Zhejiang, to Hangzhou, Ningbo, Wenzhou and intervening places in June and July carried them by sea-going junk to Taizhou, and from there over the hills to Henry Taylor at Jinhua and in August to Qü Xian on the Qiantang River (see also map p 214).[18] These were old haunts. From Jinhua he wrote revealing to Jennie his proposition that from Shanxi they should visit each of the far western pioneers, in Shaanxi, Gansu, Sichuan, Guizhou and Yunnan. From there they could cross into Burma and make a very necessary visit to Britain, or return by way of Yichang. To the last this was his hope, but although some of the most serious problems were developing in Shanxi, one predicament after another prevented his reaching even that province.

As if he was still a young man, he decided at Qü Xian to break new ground, cutting across Jiangxi to the Yangzi (map p 397). They made for Yüshan, passed down the Guangxin River through Guangxin itself, now the great city of Shangrao, and through Guixi and the Poyang Lake to Cardwell's home at Dagutang on a hill overlooking the lake near Jiujiang. Hearing that several of the Pearse family were ill at Anqing, they hurried on, too late to do much. Mrs Pearse had been ill with dysentery and the eldest child with whooping cough, but the baby, only just alive when he arrived, died in Hudson Taylor's arms. Years later Mrs Pearse recalled, 'Anyone who knew dear Mr Taylor would understand how truly he entered into our sorrow . . . He seemed to lay aside everything else for the time being to be as a *father* to us.' He was not ashamed to shed tears with them.[19] He could only stay to give advice on how to use the medicines they had. Edward Pearse stayed with his wife and children until they could travel with Jennie to Yantai, while Hudson Taylor went on, taking the little coffin in a packing case as his own personal luggage, for burial beside his own children and Maria.

15,000 MILES: HUDSON TAYLOR'S TRAVELS

Another visit to Ningbo had to be fitted in before he returned to Yantai in September, until February 1881. But then from March until May it was Shanghai, the Yangzi region and Zhejiang all over again. The hottest months he spent working at Chefoo (Yantai), and in November and December he was back on the Yangzi for some historic conferences. Apart from a few weeks in Chefoo during 1882 he travelled extensively again, always hoping to get to Shanxi, but drawn by painful necessity from place to place up and down the Yangzi and through the trouble spot of southern Zhejiang. At last the opportunity to go up to Shanxi arrived, and on November 4, 1882, he left Yantai for Tianjin – only to be thwarted at Baoding. The man he most wanted to meet had left Shanxi and passed him on the road. By the time Drake returned from Yantai, married, it was too late to attempt Shanxi again. After one more conference at Anqing and a final winding up at Chefoo (Yantai), Hudson Taylor sailed for Britain on February 10, 1883.

By computation with dividers, journey by journey, he himself had travelled fifteen thousand miles since landing on April 22, 1879. The true mileage must have been far in excess of that. Yet in none of the maps which he painstakingly annotated to show the journeys made by others, did he include his own. After 1880 no map of China could bear the routes of more than a few travellers without hopeless confusion. The folding map in the *Millions* of 1879 had all it could take. James Cameron's 'cat's cradle' had to be shown in isolation, but after that it was not itineraries but footholds, 'stations' occupied in every province, that took pride of place. The distances covered were sometimes accurately recorded, amounting to thousands of miles, but the days, weeks and months on the road more graphically convey the toil and endurance of men and women who walked so that they could talk with fellow-travellers, and were in no hurry to move on, so that they could preach Christ and sell Gospels in every city, market town and village. The travels of Hudson Taylor and his team formed only the framework of their true activities. Men led the way, assessing the safety, but as soon as that appeared to offer reasonable hope of foreign women being unmolested, he also gave them full scope.

Cameron's cat's cradle: the south — *January 1878–June 1879*

The tall highlander, James Cameron, was not content to enjoy the pleasant company of Henry Soltau and John McCarthy in Bhamo in January 1878 (p 151) simply hoping that the British-Indian government would relent and allow them to re-enter China. If he could not complete his planned itinerary of Yunnan from the Burma-Dali direction he would try from Guangxi in the south-east. 'I left without loss of time,' he reported very typically, and instead enjoyed three weeks of enforced idleness chugging down the Irrawaddy in the old steam-launch for nine hundred miles to Rangoon. From there to Singapore and Hong Kong was straightforward. Neither uncharted rocks nor typhoons broke his journey. He called on the German and American missionaries in Hong Kong and Canton, enquiring about the extent of their work and his best route

G F EASTON

JAMES CAMERON

ahead, and it seems that in Hong Kong he met John Shaw Burdon, Bishop of Victoria, (Maria Taylor's brother-in-law).

Following Alford in that see (1874), Burdon was suffering the same frustrations imposed from London in 1872 by the division of territory with W A Russell taking 'North China'.[20] Burdon, 'an able and large-minded man' and always an evangelist, saw the Church in Fujian undergoing fiery persecution (p 31), and doubling its strength while various American and European missions continued under fierce opposition among the Cantonese and Hakkas of Hong Kong and Guangdong. So he pioneered a virgin field of evangelism at Beihai (Pakhoi) on the most southerly tip of what is now Guangxi province, staffed it with Christian Chinese and at Hong Kong trained theological students for future Church leadership.[21]

When Cameron arrived, John Burdon provided one of his Chinese students as a companion on the next adventure, and put his Beihai premises at his disposal as a base for penetration through Guangxi to Yunnan and Guizhou. Cameron made his way to Beihai, trans-shipping at Hainan Island,[22] and at once recognised

CAMERON'S TRAVELS: EIGHT YEARS ON THE GO

the importance of the little port of '12,000 souls, besides a large floating and moving population'. At that time part of Guangdong province, it was the entry point for western Guangxi and Yunnan. 'Were the Gospel to have decided triumphs in Pakhoi [dialect for Beihai] the knowledge of salvation would spread far and wide,' Cameron wrote – among ethnic and social observations of a highly professional standard which he made as he travelled.[23]

On June 11 he and the student were off on the road to join the great West River near Nanning. Cameron could find few people who understood Mandarin, and the student was still 'too timid to preach much' in his native Cantonese, until they reached the river. There more people were bilingual. But the Nanning literati 'seemed determined on a riot', so after four days of 'much opposition' to their preaching, 'and a great amount of hostile feeling', they headed up-river, preaching at villages with 'unusually good audiences'. At Bose (or Peh-seh) he was told about Clarke and Fishe having been there, and was also generously helped by the local officials. They crossed the Red River on the border of a small tongue of Guizhou, and after little more than thirty miles, through Xingyi, left Guizhou again, to enter Yunnan. Here one of their carriers absconded with his load, taking a long detour over a rocky hill, back to their starting point. But Cameron was not a highlander without some knowledge of following a spoor. He caught him red-handed. 'Although I did not accuse him of trying to run off or even scold him, he was quite frightened, and at the nearest village the natives wanted to give him a beating, but of course they were not allowed (to).'[24]

They reached Kunming, the provincial capital of Yunnan, on August 17 and found themselves 'in the very inn and room Mr McCarthy had occupied . . . on his way to Bhamo'. The people were 'quiet and very civil' and after his preaching some came to talk with Cameron in his inn, confirming McCarthy's impression that Kunming would be a good mission centre. The Roman Catholics already had an imposing 'foreign-looking edifice' (in Hosie's words 'a handsome palace') in Kunming, and 'evil reports in circulation about them' were so manifestly false, that Cameron defended them, without effect on the critics.[25] Those were still the days when Catholics regarded all Protestants as dangerous heretics and the average Protestant of the time saw Roman Catholics as anti-Christ, propagating a false gospel. At best they disregarded or grudgingly admired each other as brave men and women, but discounted what they taught as inadequate and schismatic. The vicar-apostolic of Yunnan gave to applicants for instruction as his summary of Christian beliefs and duties, 'to believe and hope in God, in one only God in three persons, to love and serve Him, to obey His law, to believe in Jesus Christ, our God and Saviour, to hope in His mercies, and to follow His counsels and to imitate His virtues.'[26]

Leaving Kunming 'about the end of August' and following the ancient road 'to Peking', they reached Guiyang in twenty days, to be welcomed by James Broumton and Robert Landale (see also map p 260). Cameron was indefatigable. 'As the (Chinese) with us needed rest, and as I wanted to see (George) Nicoll, I set out for (Chongqing) in Sichuan accompanied by Landale . . . a hard journey both ways.' At Chongqing they met the newcomers Riley and Samuel Clarke, and heard from Colborne Baber himself about his journeys – the circuit of the Daliangshan ahead of Nicoll, while Cameron was on the borders of Tibet, and most recently his journey from Chongqing to Kangding from which he had been back only a few weeks.[27] Cameron was already known to Baber by his epic adventure with 'one man and a mule', and a change of attitude towards the CIM is noticeable from around this time, even in Sir Thomas Wade, the minister. 'The wet season having set in', Cameron's little 'detour' of four hundred miles on foot had to be completed by the main road instead of by another route as intended.

When they reached Guiyang again a new complication faced them. One of Cameron's men from Guangxi had been so ill that he had to be taken home by mountain chair and, where possible, by river. James Broumton went with them, from November 4 to December 11. Their route took them again through Miao tribal territory, his special interest. At Guilin (Kweilin) Cameron wrote 'We might have had trouble, (but) being men of peace, we only spent two or three days', as always preaching and selling books to the 'bold and fearless' people. Then at Liuzhou they parted, Broumton heading back to Guiyang alone. Cameron had to pass through a robber-infested region. 'At one place a woman and the household effects had been carried off the night previous. At another . . . one or more travellers had been killed, a day or two before. But I saw nothing alarming and reached Pakhoi in safety on Christmas Eve, finding such a bundle of letters – eighteen months' correspondence – awaiting me. So I was happy indeed, and thankful to my Heavenly Father for journeying and other mercies.'[28]

It would seem that Cameron made a good impression at Beihai (Pakhoi) on the consul, W G Stronach, for he wrote to Hudson Taylor suggesting that he buy premises and establish a mission base there. But although nearer in miles, the journey from Beihai to Guizhou or Yunnan had proved more difficult than by other routes. Cameron himself was ready to move on. 'As soon after their (Chinese) new year (1879) as men could be engaged to carry my luggage' – the indispensable loads of books – Cameron set out again, overland to Canton. He had been learning Cantonese and could speak now of 'supplementing' his 'slight knowledge' of the dialect with Mandarin. He was always learning. This time he found that by using his daylight hours 'working' in the towns and villages when people were gathered at markets, he could sleep on 'passage boats' at night and wake at the next busy place. In this way he found here and there to his joy and theirs, evangelists and members of several mission churches. 'I expect the whole province will soon be occupied in this way, and that they will extend their operations into those parts of (Guangxi) where the Canton dialect is spoken.' This was in fact the strategy of the southern missions, and determined the policy of the CIM to leave Guangdong, Guangxi and Fujian to them.[29]

On the way Cameron fell ill and for a month was cared for by the Canton missionaries[30] learning of the bitter persecutions 'that tested the genuineness of the work', and the steady expansion of the Church resulting from it. Then on March 18, 1879, he was off again, with a Hakka Christian companion, and found too late that the river boat he engaged was already carrying two cases of smallpox and two of high fever. In spite of this contagion, at Shaoguan two Methodist missionaries (Selby and Hargreaves) insisted on his joining them for a few days, and delighted him with their daily preaching and discussion of the gospel in the city, in the CIM manner.

April 5 saw him crossing the thousand-foot Meiling Pass into Jiangxi, for a taste of old-fashioned harassment at Nangang by a mandarin who set his *yamen*-runners on to badgering the inn-keeper until Cameron obligingly moved on. But at the next city of Ganzhou the innkeeper was beaten for 'harbouring a foreign devil'. This was no journey from one end of the province to the other. It was true 'itineration'. 'I visited all the cities in the eastern part of the province . . . as I thought those cities had less chance of being visited (with the gospel) by others . . . The road was bad for walking.' His reward was to find 'very civil' people who listened attentively to him. From there he crossed the mountains into Fujian and visited the missionaries and church at Shaowu. 'Mutual love to the Lord Jesus soon draws people together and makes Christians feel like old friends instead of acquaintances of yesterday . . . Such (experiences) cheer and encourage wanderers like myself . . . Parting with (them) filled me with sorrow.' He was very human, not immune from loneliness and depression in his prolonged isolation.

Striking north, back in Jiangxi again, 'We found wheelbarrows in use. I hired one to carry my baggage and coolie as he had hurt his foot.' It is not difficult to see why Cameron himself was well treated almost everywhere he went. Words flow, and he wrote as if his legs carried him swiftly from place to place, but crossing the 'rapid and dangerous' rivers was not so easy. On the edge of Cardwell's

SKETCHING OR PREACHING, SURE OF A CROWD

stamping ground at Hekou (now Yanshan) and the Qü Xian outposts of Shangrao (Guangxin) and Yüshan where he knew there were Christians, he could not find them (map p 397). But at 'Singkeng' 'I had a hearty welcome from an old farmer and his family. The news soon spread, . . . so the Christians gathered . . . We soon sat down to a sumptuous supper and . . . I had the best room given to me. For a long time after I could not sleep for joy . . . In every village . . . on our way to the next city, many had a very intelligent knowledge of the gospel.' Little by little it was taking root.

He reached the Douthwaites at Qü Xian on May 15 and could not bring himself to go on, he 'liked the people and place so much'. 'In my life, parting seems to be the rule, and yet one never feels (able) to get used to it. On the way to Shaoxing I felt very lonely . . .' Now he was in James Meadows' well-worked territory. He hurried on by night-boat to Hangzhou, and by foot-boat (Book 5, p 193) to Shanghai where he found Robert Landale, his companion on the Guiyang-Chongqing detour, and sailed with him for Yantai. Once there, he confessed, 'I found I was more run down than I was aware of.'[31]

Cameron's cat's cradle: the north-east[32] *June 1879–December 1882*

Before Hudson Taylor left Yantai on July 30, 1879, and headed into the typhoon, he and Cameron had ample time to plan another great itinerary. In 1869 the Irish Presbyterians had responded to William Burns' deathbed appeal for Manchuria to be given the gospel (Book 5, p 67). Hugh Waddell and Joseph Hunter MD occupied Yingkou (Niuchuang) and the church they planted had spread and taken root against opposition in Shenyang (Mukden) and south-eastern Manchuria almost as far north as Harbin.[33] They had not been the first. Alexander Williamson had been through the region in 1866–68, and John Ross of Yantai followed in 1872. However, apart from the natural extension of these churches, vast areas of Manchuria (now the provinces of Liaoning, Jilin and Heilongjiang) were without the gospel. First-hand knowledge of the region was needed, as well as of the most northerly parts of Shanxi and Shaanxi provinces, bordering Inner Mongolia.

Cameron accepted this challenge, and the arrangement with the B&FBS worked out with Alexander Wylie's help in London offered an opportunity for Cameron to have travelling companions financed by the Bible Society. The plan was for Wylie's successor as Agent in China, Samuel Dyer (Maria's brother), and two Bible Society colporteurs Guang and Wu to go with him in August, taking a large supply of Bible portions and collecting more at various rendezvous. Hudson Taylor, in Zhenjiang by then, obtained passports for them. But this plan fell through, and T W Pigott, who had arrived in China with Hudson Taylor only four months previously and was learning Chinese at the Chefoo Bluff, took Dyer's place at short notice.[34]

Pigott had no more experience of the Chinese way of life than he had acquired in Yantai, and none of travelling. So Cameron first took him for a trial ten-day circuit of the Shandong promontory to the east of Yantai, all on foot, with books and bedding on pack mules. Each day from September 4 to 13 they walked twenty or thirty miles, preaching the gospel at every resting place except in the bigger towns, where they worked for part or all of a day. On the last day, lightly laden, they capped this achievement by covering 120 *li*, about forty miles, reaching Chefoo 'late' in the evening. Pigott had proved himself. He did not realise that Cameron had found it a depressing tour of down-at-heel places with illiterate people slow to understand. His Nanjing mandarin was not to blame; it served him well in most of China.

Cameron, Pigott, Guang and Wu arrived at Tianjin by ship on September 30, 1879, and while Pigott and Colporteur Guang took the main bulk of books by steamship to Yingkou, Cameron and Wu began selling and preaching, first in Tianjin itself and from October 10 north-eastwards to Shanhaiguan where the Great Wall runs down into the sea (map p 210). Beyond it lay Manchuria and Shenyang ('Mukden'). They hired a cart and covered long distances on the busy highways. After Jinzhou they turned south and in

CAMERON'S NORTH-EASTERN JOURNEY

November reached the United Presbyterian Mission at Yingkou. Pigott had bought a cart and team of animals and was away testing them, on a visit to the churches with James Carson of the Presbyterian Church of Ireland.

Ten days later they 'set out in high spirits' with their companions, travelling southwards down the west coast of the Liaodong peninsula – into a snowstorm that took many lives. Their cart turned over, as was happening frequently, and by the time they had it upright again it was too late to go on. So they shared out what food they had with them between the two colporteurs, the carter and themselves, enough for perhaps one quarter of a meal each, and huddled together in the cart from Thursday until Saturday morning. Cameron and Pigott tried and failed during the storm to reach the nearest town, somehow finding their way back to the cart after becoming lost. But when their companions became distressed they tried again. The air had cleared and the town lay only a few hundred yards away. They found men and animals to help, and returned to find the cart and all its contents forsaken, but still unrifled. Safely reunited at an inn they gave thanks that not even the life of an animal had been lost, but they all had frostbite. So miraculous did their escape strike the townsmen as being, that crowds listened attentively to the gospel as long as they were there. 'They often said we *must* be good people to have escaped so.'[35]

Wu and the carter had to be shipped home to Yantai from the nearest port; Pigott and Guang took the cartload of books to Shenyang (Mukden) by the main roads (maps pp 217, 223); and Cameron with a pack mule worked his way up the east coast of the peninsula alone. Pigott fell ill on the way but reached Shenyang on January 17, less than nine months since he arrived in China.

The consul at Yingkou had extracted a promise from Cameron not to enter Korea, for he could have done so without difficulty. He walked through Dongguo to Dandong on the Yalu River, and on to 'the Corean gate' where he stayed for several days, talking and leaving books with Chinese-speaking Koreans. For two days he had travelled through 'neutral' territory, a Chinese buffer-zone, drawn to the 'forbidden land', but having to keep his rendezvous with Pigott at Shenyang (Mukden). Their welcome by the sixty or so Christians of Shenyang, Manchus among them (mostly Ross's converts), and the warmth of their send-off on January 23 foretold a strong Manchurian Church. Even the mandarins sent a military escort to see them on their way.[36] Thousands of miles apart, in the

A NORTH CHINA PEASANT, INURED TO HARD WINTERS

extremities of the empire, the roots of the Church were striking deeply. No one, without exception, could testify to this as James Cameron could.

They travelled north through Changdu, and a hundred miles on reached Changchun, thronged for Chinese New Year, the perfect opportunity for preaching and selling to people from far and wide. Meeting Mongols as well as Manchus from Heilongjiang, they found convincing evidence that most people were Mandarin-speaking immigrants. 'It would almost seem as if, through becoming rulers of China, the Manchus had lost their own language and country. They will indeed have no country to return to' from the hundreds of garrison towns they occupied throughout China.

On February 16, 1880, they resumed their journey into Jilin[37] and made for the provincial capital, also called Jilin. Here too they drew large crowds and quickly sold two thousand books and tracts. But what was that among '200,000 souls, yet no one to tell them of Jesus!', apart from occasional visits by the Presbyterians? 'They found the French Catholic priests hard at work here, as in almost every other part of the Chinese Empire, far ahead of the Protestants.'[38] Officials and people were 'most civil', the climate 'dry and bracing', but supplies were nearly exhausted and on February 23 they had to start back to Peking to restock with books.

Following a different route, through Shuanggang and Yitong, they 're-entered the stockade' (a token line of defence) and on March 4 reached 'the Mongol gate' of Faku (Fahkumen). By then they had used up what was left of their stock so, leaving their companions to rest at Xinmin, Cameron and Pigott made a detour to Yingkou to borrow enough books to see them to Peking. The hard journey took them sixteen days, and when they resumed the trek to Peking, Pigott's journal re-echoed much of what they had experienced for months already: '26th to 29th progress very slow; the cart perpetually sticking fast in the mud.' Often it had been 'up to the axles', and even 'to the shafts', with their shoulders and brute force needed to get them through. On April 1 'an unruly crowd threw mud and stones at us', but this was exceptional, and on the 12th they 're-entered China Proper' at Shanhaiguan.

American Board missionaries compelled them to spend a few days at Tong Xian (T'ungchou), and at Peking W H Collins of the CMS received them royally, by long-standing invitation. Other missions also went out of their way to welcome them, for in eight months of rough travelling and rough living they had sold more than

20,000 Gospels and other parts of the Bible, distributed thousands of tracts, and preached to tens of thousands of people.[39] Colporteur Guang stayed to work faithfully with Cameron for two years, until December 1881 when their agreement with the Bible Society ended. And Cameron went on into the summer of 1882. Such gargantuan effort must reap its rewards.

Cameron's cat's cradle: the north-west[40] *May 1880–August 1882*

If the reader needs tenacity to follow arid records of these travels, the men who made them needed all the resolution they could muster. Few persevered for long. James Cameron did little else for seven years, but by the end had had enough and called a halt. The last year of his north-western journeys needed strength of will. Even with maps to follow, dry records make dry reading, but the sheer scale of his exploits illuminates his achievement.

The working interval at Peking was soon over. On May 20, 1880, they resumed the travelling which for Cameron was not to end until August 1882. They intended no less than to visit, with A G Parrott, 'every city in (Shanxi) and the adjoining (province of Shaanxi) together with any neighbouring cities of (Gansu).' The ambitiousness of the plan in almost anyone else's hands would have been unrealistic. As it was, Pigott could only give two months before returning to Yantai. To replenish their stocks during the first itinerary of over a thousand miles, they sent a consignment of books ahead to await them at Kalgan (now Zhangjiakou) north-east of Peking and near the Mongolian border (maps pp 85, 217). On the northern arm of the Great Wall where it is doubled for two hundred miles, enclosing many towns and cities, Kalgan was the strategic base held by Chauncey Goodrich of the American Board, for evangelism in Mongolia, but the key to the region of Shanxi between the walls was Guangling. So to Guangling they went, over a high mountain pass, leaving Zhili through Yu Xian.

Surviving reports and journals from this point are briefer and almost devoid of dates, but take them westwards across the northern tip of Shanxi, through the Great Wall into what is now Greater Mongolia, following close to the great northern loop of the Yellow River enclosing the Ordos Desert, to Togtoh and Baotou. Returning eastwards they came to the city of Guihuacheng (now known by its original Mongol name, Hohhot).[41] Including a Manchu quarter this large and prosperous city of 10,000 families lay at the eastern end of a fine plain in Mongolia, with four other good-sized places within a hundred miles. They were impressed by its size, activity and intelligent, courteous people. 'There is probably no city north of (Taiyuan) more important for us to occupy than this,' for work among Mongols and Chinese, Cameron reported to Hudson Taylor, who said at the Shanxi conference in July 1886, 'We had determined in 1880 to work that city (Guihuacheng) and the prefectures of Soping and Datong.'[42] But men of the right spirit were hard to find. After trial periods by several members of the Mission, George Clarke of Dali occupied Guihuacheng in 1886 and others settled at Baotou.

Cameron fell ill with fever after returning through the Great Wall at Shahukou, but as soon as he could keep his balance on a mule travelled to Datong where they had arranged to meet the colporteurs and on to Zhangjiakou (Kalgan). Seeing Cameron's condition, Chauncey Goodrich kept him for a month to regain his strength.[43] Then on August 17, 1880, with fresh stocks of books, they crossed the mountains southwards and, denying themselves a visit to the scenic holy mountain of Wutaishan, divided up in pairs and zigzagged from city to city east of Taiyuan, and countless towns and villages between them. Cameron was the last of the team to arrive at Taiyuan, and the first, with the faithful colporteur Guang, to set out again, working their way down the Taiyuan plain until they came to Linfen (Pingyang).[44] A G Parrott joined him briefly on his return journey northward.

The matter-of-fact, deliberate style of Cameron's journal – 'We now turned (on October 26, 1880) to the north-east and east (for) two months . . . in this part of (Shanxi), as also several cities in (Henan)' – reveals again the spirit Hudson Taylor loved so strongly in this man for his entire commitment to taking the gospel to every corner of the land. 'We visited altogether twenty-nine cities (and) of course all the market towns and villages . . . along the route.' Up into the hills as far north as Heshun and everywhere down to Lucheng and Changzhi (Lu'an, Lungan) in November, they found the population reduced by famine to one third of what it had been, and wolves more numerous and fearless than ever. 'We saw not only ruined houses but half-ruined cities and villages, and . . . the people seemed to have no heart or hope left.' Steeply up the Hanling range and as steeply down into Henan, they covered the cities north of the Huang He (Yellow River) from Anyang (Zhangde) near the Zhili border southward to Weihui near Fenqiu and then westward to climb into Shanxi again.

Back at Linfen for the Chinese New Year of 1881, Cameron enjoyed the rare experience of working with the first men to be baptised there, and other new (un-named) believers who from his description included the famed future pastor Hsi. But only briefly, for on February 8 he left for Taiyuan again with A G Parrott, and on March 14 resumed his partnership with Pigott. Parrott was systematically working through the western hill cities so, after nine or ten months largely given to Shanxi, Cameron crossed the Yellow River into Shaanxi, climbed up to Suide on March 28, and went on to Mizhi, Jia Xian and Shenmu (map p 85). The thoroughness of these journeys, penetrating the remotest regions, surprises anyone investigating them in detail. No inns existed fit for moneyed merchants, but caravanserai for muleteers and camel drivers, with brick beds and coarse corn or millet and steamed bread for daily food, were the luxuries enjoyed after long dusty days. At Shenmu on a main road 'to Peking', Cameron wrote, 'I had a stirring time' contending with drunkards – meaning that they had pestered and molested him and Pigott, taxing all his ingenuity to quieten and get rid of them.

They were close to the Great Wall again, and to the Ordos Desert beyond, crossing and recrossing the ruins of the wall as they moved south-westward along the desert edge for fifty miles to Yülin. 'We were astonished to find that the surrounding sand was almost level with the (city) wall. Some (dunes) were . . . already higher . . . (all formed) within the last twenty years.' After another week Pigott fell ill but Cameron pressed ahead through 'Ordos country' to Jingbian, about sixty miles from the present Ningxia (map p 80), and only three hundred from Lanzhou 'as the crow flies'. Finding a Catholic priest near a 'station' with three more in residence, he felt ashamed. 'The Romanists certainly put Protestants to the blush; for where now is the heathen land they have not occupied or attempted to occupy?' Rejoining Pigott after a week, a sweep to the south brought them to Yan'an, a lethargic place of loess caves, due to be Mao's headquarters sixty years later. But Pigott's two months were up, and they parted company at Qingjian, he to reach Taiyuan by a ten day journey on his own, and Cameron to arrive at the ancient capital of Xi'an, on the same day May 25, 1881.

With no books left and his new stock not yet arrived, he waited 'and found the people quiet except when I preached on the street – then they opposed'. But he met a National Bible Society of Scotland colporteur who spared him a few hundred Gospels, and with this armament he criss-crossed between cities across the plains south-eastwards, then over the Qinling mountains, and at Jingziguan where Shaanxi, Henan and Hubei meet he found a cache of books left by Parrott (map p 94). This fact alone indicates the degree of penetration being achieved. Instead of gliding peacefully by boat down-river to Xiangyang and Fancheng (Xiangfan) and the comforts of a CIM outpost and Chinese Christians, Cameron struck across country to more cities of Henan on the way to Nanyang. There again, instead of taking a river boat he chose to turn south-westwards, preaching in market towns and collecting in Fancheng a large consignment of books for the next phase.

He took his load of books by boat to Xing'an (now Ankang), furthest point on the Han River reached by Baller and King in 1876, and used it as a base for evangelism in accessible towns. At one market town the headman ordered him out, threatening him with a beating; but instead of turning people against him this made them more obliging, for fear of repercussions from the city mandarins. While the boat 'tracked' slowly up the winding river Cameron walked overland to Hanzhong to collect the first home letters he had seen since March in Taiyuan.

In the two years since George King had begun work in Hanzhong a church of forty or fifty Christians had come into being, nearly all natives of Sichuan. It was August and Cameron deserved a rest, but he denied himself the pleasure of their company. To rendezvous with his boat and supplies he took a mountain short cut to Ziyang and soon regretted it (map p 80). Thrown off balance by striking a jutting rock, his loaded pack-mule crashed head over heels for several hundred feet down the steep hillside. Stone dead, 'the last relic of Manchuria' became quick income to a countryman who bought the carcase for a song and sold its flesh pound by pound in the nearby village. Cameron had become too fond of it to join in the meal put on by his innkeeper.

A difficult detour to Hanyin and back to Xing'an led him on a northward march to Xi'an again on October 8.[45] From there he worked his way north-westwards from city to city, crossed into Gansu and for ten days moved southwards, leaving no big place untouched, as far as Tianshui. George Parker was away, so Cameron stayed only one day and made for Hanzhong again, his books nearly all sold. The three last cities of Shaanxi were soon visited, and then he swallowed up the final seventy miles in two days' forced march. 'I was indeed glad when I had reached the last city, and had disposed of my last Gospel. I felt much the need of rest, and I then thought of taking up settled work . . . I arrived in (Hanzhong) on November 11th, just in time to sit up with poor Mr (George) King as he watched his little boy, who died on the morning of the 12th.'

There was to be no rest. An educated Christian named Ho, the first believer in Hanzhong (p 260), invited Cameron to go with him to preach the gospel to his clan in Sichuan, at their request. 'A revulsion of feeling' was Cameron's reaction, so weary of travelling had he become. But he could not reject so God-given an assignment. For eight days they trudged the two hundred miles in pouring rain, fording flooded rivers, drying out by charcoal fires at night, preaching and pasting up gospel posters in the towns and villages. On arriving at Nanjiang and at one village after another, crowds of 'relatives' gathered to greet them. Mr Ho rose to the occasion, reminding them of how religious he had been, loyal to their ancestors and going on to tell how he had found no foreign doctrine but the universal answer to man's needs. His own family responded and, led by him, burned their idols and ancestor tablets – the beginning of a new church in northern Sichuan.

Cameron returned to Hanzhong until the end of the year 1881, and then travelled by stages, still preaching where he could, back to Wuhan, Anqing, Zhenjiang and to Shanghai for two months' work before returning to his September 1879 starting point, Yantai, for the summer. Only one province, Hunan, had escaped him – and the outlying dependencies of Tibet, Xinjiang and Taiwan. Finally, 'In August, 1882, I left for England, having finished almost seven years' work in this vast empire.'

At the annual meetings in London, 1883, he paid a glowing tribute to those in other missions who were like brothers and sisters, mothers and fathers to him on many occasions. And to the Chinese, not only Christians. Time and again 'literary men' would sit for hours talking with him at his inn. To encourage them to buy his books he would say, 'Take these home – look them through, and bring them back.' Trustful friendliness won him friends. And mandarins too, 'there were very few who were not friendly and somewhat kindly in their manner . . . I liked to come in contact with them . . . and to speak the gospel to them in their own homes.'[46] Many remarkable things were being done in China by many remarkable men and women, but perhaps none comparable with the 'itinerations' of this calm, courteous Scotsman, preparing the way always self-effacingly for others to reap where he sowed.

CHAPTER SEVEN

WOMEN INLAND
1879–82

The women pioneers *1879*

Hudson Taylor's revolutionary ideas had one explanation among others, his early isolation in China as the first 'agent' of the ineffective, incompetent Chinese Evangelization Society. Forced to make his own observations and choices, he very early saw that Chinese women were largely out of reach of the gospel unless it could be brought to them by Christian women. He pleaded with his sister Amelia to come and do this. In Ningbo, 1856–60, the effectiveness of Mary Gough, Maria and Burella Dyer and of Mary Jones confirmed him in this conviction.[1] After Maria became his wife the value of her work among women could be proved incontrovertibly. But not only among women. Educated Chinese men admired and respected her knowledge and ability.

When the *Lammermuir* party arrived at Hangzhou on November 21, 1866, Maria's strong leadership and example were felt by the young women and also by Hudson Taylor and the men of the party. Her example set the pattern and the pace of evangelism among the women of Hangzhou, which Jennie Faulding and Mary Bowyer at once took up. The church in Hangzhou came into existence as much from their work as from that of the novice pastor, Wang Lae-djün, Hudson Taylor, Judd or McCarthy. Then when the Taylors made their bold advance to Yangzhou, Jennie stayed with the McCarthys and Lae-djün, at twenty-four carrying responsibilities normally borne by mature missionaries. Hudson Taylor wrote to her on June 24, 1868, as he might have written to a young man in an equivalent position,

> You cannot take a pastor's place in name, but you must help Lae-djün to act in matters of receiving and excluding (candidates for baptism) as far as you can. You can speak privately to (them) and can be present at Church meetings and might even, through others, suggest questions to candidates. Then after the meeting you can talk privately with Lae-djün . . . so he may have the help he needs, and yet there will be nothing which any can lay hold of and charge as unseemly . . .[2]

– unseemly, that is, for a woman among men, and for a woman in what was conventionally the preserve of a male missionary. Some critics would leap to rebuke her on either score, but Hudson Taylor saw women as 'the most powerful agency' for carrying the gospel into China's homes.

On May 24, 1870, he had written to Emily Blatchley (HTCOC Book 5, pp 231ff) when she had barely arrived back in Britain with his children. At only twenty-five she was to represent him, unofficially, by quiet influence upon his well-meaning but uncomprehending official representatives. For she was not only naturally capable but more closely one in mind and spirit with him and Maria than they. Hudson Taylor's confidence in her was complete, so he wrote (in her own poetic style),

> May He make you so conscious of His indwelling . . . that you may realise . . . that in Him the weak is strong, the ignorant wise, the mute eloquent, the incompetent all-sufficient, and that *in Christ Jesus* there is no male or female, that so far as moved *by* Him, and acting *for* Him, you are no longer a girl whose place it is to keep back, retired and silent, but His instrument, called to adorn Him who is your adornment.[3]

Some account of her success has been given in *Refiner's Fire*.

Now, in 1879, nine years later, Jennie had also come through an extreme test, that of leaving her children and him, to be the first Western woman to go deep into inland China, at a time of extreme famine, to show the love of Christ in action. In courage and ability she and her companions had proved him right. With plain evidence multiplying that in most of the empire it was safe for foreign men to travel, and in some places to live unmolested, he was convinced that the time had come for what would be 'a great step in advance', the most dangerous innovation yet attempted. The only comparable venture, 330 miles into the 'interior' had been made in Shandong by Mrs Alexander Williamson in western clothes, to Wei Xian in 1875, and via Weifang (Tsingchou) to Jinan in 1876. Travelling with her husband by mule-litter, they had dispensed medicines at each stopping place on their journey.[4] Without doubt in their own minds Hudson Taylor and Jennie believed that the will of God was for women to be at the forefront with the men – and even without them. (*See* Appendix 5 Pioneer Women.)

In Yantai he discussed with Jennie whether the well-proven pioneers, George King, George Clarke, George Nicoll and others, might now marry, as some were 'impatient' to do, intending to take their brides far up-country with them. To one impatient newcomer pleading his 'special case', Hudson Taylor replied,

> None can be more earnest than myself to see woman's work commenced in the interior of the various provinces; this has long been the consuming desire of my heart. . . . I truly joy in the joy (of the happily married) and I share in deep sympathy in their loneliness before marriage. But it is required of stewards that they be found *faithful*; and if, without adequate reason, I were to set aside (to the detriment of the work and yourselves) the stipulations agreed upon, I should feel that I was not guided by fidelity to principle so much as caprice of feeling.[5] [And to candidates in general] Unless you intend your wife to be a true missionary, not merely a wife, home-maker and friend, do not join us.

He failed to hold them to the highest, and they resigned.

Conditions were better than when he took his own family to Yangzhou. Famine relief admittedly was exceptional, and the route to Shanxi was used and guarded by Peking officials. But for two or three years he had been preparing for this moment. For a few months, while the *Lammermuir* women were on furlough in Britain, only one unmarried woman of the CIM, Emmeline Turner, had been left in China. But on the heels of 'the eighteen' men pioneers, he had sent out seven women in 1876–77, none married, and fourteen more in 1878, of whom twelve were single.[6] Before leaving Britain himself in February 1879, his editorial in *China's Millions* had stressed the importance of *Women's Work*,

> The early religious and moral education of the whole rising generation, and the strongest and most constantly operating influence that is brought to bear upon the male part of the population through life, is in the hands of the women; and . . . these women can only be effectively reached and instructed by their own sex. . . . The Lord increase the number of lady workers in China tenfold![7]

At the General Missionary Convention of October 1878 in London, George Smith of the English Presbyterian Mission had claimed that the work done among women made an important contribution towards his society's objective of 'establishing in China a self-supporting, self-ruling, self-propagating Church'. The significance of his speech lay in its divergence from current opinion and practice. For years almost the only place for Western women in China had been in education. But the CIM's *Lammermuir* party had set a new pace, and a decade later there were sixty-three unmarried women missionaries of all societies in China, when the General Conference met at Shanghai in May 1877.[8] It appealed for women as well as men, with poor response except in the CIM.

Griffith John, whose wife had died at Singapore on the way back to China, had married again in 1874, a person whose addition to the missionary body in Wuhan soon resulted in many more Chinese women and whole families joining the Church. Yet he wrote to the directors of LMS in 1875, 'I am not a strong believer in unmarried female agents in China.'[9] Like so many he was watching 'with considerable anxiety and hesitation' the experiment being made by 'another mission'. He could only have meant the CIM. A few months later his words to the directors were even stronger. 'I feel sure you are going to *waste* a good deal of money and introduce elements of discord into missions.' Yet in April 1877 when the only single woman in the LMS in China was the Goughs' one-time governess, Miss Bear, on a temporary assignment, he could say, 'I thank God for the CIM.' He was coming round.

In pursuing his unconventional course, Hudson Taylor faced a choice. Jennie's adventurous penetration into Shanxi, and her companions' peaceful residence in Taiyuan, while Henan, Shaanxi and Hunan would not tolerate foreign men, could be left as an isolated achievement or developed to whatever extent proved possible. The die was cast. On August 2, 1879, when he reached Shanghai he discussed the proposition with Charles Moore, a godly intellectual, and on the 11th told Jennie his plans for the western provinces. As a first step married couples would attempt to settle in Shaanxi, Gansu, Sichuan and Guizhou. Later one couple and single men would move into Yunnan. He hoped he and she would be able to go and see these place for themselves after meeting Cameron and Pigott in Taiyuan. They never succeeded in doing so.

George King had married earlier in the summer of 1879 and taken his bride Emily to Wuhan. At twenty-three he had already packed a wide experience of China into four years. Hudson Taylor had confidence in him. But she had only arrived in late November 1878, and had little language or experience. The historic letter was sent. Would they be the first, and to join Easton at Tianshui in Gansu, taking eighteen boxes of books. The answer 'Yes!' arrived without delay, and on September 18, 1879, they were on their way up the Han River rapids, a two to three month journey. By the time they arrived at Hanzhong in southern Shaanxi, he had to break the journey for a few months there for his wife's sake. 'Who is this foreigner?' the magistrate enquired. King sent his 'card'. Remarkably, they had met and become friends at Xi'an. The magistrate told him to choose the the house he would like to rent, and the contract would be approved.[10]

A QUIET REACH ON THE HAN RIVER

Hudson Taylor's policy of letting the men plunge in with little of the language had paid rich dividends in fluency. Now he was placing equal confidence in the young women. What if their husbands were to die? They would have Christian Chinese colleagues with them, but how would they stand up to the strain? And what would the critics say then? He chose to be guided by Scripture, 'He that observeth the wind shall not sow; and he that regardeth the clouds shall not reap' (Eccl 11.4). In the event it was Emily King who died after only two years, from typhoid, a disease as common at the coast. By then what mattered more was that women had found their place, had made a start. In time they were to outnumber the men by two to one.

The first women to the west *1879–80*

Emily King was the first foreign woman to go into the far west of China, since any in Marco Polo's day. After George Clarke and A G Parrott had been driven out of Jincheng (Tsechou) in Shanxi (p 183) and went to Linfen, Parrott stayed but Clarke moved on to Yantai. He, Cameron and Nicoll had reached China in 1875 shortly after King, and were fully as experienced as he. Hudson Taylor's proposition to Clarke and Nicoll matched their own thoughts, to marry without delay and travel together up the Yangzi gorges to Chongqing. There Clarke would leave the Nicolls and go on with his Swiss bride, Fanny Rossier (one year in China), to join James Broumton at Guiyang. When others took their place they would move on, far into Yunnan.

When they reached Shanghai in early September, Hudson Taylor was there, 'dangerously ill' again but recovering enough to be taken back to Chefoo. The Clarkes and Nicolls were married on September 15 in Shanghai, and on November 3 set out from Wuhan on their hazardous journey. Its dangers they knew, from rocks and currents in the many Yangzi rapids, from possible encounters with river pirates, and from angry mobs in Sichuan whose attacks on Roman Catholics might be turned on them too. A greater hazard, more capable of ending the whole project at the start, was intervention by the consuls or minister, Sir Thomas Wade, if they heard of it. No question of legality could arise, but while being as harmless as doves, they needed the wisdom of serpents. To say nothing in Wuhan about going to Chongqing, when starting for Yichang, would arouse no suspicions.[11]

Yichang was the normal place for transferring to smaller boats for the gorges. In advising them about this, Hudson Taylor also sent Nicoll instructions about reporting his movements. Although a schoolmaster by profession he had been less systematic than others with less education (including Cameron and Clarke). Every journey in new territory was a reconnaissance to benefit colleagues. So places should be named and described or assessed, distances noted, the attitudes and characteristics of the people and officials also; inns should be recommended, and accounts given of the duration and kind of work achieved. He mentioned trades, but not mineral resources or commercial matters of interest to geographers or consuls. They were taking their wives far from medical aid, so he taught them the essentials of treatment for the diseases they were most likely to meet and, presumably, how to help at the birth of a baby.

The courage of those first pioneers deserves more praise than they would have tolerated in their day. K S Latourette allowed space in his mine of information to pay this tribute: 'Between 1878 and 1881 he (Hudson Taylor) began to send them alone into the interior provinces, a policy whose success testified both to the courage of the women and to the character of the Chinese.'[12] Indeed Mrs C W Mateer testified that women were far safer in China than in New York or London, and Elizabeth Wilson who later spent years in Hanzhong and Gansu only once in her long experience had any anxiety for the young women she was escorting.

Slowly the trackers towed their boats upstream, day after day, until on December 17 George Clarke recorded,

> In ascending the rapids we have been exposed to danger. Whilst waiting at one of these for a day and a half . . . two boats like our own were crushed (but) we only sustained a little damage. Boats waiting [their turn] to ascend are exposed to injury from . . . the current or swell, and (from) large boats . . . between which there is a danger of getting jammed like a nut in a nutcracker. The crashing sound is anything but comforting.
>
> At Wushan we found a boat waiting for us from the *yamen* (displaying) a flag (with) white characters on a red ground, 'To receive and escort the foreign travellers' . . . I have not seen the same respect shown before.[13]

The Yichang mandarins had sent word ahead of them. Two days before Christmas, however, 'the most trying of all my travelling experiences' happened when they were wrecked. Their boat was holed on a rock, fortunately close to land. They got their wives ashore and threw or carried to them everything that could be saved. 'The boat was filling fast and going down.' Of eleven boxes of books only four or five were rescued dry, so Christmas Day was spent drying books and possessions, spread out on the rocks. A tent made from masts, oars and mats gave some shelter from the 'piercing cold', but the risk of a foray by looters was their main anxiety. By the 29th the boat had been raised and repaired, and they made another attempt 'into the teeth of a small rapid'. This time the tracking cable and ship's mast snapped, and they were swept downstream. Clarke and Nicoll at the oars caught a back current which brought them to their camp site again. If this accident had happened at a major rapid, boat, goods and lives might well have been lost.

The first foreign women to enter Sichuan reached Chongqing on January 13, 1880, to learn that the Roman Catholics across the river had been attacked. 'Maybe our Father saw fit to detain us,' Mary Ann Nicoll wrote, 'that we might arrive here in safety. Not even a crowd gathered when we landed.' The crowds were soon to come. A month later, after the Clarkes had gone, 'As soon as it was known . . . the women flocked to see her. (At first) we had from 100 to 200 women daily . . . but since the (Chinese New Year, except when it was raining) we have had from 200 to 500 women daily. We receive the men in the front of the house, and the women in the inner hall.'[14] An elderly military mandarin himself came to take them to a feast in his home, and a motherly old lady, 'knowing how weary she (Mary Ann) must be, used sometimes to send her (sedan) chair' to bring her to her own home, put her to bed and quietly fan her till she fell asleep. When she woke she was given a good meal before being taken back to her husband. For two years she saw no other Western woman, and then only in transit.

George and Fanny Clarke stayed only a week at Chongqing before going over the mountains to Guiyang. In seventeen days of travelling only two were dry and sunny, so the trails were dangerously slippery. 'The men often let her (mountain-chair) fall . . . she would rather travel up all the large rapids of the (Yangzi) than take this journey. . . . She was such a good traveller though.' On February 5, 1880, they joined James Broumton in Guiyang, and the first Western woman in Guizhou began her strange new life. Eleven weeks later, on April 20, two more arrived, overland all the way from Wuhan.[15]

The first unmarried one *1880*

When Hudson Taylor arrived in Wuhan with Frank Trench on February 9, 1880, he kept his intentions secret. Disapproval of them was so predictable that he avoided contact with members of other missions who might question him. 'None know of our plans.' The fact of young brides having gone to Chongqing and Guiyang would be known, and he had come, as Elizabeth Wilson said of this occasion in particular, like 'a bombshell scattering us' again.[16] But this time young unmarried women were involved. Two struck Hudson Taylor as suitable. Jane Kidd, as playful 'as a kitten' (in Hudson Taylor's phrase) but an effective missionary already, was fluent enough after one year in China to keep up an animated conversation; she was to go with William McCarthy's widow to join the Clarkes at Guiyang. And 'Miss A L Fausset' after nearly two years in the country, 'truly devoted and most unselfish', was to go up the Han River with Elizabeth Wilson to the Kings at Hanzhong (map p 94).

For a week after his arrival at Wuhan Hudson Taylor prepared the travellers for whatever lay before them, combining daily sessions of prayer and study of the Bible with practical advice and business matters. The words Jane Kidd most took to heart were his powerful farewell reminder, 'You have only the great GOD to take care of you!' They summed up his own confidence in the omnipotence and faithfulness of the One they served.[17] He had chosen Frederick Baller as 'the best possible escort' for Ellen McCarthy and Jane Kidd. And Frank Trench, the competent man of independent means who had been proving himself by thorough itineration of the cities of Anhui, was to go with them on his way to Yunnan. An evangelist named Yao, the Bible Society's colporteur Lo, and a Christian woman made up the party.[18]

Instead of the Yangzi route through Chongqing they were to cross Hunan, the hostile province where the people on this route to Guiyang had burned Augustus Margary's boat, and stoned other travellers, yet treated Judd, Broumton and Clarke at different times with respect. The rapids on the Yuan River by comparison were small hazards on 'the first visit of ladies to such a rowdy province'. But five years had passed since Margary and Judd were there, and Hudson Taylor also 'wished to have (Baller's) judgment as to the preparedness of the province for settled work'.

They left Wuhan on February 19 in a house-boat captained by a member of Griffith John's church, reached beautiful Yueyang at the mouth of the Dongting Lake on the 27th and anchored for the weekend to ride out 'a perfect hurricane'. Men and women came aboard to visit them, and the *laoban* (captain) and his wife proved to be as 'ready with a word for the Lord Jesus' as his passengers. 'There was a boldness and frankness about (the people of Hunan), an absence of hollowness, and a reality. . . . It was a treat to preach to them.' The women were delighted to see foreign women and 'stroked their hands and stroked their cheeks', saying they were beautiful.[19]

Safely across the lake and working up into the Yuan River the widely travelled Baller said of the well-wooded pastoral scene, 'This province is one of the finest, if not the finest, in China.' Then, moored for the night, men and women went ashore, to be 'received with the greatest kindness'. 'An attentive listener' invited Baller and Trench to explain the gospel to him more fully, and his boys took their hands to lead them to his home. Then they preached for an hour to a roomful of people. So far so good.

The next night some men the worse for drink tried to pick a quarrel and pelted them with clods of earth. But the weekend at Changde was peaceful, with good audiences, and as the river narrowed, fierce rapids several miles in length were safely negotiated. At place after place without exception women flocked to welcome 'the ladies' and listen to the gospel, until they reached Qianyang near the Guizhou border. There 'our old enemies the officials' stirred up the riff-raff to snatch away the books people had bought, and forced the travellers to move on. Even so, people followed in boats asking for more, and 'one decent man' showed that he had read over and over again the books brought from Wuhan by a friend. The steady penetration by the gospel was thrilling to observe. Their boat was battered and tossed about day after day until, badly holed by a rock in one rapid at the provincial border, they kept afloat only 'by dint of hard baling' and plugging the leak while they limped to where they could tie up and effect repairs.

After seven weeks by boat, nine more days spent crossing the high mountains brought them to Guiyang and the Clarkes, on April 22. Jane Kidd had made history, the first single girl to enter the far western provinces of China. Three days earlier, to their surprise they had met James Broumton on his way to a festival of Miao tribesmen of various tribes, so good was his rapport with them. For learning the Miao language, this opportunity for comparing their dialects was too good for him to miss. Trench and Yao came in behind the others a few days later, having begun their colportage of Guizhou at the city of Guiding. As soon as Broumton was free in May they were to make a major assault on Yunnan together, including Kunming the capital.[20] After a few days Baller left with Lo, travelling by Chongqing and the Yangzi gorges to take charge at Wuhan. Faith and courage had been vindicated once again.

Women 'alone' against the current[21] *February–November 1880*

When Jennie Taylor and 'Miss Fausset' arrived at Wuhan on February 20, the day after the Guiyang party left, Hudson Taylor discussed his next plan with them. A new kind of courage was involved. All available missionary escorts and even Chinese Christian companions were away on other ventures, and none could be borrowed from other missions. Griffith John had already provided two colporteurs for Shanxi. But George and Emily King at Hanzhong intended to complete their journey to Gansu after their child was born. Someone must care for the growing number of Christians at Hanzhong (maps pp 80, 94).

Elizabeth Wilson had begun life in China at the late age of forty-six, and after four years could make her meaning known in Chinese only with difficulty. But her greying hair was an advantage in a Confucian society that respected age, and her cheerful, outgoing way with Chinese women won her friends. She employed a cook named Zhou, witty and conceited, with shortcomings that made him a doubtful asset. If she and young 'Miss Fausset' were to ascend the Han River with its rapids, they must at least have a reliable Christian escort. The only one who answered to this description was Huang Kezhong, one of Charles Judd's converts, who lived in a shack on his own, because he had leprosy.

The two women were game to go, and Hudson Taylor had confidence in them. His sense of God's guidance in these circumstances made him willing to add risk to risk, in human terms. Shipwreck could come to anyone, even a Baller or Cameron, but what of the wickedness of men? A good *laoban* with his wife on board, Huang Kezhong as a standby, and 'the great GOD' in full control seemed insurance enough against any calamity. So it was decided. They would go.

A few days later Hudson Taylor and Huang Kezhong went out to hire a boat, and slept on board that night. In the morning 'the ladies' joined them, and noticed at once that Huang's bedding, a wadded *pugai*, stank offensively. Hudson Taylor had slept alongside him without complaining, but now he arranged for it to be exchanged for a clean one. He travelled with them for several hours before going ashore, returning with a basket of eggs and lard. 'Miss Fausset' then recalled that she had commented on vegetable oil having spoiled the flavour of some meat. This was his parting present. He prayed with them and left to return to Wuhan. Elizabeth Wilson felt cared for, supported by his attentiveness on many occasions. Her travelling boxes still bore her name stencilled by him in London.[22]

On May 21 they arrived at Hanzhong, one thousand miles upstream and nearly three months from their starting point. Huang

'EYE OF A NEEDLE': THROUGH THE HANZHONG CITY WALL

Kezhong had been all they hoped of him, talking to people at every opportunity about Christ, and bringing women and girls to hear more from the missionaries. The *laoban* took them to visit his own home, and brought his crew to listen when the four Christians had their daily Bible reading and prayer. He tried to keep them hidden in potentially hostile places, and their only alarm was to wake one morning to find their bedding and some clothes missing, stolen by thieves while they slept. But their passports and money were safe. Once a crowd cut the boat's mooring ropes, simply hoping the excitement would bring the foreign women out where they could see them again. Elizabeth Wilson called it 'a straightforward boat journey' with little to report. 'Miss Fausset' had been 'always ready for work', showing 'excellent judgment'. From the moment of arrival they were swept into the work of the 'station'.

There was more than enough to do. George King was exhausted, pressed to the limit of his strength by the demands of his work and by opium addicts clamouring for treatment. On their one street alone they counted two hundred places where opium was on sale. On the 18th he had been threatened with eviction, but the magistrate, the acquaintance from earlier days in Xi'an who had welcomed him to Hanzhong, nipped trouble in the bud. Two days after the women arrived, George Easton turned up. Hearing of King's need of help he had covered the 150 miles from Tianshui in three days. By the end of 1880 there were twenty baptised members of the church. And Zhou, the cook, and Huang Kezhong (forced to live in isolation outside the city) had shaped up so well that they were ordained deacons.

Somehow Elizabeth Wilson acquired the reputation of being the first unmarried woman to the 'unoccupied' western provinces, but must yield the honour to Jane Kidd by a difference of one month (April 22–May 21), or share it with Jane and 'Miss Fausset'.

Gansu before the brides arrived *1878–82*

The story of the far north-west of China is the tales of the *Arabian Nights* set in the Celestial Kingdom. In the days of the Great Silk Road what are now Shaanxi, Sichuan, Gansu, Ningxia and Xinjiang were all administered from Xi'an, or Chang'an as the old capital was called. Mountains and deserts stretched endlessly westwards into Tibet on the southward side and into Mongolia and the Gobi Desert in the north. Intense heat, intense cold and long tracts without water characterised the western half, but in the eastern half grain, fruit and wild animals abounded. People of many origins shared the natural wealth, Chinese from every province, Tibetans, Mongols, aboriginal tribes and Turqis, with a preponderance of Muslims.

Before the great conquest of the Muslim rebellion by Zuo Zongtang (p 135) Gansu extended 1,500 miles to the Afghan and Russian borders. But in 1877, 1882 or 1884 (as variously stated) the period we have entered with the pioneers of the CIM, this administrative territory was halved, to create Xinjiang and a more manageable Gansu. The capital of Gansu, Lanzhou, stood at 5,000 feet, seventy-two days travel from Wuhan and the same again from Urumqi, capital of Xinjiang. But Tianshui (Tsinchou) at 3,300 feet, halfway between Lanzhou and Xi'an and on one of the main trade routes, commanded the most populated and productive part of the province. Only one hundred and fifty miles from Hanzhong (an excellent staging post on the navigable Han river in southern Shaanxi), Tianshui was the strategic city for occupation by the Mission. That a Hunan military mandarin should provide the premises when the right time came was wonderful but true.

We saw (p 81) how G F Easton and George Parker first entered Gansu on December 28 or 29, 1876, and reached Lanzhou on January 20, 1877, after travelling for five months, to occupy Tianshui in 1878. The year 1885 was to see missionaries settle in Xining, at 8,000 feet the key to the Tibetans of Qinghai province, and at Ningxia in the north-east among Muslims and Mongols (maps pp 80, 210). But in the first few years not only Parker and Easton but women were to share in the travels over thousands of miles. They took the gospel to towns and cities over wide areas, and left Christian books with the people.[23]

While Parker and Budd attempted to gain a foothold inXi'an, and after being forced out worked by boat up and down the Han River for several months, Easton returned to Gansu and travelled the Qinghai border from March 15 to April 19, 1878. Records are vague, and dates confused, as individuals lost count or simply failed to name the month or year in their letters. But in the summer, after visiting Chongqing, Easton was on his way back alone to Gansu when he fell ill with smallpox at Langzhong (Paoning) in north Sichuan. Seeing his employer so ill, Easton's hired carrier decamped with his possessions. So Easton had to retreat all the way back to Chongqing. By November 15 he was well enough to try again, this time with George King, taking twenty-six days to

Tianshui, and embarked on more itinerations in Gansu. But King was to marry in 1879 (pp 235f) and left the next day for the coast.[24]

It was while Easton was alone for the first half of 1879 without any Christian companion, that he discovered in the Tianshui city and countryside the desperate plight of almost naked refugees from the Shaanxi famine (p 186). Debarred from entering some premises, he was told that the occupants had sold their clothes for food. At once he bought secondhand clothing and sacks of corn, distributing them from the inns he stayed in temporarily, while waiting for advice from Hudson Taylor.

Throughout June and July he travelled more extensively, visiting the Qinghai borders and tribal peoples, the city of Xining and the provincial capital of Lanzhou.

> To my surprise, at Sining I found Count Béla Széchényi, a Hungarian nobleman (and two companions) on a scientific journey to Lhassa, and on to India. . . . Colonel Prejevalsky and eight other Russians are on their way from Russia via Ili, and are expected in (Lanzhou) and Sining about October; they intend making for Lhassa. . . . Széchényi intends reaching Lhassa 'dead or alive' . . . Five Germans arrived (in Lanzhou) to commence (a) cloth and woollen works, but one of them has since committed suicide.[25]

Therefore the CIM delayed attempts to occupy Lanzhou until excitement over the advent of so many armed foreigners had subsided.

Easton waited until late autumn for the Kings, but hearing from Hudson Taylor that thousands of taels of silver were available for famine relief, went down to Hanzhong and returned with 2,500 secondhand garments on pack mules for the destitute in south-eastern Gansu. On February 3, 1880, he reached Tianshui and by the 23rd had verified the need of individuals and issued all he had brought. George King sent five more mule-loads with 1,400 garments for children, and from two rented shops in which he organised his work, Easton distributed clothing and grain within a radius of about twenty miles. All his labour and sympathy probably received no more notice than a passing sentence in any report of the famine.

In May 1880 he made the forced march in three days to help George King in distress at Hanzhong (p 244), and was travelling again after the summer. But in early 1881 his place in Gansu was taken by George Parker, and we find Easton waiting at the coast for his fiancée Caroline Gardner to arrive from Britain. Steamers were plying the Yangzi and along the China coast, but all travelling elsewhere had to be by slow river and canal boats, by pony or mule-back, by cart or litter or wheelbarrow, or more often on foot. The wonder then is that some of these men and women covered such great distances, treating months and weeks as we do days or hours, spreading the truth, 'Christ died for sinful men and women', and leaving books, leaflets and posters to reinforce their words.

Finding that his fiancée was not due until April, Easton escorted Robert Landale and his bride and two single girls overland via Jinan, Shandong, to Taiyuan in Shanxi. From there he visited Gansu again, in time to take Elizabeth Wilson to the bedside of Emily King, dying of typhoid at Hanzhong. And on the way back to Yantai he helped Henry Hunt, ill at Runan in Henan. At last in August he married Caroline at Chefoo. Together they took a new missionary, Hannah Jones, with them to Hanzhong. But the plot thickens, and other threads must be picked up before Hannah Jones is with the Tibetans of Qinghai.[26]

Women on the borders of Tibet *1879–82*

Just when George Parker and Shao Mianzi, the Chinese schoolgirl at Yangzhou (p 74) fell in love is not mentioned in the documents we have. Hudson Taylor was in London when indignant letters began to reach him from the missionaries responsible for her. She was a fine girl, intelligent and active as a Christian, well suited to be a pastor's wife in a year or two. But Parker was determined to marry her, and nowhere is it suggested that the wish was not mutual. There were, however, strong reasons why George should think again. On July 5, 1878, Hudson Taylor wrote to him as candidly as he ever did, saying that his mother was in tears, pleading that he should change his mind for serious practical reasons. Chinese culture, attitudes and family ties were so widely different from European ones in those days that many marriages between the races foundered over the inability of partners to adapt to each other. Adaptation between two people of the same background and upbringing was difficult enough, but he would be marrying a family, not only a wife. All the social obligations towards her parents and relatives, that a Chinese husband would take for granted, would be more than he could take.

No objection was raised to an inter-racial marriage *per se*. Yet even adaptation was a minor matter beside the fact that Mianzi had entered the mission school soon after the upheavals at Yangzhou in 1868–70. Following custom, a contract had been drawn up between her parents and Charles Judd for the Mission, with Hudson Taylor's help. Among the usual terms, after educating and caring for her over the years the Mission was to have the right to arrange her marriage. Only so could a Christian girl be saved from betrothal to a pagan, and certain persecution when she refused to perform the ancestral rites. Hudson Taylor's letter to George Parker said,

> When I proposed to the parents to give (the Judds) the right of betrothal (to a Christian husband) they objected, lest she should afterwards be married to an Englishman or taken (abroad). I promised them most solemnly and absolutely that she should only be married to a Chinese Christian and should not be taken away from China. . . . No amount of subsequently purchased consent would ever satisfy the parents that all we had said was not false, and that the intention from the beginning was not what they had objected to and feared. (To break this undertaking would ruin the Mission's schools.) (I) entreat you to abandon the thought (and to trust God to provide you with) a true helpmeet suited to you.[27]

A many-sided correspondence followed. The contract was the crux. Theodore Howard thought Charles Judd too hard on Parker. Hudson Taylor judged that half a dozen of George's friends were ready to resign if in their opinion he was disciplined or forced to yield. Frederick Baller, in charge at Yangzhou, was receiving daily visits from Mianzi's father, an opium smoker out to make trouble but talking only of the financial loss to his family if he surrendered Mianzi and his rights. Soon all was settled; indeed before Hudson Taylor from a distance could take any further part in it. Mianzi's father himself volunteered an acceptable solution, simply compensation for his expenditure on her since her birth. He willingly signed a document agreeing to the marriage, and absolving George from all claims. On June 10, 1879, Judd informed Hudson Taylor that all had been satisfactorily settled, and eight months later 'Miss Minnie Shao' married into the CIM at HBM Consulate, Yantai, the first Asian member.[28]

They travelled up the Yangzi and Han Rivers to Hanzhong, delaying at Fancheng to be with Emily King through her confinement, before continuing the long journey to Tianshui in December. Elizabeth Wilson went with them from Hanzhong, perched above her baggage on a mule – the first missionary women in Gansu.[29]

She and 'Minnie' took Tianshui by storm, visiting the women in their homes, especially after Minnie's first child 'Johnnie' was born in February 1881, and soon there was 'hardly a lane or courtyard' where they were not known and welcomed. But in May word came that Emily King had typhoid. Elizabeth Wilson started back to Hanzhong immediately with G F Easton, but in vain, Emily died, and six months later her child died of dysentery – on November 12, 1881, when James Cameron was there to support George King in his renewed grief.

In February 1882, King took Elizabeth Wilson yet again to Tianshui, this time with twenty-three-year-old Hannah Jones as well, setting George Parker free to leave on the 21st, on a five-month journey through north-eastern Gansu and Ningxia. Pioneering was in his blood. Hardly had he reached home than he swept his wife and Hannah Jones away, to take the gospel to Tibetan women and mandarins' wives on the Qinghai border, while Elizabeth Wilson and A W Sambrook from Henan held the fort at Tianshui.[30] Leaving Minnie and Hannah at an inn, Parker himself went on to Labrang now Xiahe, only inferior to Lhasa, and to Huozhou (or Hezuo) 'the most important Mohammedan centre in China'. Welcomed at each place, he was rebuked for not bringing Arabic Bibles. 'I could have sold a large number of Arabic and Persian Scriptures,' he wrote in his diary, 'but few can read Chinese.' They returned to Tianshui on September 26, completing a distance of one thousand miles in seventy-eight days, roughly the same time and distance as on another of his journeys. He had sold 25 complete Bibles, 183 New Testaments, 685 'quarter testaments' (a Gospel, Acts and some epistles) and 5,732 single Gospels, and was asked for more in different languages.

Their return set the intrepid Elizabeth Wilson free to go back to Hanzhong, taking seventeen days in bad weather. Once her mule very nearly went over the precipitous edge of a narrow mountain trail. Another time it bolted, throwing her and its paniers, 'my heavy tin box on top of me,' she wrote, grateful that 'God had provided a soft bed of sand . . . Head and chest were bruised but no bones broken,' and she had 'only' four more days' travel in that state on the same mule. Not least among the qualities shown by these men and women, Hudson Taylor's 'joy and crown', was their willingness to risk injury, illness and the malice of evil men when

HAZARDS ON THE HANZHONG–TIANSHUI ROAD

hundreds of miles apart from each other and distant from any skilled medical help.

For twenty years Hudson Taylor himself had been almost the only doctor in the Mission, in spite of many prayers and pleas to the profession. But at last, in January 1880 Dr W L Pruen arrived, and on April 7, 1880, the highly qualified surgeon Harold Schofield left home with his wife to join the CIM in China. Then on August 16, 1882, two more followed him, E H Edwards and William Wilson, Elizabeth's nephew.[31]

We shall hear more of George and Minnie Parker but may be forgiven for looking ahead to their old age. He only returned to England twice, in 1890 and 1907, and twice at least they lost all they possessed, by looting in 1900 and 1914. He died in Henan on August 17, 1931, the Mission's doyen of active members, with fifty-five years' service to his credit. Of all surviving active members, his widow Shao Mianzi was then the most senior. Her son, the Chief Electrical Engineer of Greater London's Underground, tramways and trolley-bus services (the latter his innovation) served the Mission on its London Council. And her daughter, Mrs Mason, became as good a missionary as her mother.[32]

CHAPTER EIGHT

'DARING AND SUCCESS' 1880–83

Trench takes on Yunnan *1880–81*

'This great explosion of Mission energy' showed no sign of slackening. Each of the Nine provinces had been crossed and recrossed in systematic 'seed-sowing'. And more than token 'occupation' of Taiyuan, Tianshui, Hanzhong, Chongqing and Guiyang meant a strong foothold in all but four of the nine. Henan, Hunan, Guangxi and Yunnan remained to be 'occupied'. Newcomers to the CIM were catching the spirit of the earlier pioneers and joining in the assault. K S Latourette referred to 'the daring and success of the Mission'.[1] For Hudson Taylor and the China Inland Mission were sweeping ahead on the momentum of one of the great epochs of the Mission's history in either century. It rose to its most *conspicuous* outcome (the advent of 'the Cambridge Seven' in 1885) but not the apogee of achievement. That had been reached by then.

After Frederick Baller and Frank Trench had delivered Ellen McCarthy and Jane Kidd safely to the care of George and Fanny Clarke at Guiyang, in April 1880 (pp 239–241), Baller returned via Chongqing to Wuhan and Trench continued his colportage in Guizhou. James Broumton returned from two weeks at the exotic Miao tribal festival (April 16–May 1, 1880) and ten days later he and Trench set out for Yunnan to preach and sell books in as many walled cities and intervening towns and villages as possible. With seven carriers laden heavily with books they trekked for five weeks and a day over the mountains to Kunming, the lakeside capital of Yunnan. 'Resting' on Sundays and at two cities on the way for three or four days of work, they arrived on June 16, to work systematically through the great city until Broumton started back towards the end of the month. 'The handsome palace of the French Bishop', as imposing as the princely status he assumed, indicated the extent and strength of the Church of eighty thousand adherents he ruled. But even ten thousand nominal Catholics in so great a city left ample scope for Broumton and Trench to evangelise among 'quiet attentive people'.[2]

Broumton reached home and his normal work on August 16, 'somewhat fagged after my 1000 mile walk,' but grateful for protection 'from all evil, sickness or violence. Most travellers in Yunnan carry arms, we had none; but we had the arm of God.' Within a few months he was engaged to marry Ellen McCarthy. Trench and the carrier he had employed at the end of the boat journey through Hunan (not a Christian and of uncertain integrity), proceeded to visit 'every city in south and south-eastern Yunnan'. He was still at it in December, enjoying the mild climate of this part of the plateau, at 3,000–5,000 feet on the latitude of Hong Kong. But illness (unspecified) and the need to collect another load of books forced him to withdraw to the Yangzi again, and to Shanghai for treatment. His whereabouts on January 21, 1881, when John Stevenson and Henry Soltau sprang their surprise, neither he nor they mention.

By April 1, 1881, Trench was ready to start back from Wuhan, intending to join James Broumton, who had married and gone ahead with his wife and others on March 26. In appalling weather they failed to find each other, and Trench duly arrived at Guiyang on May 31, well ahead of the rest, only to suffer a relapse of his symptoms. He worked within reach of Guiyang hoping to recover and to leave for western Yunnan province, but in September he had to capitulate and return to the doctors at Shanghai.[3]

In the *Reports of Her Majesty's Consuls in China*, published as a parliamentary blue book, Challoner Alabaster, the consul at Wuhan, the hub of the CIM's movements, wrote,

> You can travel through China as easily and safely as you can in Europe when and where you leave the main road.
>
> Apart from this increased care on the part of the mandarins, this improved state of affairs is due to the fact that the natives are becoming more accustomed to the presence of foreigners among them, much of the credit of which belongs to the members of what is called the China Inland Mission, instituted by the Rev. Hudson Taylor MRCS, some dozen years ago.
>
> Always on the move, the missionaries of this society have travelled throughout the country, taking hardship and privation as the natural incidents of their profession, and, never attempting to force themselves anywhere, they have managed to make friends everywhere, and, while labouring in their special field as ministers of the Gospel, have accustomed the Chinese to the presence of the foreigners among them, and in great measure dispelled the fear of the barbarian which has been the main difficulty with which we have had to contend.

> Not only do the bachelor members of the Mission visit places supposed to be inaccessible to foreigners, but those who are married take their wives with them and settle down with the goodwill of the people in districts far remote from official influence, and get on as comfortably and securely as their brethren of the older Missions under the shadow of a Consular flag and within range of a gun-boat's guns; and, while aiding the foreign merchant by obtaining information regarding the unknown interior of the country and strengthening our relations by increasing our intimacy with the people, this Mission has, at the same time shown the true way of spreading Christianity in China.[4]

Little did either Alabaster or Hudson Taylor anticipate the hostile innuendoes later to be made, that missionaries deliberately sought information for the merchants. Only ten years previously 'the devil's growl' in the press and the House of Lords had been focused on Hudson Taylor, this 'flea in a blanket', this 'incurable idiot' and his troop of novices. At least that had changed, and more was to happen in the few years before a flare of undreamed-of publicity was to levitate the humble Mission to almost dizzying heights.

Stevenson and Soltau: first from west to east *1879–81*

John Stevenson and Henry Soltau had arrived at Bhamo in October 1875 expressly to open up a route into remote south-western China. Since then the British–Indian government had persistently obstructed them. But in Bhamo, once the antagonistic Burmese governor was replaced, officials and people were only friendly. The clinic was valued, and (in spite of his irascible manner) while Dr Thomas Harvey was there it acquired a reputation extending to Dali and beyond in Yunnan. They survived the cholera that took the life of the governor and Roman Catholic priest, and many visits to the bellicose Kachins in the hills. One night when Stevenson was unwell and stayed at home instead of going as usual to the clinic, a man was killed by a tiger on the road he would have taken, and another mauled. Fire destroyed the house next door but left their thatched house unscathed. But still not one of the many Chinese and Burmese to whom they preached the gospel showed more than a polite interest.[5]

After the ghoulish Thebaw succeeded his father, King Mindon, at Mandalay, atrocities multiplied and relations with the British rapidly deteriorated. On October 3, 1879, a steam launch arrived at Bhamo with a message for Stevenson and Soltau. T T Cooper, the Resident, had been murdered by his own sepoy guard, and his successor had been withdrawn as the dangers increased. The British representative in Mandalay was himself withdrawing to Rangoon. 'Leave by this steamer,' ran the message. 'It is the last.'

Stevenson and Soltau 'decided not to leave their posts', and the American Baptist missionaries to the Burmese stayed with them. Not to be always under the Resident's eye was a relief. A month later the dispensary was still in full swing, Soltau reported. Attendances often lapsed at the merest hint of rumours against them, but otherwise all were as friendly as ever. The Kachin chiefs whose homes they visited from time to time were among their best friends, and whenever they chose to go into the hills they had no lack of escorts. Stevenson decided to make a reconnaissance into China as a guest of the Kachins, knowing that the Chinese merchants and muleteers had spoken well of him in the plains beyond the border.

He left on November 18, 1879, with Kachin escorts, and while Hudson Taylor and J J Coulthard were travelling by mule litter from Yantai to Yangzhou, John Stevenson penetrated more than a hundred miles into Yunnan, to the city of Yongchang (now Baoshan), between the Salween and Mekong Rivers, less than a hundred miles from Dali. Not only the medical work but the Gospels and tracts distributed in Bhamo 'had affected a wide area'. Not even the Chinese authorities were surprised to see him, the first European to enter China from Burma since Margary's murder. He returned safely to Bhamo, reassured and planning next time to keep going eastwards.

Hudson Taylor was less sanguine when he heard the news. Sir Thomas Wade had received adverse reports from some consuls about 'unwise' missionaries in their areas, and applications for 'passports' (travel passes) were being denied on flimsy grounds. 'I hope Stevenson's crossing the border may not occasion serious trouble,' he wrote to Benjamin and Amelia on March 12. But apparently any repercussions took only time to be resolved, and work in Bhamo proved too satisfying to forsake, for Stevenson and Soltau did not leave until November 29, 1880, after the monsoon rains. Count Béla Széchényi, after meeting George Easton at Sining and failing to enter Tibet, had been forced like all others before him to opt for Burma instead. But his ill wind blew good to the Mission in Bhamo. He presented his well-proved ponies to Stevenson and Soltau.[6]

A new commercial caravan route through friendly Kachin territory provided the opportunity, but it looked as if the Burmese deputy-governor would forbid them to go. That night an attack was made by Kachins on merchants camped outside the Bhamo city walls, and when the deputy himself came to the Mission next morning prospects looked bleak. But he had simply come to assure them that he would protect the Mission property in their absence.[7]

Travelling in Western clothes, with Kachins carrying loads of books and medicines for their work along the way, they joined a long train of 600 animals and 400 men filing out towards the hills. Kachin chiefs and Chinese merchants led the way, Chinese, Shan and Kachin muleteers followed with three pack animals each, guarded by Kachins armed with spears, matchlocks and tasselled machetes ornamented with silver. Over forty chiefs representing one hundred Kachin families formed the escort among whom Stevenson and Soltau brought up the rear.

In tense silence broken by the jingle of harness they marched hour upon hour. An attack by rival chiefs could be expected, as their way of collecting 'road-tax'. But nothing happened until on December 1 at the midday halt half a dozen Kachins tried to make off with the Széchényi ponies and the missionaries' pack-loads. When Soltau stopped them, they 'drew their frightful-looking sword-knives and flourished them over my head as if to cut me down. The Lord kept me perfectly calm . . . My composure baffled them, and they seemed afraid to strike.' At this point friendly chiefs came to the rescue and in the fight that followed, 'with the backs and not with the blades' of their short-swords, Stevenson and Soltau were dragged to safety at the far end of the camp. Their animals and possessions were recovered, and after some firing of guns and wild cursing, the rival chiefs settled down together to parley over pipes and alcohol.

It transpired that a Kachin chief had disappeared at the time of Major Sladen's expedition in 1867–68, and although the matter had been amicably settled, this was a plot to have the blood of Englishmen, or failing that to collect a ransom. By nightfall a settlement of just twelve rupees had been agreed and, in celebrating, the chiefs of both sides were 'considerably intoxicated', with 'bullets whizzing about among the trees, so that we became more afraid of our friends than of our enemies'.

This was not the last of such excitements, but on December 4 they emerged from the hills into peaceful Shan territory, and from then on travelled in peace, broken only by calls for medical treatment wherever they went. Passing through Tengyue (Momein), Tengchong, Baoshan and Xiaguan, they reached Dali, the old capital of western Yunnan with its marble and granite temples and bridges, on December 31. Influential men who had met them in Bhamo introduced them to the mandarins, and until January 6, 1881, they were kept busy talking, preaching the gospel and selling books.

The direct route to Kunming took them through beautiful country bedecked with rhododendrons and camellias, and inhabited by 'Lolo' tribal people. But they also travelled through untended agricultural land, mile upon mile, with endless evidence of desolation from the long Muslim (so-called 'Panthay') rebellion. Kunming, '496 miles from Bhamo', was reached on January 21, but they met with no trace of Trench. Leaving the imperial road to Guiyang, they turned north through Dongchuan to Zhaotong, on February 4.

Soon afterwards 'we were met by two extraordinary objects [Miao tribesmen] . . . leading a goat' – 'far wilder-looking than any men or women we have seen among the (Kachins)'. It seems not to have struck them that two apparitions in European dress were far more 'extraordinary objects' on the hills north of Zhaotong. Here 'narrow tracks that skirted dangerous precipices, steep ravines, and narrow ledges cut in the face of the rock' were too narrow for pack-loads to pass and too broken for travellers to stay mounted. They were in Baber's region of the Sun Bridge (p 143).

At last they reached Laowatan, '756 miles from Bhamo', sold their animals, shot the rapids of the Heng River, and entered Sichuan on February 14 (map p 123). Seventy-nine days after leaving the Irrawaddy River, '1000 miles from its mouths, we entered the muddy waters of the (Yangzi) 1756 miles from its mouth'. And on February 22 they arrived at Chongqing. In more than 1,000 miles of travel they had met no other missionary.

They rested for only a few days. Late one night on their way to Wuhan, when anchored a mile above Wanxian, they were surprised by a messenger from the city magistrate. A friend of General Mesny and of James Broumton with a photograph to prove it, he declared that a boat would attend them in the morning to bring them to breakfast in the *yamen*. Sure enough they became his honoured guests. 'Throwing off all reserve, he chatted with us in the most friendly manner,' before returning them to their boat. Such a far cry from the attitudes of the literati and mandarins of even five years before, fully vindicated the policy of seeing and being seen widely throughout China.

Descending the Yangzi gorges without mishap, they reached Wuhan on March 25, and took their time to complete the journey to Zhenjiang and Shanghai. The first successful attempt by Westerners to cross China from west to east was headline news and they were lionised. But astute readers of *China's Millions* in China, Europe and the States recognised the unsung itinerations of others as being of equal or greater value.

Stevenson was back in Bhamo, via Rangoon, on July 26, 1881. He immediately went down with 'jungle fever' for three weeks but recovered, to hold the fort for two more years, with an evangelist. Free to enter Yunnan at any time, his opportunities in Bhamo were too many to allow him to leave. Soltau returned to Britain to study medicine, becoming fully qualified. He married and brought his bride to Bhamo in November 1883, only to be driven out in 1884 by a revolt and the sacking of the town.[8]

After several failures by government expeditions, their west to east adventure deserved publicity and was reported in the *Proceedings of the Royal Geographical Society, 1880–81*. It had, however, followed in reverse the well-documented route taken by other travellers from east to west. Its lasting value lay rather in the fact that the mature John Stevenson endorsed John McCarthy's and Broumton's judgment that Kunming would be a valuable centre for the Mission in Yunnan, and McCarthy's and Cameron's that Dali held the key to western Yunnan and the border tribes. The eventual opening of the southern route and railway from Tongking (North Vietnam) ended attempts to develop access from the west, until World War II. But that was far ahead. France had been annexing more and more of 'Indo-China' since 1787, and her invasion of Tongking in 1882 precipitated the Franco-Chinese war of 1884–85.[9]

A firm foothold in Sichuan *1878–81*

Henry Soltau's description of their arrival at Chongqing on February 22 opens a window on life in this 'city set on a hill' with battlements and parapets along the edge of a cliff above a long line of junks at anchor. The man they sent to find the CIM and say where their boat was moored came back with a stranger in Chinese dress.

After his exploratory journey round the Daliangshan in October–November 1877 (pp 151–3), George Nicoll had written urging two candidates in Britain, Samuel R Clarke and J H Riley, to consider taking the gospel to the Nosu. Hudson Taylor approved, and in October 1878 they had joined Nicoll at Chongqing. Within a year they were pulling their weight in a thriving work in the city and Sichuan countryside.

Surprised to find John Stevenson and Soltau in foreign clothes, and anxious not to draw a crowd on their way through busy streets to the CIM Mission house, young Samuel Clarke hired sedan chairs to hide them in and followed behind them. Fresh from unresponsive Bhamo and their long journey without meeting a Christian, they found the contrast at Chongqing exhilarating. Opposite the entrance to the premises they first saw a mandarin's proclamation,

> The place where the Gospel is preached is a solemn place; everything must be quiet and reverent. Men and children must listen in the outer hall, and women in the inner. Let there be no noise or uproar. All idlers are forbidden to enter and loiter about. There are to be no crowds round the doors. Everything must be done according to order, and if anyone dare disobey, let him be immediately bound and sent for punishment.[10]

Then they were being greeted by more Chinese and Europeans ('pale and thin') than they had expected to see.

George Nicoll was ill, and away for a few days with his wife. But Riley and a colporteur of the National Bible Society of Scotland named Wilson were at home, and four Chinese colleagues. The B&FBS colporteur, Mollman, an older man, made the CIM his base but was also away. Across the central courtyard beyond the big hall used as a chapel, stood the main two-storey building. On the ground floor the formal reception room where literati were entertained was flanked by store rooms and the Chinese staff's own rooms. Above were bedrooms for Riley, Wilson, Mollman and guests. Flanking the courtyard, on the right a noisy school was in full swing, with Samuel Clarke's room beside it, and on the left the communal dining-room and kitchen, with the Nicolls' private quarters. One of the Chinese, from the LMS in Wuhan, was working for the American Bible Society; another, a Wesleyan, for the B&FBS. The senior Sichuanese evangelist had been converted through the American Presbyterians in Canton, and his son worked with him. Denominational differences were forgotten in their essential unity.

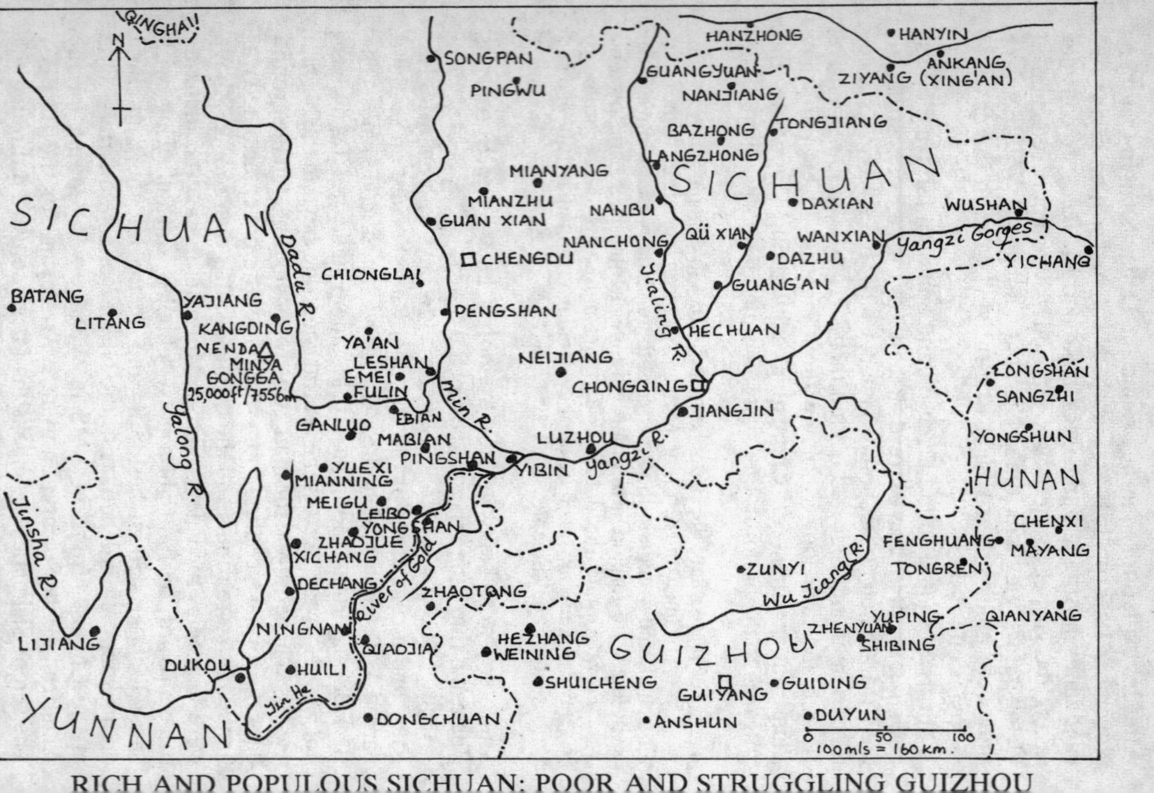

RICH AND POPULOUS SICHUAN: POOR AND STRUGGLING GUIZHOU

Chinese visitors kept coming in, and frequent meetings drew fifty or sixty at a time. It was in this place that Nicoll's bride had coped week after week with crowds of women callers after her marriage in September 1879. She was still the only foreign woman in the province, so populous that a hundred Christian missionaries deployed among its cities would be none too many. Although the first believers were not baptised until June 1880, 'the large, quiet, orderly congregations on the Lord's day might give a stranger to suppose the station had been opened fifty years'. In that comment by Hudson Taylor we see the sapling start of a Church in Sichuan which today is a great tree.[11]

From July 21 to September 19, 1879, Riley and Mollman had travelled, preaching and selling Gospels, to Emei (Omei) city and its sacred mountain, crowned since the Han dynasty in AD 200 with beautiful Buddhist monastery-temples where their books would be read with interest. From there they went to Ebian (Opien) city on the northern flank of the Nosu homeland to reconnoitre, intending to go to Mabian to find a place for Riley and Samuel Clarke to settle. The Ebian magistrate was anxious, however, lest they come to harm from wild Nosu on a foray – 'fine stalwart fellows', Riley called them. So they had to be content with hiring one Nosu, called Niko, to return to Chongqing with them. From him they learned more than his language – Niko schemed to take a beggar-boy with him when he returned home, to sell him to the Nosu as a slave.[12]

Samuel Clarke then took a turn with Mollman, making another five hundred mile figure-of-eight tour of cities along minor roads to Chengdu, the provincial capital, and beyond. Starting on October 6 they were not back until November 25, drooping with fatigue from travelling and preaching at every place of any size. At night they had been objects of insatiable curiosity, or were kept talking until late by enquiring people.

In the spring of 1880, from March 8 to May 8, Riley and Samuel Clarke with Niko as interpreter, made a second reconnaissance of the Nosu border. Captain Blakiston had gone up the Yangzi to Yibin (Suifu) in 1868 and beyond to the next walled 'town' or fort of Pingshan.[13] And Riley and Mollman had come down the Min River from Leshan (Jiading) to Yibin when returning to Chongqing. So this time the goal was Leibo (Luipo) at the mouth of the Valley of the Beautiful Maiden beneath the towering Dragon's Head and Sun Bridge seen by Baber from twenty miles to the east (p 143).

By the time they reached the village of Huanglang on April 13, they were running out of silver. While Clarke went back to Chongqing for more, Riley pressed on with Niko and the young Sichuanese evangelist. On the 18th they heard that a man had escaped from a Nosu attack only after they had stripped him naked, but a woman and child had been carried off. Even Niko was sick with apprehension, but Riley insisted on going on, and Leibo was reached on April 24. Two days later fifteen Chinese were caught and killed nearby. Reluctantly Riley wrote, 'As the Lolos in this neighbourhood are so much given to plunder just now, I think this is not the best time to seek an entrance among them.' Ebian had been more promising. He withdrew to Yibin, met Samuel Clarke there, sent Niko home, and waited for a more propitious time. Between these expeditions and others into the province in other directions, they worked among the two or three hundred thousand inhabitants of Chongqing itself.

George Nicoll's protracted ill-health was thought to be due to heart disease, and during a time of political excitement after Stevenson and Soltau had gone, when a consular representative was attacked (on June 3, 1881) and a house destroyed, he took his wife to the coast. He was still recuperating at Chefoo six months later, but recovered enough to return to Chongqing and struggle on, still hampered by ill-health, until sent home.

A Swiss girl first in Yunnan *1881–83*

Ellen McCarthy and Jane Kidd had not been in Guiyang long before James Broumton, back from his thousand mile working tour of Yunnan, carried Ellen off again to marry her at Wuhan early in 1881. George and Fanny Clarke had hesitated to go five hundred miles away from fellow-missionaries, to Dali, until their first child was born and strong enough to travel. But the child died. Through their grief they saw the hand of God freeing them to occupy a house at Dali rented from the consular 'writer' in Chongqing. In Broumton's absence they could not leave Jane Kidd alone in Guiyang, so Samuel Clarke gallantly came from Chongqing to take charge until the Broumtons returned, and the George Clarkes set off on May 16, 1881.[14]

A Swiss girl therefore became the first foreign woman to enter Yunnan, and the first to die there. 'A prosperous journey' brought them to Kunming on June 7, where they found the people 'not curious or troublesome'. Before the end of June they were in Dali, farther from other Westerners than were any other foreigners in China. No mail service existed and communication even by public courier was difficult and expensive. The occupants of the Chongqing writer's house refused to move out, and the Clarkes had to make shift for five months without even a proper room of their own. They had no Chinese Christian with them, and found themselves under suspicion of ulterior motives in coming. 'I don't suppose any station has been opened under such difficulties,' George wrote. His wife found reminders of Switzerland in the snow-capped, 15,000 foot mountains she could see. Like Daniel's three young men in the burning fiery furnace, she wrote, they were content to wait for the Lord's deliverance. The only domestic help they could get was from a woman and her child escaping from her opium-sot husband who had already sold two of their children. He soon tracked her down, to sell her too. 'This is a terrible place; Sodom and Gomorrah could not have been much more wicked . . . Our neighbour was going to kill his wife and child. My husband and three women held him.'[15]

At last they found a house to rent, employed a teacher and opened a small school with seven pupils. In what he called his spare time, during the first year George hand-printed 6,600 'Gospel books' under twelve titles, totalling 48,700 pages with 3,000 maps. His working hours he spent distributing them and trying to get a hearing for the gospel. More months went by, until on May 21, 1882, two sick explorers, hungry and dishevelled, stumbled into Dali and found an inn.

Archibald R Colquhoun, an Indian government engineering administrator, and his companion Charles Wahab, had started out from Canton on an exploratory survey of southern China, crossing from east to west close to the Tongking and Laotian borders. All that could go wrong did so. Dysentery, fever, the disloyalty of the interpreter, and obstruction by a high mandarin forced them to make a major change of direction without enough money to complete the journey. Wahab was too weak to ride an animal and had to be carried. Even Colquhoun 'reached (Xiaguan) in a famishing condition', but after resting managed to cover the last eight miles to Dali. 'I was too fatigued to walk, and this part of the day's work [clinging to his mule on a very slippery stone causeway] wearied me terribly . . . Torn clothes, broken shoes, unkempt hair and weariness nearly amounting to prostration must have given me a more than usually seedy appearance.'[16]

When planning his journey in England he had consulted John

COURTESY CALL: THE MANDARIN, PÈRE VIAL, WAHAB AND COLQUHOUN

McCarthy and Stevenson, and was carrying a note of introduction from Benjamin Broomhall, though he had had no intention of passing through Dali. While he cleaned himself up, his interpreter made enquiries and arrived back at the inn with George Clarke. The French priest was away, and these were the first Europeans the Clarkes had seen for more than a year. They insisted on Colquhoun and Wahab moving in with them until well again. 'The very fact of finding a highly-educated lady in this faraway land – where so many missionaries have already met their deaths – speaks volumes for their self-abnegation and zeal . . .' Colquhoun later wrote. 'I felt unwell and would have been seriously ill' but for the 'unbounded hospitality and generous assistance' provided.

By May 30 he was strong enough to go on, Wahab could ride an animal, and Clarke had been able to lend them some silver for the remaining stages to Bhamo. So they went, only to find themselves in dire straits again until they encountered Père Vial, a Catholic priest who accompanied them to Bhamo. There the American missionaries supplied 'a good large tub, with plenty of delicious soap' and a breakfast about which they could not stop talking when they met John Stevenson afterwards. 'Mr Stevenson . . . immediately set about sharing everything he had with us. His house, his clothes, his food, and the last half-penny of the small stock in his purse, he placed at our disposal.' Wahab recovered enough to be shipped home to Britain, but died before Colquhoun's two volume travelogue was published.[17]

During the days spent together in Dali, George Clarke translated for Colquhoun 'a Manuscript Account of the Kwei-chau Miao-tzu', written in about 1730 after their subjugation. Eighty-two different tribes or clans of minority peoples, including the Nosu – 'their customs are devilish and their place is termed "the Devil's Net"' – the Zhong Jia, Yao and many kinds of 'Miao', were described.[18] Then George and Fanny were alone again until Arthur Eason, a newcomer to the ranks of CIM pioneers, visited Dali for a few days in the last week of June, 1882. This was the first opportunity for 'Christian fellowship' they had had since parting from Samuel Clarke in Guiyang on May 16, 1881. They thought they had been away for 'eighteen months'.[19]

Adam Dorward: 'though it be by my life' *1878–83*

The action continues, the pageant moves on, a succession mostly of *young* men and women taking risks 'beyond the call of duty'. That they were making history, while their leader battled with adversity of other kinds, few could recognise at the time. They all knew Hudson Taylor's master plan, to put down roots in the nine provinces, and each played his or her part 'for the glory of God'. For some that part was to mean long years without house or home; for others death or bereavement. Where fiction would bring in more variety, stranger reality demands that we stay with these pioneers a little longer, to meet three more.

In 1875 six outstanding men had come to China, Cameron, George Clarke and Nicoll; Broumton, Easton and King. Elizabeth Wilson and George Parker followed the next year. 1878 brought Trench, Riley, Samuel Clarke and Adam Dorward, and 1881 saw George Andrew and Arthur Eason arrive. These last three now come into focus.

Adam C Dorward stands out, unique in that he took on the most dangerous province and for eight years worked in it, often alone and homeless, until he died. 'As Lhasa to Tibet, so has Hunan been to

China.' The hostile literati denied him a foothold. Source throughout the century of scurrilous and obscene attacks upon Christianity as much as on foreigners *per se*, they succeeded in making Hunan the last province to yield to the tenacity of the pioneers.

Dorward had given up good prospects in his uncles' tweed mills to go into training at Harley House. Under Grattan Guinness for three or four years, he shared a room with James Fanstone, the future apostle to Brazil. As Hudson Taylor in his youth had seen remote central Asian Ili as his goal, Dorward set his heart on Tibet, the greatest challenge he knew. He reached China in June 1878 and after a short introduction to the language chose to live with Chinese, away from fellow Europeans. Datong in Anhui became his home for a year with an evangelist and a colporteur. While they learned more from his example than his teaching, he became a Chinese to the Chinese with their help. Then, with his base at Anqing (map p 397), he embarked on three ambitious journeys through different parts of Anhui province. For six weeks they moved from city to city (August 6–September 17, 1879) until their stock of books was exhausted. In trying his wings he could not have wished for a better companion than John McCarthy's ex-soldier friend Yang Cunling. They matched each other. 'Endowed with a strong will and firm resolution, (Dorward) was at the same time one of the meekest and least self-assertive of men.'[20]

In December, and January 1880, and again in March with another companion, Dorward 'lived rough' and proved his fitness for a hard life. In eight months he walked 1,200 miles, and travelled 500 by boat. To Hudson Taylor when he met him at Shanghai in June 1880, he seemed 'young and alone' but the right man for dangerous Hunan, so he offered him the honour. Dorward accepted. In the heat of mid-July he walked from Yangzhou to Yantai (map p 214), Hudson Taylor's overland journey of 500 miles in reverse, and after a holiday by the sea was 'very impatient to get off to Hunan'.

> I feel unfit for such glorious work and unworthy of such an honourable position in the Lord's service, but . . . if only I can by my efforts, trusting in God's blessing, lead a few of these perishing souls to the knowledge of Christ Jesus, and in any way hasten the opening of that province to the gospel, though it be by my life, I shall be satisfied and my coming to China shall not be in vain.

He could have had funds guaranteed by the Bible Society in return for his work for them, but preferred to do without, in order that he might 'have to look to God for it'.[21]

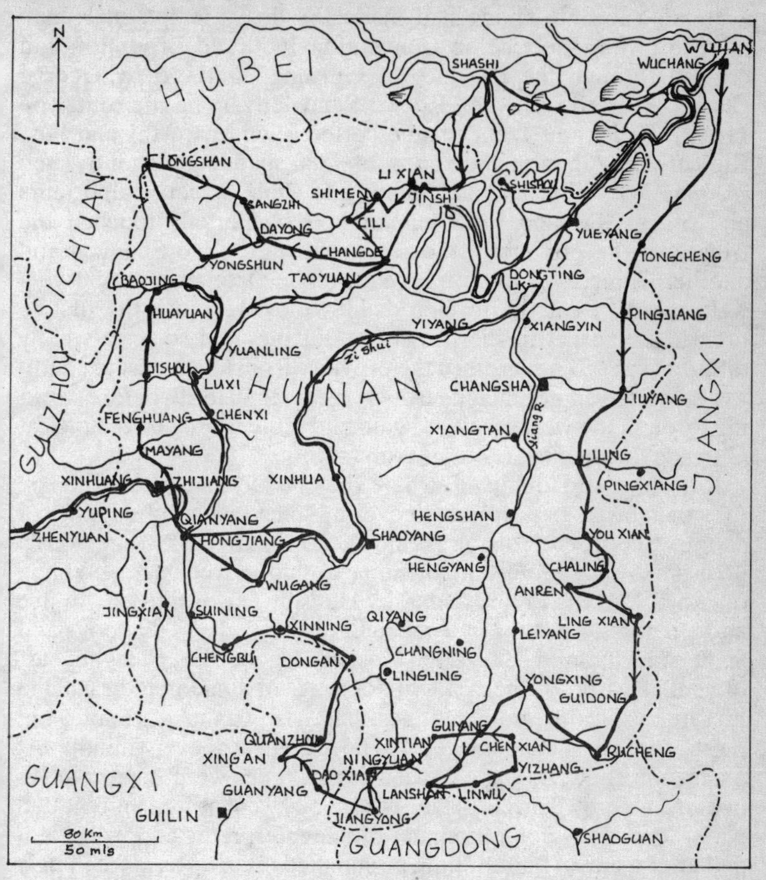

DORWARD'S HUNAN: 'THOUGH IT BE BY MY LIFE'

Judd, Yao and Zhang had made the first attempt on Hunan in 1875. After the Chefoo Convention Judd and Broumton had crossed through the province to Guiyang, followed by George Clarke, Edward Fishe and Robert Landale, varying the route (pp 118–9). Baller and Trench had escorted Ellen McCarthy and Jane Kidd from Wuhan in the spring of 1880 spending a month (Feb 27–Mar 31) within Hunan. Meanwhile Bible Society colporteurs and other CIM and LMS missionaries had briefly touched the fringes of the province.[22] So when Dorward, Yao Shangda and another Chinese set foot on Hunan soil on October 27, 1880, to a welcome of 'Beat the foreign devil!', they were not the first to preach the gospel in the province. But they did so on a wholly different scale. They crossed the province from north-east to south-west, and stayed in Changde from November 16 to 29, before working through the western cities again and replenishing their funds at Guiyang, by then nearer than Wuhan.

Returning to Hongjiang, where they had left a cache of books, they then broke new ground, 'covering some two hundred miles of country (between Hongjiang and the Dongting Lake) previously unvisited by any Protestant missionary', and arrived back at Wuhan on April 1, 1881, to be greeted by Hudson Taylor himself. In five and a half months they had sold and distributed 30,000 books and leaflets, including 1,700–1,800 Gospels, a good start to eight years of similar work.[23] The *yamen* underlings of some mandarins and literati, suspicious of his motives, had tried to make trouble, but most people they encountered had been neutral or even friendly. At Yuanzhou (now Zhijiang), when some stones were thrown at his boat from a crowd on land, Dorward coolly went ashore and chatted with them. 'He's not a foreigner but an interpreter', they decided, and after a day of book-selling he summed them up as 'exceedingly good'. Where Henry Taylor had failed by stolidly trying to hold his ground at Queshan in Henan, until his own courage cracked, Adam Dorward was using the Biblical alternative advised by Hudson Taylor, of tactfully moving on from place to place before opposition could build up.

At Wuhan Hudson Taylor had been seeing James Broumton and his party off on March 26, across Hunan to Guiyang, and was himself about to leave by river-steamer. So instead of resting, Dorward joined him on the boat to report on his travels and at Anqing to enlist Yang Cunling for his next foray into Hunan. By hurrying he hoped to overtake Broumton's party and help them through the dangerous rapids of the Yuan River and the cities that had been most hostile to others. Without help Broumton could be put under intolerable strain – exactly as happened.

Director in action *March–June 1881*

After meeting the surgeon Harold Schofield and his wife at Shanghai on June 30, 1880, Hudson Taylor had made his own long journey through southern Zhejiang and the Guangxin River region of Jiangxi (p 214). He then returned to Yantai for four months (October 1880–February 1881), and on February 24 was in Shanghai again to meet the French Mail bringing George Andrew and Arthur Eason. Time and again he had written, in letters to Jennie, Theodore Howard, Benjamin and Amelia, 'We need more *good* men.' He was having ceaseless trouble with some disappointing men and a few gross failures. In Schofield, Andrew, Eason and others in the next five years his prayers and hopes were to be fulfilled.[24]

He firmly believed in establishing a personal friendship, beyond mere personal acquaintance, with each individual. George Andrew never forgot how Hudson Taylor took him by the hand after they had had a long talk together, and 'expressed his thankfulness to God for bringing me to China'. '"Remember," he said, "that the work of the Lord is the LORD's work," emphasising that I was not an agent but an instrument.'

On his part Hudson Taylor was impressed by the quality of both men, Andrew and Eason. In fact, of recent arrivals, he wrote to Benjamin when he reached Anqing with Dorward, 'Six of the seven are treasures indeed. I am at my wits' end to know what to do for six more like them.' The scope for deploying them was so great. Advances in every direction, beyond expectation, were needing to be secured by occupying intermediate 'stations' along the routes, if perilous beginnings were to be consolidated. They were learning that one man, perhaps with more than one woman missionary, in any location, needed to be able to call on the help of another in emergencies. A minimum of three men to two mission centres was proving necessary. Less enterprising men would have to be content with advancing one step at a time. The long stride had succeeded too often to be abandoned now.[25]

He took the bold (but not unprecedented) step of asking Andrew and Eason after only a month in China to join James Broumton, his bride and Charlotte Kerr, a nurse who was to join Jane Kidd, on their imminent departure to Guiyang. With little knowledge of the language or of things Chinese, they were to face 900 miles of primitive travelling conditions and the possible malice of literati and mobs. J J Coulthard took them up the Yangzi to Wuhan and thought them 'stirling missionaries, prepared to endure hardness'. They were to study Chinese in the dialect of Guiyang instead of at Anqing. Frank Trench was also on his way back to Yunnan after treatment in Shanghai. He was to start a week after the Broumton party, to catch them up at the far side of the Dongting Lake and travel with them.[26]

All were ready on March 18 when Hudson Taylor himself arrived at Wuhan to see them off. Finding the Ballers in poor health he sent them to take charge at Chefoo while he and Jennie made their projected journey to Shanxi and the western provinces. This vital business centre of Wuhan had to be reliably manned, and he could only use available men, so he confidently appointed his personal secretary to replace Baller. The position involved handling and transmitting large sums of money, and signing documents in the name of the Mission. 'I was barely 21 years old at the time,' Coulthard wrote. 'He felt he had got men from the Lord and that God trusted them. . . . If anyone raised a prejudice against them it did not affect him at all.'[27]

Finally Hudson Taylor invited members of other missions to a commissioning service before the Broumtons left, and notes taken by Mrs Bryson of the LMS caught the atmosphere. He applied Psalms 123, 124 and 125 to the travellers. Relying only upon God and his enabling, 'they must not be surprised if their message were to be received with scorn and contempt'. On their difficult and dangerous route through hostile Hunan, quite possibly 'men would rise up against them'. In the many river rapids they would see the wrecks of other boats and might experience disaster themselves. They should remember the psalmist's words, 'The water had overwhelmed us, the stream had gone over our soul', and that their hope was 'in the name of the Lord who made heaven and earth'. They knew that he lived by these precepts himself. From Deuteronomy 4 he showed that obedience and entire consecration to God are prerequisites of success; and from Joshua 1 that undeviating courage with constant dependence on the Word of God were conditions of the promises 'I will not fail thee nor forsake thee,' and 'Then shalt thou have good success.' He urged them to preach and teach gently, not by argument, which alienates the one who is worsted. By

Christlike living and loving while delighting in him, they would 'bring forth fruit in due season'. The stark possibility that those present on this occasion might never meet again, added solemnity to the communion service.

Then Hudson Taylor spoke individually to each traveller. To George Andrew he said after encouraging remarks about his own experience of being unable to speak Chinese at first, 'Your faith will doubtless be tried; sometimes, it may be, your supplies will fail altogether and you may not know where to turn for help. Then, in your extremity, you need fear nothing, for the Lord will be with you . . . and will be your helper.' To Charlotte Kerr he spoke frankly of facing up to loneliness, such as Jesus had experienced, that she might be a comfort to Chinese women as well as to her colleagues.[28]

On March 25 a surprise and 'great excitement' almost eclipsed the elation they already felt as boats were hired to cross Hunan: Stevenson and Soltau arrived with their story of 1,990 adventurous miles from Burma, and of having rented a house in Dali. Hudson Taylor's delight overcame his concern that they had unwisely made the journey dressed as foreigners. Due to start on the 22nd, Broumton's party had been delayed by the officiousness of a mandarin, but on March 26 they were away, heading straight into trouble.

Frank Trench left on April 1 to overtake them. He was to rent premises in Kunming, to occupy Dali if George and Fanny Clarke were not there already, and to go on into the Shan States of western Yunnan if he could. Adam Dorward arrived on April 1 from his five and a half months' absence, 'very pleased with Hunan . . . the right man for that province', Hudson Taylor told Jennie. 'God is evidently so arranging things as to make the most of my visit . . . So many are now meeting me and so many arrangements are being made.' He and Dorward boarded the steamer on April 4 for Anqing, and by the 7th Dorward and Yang Cunling were on their way back to catch up with the Guiyang party.

Until something came of these bold moves, it was important not to stir up criticism. 'No statement (is) to be published prematurely,' Hudson Taylor instructed London, 'it might defeat us and defer success. But the more prayer the better.' Those in the know held their breath as days lengthened into weeks and no news of the travellers arrived.

WUHAN: WHERE THE HAN RIVER JOINS THE YANGZI
Hankou (l), Hanyang (r) and distant Wuchang

Broumton's ordeal[29] *March 26–June 21, 1881*

The mouth of the Han River gave more shelter to shipping than the shores of the Yangzi, so James Broumton and his wife, Andrew, Eason and Charlotte Kerr had first to cross the great river from the Wuchang side to join their hired house-boat. They found the Han 'completely blocked with boats'. Working their way through the log-jam took time, and an adverse wind forced them to tie up not far from their starting point, the Mission home at Wuchang again. In spite of dawn starts, day by day, each night fell when they had made a mere twenty miles upstream against strong Yangzi currents and headwinds. By April 2 they had only covered a hundred miles. This was gentle training in patience for what lay ahead. The explanation was to come after ten days of high drama.

They pulled into a winding creek and tied up near the small village of Luqikou for a quiet Sunday. Early that afternoon a thunderstorm suddenly broke over them. More and more boats left the Yangzi to shelter in the creek, and when the steep banks were lined with junks packed closely side by side, still more anchored in midstream. Rain fell all through the night. By Monday afternoon the swollen tributary was a raging torrent. Anchors dragged, cables snapped, and boat after boat was swept towards the Yangzi, colliding with others, dragging them loose and turning turtle. In the dark the crashing and cries for help went on and on, but for the present the Broumtons' boat was unaffected, moored to the lee bank of a wide curve. Those on the outer curve were being swept away. Broumton found a shack on shore where the women could shelter with George Andrew for support, and himself returned to guard their baggage with Eason. A heavily laden coal-boat lay alongside, being forced against them by the current. Suddenly, near midnight, with a deafening crash, one side of their hull and cabin caved in. They leapt ashore, assessed the damage and slaved hard to haul their possessions and the ship's fittings to safety up the bank. As Broumton, Eason and Andrew in turn kept guard, along both banks fires were lit by other marooned people and 'threw a lurid glare' on the raging torrent and the devastation ashore.

The storm passed over and repairs began, but twenty large boats and a hundred lives had been lost. With daylight the news spread that foreign women were among the survivors. Threatening crowds 'forced their way in everywhere' to stare interminably. Lost sleep and the strain of keeping calm and courteous hour after hour made the women 'almost ill', until Broumton found 'an old shop', semi-derelict but 'almost a palace . . . we did not mind the dirt.' After dark they took possession, the women hiding in the loft for four days while carpenters made their boat safe to go on up the Yangzi. On the 11th another storm lashed them at anchor in a sheltered cove, halting them for two more days. But at last on the 13th they reached Yueyang at the entrance to the Dongting Lake. There Yang Cunling found them. In four days he and Adam Dorward had come as far as they in nineteen. Together they entered Hunan.

More storms made hazardous the crossing of the lake, and one of Dorward's crew was lost overboard. But at one anchorage a man who had welcomed Baller to his house saw Dorward when they tied up for the night, and invited him in. 'Scarcely a day passes but we are brought through some fresh difficulty,' Broumton wrote on April 26. At last they were safely in the Yuan River and near Changde. This was where Adam Dorward had planned to strike off overland, but the rapids still lay ahead of Broumton's inexperienced party, and Trench, who was to have escorted them, could not be found. Reluctantly Dorward decided not to leave them.

George Andrew then fell ill with smallpox, and Dorward nursed him, isolated at the stem of the river-boat, day and night for week after week. Charlotte Kerr was busy doctoring the women who heard about her from the boatmen, and suffering herself from 'ague'. But the Hunan people were friendly, and even the men who demanded to see the foreign women were content when Ellen Broumton, blonder than Charlotte, consented to show herself. 'Mr Dorward's intense *delight* as to the *wonderfully good behaviour* of the Hunan people' amused the others. In this change from violence to mere curiosity he saw hope, a promise of the province accepting him.

More than a month of travelling and hairbreadth escapes still lay ahead of them. On May 4 the boat's bamboo towline broke on the way up a rapid, and they nearly came to grief. But on May 18, beyond the city of Hongjiang near the Guizhou border, they were holed by a hidden rock and quickly filled with water. The sick man Andrew was carried in a sheet slung from a pole to a house on the mainland. And once more their sodden baggage was landed, at first on an island in midstream. Cunling, Dorward, Eason and Broumton were wet through all day long, salvaging all they could. Slowly they moved their saturated books and personal possessions from the island to the river bank, only just in time. By the 22nd the river had risen thirty or forty feet, covering the island.

Again, the people of the hamlet of Losiping treated the foreigners well. With charcoal fires and two days of sunshine everything was dried, and in return for her 'doctoring' Charlotte Kerr was given more than they all needed of vegetables and meat. The villagers listened for hours to Cunling's preaching, and welcomed him and Adam Dorward when they returned from Guiyang.[30] 'The whole village turned out to see us start' – overland on foot and by mountain chair. At Yuanzhou men tore down the inn windows to get an unimpeded view of the strangers. And Zhenyuan in Guizhou (where Margary's boat was burned) lived up to its reputation for rowdiness. Only when the two women came out of their inn rooms to stand on show before a crowd of men could quiet be restored. By enduring hardships at many points along the way, they left a good impression of the maligned 'foreigner', and helped to destroy prejudice.

Frank Trench had reached Guiyang a full month before, growing more and more anxious about their safety. When he came upon them 'three stages' – about ninety miles – out from Guiyang, it became a triumphal entry of the five men and two women who rejoined Jane Kidd on June 21, almost three eventful months since leaving Wuhan. To meet the first-ever Miao tribal Christian, a woman, on their arrival was reward enough. Now there are tens of thousands of Miao Christians.

When the news reached Hudson Taylor, he too was jubilant.

> Curiosity is being appeased; hostility removed [his editorial in the *Millions* read]. The stay of missionary ladies in the heart of Hunan for a fortnight in one place [Losiping], the journey overland to the notorious city of (Yuanzhou), and a night spent on shore there at the inn; the not less rowdy city (of Zhenyuan), visited by ladies, who slept there also, and departed without any insult or danger – all point to the conclusion that *China is opening* . . . far more rapidly than Christian Missions are prepared to follow up. . . . Were the Lord to grant us double the number of workers, and double the means, within twelve months we could have them allocated and at work.[31]

Sequels in summary *July 1881–1883*

This real life story took unexpected turns soon after the long journey ended. After six days Adam Dorward and Yang Cunling walked back to Hongjiang in Hunan, preaching the gospel as they went and spending half a day at friendly Losiping (above). Frank

Trench had reached Guiyang in sixty-one days, unhindered by officials but shown 'bad feeling' by fellow-travellers influenced by current Russian aggression at Ili. When preparing to take Arthur Eason as his companion on a marathon itinerary of western Yunnan, Trench fell ill again with the same complaint as had taken him to Shanghai. Charlotte Kerr's attack of 'ague' became 'severe and all but fatal'. Soon after reaching her place of work she too had to face returning to the coast for treatment. This meant Jane Kidd handing over her school and women's work to Ellen Broumton, and escorting Charlotte with Trench to Chongqing and down the Yangzi, at least another month of travelling.

When they arrived at Chongqing in October 1881, and while Trench and Charlotte Kerr rested before braving the Yangzi rapids, Jane Kidd threw herself into work among the women of Chongqing. The Nicolls were away and Riley had more on his hands than he could manage. 'Suicide (by opium) is terribly common here. Last month we had twenty-six cases, twelve men, twelve women and two girls. . . . All, I believe, except four, were brought round,' he wrote to Hudson Taylor as soon as his visitors had gone.[32] Could Miss Kidd not be spared from Guiyang to work in Chongqing. She was 'well understood and has a very winning way of speaking to the women'. Hudson Taylor understood! And probably consulted her. For he told Riley to rent another house for women's work, and sent Jane back to Chongqing, escorted by David Thompson, a new colleague for Samuel Clarke at Chengdu. Within three months she and Riley were married at the Yichang consulate.

George Andrew, convalescent, and Eason settled down to language study at Guiyang, but before long heard from Hudson Taylor. With Trench unable to occupy Kunming and support the Clarkes at Dali, would they do so instead?

> I have, after mature thought, concluded to ask you both to go there . . . I should advise your securing accommodation in (an) inn, and not attempt . . . to rent a house until you have been there some time . . . and have made some friends in the place. I would suggest . . . you go out in turn on missionary journeys (with a Chinese companion) . . . There should always be one of you (in Kunming, so that remittances) may not be lost. I would advise your taking as little baggage with you as you can . . . Much baggage would be a source of danger as well as expense. . . . I should be thankful if you will aim at selling Scriptures and preaching the gospel in every city in Yunnan which has not been visited . . . and in as many market towns as possible.[33]

On January 20, 1882, within eleven months of reaching China, they left Guiyang and established themselves in Kunming (where they met but were unable to help Colquhoun and Wahab in their plight). They worked through every city of Yunnan east of Dali, and Eason visited George and Fanny Clarke at Dali before himself returning to Wuhan to get married. George Andrew changed places with the Clarkes at Dali, giving them some months in Kunming for 'a wonderful time' of street preaching, and was host to Alexander Hosie at Dali in March 1883.[34]

Hudson Taylor's impressions of Andrew and Eason when they arrived in China had been right. They had quickly shown their mettle and maturity as trail-blazers.

An attic in Hongjiang — *July 1881–December 1883*

Adam Dorward and Yang Cunling had walked from Guiyang to Hongjiang in Hunan, preaching the gospel as they went. There they tried and failed to rent even the humblest foothold, but by living inconspicuously at inns and a 'policy of perseverance and conciliation' made friends for the future. Then in a series of cities on a loop northwards through Fenghuang to Baojing near the Sichuan boundary and back to Changde, they had a mixed reception. At some 'the *yamen* people' would not even let them through the city gates, but work with few encouragements drew from Dorward the remark, 'If our work is true, "we are labouring together with God"; and that means that success is . . . an absolute certainty'.[35] Yang Cunling had to return home, but after several shorter journeys Dorward set out from Wuhan with another evangelist on December 1, ascending the Zi Shui through Yiyang to Shaoyang and meeting stiff opposition, before circling westwards to reach Hongjiang again on January 1, 1882. This time they succeeded on the 20th in renting an attic under the tiles; this the evangelist occupied while Dorward judiciously withdrew.

In March he went to consult Hudson Taylor in Shanghai. 'How Father loved him!' 'Joe' Coulthard exclaimed (after Dorward's death and his own marriage to Hudson Taylor's daughter Maria). By April 2 Dorward was on his way back to Hunan, making Shashi his base, and set off from there on May 4. June 17 saw him in Hongjiang again, and 'working quietly' he managed to stay unchallenged for three and a half months, breaking the opium addiction of two or three men at a time until forced out by the literati in October.

Friendly people presented him with parting gifts of 'pork, ducks, grapes, pears, bamboo shoots, and about a dozen packets of confectionery' and 'at least six or seven appeared interested in the Truth'. The seed of a church in Hunan was germinating. A year later he was writing of his landlord's brother being truly converted, and eleven or twelve cured addicts remaining free.[36]

Although himself expelled, he left two evangelists at Hongjiang, so when they turned up at Wuhan he was deeply disappointed and without waiting set off by boat on December 5, 1882, to regain lost ground. Taking yet another route through the Dongting Lakes to Anxiang and Li Xian in the north, south of Shashi (map p 267) he found friendly people who helped him to engage carriers for an overland journey through Cili to Changde. And on January 1, 1883, as he turned westwards he rejoiced in his diary at the ease and comfort of travelling conditions (that is, without harassment, a far cry from even two years previously) for he was still sleeping on straw or table tops or whatever an innkeeper could offer him. He foresaw 'permanent settlement among the people' but it was never to be his own lot.

This time he was penetrating the far north-western corner of the province. At Yongshun he met two Koreans and took unhurried time to tell them the gospel before making for the remotest city of Longshan, close to the junction of the Hubei, Sichuan and Hunan borders. Even the opium-besotted officials treated him well, and he sold more books than in some larger cities. At Sangzhi and Yongding (now Dayong), however, the presence of a foreign copper-mine prospector in the region had filled the people with suspicion. Here he learned that Griffith John and John Archibald of the National Bible Society of Scotland were in the vicinity, but could not find them. And on February 10 he was back at Wuhan from what had been 'the most encouraging tour he ever took in (Hunan)'. He had walked 500 miles and sold 1,600 Gospels and booklets.

In May 1882, on his way from Shashi to Changde and Hongjiang Dorward had opened his heart in a frank letter to Hudson Taylor. In the deafening noise of his inn, with no privacy in which to pray, he wrote, 'I feel my soul to be very dry and parched, and sometimes I think I shall not be able to continue much longer at this isolated kind of work.' Not only loneliness but the pressure of unrelieved 'heathenism' around him were as much as he could stand. He felt the need of being 'alone with God . . . to spend a few days in a room by myself . . . apart from all noises and distractions (to) pour out my soul to Him, and hear His voice speaking to me.' 'Fellowship with the Lord's people' would be reviving, but 'there is nothing I would like so much as a heart wholly occupied with God – a pure, holy, consecrated heart'. Saintly he certainly was, but another kind of life was not to be. He was still travelling, often alone, six years later.

Before he ventured on his longest and most daring journey, through Jiangxi into eastern and southern Hunan, through north-eastern Guangxi and up to Hongjiang again, from April to July 1883, he learned that Griffith John and Archibald had been 'badly mobbed' at the city of Longyang, south of Changde.[37] A Roman Catholic priest had been forced out of Changde for trying to buy a house, and orders had been issued that he was not to be allowed to land anywhere along his escape route. It happened that his boat was at anchor off Longyang when Griffith John arrived and, ignorant of the priest's presence, tried to go ashore. Mistaking his identity, the people vented on Griffith John and Archibald the venom intended for the priest. Dorward admitted to some trepidation as he left his friends on April 2, 1883. He was not to see them again until he had walked 1,300 miles on the outward journey alone; had sold 7,000 books and 1,500 Gospels; and lived again for five months at Hongjiang, from July 29 until about December 20.[38]

All through these epic years of 1879–83, Hudson Taylor longed to join in the pioneering, the actual travelling in untried areas. He succeeded in making a few exploratory journeys, but recurrent ill-health, and administrative pressures which all but broke his spirit, largely anchored him to the circuit of Yantai, Shanghai, Zhejiang and Wuhan. Hardest to bear was 'the Shansi spirit' of complaint and loss of conviction and purpose. At its heart lay the attitudes to compromises which had been voiced at the Shanghai Conference in 1877, and new theories on how best to 'Christianise' the nation. Mass 'conversion' achieved by muting the gospel until the literati were won over, the proponents maintained, could be brought about by emphasis on the similarities between the Chinese classics and many Christian beliefs, while head-on conflict between the gospel and Chinese cultural practice would harden opinion and opposition. Hudson Taylor found himself cast inescapably in the role of opponent of these views, and champion with others of preaching 'Christ crucified' – a harder battle in some ways than front-line pioneering might have been. (1 Cor 1.18,3)

PART 3

CRESCENDO

1877–87

CHAPTER NINE

'J'ATTAQUE'
1877–85

The ancestor controversy *1877–85*

The penetration of China was more spiritual than territorial. The whole purpose of long journeys and encounters with danger was to 'rescue the perishing', 'to snatch them as brands from the burning', to challenge Satan's hold on China's millions. None expected to emerge unhurt. Hudson Taylor's constant warning to his members not to neglect their intimate fellowship with God sprang from personal knowledge of the debilitating, destructive effects of close contact with paganism, vice, dissension between Christians – and latterly the Trojan horse of the 'new theology'.

Timothy Richard's increasing propagation of his views had its effect on those whose intellect and convictions were weaker than his own. He protested that the gospel of ' "God so loved the world that He gave His only begotten Son that whosoever believeth in Him should not perish but have everlasting life" is only the thought of the most romantic of missionary tyros'. Chinese beliefs and practices, he claimed, also expressed God's truth. 'Moral teaching is another forte of theirs.' Virtuous example is often to be found. 'What then are the myriads of temples, these clouds of incense, their incalculable heaps of paper-money, and these innumerable instances of answered prayer (proof of the living power of their gods) but the evidence of a faith that is all-pervading from the Emperor to the beggar.'[1] Nebulous 'faith' instead of faith in 'our God and Saviour Jesus Christ'? As was to be expected, where he lived and mixed with other missionaries his ideas were most expounded and 'the Shansi spirit' went deepest, deflecting and destroying the Biblical faith of some. To Hudson Taylor and the rest of the CIM Timothy Richard and his friends were on a false trail.

W A P Martin's advocacy of a liberal attitude to ancestor worship fell into the same mould, although he remained theologically conservative. After the General Missionary Conference of May 1877 in Shanghai, W A P Martin had quietly continued to press his views. Confucian philosophies and 'ancestor worship' became major topics of debate among missionaries and Chinese Christians, as among Chinese and Westerners who understood only the philosophical issues. Because some members of the CIM were confused by the arguments to the extent of resigning and fomenting discord, a brief summary of this far-reaching subject is essential, leaving it to be amplified in connection with the General Conference of 1890.

This rite of 'ancestor worship' is as alive today as in the nineteenth century. The practice has two inseparable aspects, two sides of the same coin. One is the commemoration of deceased parents and other forebears – a family event expressing respect and gratitude. The other, animistic in origin, concerns communication with the spirits of the dead and placation of vengeful ones. The first can be a joyful reunion of members of a family, akin to Thanksgiving or Christmas festivities. The second merges imperceptibly with the first, so that candles, flowers, decorations, memorials, bows and declarations become inseparable from outright idolatrous practice.

In valuing the first, dutiful sons and daughters are involved in ancient customs associated with the second. Expressions of respect and veneration merge into prayers of confession and supplication. 'Announcements' become petitions, decorations become offerings, bows become prostrations, awe becomes fear, petition becomes placation, and veneration becomes worship. An attempt to retain the first innocuous, admirable intentions becomes entangled in the practices of the second. From the beginning of Biblical Christianity in China (as distinct from deviant forms) Chinese believers have recognised the differences and renounced the custom rather than compromise. A dogged minority have followed Matteo Ricci and Martin in searching for ways of retaining the customs while denying the idolatry, without success. Failure has always lain in the impossibility of doing so without compromise or the appearance of it. Hope lies in an unmistakable substitute for the pagan practice. The search during the days of the Open Century concerns us here, but it also is still active.

Based on a belief in the existence of two worlds (the world of light, known by experience, and the world of darkness after death) the practice of 'ancestor worship' attempted to harmonise the two. The dead, it was believed, still depended on the living to provide for them. By burning replicas of all they needed in the after-life, the living could supply them. But neglected ancestors or spirits with no one to care for them took revenge by causing disease, death and calamity. Rituals performed after a death – connected with the

CALLIGRAPHY USED AS A SUPERSTITIOUS CHARM

burial, with a memorial tablet, with annual sacrifices at the graves and at ancestral halls – were thought necessary to keep the spirits quiet and to protect the living. Ancestral tablets carried the name and dates of birth and death of parents and grandparents, and twice daily the family worshipped by prostrations, incense burning and offerings to the spirits believed to occupy them. Sickness in the family drove them to pray to the ancestors for help, and 'paper money' was burned to appease malevolent spirits. Death set in motion all the rituals to honour the dead person and prevent him from returning to avenge the injuries done to him in his lifetime.

At death one of the three souls of the deceased was believed to be seized by the ruling demons of the world of darkness for torture and punishment by an endless variety of terrors, unless extricated by the efforts of the living. Of the two other spirits, one stayed with the corpse and the other entered the tablets. This purgatory could be relieved but never ended. A blood relative must maintain the ancestor worship and bear sons to perpetuate the practice. Should an only son become a Christian and repudiate ancestor worship, the whole community would anathematise him, believing that he would

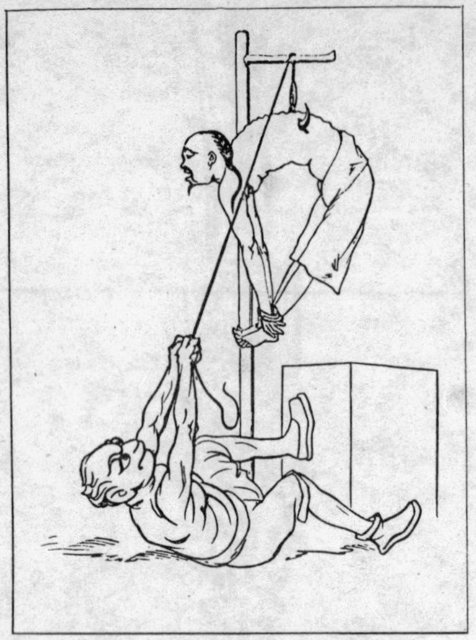

FROM A HANZHONG TEMPLE:
THE TORMENTS OF HELL

consign his ancestors to spiritual destitution as victimised spirits. Deep conviction and moral courage were needed by believers.

Twice every year, in the spring and autumn, festivals at the public cemeteries or private mausoleums brought families together to renovate and decorate the graves, offer sacrifices and present more paper effigies by burning. The family prostrated themselves in the *ketou*, precisely as they did before the temple idols, for the form, manner and intent were the same. What was done to gratify the ancestors was also done to appease the demon-spirits. 'If worshipping at the tombs and before the ancestral tablets is not worship, then the worship of their idols is not worship.' Of the three compelling motives, affection, self-interest and fear, fear was the strongest. Ancestor worship is 'the very last thing they are ready to give up'.[2] It was and is therefore the greatest obstacle to acceptance of the gospel which admits of 'no one else', 'no other name' than 'Jesus' as the 'one mediator between God and men'. The undermining of ancestor worship by twentieth-century atheism has therefore paved the way in one respect for acceptance of the Christian gospel, as the return of the old customs has faced Christians with the need to declare their loyalties. But in the nineteenth century ancestral rites were observed by all, from emperor to pauper.

Where Westerners think of their ancestors historically or as living souls in a world apart, the classical Chinese concept is of the soul or souls of man continuing their existence with enhanced power in the unseen world after death. Such a belief became a fear, fear a cult, and the cult a religion.[3] A 'dear old grandfather' as soon as he died was feared as a *gui shen*, a spirit to be dreaded. But filial piety apart from such beliefs resulted in a son's preparation of coffins for his parents years before they needed them – a comfort and reassurance to them. It led also to a general recognition of the sanctity of graves, though fear of the spirits was at least as strong a factor in this. *Worship* was distinguished from respect and veneration, by sacrifices, never made to the living. And sacrifice was intended to establish communication (even communion) with the dead, not a commemorative rite but real dealing with spirits. It became a placation of the departed or of demon impostors.[4]

Christian attitudes to ancestor worship were mentioned in the first book of this series (Book 1, pp 64–5, 71–5). The weakness of the Jewish communities and the Nestorians, that of compromising their beliefs by accepting the ancestral rites, reduced them to bare survival. Matteo Ricci's compromises, allowing participation in the rites if a cross or crucifix were concealed among the objects of worship, not only met with the opposition of the Dominicans and Franciscans but of his fellow Jesuit successor Longobardi, and ultimately of the Papacy. Mezzabarba's concessions based on loopholes in the papal bull were swept away by the Pope in 1742, and the notorious 'rites controversy' ended to the satisfaction of the Greek Orthodox Church and the Protestants. Robert Morrison, William Milne, Walter Medhurst, Elijah Bridgman, David Abeel, William Boone, all the truly learned divines and also the Sinologists John R Morrison, Sir John Davis and Samuel Wells Williams agreed.[5] Missionaries of all societies shared the same view until W A P Martin began to return to Ricci's reasoning. A few others followed him, most significantly Timothy Richard, Gilbert Reid and Young J Allen. But, as the General Missionary Conference demonstrated in 1877 and again in 1890, the overwhelming majority were unmoved. (The recent reversal of the Papal stance reflects the conflict between principle and expediency.)

Writing in 1846–47 when Protestant Chinese Christians numbered less than a hundred, Wells Williams said, 'The few Chinese who have embraced the doctrines of the New Testament . . . regard the rites as superstitious and sinful.' Without question it was worship and as such it was idolatry. To distinguish between cultural commemoration and idolatrous worship was impossible, for commemoration was by sacrificial worship. Biblical Christianity had no place for it except 'Come out from among them and be ye separate . . . touch not the unclean thing.' But the price of faithfulness was often persecution and ostracism, expulsion from the family. They were prepared to pay it. Yet that is not all. A Christian expression of affection and honouring the family's forebears was and is right, just as admiration and emulation of all that is good in Chinese culture and morals was and is to be encouraged, *short of compromise.* This was where Martin and Richard parted company from their colleagues.

Timothy Richard and 'the Shansi spirit' 1879–83

This period of five years, Hudson Taylor's fifth in China, was so eventful as to need separate handling of each main feature. Every advance was matched by particular difficulties for Hudson Taylor himself. They are pertinent to the advances made. His recurrent ill-health was enough handicap, but well or ill he had to keep the administrative wheels turning. A touch of the oiled feather (Jennie's phrase) was often enough. But broken wheels were another matter. While the success of venture upon venture, as already described, buoyed him up and led him on to attempt more, all was against forces of resistance which could have stalled the Mission and wrecked it. He personally was tested as he had been at every phase of his lifework and, until men of the right spiritual calibre and natural ability matured in experience, he had to handle the frequent (and often concurrent) adversities largely alone. Such men were at last emerging.

The story of Shanxi cannot be complete without this painful episode. A phrase 'the Shansi spirit', found in a few letters, described a whirlpool of complaints, misunderstandings, derelict spiritual morale and finally resignations from the CIM and BMS. At the vortex was the remarkable personality of Timothy Richard, still young and developing but intellectual, original and inevitably influential. K S Latourette, from the high ground of his immense knowledge of 'Christian missions in China' could not only call Richard 'one of the greatest missionaries whom any branch of the Church . . . has sent to China,'[6] but, 'like Hudson Taylor, Richard dreamed and planned in terms of all China. He, like Taylor, laid comprehensive plans for preaching the Gospel to every Chinese.' Unlike W A P Martin, however, Richard's 'Gospel' was different, a broad concept of the Kingdom of God on earth – 'how by the grace of God we may be able to save the world in this generation from the wicked ones who tyrannise over the poor and needy'. Much depends on what is meant by a word. Precision and definitions mattered immensely in this context. He foresaw 'the danger of the conversion of China from her traditional teaching of the superiority of the moral and intellectual to primary dependence upon physical force'. 'He held that it was possible to find approaches which would win for Christianity the sympathy and co-operation of all the Confucianists, Buddhists, Taoists and secret sects . . . He held that God had been at work in each of these religions, and that pointing out the similarities of each to Christianity, contacts would be established which would win their adherence to the Christian faith.'

He therefore sought out the contemplative sects in each religious discipline, to find and influence those who were seeking higher truth. And to fit himself for this he devoted much of his time to studying the Chinese classics and religious pamphlets. He adapted Chinese dissertations on ethical themes by eliminating pagan concepts and substituting the worship of God. As early as his first year as a novice in China, when a colleague showed Richard an ancestral tablet which a converted Chinese was going to burn, Richard said, 'I suppose you will at the same time burn your parents' photographs.' He did not change. 'Such was his attitude towards ancestor worship, as towards Chinese religions in general' in later years, his biographer W E Soothill, professor of Chinese at Oxford, commented.[7]

By the time Richard retired in 1915 he could see immense changes in the Chinese way of life. Partly from his own great influence, the changes also sprang from many other factors, especially the need to match the growing threat of Japanese Westernisation. So Richard lived to see China converted to the Western science and Western education he had worked so hard to convey in lectures to officials and scholars, and by a flood of publications. He had set his sights on the 100,000 literati, saying, 'When these are won to Christ the whole nation will follow.' But what he meant by 'won to Christ' was 'in striking contrast' to what Hudson Taylor and his missionaries meant and taught. Soothill wrote that Richard 'came out of the horror [of the Shandong-Shanxi famine] with the one word "Education" branded into his soul, a word which became the key-note of his life . . .'[8] Education would enable China to cope with such disasters. Hudson Taylor gave spiritual regeneration a higher priority.

More than a year before Richard went to Shanxi for famine relief, J J Turner and Francis James had criss-crossed the province with colporteur-evangelists – on the three-month reconnoitring journey of 1,700 miles from Wuhan in 1876. And after 'settling permanently' in the province with Taiyuan as their base, from April to November 1877, Francis James had fallen ill with typhoid, forcing them to withdraw temporarily to Wuhan again. When the famine died down, David Hill, Turner and James intensified their preaching of the orthodox gospel and distribution of Scripture and soon were reinforced by Jennie Taylor, Anna Crickmay, Celia Horne, Elliston, Drake, Pigott, Parrott and for a time James Cameron, George Clarke and their Chinese companions, followed by Robert and Mary Landale, Emily Kingsbury, Agnes Lancaster and Dr and Mrs Schofield. Yet Timothy Richard who did not come to Shanxi until late November 1877, opposed their methods as counter-productive and strongly advocated his own.

David Hill of the WMMS found himself having to choose between the two. After his first dealings with Timothy Richard in 1878 he wrote to his brother Edward about missionary methods, 'probably in the first place this is better – finding out, making selection of the worthy men of a place and working out from them, though not to sound abroad the gospel differs from my plans in the past, and I am not exactly satisfied yet which is the better to begin with' – 'a faithful reflection' of Richard's influence. But three years later David Hill said at the fifteenth anniversary meeting of the CIM in London, 'I feel almost like a missionary of the China Inland Mission.' Well before he left Shanxi in May 1880, he had rejected Richard's policy.[9]

Timothy Richard had met a kindred spirit in Shandong, the Scottish Presbyterian missionary Mary Martin. After marrying in October 1878, when he had been ten months in Shanxi, they made their home in Taiyuan. Relations between all these people, and the 'Oberlin Band' of the American Board when they also came to Taiyuan in 1881, were cordial. For all were agreeable people, willing to differ amicably. But from the beginning the attractive and persuasive nature of the Richards led to one and another of the CIM missionaries being won over. Mary Martin 'had also been growing away from the stern dogmas in which she had been trained', and replied to her brother's exhortations, 'If you had travelled over the world as I have, and seen the millions (of Chinese) you would, like me, feel it such a joy to be able to lay for ever aside that doctrine we were taught as Bible truth in Scotland' – the Westminster Confession and its Biblical authority.[10]

As early as August 15, 1878, Hudson Taylor confided to Lord Radstock, 'The faith of one brother has quite broken down, under the unhelpful influence largely of other missionaries, and we shall have to recall him.' Others were succumbing, and in March 1879 Francis James was talking of resigning from the CIM to look for a regular salary such as other missions provided.[11] By August when George Clarke arrived at Yantai (after three months in Shanxi following his expulsion from Jincheng) (p 183), even he was 'a faithful reflection of the Shansi state of mind'. On March 6, 1880, Hudson Taylor named in a letter to London those who were unshaken by Richard's arguments. '(His) presence in Shansi causes me great anxiety for some of his views are so Romish [an allusion to Ricci], and his personal influence so strong that the CIM has no existence, scarcely, or place, or work or claims in the minds of (two of the CIM missionaries). This is not necessarily Mr R's fault; it is rather the inevitable result of a strong and attractive character over weaker minds.' Turner and Drake were so convinced of the rightness of Richard's policy that the persistence of the rest of the CIM Shanxi team in 'Scriptural colportage' and evangelism was driving them to resign. Hudson Taylor commented, 'Richard is driving a good theory to death. He refuses to preach to the masses, is for circulation of moral and theistic tracts, not containing the name or work of Christ, to prepare the way, as he thinks, for the gospel . . .' By May, Francis James had resigned, and at his request Hudson Taylor wrote to the BMS in London endorsing his application for a transfer of membership and referring them to Timothy Richard for his opinion.[12]

When the Oxford graduate Robert Landale married Mary Jones of Ningbo, step-daughter of Frederick Gough, Hudson Taylor gave them the choice between Wuhan and Taiyuan as their sphere of work. They chose Taiyuan. So did the surgeon Harold Schofield and his wife after four months of language study at Yantai. All four were sufficiently at home with Christian theology and mission strategy to be unaffected by Richard's views.

Until 1881 the CIM avoided separating their work from Richard's, but Chinese Christians could only be confused or harmed by the conflicting teaching of the missionaries. What was to be done? When the admirable J J Turner himself arrived at Yantai 'utterly down in body, soul and mind', the price of co-operation had become too high. Hudson Taylor at last advised a parting of the ways. Let Timothy Richard pursue his policy, and the CIM their own. Being first in the field of Shanxi and Taiyuan justified this action, however regrettable it might appear to be. The precedent had been set by the apostle Paul in writing to the Galatian church (1.6–9) and by Jude, 'I . . . appeal to you to join the struggle in defence of the faith which God entrusted to His people once and for all. It is danger from certain people . . .' (Jude 3, 4 NEB).[13] Quite independently, in Shanghai the Union Church had acquired a minister whose 'liberal' teaching and admission of 'the uncoverted and immoral to the Lord's table' incensed members of his congregation. A nucleus of them, including Weir, Cranston and the Hodsons (Book 5, pp 397), established the Free Christian Church and invited Hudson Taylor to advise them. Edward Pearse served briefly as their first pastor, followed by Judd, Hudson Taylor and other CIM missionaries when available.

A united church was however so important to Richard, overriding theology, that he travelled to Yantai to persuade Hudson Taylor. Turner returned to Shanxi with him, resigned from the CIM, and was later followed by two or three others. Timothy Richard played an immense role in China during the next few decades, in touch with some of the highest mandarins of the land. But his role in Taiyuan ended in 1886 when he returned from a disappointing visit to Britain. The Committee of the BMS could not see their way to adopting his scheme for a college in each provincial capital of China. 'He came home in anguish,' his wife told her diary. During his absence, orthodox BMS missionaries came to Taiyuan, and when Richard returned and tried to resume his old methods, his own colleagues protested. As he could not be dissuaded, 'they sent a long letter to the Committee, censuring me in regard to both my theological views and to my methods of work.'[14]

Richard decided to leave Shanxi and moved to Tianjin and then Peking. He petitioned his mission to be allowed to establish a college at Jinan, the capital of Shandong, and on being advised to rejoin his Shandong colleagues in conventional 'church-planting', chose to resign and engage in literary work. He edited *Shi Bao*, '*The Times*' of North China and, after Alexander Williamson died in 1891, became the director of 'the Society for the Diffusion of Christian and General Knowledge among the Chinese', later called the Christian Literature Society. 'Instead of writing goody-goody tracts . . . we decided to enlighten China on the world's progress and put her in a fair way of saving herself.'[15] In this second phase of his life he earned his great reputation among Chinese and foreigners until his name was familiar to emperor and schoolboy.

In Shanxi the CIM and BMS worked in close harmony through the decades that followed and, returning to their former convictions, the CIM missionaries who had resigned served in other missions for many years. But these were not the only resignations during those momentous years, nor the major problems Hudson Taylor faced.

'My face like a flint' *1879–83*

Like windows into Hudson Taylor's soul, his editorials in *China's Millions* reveal his train of thought. In January 1880 he headed his New Year greetings with the words of Isaiah 50.7, 'The Lord God will help me; therefore I shall not be confounded; therefore have I set my face like a flint, and I know that I shall not be ashamed.' What was good for the Servant Son of God was good for his servants. Adversity was to be expected and endured. More positively – *this was the road to success.* In the *Millions* of 1878 he had written, 'Sometimes a longing indescribable comes over me to be with some dear brother and encourage him when depressed.' He himself often needed such encouragement. He had learned to draw upon 'the encouragement of the Scriptures', but being frequently under assault caused him acute suffering. His thorn in the flesh, 'dysentery', dragged him down, magnifying the problems he faced.[16]

He had arrived back in China in April 1879 weak from a life-threatening attack on the voyage. Relapsing in Shanghai he reached Yantai fit only for bed. But his resilience made possible a visit to the Yangzi region, until his anxious companions had to take him back again. Up and down in health as he recovered strength in the invigorating climate of 'Chefoo' and set off again to Zhejiang or Yangzhou or distant Wuhan, he frequently fell ill again. By July 1881 Jennie had been more than three years away from her little children and longed to be with them again. But Hudson was not well enough to be left and parting was too painful to contemplate. She stayed until the autumn.[17]

A fast-growing mission meant more and more administrative correspondence and problems to resolve. The council in London were still learning. Some newly arrived missionaries showed that they should never have come. In the process they damaged relations with Chinese, consuls and fellow-missionaries. Two revealed that they were epileptics who had thought themselves cured, until new stresses proved they were not. Two others showed that they were mentally ill, not only 'unbalanced', and had to go home. Another had 'a morbid conscience' and needed 'careful handling'. One new arrival made no attempt to learn the language and Hudson Taylor sent him back as 'a thoroughly good-for-nothing fellow'.

Henry Taylor, 'broken' by the rough handling and 'deep hate' he had encountered in Henan, tried to find a niche in Zhejiang. Resentment made him incapable of a new start. He quarrelled bitterly with his Chinese colleague at Jinhua, and resigned from the CIM to take up a lucrative post in the Customs service. To dare to invade Satan's domain in the hearts of men was to invite attack, and he fell wounded emotionally and spiritually. So 'pray for those you send, shield them by prayer,' Hudson Taylor urged upon the Mission's friends. The first pioneer to penetrate the first of the nine unevangelised provinces had become the first such casualty. And not only he. His newly comfortable circumstances became a strong inducement to some colleagues in Zhejiang, where loyalty to the Mission's principles had too often been half-hearted. Close proximity to other societies with foreign life styles strengthened the temptation. In March 1882 'nearly all' were affected, and Hudson Taylor almost wished they were not his responsibility.[18]

International tensions in south China and Indo-China threatened the rest of the empire, like a menacing cloud over whatever else was happening. The sudden death of the co-empress regent, Ci An, by the hand of Ci Xi it was believed, signalled the presence of a most unscrupulous person still at the seat of power. In this climate Hudson Taylor was sending out not only men but women too into the remote provinces.

He built up the 'sanatorium' and school complex of premises at Chefoo, and because W L Elliston proved such a good master, other missions, merchants and consuls used 'much solicitation and pressure' to persuade Hudson Taylor to open the school to their children also. Simply making 'Chefoo' what it became, with constant staffing problems, demanded much of him. The administrators he needed were slow in coming. One capable individual in Britain was suggested, but Hudson Taylor knew him too well. He would continually be in hot water through inability to stand being reviled as a 'foreign devil'. 'No more hinderers' were wanted; Satan was 'enough already'![19]

The illnesses of one after another, and the deaths of missionaries and their children weighed upon him. Again and again C G Moore's wife was 'dying' of self-imposed 'hysterical' starvation (anorexia nervosa), consuming the time, sleep and energy of others, 'a great care'. Her distraught husband, capable and influential, hung around, dissatisfied and unable to work until he could take her home to Britain and join the staff there. Then in May 1881 Emily King died of typhoid in faraway Hanzhong, and soon 'everything at once' seemed to happen. Hudson Taylor's mother suddenly 'fell asleep while sitting in an armchair' in July 1881; Jennie's mother died of cancer in August, and in November Hudson Taylor's father collapsed while giving instructions to some workmen in his garden, and died.[20] Feeling 'orphaned', he and Jennie could see no alternative to parting from each other. One of them must see to family affairs at home. She sailed from Yantai on October 13, 1881. Without her and desperately longing, as his love-letters show, he stayed on until February 6, 1883, for he was needed more in China than in Britain.

Mrs E C Lord and the Judd baby were under his medical care that August. But both died. Then he himself went down with 'choleraic (dysentery)'. Caroline Kerr arrived from Guiyang, still very ill, 'nearly fatally'. News came of John Stevenson with jungle fever in Bhamo, where the Catholic priest had died of it. And in giving birth to her first child, Mary Landale died at Taiyuan. She was like a daughter to Hudson Taylor – the child of his close friends John and Mary Jones of early Ningbo days (Book 3, p 337).[21] A very promising Scotsman named William Macgregor arrived in April 1882 to pioneer in Guangxi after two years with George Clarke at Dali. He set himself to master Chinese rapidly, and was learning every character and the meaning of one chapter of the Chinese New Testament each day. But in October he contracted virulent smallpox and died.

Jessie Murray had written to Jennie in October 1881, telling about a Christian schoolgirl who died in her school at Shaoxing. Towards the end 'it seemed as if she had been . . . to the very door of heaven'. 'Inexpressibly *happy*,' she had said to those around her bed, 'You must not weep. I have *seen* the Lord! I have *seen* heaven. It is *very*, *very* good. . . . I wish you could come – there is *nothing* to fear.' And Jessie Murray added, 'It is not death to die. How glorious!' '*It is not death to die*' put things into perspective.[22]

All through these five years the Mission's receipts continued painfully low – £1,000 less in 1881 than in previous years – although other British missions reported an increase.[23] But this was not Hudson Taylor's chief concern. Even when funds were in hand in Britain, they were not being regularly remitted to him. With so much on his mind, he extended his habitual hours of prayer and fasted more than usual. What was God saying to him through all this testing? 'What if the presence of men like (X and Y) is the cause of God's favour being withheld?' 'I am in great straits for funds. I am happy about it. The Lord may take away all our troublesome people through it and give us true-hearted ones instead' – those who would look, as most did, to God instead of to 'the Mission' to supply their needs.[24]

On December 23, 1881, he wrote, 'We had to win from Him by daily prayer and trust the funds to make remittances (to individuals). We did not ask in vain, for 4/5ths of the last month's income for general purposes was received in China' (instead of from Europe), including sizeable gifts from a consul and the parents of a non-CIM child in the Chefoo school. Some might forget their intentions when they joined the Mission, and take to grumbling. The true spirit was reflected in the missionary's letter comparing herself to King Saul's lame son Mephibosheth, '*fed at the King's table*'. As guest of the King she would always be content. Elizabeth Wilson also drew attention to the difference between looking to God and relying on 'the Mission' to supply recurring needs, when she wrote from Hanzhong on November 26, 1880, 'Our confidence must be in God, who has never failed those in the Mission who trusted in Him', implying that the complaints of 'passengers' were self-explanatory.[25]

The 'trouble' was not only over money and men who should never have joined the CIM. A wave of indiscipline swept through the Mission, affecting even some of the best members. Perhaps Hudson Taylor's immobilisation by illness, and by the need to be on hand to distribute funds when they came, gave them an impression of independence from him. One after another did what he thought right or simply wanted to do, without consulting their leader. Others rejected his advice and even his instructions. One of the epileptics, strongly advised by Hudson Taylor and the LMS doctor in Shanghai to defer his marriage, secretly arranged it with the Settlement chaplain and announced a *fait accompli*. Another declined to wait until he and his fiancée had fulfilled their language study and period of adaptation to the climate and the customs of

China. When held to their promise they resigned. He joined another mission and went on to win the Order of the Double Dragon for services to the Chinese empire.

'In matters of the heart few accept advice,' Hudson Taylor wrote. Even one or two of the best pioneers married without consulting him. 'I see the importance of being firm, more than ever,' he added. Far from being autocratic, he treated them as friends and expected and usually received loyal co-operation. When it involved taking young brides far upcountry they could not afford to act independently. One of his trusted assistants fell so deeply in love with a newcomer, almost at first sight, that they could neither be together nor separated without emotional stress. He took the poor swain away with him on a long journey to calm down, and made an exception to his own rule by allowing them to marry at the first opportunity after his return. He believed in a minimum of rules, and that they should be servants, not tyrants. But liberal control depended on willing concurrence.[26]

Jackson the incorrigible had incurred large medical bills when his wife was ill and died. Refusing to pay he was sued at the consular court. Hudson Taylor intervened and at long last sent him home to Britain, not to return – unless showing great improvement! On August 26, 1884, the London Council meeting with Hudson Taylor minuted that Jackson's connection with the CIM was to end, after nineteen years of patience.

Truancy was another failing of indisciplined missionaries. Forsaking their work and the employees who depended on them for daily or weekly wages, they sometimes went to a neighbouring 'station' or farther afield for a change, or to find a wife. It was understandable; they were unexceptional people. But if this happened, binding rules and regulations would have to be introduced. 'It is reported that CIM missionaries have nothing to do and do nothing,' Hudson Taylor groaned to Benjamin about one district. He had to treat some young men as immature, but how should he deal with one or two senior missionaries with humble origins whose life style in 'fine houses with fine tables' not only suggested no lack of money but set a bad example?

'Prickly' and 'rude' missionaries also needed more than the 'oiled feather' to lubricate their troubled relationships. One undertook the task of business manager at Shanghai, as Mission buyer and travel agent.[27] Inevitably he was asked to make private purchases for individuals inland, and grudgingly obliged, but he seldom rendered an account. Appeals to Hudson Taylor fell as heavy straws on the overladen camel's back. Far worse were those few given to tongue-lashing the Chinese or even striking them. Carriers or tradesmen so treated could well stir up a riot. The consuls protested. At Chongqing it transpired that a visiting missionary of another society, using the CIM premises while dressing and behaving with colonial arrogance, was chiefly to blame. At Consul Baber's urgent request his society withdrew him. But one of the CIM men aped the older man and was slow to reform. When yet another had to be dismissed 'the shock to the Mission' was as great as if ten had to be dismissed later in the Mission's history.[28]

Reports of such incidents reached Sir Thomas Wade's ears in Peking, and through him the Foreign Office in London. They are still on file at the Public Records Office. Wade instructed the consuls to restrict as far as possible the issue of passports. But the risk of passports for travel and residence in China being denied to all CIM missionaries became so grave that Hudson Taylor wrote urgently to everyone. If overbearing behaviour towards Chinese continued, all might be required to register in person at consular ports involving great difficulty, expense and waste of time, let alone danger en route. That ended the emergency. Four good men (Elliston, Parrott, Stevenson and Turner) whose passports had been withheld then received them.

It was reasonable that missionaries of different societies should live and work together, or receive each other in transit. But dilemmas arose when some in foreign dress and carrying firearms made themselves at home in CIM premises in the absence of the resident missionary, rather than go to an inn. Evangelists and employees were unaccustomed to being treated impersonally. The problem of returning hospitality with hospitality defied solution for many years. At other times, as different societies moved into cities already occupied to plant churches of their own denomination, rivalry sometimes developed. Except in large cities and business centres, Hudson Taylor preferred to move away to new territory.

Problem followed problem in the director's mail, and he learned to meet them by 'living one day at a time rather than carry tomorrow's problems today'. 'The Lord God will help me; therefore I shall not be confounded.' On November 14, 1881, the day he received Henry Taylor's resignation, he wrote, 'Almost a storm of business to be done today.' This, after spending the whole voyage from Yantai to Shanghai dictating letters to Parrott. When two other couples resigned in the same fortnight, Hudson Taylor wrote frankly in *China's Millions* about this epidemic; 1881 had been 'a year of trial' unlike any other.[29] J J Coulthard, his personal secretary during much of this time, recalled,

> It was his habit to rise before us, very early any time before dawn, and by candle-light read his Bible . . . He valued despatch and prompt execution in correspondence, remittances, etc . . . At some of the stations there were a great many difficulties to be met, but he never trusted to anyone's advice, he always prayed about the work; some said he was able to get his own way by his personal magnetism, but he always prayed about everything. His way of living was so simple. He would take such notice of (a little child) and win the mother's heart. Then (he would) read the Bible with (the missionary in difficulties or disaffected), and would give such helpful talks (about the passage), and invariably the difficulties were settled.[30]

But the obverse of the coin held a very different image. Trouble was the exception to the steady, faithful, costly part being played by most of the Mission. The Broumtons and Camerons, the Clarkes and Dorwards and Eastons of the CIM were penetrating ever farther into the interior. The seldom-mentioned men and women were building up strong churches in obscure places. Louise Desgraz, who married Edward Tomalin in 1882, was one of these. '(There was) never a leader with more cause for thanks for loyalty than I,' he assured her. Friends of the Mission at home were unruffled by the squalls. The Earl of Shaftesbury who in ignorance had belittled the CIM (Book 5, p 170), as chairman of the annual meeting now said, 'I like this society very much.' And Lord Radstock, enclosing £100, wrote to Jennie, 'The labours (of your dear husband – highly honoured is he) are not only owned of God in China but for the strengthening of the faith of many in England.'[31]

The Seventy — *November 1881–82*

A more difficult year lay ahead. The greatest advances seemed always to be accompanied or followed by counter-attacks from the great 'adversary' of 1 Peter 5.8. By this yardstick the 'daring and success' of Hudson Taylor and his pioneers deserved a major onslaught. But they had only begun their invasion of inland China. The missionary community and the Churches at home were about to be startled by yet another 'bombshell'. Adversity aroused him. It spurred him to stronger effort. But not defensively. As in the first world war Foch's famous despatch read, 'My centre is giving way, my right is in retreat, situation excellent. I shall attack!'[32] so now, low income and disarray in the Mission had to be seen as distractions from the prime objective, the gospel to every corner of the empire, and so to every man, woman and child.

While Jennie was on the way home to Europe, Hudson Taylor and Parrott went up the Yangzi to Wuchang, visiting stations en route. At Anqing on November 21 he wrote to her, 'God is greatly helping me . . . to rejoice in our adverse circumstances, in our poverty, in the retirements from our mission.' And quoting her, 'All these difficulties are only platforms for the manifestation of His grace and power and love.'[33] 'Joe' Coulthard was in charge as business manager at Wuhan, and Jane Kidd, Adam Dorward, Trench and Pigott, five of the best type, were passing through. Whenever he was among his missionaries, Hudson Taylor seized the opportunity to lift their spirits above the earthy everyday things of life to the spiritual level, by singing, praying and sharing with them the truths he himself was learning daily from his feasting on the Bible. During the week they were together, they spent time doing this each morning and evening, and discussing the working out of the Principles, the shortage of funds, and the inadequacy of their present numbers.

This last subject seemed most urgent. In province after province and city after city more fully committed men and women were needed. In October he had sent home his short editorial for the December *Millions* about 'Western China opening'. 'Were the Lord to grant us double the number of workers and double the means, within twelve months we could have them all located and at work . . . Who will "come to the help of the LORD"?'[34] The CIM already numbered ninety-six missionaries, twenty-six of whom were wives and mothers with limited freedom for activities among Chinese outside their homes; and in addition about one hundred Chinese colleagues. But the size of the task and the policy of most other societies to base their work on the treaty ports left the CIM little choice but to expand their effort, and therefore their numbers.

The Mission house in Wuchang (the southern city of the three which with Hankou and Hanyang now comprise Wuhan) stood near a little hill crowned by a Yüan dynasty (1280–1368) pagoda. (The approach to the great twentieth-century bridge across the Yangzi River now makes use of this Snake Hill, and the pagoda has been rebuilt farther to the south.) On Friday afternoon, November 25,

Hudson Taylor and Parrott were strolling together on the grassy hilltop, discussing the need to expand the Mission. Financing it was no problem. If God was saying to them, 'Enlarge the place of your tent . . . do not hold back; lengthen your cords, strengthen your stakes. For you will spread out to the right and to the left . . . Do not be afraid,' he would provide for those he sent. Then how many were they talking about? By rough computation fifty-six could already be placed. Allowing for losses by illness and resignation, and for more and more Christians needing to be taught, as many as seventy would be a realistic number to pray for. They realised that they had been praying only vaguely for reinforcements. In the six years 1876–81 about seventy had come to China. An average of ten or a dozen each year was too few. Seventy more were needed soon. However out of context the thought, 'seventy others also' had been the number Jesus had sent out on one occasion. A cheerful irrelevance? Should they pray for so many now? As they walked, Parrott's foot kicked a string of 100 brass cash in the grass (*see* Book 2, p 130). A coincidence? At least it reminded them that 'all the silver and the gold' was the Lord's. He would meet the cost.

By Sunday they were convinced that God was guiding them. Over tea they consulted Coulthard and Trench, who agreed. Across the table they promised each other to pray for 'seventy more' until they arrived. Dorward was leaving for Hunan again on Tuesday, 29th, and Jane Kidd with her Chinese companion and David Thompson for Chongqing, so Monday evening was given up to prayer. With all the household present, Hudson Taylor prayed specifically for 'seventy', and one of those present wrote in his journal afterwards, 'I quite believe he prayed the prayer of faith tonight'. To explain to the others how he reached that number, he worked it all out on paper, province by province, city by city – '42 men and 28 women for our work, and large reinforcements to all the evangelical societies'.[35] On the Wednesday night someone suggested, how good it would be to meet again to praise the Lord, when the seventy had all come. Why wait? said someone else. To be able to get together was unlikely. So that evening they praised God in advance.

At the time they mentioned no date by which the seventy should come. Interviewing, training, equipping, accommodating and introducing to the language and land of China would limit the number who could be handled at any one time. But the need of them was already pressing. Spread over three years seventy would not be too many. Later 'within three years' became the goal of their prayers, twice as many per annum as usual. On December 1, Hudson Taylor was on his way down to Zhenjiang and writing to Jennie. He was inviting the Anqing staff and language students to join him at Zhenjiang for a similar informal conference.

> God is faithful and expects us to walk by faith [he wrote]. This month the home remittance was [worth by exchange] taels 300 perhaps; the contributions in China exceeded taels 1200. At the beginning of the month *I* did not know what *I* could do; *He* knew what *He* would do . . . [with so little for so many].
>
> We have our definite lines of work; we must not leave them nor get weary of them. If any leave us on account of them, they not we are the losers. If any members of our home Council cannot go along with us, they too will sooner or later need to go. God remains faithful. Do not be cast down, Darling, if you meet with difficulties at home. All things are working together for good, as in due time we shall see. Pray much for me . . . Satan is a terrible reality and so is the flesh; but more is He who is with us.[36]

Missionaries of the American Episcopal Church and a customs officer were present as guests at the Zhenjiang conference, December 3–9, where agreement was again unanimous. He wrote to all members of the Mission inviting them to join him and each other in praying for 'seventy' if they felt able to do so. Without the background knowledge all could not be expected to agree at once. Nor did they. Even protests were predictable. If the Mission's income was so low, not keeping pace with the Mission's growth (£8,119 in 1875–76 and £8,692 in 1879–80), how could they nearly double the membership? There was nothing secret about all this. Soon critics within and outside the CIM were questioning and condemning the latest irresponsibility.

At Shanghai Hudson Taylor met his son Herbert, arriving from England to join the teaching staff at Chefoo; he took him to see his mother's grave at Zhenjiang and the scene of the Yangzhou riot. Then he went on to Ningbo and the Zhejiang region. Once again the question of re-baptism had arisen, and he agreed to baptise Pearse and Parrott as 'believers'.[37] At Ningbo on January 7, 1882, he drafted an appeal to the Churches in Great Britain and Ireland,

> 1. To unite with us in fervent, effectual prayer (for) more labourers in connection with every Protestant missionary society on both sides of the Atlantic.
> 2. . . . for forty-two additional men and twenty-eight additional

> women, called and sent out by God . . . We are not anxious as to the means for sending them forth or sustaining them . . . urging such to count the cost . . . to ask themselves whether they *will* really trust Him for *everything* . . . Mere romantic feeling will soon die out in the . . . constant discomforts and trials of inland work . . . when severe illness arises, and perhaps all the money is gone. Faith in the living God alone gives joy and rest in such circumstances . . . He is supplying, and ever has supplied, all our needs; and if not seldom we have fellowship in poverty with Him who for our sakes became poor, shall we not rejoice . . . that we have been (like Paul) 'poor yet making many rich' . . . ?[38]

He would set no standard by which God should be expected to provide; only the absolute standard of the immutability of His promise.

This appeal was circulated among the active members of the Mission for optional signature, and took months by the slow postal system to be completed. A letter written by Hudson Taylor at Wuchang on November 26, 1881, and published in the March *Millions* naturally made no mention of it.[39] Thanking supporters for donations during the year, he referred to the extreme limitations of income only by saying, 'Though our needs have been many and great, I can again testify that God has supplied all our real needs, though oft times more sparingly than, had we had our choice, might have been done. But for all the trials of faith we can thank and praise Him; doubtless He sees them necessary'.

His letter to the annual meeting at Mildmay on June 6, 1882, also remained silent on the subject. And Theodore Howard, the director in Britain, made no reference to it in his address. Lord Shaftesbury as chairman in the afternoon this time went further than before in saying of the CIM, 'This is one of the nicest and snuggest little societies I know . . . small in magnitude and yet it is very vast in operation. . . . I would be very sorry if it went beyond the power of the superintendence of Mr Hudson Taylor.'[40] And in the evening Lord Radstock, a sacrificial donor, added, 'Christians in England are not half awake about China. I consider that the income of this Society is a contemptible income. . . . There is no country where Christians allow themselves so much self-indulgence as in England.' From extensive knowledge of Europe he spoke with authority.

This malaise among Christians had been troubling Lord Radstock. In the May meetings of the previous year, in the Exeter Hall, he had said,

> I believe that our great failure in England arises from what I should call a comfortable religion . . . . that there are more Christians that are injured by comfort than by anything else. Comfort seems to paralyse work on all sides. . . . There is a circle of habit which enchains most Christians. . . . When they get beyond that circle into utter abandonment to God, they have a revelation of Christ's presence and Christ's joy which those who remain within that wall never experience. . . . It requires faith for a man to go out to China simply with his passage paid. . . . They will not tell you when they are in need, and if you want to find out . . . the only thing is to pray about it, and in your prayer God will direct you.[41]

That was true of material needs, but from the beginning Hudson Taylor had believed that the Church, disabled by comfort, should be challenged to face her obligation to 'preach the gospel to every creature'. To appeal in 1875 for eighteen for the nine unevangelised provinces had been dramatic. So soon afterwards to appeal for seventy would strike a complacent public as irresponsible unless presented with the right support. Even the Mission's referees might balk at this. The individual signatures of those who would have to divide the Mission's income with the newcomers, were worth waiting for. So in June 1882 it was still China's general need and not the specific appeal which was publicised.

At long last, in the February issue of *China's Millions*, 1883, the full text was followed by facsimile signatures of seventy-seven missionaries, beginning with 'J. Hudson Taylor, 1854' and ending with 'H Hudson Taylor, 1881' – Herbert, at the age his father had been when he first reached China. Some others had objected to enlarging the Mission while the funds were low, and some of naming 'seventy', though promising to pray in general terms.

By then a whole year had passed. And only eight had arrived. For the rest to come within two more years would tax the accommodation and smooth running of the Mission. By the close of the financial year, 1882–83, only a maintenance amount of £10,840 had been received, and one gift of £3,000 towards the advance.[42] Instead of answered prayer in the form expected, resignations and the death of one valued worker after another had to be reported. The whole of 1882 also deserved its epithet, 'a year of trial'.

'Our mismanaged mission' *1882*

To mark the twelfth anniversary of the sailing of the *Lammermuir* in 1866, Hudson Taylor stated in 1878,

> Of all who have offered for China, not one of whom we have had reason to believe to be qualified has ever been refused; and funds have never failed to come for the outfit and passage of all who have been accepted, and for the subsequent support of all who have gone forth . . . The contributions from year to year have sustained the work adequately, though not without faith being at times considerably exercised. But we have never had to leave an open door unentered from lack of funds.[43]

The same could have been said of the next four years. Marked progress had been in the face of minimal resources. William Berger had been a faithful donor, even though never able to contribute really large sums. At the end of 1881 when he finally surrendered his directorship in the starch factory at Bow, he wrote to tell Hudson Taylor that as his income would become one third of what it had been, his ability to help would be correspondingly less.[44] 'Put not your trust in princes' had a firm place in Hudson Taylor's thinking. His dependence on 'God alone' was strengthened. And when his own father's death provided Amelia with the income from five houses in Pyrland Road, secured to her and her children, it may be surmised that Hudson was also a beneficiary.[45] In the summer of 1882 so little Mission money was being forwarded from Britain that he had to stay in Yantai for more than three months, simply to be available to distribute at once whatever might be received. The last three months of the year were as trying. In August 1883 he told the story in full.

> In the months July, August, and September [1882] we had received from home besides special donations, over £2000 for the general purposes of the Mission; but during October, November, and December only £393 19s 6d was received for these general purposes, a sum very far from sufficient for the wants of any one month. In October . . . moneys for the expenses of long journeys seemed needed; and when we . . . found, instead of the hoped for £700 or £800, or more, only £96 9s 5d, . . . locking the door, (we) knelt down and spread the letter before the LORD, asking Him what was to be done with . . . a sum which it was impossible to distribute over seventy stations in which were eighty or ninety missionaries (including the wives), not to speak of about 100 (Chinese) helpers and over 100 (Chinese) children to be boarded and clothed in our schools. Having first . . . rolled the burden on the LORD, we then told the need to others of our Mission in Chefoo . . . but let no hint even of our circumstances be given outside.
>
> Soon the answers (to prayer) began to come, in local gifts from

> kind friends . . . and ere long all the needs of the month were met . . . We had similar experiences in November, and again in December.[46]

One day, coming across Mary Ann Nicoll in the house in Chefoo, Hudson Taylor asked her, 'What would you do if you had a very large family and nothing to give them to eat?' She knew it was his way of explaining why he spent so much time alone in his room, 'waiting upon God'.

His confidence in the Lord to supply in one way or another was one thing. The reliability of the staff in London to remit funds was another matter. Charles Moore had taken his famished wife home and succeeded William Soltau as cashier-accountant at Pyrland Road. But his distraction by his wife's condition continued, and there was no improvement in the state of affairs he had gone to remedy. In January 1882 Hudson Taylor was exasperated. Moore was not sending telegraphic remittances as instructed. 'I have written till I am tired and sick of the subject,' Hudson Taylor confessed to Jennie. By April that had improved, but even the Mission treasurer was not answering letters and Hudson Taylor felt in the dark. But for letters from Jennie and one or two others, 'my knowledge of England would be mainly geographical'. Neither Theodore Howard nor Benjamin were intervening to put things right. Jennie's personal legacy was available to pay the ocean passages of ten of the Seventy, about £300, but how did the Mission's finances stand? Were letters going astray or being stolen?

In September he was still starved of information. Theodore Howard occasionally replied but did not answer his questions, and Benjamin did not give enough information about the new men and women he was sending out. Even Jennie seemed too busy, writing briefly about business while Hudson pined for deep communion with her. 'It just seems as if nobody cares for me,' he groaned. 'The constant uncertainty and no tidings from home is a painful contrast to Mr Berger's administration.' At last it transpired that letters were being sent via America and both being delayed and going astray.[47]

He badly needed to go to Shanxi to sort out the deepening troubles between the missionaries, but could not leave the helm. At least Joe Coulthard was coming to take over the accounts, and Douthwaite to act as an assistant editor, dealing with material from sources in China. By October there was barely time to get to Tianjin before ice would close the port to shipping. 'A long, cold winter's journey (overland) is the alternative, all caused by want of compliance with my reasonable directions . . . I have asked again and again for lists of the missing vouchers, but McCarthy sends me no reply.' 'I have no one but you (on earth) to tell some of (these things) to.' 'It is only through God's special care that our mismanaged mission does not come to nought.' He was at 'a complete standstill', unable to travel or to manage the Mission. 'There are two aspects of these things – the one, God's purpose in *permitting* it, the other the incompetence or disobedience of those who ought to be carrying out my instructions.'

When a fortnightly mail boat came with nothing for him, he left for Tianjin and Shanxi – on the occasion when the one he most needed to meet had left his work and gone to Chefoo. 'I am very, very sorry for this. The Mission will come to an end if this lawless running away from work . . . is to go on.' So Hudson Taylor visited the other missions. In Peking 'Dr Edkins, the first missionary that I met in China,' chaired a meeting at which Hudson Taylor explained 'the rise and progress' of the CIM. W A P Martin showed him over his college, and the Hon T G Grosvenor (of the Margary investigation), chargé d'affaires at the legation, 'advised me *privately* by all means to "press forward (towards Tibet via Gansu), but *carefully*"'. Then the truant and his bride returned bringing a missing transmission of money for immediate distribution and Hudson Taylor 'got them away' to their work again.

Now he could see that he must return to Britain, to get the machinery turning smoothly again, and to have a hand in the selection of the Seventy. On the last day of 1882 he told Jennie that £350 had been telegraphed from London, 'but £750 *seems* needed'. And paradoxically, 'I can't tell you how happy I am amidst it all.' 'Now we shall see what GOD will do,' spiced every turn of events.

Despair *1882–83*

Looking for the firm ground of God's promises in the quicksands of despondency had become habitual for Hudson Taylor. His survival would have been remarkable, but 'to walk on the water' when he 'was assailed by such depression, loneliness and forebodings, due in part to illness,' surprised those who knew how he was suffering. In his *History of Christian Missions in China*, K S Latourette's reliance on secondary sources led to his misunderstanding of the facts when he wrote, 'at last his hopes (of seventy additional missionaries by the close of 1884) were to be frustrated.'[48] His 'depression and foreboding' were at no time due to that. An appeal had not yet been publicised. Signatures were being collected. He was not shaken by such things. Every reference he made to the Seventy assumed fulfilment. It was the spiritual failure and disloyalty in Zhejiang and Shanxi, and 'the utter inadequacy of existing arrangements' in London which shook him to the core. His protests through the past year had shown it. He had no one but Jennie in whom to confide, and she kept his letters. The Howard Taylor biography highlights his spiritual resilience, a lesson in 'overcoming', but the need for resilience is as revealing.

He and Jennie had *suffered* so much separation for the sake of the gospel, the Mission, the famine and the family, almost more than he could bear. At Ningbo early in January he stayed with his old friend, the recently widowed E C Lord. A restless companion so prevented him from sleeping that he got up at 1.00 a.m. Looking at his photograph of Jennie and the children by candlelight decided him to write. 'I don't like these nice bedrooms with their sunny sheets,' he confided to her. 'They seem to want you. In *rough* places I am glad you are not there to share my discomforts.' On the way to Wenzhou in February (trouble-shooting) he called their separation 'a time of great trial; I seem unable to rise above it as I should. The Lord knows my heart and my determination by His grace to make His work the *first* thing.' And a few days later, the flippancy of some missionaries in southern Zhejiang, lacking spiritual life and power, drove him to say, 'These things almost break my heart . . . Blessed Jesus! . . . make *me* more like Thyself.'

In mid-March he was in Shanghai, feeling too ill to write, lying on his bed doing nothing, scarcely able to bear the separation any longer, grieving for Robert Landale over the death of his Mary, and for F F Gough, her widowed step-father. 'I feel as if my journeying days were almost over; the last journey tired me more than I have ever felt a journey do.' On April 2 he was almost at the end of his tether. Except for Jennie and China he would long to die, he said. 'Sometimes I feel the Lord will soon say Enough, and call me to the only true rest . . . Perhaps I may stay here to see the Seventy out and settled, and then return to England for good. Or, I may never return . . . I must get to Chefoo, I think, and see if I can brace up for a little more work . . . My heart feels ready to break.' Still at Shanghai four days later he wrote that he was still needed in China and she in Britain, so they must go on enduring. He was carrying on his work in spite of how he felt, and these were often asides in business letters to her. 'Cheer up and trust,' he wrote to John Stevenson, adding, 'myself far more'.

On the way to Chefoo he felt that he and she were very unlikely to meet again on earth. And safely there, 'You've got my heart so tight that I must gasp for breath on paper every now and then for sheer relief.' 'The very thought of six or eight months more of this separation seems overwhelming.' But Chefoo held 'a large and happy family' of missionaries, and soon he was buying the land between the 'beanfield' and the sea, and getting estimates for another building, a school for Eurasians and a 'medical college' (to train missionaries) under Douthwaite and others. Adam Dorward was a great cheer to him.

He picked up so well that he could not understand why Jennie's letters showed she was anxious about him. He had forgotten his depression when he replied, 'I have not been so well for years.'[49] Then he was off to Shanghai again with Parrott, his Corresponding Secretary, to meet 'many and serious difficulties'. 'Most friends are disappointed that at least a quarter of the Seventy are not in China already.' They went on up the Yangzi to Anqing, where he revealed that through these months of suffering he had been feasting on the *Song of Solomon*.

From June 24 when he arrived until July 1 when he and Parrott had to leave, all who could met daily from 7.00 to 9.00 each morning and evening to hear him expound the 'Song of Songs', and Mission principles. 'The Holy Spirit seemed to fill us this morning till several of us felt as if we could not bear any more . . . So long as God gives us such times as these, we will not be cast down, however great the difficulties and trials.' 'We were all melted by the contemplation of His love, and felt how great the dishonour done to Him by distrust in any of its forms.' 'If you want blessing, make room for it' – set aside counter claims and attractions; take the time. They spent the last day in fasting and prayer,[50] and they hugged each other goodbye. Those studies in the Song of Songs were published in the *Millions* and under the title *Union and Communion*, reprinted time and again.

Briefly feeling well again he went down to Ningbo and neighbouring cities. At last the temptation to follow Henry Taylor into lucrative secular employment was losing its attraction for some who should have been immune to it. 'There is such a lack of sustained spiritual power among us that one fears to be long away or far away from the field.' And yet in September the administrative failures in Britain led him to write, 'If God were not God indeed, the Mission would have been in ruin long ago.' Worse still, a whole packet of letters and documents fell (or were taken) from his own pocket in the road, and were never recovered. One of the Shanxi malcontents arrived in a deplorable spiritual state, making trouble. Another got married in Peking expecting to 'claim' costs afterwards, and Hudson Taylor feared he would never be able to get away from such entanglements. 'Shall I never get to Shansi?' – to deal with that festering wound – became a recurring theme.[51]

October came. 'I am getting old and feeble, and incapable of much work.' He was fifty but burning out. 'May God . . . help a weary, fast-failing old man – for if not in years, in constitution I am such.' Yet at Tianjin, Tong Xian, Peking and Baoding in November he was riding high and by invitation preaching in other missions' chapels. By the end of these four years in China he had covered 23,800 kilometres, reckoned by map and dividers. Equivalent to 15,000 miles, it was a gross underestimate in terms of actual travelling.

On January 6, 1883, he was in Yangzhou, tempted to pack up and go home, 'but I try not to give way to the tempter', and on the 17th a flimsy letter from Jennie almost broke his resolve. 'I feel as if my heart would break soon if I don't have *you* yourself. I was almost in a mind just to run off by today's P and O, leaving my foreign clothes at Chefoo, and papers and books . . . Though the tears will come into my eyes every few minutes, I do want to give myself, and you too, darling, for the life of the Chinese and of our fellow labourers . . . An easy-going non-self-denying life will never be one of *power* . . . Pray for me, my own heart's love, that neither my faith, nor my patience fail . . . I have been so pressed and wearied. The strain is very great.'[52] Without doubt it was time he went. Coulthard, Parrott, Douthwaite, Baller – younger men could manage in China while he tried to put things right in Britain.

At last another long-delayed transmission from London allowed him to sit up most of the night with Joe Coulthard despatching remittances. And on January 23 he cabled to say 'Coming'. More and more were afraid that he had gone too far over the Seventy. Didn't low income show it was folly to double the Mission in size? He answered, 'We can afford to be poor with so rich a Father.' A few days before he sailed from Yantai on February 6 to catch the French Mail at Hong Kong, he and some others asked God 'to set a seal on this matter', to lead one wealthy Christian 'to make room for a large blessing for himself and his family' by giving liberally towards the Seventy.[53]

On the French ship in the Saigon river he wrote, 'I am quite clear, thank God, that my love for you has not caused me to hurry home before His time.' His only fear was lest being with Jennie again should weaken their love for God.[54]

Big waves have deep troughs. Though he did not yet know it, he had set a tidal wave in motion. If he still needed encouragement, it was waiting for him at Aden – news that on February 2 an anonymous donor had contributed £3,000, to be thought of as well over £100,000 today. In 1884 it was followed by another £1,000 from the same family. God's seal had been set on the Seventy. Fifty years later it came to light that this donor was the publisher Robert Scott, of Morgan and Scott.[55]

Pause to take bearings *1878–85*

If great things had been happening for missions in China, there was plenty in the outer world to shake complacency. The climate of the day is relevant to the narrower events of Hudson Taylor's story. Queen Victoria might be declared Empress of India (to strong protests by Lord Shaftesbury, prophet of Justice), and the Transvaal be annexed to the British Empire, but it took more to satisfy the spirit of conquest. The year 1878 had seen war with Afghanistan and massacre in retaliation, and 1879 the abortive occupation of Kabul. The Zulu war in the same year, with the shock of defeat, the death of Prince Louis Napoleon, and the answering slaughter at Ulundi when 20,000 Zulus were mown down by modern firearms, were a costly price to pay. Clashes with the Boers had followed in 1881, the year the West trembled over the assassination of Tsar Alexander II by a grenade thrown by members of the Peoples' Will; and of President Garfield. Marx and Engels saw the Russian crisis as ushering in the Commune of their dreams. But Tsar Alexander III reacted energetically. Lenin was a schoolboy when his brother was executed. Britain defeated Egypt and occupied the Nile Valley and the Sudan. Although in 1883 the Mahdi overcame a British force, General Gordon was sent to Khartoum. (His journey to Peking had been in 1880.) Lord Wolseley led an expedition to support him, but it came too late. He was killed on January 26, 1885. The epic story of Gordon happened therefore to coincide with Hudson Taylor's departure from Yantai on February 6, 1883, until he was on his way back to China again. During his time in Britain (in fact, from 1880 to 1885) Parliament was taken up with the intractable Irish question, following the assassination of Lord Cavendish and Mr Burke at the Phoenix Park, Dublin, in 1882.

In East Asia comparable events were taking place. The empress dowager Ci An had died mysteriously on April 9, 1881, leaving Ci Xi, the invulnerable Yehonala (in Manchu, Yehe Nara) as the young emperor's sole regent. On March 25, 1882, France had occupied Hanoi, and in May Korea signed a treaty with the United States. Back in 1876 Japan had demanded direct dealings with Korea as an independent state. An anti-Japanese riot in July 1882 increased the tension. When the French Chamber approved the expense, on May 15, 1883, and France sent an expeditionary force to Tongking (North Vietnam today), Annam in the south accepted the French 'protectorate' after a decade of encroachment.

China had had enough. There was rioting at Canton on September 10, 1883. Houses on Shamian 'island', the foreign concession, were burned. But on December 16 France challenged China by taking the border town of 'Sontay' from its Chinese garrison. Throughout southern China attacks were made on foreign property. More than eighteen Protestant chapels were destroyed. Thousands of refugees flocked into Macao and Hong Kong. But trouble was not only in the south. In the south-western provinces and in Shaanxi and Shanxi placards threatened extermination and mandarins became hostile, especially to Catholics. For a fourth time Prince Kong was degraded and dismissed from office as foreign minister, this time for ten years. Instead, Li Hongzhang's star entered its ascendancy. But on July 12, 1884, after a French defeat, an ultimatum was delivered at Peking. In August French ships destroyed the Chinese fleet and docks at Fuzhou, and attacked the forts at Jilong on the northern coast of Taiwan, blockading Taiwan in October. Understandably Chinese turned upon all foreigners and Christians.[56] The Chinese strong man Yuan Shikai had become Resident at Seoul in the spring of 1883. On December 4, 1884, a coup d'état and riot at Seoul, followed the next day by a clash between Chinese and Japanese guards, showed the way the wind was blowing. Once more the Grand Secretary Li Hongzhang was called to the rescue. His Sino-Japanese convention on Korea, signed at Tianjin on April 18, 1885, only postponed war.

Missions in China had faced the usual considerable difficulties before the Franco-Chinese war erupted. The CMS in Fuzhou had lost five missionaries, three by death, leaving only a new arrival, John R Wolfe, to carry on there and at three or four cities with resident evangelists. In 1866 the first two baptisms had been recorded, but in *China's Millions* of January 1885, a page was devoted to celebrating, among other things, the 1884 report of this sister mission. Wolfe's policy of working through Chinese colleagues as far as possible had resulted after eighteen years in 5,414 believing adherents of whom 1,587 were communicants in 120 towns and villages. Seven Chinese clergy, of whom three had died, 107 catechists and about 100 lay workers served nine churches, seventy preaching chapels, a theological college, a medical mission and boarding schools. Yet at the height of this work Wolfe had only seven Western colleagues. Persecution and the martyrdom of one Christian had been the climate in which this growth had taken place. After the bishop W A Russell had died on October 5, 1879, his territorial diocese was divided at the 28th parallel. C P Scott of the SPG became Bishop in North China, and G E Moule in 'Mid-China'. Bishop Burdon of Hong Kong succeeded in persuading the CMS in 1882 to give China 'a much more prominent position' in its sympathies. And a gift of £72,000 (*sic*) came to the CMS for training and supporting nationals as evangelists in China and Japan.[57] At the annual meeting of the CMS in 1885, Canon Hoare declared, 'All England is ashamed . . .' that the government had failed to relieve Khartoum before Gordon was killed. The audience roared and cheered. Then Hoare went on, 'You did not let me finish my sentence. You sent my dear son to China; are you going to leave him alone there?'

The LMS page in the February *China's Millions* told of chapels filled to overflowing, but of few baptisms. Griffith John, however, reported a church membership at Wuhan and district of 777. The Amoy area, with twenty-two outstations, had 883 members and over 400 more adherents, while in the whole of China this society alone served 2,924 church members. Had Robert Morrison (Book 1, pp 112–228) foreseen even these results his joy would have known no bounds. Seventy-seven years after he arrived in China, they demonstrated the continuing difficulty but also the increasing tempo of success. A century later the count is in millions, devoid of denominational labels.

Already a decade of religious liberty in Japan had by 1883 allowed 145 missionaries to enter the country. An influx of 5,000 Japanese into the Protestant Church regrettably resulted in newspaper discussions of the possibility of Japan becoming a Christian country. Immediately a revival of Buddhism and the expenditure of vast sums on temples and colleges created an effective barrier to Christian advance.[58] The vigour of Japan in every sphere threw into contrast the comfortable lassitude of China, wearied by tens of centuries of ponderous progress. China seemed to want nothing but to be left to get on with her old ways. The pressure of expanding forces from West and East made that impossible. The scramble for colonies had begun. Li Hongzhang, Zhang Zhitong (Chang Chih-t'ung) – promoted from governor of Shanxi to viceroy of Guangdong and Guangxi and then of Hunan, Hubei and Anhui – and others recognised the need for reform and modernisation and did what they could. But with Ci Xi in power that could only be with extreme caution. If the powerful were hampered, what of the weak and alien?

Harold Schofield: a seed in the ground[59] *1880–83*

The arrival of Harold Schofield and his wife at Shanghai on June 30, 1880, opened a new era in the history of the CIM. Among the predominantly yeomen types making up the Mission were a handful or two of men and women from more educated and well-to-do backgrounds. John Stevenson and Arthur Douthwaite had set aside their professional training to go to China. Robert Landale, an Oxford MA, had been encouraged by his barrister father to go first as a 'traveller', to see for himself before sacrificing his prospects. Trench also moved cautiously at first. They had both done well and returned from home leave as full members of the Mission. Robert Landale had been 'impressed' by the quality of Hudson Taylor and the CIM and was a good companion for the Schofields on the voyage out. But Robert Harold Ainsworth Schofield was a new phenomenon.

He was twenty-nine and already widely experienced. For his wife he jotted down the scholarships he had been awarded.[60] Having qualified MA and BM, Oxon, both in December 1877, he went on to be elected FRCS England in May 1878. With his travelling scholarship he proceeded to Vienna and Prague for specialist studies, and on his return served as 'house-surgeon' for a year and 'house-physician' for six months at St Bartholomew's Hospital, London.

When war broke out between Turkey and Serbia, Schofield

offered his services to the Red Cross Society. He was given charge of a hospital at Belgrade for one month, and in a similar capacity for two months in the Turkish army during the war with Russia. On his return, he 'associated himself with the China Inland Mission', and faced the expected protests. Some of his best friends tried to dissuade him, 'on the plea that "there was so much need at home". How I wish [he wrote from China] that they and all who use this argument could just live here for a while, and see and feel the need for themselves; they would then be disposed to ask . . . whether they themselves had a special call to stay at home.' Again 'I cannot for a moment think that home is my sphere, especially as natural inclination is all on that side, as well as prospects of worldly advancement.' As a medical student three years before qualifying, he had read the life of Dr Elmslie of the CMS in Kashmir, and consecrated his life to God, to serve him abroad. Nothing deflected him from this resolve.

Hudson Taylor met them on arrival at Shanghai and found them 'pleasant but distant'. The shock of meeting him in Chinese clothes, described by many as 'unimpressive' on first acquaintance, was enough to account for that. He found he had to move carefully. They agreed first to go to Yantai for language study. He had arranged for them to live as paying guests with the Ballards of the Customs service – two miles from the English speaking CIM community of 'Chefoo'. They would take their time to decide about going into Chinese dress themselves. That would determine where they worked, he explained, for everyone in the CIM away from the treaty ports now regarded this as necessary.[61]

Back in January Hudson Taylor had replied to Benjamin's first letter about Schofield, 'If he be the *right* man he will be a treasure indeed . . . But has he faith in God? Is he willing to endure (and see his wife endure) the indispensable hardships of a pioneer worker?' He would be useful in Zhejiang in foreign clothes, but ten times as useful in Chinese clothes upcountry. But by January 20 he was putting it more strongly. Nearly every post suitable for a missionary in foreign dress was filled. The Schofields *must* be in full sympathy with the principles of the Mission. They satisfied the council that they were and, once settled at Yantai with opportunities for long conversations with Hudson Taylor, they clearly showed that they were with him heart and soul. Afterwards their correspondence revealed their spiritual maturity. 'The secret of it lay, I think,' his wife was to write, 'in a heart and life given up to God and His service, unclouded faith in God as Father and in Jesus as a Saviour from the *present* power of sin . . . He was in fullest sympathy with Mr Taylor's principles and work . . . in perfect confidence that God would supply, not only all spiritual, but every temporal need of the Mission.'[62]

For three or four months the Schofields worked hard at Chinese and fitted in well at Chefoo. They undertook to join Robert Landale in the Taiyuan team, and travelled third class on the coaster to Tianjin – but the captain insisted that they have their meals in the first class saloon. From arrival at Taiyuan late in November they made their mark, getting on well with Timothy Richard. Schofield developed his medical work carefully, at first reserving time for language study. He surprised the others by his progress, soon joining in street preaching. He even kept a diary written in Chinese character, and would sit for half an hour with his patients, talking about their families and farms. 'He had a large vocabulary which enabled him to speak without hesitation, and thus he made many (Chinese) friends.'[63]

In the first eighteen months he treated over three thousand patients and performed eighteen operations under chloroform. Tragically, Mary Landale died a week after the birth of her firstborn, and Robert had to take his child home to Britain, after helping the Oberlin missionaries look for a city to settle in. T J Pigott became a patient after tackling an intruder in the night and receiving 'a number of severe and dangerous wounds (from) a large carving knife'. Only the high collar of a Chinese jacket saved him from having his throat cut.

Harold Schofield wrote in February 1883 appealing to medically qualified men and women to come to China. 'There are already eight American ladies (doctors) . . . One American mission alone has five such ladies in the field.' In his second full year he had treated 6,631 patients including many cases of lacerations by wolves, and performed 292 operations, 47 under chloroform. But in July, 1883, a very ill man with virulent diphtheria was brought in. During the few hours before he died Schofield personally cared for him – and from infected body-lice himself contracted typhus. Timothy Richard heroically nursed and treated Schofield on the instructions he gave until he could no longer speak. He died on August 1, 1883, at the age of thirty-two.[64] The shock to the whole Mission and far beyond was intense. Why? Why he of all promising people? What great developments in China might he not have brought about? 'Tell Mr

Taylor and the Council . . . that these three years in China have been by far the happiest in my life,' he had said to his wife. Together they had been praying, she told Hudson Taylor, 'That God would open the hearts of the students at our Universities and Colleges to the needs of the Mission Fields of the world.' 'He longed and prayed so earnestly for the best men in all respects to be sent to China.' And Hudson Taylor added 'I have sometimes thought, that in those prayers the greatest work of Harold Schofield was accomplished, and that, having finished the work that God had given him to do, he was then called to his eternal reward.' His widow took their two children home. One was hardly ten weeks old. 'On the morning before he passed away,' she recalled, 'his face was so radiant with a brightness not of earth, and since then I have often thought those lines were a true description of him,

> "Jesus Himself, how clearly I can trace
> His living likeness on that dying face."

A short time after that he looked up, smiled, and said, "Heaven at last", and seemed as if he had recognised someone.' Some of the most influential lives have been brief, Henry Martyn, Samuel Dyer and Bishop Hannington of Uganda among them.

How Harold Schofield's prayers were answered is the continuing story. On the day Hudson Taylor received news of his death, he also received the first enquiry from a growing flood of men and women of that type. It came from Dixon Edward Hoste, Lieutenant, Royal Artillery, who was to succeed him eventually as General Director.

Medical plans for the CIM — *1880–1900*

The vast ocean of physical suffering that was China could not be relieved by a few doctors and amateurs doing their poor best with a few simple remedies. In the 1880s scientific medicine was still in its infancy. The best known treatment of typhus was aconite, quinine and 'cold packs to the torso'. Harold Schofield with his array of qualifications was a child of his times. An hour after examining the dying diphtheria patient he had told his wife 'at dinner', 'that diphtheria could produce typhus, and typhus diphtheria' (so she understood). In the report on his first year's work he had written of the Shanxi climate, 'even in the winter months the effect of the sun's rays is very powerful and it is unsafe to go out bare-headed'.[65] Preventive medicine was in its infancy. European medical colleges taught what they knew, and much besides but, as an editorial in the *British Medical Journal* (23 November 1985) (*sic*) began,

> A century ago in the United States scientific medicine scarcely existed . . . The foundation of the Johns Hopkins Medical School in 1889 . . . led to a scientific revolution in medical academic circles that was to establish the United States as the world leader in biomedical science in the modern era.

Medical schools still taught the accumulated practical experience of centuries, surgical, obstetric and medicinal. Much of it could be conveyed to students in a short time. In 1887 Hudson Taylor had considered travelling via the States to find a short medical course for suitable missionaries, and with the London Council decided to help them financially to obtain a recognised qualification. In 1883 James Cameron, his arduous travelling days over, crossed from Britain to New York and less than a year later was listed, in September 1884, as James Cameron MD (USA). On his return to China he became superintendent of the mission in Shandong and worked as a doctor at Chefoo. A W Douthwaite also completed his medical course, at Vanderbilt University, Nebraska, cramming the work of three years into one year, to qualify MD (USA) in nine months. Cameron then married the widow of a Shanxi missionary named Rendall, who had died at Taiyuan after only two years in China, and practised medicine at Chongqing until he himself died on August 14, 1891. Horace Randle also became MD (USA), and Frank Trench began the study of medicine at Edinburgh in 1884, followed by George King.

Well before then, the long years of being the only available doctor in the mission ended for Hudson Taylor with the arrival in China of W L Pruen, LRCP, LRCS (Edinburgh) in January 1880, and Harold Schofield in June. Henry Edwards and William Wilson (Elizabeth Wilson's nephew) arrived together in October 1882. Edwards reached Chongqing on his way to Yunnan, but was recalled to replace Schofield at Taiyuan, and Wilson after failing to gain a footing in Xi'an by medical means set up a hospital at Hanzhong.

William Wilson earned notoriety during his eleven years (1884–95) at Hanzhong by his skilled use of local cotton products for surgical dressings, and of Chinese chemicals by refining and transmuting them. He distilled local spirits to obtain alcohol, and made extracts of botanical drugs. He also converted the zinc linings of packing cases into zinc oxide.[66] After a period at Chefoo, Pruen succeeded Cameron at Chongqing and then pioneered the medical work at Chengdu and Guiyang, while the Chengdu hospital work was taken over by Canadian missions. Two of the Seventy, Wilson and Edwards were followed in November 1884 by a third doctor, Herbert Parry, first of another family to become pillars of the Mission. Most members therefore were within a few hundred miles of medical aid, and Hudson Taylor still helped when he could.

Dr John Kenneth Mackenzie of the LMS here comes into the CIM's orbit as a close friend. Because of his wife's ill-health, he took her from Wuhan (where he had spent four years with Thomas Bryson after reaching China in 1875) and began again at Tianjin. There his medical reputation became known to the great Li Hongzhang. At the annual meetings of the CIM on May 31, 1883, both Bryson and Mackenzie gave major addresses. 'One day there came a courier,' Mackenzie said, 'calling us to go up to the palace of the Viceroy whose wife was at the point of death. The native physicians had said there was no hope . . . Gradually she became better, God blessing the means for her recovery . . . One day the Viceroy said to us, "I believe that Western medicine and surgery can achieve what Chinese cannot. There is a temple there; you can have it for a dispensary." '[67]

The temple was 'close to the busiest and best part of the city,' Mackenzie had told Cameron and Pigott in 1879. The Viceroy handed him a generous amount of silver 'and promised to bear all expenses and pay for all medicines . . . A great wall of opposition seemed broken down . . . The dispensary was crowded with patients daily (and) numbers of the highest classes, from Li's own family downwards, came to be treated . . . He thus is enabled frequently to set the Gospel before them, and to remove many mistaken ideas (about the mysterious foreigner) from their minds.'

With funds contributed by Li and other Chinese, a hospital was built in 1880, and Mackenzie began a medical school, training doctors for government service. The importance of this man to the future of relations between China and the West, as well as missions in general, could hardly be exaggerated. When Mackenzie had to take his wife home to Britain, Hudson Taylor offered him the hospitality of the Mission at Pyrland Road and wrote to Jennie on December 5, 1882, 'Dr Mackenzie is one of the *best* and most important men in China. Take him in, if he comes, at almost any cost.' But Mackenzie died in 1888 and official support was withdrawn from the hospital.

On August 6, 1880, when Hudson Taylor was travelling slowly by boat towards Qü Xian near the Zhejiang–Jiangxi border, he outlined to Theodore Howard the plans he intended to discuss with Douthwaite, the medical student. 'Something as follows:' included a central hospital in which to give doctors experience and to train others in basic medicine; an attached opium refuge for addicts, for training missionaries to treat them; an opium refuge in each inland station, at which a range of medicines would be stocked for sale to the public with instructions in their use; and trained Chinese medical assistants with evangelists at each out-station – a rural health service. Initially it would cost £2,500 (at current values) rising to £4,000 for premises and stock. Douthwaite moved to Wenzhou for two years and treated more than four thousand patients in his first year, and then to Chefoo in April 1882, to recover from bronchitis.[68] This was his niche. Ideal as the leader of the community and popular as the doctor, especially after returning from the States with his MD, he established a hospital and a 'fever (isolation) hospital' (in memory of his wife when she died of 'typho-malarial fever') and began teaching. When Korea became open to missionaries by the treaty of 1883 he reconnoitred there in the winter of 1883–84, in response to an invitation from Sir Harry Parkes and at the request of Alexander Williamson of the Bible Society of Scotland. Hard on his heels came the first missionaries of the American Presbyterian Mission (North) and Methodist Episcopal Church, in 1884.[69] The evidence strongly suggests that Dr Douthwaite was the first to enter Korea at this time.

Hudson Taylor also discussed his plan with Harold Schofield, for him to consult Mackenzie on his way through Tianjin. Mackenzie made Schofield thoroughly at home and impressed him with the wisdom of how he ran his dispensary in the temple and had built his new hospital. Both were thoroughly Chinese, with brick *kangs* in place of beds. But after a débâcle in Peking in which medical assistants with medicines for sale had feathered their own nests, he 'disapproved in *very* strong terms of that aspect of the plan'. The temptation it created was too great.[70]

Within twenty years, when there were 120 medical missionaries of all societies in China (of whom 61 men and 2 women were British and the rest American and German) the CIM had 14 fully qualified doctors in seven hospitals with oversight of sixteen branch dispensaries and numerous opium refuges.

CHAPTER TEN

A WAVE OF POPULARITY 1883–85

The rising tide in Britain *1883*

When the Marseilles boat train steamed into the Gare de Lyon, Jennie was on the platform to meet Hudson Taylor. The pain of anticipation had felt almost intolerable. Their reunion was beyond words, though they had so much to say. In the cab, trotting through the Paris streets to their favourite hotel, they held hands in silence.

He had reached Marseilles on March 17, 1883, and gone straight to the Bergers at Cannes for the weekend. William Berger had written, 'Kindly let me know more about the CIM and its needs – new missionaries – claims in China – if danger from the present state of France and China.' And later, when sending a cheque for £500, 'My heart is still in the glorious work.' 'Most heartily do I unite in praying for the seventy more workers! But I do not stop at seventy. Surely we shall see greater things than these.' He saw himself as still part of the Mission, more than a supporter, when he wrote, 'And if legitimate and great need should arise I would do more. Keep me *au courant*, SVP.' He had come far from advising caution and consolidation of existing work in China, as he did in 1875.[1]

After eighteen months apart (October 13, 1881–March 23, 1883) the Taylors had only the weekend to themselves. But it could not be all holiday. He needed to be briefed on the state of things in Britain. After the administrative hitches there was a great deal to put right. A note from Benjamin welcomed him with, 'I have no more cherished desire than to help you and to do so to your own satisfaction; if I cannot do this I would rather retire. I have had respect and favour both in the Mission and outside altogether beyond anything I could have expected, and far exceeding anything I have deserved, for I have fallen sadly short of satisfying myself.' Now Jennie could explain. All the staff in London had been stretched to their limit. Anxious friends of the Mission had questioned the wisdom of appealing for seventy more members when funds were barely enough for current expenses, and it had not been easy to answer them. With full steam ahead a ship must expect a bow wave. But at last the 'folly' was vindicated. The April issue of *China's Millions* was in print, announcing the stupendous gift of £3,000. Ample funds could at once be remitted to Coulthard.

Crossing the Channel and reaching London on March 27, Hudson Taylor was delighted with what he found. He had been away four long years. His son Howard had become a young man of twenty and Maria sixteen. Two of Benjamin's and Amelia's family were over twenty and three others over sixteen, maturely in sympathy with the Mission. Maria Taylor and Gertrude and Hudson Broomhall were hoping to be among the Seventy. Others hoped to follow later. But better still, on arrival he noticed 'the new position accorded to the Mission in the esteem of the Christian public'. The half had not been told him. The incessant journeys and industry of the pioneers had caught their imagination. In 1883 twenty more of the Seventy were to be sent, and applicants to go in 1884 were multiplying. 'The eight years of Mr Broomhall's unwearied labours had told especially in the direction which was his forte – that of inspiring confidence and making friends.' It resulted in accumulating invitations to address meetings or to send representatives of the Mission.

Meeting his own old friends, Hudson Taylor was even more encouraged. He came across Lord Radstock at Mildmay and spent an evening with him at Portland Place. He had no truer friend, not even the ageing William Berger, John Eliot Howard or George Müller. 'I pray at least once a day for CIM,' Lord Radstock wrote. 'You are a great help to us . . . by strengthening our faith.'[2] Hudson Taylor spoke at one of Spurgeon's meetings, convened the council twice, spent an afternoon with James Cameron whom he respected so highly, met the Bible Society secretaries one day and attended their committee a few days later, and spoke at Annie Macpherson's Home of Industry where he declared, 'There are three truths, 1st, That there is a God; 2nd, That He has spoken to us in the Bible; 3rd, That He means what He says. Oh, the joy of trusting Him!' In his June editorial in the *Millions* he went on 'The missionary who realises these truths . . . knows that he has solid rock under his feet whatever may be his circumstances.'

Then an evening with the Grattan Guinnesses at Harley House, at Tottenham with the Howards, and at a farewell for George Nicoll (returning to China in restored health), and Marcus Wood, a strong new member with his eye on Guangxi. Hudson Taylor preached for the Open Air Mission, addressed the annual meeting of the Anti-Opium Society, agreed to address the Rev John J Luce's conference at Gloucester, and attended May meetings of the Salvation Army, the LMS, the Bible Society, the Evangelical Alliance, an Anti-Vice organisation, the Religious Tract Society, the YMCA, and on May 31 the CIM's own annual meetings. Apart from these he spent an afternoon at the Earl of Shaftesbury's home at 24 Grosvenor Square, met George Müller who was to speak for the CIM, and stayed a night at the home of Mr Stoughton the publisher, a generous donor, and on another occasion with Mr Hodder. So it continued, month after month, superimposed upon routine Mission business and the interviewing and sifting of candidates. Benjamin's life was as full. But still the demands piled higher so that in June Amelia offered her brother a bedroom and study in one of the houses she owned in Pyrland Road, as an escape from interruptions.

All the temptations and sufferings of the past year could at last be seen at their true value. In a twentieth-century translation 'Every branch that does bear fruit He trims clean so that it will be even more fruitful.'[3] The 'man of God' must expect the pain of the pruning knife. The presence of the Holy Spirit at the Wuhan and Anqing conferences before he left China had thrilled those present with the joy of the Lord, so that Hudson Taylor could write to Jennie before leaving China, 'I too have done more (I think) for our people here this year than in any former one.' A change of location must not lower their standards. 'May God bless our meeting (each other) and ever keep JESUS first. I feel almost afraid . . . I want *you* so, and *He* has been so near to me during your absence.' And again from the ship, 'I feel almost afraid, darling, lest I should have less of the manifestation of His presence, which has been so real and vivid in your absence.'[4]

He need not have feared. He was 'filled with the Holy Spirit' as he travelled round Britain. When he spoke at the Gloucester Convention and afterwards in an adjoining room with twelve individuals, John Luce, the convener, recalled,

> I can never forget the overwhelming power of that little meeting in my own soul. I was so moved that I had to ask Mr Taylor to stop; my heart was broken, and I felt, as never before, that I had as yet given up nothing for my Lord. . . . Three (of the twelve) went to China as a result. [And again,] It was the influence of the man on one's soul – the character on my life.[5]

From Gloucester he travelled to his friends in Bath and Bristol, where he interviewed candidates and preached twice. Then to

Cheltenham for two meetings in the Corn Exchange, and back to London to speak at the Eccleston Hall near Victoria and the YMCA in Aldersgate Street. Going straight on to Southampton, to a private conference of Canon Wilberforce, Lord Radstock and their friends, only to be asked to return for a week of public conference in August, he returned to address the Mildmay Conference, June 27–30. July saw him back at Gloucester, at Bishop's Stortford, at the Keswick Convention, at Kendal and Rochdale. For ten days or so he dealt with mail and interviews in London, meeting Dixon Hoste for the first time, and then off again. Through the past twenty or more years of his friendship with Lord Radstock and his relatives the Beauchamps and the Hon Miss Waldegrave, he had known the Hon Granville Waldegrave, Lord Radstock's eldest son, as a child and growing schoolboy. Since then Granville had been a pillar of the Christian Union at Cambridge and a strong influence on Montagu Beauchamp and others soon to enter this saga.

Granville introduced Hudson Taylor to Lord and Lady Tankerville, who invited him to Chillingham Castle, Northumberland, in mid-August, to speak at a drawing-room meeting for neighbours and to preach in the parish church. And Granville was there when the news arrived of Harold Schofield's death and 'a violent sick-headache' laid Hudson Taylor out on Sunday morning.[6] 'We feel sure that there is *much* love (from God) in it,' Hudson Taylor observed prophetically, not yet knowing of Schofield's prayers, 'and somehow or other much blessing to follow.' Then back to London with Granville, via Cliff House, the Grattan Guinness family home. There he gave an address on 'Unfailing springs of the water of Life' (Isaiah 58.11; Rev. 22.17) through which Geraldine Guinness 'received her call' to China. And on to Southampton for the general conference 'for the deepening of spiritual life'. In the last week of the month he 'farewelled' three groups of the Seventy leaving for China, and another group of three a fortnight later.

September was as full of meetings and conferences, while his whole family had the run of the Radstocks' Richmond home for a month while they were away. He met the committee of the Society of Friends on September 6 and helped them to send their first representatives to China, under the wing of the CIM; and went up to Scotland to address conferences at Perth and Dundee. John Stevenson arrived with Henry Soltau on September 15 from Burma and rejoined his family in Scotland after almost eight years of isolation from them and from the rest of the CIM. His coming was most timely.

Returning through Edinburgh and Leicester, Hudson Taylor was joined by Thomas Barnardo for a private conference in Salisbury, in the home of Canon E N Thwaites of Fisherton, who had been at the Gloucester Conference. Leading Christians were asking Hudson Taylor to expound Scripture to them. Yet it was not so much what he said as the presence of God in the meetings that drew them.[7]

Mrs Thwaites had been going through a period of 'great (spiritual) darkness', her faith imperilled by her own rebellion against God. 'What most appealed to me,' she admitted, 'was intellectual power and enthusiasm in (parish) work.' As Hudson Taylor spoke, a deep sense of calm came over her – 'a fresh revelation of God coming down and meeting human need,' was how she put it. 'I began to yield myself to God.' Her drawing-room was packed at one meeting, 'and the power of the Holy Ghost was so intense.' As a result of this two-day conference fifteen or sixteen offered themselves to God, to serve him abroad. Rosa Minchin was a fifty-two year-old, accepted to run the Chefoo sanatorium. She was to die within eight months of reaching China. Emily Whitchurch of Downton was bludgeoned to death in the Boxer Rising of 1900. Some, when confronted with Jesus who 'emptied Himself and became of no reputation' for their sake, gave up jewellery, symbols of their self-centredness. John Luce was present and wrote that 'People felt they had received so much . . . (they) would give anything'. 'Rings, chains, two watches and a whole jewellery case (were) sent afterwards.' Yet it was not oratory or about the CIM, but with 'beautiful, gentle, loving simplicity' that Hudson Taylor spoke, 'always bringing us to God first', before talking about China or anything else – 'always so glad to say a good word for others, for other missions and Christian enterprises'.[8]

In October he had meetings to address on most days, in and around London, in Norwich and at a conference at Leicester where the convener F B Meyer was as hungry for God as were his congregation. From November 14 until December 18 Hudson Taylor was away in the north, sometimes 'tired out'. But William Sharp, the new solicitor member of the London Council, was more anxious lest Benjamin's health should break under the strain of his overwork. As executive secretary 'BB' was handling Mission correspondence about the council's affairs, all business with scores of candidates until and after meeting the council, outfitting them and arranging the farewell meetings and the departure of old and new missionaries, and producing the monthly *Millions*. All the staff were stretched to the limit by the Mission's growing popularity. Sharp was to say of Hudson Taylor,

> His restful spirit and simplicity of faith were all-inspiring; his entrance into any assembly was to make those present conscious of a peculiar atmosphere of spiritual power.
>
> When in Council, with some difficult subject . . . to which our united wisdom brought no apparent way out, he would . . . call us to go on our knees, confessing to God our inability and want of understanding, and asking Him in the fewest and simplest of words to show us His will. Thus the expression of his habitual intimacy with God became a wonderful experience in one's *own* life.[9]

On his tour of the north Hudson Taylor went first by night train to St Boswells, Roxburgh, just over the Scottish border, as guest of Lord Polwarth. There he found William Hoste, 'the one who was at Cambridge, not the soldier', engaged as tutor to the family. 'I should not wonder if he should not go to China too. His youngest brother also desires to be a missionary.' Lord Lichfield's son was in the party. God was bringing the claims of China before a new stratum of society, and using Hudson Taylor to influence them.

He was staying with Dr Halley of Edinburgh, 'very active among students', when word came of the death of John Eliot Howard, FRS, Hudson Taylor's intimate friend and supporter since 1850. 'The shock made me feel quite ill' from Friday until Sunday, he wrote. The Howards wanted Hudson Taylor to conduct the funeral at Tottenham, but although he telegraphed to Dr Andrew Bonar in Glasgow, it was too short notice for him to be released from the many meetings arranged. So he was spared what would have been an ordeal. Benjamin wrote after the funeral of 'an immense concourse . . . between one and two thousand. Among them W Fowler MP for Cambridge and R N Fowler, the present Lord Mayor of London'.[10]

In view of the phenomenal turn in events soon to take place at Edinburgh, it is interesting to notice that during his ten days there, Hudson Taylor preached four Sunday sermons and spoke at two meetings for students, three times for the YMCA and once at the annual meeting of the Edinburgh Medical Missionary Society, preparing the ground for the most memorable meetings among students yet known in Scotland. At Glasgow, too, he and John

McCarthy had students' meetings, and interviewed several 'promising men'. Two joined the CIM as a result.

It was the same at Aberdeen – too many meetings and sermons for his own good, but insatiable audiences in the United Presbyterian Church of Scotland and the Free Church, YMCA and college circles, and at Montrose, Dundee, and Dumfries. The very simplicity of his style and subjects made him intelligible to anyone who listened. What they heard they recognised as old truths suddenly become alive and relevant to them as individuals. Or new to them in every way as God's message, demanding a response. Or more profound than rhetoric could make it. Laymen and 'divines', students and professors heard the voice of God and were hungry to hear more. They responded by repentance and deep dedication of their lives and substance.

He was also writing a long article on the Opium Trade, and speaking here and there for the Anti-Opium Society, whom McCarthy thought to be under the influence of opiates! He found time to visit Adam Dorward's mother at Galashiels. Unknown to them, Adam was at that time being driven out of Hongjiang after five months' 'occupation', and the French were driving the Chinese garrison out of Sontay. After Dumfries and Carlisle, back to London for a council meeting as soon as he arrived. To every host and hostess he sent a bound and gilt-embossed annual volume of *China's Millions*. Then away again to Weston-super-Mare. The Earl of Cavan, a friend for many years, had invited him to stay, but as his place was some distance out of town Hudson Taylor simply went for lunch. On the same evening he visited Augustus Margary's mother. The year ended with the customary 'day of prayer' – and a letter from the Leeds philanthropist Robert Arthington inviting Hudson Taylor to visit him.

During 1883 twenty more of the Seventy had sailed to China, leaving forty-two to follow in 1884 if the full number were to go within the arbitrary three years.[11] Then 'about the end of 1883' a Cambridge graduate named Stanley Smith, eldest son of a Mayfair surgeon, Henry Smith, FRCS, of John Street, Berkeley Square, wrote to the CIM, and on January 4, 1884, arrived at Pyrland Road for an interview with Hudson Taylor. A friend of William Hoste, of Granville Waldegrave and of Montagu Beauchamp, Stanley Smith was the next link in a remarkable chain being forged for China and the CIM.[12] John R Mott was to call it 'the germ of a world movement.'

D L Moody and the 'Cambridge Band' *1867–82*

The seven men who came to be known as the 'Cambridge Band' and later as the 'Cambridge Seven' in fact included one, Dixon Hoste, who had not been to Cambridge but to the Royal Military Academy, Woolwich, and was a lieutenant, Royal Artillery. Cecil Polhill-Turner of the same rank in the 2nd Dragoon Guards, the Queen's Bays, had been for a year or more at Jesus College when he was commissioned first to the Bedfordshire Yeomanry in 1880 and then to the Queen's Bays in 1881. The Royal Dragoons were the resplendent heavy cavalry seen in glittering cuirasses in royal processions and the 'changing of the guard'.[13] Only in 1884–85 did the seven men gradually come together through their links with the CIM. Before that some had been acquainted through mutual friends or relatives. Each was outstanding in his own way, and individually two or three had already become famous as sportsmen in 'a generation which set much store on social position and athletic ability in an aristocratic age', as John Pollock put it.[14] If the attention paid to them appears excessive today, it was not in 1885. Only a full account can do justice to the spirit of the time. Giving up wealth and prospects to become missionaries, and doing so all together, to bury themselves in China with the little known CIM, was highly sensational. Not until February 1885, on the eve of departure, did all seven combine to be 'farewelled' and to travel together; but by then, in groups of two, three or four, they had taken the country by storm.

Their story is as much the story of the American evangelist D L Moody as of themselves or the CIM. They were only children when he first came to Britain in 1867. The eldest by three months was W W Cassels (born on March 11, 1858) and the youngest, Arthur Polhill-Turner (February 7, 1863). In 1872 Hudson Taylor had shared the platform at Mildmay with Moody before he was well known in Britain. But in 1875 when Moody filled the Agricultural Hall in North London with 15,000 seated, and Gladstone (shown to his seat by Eugene Stock) said, 'I thank God I have lived to see the day', any or all of the Seven could have been present.[15] Moody's mission to Cambridge in 1882 (November 5–12) and following it in the Dome at Brighton, netted some remarkable fish for the future of missions to the world, among them some of the seven. When he returned for eight months in London in 1883–84, many of his most valuable assistants were the maturing converts of his earlier visits.

Up and down the country where Moody had prepared the ground by making new and older Christians hungry to learn more and to know how to serve God, preaching by members of the CIM and by the evolving 'seven' met with enthusiastic response. Hudson Taylor, filled with spiritual power since God's pruning knife had done its work on him in 1882; John Stevenson, John McCarthy and Robert Landale, each refined and brought closer to Christ by sickness or bereavement or other distress in their families, were making a strong if quiet impression.

Stanley Smith, before any formal connection with the CIM, was rousing audiences by infectious devotion to Christ expressed through a remarkable gift of oratory. He had been a practising Christian since 1874. At Repton, his public school, Granville Waldegrave had shepherded him along. And Granville's cousin Montagu Beauchamp, a year older than Stanley, had become his good friend. Then a serious illness had removed Stanley Smith from school for a year before he went up to Cambridge, to rejoin them in 1879. Stanley's father, the godly London surgeon, and Montagu's ultra-Christian home circle gave them more than Repton in common, the inestimable heritage of a childhood steeped in devotion to Christ. They attended meetings of the fledgling Cambridge Inter-Collegiate Christian Union and helped with meetings for slum children. Both Montagu and Stanley joined the Trinity College rowing club.

Granville had been at St Petersburg with his father for an evangelistic mission among the aristocracy of Russia. When he came back in April 1880 he lost no time in facing Stanley with the need to be more than a dutiful but half-hearted Christian. It touched the right 'nerve'. It was all he needed to bring him back to true dedication. He threw himself into evangelism in Mile End, Stepney and other parts of London, and among soldiers at Aldershot. But others could do that. He saw a greater need far overseas and wanted to go, but vaguely, not knowing where.

One of Stanley Smith's friends at Trinity was William Hoste, from Clifton College, Bristol, a Christian and also a rowing man. Yet another oarsman, better at rugby and 'association' football but unfortunate to miss his 'blue'[16] by breaking a leg, was William Cassels – 'William the Silent', two years ahead of Smith and Beauchamp at Repton and therefore less in touch with them. He took his degree in 1880 and was reading for Anglican ordination when a closer friendship with Stanley Smith developed. Also at

Trinity were two Etonians, George 'G B' and Charles 'C T' Studd, joined by their elder brother Kynaston 'J E K' when he came up to university after having first gone from Eton into business.

By the autumn of 1881 Stanley Smith was captain of his college boats, and both he and Montagu Beauchamp rowed in the university trial eights. On a holiday in Normandy with Lady Beauchamp, her family[17] and the young Waldegraves, 'SPS' had the disappointment of not being chosen for the 'varsity boat when 'Monty' was selected. Yet back again in England Stanley was called, and in the Lent term confirmed as stroke oar, winning his blue, when Montagu was dropped. He set out to win all his crew for Christ, as C T Studd was to attempt for the all-England cricket team. Smith took his degree in 1882 and while he thought about his future and filled in time before starting to teach in the autumn, he went as a holiday tutor to the younger brother of a college friend, the Burroughes of Burlingham Hall in Norfolk, cousins of the Hostes. There he met an elderly gentleman who on a second visit showed him the difference between living as an average Christian and living altogether possessed, set free from the domination of personal sin and used by the Holy Spirit of God. He learned to take at face value and to act on the truth, 'He died for all, that those who live should live no longer for themselves but for Him who died for them and rose again', and 'Present your bodies a living sacrifice, holy, acceptable unto God'. From then on, this attractive, athletic, handsome young gentleman possessed not only oratory but power to preach and testify for Christ. He stood in the market places and at Speakers Corner in Hyde Park, well able to hold his audience of 'curious gentry and casual strollers'.

The Studd brothers[18] were unique, not in their luxurious upbringing but in sport and in their outspokenness as Christians. Their father, Edward Studd, a retired jute planter, owned the palatial Tedworth (now Tidworth) House in Wiltshire, kept a stable of about twenty horses and his own race-course, won the Grand National with Salamander, was Master of Hounds, laid out his own first-quality cricket ground, in the days when country-house cricket was at its height, and had his world at his feet. Then Moody and Sankey came in 1875 – Sankey to sell organs and Moody to sell hymn books, the cynics said. The papers so abused them that Edward Studd went to see for himself, and came home 'a new man in the same skin'. 'But it did make one's hair stand on end,' his son C T declared. 'Everyone in the house had a dog's life of it until they

TEDWORTH HOUSE – AND STUDD'S CHOICE

were converted.' The three brothers were at Eton, and all three in the cricket XI when they beat both Winchester and Harrow. But the 'dog's life' ended in the thoroughgoing conversion of each boy on one summer's day at home. A visitor took their 'cruel practical joke' against him so well as to earn their respect and a hearing when he talked with each of them on the quiet about the meaning of Christ's death for them. For such leading athletes to begin a Bible study class at Eton could not fail to influence others.

George and Charles went up to Cambridge, 'C T' an 1879 freshman with Stanley Smith, Montagu Beauchamp and William Hoste. 'C T' at once won his cricket blue and went on to play for the university for four years. George captained the XI in 1882, 'C T' in 1883 and Kynaston in 1884, an unbroken family record. In 1882 'C T', in his third year and aged twenty-one, attained national fame when Cambridge 'defeated the unbeaten Australians', and in August played for England in the historic match that created 'The Ashes'.[19] His all-round brilliance ensured his going to Australia to win back The Ashes in 'one long blaze of cricketing glory'. The name of C T Studd was on everybody's lips. But while Kynaston was unashamedly a Christian, working to show other men the way to Christ, 'C T' although idolised and influential went little further than inviting them to meetings, a 'proper' Christian but by his own admission 'no obedience, no sacrifice'.

Moody for town, gown and army *1882–83*

Kynaston Studd as an older man dropped naturally into the role of university cricketer and leader of the Christian Union. In February 1882 he organised and sent to D L Moody in Scotland an invitation signed by undergraduates, clergymen and dons[20] (including Handley Moule, Principal of Ridley Hall) to conduct a mission to the townsfolk and students of the university. Moody accepted for November 5–12, eight days beginning on a Sunday which happened to be Guy Fawkes Day ('of gunpowder, treason and plot'), celebrated by fireworks and high spirits. 'There never was a place,' said Moody, 'that I approached with greater anxiety than Cambridge.' When 'J E K' later met and heard this broad American of rough un-English speech and manners his heart sank. What fiasco or disaster were they in for? A marked man, he had already personally signed an invitation to every one of the 3,500 undergraduates.

Seventeen hundred undergraduates were counted entering the

great Corn Exchange, 'laughing and talking and rushing for seats'. Some started building a pyramid of chairs. A firework exploded against a window, outside. Dons and clergy led Moody and Sankey on to the platform to a chorus of 'hoots and cheers'. Sankey's sacred songs were greeted with cries of 'encore!' after each verse. Moody started speaking about Daniel and was heckled with shouts of 'Dan'l, Dan'l!' from the rowdies. He kept his temper and his bluff humour. The majority were listening. At the end he asked any who wished to pray to stay behind – and four hundred stayed.

The following morning, Gerald Lander of Trinity, the leader of the uproar, arrived at Moody's hotel with an apology signed by his fellow-culprits. On the Wednesday night in a full gymnasium hall Moody said, 'I feel sure many of you are ready and yearning to know Christ.' And he asked them to climb the central iron staircase 'in full view of all' to the fencing-gallery where he and Sankey would talk with them. Fifty-two went up, among them Gerald Lander. On Thursday night when thirty more climbed that staircase, one who should have joined them crept away to count the awful cost of burning his bridges if he did turn to Christ unconditionally. Arthur Polhill-Turner had not been one of the pyramid builders and hecklers, but felt 'secure in his destiny as a clergyman', the comfortable profession for which he was training at Trinity Hall. At that Thursday meeting and on Friday and Saturday Moody's denunciations of sin, 'always balanced by the wonderful love of God' broke his rebellion.

Back in the Corn Exchange on the final day, the 12th, D L Moody faced nearly two thousand university men without a 'shadow of opposition, interruption or inattention'. The lives of too many men of the fast set, the pubs and racetracks, had been changed before their eyes in college after college. When he asked all 'who had received blessing' during the week to stand, two hundred rose to their feet, Arthur Polhill-Turner among them.

Cecil and Arthur Polhill-Turner were the second and third sons of the late Captain F C Polhill, formerly of the 6th Dragoon Guards, Member of Parliament for Bedford, a Justice of the Peace and High Sheriff for the county in 1875. With a wife who was a Barron, three sons and three daughters and all he could desire, life for Captain Polhill and the family at Howbury Hall had been carefree, until Alice his eldest girl exchanged nominal Christianity for true faith in Christ and became 'the talk of the hunting field'. He died in 1881 at only fifty-five.[21]

Cecil had joined his new regiment in Ireland, but was on leave, hunting and shooting, when Arthur arrived home from Cambridge. To Cecil's alarm his brother talked 'of going to preach in China'! What madness was this? How Arthur had come to the idea is not clear; perhaps through Montagu Beauchamp or William Hoste to whom Montagu had lent copies of *China's Spiritual Need and Claims*. Since Moody's mission 'the old life of theatres, dancing, racing and cards' had given place to friendship with maturer Christians, with Kynaston Studd, Beauchamp (no longer half-hearted) and others whose passion in life was becoming 'the gospel to the world'. Of the Seven, Arthur's remark to Cecil in the winter of 1882 appears to have been the first mention of China. Cecil had to admit to himself that Arthur's experience was the genuine article, 'I knew he was right.' His regiment moved to Aldershot, and he went with Arthur to two of Moody's meetings in London. But all through 1883 he knew that becoming a Christian would alienate him from his fellow-officers and perhaps cut short his intense enjoyment of life in the cavalry with its immaculate drill, its polo and camaraderie.

William Hoste's position was strangely similar to Arthur Polhill-Turner's. After the Cambridge Mission, D L Moody had gone on to Oxford and then to Brighton. When the Cambridge term ended and William Hoste returned home to Brighton, his brother Dixon was there on leave from his battery at Sandown Fort in the Isle of Wight. The Hostes were a Norfolk family, staunchly Protestant since the early Reformation. Jaques Hooste was sheriff of Bruges in Flanders in 1345, as were six of his family successively during the next seventy years. But persecution drove many of the Dutch nobility to England. A Hooste relative, a girl of eighteen, was burned at the stake. So a later Jaques Hooste moved to England in 1569, was naturalised and granted wings to his coat of arms and crest in recognition of his flight. By 1675 the family were settled in Norfolk. Around 1686 James Hoste, Member of Parliament, bought the Sandringham estate, and it remained their home until 1834. His brother's son, a sporting parson more in the saddle and in debt than in the pulpit, had two sons, among other progeny. William attained the rank of captain, Royal Navy, under Nelson, and for gallantry and a famous victory off Lyssa in the defence of Portugal in the Peninsular War was honoured with a baronetcy. George his brother, a colonel in the Royal Engineers and later knighted for his part at Waterloo in 1815, became Gentleman Usher to Queen Victoria, and in time the grandfather of William and Dixon Edward Hoste. Their father was

Major-General Dixon Edward Hoste CB, Royal Artillery, living at Brighton since retiring in 1881.[22]

Uncompromising Christians, the general and his wife had brought up their family of four daughters and six sons with the Bible 'almost from end to end implanted on the mind for life', and to remember the needs of missions, especially the CMS. The family were neatly arranged in two symmetrical groups of five, three boys with 'a sister at the head and another at the tail of each group', Dixon liked to recall. He was the second son, in the middle of the first set. But his personal Christianity was no more than head knowledge and the public school churchmanship instilled at Clifton College. For three years in his regiment he shrugged off all but garrison religion in any form, although he knew at heart that the Bible was true and he was wrong. The price of being a Christian was more than he was prepared to pay. His goal was progressive promotion for dedicated efficiency as a soldier.

So when he found his family attending the Moody mission near his home, he declined his mother's invitation to accompany her and settled down for the evening. But William, straight from the Cambridge and Oxford missions, said 'Come on, Dick! Put on your wraps and go with me!' Despite himself, Dixon went, and to his surprise met with God. First, Moody *talked* to God, as if He were there, a friend. Then Moody warned his audience to 'flee from the wrath to come'. 'A deep sense of my sinful and perilous state laid hold of my soul with great power,' Dixon was to record.[23] For two weeks he went regularly to the Dome but resisted in agony while his mother and William and others prayed for him in his struggle. The last night came and he knew it was now or never – what he knew to be right, or short-term indulgence – Christ or career. If Christ, then it must be as completely as he had given himself to soldiering.

He was at the back of the hall. 'I shall never, in this life or the next, forget how, when under conviction of the sin of my ungodly life, I knelt at the back of the hall in Brighton and placed myself, my whole being, unreservedly at the disposal of the Lord Jesus . . . thankfully receiving the salvation offered so freely through the sacrifice on Calvary'. To his amazement peace and a sense of having been forgiven filled him. When Moody called for those who had responded to confess their faith by coming to the front, his family saw to their delight his tall, soldierly figure making his way forward with the look of a man who has won.

Within two weeks Hoste knew that nothing now mattered so

much as taking this gospel to 'where Christ is not known . . . I want to give my life to this.' General Hoste would not hear of his resigning his commission until he had taken time to weigh it up more calmly. Dixon decided to say no more until his father raised the subject again. He was disciplining himself to overcome a strong streak of shyness. He returned to his battery at Sandown Fort and on the first evening told his commanding officer and fellow-officers in the Mess that he had become a Christian. To his surprise they took it calmly, impressed by his conviction and fearlessness. 'He was on fire with it all . . . which to this day I reverence,' a brigadier who had been his junior in 1882 was to recall in 1946.

So back he went to the life he so enjoyed, the battery drill, the polo and the friends he had made, for a year and three months until he resigned his commission. His brother William fed him with books, among them some from the CIM, *China's Spiritual Need and Claims* and probably *China's Millions*, for he had once admired the 'simple and direct faith in God for temporal supply and protection, and also the close identification by the missionaries with the Chinese social life'.

In May 1883 General Hoste wrote to say that if Dixon still wished to become a missionary he would no longer stand in the way. By then Dixon had been impressed by the demanding standard of the apostle Peter's injunction, 'If any man speak, let him speak as the oracles of God', that is, 'as one speaking the very words of God'.[24] Set on maintaining the highest standards in his life as a Christian no less than as an officer, he resolved to pray and to 'wait on God' until sure he was being 'led by the Spirit', before he took action, wrote a letter or attempted to preach. If he often appeared cautious, deliberating before taking action, this lay at its root. On July 23 he wrote to Hudson Taylor,

> Sir; I have for some time been thinking about offering myself for the China Inland Mission. . . . My time is just now, in the drill season, very much taken up with my duties . . . This must be my apology for asking whether I can see you on Friday or Saturday next: I have the honour to be, Sir, your obedient servant, D E Hoste, Lieut. R A.

Three days later an inspection of troops made him postpone his visit.

With Hudson Taylor away on tour in the north, Benjamin Broomhall acknowledged the letter, and on August 1 (the day Harold Schofield died) Hudson Taylor read it on his return. Years later, when D E Hoste was Benjamin's son-in-law and General Director of the Mission in Hudson Taylor's shoes, he wrote (with the humility that required references to himself to be in the third person) that Hudson Taylor,

> was careful to set before him the real character of life and work in inland China, telling him quite plainly that it involved isolation, privation, exposure to the hostility of the people, and the contempt of his own countrymen, and also many trials of faith, patience and constancy. . . . (He) went away deeply impressed with the character of the man . . . and with his heart more than ever set on becoming a missionary in China . . . more and more impressed with the need of the utmost care and caution lest he should presume to enter so privileged a life and service . . . without having been called and appointed thereto by the Lord.

Hudson Taylor had advised him first to mature as a Christian and then to gain experience of evangelism. He accepted the advice, and drew upon his parents' faithful teaching over the years.

> One day I was in my room, tilted back in my chair with my open Bible before me. I had begun thoroughly to enjoy the Word of God. As I read I smoked, and raised my head occasionally to blow the tobacco smoke over the open pages before me. All at once the thought came to me – 'Is this honouring to God . . . ?' I at once stopped smoking, and from that moment have never touched tobacco.

In another jotting the informal DEH comes through: '(the CIM) thoughtful, sober-minded, feet on the ground: this gained *my* confidence. So much cackling *before* they have their egg! (CIM) show the *real* thing.'

From time to time as he was able he came to Pyrland Road, and became acquainted with those regularly at the Saturday prayer-meetings. On one of these occasions as he entered he saw Benjamin's petite daughter Gertrude at the piano and said to himself, 'I shall marry her one day.' She and her brother Hudson left for China among the Seventy on September 24, 1884, while Hoste let God guide him and bring them together in due time.

'Sporting hearties' for the CIM — *1883–84*

Meanwhile Stanley Smith, unsure of where God was leading him, considered a variety of possibilities in Britain. Back in 1880 he had applied to himself the words of God addressed to Ezekiel: 'Thou are not sent to a people of strange speech.' But on November 30, 1883, the commission given to Isaiah impressed him: 'I will also give thee for a light to the Gentiles, that thou mayest be my salvation unto the ends of the earth.' His use of Scripture may have been shaky, but 'I got set free,' he said, from the sense of restriction, free to act on a growing estimation of the CIM. A month later, 'about the end of 1883 I wrote to Mr Taylor, telling him I wanted to come out to China'.[25] Five months after Schofield's death, a second man of the type he (Schofield) had had in mind (when pleading with God to send the most deeply consecrated and gifted types to China) had approached the Mission. On January 4, 1884, a long evening with Hudson Taylor took Smith to the point of saying, 'I hope to labour for God there soon.'

William Cassels was ordained on June 4, 1882, and went as curate to the overflowing working-class church of All Saints, South Lambeth, under Allen Edwards. The pews, the aisles, even the chancel and pulpit steps were packed with people on Sundays, and three thousand children filled six Sunday schools. Edwards and Cassels heard people say in the streets 'There go David and Jonathan,' so one were they in partnership. This training for the future could scarcely have been better as during the next two years he thought more and more about going overseas. His forebears, named Cassillis, had been ship-owners on the Firth of Forth and his grandfather a physician in Kendal and Lancaster. His father had become a merchant in Lisbon and Oporto where he met a West Country mill-owner's daughter whom he married. Of their thirteen children William Wharton was the ninth, and the sixth of seven sons.[26]

His family background with a vicar uncle and Repton schooldays had led on easily to ordination and the intention to join the Church Missionary Society. But when he 'expressed a strong desire for work in inland China' and was told that the CMS had no plans to go there, he turned his attention to the CIM. In February 1884 Stanley Smith took part with Cassels in an evangelistic mission in Clapham, between South Lambeth and the school at Newlands where 'SPS' was teaching. They talked together about China. Then in March Stanley Smith joined in Moody's London campaign, earning Moody's admiration for his zeal and ability in the 'inquiry room'. After the afternoon campaign meeting on March 26, Stanley took his mother to tea with Moody and was invited to come to

Massachusetts to help in training converts at Moody's training school. From Moody they went home to 13 John Street, Mayfair, where Hudson Taylor joined them for dinner and discussed Stanley's future. That settled it. He walked part of the way back to Pyrland Road with Hudson Taylor, and the same night wrote, 'decided to go to China with Hudson Taylor . . . and to go, D V, via America to see Moody's training home.'

On February 26, 1884, the day before the two Salisbury women (Rosa Minchin and Emily Whitchurch), two other women and two men sailed for China, making forty-two of the Seventy, D E Hoste had met the CIM council informally, as he was still not sure that it was God's will for him to resign his commission to go to China. But by April 15 he had already acted, as he told Hudson Taylor in characteristic prose,

> I have been with my battery for the last six weeks, having been recalled by telegraph, on 4th of March, and am now come on leave, pending my name appearing in the Gazette, as retired from the army. . . . My own feeling is now that I should go to China, and if so I would esteem it a most blessed privilege to go under the auspices of the China Inland Mission.

He still distinguished between his own sense of what would be right, and an assurance that this was God's will for him. It depended after all on the CIM's view also. On Hudson Taylor's advice he was hoping to gain experience as a counsellor in Moody's inquiry room as Stanley Smith had done.

By then Stanley had had his formal interview with the London council, on April 1, following a public meeting of the CIM in the Mansion House, presided over by the Lord Mayor. His offer to serve in China with the CIM had been 'cordially accepted', and the first of what George Woodcock called the CIM's 'sporting hearties' was a probationer of the Mission, to Dixon Hoste's delight. But,

> It was not SPS at all – to begin with [Hoste was to recall]; Studd came through McCarthy, Beauchamp had known JHT for years, SPS was a percussion cap! – the gun already loaded in many cases. Oh! so attractive! Brilliant fellow. (And why the CIM? So practical. So sane.) We young fellows notice how much they (the CIM) *pray* for the safety of their people, and for the money to *reach* them.

The council as well as Hudson Taylor and the general secretary were kept extremely busy, interviewing and advising many candidates at frequent meetings all through 1884. On August 4 the future pioneer of Tibet, Annie Royle Taylor, 'Lady Probationer, London Hospital' was 'cordially accepted'; the acceptance of Gertrude and Hudson Broomhall, future treasurer in China, both well known to the council, was 'agreed'; and 'Jeanie' Gray (later to marry Herbert Hudson Taylor) was interviewed. The minutes of October 7 record that the Rev W Cassels was 'cordially accepted', and 'Mr Hoste' accepted subject to his references proving satisfactory. Already Cassels' six brothers had gone overseas, and in agony of heart his mother had pleaded with Hudson Taylor not to take William. To her joy he 'assured her that he held a parent's wishes sacred and would not encourage William if she opposed' his application. But on October 1 a letter from her withdrew her objection lest she should prove 'a bad mother to one of the best of sons'.

Dixon Hoste could have fallen at the council fence, for the vicar of Sandown grudgingly characterised him as shy and reserved, 'not naturally enterprising' and 'not naturally fitted for (missionary) work, but I may be mistaken'. And then, significantly, 'I should have liked him to have remained in the army'. The council understood. They themselves saw humility, sincerity, wise judgment, character, courage and self-sacrifice. More than mere assessment was involved. Now there were three 'sporting hearties' and talk of them sailing with Hudson Taylor in December, with a schoolmaster for Chefoo, Herbert L Norris, for good measure. For fast growing numbers of raw probationers learning the language in the Yangzi stations needed Hudson Taylor's presence to deploy them appropriately, in terms of the greatest needs for reinforcements, of denominational preferences, of physique and aptitude.

In the spring of 1883 C T Studd had returned from Australia with 'The Ashes', the best all-round cricketer in Britain for the second year running, but spiritually at low ebb – until in November his brother George was hovering between life and death.[27] Fame and wealth no longer meant anything to George. At the gateway of 'eternity' in their London home, No 2 Hyde Park Gardens, 'he only cared about the Bible and the Lord Jesus Christ'. Watching him and waiting on him hour after hour, 'C T' saw the transience, the emptiness of all this world could offer. 'God brought me back' to consecration, as he brought George back to life. And at one of Moody's meetings '(God) met me again and restored to me the joy of my salvation'. 'My heart was no longer in the game,' of cricket. What mattered now was to serve and to lead others to Christ. He took members of his Test team to hear Moody, and thrilled to see them turn to Christ, especially A J Webbe, H E Steel and the captain, Ivo Bligh, the future Lord Darnley. But he could not fathom what he was to do with his own life now that he had taken his degree. He decided to read law. The *Daily Telegraph* was to indulge in hyperbole about his sacrificing a brilliant career at the Bar to become a missionary. But he knew that for him the Bar was wrong. He must spend his life for Christ. He read Hannah Pearsall Smith's *The Christian's Secret of a Happy Life*, in a word, abandonment to Christ and 'absolute faith' in Him. 'Christ's love compels us . . . He died for all, that those who live should no longer live for themselves but for Him who died for them and was raised again.' He knelt and prayed in the words of F R Havergal's hymn,

'Take my life and let it be
Consecrated, Lord, to Thee!'

He was ready at last for marching orders and was not kept waiting.

On Saturday, November 1, Stanley Smith called at Hyde Park Gardens on his way to Pyrland Road. Too many claims in Britain had decided Hudson Taylor to ask John McCarthy to deputise briefly for him in China. McCarthy was being 'farewelled' at the weekly prayer meeting, so 'C T' went along with Stanley. Listening to McCarthy tell about his own call by God when Hudson Taylor came to Dublin in 1865,[28] and to Stanley Smith and Robert Landale, 'all (of whom) spoke splendidly', Studd knew without doubt that God was sending him to China. On the way back he told Stanley Smith, and at home broke his news to Kynaston and their mother. They knew him too well not to be alarmed, a Roman candle, impulsive, unpredictable, even unbalanced. Mrs Studd was distraught, for two days imploring him to wait at least a week 'before giving himself to H Taylor'. When Montagu Beauchamp called round he found Kynaston in the depths of depression. 'C T' was 'a fanatic'. But 'C T' could not be budged: he went back to Pyrland Road on November 4, was interviewed by members of the council and recommended to 'consider the question . . . more fully and . . . if he still wished to go, to write definitely offering himself'. This he did, and was taken at his word and accepted.

Since Montagu Beauchamp was a child of five, playing with Hudson Taylor's chopsticks and (detached) pigtail, they had often been together and knew each other well. In September 1878 as the guest of Lady Beauchamp and the Hon Miss Waldegrave in the Engadine and on the Pontresina glaciers, Hudson Taylor had shared their concern for the Beauchamp sons. Montagu, the fourth, was eighteen and still at Repton. There and at Cambridge he trailed behind the others, especially Stanley Smith, as a Christian. Hudson Taylor went on praying for him. Late in 1881 Montagu wrote to tell Kynaston Studd that at last he had 'yielded all to Christ', and came up to Trinity 'so full of zeal instead of his coldness and lukewarmness'. When Stanley lapsed into smoking again, it was Montagu's influence on the family holiday of the Beauchamps and Waldegraves in Normandy that rallied his spiritual discipline.

After taking his degree in 1883 Montagu had started on an ordination course at Ridley Hall, but without conviction that he should be ordained. He withdrew and in 1884 went through a spell when his faith was shaken, until his eldest sister helped him back to a 'very deep spiritual experience of reconsecration to God'. In the autumn the talk of his family (at their home, 4 Cromwell Road, opposite the Natural History Museum) was of Stanley Smith's impending departure to China. Lady Beauchamp had often said that it would give her great joy to have a missionary son. When Hilda Beauchamp's engagement to Kynaston Studd drew the two families together, and Montagu saw the Studds' distress over C T's decision to go to China, his own conscience was needled into writing to his mother (to quote Pollock), 'If Charlie Studd was willing to go in spite of his family, ought a man to hold back whose mother would "rather encourage than hinder"?'[29] One day Stanley and Montagu were in a restaurant opposite Victoria station, talking about China, when Stanley said, 'If you saw two men carrying a log of wood, one end much heavier than the other, which end would you help at – the heavier or the lighter?' Montagu went home and thought about it, and as he prayed became convinced 'that not only was I to go but to induce others to go too'. The mothers of the seven were being drawn in, some despite themselves.

A 'big go' for China — *1884*

From the emerging 'Cambridge Seven' we revert to Hudson Taylor in another strenuous year. Two quarto letter books of 1884 in his and Jennie's handwriting have been preserved. One records the source, contents and date of reply to 997 letters from China by

October 13, and the other 1,992 personal letters from correspondents in Britain by October 25.[30] On January 1 alone he replied to seventeen from China. General Mission letters were handled by others. In the year, he dealt with about 3,200 personal letters between and during his frequent journeys, meetings and interviews. By January 19 'Benjamin B' was writing that Hudson was 'prostrate'. Splitting headaches immobilised him. The pace was too great. Already in January he had taken part in fourteen meetings in London, Andover and Southsea.

After five days' rest at old Mrs Robert Howard's home in Tottenham he was on the welcome treadmill again. Farewell meetings for the Salisbury ladies followed in February, with lectures at Harley House and to students of the Presbyterian College, at Spurgeon's Tabernacle and the YMCA, as well as in a variety of churches. Dixon Hoste met the council, and from Glasgow, before he left for China, John McCarthy reported serious consultations with men of the first quality. If office routine had not been McCarthy's forte, personal counselling at a high spiritual level was another matter. C T Studd's dramatic decision was not made until November 1 of that year, 1883, but on February 2, 1884, McCarthy wrote that he was staying at the home of 'a fine young fellow, very wholehearted for God. He has been to China and Burmah (and) seen a vision of a needy world.' He was also very wealthy. Archibald Orr Ewing and his friends, Walter B Sloan and Campbell White (Lord Overtoun), had talked with John McCarthy the previous day. Orr Ewing and Sloan were not only to go to China together a year after the Seven, but also to become stars in the Mission's crown.[31]

On March 5 Hudson Taylor crossed over to Belfast for a week of meetings arranged by the YMCA, and to reap more 'good, reliable men,' 'valuable candidates'. No one realised that he was not fit enough to stand from 8.00 to 9.40 p.m. and then to perch on a backless bench before his turn to speak. He confessed to Jennie that he was 'too tired to do well . . . a pity . . . for it was a magnificent meeting'. Like a snowball he gathered work as he went. On March 13 he met the theological students, 9.00–10.00 a.m.; working women 2.00–2.30 p.m.; ladies, gentlemen and ministers, 3.00–4.30 p.m.; and 'candidates to China', 4.30–5.30 p.m.[32]

At Nottingham the next day he was disappointed to hear from Benjamin who had personally arranged the meetings that 'some magic lantern business' had been introduced and should be eliminated. Hudson Taylor agreed. They drew the wrong people in the

THE BRITISH ISLES: INSATIABLE

wrong spirit and offended some supporters. To 'exalt the Lord', and to do his will, created the right atmosphere and results. Eugene Stock stated that this emphasis was the CIM's great contribution to the Christian Church at this period.[33] The 'happiest hours' were spent at the Congregational College. Then back to London, and Mrs Robert Howard sent a carriage to bring him and Jennie to her home for the weekend. Then to Reigate and the home of Florence Barclay who was soon to join the Mission. (In 1892 she married Montagu Beauchamp), 'I do not know anything so encouraging as insuperable difficulties,' Hudson Taylor said to them. 'There is a POWER behind us that can lay low every mountain in its pride.'[34] The philanthropist Robert Arthington, 'emphatically' enthused, reminded Hudson Taylor of his interest in the aboriginal tribes and Tibet.[35] Together Hudson Taylor and Benjamin revised and issued a large illustrated 5th edition of *China's Spiritual Need and Claims*. It sold fast and well. *China's Millions*, an unrelenting labour, was also in greater demand, with news of French action in Indo-China and increasing persecution of Christians in China. But there were many conversions to report, and Cameron's travels were still big news.

From Xi'an George King wrote that for his work in Shaanxi province and Xi'an its capital, 1,500 preachers of the gospel would not be too many. 'Were I in England again, I would gladly live in one room, make the floor my bed, a box my chair' if it would help to get the gospel to those who 'perish for lack of knowledge'. The Church at home must *care* more about the Christless. With the Eastons and then George King and Dr William Wilson hounded out of Xi'an, and the landlords of the inn they used and of the house they rented being beaten and imprisoned, it was still an uphill fight. The danger to their Chinese colleagues had become too great, so they withdrew and King and Wilson went straight back to Xi'an. 'No sorrow seems great, no trial severe, after my having lost my dear wife and boy,' King wrote. Then came the news from George Clarke that his wife had died in Dali on October 7, 1883. 'The last foreign sister she saw was on May 16, 1881 . . . I have been burying my sorrow by preaching in the open air.'

May, with a long list of meetings, ended with the CIM's annual meetings, chaired by Robert Scott the publisher when Lord Shaftesbury was detained at the last minute. Of 428 Protestant missionaries in China, 126 were now members of the CIM, thirty-three of them unmarried women. But 'Scotland has 3,845 ordained ministers' and Glasgow more than in all of China![36] Looking out over the audience Hudson Taylor recognised friends who were praying for China before he first went out, thirty-one years before. One friend had missed only one of the weekly prayer meetings in nineteen years. The family atmosphere was strong. The year before, both John Eliot Howard and Lord Congleton had been on the platform. Both were 'with the Lord'. It was good to see so many Christians in the audience, but 'one is almost tempted to wish a persecution could come after the work of Moody and Sankey, to scatter us all to some dark parts of the world'.

June 25 saw the Mildmay Conference with Bishop Hannington of Uganda and Professor Drummond of Edinburgh speaking. Then on the 27th Hudson Taylor gave the closing address. The great audience had sung the hymn 'Waft, waft ye winds the story' when he rose to his feet, led in prayer and said, 'It will not do to sing (that). The winds will not waft the story. No! Mothers must give up beloved sons; fathers must give up precious daughters; brothers and sisters must cheerfully yield one another to the Lord's service . . . It is in the path of obedience and self-denying service that God reveals Himself most intimately to His children.' At the Salisbury conference in September, Bishop Hannington said that his own call to be a missionary had come from China, and he 'chose to forget Africa for a while to pray for China'.

By invitation of the Lord Mayor of London, Alderman Robert N Fowler (who in 1860 had been treasurer of the ill-fated Chinese Evangelization Society), another CIM meeting was held on July 8, 1884, with the Lord Mayor himself again presiding. He held up Consul Alabaster's report (p 253), presented to Parliament a few days before, and read out its compliments to the CIM. But three days later the French ultimatum was presented at Peking and war was declared. Public attitudes were volatile. Criticisms of Hudson Taylor increased, for sending out more and more young missionaries including mere girls in these circumstances. Henrietta Soltau heard someone expostulating at the madness of running such risks, and Hudson Taylor's quiet humour in reply, 'I have never found in my Bible that the Lord says the Gospel was not to be taken to China when there was war with France.'[37]

At least three donors had seen how tired Hudson Taylor was and sent gifts to pay for a good holiday. So he, Jennie and Maria were at the Keswick Convention together when Walter B Sloan went on his knees in the great marquee and put himself at God's disposal, 'for China'. Not yet eighteen, Maria sailed on August 27.

Thanking Miss Arthington in August for a donation, Jennie said, 'The very prosperity that the Lord is giving us just overwhelms him (J H T) with work.' But it was better to be overwhelmed than to let the opportunities go by. D J Findlay of Glasgow telegraphed, 'Tent conference fixed for 27th Sept on your account. Do not disappoint us. Want you for 28th also.' And he wrote 'We want to make our conference a big go for China and of course you are indispensable. We also want McCarthy, Stevenson, Landale, and as big a contingent as possible.' What could he do but go? He enlisted Stanley Smith for the first of six weeks of meetings he was to have, and as soon as he could get away from the Salisbury conference Hudson Taylor and Benjamin joined the others at Glasgow. Instead of being exhausted at the end, he felt '*rested*', he told Jennie, so uplifting had the meetings been, reaping the harvest of Moody's campaign of 1882.[38]

October was fuller still. After Glasgow and Greenock came a great meeting on October 2 in the United Presbyterian Synod Hall, the largest in Edinburgh, with the same four stalwarts to support him, reinforced by Trench; and another in the Free Assembly Hall chaired by Lord Polwarth. Frequent applause greeted their reports of 22,000 converts in all of China in the past year; and of £130,000 having been received by the CIM since its inception. Then he himself had a big meeting at Chillingham Castle on the way back to London. A letter followed him from the Earl of Tankerville's staff, thanking him and enclosing a donation.

He had already been to Belfast. Dublin wanted him too. With Smith, Cassels and Hoste already in the Mission he was planning to take them to China by 'the first boat in December'. It meant leaving Jennie behind again, but with such scope for influencing the Church in Britain he hoped to be back after only a brief absence.[39] Time was short. Eight others sailed away on October 8, and on the 10th he and Stanley Smith crossed over to Dublin. Hudson Taylor's SOS shows the tempo of life. 'I've got the wrong trousers on. Send my best.' All went well except that few opportunities were given for the still unknown Stanley Smith to speak. However, on the 14th 'we had a wonderful audience tonight. I have seldom seen such a sight.'

A cable arrived at Pyrland Road from China, 'Trouble inland, impossible forward arrivals . . . send no more till way clear.' *The Pall Mall Gazette* of October 13 reported riots at Wenzhou on the 5th and most foreign premises burned, including the Stotts' but excluding the consulate and Customs house. Repercussions of the French attacks on Fuzhou and Taiwan were spreading. Deciding with Benjamin that 'in quietness and in confidence shall be your strength', Jennie sent the cable on by post instead of telegraph. 'I expect, darling, that you are remembering that Maria is due in Shanghai this week' – in the dangerous Taiwan straits as she wrote. The Chinese were fleeing from Ningbo, sure of attack soon. And Hudson Taylor began hearing of 'destruction and damage in different stations'. He prayed about the cable and disregarded it. Seventeen more were en route in two ships anyway, Amelia's son and daughter (Hudson and Gertrude) among them. The next group would sail as planned. It included six Glasgow women, the Murray sisters, widely experienced and in their thirties, going at their own expense, and Kate Mackintosh, soon to become a pioneer of 'women only' outposts. 'One of the best parties that ever went to China.' One effect of the attacks on Taiwan was that Eleanor Black, designated to Taiwan, did not go, and the CIM did not work in Taiwan until 1952.[40]

He was back in London in time for the Saturday prayer meeting on October 18 before their departure. The Seventy had been exceeded. 'The room was crammed and thirty or more people were standing in the halls,' Jennie wrote to Maria. It was 'as if the world were moved . . . more power with God was felt than ever before . . . I felt that eternity would show the result.' After the farewell communion service on the day before they joined their ship, the council minuted their opinion that women should carry equal weight with men in deciding 'station' affairs. (The suffragette movement began early in the twentieth century, winning suffrage for women of thirty in 1918 and equal suffrage a decade later.)

Stanley Smith's letters to Hudson Taylor convey the warmth between them, almost as father and son, since being in Glasgow, Edinburgh and Dublin together. 'Enclosed is a photo with love.'[41] From Cambridge where he was busy with many college meetings he wrote of trying to arrange three meetings each night for a team led by Hudson Taylor. 'I have met with such love; and I believe a warm welcome will await you.' 'I have engaged the Alexandra Hall every night from November 12–17 and a friend of mine has offered to defray all expenses.' Robert Landale was busy in the same way at Oxford and 'much encouraged' although his meetings were 'not so large or numerous . . . SPG (the "high church" Society for the Propagation of the Gospel) is more the article for Oxford than CIM or even CMS.'

November (not March) came 'in like a lion' and roared its way through, more eventfully than October. The Saturday prayer meeting on November 1, far more than an institution at any time, was honoured by the presence of Reginald Radcliffe, the veteran evangelist, now throwing in the weight of his effectiveness to help the CIM. Hudson Taylor was with the Kemp and Pigott families for meetings at Rochdale, but John McCarthy was taking leave of the United Kingdom, to sail on November 6. This was the occasion of C T Studd's 'resolve' to go to China, and its immediate effect on Montagu Beauchamp, confirmed after a 'chance' meeting and journey with Stanley Smith on the smoky 'Underground' to Victoria and that memorable cup of tea (p 342). Charlie Studd's mother came in distress to talk with Jennie at Pyrland Road and left satisfied. Lady Beauchamp also consoled her, and despite herself she began to find their enthusiasm infectious. Hudson Taylor was away again when Montagu's mother came to see Jennie. Glad that Montagu was going, 'She would like (him) to go out with you that he may drink into your views – a *very* satisfying talk'.[42] In China Hudson Taylor was to honour her wish. They made long journeys together and developed an ever closer friendship.

Passing over the Oxford and Cambridge meetings for the moment, it may help understanding to get the perspective of November, December and January from Hudson Taylor's point of view. Illness on his return from Rochdale delayed his joining the team at Oxford, but he played a full part at Cambridge and went on to Ipswich – in the Town Hall, with the mayor and aldermen complete – to Nottingham with Studd and Hoste, to Leicester with Studd and Smith, for two meetings in F B Meyer's Melbourne Hall, and for Lord Radstock two meetings at the Eccleston Hall in London with Smith, Studd and Cassels. The Leicester meeting was historic, for early the next morning the minister himself, F B Meyer, came round to ask Smith and Studd, 'How can I be like you?' 'The talk we had then was one of the most formative influences on my life,' the future saint and Biblical expositor was to claim. In a different key, one of the audience sent a gift of underwear for Hudson Taylor, Smith and Studd; and another promised a Stilton cheese for every new missionary who would accept it.[43] The outcome was hilarious (p 374).

Not surprisingly, other missions, denominational Churches and other countries were not only hearing of but being influenced by what was happening in Britain. The Methodist Bible Christians, and the Friends' Foreign Mission had consulted Hudson Taylor and invited him to address their annual meetings, in May, with the direct outcome that they sent missions to China from each body, under the wing of the CIM.[44] Approaches from Scandinavia led in time to another associate mission of the CIM sending Norwegian candidates to London for training. And a visitor from the United States, also in July, was the first hint of the unplanned future international nature of the Mission. On August 13 Major-General Haig of the Kabyle and Berber Mission, initiated by Hudson Taylor's old friend George Pearse and parent Society of the North Africa Mission, consulted Hudson Taylor on administrative problems. In November the first links with Sweden were forged by a request from a Pastor Holmgren for an article from Hudson Taylor. And in December a Professor Tauxe of Aigle proposed an *Occasional Paper* on China for French Switzerland.[45]

In mid-December Hudson Taylor discussed his plans for administrative reorganisation in China, and worked on three monthly issues of the 1885 *Millions* in preparation for leaving Britain on January 20. With such momentum as had built up during the last few months, and with John Stevenson home from Burma, 'filled with the Spirit' in a way he had never experienced before, and proving to have a strong gift for administration, Hudson Taylor could afford to leave for a while. The need for the general director to be in China had become paramount. Through all the long years of overwork, crying for delegation of duties, a potential lieutenant had been within calling distance. But Stevenson had been dour and withdrawn, until he put himself at God's disposal. Apart from the Franco-Chinese war in the south, the coup d'état and anti-Japanese riots in Korea had precipitated a new crisis in the north. Hudson Taylor could delay no longer.

'An expanding circle of action'[46] *November–December 1884*

Some wild things have been written about Hudson Taylor and the so-called 'Cambridge Seven', best answered by the facts. Apart from the biographies of Cassels, Hoste and C T Studd, the story of the Seven and their dealings with him has usually taken them as far as China. More light can be thrown on this early period and on their later history, instructive from the way they turned out.

When the first CIM meetings took place in Oxford and Cambridge in November 1884 there was no 'Cambridge Seven', not even a Cambridge five. As an Oxford graduate Robert Landale had tried to stir up interest in his own university, and Stanley Smith had been well received. But his warning that the climate was unfavourable proved true. News of C T Studd's decision to go to China was to create a great stir in the cricketing and university world, but his presence in Oxford from Wednesday, November 5 to Monday 10, could not have been planned. On the heels of deciding on November 1 and meeting the CIM council for the first time on the 4th, he at once joined Smith and Hoste to go there on the 5th. Beauchamp turned up on the 7th. Hudson Taylor's illness kept him back until Saturday the 8th, which was also the earliest day Cassels could manage although billed as a speaker. After the first meeting attendance was poor and the team disheartened, but on the 11th an Oxford donor wrote 'greatly rejoicing' that God 'so marvellously helped' them. They had given of their best. And on the same day Hudson Taylor told the council that he expected 'some of those present to become missionaries'.[47]

Cambridge was entirely different. The lively Christian Union had prepared for six days of activity on behalf of the CIM and other missions. 'Extraordinary interest was aroused' by the news that C T Studd, ex-captain of the Cambridge XI and England's most outstanding cricketer of the day, still at the height of his powers, with S P Smith, stroke oar of the University Eight, and Montagu Beauchamp who had narrowly missed his place in the same boat, were about to tell the university why they were going to China of all places and in wartime. 'The influence of such a band of men . . . was irresistible,' Eugene Stock said in his *History of the Church Missionary Society*. 'No such event had occurred before; and no event of the century has done so much to arouse the minds of Christian men to see the tremendous claims of the field, and the nobility of the missionary vocation' – strong words, for David Livingstone's appeal to the universities in 1857 had given rise to the Universities Mission to Central Africa.[48]

Concerned not to fish in other societies' waters, Hudson Taylor had asked the CMS to send representatives to take part in the meetings. In thanking him for this 'kind and brotherly invitation' Stock himself lamented that he had four other engagements that could not be shelved. And in his history he said, 'The gift of such a band to the China Inland Mission was a just reward to Mr Hudson Taylor and his colleagues for the genuine unselfishness with which they had always pleaded the cause of China and the World, and not of their own particular organisation.' Prospective CMS men supported the mission and testified from the platform with the team. One of them was Arthur Polhill-Turner, 'two years to the day since his conversion'. As a result more offered their lives to the CMS. Cynical dons and facetious freshmen had their say, but they were merely the losers.

The meetings ran from November 12 to 17, with Dr Handley Moule, Principal of Ridley Hall and later Bishop of Durham (brother of G E and A E Moule of Hangzhou) presiding at several, and Hudson Taylor speaking at each except on the Friday, 'mail day'. Smith's charm and fluency, Studd's down to earth colloquialisms, Beauchamp's straightforwardness, Hoste's laconic, military directness, and each one's transparent love of Christ and costly sacrifice shook their audiences. Utter consecration, in athletes of the best type, each confirming the reality of the others' experience, challenged the mediocrity of everyone's life. 'Mounting enthusiasm' (so different from Oxford) and many long personal conversations filled their days. On Sunday afternoon a 'very remarkable' meeting (in Handley Moule's words) was open to townsfolk as well as the university. That evening fifty men stood to declare their willingness to serve God overseas, and the next day when Stanley Smith asked 'all who intended to become missionaries' (not specifying where or how) to stay behind after the last meeting closed, forty-five stayed, Arthur Polhill-Turner among them.

His brother Cecil had faced up to the loss of all he so greatly valued, in the Guards and hunting field, and to his mother's rebuke. His Roman Catholic bachelor uncle, Sir Henry Barron, 'British Resident at the court of the Kingdom of Württemberg' had made him his heir. The odds on being disowned were considerable. But after a winter leave spent with him Cecil returned to his regiment 'with a mind fully made up. I had yielded to and trusted in Jesus Christ as my Saviour, Lord and Master' – without any reservations. He had shown himself 'too good an officer to be treated with disrespect' when he told the Mess what had happened, and now played polo and cricket 'for Christ'. Many high-ranking officers of the first quality were dedicated Christians. He could be the same. But he went to a 'China missionary meeting, and from that time I made up my mind to engage in the Lord's work in China'. On December 1 a memorable meeting of the CMS in Cambridge fed the enthusiasm aroused by the CIM, and both societies reaped the benefits. Cecil spent three days with Arthur, talking and praying together, so far had they travelled in a short time.

Reginald Radcliffe had recognised the power in the young men around Hudson Taylor and convinced him that before they sailed away the universities of Scotland should be visited also. Radcliffe consulted Professor Alexander Simpson of Edinburgh and an itinerary of Glasgow, Dundee, Aberdeen and Edinburgh was quickly arranged. After the Eccleston Hall 'farewell' meetings 'C T' and 'S P S' took the night train to Glasgow just as they were – Studd, to his mother's distress, without even a change of clothes. Hudson Taylor asked that a parcel might be sent after him. They were 'in a mortal funk' about meeting unknown students. They need not have feared, though uproar was a Scottish way of life.

From Dundee, where Stanley Smith was left after the meeting to talk with students while Reginald Radcliffe, Robert Landale and Studd went on to Aberdeen, 'S P S' wrote to Hudson Taylor that Mr Radcliffe proposed a repetition of the tour from January 10 to 22, to Liverpool and other cities in England.[49] 'Could you come? If not, may we go?' It would mean deferring their departure to China until late in January. He agreed, although it would mean separating, Hudson Taylor himself having to go ahead on January 20. (Cf p 340). Already he had cancelled the December sailing, although a small army of new missionaries learning the language in China needed his decisions on their deployment.[50]

John Stevenson had played a major part in the preparations in Scotland, and after the Edinburgh meeting called it 'a most remarkable one'. 'S P S' was scintillating, 'simmering'. A committee of professors and students had taken the Free Assembly Hall holding one thousand, and advertised the occasion very enterprisingly. Students packed the hall, singing and beating time with sticks. Compared with Smith's inspired eloquence, Studd was prosaic, but such sincerity and devotion 'if anything, made the greatest impression'. They cheered him to the echo, and at the same time were 'spellbound'. When the meeting ended a stampede of men crowded around them to say goodbye, showing on their faces that the message had gone deep. A hundred saw them off at the station, when they left for London to be at Kynaston Studd's marriage to Hilda Beauchamp.

The last half of December went in smaller meetings in the south and midlands. John Stevenson travelled with Hoste and Cassels to the Isle of Wight, the first of a continuous round of meetings which occupied him until March 1885, many of them in Devonshire. He was famous as the first Westerner to cross China from west to east, as McCarthy had been from East to West. But the taciturn Scot had become a new man, with richer experiences ahead of him at Keswick in 1885. He and 'Benjamin B' made the most of the flood of requests for speakers. 'We had *heaps* of money' for it, with costs covered, over and above generous donations. Funds had flowed in, but no more than were needed for the Mission doubling in size. The balance in hand as the year closed was £10. 'Nobody else had such a story to tell about China as we had in those days.' 'JHT was very bright, full of enthusiasm, well and strong, travelling at night, speaking so powerfully, so clearly, always simple and telling . . . overwhelmingly busy, full of hope and courage – fifty-two, in his vigorous prime. Mr Broomhall too. No friction anywhere . . . enthusiasm itself about the Seventy and the Cambridge Band.' Where was that 'fast-failing old man' of 1882?

Smith, Studd and Cassels spoke on Christmas Day at the YMCA headquarters in Aldersgate before joining their families' festivities.

Hoste writing to Hudson Taylor on December 30 signed himself 'affectionately yours in Christ' – gone the remote 'Sir', of early in the year. He arranged for meetings in Brighton in mid-January, with Hudson Taylor the guest of his parents. The Cambridge trio Smith, Studd and Cassels were there on December 29, before Hoste and Stanley Smith spent the last day of the year at Pyrland Road in fasting and prayer. Neither Montagu Beauchamp nor Arthur Polhill-Turner had yet joined the Mission, and Cecil Polhill-Turner had still to make his first approach.

Then there were Seven — *January 1885*

After the high points of November and December who could have thought they would be exceeded? The receipts in January alone were more than the income for the financial year 1866–67; and the income for 1885 became double that of the painful period of 1881–82. New donors included a senior administrator of the Bank of England, Hammond Chubb, who later joined the CIM council. With a gift of £200 (several thousands today) old Mrs Grace (p 40) asked, Why stop at the Seventy? Ask for seven hundred, a thousand. That was the spirit. 'All in good time' was the reality. Lord Radstock, never failing to contribute to Hudson Taylor personally when sending larger sums for the Mission, wrote from Calcutta that he had met a leading 'wine and spirit' merchant named Stark, 'a complete man of the world', self-styled a 'sceptic and freethinker' when he boarded the P & O *Chusan*. Two young women had attracted his attention, standing at the ship's rail softly singing together. Afterwards 'Gertie' had passed the time of day on deck with him, drawing from him that he was the only unbeliever in his family. It unsettled him. He began to sit behind a partition where he could hear them having daily 'devotions' together. Nothing of mere formality spoilt it. Every word was real to them. Then, after long talks with Gertie's brother he had turned to Christ and destroyed his 'infidel' books and papers. In Calcutta he could not stop telling other people, and wrote offering his services to the CIM.[51]

Hudson Taylor had agreed to visit William Berger at Cannes, leaving London on January 20. His days until then would be full. A party of six men including his personal secretary W J Lewis sailed on January 15. He was to join them at Suez. On January 1 Reginald Radcliffe himself wrote listing the many cities in Scotland and England in which he was to hold meetings with Stanley Smith and

Studd, this time from January 9 to 25.[52] He would like to keep the men until February 9 in Bristol. Hudson Taylor replied by telegram. Manchester and Leeds on January 26 and 28 must be the two men's last. Until January 8 and on each day after the 29th they had farewell meetings to attend until they sailed on February 4.

Cecil and Arthur Polhill-Turner were in close touch with the others. They arranged for Stanley Smith to speak in Bedford on Friday, January 2, and for C T Studd to join them on Saturday for a drawing-room reception at Howbury Hall, for thirty-five county neighbours. Sunday they spent together. As a result, as soon as their friends had gone, Cecil sat down and wrote to Hudson Taylor as a stranger, 'Jan. 5th, 1884 Dear Sir,' asking for a personal interview. Jennie stamped it 'Received 6 Jan 85'. On the 7th (dating it December 7th, 1884 and received the next day, 8 January 1885 – his world was upside down!) he wrote that he and his brother would come to Pyrland Road at 1.00 p m on the 8th (to lunch?), hoping to attend the big farewell meeting afterwards.[53] Their friends would have forewarned them, but the austerity of what they found confirmed the impressions they already had of the CIM and of what lay ahead of them: combat, not comfort; sincerity, not emotion. Hudson Taylor was pleased with what he saw, and invited them to meet the council on the 13th. But he was sure enough of the outcome to have them on the platform with him that evening of the 8th at the Exeter Hall in the Strand.

An audience of three thousand streamed in to give Hudson Taylor, twelve new missionaries (over and above the seventy-six of the Seventy) and the 'Cambridge Band' of four or five a worthy send-off. Even to some of the five the eleventh hour addition of the Polhill-Turners to the platform party must have been as great a surprise as to them themselves. But this was what pleased Dixon Hoste, no beating about the bush. The February *Millions*, already at the printers, came out with the announcement that Cassels and Hoste were to sail on January 28, and Studd, Smith and Beauchamp to join them at Suez. In the end two parties left on January 15 and 28 but demands on the Seven kept them back to leave together on February 5. At this long meeting on January 8 all were introduced to the audience and probably made a few remarks. The Polhill-Turner brothers explained briefly how they also came to be there, and Stanley Smith gave the final address.

Ones and twos of their type had been 'farewelled' before. Harold Schofield had created a stir, but seven such conspicuous exceptions

THE SEVEN COMPLETE

to the rule presenting themselves together shook the placid waters of the evangelical pond. The twelve others were almost lost in the glare of publicity surrounding the seven. Yet few had any inkling of the effect this galaxy was about to have on Britain and the world scene. The secular press took up the excitement and they became the talk of the town: Studd, Britain's best cricketer; Smith of the Cambridge Eight; Hoste, a Royal Artillery officer; Cassels, a footballer and clergyman; Beauchamp, son of a baronet; Cecil Polhill-Turner, still in the Dragoon Guards; and his brother, of Eton and Cambridge. This was 'news'. None had a 'first' or would claim to be an intellectual, but all had renounced wealth or prospects of advancement or both, for Christ and for China, at a time of war in the East. Directly after the Exeter Hall meeting a Harley Street specialist wrote to Hudson Taylor that he too was 'determined upon giving up the pleasures of the world' and asked for an interview. Only three weeks remained before the seven were to sail. Called 'the Cambridge party' at first, and then 'A Cambridge Band', the popular term 'Cambridge Seven' came into use after they had gone.

When Smith and Studd joined Reginald Radcliffe at Liverpool on January 9 they found a crowd of twelve hundred young men ready for 'revival'. Many responded in tears to their call for surrender to Christ, and seventy or more were 'awakened'. Hudson Taylor spent the 12th with Dixon Hoste and his parents at meetings in Brighton; and on the 13th informed the council that he had interviewed and accepted Montagu Beauchamp. It was short notice, Cecil Polhill-Turner was young as a Christian, but with refreshing freedom of action and lack of 'red tape' the council also welcomed the two brothers to proceed to China with their friends, with or without formal identification with the Mission, which could follow 'after a time if on both sides it seemed desirable'. Beauchamp sent in his signed copy of the Principles and Practice that same day, adding in his strong, cultured handwriting, 'I fully agree to the same, and should like to go out to China with the party leaving London Feb. 4th, 1885.' Arthur Polhill-Turner wrote on January 14th to say, '(Cecil) has sent in his [army] Papers and is now like myself at your service.'

Things were moving fast, and the impending separation from their sons was tugging at maternal heart-strings. Mrs Studd had already been asked to dispose of Charles' 'goods and chattels' and had sent a cheque to the CIM,

> which I am almost sorry Mr Taylor did not keep. . . . I am most thankful that Mr Taylor's advice as to his wearing proper clothing has been heeded – dear fellow! He is very erratic and needs to be with older and more consistent Christians! [And to Jennie on January 5] A few lines to ask you to impress on him the necessity of taking what is *necessary to be comfortable*. He seems inclined to take so *very little*, hardly enough to last him, to say nothing about cleanliness in the hot climate . . .

After Hudson Taylor had left Britain on January 20, Jennie wrote to him, 'I am afraid Mrs Studd is going too far in carrying out your suggestions . . . They told me that a case was going to (Hanzhong) to be unpacked before he arrived that he might find a room ready prepared with curtains . . . knives and forks, table napkins etc, etc . . . to him unknown provision.' – for 'C T' of all ascetics![54] If they reached him in China he certainly disposed of them at once.

Crescendo of influence — *January–February 1885*

The last farewells were over, apart from a few local meetings, Reginald Radcliffe's tour, and a return to Oxford and Cambridge. Two days before Hudson Taylor crossed to France, the first signs of unusual excitement appeared in Edinburgh. Radcliffe, Studd and Stanley Smith had had small but packed meetings at Aberdeen, Perth and other towns in Scotland, with Landale, J E Mathieson the evangelist and Major-General Haig taking part in some. But on Sunday, January 18, more students than had ever been known to come together, 1,500–2,000 of them, filled the Synod Hall. Not China or consecration to Christ but 'Christ crucified' was each speaker's theme this time. Half the audience stayed on afterwards and on Monday a stream of students came for personal conversations with the team. 'Wonderful times. It is the Lord,' Stanley Smith told Jennie Taylor.

In the Glasgow area the story of many conversions and surrenders to the Lordship of Christ was repeated. They made Archibald Orr Ewing's home their base until the Friday when they returned to Edinburgh, to find 'all the signs of true religious revival'. The men converted the previous Sunday were helping their friends to yield to Christ. The last meeting excelled the others, with professors and students in tears, three or four hundred staying to ask 'how to be saved', and Christian professors and students going from man to man to show them the answer.[55] After that, Leeds, Manchester, Rochdale, and finally Liverpool again. And the same experience repeated, with 'huge' after-meetings, but for all social classes. People came to hear leading athletes, but God himself met them. And these rich young men learned lessons too,

> finding out so much about . . . the poor in . . . the great towns has increased my horror at the luxurious way I have been living [Studd wrote to his mother]; so many suits and clothes of all sorts, whilst thousands are starving and perishing of cold, so all must be sold when I come home if they have not been so before.[56]

The night train from Liverpool brought them back to London in time for the 'final' meeting on January 30 at the Eccleston Hall, with all the Seven present. Many had to be turned away. Even before that the YMCA's leaders had been thinking ambitiously. The 'Cambridge party' were due to leave Britain on Wednesday, February 4. Benjamin B and John Stevenson had 'moved heaven and earth' to arrange meetings for them in Bristol on the 1st, Cambridge on the 2nd and Oxford on the 3rd. If their departure could be postponed just one day, the YMCA would take the great Exeter Hall for one supreme 'last night' meeting.[57]

After the long separation from October 1881 to March 1883, Hudson and Jennie Taylor dreaded parting again for a year at the least. But it had to be. This was the young men's hour, and he himself was needed in China. Dixon Hoste saw him as humbly 'slipping away' without stealing any thunder on their field-day, or diluting the impact of the young upon the young. He left on January 20, apparently by cab from the door of 6 Pyrland Road. 'After you left,' Jennie told him, 'I went in for a minute (with the children) and back to the study. Dear Amelia came in and cuddled me up for a little while.' Each parting could so easily be the last, with no return. Then on to business. The YMCA had made their urgent propositions. Both she and Benjamin at first thought it unwise, but he consulted the P & O. The Seven could join their ship at Brindisi, as Hudson was doing, without additional cost.[58] George Williams of Messrs Hitchcock, Williams at St Paul's Churchyard, founder of the YMCA, was 'not willing that we should be at any expense' for the Exeter Hall or emergency advertising of a meeting. So Benjamin went ahead. A letter was widely circulated, notifying everyone of the arrangements and asking for prayer that it would be what the Seven 'shall long remember with gratitude to God . . . (and) memorable for ever in the experience of many a young man as the time when he was led to decide for Christ.' Even that was to be a pale understatement of what transpired.

By January 30 some of the YMCA leaders 'hung fire . . . and wished to back out of it', until Benjamin removed all doubt with 'We shall go on whether you do or not.' Stevenson was backing him 'splendidly'. But in the thick of it all the Mission stalwart, A G Parrott, at home on leave, talked of resigning. Counter-attacks were as ever to be expected, but to lose Parrott would be deplorable. He stayed for a time on the London staff. Worse still, news came of Khartoum being captured by the Mahdi on January 26, and General Gordon being left isolated by the dilatory progress of the relieving column. Was interest to be deflected from China as so often before?[59]

Between them Benjamin and John Stevenson were supervising all arrangements at Bristol, Cambridge and Oxford. Professor Babington the botanist would preside at Cambridge; Mrs Babington wanted Montagu Beauchamp to be their guest; J H Moulton, the classics scholar, regarded the phenomenon of these seven men forsaking all to follow Christ to China as 'a most remarkable thing in itself and in its influence upon the university'. The Guildhall would be too small, so an overflow meeting was being arranged for.

Hudson Taylor left the Bergers and Cannes on January 24. At Genoa a porter commissioned to collect his registered baggage returned as the train pulled out, saying he could not do it in time. Without his documents enforced idleness on the voyage would once again give him needed rest – but meant there would be a large backlog of work when the Seven arrived in China, bringing the vital boxes of papers and medicines. Instead, when he joined his ship at Suez he at once started teaching Chinese to the six men of his party. By February 4 they had learned three hundred characters. At Colombo, Singapore and Hong Kong he arranged meetings for the Seven when they arrived, giving them the option of coming on by a later ship if they judged that more time at Singapore would be profitable.

Studd and Smith made a quick dash to Bristol, where the crowd was too great for the Colston Hall, and were back at Cambridge the next day. There too 'every corner – floor, orchestra, gallery' of the Guildhall was crammed with people. Professor Babington led off as chairman, followed by 'Benjamin B', Stevenson, Landale and then Stanley Smith on the love of Christ constraining them 'to go out to the world'. 'Unless we spread abroad the light, we will find in England . . . that we cannot hold our own with the powers of darkness'. Then each of the Seven testified to their allegiance to Jesus Christ as their Lord and Master: Beauchamp, tall and powerful, with a 'capacity to extract enjoyment from anything'; the soldiers erect and to the point but no orators; Studd's fire glowing through his quiet conviction – 'God does not deal with you until you are wholly given up to Him' (but then he shows you that fame and wealth and self-centredness are trash compared with being given up to him); and finally the two theologians, Arthur Polhill-Turner and W W Cassels, no less straightforward, practical and profound.

The 'Cambridge Correspondent' of *The Record* – Handley Moule in fact – judged it 'the most remarkable missionary meeting held within living memory at Cambridge', which was again to say a great deal. In the same issue a correspondent went deeper. Why had this Mission drawn to it man after man of this influential type? For one essential reason:

> The uncompromising spirituality and unworldliness of the programme of the Mission, responded to by hearts which have truly laid all at the LORD's feet, and whose delight is the most open confession of His name and its power upon themselves. I venture to pronounce it inconceivable, impossible, that such a meeting should have been held in connection with any missionary enterprise of mixed aims, or in which such great truths were ignored, or treated with hesitation, (or) did the work not demand of the workers very real and manifest self-sacrifice and acts of faith.[60]

After the tepid welcome to Oxford in November, it had required some faith for 'Benjamin B' to book the Corn Exchange, with the city's greatest seating capacity. He need not have feared. 'With so many undergraduates present', even if fewer than at Cambridge, and enough townsmen to fill the place 'to overflowing', many standing, this meeting on February 3 also earned the comment 'of almost unparalleled interest'. Theodore Howard as chairman 'spoke *admirably*', after himself having been stirred at Cambridge the previous day.

'A blaze of publicity' — *February–March 1885*

Wednesday, February 4, saw the grand climax at London's Exeter Hall, in the meeting that might not have been. London's daily and weekly papers, including *The Times*, and religious periodicals, reported the occasion at length. Sheets of rain pouring down on the crowds who pressed into the hall deterred no one. When the great hall was full, with 'platform, area, galleries, every nook and corner . . . crowded', the lower hall filled and overflowed. 'Even then many were turned away at the doors.' Three thousand five hundred found places. The young men for whom the meeting had previously been intended were equalled in number by young women and people 'of all sections of the Church and grades of social life'. 'People of note and title had to get in anywhere and be thankful if they got in at all,' Benjamin wrote afterwards to Hudson Taylor.[61] 'Mr Denny, Mr Howard, Dr Barnardo . . . had to stand nearly all the time. It was almost impossible to reserve room on the platform for the speakers. Miss Waldegrave came beseeching a seat for Lady Beauchamp . . . Happily we could get her in beside her daughter' – at the organ. C T Studd's mother was there with Kynaston and his bride, Montagu's sister, and the Christian Polhill-Turner sisters had brought their reluctant mother. A large map of China formed the backdrop of the platform; beneath it were ranged forty Cambridge undergraduates dedicated to become missionaries, led by J C Farthing of Caius, the future missionary bishop, who spoke as their representative.

George Williams (Sir George to be) led the 'platform party' out to their places, to a roar of cheers and clapping. After a spirited hymn he presented each of the Seven with a Chinese New Testament, gift of the Bible Society on whose committee he served. The CIM, he said, was the only society working overseas 'on an undenominational basis'. Benjamin briefly described the Mission and its principles, and introduced the Cambridge contingent. Robert Landale spoke as an Oxford graduate and law student who had already spent seven years in China and knew that it was 'no light thing' to leave all and bury oneself in an often hostile land – not to be done on 'human enthusiasm' but only by those with hearts 'full of love to God'.

As at Cambridge, Stanley Smith then gave the main, spellbinding address. It cannot be read without conveying the atmosphere in that hall. Neither the apostles nor their successors today were charged with the 'milk and water of religion but the cream of the Gospel'. William Carey on leaving yet another meeting of colleagues in Britain to discuss 'the Gospel and the World', had protested, 'Are we going to separate again, and is *nothing* to be *done*?' 'If David Livingstone could leap to life (again) what would he say? "Do not follow my body home to this cathedral, but follow where my heart lies. . . in Africa."' The five thousand would never have been fed if the apostles had served only the front rows again and again. Then seizing on the indignation of the hour, 'a greater than Gordon cries from Khartoum . . . the voice of Christ from the Cross of Calvary. . . . "I thirst!" . . . He thirsts for the Chinese, for the Africans, for the Asiatics, and for the South Americans. . . . Would you pass by that Christ? . . . There is "sin in the camp"', the infidelity of Achan thwarting the victory of God's people, the triumph of the gospel.

While Smith went down to the Lower Hall and Studd made his way up, Montagu Beauchamp called for many to put themselves at Christ's disposal. Dixon Hoste told how in the army he had been blind until Christ opened his eyes to see him and his command to 'Go! and preach the Gospel.' William Cassels saw the need for 'more heroism' in Christians. 'Oh, for shame, that He who gave His own life on the cross should still be crying for helpers.' Cecil Polhill-Turner, his resignation not yet gazetted, so still the serving officer of his crack cavalry regiment, simply told how his own life had been transformed and redirected. Arthur was three days from his twenty-third birthday. Leaving home to go to the unknown was not proving hard but 'like that of a bird when let out of a cage . . . very glorious'. J C Farthing spoke before Studd. After the Guildhall meeting, he said, 'I saw this; that we were to take up our cross and follow CHRIST; that there was to be no compromise, however small; that there was to be nothing between us and our Master; that we were to be wholly for CHRIST.'

C T Studd then told frankly about his conversion and slow progress and backsliding before his brother's near-fatal illness. 'I had formerly as much love for cricket as any man could have,' but after he yielded to Jesus Christ as LORD, 'my heart was no longer in the game.' He read what an atheist had written, 'If I were a thoroughly consistent Christian, my whole life should be given up to going about the world preaching the Gospel.' Then how he went to John McCarthy's farewell prayer meeting and knew that GOD was sending him to China. 'Choose who is to be your God!' – the true God or your own substitutes. Then obey Him.

Two hours had passed. The Rev Hugh Price Hughes, billed as the final speaker, suggested to the chairman that he should not speak at all, but the audience were wanting more. He faced them with the need to 'submit to Christ' – to offer themselves to God as a living sacrifice, declaring 'There is enough power in this meeting to stir . . . the whole world.' This very thing was beginning to happen. In the first missionary book she ever read, a young woman saw a report of this meeting and was 'drawn in spirit' to the one who had 'counted as loss all that life as an officer of the Royal Artillery would have meant.' Amy Carmichael of South India went on to influence thousands in her lifetime. But she was only one so influenced.[62]

The 'boat train' left Victoria at 10.00 the next morning, February 5, the very day news of Gordon's death reached London. Sober Cassels, 'the old man of the party' a month short of twenty-six, had pasted red labels saying 'God First' on each piece of his baggage. They travelled by Brindisi to Alexandria and by the desert train to join the *Kaisar-i-hind* at Suez.[63] On board and sharing their second class accommodation ('fit only for servants and dogs', it had been said, but at a twenty-five per cent discount to the CIM for many years), they found a drunken, hard-swearing sea-captain of an Indian ship, already notorious among passengers and crew for his behaviour. Hoste at once got talking with him and was soon reading the Bible – 'all rot' – and discussing it with him. Another of the party took a turn a few days later.

Alone in his cabin that night the captain cried to God to forgive and save him. He soon revealed how much he knew. 'He seemed to be a fullgrown Christian at once,' telling the ship's company and passengers, 'It's so simple; it's only trusting.' After that several of the crew and other second-class passengers were converted and joined the Seven for daily worship. Changing ship at Colombo, and after meetings there and at Penang, Singapore and Hong Kong (where they also visited the barracks in each place) they were met at Shanghai on March 18 by a Chinese they did not at first recognise, Hudson Taylor. He had arrived on March 3.

The teeming city crowds made the work ahead of them seem overwhelming, but for the present more meetings for foreigners had been announced, for all nationalities and types; for cricket and rowing club athletes; in the Royal Asiatic Society and in the Lyceum Theatre. Not even standing room could be found after the first day's meetings. The *Shanghai Mercury* gave full and sympathetic reports. But the community was shaken from any complacency when at the largest meeting of all the port chaplain, the Rev F R Smith, incumbent of the cathedral church, came forward after Charlie Studd had spoken, and said that if he had died in the night he would have been a lost soul. He had never before understood the difference between being 'a Christian' and clergyman by duty and his own effort, and being made one by the Saviour in response to real confession and faith in him. After a miserable night he had consulted a young CMS missionary, Heywood Horsburgh, on an early morning walk, and had been helped to commit his soul to Christ. Some would ridicule him, but he implored all who were in the position he had been in to put it right with God as he had just done.[64]

The Seven's final weeks in Britain had been too full to allow much time with their families, to their mothers' distress. Mrs Studd had offered to pay the costs if only her son could stay a day longer and give her a few hours of his company. What did outfits matter? was the men's attitude. They were going into Chinese dress at the end of the voyage. 'I am deeply grieved to trouble you,' Mrs Smith wrote to Jennie late in January, 'but Stanley . . . gives no thought to temporal affairs. (Please) write by return of post and tell me what is *absolutely* necessary for (his) outfit as . . . he fancies he needs nothing and has sold or given away all. . . . Also kindly tell us *the name of the vessel*.' But after the last Exeter Hall meeting, her maternal flutters subsided. 'Never shall I forget; it was a glorious ending to their labours in this country.' And three days later she wrote again. The mothers and families were going to meet in Mrs Studd's large rooms weekly or fortnightly to pray for the men and for missions in general. Would Jennie or Amelia or both come and show them how to go about it?[65]

When the boat-train had steamed out of Victoria Station, the Pyrland Road family returned to a new welter of work. Letters to Hudson Taylor came first.

> Exeter Hall last night – what shall I say? [Benjamin scribbled in his fast flowing hand.] Such a meeting! I question if a meeting of equal significance and spiritual fruitfulness has been held in that building during this generation. Its influence upon the course of Missions must be immense – incalculable. [He was not mistaken.] I am filled with gratitude . . . It was a most magnificent success. . . . *The Times*, *Standard*, *Daily News*, etc, etc all had good articles. . . . It seemed as if the influence for good of the CIM for the whole of its existence was focussed in that one night's meeting. We cannot praise God enough. . . . That meeting will be the talk of England . . . the Halls were given to us free.

Theodore Howard had written very warmly, but said he was too busy to do more than chair the council meetings, so Benjamin would have to carry the main weight of the work in Britain. In the circumstances that was sheer joy, except for the 'teething troubles'.

> You will hardly believe how much the meeting has been noticed (in the Press). The CIM seems to many to have emerged all at once into a very blaze of publicity, and we may be sure that it will provoke much comment, some very friendly and some very otherwise (from denominational viewpoints). [And on February 20]: A writer in *The Cambridge Review* speaks of support to unattached missions as the disloyal weakening of the older missions. I trust what I have written [for the Press] will be useful to counteract such notions.[66]

Benjamin was printing an extra 22,000 copies of the *China's Millions*, increased by another 10,000 a few days later, describing the meetings which 'would have been worth £10,000 to the cause of Missions had they cost so much.' But in fact donations stemming from the meetings themselves had more than paid for everything. At the later May meetings he reported that few copies remained of 50,000 and 'we must without delay print more'.

'The Cambridge party' (as they were still being called) had won a place in the minds of Christians which remains unique a hundred years later. In 1899 Eugene Stock looked back and said 'The influence of such a band of men was irresistible . . . No such event had occurred before . . .' Archbishop Benson called it 'one of the good signs of the times'.[67] And Stock again: 'Although all English Societies, and preeminently the CMS, felt the influence of the uprising of missionary zeal for which their outgoing was the signal, the China Inland Mission naturally felt it most. Its energetic Secretary . . . and his colleagues . . . were quite overwhelmed by the multitude of applications for service.'

CHAPTER ELEVEN

BUILD-UP FOR EXPANSION 1885–90

The China the Seven reached *1884–85*

The great empire of the Manchus was rotten at its heart and breaking up at its extremities. The Peking court in Ci Xi's hands had become more than ever a place of intrigue, extravagance and corruption, while foreign powers strengthened their grip on Manchuria, Korea, Burma and Indo-China. Ever since the eunuch Li Liangying had stolen the imperial seal for Ci Xi to thwart the Jehol plot (Book 3, p 259) and secured himself in her favour, he had feathered his own nest, becoming one of the wealthiest and most powerful men in the nation. Permitted to speak without first being spoken to by his imperial mistress, a privilege denied even to the Grand Secretary and the child emperor's father, he took to referring to her and to himself as '*Zamen* – we two'.

Prince Kong detested him. But Ci Xi felt insecure while Prince Kong headed the Grand Council of Ministers. By a surprise decree in 1884 she had admitted that 'Our Country has not yet returned to its wonted stability, and its affairs are in a critical state . . . There is chaos in the Government and a feeling of insecurity amongst the people.' This understatement covered far more – riotous unrest in the southern provinces and whispers of rebellion among the secret societies.[1] Addressing Prince Kong and his colleagues of the Grand Council, on their knees with downcast eyes before her Peacock Throne in the great Audience Chamber, she declared that he and two others were forthwith deprived of office and fortunate not to be decapitated. Not until ten years later was he recalled, when she could not manage without him. She forcibly married the boy emperor to a cousin whom he hated. This daughter of Ci Xi's younger brother became her spy in his closest circle. And the Pearl Concubine whom he loved met with a 'fate even more horrible' than Alude's (Book 5, p 488).

Into this situation the indispensable statesman Li Hongzhang was brought again, charged with the protection of China from attack on her sea coasts. As viceroy of Zhili he had already ordered six

PRINCE KONG, CHIEF MINISTER, SENIOR GUARDIAN OF THE THRONE

gunboats from Europe, but they were laughable without trained commanders and crews. His Sino-Japanese Convention (signed on April 18 exactly one month after the Cambridge Seven landed at Shanghai) (p 312) could only postpone attack by Japan, rapidly modernising. The surrender of suzerain rights in Annam and Burma (1885–86) proclaimed to the world the weakness of China, offering too great a temptation at a time of foreign imperialism. France's ambitions in East Asia demanded a countermove by Britain, and the annexation of Upper Burma in 1886 was the logical step.

When Britain's hero-envoy to Peking, Sir Harry Parkes, died at his post on March 22, 1885, Sir Robert Hart was invited to succeed him. 'While his (Sir Robert's) entire loyalty to the Chinese government was never doubted, his guiding hand in the (British) legation had worked for the good both of China and of England.'[2] But who could succeed Hart as Inspector General of the Chinese Customs? He trusted his own brother James, efficient and popular, to maintain the standards of integrity. And after an attempt by the Chinese government to instal W A P Martin, an educator without the essential administrative experience, James Hart was appointed. Martin instead was honoured with the rank of Mandarin, Third Class, for his work as President of the Tong Wen Guan.[3] For the brother of the British minister to hold such a high rank in the Chinese Civil Service was too much for Li Hongzhang, always with an eye to the main chance, and Hart's irreconcilable rival. He manoeuvred to have James Hart replaced by the German Gustav Detring, 'a man of brilliant intellect and great diplomatic ability' who had been Li's own right-hand man since the Chefoo Convention of 1876 (pp 67–8). With Detring owing allegiance to Li 'of the itchy palm', the integrity of the Imperial Maritime Customs would soon have passed beyond his control. Sir Robert therefore resigned his position as Her Majesty's envoy in August and resumed duty as Inspector General to the satisfaction of all, including Germany, for Detring had never been as co-operative as his own countrymen wished.

The close link between France and Roman Catholicism in China, the French 'protectorate', naturally led to hostility in Guangdong against missionaries and Chinese Christians. Thousands of refugees fled to Hong Kong and Macao. In Yunnan, Guizhou, Sichuan, Shaanxi and Shanxi officials became hostile and placards threatening extermination appeared on city walls. Only after peace with France was concluded in September 1885 and copies of the imperial edicts of toleration (of 1884) were prominently displayed, did calm return. Protestants could not expect to be exempt. But when in the glum mood of the 1884–85 United States Depression a mob in Rock Springs, Wyoming, attacked innocent Chinese residents, killing nineteen, wounding many and driving hundreds from the town, violent protest in China could not be halted by mere compensation to the victims.

Catholic priests were flooding into China. The 250 in 1870 had become 488 by 1885. All, whatever their nationality, still carried French and Chinese passports. The towers of the Beitang, the North Cathedral at Peking, still overlooked the imperial palace in defiance of Ci Xi's repeated requests for the Lazarists to yield the site. In exchange for land farther away and the construction costs of a new building, it was at last incorporated in the palace gardens in 1888. As a diplomatic gesture, Père Armand David's remarkable natural history collection was simultaneously conveyed to the government.

Farther afield, the birth of the Indian National Congress gave evidence of new stirrings which in little more than sixty years' time would win independence for the subcontinent again. Karl Marx had died in 1883 but Engels completed the second volume of *Das Kapital* in 1885 (and the third in 1894), promoting the idea of class struggle by violence to bring to workers the full reward of their labour. Oblivious of the dawning of the political polarisation between 'east' and 'west', let alone of a Marxist day in China, Gladstone was still preoccupied with the intractable Irish Question. On October 10, 1884, King Mtesa of Uganda had died and in January 1885 his son Mwanga had begun the torture of Christians by sword and fire. Bishop Hannington and all but four of his fifty companions were massacred by Mwanga's orders on October 29, 1885. More deaths followed, from violence and disease. The faint-hearts as usual cried, 'Abandon the attempt!' Mackay, all alone, wrote: 'Are you joking?' Hand Africa over to Mwanga, to slave-traders, gun-runners and gin merchants? '*They* make no talk of "giving up" *their* respective missions!'[4] The Church in China and worldwide took note. God did not always deliver his servants from the sword.

The Mission the Seven had joined — *1885*

Doubled in size during the past three years by the addition of the Seventy, the membership of the China Inland Mission stood at one hundred and fifty when the Cambridge party reached Shanghai. By the end of the year it was nearing two hundred. Unrest might interrupt but did not prevent progress. *China's Millions* carried reports of other missions' personnel and work, the CMS, the LMS, the Presbyterians and Baptists, side by side with the CIM's. Seldom in the news, the rank and file missionaries worked faithfully on in their allotted spheres. Preaching night and morning in their 'street chapels', visiting in homes or receiving guests, much as in the early days at Ningbo and Hangzhou, or tramping doggedly through the provinces 'scattering seed', they allowed themselves to be seen, the harmless 'exhorters to virtue'.

Steady teaching of the Christians led to some going out to sell books or as 'helpers' to work with evangelists or missionaries in outposts; or even on the road as carriers. Growing experience and proof of having a gift of preaching or teaching made them 'fellow-workers in the Chinese Church' and missionaries to distant regions. Wang Laedjün had become, by natural growth of the Hangzhou church, the superintendent-pastor of a wide network of local churches planted and fostered by himself and his helpers. His wise relationship with the other missions in Hangzhou often brought them to seek his advice. Others were, like him, glad of the missionaries' greater knowledge of the Bible, but well able to care for the churches in their absence.

The Broumtons had seen proclamations promising protection of foreigners, and set out from Guiyang to Chongqing when James Broumton fell ill. Nevertheless on the way they were repeatedly robbed on the road, and in a wayside inn where they took refuge were stripped of all but their underclothes and left destitute; they hid in a loft there for a week before officials sent them on under escort.

Henry Soltau, in lower Burma with his wife and child, had learned of an attack on Bhamo in early December by hundreds of Chinese and Kachin rebels who had put the town to the torch. He had set off at once by steam-launch and arrived in time to rescue the American missionaries and Christians, under rifle fire. The Kachin rebels begged him as a friend to stay and support them in negotiations with the Burmese, but to take sides politically was unthinkable. Bhamo was retaken in March. So came, in his words, 'this terrible ending to the first volume of Bhamo history. May the second be brighter.' The CIM returned there in 1887 but not the Soltaus.[5]

Hudson Taylor's report from China to the Annual Meeting in London was written while the Seven were still in Shanghai, almost daily addressing packed audiences.[6] They 'have more thoroughly affected Shanghai than any series of meetings that have ever been held', one report read. The editor of the *Courier* and his wife were among those converted, and scores of others in the Lyceum Theatre, the Masonic Hall and at special receptions for athletes. John McCarthy had already dispersed the accumulation of missionaries at the coast, waiting for more peaceful conditions upcountry. So the news was of parties of them pressing up to the north-west, and others going to Guiyang, Kunming and Dali, in the far south-west, from which two cities the first baptisms had at last been reported. George Parker had secured premises in Lanzhou, the capital of Gansu, and Riley in Chengdu, the Sichuan capital. Progress under persecution made Hanzhong a promising place for one party of the Cambridge men to start in, and Shanxi for a second group of them. Henan, one of the toughest provinces to crack, had at last allowed Sambrook to settle at Zhoujiakou with two others, but not for long. Soon they were to be driven out and like Henry Taylor before him, Sambrook dropped out of the battle utterly broken in spirit.

Meanwhile the older churches in Zhejiang, Anhui and Jiangxi had struggled on through 'periods of excitement', a euphemism for persecution and riot. One highlight in Zhejiang had been response in 'revival' proportions to aggressive evangelism by the CMS. It was even possible to write of scope for more and more women in the areas of China already opened up. But Hunan remained impenetrable. With their base at Shashi on the Yangzi in Hubei, Adam Dorward, Henry Dick, Thomas James and Chinese colleagues were quietly holding an outpost at Jinshi across the Hunan border, and making surreptitious journeys into the province. But even the freedom to travel in turbulent Hunan which Dorward had earlier known was for the present being denied to them.

Ever since he himself landed on March 3, Hudson Taylor had been swamped with work that could not wait to be done, including 120 letters to be answered without delay.[7] A missionary charged with conducting the Mission's business in Shanghai had rented premises in his own name and after defecting, to run them as a private boarding house, was claiming them for himself. Hudson Taylor found two other houses in the Yuan Ming Yuan Buildings 'a stone's throw from' the British consulate. Their simplicity and down-to-earth practicality met with the Seven's approval. They had not come looking for luxury. He designated No 5 for offices and No 6 as a home for transients, ready in time for the next influx of newcomers. Within a few weeks, on May 4, he cabled for thirty more men to be sent from Britain, and twenty-nine set sail. J E Cardwell, often disaffected, had resigned but found life outside the Mission less than rosy. So he swallowed his pride at Hudson Taylor's suggestion, rejoined and took charge of business affairs, with John McCarthy staying at Shanghai to handle Mission accounts and remittances.

There were now so many more missionaries to provide with accommodation at Shanghai, and so much coming-and-going between China and Europe, the coast and the interior, often in ill-health and needing special care, that serious thought had to be given to acquiring more suitable permanent quarters. To rent them would be a constant heavy drain on resources. To buy a site and build would be immensely costly, involving a leap of faith. Yet from this time Hudson Taylor kept it in view. His vision of the Mission's expansion and extension throughout China was itself enlarging beyond what he could yet share with others – far exceeding anything yet seen in the missionary world anywhere. At Colombo on his way out he had met and consulted the explorer Ney Elias (Book 5, pp 423, 430), serving as British political agent at Kashgar, about Turkestan and Tibet. The evangelisation of the whole empire would need hundreds. His mental picture of the premises needed would have alarmed even his closest colleagues. But he was level-headed. Two years later he telegraphed £1,500 from Britain to be put on deposit for a chosen site on Wusong Road to be levelled and built up above flood level, ready for ambitious development.[8]

His plan for the Cambridge men had been that all seven should pioneer the great province of Sichuan, apart from the river region between the already occupied cities of Chengdu and Chongqing on the Min River and the Yangzi (Maps pp 210, 260). Rich and teeming with millions of industrious people, Sichuan extended 600 miles westwards from the gorges near Yichang to the Tibetan marches, and 500 miles 'as the crow flies' from the mountains south of the Han River plain and Hanzhong to the southernmost loop of the Jin He, the River of Gold, dividing it from Yunnan. Each man was nominally an Anglican, even if only Cassels and Arthur Polhill-Turner favoured planting the Anglican Church on Chinese soil.[9] The principle of arranging for missionaries of the same denominational outlook to work together, pointed to their forming a strong team in this strategic region.

But discretion required a careful approach. Seven athletic young men, among them two of undisguisedly military bearing, could arouse misplaced suspicion. So Hudson Taylor split them into two groups of three, for the present keeping Montagu Beauchamp to travel with him (as Lady Beauchamp had requested).[10] He proposed to go himself on a preliminary reconnaissance of Sichuan. C T Studd and the Polhills he sent up the Yangzi in Chinese clothes, with John McCarthy as escort-interpreter, and Montagu for the experience as far as Anqing. As Griffith John's guests at Hankou and by his arrangement, they addressed audiences including consuls, customs officials and merchants on three successive nights, for their message was Griffith John's own – 'the power of the Holy Spirit daily renewed for Christian service'. '(We) greatly astonished the resident missionaries', the Polhill brothers commented enigmatically. From there they ascended the swollen Han River rapids, with Dr and Mrs William Wilson in another boat, three Etonians on 'a continuous picnic', taking until mid-July to reach Hanzhong. At first their river days were filled by studying Chinese with a language teacher, relieved by walking on the trackers' towpath and swimming in the river. Plagued by an invasion of rats, they remembered the Leicester donor's Stilton cheeses and proved their guess right by presenting them to the Wilsons, for the rats changed boats.

Stanley Smith, Hoste and Cassels were sent by ship via Yantai to Tianjin, and on through Peking to Shanxi, there to learn Chinese and join in the work of which David Hill's convert Hsi (known as Xi Liaozhih or 'Shengmo') was becoming the remarkable leader. This would give the foreign communities in Tianjin and Peking an opportunity to hear them. A few days before sailing with them, J J Coulthard told Hudson Taylor that he had 'found almost by accident his own love for Maria to be reciprocated'. Might they become engaged? Yes, he replied, delighted, but they must wait three years until she reached twenty-one before marrying. So he found a substitute escort for the Cambridge men in David Thompson of western Sichuan.

The immediate effect of their visit to Yantai was the drawing together of the different missions in the community for united communion services, previously neglected. And after they had left Peking all missions were meeting daily to pray for 'the baptism of the Holy Ghost on our own hearts' and for 'the outpouring of the

Spirit on China'. Twenty-five missionaries and others signed a joint letter, sent to missions everywhere, saying what the newcomers had done for them and inviting them to adopt the same prayers.[11] By then the Cambridge men had gone on overland, enjoying the physical exercise and 'roughing it'. The commander of a Chinese cavalry regiment at Taiyuan invited them to a meal. And everywhere they were well received as they travelled on to Linfen (Pingyang), Hsi's home area in south Shanxi, meeting their American counterparts, the men of Oberlin College, at Taigu.

The pressure of demands upon Hudson Taylor at the coast, keeping him at his desk until midnight, day after day, forced him to forsake his Sichuan journey. So he sent F W Baller and Montagu Beauchamp to join the others in Shanxi, and in response to urgent letters from Chefoo himself went there immediately to talk with some members affected by the 'Shanxi spirit' (pp 288ff). Although Timothy Richard's own colleagues in the BMS had rejected his theses as 'another gospel', among those whom he had convinced these few members of the CIM were propagating his views.[12]

At the end of May Hudson Taylor was back in Shanghai, wearied by the difficulties he had faced and late night consultations, when word began to come of problems with the Cambridge men. He had hoped that Baller, an experienced, capable missionary but dry at heart, would absorb the spirit of his companions. Instead, he wrote, he was repelled by their extreme piety. Stanley Smith and Hoste in his opinion were damaging their health by excessive prayer and fasting.

News from the Hanzhong party was more disturbing. C T Studd and the Polhill brothers had thought language study a laborious substitute for what they saw to be the Biblical way of acquiring a foreign tongue. On the slow journey up the Han River they had put away their books and 'given themselves to prayer' for a Pentecostal gift of speech in Chinese. If anyone should have received it, surely men who had forsaken all and followed Christ could expect it as a mark of God's approval. Arrived eventually at Hanzhong, they persuaded two of the young missionary women there to do the same. But before October ended they saw their mistake, knuckled down to study and in time became fluent. 'How many and subtle are the devices of Satan,' Hudson Taylor wrote, 'to keep the Chinese ignorant of the gospel.' 'If I could put the Chinese language into your brains by one wave of the hand I would not do it,' he took to saying to new missionaries. Unadapted foreign thought and idiom merely translated into Chinese could do more harm than good. Months of submission to a Chinese scholar while watching and listening to evangelists and experienced missionaries taught wisdom as well as language.[13]

Within the same period in Shanxi the other Cambridge men were carrying on simple conversations and telling the gospel in memorised sentences. Stanley Smith, the orator who 'could hold the Sunday throng at the Achilles Statue in Hyde Park' swept ahead of the others. Once he could speak freely he held his Chinese audiences in the same way, and over the years, Cecil Polhill recorded, 'thousands have believed through his preaching.'[14]

Dixon Hoste in his periodic letters to Hudson Taylor mentioned 'some rather rough assaults by the "prince of the kingdom of China" (meaning Satan) who now that we are here, does all that he can to keep our lives from really getting mixed up with that of the Chinese.' No one complained that Baller kept too tight a rein on them, but later protests from language students at Anqing that he was by far too authoritarian for mature men to tolerate may explain Hoste's veiled wording. Discord among missionaries, and keeping them out of touch with the Chinese were two of Satan's favourite devices. The utter genuineness of all that Hoste wrote impressed Hudson Taylor. Nothing he said was for effect but revealed the true man. He chose to spend several months each year living in the villages or market towns with an evangelist, preaching at country fairs far from fellow foreigners. He enjoyed having his 'utter rawness rubbed off', while seeing the need of constant 'forbearance and willingness to be the inferior' if the cultural gulf between Westerner and Chinese was to be bridged. 'Little acts of rudeness and contempt' for the alien by passers-by were a salutary lesson in humility. Less than two years after Harold Schofield died praying for his place to be taken by like-minded men, they were there. And soon Hsi Shengmo was to find in Dixon Hoste the wise adviser he as a Christian beginner most needed.[15]

A trap for the leaders *1885–86*

The Cambridge Seven had departed at a high point not only of the CIM but of all missions. No send-off had ever been so stirring, and no heart-searching so deep or widespread among Christians. 'In one short week, the China Inland Mission has been suddenly lifted into unusual and unexpected prominence and even popularity . . . The hour of success is often the time of danger . . . a snare and not a blessing.' Benjamin Broomhall's statement had its echo in many forms. John C Thompson, a graduate of Edinburgh, called it 'a movement perhaps more wonderful than ever had place in the history of university students . . . The work is spreading itself in all its depth and reality throughout the whole country.' Thirty-five men applied for training to the Edinburgh Medical Missionary Society alone.[16]

In the remarkable *History of the Church Missionary Society*, 1885, '86 and '87 were named 'Three Memorable Years'. At the invitation of the YMCA another great 'memorable meeting for men' was held at the Exeter Hall on March 24, 1885. Parties of men from the universities, including fifty from Oxford and Cambridge, others from the Islington and Highbury Theological colleges, and three hundred from the City, packed the hall and overflowed into King's College. 'Ladies were banished to the west gallery,' but 1885 saw the foreshadowings of CMS women's work. Offers of service from men began to multiply. After the Seven's meetings thirty-one more students offered themselves to the CMS. By 1893 offers had reached 140, making Handley Moule implore the Christian Union not to forget the needs of the United Kingdom. In October 1885 the largest valedictory service within living memory was held. And the CIM's own annual meetings in May were 'unequalled for blessing by any we ever had'. Gone were the days when an unknown 'small independent body of men' had been written off in those words by the great friend of the downtrodden, Lord Shaftesbury. Whenever he could he presided now at CIM meetings, saying 'I *like* this Mission.' But in 1885 Theodore Howard had to deputise for him at the May meetings, and in mid-October the London Council noted his death, at eighty-four.

Not only were 50,000 copies of *China's Millions* with the story of the Seven too few to meet the demand, but when Benjamin republished it in book form with photographs, maps and recent news of the Seven, amplified to 250 pages by an anthology of articles from many leading churchmen and public figures of the day, 10,000 were sold within a few months. This second edition had to be followed by a third in 1890 making 20,000 in all. First called *A Missionary Band: a Record of Missionary Consecration*, it was renamed *The Evangelisation of the World*, with sections on Africa and India as well as China. Queen Victoria accepted a copy of the gilt-edged edition, and others circulated by Sir George Williams profoundly affected young men in the YMCAs of Britain and the United States. Robert Speer publicly stated that, apart from the

Bible no books had so influenced his life of dedication to the cause of student missionary volunteers as Blaikie's *Personal Life of Livingstone* and *The Evangelisation of the World*. Robert P Wilder, John R Mott and other leaders of the student movements paid tribute to its impact in both continents and on their own lives.[17] But 'the time of danger' and the 'snare' lay not only in temptations for the Seven in the heart of China to despair and to question the rightness of what they had done, but in assaults on the leading men of the Mission.

For ten years Benjamin had been the chief and almost the sole executive administrator of the CIM in Britain. Others had played their considerable part as honorary director, treasurer and advisers, and had borne the ultimate responsibility in channelling funds and approved reinforcements to China. But Benjamin had carried the burden of correspondence, of public relations, of organising annual and farewell meetings throughout the country, and directing the activities of missionaries on home leave. He had managed the office in Pyrland Road with its missionary assistants and employed staff, edited the *Millions* in Hudson Taylor's name, using 'copy' sent from China, and guided those who offered to go as missionaries from tentative enquiry and initial interviews through to formal application and appearance before the council. Although Amelia ran the home with its changing population of candidates and missionaries, in transit or residence for varying periods of time, Benjamin had the oversight and presided at meals and meetings. He was in his element. But danger lay in the rapid growth of the Mission. It was no longer possible for one man to carry so much.

Before leaving the country Hudson Taylor had arranged for some responsibilities to be delegated to experienced members of the Mission detained at home by their own ill-health or their families'. C G Moore became Deputation Secretary, Charles Fishe the Financial Secretary (or cashier-accountant), Cardwell, Benjamin's personal assistant, and Robert Landale (followed by Jennie Taylor) edited the *Millions*, while the Auxiliary Council of Ladies interviewed women candidates; this meant that Benjamin was freer to exploit his *métier* of public relations. Revealed through his management of the Cambridge Seven's whirlwind tour of the country, this gift had become of unique value to the Mission.

In his early days Benjamin had been secretary to the Anti-Slavery Association and being naturally gregarious had a wide circle of influential friends. An 'alert and discerning observer of the trend of things . . . he had the gift of the effective word, the helpful suggestion, that brought him into touch . . . with a large number of England's leading men', especially in later years. Like his father, both Anglican and Methodist at heart, and regularly taking the periodicals of the leading Churches, he was eirenic in his attitude to all. 'Unperturbed in spirit, never hasting and never resting, he continued at his desk regularly until midnight and sometimes beyond.' He travelled extensively and opened the way for the Mission's representatives to be welcomed to speak about China.[18]

Letter-writing was one of his greatest gifts, always in his own flowing hand and as warmly to the donors of small amounts as of larger sums. Very often it was the working man's donation or the widow's letter that he cited in the *Millions* or from the platform. But it was 'the astonishing energy and practical wisdom with which he directed the burst of missionary zeal' at the time of the Cambridge Seven, that most impressed Eugene Stock and John Stevenson. This energy Benjamin now applied to the task in hand – and fell into a trap for the unwary, attempting too much.

In China, Hudson Taylor was giving himself without reserve until he too fell prey to the same unsuspected danger. By October he was commenting to Jennie that he needed to hear more often and more fully from London. Forty new missionaries, accepted from among many more offers, went out to China during the year. Others were in the pipeline. Advance information about them and plans for their despatch made arrangements for their reception at Shanghai and upcountry so much easier. But between Benjamin and Cardwell in the pressure of work and the dependence of plans upon the funds coming in, details of who would sail and when tended to be held back. Even uncertain probabilities, qualified by 'funds permitting' would have been preferable to silence, Hudson Taylor pointed out. In response to his plea this phrase was adopted, and a century later is still a current cliché in the Mission.

His own strength and tolerance were being undermined by bouts of his old enemy, dysentery. And he was pining again for Jennie. He and Benjamin had been good friends since boyhood, accustomed to forthright speaking of their minds. Warm friendship within the family circle did not prevent them from holding different views on some practical issues. Where letters to others would be more carefully worded, they tended to be outspoken between themselves. It only needed the stress of work and circumstances to make ill-chosen words give rise to misunderstandings, or silence to appear negligence. After the exhausting heat of summer Hudson Taylor felt aggrieved and wrote to Jennie that Theodore Howard and Benjamin were disregarding him, starving him of information. In a sense it was true, but explicable. Expansion and popularity were new, uncharted waters.

A young Canadian named Jonathan Goforth, one of the future great missionaries to China, wrote from Knox College, Toronto, to Hudson Taylor saying he had written to London in 1882 asking to be sent as one of the Seventy but had had no reply. 'He found out, later, that his letter had gone astray. Nothing daunted he wrote again,' his biographer explained. And Hudson Taylor advised him to consult his own Church before joining the CIM. When his fellow-students at Knox learned that their own Presbyterian Church of Canada were unwilling to add China to their undertakings and declined to send him, they roused the college alumni and raised the funds to support him. Goforth himself bought hundreds of copies of *China's Spiritual Need and Claims* and distributed them to the ministers of his Church. The Church relented and he established a successful mission in Henan.[19] Meanwhile at the Niagara Conference of 1885 his zealous advocacy of China's claim on the Church, with 'the face of an angel (and) the voice of an archangel', won to the cause a young American businessman, Henry W Frost, of whom a great deal more was to be heard.

By honouring the responsibility of a young man to his own denomination, rather than welcoming him to the CIM, Hudson Taylor had won a faithful friend, and the Canadian Presbyterian Church in 1888 sought his advice on starting their mission in Henan.[20] Years later, in 1911, Jonathan Goforth, a leader of the great Manchurian revival movement, approached the CIM again with the hope of at last becoming a member. He had been the first North American applicant to the CIM. But in 1885 a young medical graduate wrote from Philadelphia, came over to London to meet the council, and on April 21 left Britain with Archibald Orr Ewing and George Graham Brown for China. Dr J C Stewart set up his pioneer medical work at Guihuacheng on the Mongolian border of north Shanxi, the city strongly recommended by James Cameron.

Organising for advance *1882–86*

With expansion of the CIM in hand, the main purpose of Hudson Taylor's return to China in 1885 was to organise the Mission to cope with growing numbers. Since 1882 and earlier, he had been experimenting with ways of sharing his load with others, and we need to go back to those days to recapture the context. He had appointed Dalziel as business manager in Shanghai, Coulthard as financial and general secretary in Wuchang for the western and south-western provinces and Parrott as 'corresponding secretary' to relieve him of purely business letters and the less personal and confidential correspondence. But still his own work multiplied as more and more missionaries consulted him and looked for personal attention. No longer could he be available to all or travel as widely to encourage the lonely and to deal with their problems.[21]

But the matter had developed a new angle. As loud as the clamour for him to delegate his duties, there had come a growing protest that the deputies were coming between him and the rank and file. 'Any delegation of Mr Taylor's authority was apt to be regarded with misgivings if not opposed through misunderstanding. . . . Much more of difficulty lay in the way of associating others with himself in these responsibilities than ever he anticipated.' No less than a constitutional crisis was brewing which came close to wrecking the Mission. His deputies suffered in the process by being grudgingly treated as favoured civil servants, until he issued a communiqué to all members: regional conferences would be held for mutual encouragement and discussion of difficulties and ideas. The Mission was a fellowship of equals, some voluntarily serving the others, from himself as their leader to the local secretaries and housekeepers. 'For love of the brethren', of the Chinese and the Lord himself, they were gladly sacrificing the pleasure of field work in a place of their own, to be servants of the rest. The Home Council were in no way different as a serving, not a ruling body, under a Director whom they 'voluntarily agreed to accept'.

For the time being he had said nothing about appointing a leader in each region to give direction to the work being done and backbone to those whose energies might flag in isolation and discouragement. In some areas each man had tended to do as he saw fit. Drift instead of direction characterised their work. The whole Mission could sink into the same state. Regional leaders were the natural answer. They could meet with him from time to time to compare experience and ideas, he himself would be kept in touch and they could agree on action to be jointly taken. He would benefit from their advice and they from his insights.[22] So ran his thoughts.

That this sound plan could be the reef on which the CIM would face shipwreck never entered his mind.

At his second meeting with the London Council in 1883 (on April 17, after reaching Britain) he had outlined this plan for supervision and accountability throughout China. Experienced senior missionaries would consult together in provincial or regional councils under the chairmanship of the appointed leader or superintendent. And these regional leaders would meet together from time to time with him or his deputy directing the whole work in China. With the London Council's approval he had then written, on August 24, 1883, to all members of the Mission, proposing the appointment of a superintendent approved by his colleagues, if necessary for each main region, and a China Council made up of the Director and superintendents. He invited comment and opinion, saying,

> It is important to secure that no contingency shall alter the character of the Mission or throw us off those lines which God has so signally owned and blessed from the commencement. But our home arrangement of assisting the Director by a Council may be introduced into the China work. . . . No new principle will be introduced, yet our work will be rendered capable of indefinite expansion, while maintaining its original character.[23]

He personally favoured allowing each able missionary to develop his or her own work in their own way, in consultation with each other. Regional leaders and councils should not hamper initiative. And this was when he secured the London Council's agreement that when missionaries conferred about their work, 'the sisters be recognised as equals'. At the time, the concept was welcomed. The problem was, who were the godly *and* competent men fitted to superintend others? And who could step into his shoes in China if he should fall ill or die? Some good men had shortcomings. Again and again over the years he had tried to train one after another, only to be disappointed. Each had his limitations. Others, very promising young men, needed time and experience and training. By learning the ropes as his assistants they could free him occasionally to go inland, or he could send them as his representatives.

In 1879 he had written to Benjamin on the role of leaders:

> The all-important thing is to improve the character of the work; deepen the piety, devotion and success of the workers; remove

> stones of stumbling if possible; oil the wheels when they stick; amend whatever is defective and supplement as far as may be what is lacking. This is no easy matter when suitable men are wanting or only in the course of formation. That I may be used of God, at least in some measure, to bring these about is my hope.[24]

Conspicuous, perhaps, in his evaluation is the absence of any reference to intelligence, initiative, energy or authority. These were only the equipment for being effective in applying the fundamental qualities he named. Whether in a team leader or a General Director, inappropriate use of the confidence accorded by his colleagues, whether by autocratic ways or unwise action, would soon result in his replacement. Hudson Taylor saw many fall by the wayside through such failings, men of whom he had been hopeful.

With his return to China in the spring of 1885 Hudson Taylor knew what he wanted if he was to convert vision into reality. A few key men were recognisable as well qualified to be leaders. After years of being too taciturn to win the confidence of his colleagues, John Stevenson (who always had the ability) had become 'a new man'. At the Keswick Convention, 1885, he had learned to submit himself to the will of God and be 'filled by the Spirit'. Welling up with 'the joy of the Lord', his strong lead was welcomed at home in Britain as it would be no less in China. He could be brought at once to Hudson Taylor's side and given a share in the administration. He arranged for his wife and adolescent family to stay in Scotland, and set out for Shanghai.

After the burst of generosity to the CIM early in the year, donors were tightening their belts and remembering the needs of other continents. Low receipts reaching China meant Hudson Taylor having to be on hand at the coast to send out monthly remittances of small amounts when quarterly allocations could not be made. The sooner a reliable man could be found to relieve him of this task alone, the better. John McCarthy, as senior as Stevenson, was keeping the accounts but lacked the ability to assess the requirements of the widely scattered mission. James Meadows, who had come out to Ningbo in 1862, was a successful pastor but uneducated and half-hearted in his loyalty to Hudson Taylor. One man had the ability and devotion to be a godly, sympathetic and efficient treasurer. Strong confidence in God was the first essential. But James Broumton's place at Guiyang would be difficult to fill.[25]

Hudson Taylor invited him to Shanghai and went over with him all that was involved in the job. At his finger-tips he would need to keep particulars of all Mission statistics, of each missionary and his growing family, his work, his Chinese colleagues, his rental of premises, the wages of employed teachers and workmen, his routine travel costs, running expenses of schools for Chinese children, and the fluctuating exchange rates in different parts of the vast country. They did the work together for a few months, and early in 1886 Hudson Taylor appointed him treasurer, the first in China. John McCarthy handed over the simple account books he kept, for them to audit, meticulously to the last cent, and at midnight, May 1, Broumton began the work he sustained for seventeen years. He left by steamer before dawn and set up his office at Wuchang, to be as nearly as possible at the geographical centre of the Mission. In February 1903 his assistant W Hayward took over.

One example of the kind of problem Broumton could face was handled by Hudson Taylor in June 1885. A few inexperienced newcomers, he discovered, were in difficulties through irresponsible use of funds. Some were laying in so many stores before setting off on journeys to the back of beyond that they exceeded their credit at Mission business centres – in effect borrowing from their more conscientious colleagues. Some had so many coolie-loads or mule-packs as to invite robbery and to involve them in excessive costs. Thoughtlessly, two women heading for Kunming bought kerosene storm-lanterns. They then needed heavy drums of fuel, to be carried hundreds of miles on men's backs. Vegetable oil and charcoal were in use and available throughout China. Two others set out for Gansu like mandarins with sixteen mule-loads and two sedan chairs. They would learn. In June, Hudson Taylor introduced a simple device: CIM credit notes. 'In issuing these Notes we deposit in the Bank the silver they represent. Members of the Mission purchasing them must do so with ready money.' Orders from upcountry or between mission stations would in future be the equivalent of cash transactions. And he drew up advice on preparations for travelling and equipping remote bases. Most necessities could be bought locally. Forty pounds-weight of baggage, half a mule load, was a good standard to aim for. The smooth running of a complex organisation was greatly helped by a uniform way of doing things, so he began to outline some of these in printed leaflets or letters.[26]

With funds so low, reinforcements were delayed in coming out from Europe, and with each postponement Hudson Taylor's hope faded of quickly completing his arrangements and returning to

Britain. At the end of June he wrote, 'The state of funds is serious. The LORD send help!' But shortages taught new lessons in economy of resources. The numerous boarding schools for Chinese children, many of them from Christian families, were costly to run and denied the children the knowledge of farming and domestic duties they would acquire at home. He arranged for them to spend the long winters at school and the summer months back in their villages. It was a major improvement, and the Christian children passed on the gospel to their families.

He had hoped to complete his enlistment of superintendents and to set up a China Council by the end of the year, but consultations also took longer than expected. Great distances had to be travelled in unsettled, dangerous times. Then what had appeared to be a setback proved to be an advantage. The more Hudson Taylor delegated his duties and responsibilities, the more whispers of protest began to reach him from old-timers. Who were these younger men to come between them and him? 'There was a good deal said that was unpleasant, and bad feelings aroused,' James Meadows was to recall. But it was true only of the few, and indignantly denied in some provinces. If the process had been less gradual, the outcry might have been stronger.

The arrival of John Stevenson on December 24, 1885, restored needed ballast. He brought with him six new men and the first two members of the Bible Christian Mission, Fanstone and Thorne, bound for Yunnan. Hudson Taylor sent Stevenson to visit two inveterate trouble spots in Zhejiang, and to Shaanxi and Shanxi to meet as many missionaries as possible. By April 1886 when he announced in careful words, 'Mr Stevenson . . . has undertaken to act as my deputy in districts which I cannot personally visit, and generally in matters requiring attention during my absence from China,' the appointment was popular. On the twentieth anniversary of the sailing of the *Lammermuir*, May 26, Stevenson wrote from Hanzhong, in conference with sixteen missionaries, including the Polhill-Turners,

> We had the full tide last night, and found it hard to break up such a glory-time. . . . I think you would not have slept much for delight. . . . The love and confidence the brothers and sisters lavish on me makes me feel humiliated (by) such a rich token of approval.[27]

Formal recognition as 'Deputy China Director' followed naturally. The Chinese Christians at Hanzhong impressed him deeply,

> some of them with most decided convictions and a dauntless courage and enterprise for the Lord. . . . I never was so hopeful as I am today with regard to the gospel in this land. . . . I am amazed and gratified at the splendid material which we have here for the purpose [of evangelising northern and western Sichuan].

By then Hudson Taylor had settled the question of whom to appoint as leaders in most provinces, with marked wisdom in some instances, and in others with unreserved admiration of the men available. For Zhejiang, with its rebellious Jackson and George Stott of pre-*Lammermuir* vintage, he named James Meadows, himself rebellious against wearing Chinese dress, with gentle James Williamson to mollify him. Responsibility as superintendent could bring Meadows to personal compliance with the Principles and Practice. Faithful John McCarthy undertook supervision of Jiangxi and Jiangsu, where the chief women's work and women's training home were located. And James Cameron took Shandong, with Chefoo as his main responsibility. For Anhui he had William Cooper, a quiet, saintly but physically powerful and mature man who had come to China as recently as 1881 but was already recognised as exceptionally gifted. The church and the men's training home at Anqing were put under his guidance, but more significantly, the task of opening up the whole province by J L Nevius' methods. Nevius had published in the *Chinese Recorder* his system for promoting indigenous church growth and government, by 'self-reliance from the beginning', with no more foreign subsidies for Chinese preachers.[28] Frederick Baller had proved himself as a pioneer and linguist. After helping Hoste, Cassels and Stanley Smith to find their feet in Shanxi, Baller returned to supervise the central provinces of Hubei and Henan, and to prepare a Mandarin Primer to simplify language study. Dorward was the unquestioned choice for the defiant provinces of Hunan and Guangxi. Easton on his return from furlough joined them as superintendent in Shaanxi and Gansu, and George Clarke for the north, in Shanxi and Zhili.[29] No one was yet available for the south-western provinces, so John Stevenson himself took the oversight of Sichuan, Yunnan and Guizhou.

The fact that nothing was made of this important administrative development in *China's Millions* or at annual meetings of the Mission, is the measure of its deliberately unobtrusive beginning. The subservience of mere scaffolding to the building being erected, the Church in China, was the simile John Stevenson used in his first general letter as deputy director.[30] The founder of the Mission whom all members had chosen to follow had asked these respected men to help him by sharing his burden. No thought of undermining his authority entered their heads.

Send more *1885–87*

One of the first impressions Hudson Taylor had received on reaching China in March 1885 was of the progress in his absence (p 371). No less clear was the cry from place after place for help. In spite of the Sino-French hostilities, the scope for preaching the gospel exceeded all that the thin line of pioneers could do. As soon as the funds permitted (on May 4, 1885) Hudson Taylor had cabled to London for thirty more men to be sent without delay. And in August, while attending the mortally ill Miss Murray, principal of the women's language school at Yangzhou, he planned and set in motion an enlargement of the premises there for the influx of women he also foresaw approaching. By November it was the men's training home accommodation at Anqing being reviewed in terms of an 'Institute'. And to friends of the CIM he wrote that newcomers were 'absorbed at once, leaving us as hungry as before for more workers. Our brethren in nearly every province are urgent in their cries for reinforcements; our sisters, were they to come out in ten times the number' would all find more than enough to do. If the veterans were losing their buoyancy, the energy of younger men and women was needed. Those pleading for help saw their own need as more urgent than elsewhere. What could not be made public until later was the fact that more and more young women were going inland, deep into pioneering situations. 'Keep it quiet,' Hudson Taylor reminded those involved, 'until success or otherwise appears.'[31] He had in mind another development as adventurous as any the women had yet undertaken, the staffing of a large region almost entirely by women.

By the anniversary, May 26, 1886, forty new missionaries had gone to China in 1885 and a further nine in 1886 of the 119 who had asked to be sent. To the London staff this represented the correspondence and interviews with one man and one woman for each working day of the year so far. The full membership of the CIM had risen to 188, with 114 Chinese colleagues supported by the Mission. The total income of £20,221 in 1885 was almost £2,000 more than that of 1884, but it had not kept pace with the costs, which included providing passages to and from China, for the correspondingly increasing number of tired missionaries needing home leave. When the chairman of the Annual Meeting, George Williams of the YMCA, commented innocently, 'Are we right in allowing those who have the charge of this Mission to have an amount of anxiety like that?' he showed unfamiliarity with CIM principles. To them 'shortage' was testing or restraint from God but would never reach inadequacy for the objects God initiated. One hundred years later the same is true. By the next annual meeting there were 215 members and 10 associate members, and of 184 applicants in the first five months of the year, 23 had already been accepted.[32]

The assessment of candidates for suitability to be CIM missionaries in China involved factors differing from selection for the denominational societies. For them it was usually for a thorough training for ordination and a pastoral or educational role overseas. For the CIM, in addition to general qualifications, sincere acceptance of the Mission's unusual principles and practical requirements was essential. Faith to trust God for the means to live, not in dependence on the Mission, could not be measured or vouched for by referees. Readiness to go inland dressed as a Chinese and deferring marriage while adapting to the climate and people could be sincerely intended and yet prove mistaken when faced with reality.[33] A sorrowing widow, convinced of her call from God to be a missionary, on reaching Shanghai could not face what was entailed. Sympathising deeply, Hudson Taylor saw that grief had clouded her judgment. She was trying to put sorrow behind her. He kept her in Shanghai and, to his joy, before long his friend of many years, William Muirhead of the LMS, a widower whose love for the CIM often brought him round to visit them, asked her to marry him.

The qualifications for being an effective missionary were more and more shown to be not natural ability or education or the qualities commonly sought by selection boards, but primarily of a spiritual nature. When thanking Lord Radstock for two hampers of vegetables from his garden in August 1878, Hudson Taylor had written, 'Would not a man, called of God, go whether with us or not? . . . I would have worked my way to China as a common sailor, had no other way opened – I dare not have accepted man's conclusion when I knew God's mind.' If individuals were in any doubt, how could the CIM settle it for them? Only in so far as membership of this Mission was concerned. The two of them enjoyed close comradeship in this way. Lord Radstock wished he could in some way be a part of the CIM himself. 'I think you would get more spiritual power in the sending out of missionaries,' he replied from Stockholm, if in some way they could be sent more by the Church and not only by the committee. . . . If all your believing helpers were not only subscribers but *spiritually* members, our power would be increased tenfold.' On this they were of one mind with each other and with Griffith John; the supreme qualification would always be daily constant dependence on the Holy Spirit for spiritual vitality and power. Yet in the end even an ideal personality would only stand the physical conditions in China if combined with the right physique. Hudson Taylor urged upon Benjamin and the Home Director that they must be firm with unsuitable candidates. 'We know – they don't!' Few knew; fewer could guess what lay ahead. The accumulating wisdom and experience of the Mission was a factor to be respected.

Progress in China *1885–86*

Mere numbers and real-estate were no measure of progress. What missionaries achieved and how they themselves developed as examples to immature Christians provided a truer indication. Members of the Seventy had used their voyage out to point crews and passengers to Christ, as converted officers and men told later travellers. In spite of unsettled conditions due to China's war with France, seven men of the Seventy had gone to the north-west, including two to occupy Lanzhou, the capital of Gansu, where George Parker had at last succeeded in renting premises. From Shanghai to Lanzhou was 2,500 miles. Three were to go further, right up into Ningxia, a Muslim and Mongolian area. Even bare rooms in a rowdy inn seemed luxury after months of gruelling travel. Parker himself had Kashgar in far distant Turkestan (later Xinjiang) in view, as far distant again as he already was from the coast. To encourage his Chinese wife, Minnie Shao, as stalwart a pioneer as he, came the news that her mother in Yangzhou had been baptised.[34]

Two more men had reached Guiyang only to find the province too disturbed for any travelling to be possible; and another two, soon to be followed by two more, reached Dali, freeing George Clarke to bring his orphaned child to Shanghai. The first baptisms had taken place at Dali and Kunming, where the lamp they lit burns on today after years of attempts to snuff it out. But when F A Steven attempted to go westwards to Bhamo he excited strong suspicions of his being a spy and was glad to escape arrest. Bhamo had to remain unoccupied. In Chengdu, the capital of Sichuan, J H Riley had strengthened the Mission's foothold with his wife, the brave Jane Kidd of Guiyang (p 241), and her young companion Fanny Stroud. But tragedy was soon to strike them.

The intransigent province of Henan had once again let A W Sambrook break his homeless travelling from place to place by renting premises in Zhoujiakou (Chouchiakou, now Zhoukouzhen), on the south-eastern waterway to the Grand Canal and Yangzi River. Two new untried companions had barely joined him when yet again they were driven out – the last straw for Sambrook's battered mind. As with Henry Taylor ten years earlier, the accumulative effect of having his devotion constantly scorned and rejected broke Sambrook's spirit and he had to be taken home to Britain as a sad casualty. But after the chief antagonist appealed for help to save a member of his family from attempted suicide, Zhoujiakou became the first permanent mission centre in Henan, followed in 1886 by Sheqidian (Shekitien), with the beginnings of a church in each. In the documents that have survived no explanation has been found of the fact that Hudson Taylor subsequently sent his own relatives, among others, to these two hard-won cities: J J Coulthard and Herbert Taylor, Maria Taylor and Herbert's wife, Geraldine Guinness and Howard Taylor, and in 1894 Dixon Hoste.[35]

In all the CIM's work during the year 1885 more than two hundred baptisms were reported, still slow progress but made in the face of opposition and persecution. Hudson Taylor in October called it 'war to the knife', 'a hand-to-hand conflict with the powers of darkness'. After a year in China he wrote of a total of 1,300 communicants throughout the Mission. Immense patience was needed, but with every advance the tempo of results was increasing.[36]

In the two parts of Shaanxi, separated by mountains, conditions were as different as could be. In the Hanzhong plain the Church was expanding, with six self-supporting voluntary preachers and lively congregations. In the Xi'an plain the only possible way to work was still to keep moving from one place to another, but covering the same territory again and again. An influential Hunanese family as relentlessly as ever prevented Christians from settling in the capital, Xi'an.[37]

The province of Hunan remained more stubbornly invincible, except by a Chinese evangelist quietly working at Jinshi (Tsinshi) not far across the border. Adam Dorward had made Shashi on the Yangzi his base, travelling inconspicuously by boat into the north-western corner of the province – until a Spanish priest suffered the anger of the people at Lizhou and further access was forfeited. Henry Dick, one of the Seventy who joined Dorward, and less of a marked man, penetrated as far as Hongjiang and Changde, with a converted Buddhist priest as his companion, preaching the gospel and selling books. Making history in May 1886, they even entered Changsha, the provincial capital, to the consternation of the authorities. A dreaded, hated foreigner had not been repulsed by the guards at the gate! When Henry Dick adopted a new tactic and paid a courtesy visit to the *yamen*, they expelled him. To angry cries from the crowds of 'Beat the foreigner!' he and the evangelist were hustled back to their boat and a gunboat saw them well away. The conquest of Hunan still had years to wait for God's time.[38]

Guangxi continued almost as difficult to enter. A A Fulton of the American Presbyterian Mission (North) and his sister, a doctor of medicine, succeeded for a while to occupy Guiping in the eastern half, but they too were expelled. As long as other missions wished to attempt Guangxi, Hudson Taylor held back his men, always bearing someone in mind for the task – Marcus Wood in 1885–86.[39]

In Zhejiang the CMS were witnessing a remarkable turning to God in the region of Chuqi in the Hangzhou area. Two hundred people turning to Christ in about twenty-five villages, within a few months, was a rare phenomenon, the kind of movement all missionaries were praying for. Fujian, where J R Wolfe had served the embryo church alone after the death or retirement of five colleagues, was outstanding in a different way: the believers in 120 towns and villages were spreading the gospel through 70 preaching chapels, against bitter opposition and with one martyrdom. Four ordained ministers, 107 catechists and a theological college were strengthening the foundations of the Church.

Towards the end of June 1885, Hudson Taylor himself made a long pastoral journey overland, with a motley party of companions on their way to their locations. He himself with his secretary Lewis were to visit Hangzhou to help Wang Laedjün with problems in the church. John McCarthy was escorting some women up the Qiantang River to Qü Xian. Maria Taylor, caring for George Clarke's motherless infant son while he visited Shanxi, was in the party too.

They travelled by canal boat to Hangzhou and on up the Qiantang to Yanzhou (to be distinguished from Yangzhou) where their various ways parted. (Map p 397). In mid-July, while McCarthy's boats went on upstream to Qü Xian, Hudson Taylor's party branched westwards up the Xin'an River to She Xian (Huicheng) in Anhui. Often when the currents were strong and rapids dangerous, the passengers would go ashore and walk along the trackers' towpath. On one such occasion Maria and her father had just crossed a headland where to trip would have meant a fall of many feet to the rocks below, when she slipped and went over the edge. At that point she fell only a few feet to a terrace and was unharmed. But the shock made Hudson Taylor ill. (The story of these months is punctuated by mishaps which added to the difficulties, as when the rickshaw he was in tipped backwards so that he fell head first on to the road.) During the long cross-country journey to Anqing, after a detour northwards to Ningguo, Maria went down with malaria and delirium. But he had seen enough of her potential as a missionary to take bold measures with her not long afterwards, sending her, though not yet twenty-one, to a pioneer outpost.[40]

The church at Anqing, scene of the Meadows' and James Williamson's early tribulations (Book 5, p 215) had become mature and reliable. Together with George King and William Cooper, Hudson Taylor ordained elders and discussed with them the need for sound future development on the principles which he had worked out with J L Nevius in 1879 (p 203).[41] With their work still uncompleted, a telegram from Yangzhou summoned him without explanation to come at once. Emergencies at Yangzhou he knew could take unpleasant forms, so he asked the redoubtable Adam Dorward, just arrived from Shashi, to go with him. This gave them hours of consultation on the way, about Hunan and reorganisation of the Mission. The crisis was not riot but that the invaluable principal of the training home, Mariamne Murray, was at death's door with dysentery. He was still on call as a doctor. After taking her and Maria to Chefoo, he returned in mid-November to Anqing and launched the Anhui church on the Nevius system for purely Chinese control, with William Cooper as their adviser. In conference with the missionaries and language students at Anqing he went over the Principles and Practice which they had signed in Britain, to make sure all understood them well, and gave a series of talks which he subsequently published serially in *China's Millions* and eventually in book form as *A Retrospect*.

A RIVERSIDE CITY GATE: COULD BE ANYWHERE

In mid-December Hudson Taylor was back at Hangzhou to visit Jinhua with Wang Laedjün. The Taylors' action in leaving Hangzhou in 1868 to pioneer Yangzhou and the Yangzi valley had been fully vindicated. An indigenous church movement had grown up without dependence on foreign oversight. Laedjün's pastoral oversight extended a hundred and fifty miles and more, over several churches with their own pastors. The country churches were going through severe harassment and Hudson Taylor's presence was timely. While he was at New Lane (Xinkailong), sleeping on the floor in what had been Jennie's room (Book 4, p 248), two persecuted Christians were brought to him. One, a Dr Zong, had been rescued from enemies after they had cut off his ears, hoisted him up by his wrists, tortured, beaten and all but killed him for his refusal to deny Christ.[42] From there Hudson Taylor went on to Shaoxing to consult with Meadows and Williamson, reaching Shanghai on December 23, the day before John Stevenson landed.

The Guangxin dream comes true[43] *1886*

Whenever Hudson Taylor was away from his Shanghai office for long, or arrived at the place he had named for correspondence to be addressed to, he faced mountains of mail. A letter of February 24, 1886, tells of his having been back to Yangzhou for a month (while Miss Murray and a language student were so ill again as to need a doctor near at hand). Desk work followed him, but on his return to Shanghai he took five hours to read half the letters and reports held over for him. He then slept from nine until midnight and returned to finish reading the rest before starting on his replies.

John Stevenson's return had raised Hudson Taylor's hopes of getting back to Britain by the end of the year, but first he had to work Stevenson in and be sure he was accepted as his deputy. While Stevenson made his long journey to Hanzhong and on through Shaanxi to Shanxi where the two of them planned to meet again, Hudson Taylor had an expedition of his own to make. Only Broumton taking over the Mission finances in China, with Baller back at Wuchang for the present to support him, set Hudson Taylor free to travel. He had a major development in mind and wished to re-examine the territory in Jiangxi which he had been through in 1880–81 (pp 213). This time John McCarthy and Herbert were with him in one boat, and convalescent Mariamne Murray, her sister and two young women Jeanie Gray of the Seventy and Mary Williams in another. Leaving Shanghai on May 4 and following the canal route he had used so often in the past thirty years since 1855, they travelled fast, to join the Qiantang River again at Hangzhou, where McCarthy left them.

While the others went ahead to Qü Xian, Hudson Taylor had a detour to Jinhua to make on business (p 391). The missionary he went to meet, Robert Grierson, years afterwards threw a pleasant light on the mundane when he recalled that on arrival Hudson Taylor said he had something to talk about in private. Grierson took him into an inner room. To hold the door open Grierson had attached a string from the door to a bookshelf on the wall. In closing the door behind him Hudson Taylor pulled the bookshelf down 'on his devoted head', and in answer to Grierson's profuse apologies replied, 'There, you see the trouble that comes from interfering with another man's arrangements.' Even at Jinhua he was catching up on correspondence when he wrote, 'The carrots go ahead however fast the donkey runs. The work however is looking up nearly everywhere.'

At Qü Xian Kate Mackintosh, also of the Seventy, took Mary Williams' place in the party, and the women pressed on to Yüshan in Jiangxi with Herbert Taylor to look after them. Hudson Taylor, joined by David Thompson (p 374) caught them up on May 24, (when Stevenson's conference was at 'full tide' in Hanzhong and the Polhill brothers joined the Mission). At once they saw that Herbert had made good use of his circumstances. As he explained to his brother Howard: in November 1885 he had been called to help with a case of opium poisoning (a suicide attempt) on which Jeanie Gray was also working, and promptly fell in love with her. But how to do any more about it in the segregated life they led, drove him to despair. His father, ostensibly seeing how run down he was and in need of a holiday, had enlisted his help on this journey. An accomplice or not, he was delighted when at the journey's end they became engaged. Herbert was twenty-five and she twenty-three, 'the best of her bunch in health, character and progress in Chinese'.[44]

Nine years had passed since Hudson Taylor had visited the Douthwaites at Qü Xian with Miss Elizabeth Wilson (in 1877), and met the redoubtable Captain Yü of Yüshan and the earliest believers in the area. In 1860 Captain Yü had heard the rudiments of a distorted gospel from Taiping rebels, and without deeper knowledge had become a devout Buddhist in a sect that, like the Taipings, denounced idol worship. Hearing Wang Laedjün and Douthwaite preaching the gospel at Jinhua fifteen years later, Yü had believed and in 1876 had been baptised by Laedjün. Members of his old sect had lived near to and across the provincial border, in Jiangxi, and Yü went at once to share his discovery with them, bringing some back to Qü Xian with him. 'For forty years I have been seeking the Truth,' one said to Douthwaite, 'and now I have found it!' Another man in the Yüshan region not only believed but soon had a houseful of fellow-worshippers, at the village of Dayang, sitting on baskets, inverted buckets, anything they could find, to hear the preachers who visited them.

Two brief references will indicate what lay behind the steady growth and deep roots of the Qü Xian and Yüshan churches. When Hudson Taylor had sent Arthur Douthwaite and his bride to Qü Xian on their first assignment, he had given them this advice:

> Spend a month there, or perhaps ten days might be long enough at first. In that way you would soon see the interest deepened I think. On going with Mrs Douthwaite be sure to give it out that you are only going to stay a few days, then no one will take fright and try to *drive* you away, or when you have left, spread a report that you *had* been frightened away. I should be glad if eventually you were able to live there and take permanent oversight of the work . . . in process of time occupying all the *xian* (or county) cities of these districts and extending into Jiangxi province. This would be the work of years. . . . Read the Word with much prayer with (your Chinese fellow-workers). Hold much holy communion with our Lord; then, fresh from His presence, minister *Him* to them. . . . Tell them what *you* are finding there. You will not be kept *long* sowing *thus* before you are rejoicing over the firstfruits.

Douthwaite had followed this advice and the Christians 'spread over the wall' into Jiangxi sooner than expected. Speaking at a conference of evangelists and church elders arranged by Wang Laedjün for the region between Hangzhou and Qü Xian, Douthwaite gave them these guiding 'Rules' to help them to develop: 1. Each was to write a comment on the daily passage of Scripture he read, sending a copy to Douthwaite, and also 2. copies of each prepared sermon, 3. a monthly record and statement of places visited, meetings held and books sold, and 4. a monthly essay on a given subject for Douthwaite's comment.[45]

Not surprisingly, by 1880 when Hudson Taylor visited Qü Xian and Yüshan again, a maturing church was sending evangelists farther afield into Jiangxi, and planting daughter churches. They

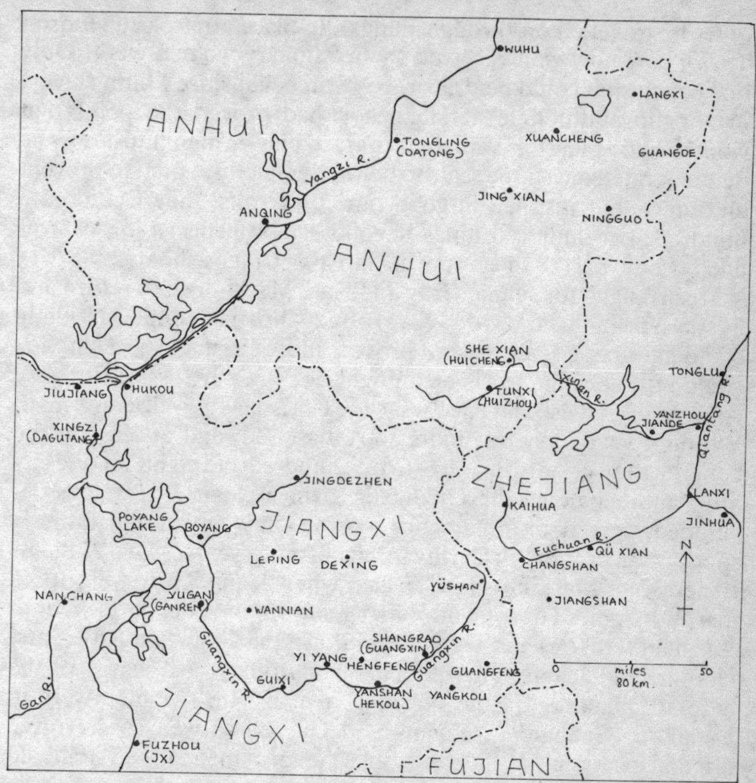

JIANGXI: THE GUANGXIN RIVER WOMEN'S FIELD

needed missionary help but who could go? At the time of his 'bombshell' he was launching unmarried women into the remotest provinces, sending Miss Wilson up the Han River to pioneer Hanzhong and Gansu (p 242). Then the key event took place in 1885. An evangelist and his wife invited Agnes Gibson, of the Seventy, a girl of only twenty who had recently moved to Qü Xian, to come and stay with them at Changshan, between Qü Xian and Yüshan. As a result, when Hudson Taylor's party arrived in May 1886, the Chinese women who for years had resisted their husbands' conversion were as much in evidence as Christians as the menfolk. They asked for a woman to be sent to live permanently among them.

As he travelled on through Jiangxi, in place after place Hudson Taylor saw how well received the missionary women were. Only one conclusion could be drawn. His firm belief since Maria (Dyer) in Ningbo and Jennie at Hangzhou had proved the point that women had at least as valuable a part to play as men, must now be demonstrated on a large scale to be valid. Quietly at first, to prevent an outcry, but justified in good time by results, they would go a hundred, two hundred miles beyond established mission centres and become part of the family in Christian Chinese homes.

He arranged for Jeanie Gray and Kate Mackintosh to return and live at Yüshan in the care of a trusted Christian couple. Nothing could have been safer or, as it proved, more satisfactory. That they could not take charge, as men might do, was pure asset. But they could teach, advise and encourage the Christians as well as any man. Within a year forty-two more were baptised, and at Yüshan the congregation grew from thirty to one hundred and eight. At one city after another down the Guangxin River a chain of churches developed, served by missionary women only, under the fatherly supervision of John McCarthy for the first five years. Mary Williams joined Kate Mackintosh in Yüshan when Jeanie Gray went to be married; Agnes Gibson and F M Tapscott, not yet twenty, went to Yanshan (Hekou) and Guixi lower down the Guangxin River, and Herbert and Jeanie Gray after their marriage took charge of the base at Dagutang on the Poyang Lake. By 1890 women were in Yangkou, Guangfeng, Yiyang and Ganren as well as the three original locations. At the same time a team of men led by Archibald Orr Ewing was opening up the south-western part of the province, first worked by J E Cardwell (1871–73) along the Gan River, the imperial route to Canton taken by Lord Amhurst and Robert Morrison. (Book 1 p 142). Thirty years later (in 1920) the church in this Guangxin region, still staffed by Chinese church leaders and missionary women in ten centres and sixty sub-centres, had over 2,200 communicant members and many more 'enquirers' and Christians preparing for baptism.

Hudson Taylor and his party crossed the Poyang Lake to Dagutang (now Xingzi) in early June 1886 – while John Stevenson was plodding over the mountains from Hanzhong to Xi'an, and the Polhills were penetrating Sichuan to rent premises at Langzhong (Paoning), and Henry Dick was heading back from Changsha, capital of Hunan, to Shashi and Dorward again. News that John Stevenson's Glasgow friend Archibald Orr Ewing (p 343) and others were expected at Shanghai any day led Hudson Taylor to go straight there without visiting any Yangzi centres. How right he was in this decision became immediately apparent.

Wusong Road and Newington Green *1886–90*

The enlarged training homes at Yangzhou and Anqing were ready none too soon. But the new Mission premises near the Shanghai consulate were already inadequate and enquiries were progressing about a site on the Wusong Road in less fashionable Hongkou (Hongkew). Hudson Taylor arrived at Shanghai on June 14, to be told that in his absence others had been bidding for the site and the option granted to the CIM would expire that very day. T W Pigott of Shanxi and his wife had offered to cover the cost until the money was available, but no donation had been received. Because the site was so suitable, Hudson Taylor prayed at the noon prayer meeting for the seemingly impossible, that the needed amount should be given in time for him to take up the option.[46] That afternoon Archibald Orr Ewing, just arrived from Britain, on hearing of the site offered a first £1,500 as a gift. It was enough. On the strength of this double assurance the deal was struck. On June 15 Hudson Taylor wrote to Jennie, 'I have today signed the contract for about 2 acres of building and garden ground in Shanghai – price £2486.9.2.'

Archibald Orr Ewing's interest in China had been aroused in 1884 by John McCarthy and fanned by C T Studd and Stanley Smith. But at the Keswick Convention in 1885 Orr Ewing had made his decision, and Stevenson wrote in September:

> This dear fellow has finally surrendered himself to God for China and the CIM. He is very wealthy and has a most prosperous business. He has asked his partners to set him free . . . and they have agreed . . . He is ready to . . . devote a large portion of his wealth to China. He feels he must spend a good deal of money yearly at the Vale of Leven where it was made. . . . His going will create a great stir in Glasgow.[47]

Orr Ewing was twenty-eight and unmarried. After a farewell meeting of leading businessmen in Glasgow he left Britain in April 1886 at his own expense, with his friend George Graham Brown and others. But his timely arrival at Shanghai only marked the beginning of his part in the Wusong Road developments. To steal a look into the future, China and the CIM in action so impressed him that he formally joined the Mission and when his business affairs in Scotland were wound up, he contributed not only the full cost of the site, but also of the extensive buildings erected on it. He served as an influential leader in China until 1911 and on the Council for the British Isles until his death on May 11, 1930.

The Pyrland Road houses had also long since become too crowded for comfort. Permission to build an extension had been refused, and Benjamin had suggested buying a house and land for building on a site available round the corner flanking Newington Green. Negotiations were begun and by July 19, 1887, a contract was agreed.

The great expansion of the CIM had begun. Numbering 163 members in March 1885, there were 409 on January 1, 1890, 621 by the end of March 1895, and 811 on January 1, 1900. So this provision came none too soon. The extensive buildings at Newington Green were completed only in 1894.[48]

Two days after Orr Ewing's arrival he was in Chinese clothes and together with Hudson Taylor, Herbert and Lewis the secretary was on a ship bound for Tianjin and Taiyuan. At long last, after many thwarted efforts to reach Shanxi, Hudson Taylor was this time to succeed. Passing through Baoding in Zhili (the only place between the coast and Taiyuan with a resident missionary, worked by the American Board), they were in Huolo (Huailu) on June 29, preparing to 'exchange our jolting carts for swinging mule litters' to scale the mountains into Shanxi. On that day Stevenson reached Linfen (Pingyang) from Hanzhong, appalled by the devastation still remaining from the great famine of 1878–79. Judging that he was too late to reach Taiyuan for the planned conference of missionaries, he stayed to give the Linfen church a feast of teaching, and spent long, never-to-be-forgotten hours with Hsi 'Shengmo'. But Hudson Taylor, Orr Ewing and the others arrived at Taiyuan to find smallpox dictating their timetable and the conference postponed.[49]

CHAPTER TWELVE

COUNTER-ATTACK 1885–87

Shanxi and Hsi 'Sheng-mo'[1] *1885–86*

The strong Church in Shanxi today owes much to its origins. After David Hill left Shanxi in 1879 to return to Hankou, following the famine, J J Turner and S B Drake had stayed on at Linfen (Pingyang), the chief city of south Shanxi (seat of the Emperors Yao and Shun before the time of Abraham). Hsi Shengmo, the converted Confucian scholar (p 374) had sometimes looked to them for help, but largely by giving himself to prayer and by force of character he broke free from his ten-year addiction to opium. What he recognised as a spiritual battle against evil forces he had won by the power of God. So he adopted the name 'Shengmo', conqueror of demons, defiantly, not arrogantly. When his wife ridiculed and opposed him and herself became convulsively demon-possessed, his neighbours challenged him to justify his boast and prove his faith. He fasted and prayed for three days and nights, laid his hands on her and in the name of Jesus commanded the evil spirit to leave her. She was cured and declared herself a believer.

From then on she worked with him in shepherding the Christian villagers and in running a medicine shop and preaching hall. He claimed that God taught him how to compound medicines with which to help other addicts to break free, and his pills became famous – the Life-giving pill, the Life-sustaining pill and the Health-restoring pill, he called them. But prayer and exhortation to trust in Jesus played a greater part. Opposition to him became stronger. When the literati failed to make him recant they prevailed upon the corrupt literary chancellor of the province to disgrace Hsi by depriving him of his degree. He refused to pay bribes or take his case to law, but Drake laid the facts before the provincial governor who saw that justice was done. Hsi's degree and honours were restored.

Vast acres of wheat land in Shanxi had been given over to the opium poppy, and 'eleven out of every ten' in the province were said to smoke or swallow the cursed 'mud'. With opium so easy to obtain, suicide also became commonplace. When village elders pleaded with the landed gentry and magistrates to eradicate the curse, they did nothing. It was their chief source of wealth. And they too were addicts. From small beginnings with one or two 'opium refuges', Hsi extended his cures to village after village and then town after town. The leader of a vegetarian sect, named Fan, grief-stricken when two sons were killed by wolves, turned to Christ, and when Drake left the district Fan took over his dispensary and opium refuge, using Hsi's herbal drugs.

Hsi and Fan were therefore respected and appealed to by growing numbers of addicts wishing to be cured. In Fan's small village fifty or sixty converted ex-opium smokers worshipped together. In 1884 there were eight or ten refuges, and Christians in each place. Hsi longed to open another at the city of Hochou (now Huo Xian), but all his available money was committed to existing work. One day his wife presented him with all her jewellery – rings, ear-rings and hair ornaments – the prized symbol of social standing, saying 'I can do without these. Let Hochou have the gospel.' Their work of a lifetime deserved all they possessed.[2]

Then in June 1885 the four 'Cambridge men' arrived – Stanley Smith, Cassels, Hoste and Beauchamp – tongue-tied in the Chinese language, but good men of striking personality. Frederick Baller, their escort, impressed Hsi by his fluency and scholarly knowledge of the Chinese classics. 'Scholars, merchants and farmers, young men and old, thronged the courtyard to watch the new arrivals and listen to Mr Baller's eloquent Chinese. "When it grows dark," they exclaimed with astonishment, "not one in a hundred would suppose he is a foreigner."'

Hsi's 'keen, commanding eyes', sharp features and masterly ways no less won the admiration of the five men. He impressed them by his profound understanding and ability to expound the Bible. Although relatively untaught by missionaries, for his home was fifteen miles from Linfen, he constantly studied it, 'comparing Scripture with Scripture'. Visiting his home they heard him preach to a mixed crowd of Christians and unbelievers on the story of Paul's shipwreck, used allegorically, and took notes of the points he made. Each point he clothed in vivid colloquial, dramatically describing the ocean and sea-going ships, of which these mountain dwellers knew nothing. Frederick Baller who had heard Griffith John and William Muirhead was to write of one of Hsi's sermons, 'The whole exposition was equal to any I have heard from a foreign missionary.'[3] The people respected Hsi and recognised in him an authority greater than his social and literary standing merited.

As for the newcomers, by dressing, living and behaving as well as they were able like Chinese scholars, cultivating the appropriate gait and manners, the men were quickly accepted among the people of Linfen, and made good progress in the language. During the first three months Baller prospected with an evangelist and found three other cities with a nucleus of Christians who would welcome the presence of a missionary. Cassels and Beauchamp he placed in Xi Xian (Sichou), near Daning in the western mountains, three or four days' travel away from Linfen. By then 'Cassels could understand more of what Chinese said to them, but Beauchamp was better at making himself understood!' And again, 'My soul was among lions,' Cassels confessed. The scorn over his dumbness, the desperate sense of a life wasted in a backwater, the fierce temptation to give up and go home, were no less than attacks by the devil.[4] Hoste chose to be alone among Chinese, and Baller committed him to the care of Christians at Qüwo in the southern plain. Later he was joined by W Hope Gill of Cambridge. Stanley Smith was making the fastest progress; Baller kept him at Linfen as William Key, the only other missionary in the area, was little more advanced and Baller himself was soon to return to the Yangzi. Outstanding as a linguist, he was to take charge of the Anqing training home, and to write his *Mandarin Primer.* C T Studd came up from Hanzhong in the autumn and, joining his good friend Stanley Smith, soon made up for time lost from language study.

Years before, a copy of Mark's Gospel had found its way into a temple outside the west gate of Daning. The early seed sown by Cameron, Parrott, Pigott and the Bible Society colporteurs was germinating. Puzzled by it, the leading Buddhist priest of the county, Zhang Zhiben, asked a scholar named Qü to examine it with him. Deeply impressed, they burned incense first to the book and then to Jesus and the twelve disciples. Somehow they obtained a New Testament and before long 'began to worship the one true God and His Son Jesus Christ'. Zhang was beaten unconscious by the order of an official who had been his friend, and Qü was three times fearfully flogged in public for refusing to join in idolatrous ceremonies. Then at last they heard of Christians at Linfen and made the three day journey to find them. A few days among kindred spirits gave them the reassurance they needed, and on their return they at once began to preach the gospel openly. At Xiaoyi, five days' journey to the north towards Taiyuan, eight families destroyed their idols and turned to Christ, the beginning of another church. With our knowledge of the Boxer Rising in 1900 these early beginnings have a poignancy and significance beyond most.

Meeting Cassels at Xi Xian, Zhang took him to Daning in February 1886, and introduced him to Qü and twenty-two families of Christians. He decided to stay, leaving Beauchamp with the Christians at Xi Xian. Each shared persecution with the Chinese when a hostile mandarin was appointed, but not because of ostentatious foreignness – the only foreign things Cassels had with him were his English Bible, a pen and a pencil, and the only daytime space he could call his own were the two square feet where he sat sharing the *kang* (the sleeping platform) in a little cave-house with his companions and visitors.

They were at a church conference in Linfen with new Christians from Xi Xian and Daning when word came of accusations against them. Cassels, for example, had destroyed an idol in the Daning temple! He and 'Monty' at once returned to face the music, arriving at dusk to find his own makeshift home barred against him. They stayed together for three weeks until convinced that the persecution of the Christians had ceased for the present, largely because of their presence.

At the conference seventy more believers were baptised, nearly doubling the membership of the Church in south Shanxi. And Hsi Shengmo took note that significant numbers of them came from the congregations that had the help of the young missionaries. The cheerful, animated personality of Stanley Smith so attracted Hsi that he asked him to help in opening a new opium refuge at the city of Hongtong, a few miles from his colleague Fan's home. Smith was to live unobtrusively in a village outside the city, quietly making himself known until premises were found in the city itself. With enough accommodation for twenty or thirty addicts and a large guest-hall for use as a chapel, physical and spiritual healing could proceed side by side. Before long ideal premises were rented. 'S P S' moved in, joined in May by Dixon Hoste at Hsi's request, while Hsi himself came often to supervise the refuge. So began a blissful period of progress with the friendship between Chinese and foreigners steadily deepening. Hoste's aphorism, 'Study without preaching would be stifling,' typified their approach to the language and the job they had come to do.

The Shanxi conferences[5] *July–August 1886*

When Hudson Taylor and his companions arrived at Taiyuan on Saturday, July 3, they found the CIM missionaries all gathered for a week's conference with them, and the BMS and Bible Society staff in Taiyuan ready to attend. Timothy Richard was away in Britain trying unsuccessfully to get the BMS to take up his educational policy. Apart from the men from south Shanxi, the CIM in Taiyuan at the time consisted of Dr and Mrs Edwards, Hope Gill, Hudson Broomhall and his sister Gertrude, and five women including Maria Taylor. Unable to be present were six from the far north: George Clarke, remarried to Agnes Lancaster, and two men at Guihuacheng; and two more at Baotou on the Mongolian border. But Adamson of the Bible Society (B&FBS) had smallpox, and C T Studd and Montagu Beauchamp were nursing him.

On July 5, 6 and 7, therefore, instead of the planned consultation Hudson Taylor gave expositions on 'The all-sufficiency of Christ for personal life and for all the exigencies of service'. Then he himself fell ill with acute dysentery, and further meetings were deferred until the 12th, 13th and 14th. 'The one thing the work needs here is a head or captain,' he wrote to Jennie on the 8th, 'not too strong on the one hand nor a weakling on the other.' (Pigott, absent in Britain, was too forceful, and Edwards too accommodating.) The one man all would welcome as their leader was Benjamin Bagnall, already thirteen years in China but under the Bible Society. And as he had already negotiated his transfer to the CIM, Hudson Taylor formally admitted him. Orr Ewing's journal also read, 'Joined the Mission, Saturday July 17, 1886 . . . Its attraction to myself was and is that it is nearest the lines of Scripture of any work I am acquainted with.'[6]

In the course of the disjointed conference Hudson Taylor as his custom was took many illustrations from his own experience to apply the lessons he was drawing from Scripture, and Beauchamp, using Stanley Smith's and others' notes, afterwards compiled the small book *Days of Blessing* often referred to in Mission literature.

The conference over and Adamson recovering, three parties set off for the south, taking two weeks to reach Hongtong, where a conference of Chinese Christians was to follow. Key, Lewis and Stanley Smith went ahead; Cassels and Hoste headed south-west for Xi Xian and Daning to bring Christians from that region; and Hudson Taylor, Herbert, Studd, Beauchamp and Dr Edwards started south on July 21. Heavy rain flooded the Fen River and prevented the western party from reaching Hongtong in time. Hudson Taylor's party struggled in the rain through quagmires and over landslides which even he 'in the saddle' found exhausting, doing thirty miles at a stretch.

He wrote of 'glorious conferences' at Hongtong and Linfen, the first on August 1. The rooms round the inner courtyard somehow provided sleeping space for a hundred men as well as the missionaries, on the *kangs*, on planks, on doors and on rushes on the floor. And Christian women filled the rooms round the outer courtyard. By day the premises somehow held three hundred, for the curious public could not be excluded. On a platform between the two courtyards Hudson Taylor glowed with happiness over such a sight in one of the 'nine unevangelised provinces', and spoke on Christ's words 'My peace', 'My joy', and 'My glory'.[7]

For Hsi Shengmo the opportunity to preach the gospel to the unconverted was too good to miss. That evening John Stevenson based his own remarks on 'The Kingdom of God is not in words, but in power', and threw open the meeting to any who wished to testify to God's dealings with them. The first on his feet was the dynamic Hsi Shengmo. He told how in his youth the Confucian classics had failed to allay his fear of death. He turned to Daoism and found it as unsatisfying. By then he was practising as a barrister, but falling ill he took to opium for relief. For eighteen months he grew worse and, expecting him to die, his friends dressed him in his grave-clothes. But in spite of the famine he recovered, except for his addiction. Then he heard of the essay competition run by David Hill and won the prize. But he did not dare to go and claim it.

> I had heard many reports that foreigners could bewitch people, and I feared to fall under their influence . . . I feared bewitchment, but I feared to lose the thirty taels. [So he took the risk and came face to face with David Hill.] One glance, one word, it was enough. As stars fade before the rising sun, so did his presence dissipate the idle rumours I had heard. All trace of my fear was gone . . . I beheld his kindly eye and remembered the words of Mencius, 'If a man's heart is not right his eyes bespeak it.' I was in the presence of a true man . . . Mr Hill led me to the gate, God caused me to enter, Jesus led me on. I remember weeping as I read how He died for me. Trusting Him I ceased to doubt.

One after another the Christians told their own story of how they had come to faith in Christ, and Hudson Taylor enjoyed every minute. His own role, unsought and unquestioned by any at the time or afterwards, was *de facto* that of a chief pastor, a bishop over other pastors and evangelists. The denominational Churches did not challenge it; the general conferences of missions tacitly recognised it, for no title or comment was necessary; and three hundred Chinese and foreign preachers of the gospel looked to him as their leader. The new churches of Shanxi contained men and women of God already playing the part of pastors, elders and deacons. On the second day of the conference Hudson Taylor and his south Shanxi colleagues ordained them to serve the various local churches. Hsi Shengmo he ordained to a general charge as 'watcher over and feeder of the sheep of God' in the extensive area he already served under the prompting of the Holy Spirit. 'He is indefatigable in visiting the sick (and) helping those in any trouble,' Hoste wrote. Hsi was in fact the pastor-in-chief, acknowledged by all to be their leader with the necessary authority. But he had been a Christian less than ten years, so a free hand without the dignity of a title as supervisor was the wisest course.[8] After the baptism of fifty-six men and women and a communion service, they scattered to their farms, for it was harvest time.

The missionaries and leading Chinese went on to Linfen for a second conference, this time with the Xi Xian and Daning Christians, and Hoste and Cassels. Mr Qü of Daning told his story of conversion and flogging, ending with the words, 'The official now wants to take away my degree, but I count it as nothing. Jesus has a greater glory in store for me.' Holding a *xiu cai* degree he could not legally be flogged. But what (corrupt) mandarin 'could stop his enemies from beating him'? He too was ordained a pastor before the conference ended.

Ahead lay the long journey from Linfen to Hanzhong but first Pastor Hsi invited Hudson Taylor, Stevenson, Dr Edwards and Stanley Smith to his home for the weekend, while Beauchamp, Studd and Herbert Taylor went on to Qüwo and returned to visit the churches with Hsi and Stevenson, on his way via Taiyuan to Tianjin and Shanghai.

At Daning, while Hsi and Qü the two literary graduates preached the gospel on the main street of the city, where Qü had been flogged, John Stevenson examined new candidates for baptism. There and at Qü's village twelve miles away, nineteen attested believers were baptised in the river. 'When it was clearly pointed out that their profession would involve them in persecution and even death . . . and it was up to them whether . . . they would still continue to be Christians, they eagerly said, "Rather let life go than Christ."' Fourteen years later Shanxi became the scene of the most appalling massacres of Christians. One of these men was among the first to suffer.[9]

'A little man to sort of steer' *1886–87*

Cassels had already been in Shanxi longer than intended. He wanted to reach the unevangelised regions of eastern Sichuan and to pioneer a new Church on Anglican principles. It troubled him to be where the established practices (of baptism, communion and ordination) were so different. He discussed it with John Stevenson after the Hongtong ordinations, but who if not the missionaries were to perform them? Two missionary couples were to be married soon, and as a minister of the Established Church his presence, all assumed, could spare them the long, taxing journey to the coast and back. He reluctantly agreed to wait while Beauchamp and Studd accompanied Hudson Taylor to Hanzhong and (John Stevenson hoped) through Sichuan. Hoste and Stanley Smith chose to stay where they were needed and welcomed in a thriving church.

Ironically, when the marriages were reported to the Registrar at Somerset House, London, their validity was questioned and registration refused by the Bishop of London also. It took William Sharp, the lawyer on the London Council, and 'learned counsel' until May 1887 to get the British Government to agree that marriages by Cassels in the interior of China without the presence of a consular official were indeed valid. But not until January 28, 1890, could the London Council finally minute the fact that the Foreign Secretary, Lord Salisbury, had assured William Sharp that he would instruct the consular service in China to recognise such marriages. The complexities of an expanding society were unavoidable. When the time came for Cassels to leave Daning in early November 1886, he could hardly tear himself away. The people were in tears. But after he reached Sichuan where he was the only licensed minister within hundreds of miles, he quickly earned his nickname, 'the Travelling Joiner'.[10]

Pastor Hsi was praying that Dixon Hoste would be appointed to Hongtong but in the autumn it was Stanley Smith who invited him to come. The way he put it, Hoste confessed, 'ruffled (me) in my spirit'. SPS let it be known that he would be the leader and take decisions. Then how about asking the directors for a younger colleague? Hoste replied, aware of the 'loss of face' involved! But 'the Spirit of God probed me.' To be unwilling would mean 'parting company with the Lord Jesus Christ, who dwells with the humble ones, those who willingly go down.' So he went. And marvelled at the spiritual power in Stanley Smith. 'He was full of the Spirit . . . The more he was willing to let Pastor Hsi keep his natural position, the more God seemed to bless him.'

In the spring of 1887 they held another, greater conference at Hongtong with 300 attending and 216 being baptised at one time – the largest number in the history of missions in China to date. But among seasoned missionaries apprehension and criticism were outspoken. Either some had been kept waiting too long, or some had been baptised too hastily, or this was a small 'mass movement', until then unknown in China. Time gave the answer. Five years later, 135 had remained faithful, 50 had backslidden mostly to opium, 20 were difficult to trace, 7 had transferred to other Churches, and four had died. Fewer than 20 had returned to idolatry.[11]

Hoste and Stanley Smith went up to Taiyuan to study Chinese for some weeks without interruption, leaving Pastor Hsi to use their rooms at Hongtong. To a few disaffected Christians this was the last straw. Good man though Hsi was, his weak points were a quick temper and a suspicious mind, both liable to alienate those who suffered as a result. Careful as Hudson Taylor had been not to make Hsi look superior to the others, jealousy of Hsi's natural authority was ready to be voiced. That he should occupy the missionaries' quarters looked like arrogance. And Hsi spoke unwisely about it. While they were away, his colleague in the opium refuge work turned violently against him. The young church, swollen by the addition of new members, was split in two, some loyal to Hsi, some 'swayed by the vitriolic fury of Fan and his adherents'.

This Satanic attack continued for several months, followed by years of trouble. Fan and an angry crowd invaded the Mission premises, Fan armed with a sword, his temper out of control. More sober men restrained him. But they drove Hsi out of the place shouting, 'Down to Pingyang!' and took him as a prisoner before Benjamin Bagnall, by then leader of the Mission in Shanxi. Surrounded by raving, angry men, 'Hsi's perfect calmness and self-control' impressed Bagnall, but for hours he could make no headway. Hsi was in mortal danger, with Fan rushing at him time and again with his sword upraised. Bagnall 'felt as if in hell', in the devil's presence. He secretly arranged for a horse to be brought, and at a critical moment himself seized Fan for long enough to let Hsi mount and gallop away.

The immediate crisis was over, but fierce opposition continued. Fan disrupted Hsi's refuges and opened rival ones of his own, close to Hsi's, selling his medicines more cheaply. He accused Hsi of every evil for which the slightest pretext could be found, and hired disreputable men to spread lies about him. A plausible young man gained access to the Hongtong refuge and administered drugs to a patient of high social standing, who died. Pastor Hsi feared all the consequences falling on his own head. He prayed and fasted before showing himself – and found not only the patient's family in a conciliatory frame of mind, but the young man who had been arrested admitting his responsibility.[12]

When Dixon Hoste returned from Taiyuan, on hearing what had happened (Stanley Smith having gone to the coast), his loyalty to Hsi made him also the butt of animosity. What should they do? Strong disciplinary action in the divided church would certainly exacerbate the trouble. They decided to ask God to vindicate the truth and demonstrate to all the rights and wrongs of the matter. Hsi turned the other cheek and gave himself to praying and working on quietly as he had opportunity. Gradually men and women returned to him. As the months passed Fan began to alienate his followers by misconduct and inefficiency, while Hsi's patient, prayerful spirit restored confidence in him. After one of his sessions of prayer he became convinced that the end was in sight. He let it be widely known that within three months the spurious refuges would all fail and close. Fan's 'whole movement sank into disrepute' and before the three months were over the last one was dissolved. This factor alone brought back many who had been deceived, and Hsi's position as the leading pastor was confirmed.

The relationship between Hoste and Hsi had through this bitter experience undergone a change. Never an easy colleague, Pastor Hsi required unfailing humility and understanding in any missionary who was to stay with him. Hoste stayed for ten years, until Hsi died. But others including Bagnall became embroiled in open ill-feeling and antagonism to Hsi in which Hudson Taylor eventually had to intervene, giving Hoste the difficult task of superintending the district. Hoste wrote:

> (Hsi) was rather an extreme case, because all the circumstances were extreme. Here was a man of exceptional force of character and organising power, and whose education and position gave him weight, a man of exceptionally deep spiritual life. . . . He had never had missionary supervision. . . . It was our place to recognise him in (this) position. Not to become his helpers . . . one of his lieutenants; that you cannot be. The missionary should . . . recognise to the full Hsi's God-given position . . . not be blind to his limitations but . . . remedy (them) . . . win his love and confidence . . . You will need grace with him and he . . . with you . . . We just grew together.[13]

Even before the Fan episode, Stanley Smith had proposed tackling the city of Lungan (or Lu'an, now Changzhi), seventy-five miles east of Linfen. On his return to Shanxi he began work there, adding Lucheng, a few miles to the north, later on. But Hoste had recognised the whole 'church' in south Shanxi as being indigenous, the fruit of vibrant spiritual life in the Chinese themselves.

> I do feel that I can only be of any use by being where the Master would have me; and that one might only go and do a lot of mischief by pushing into work which the Lord wanted to do through (the Chinese).[14]

Stanley Smith had had a very different approach to Pastor Hsi and Hongtong.

> He was the missionary in charge; I was just helping him at first, [Hoste wrote]. While he is a man of great vigour and great momentum, he isn't the man to run a big thing; he hasn't got that sort of mind. (His bright, cheery, genial, winning way was so necessary in order to warm up the people and restore them to a measure of love and confidence in a foreigner.) . . . He is such a sweet-tempered man . . . he wouldn't want to drive anybody, but he plunged along [he acted precipitately] and Pastor Hsi looked rather grim, but still he loved and appreciated him . . . The Spirit of God seemed sometimes just to fill the place when he was preaching . . . He is a stroke [the pace-setter in the university boats] rather than a cox. It was a cox that was wanted, because Pastor Hsi was perfectly well able to stroke the boat . . . What you want is a little man to sort of steer [while Pastor Hsi did the work].
>
> I thoroughly saw, right from the beginning, that the man [Hsi] was a bishop (as the other church leaders recognised in time) and Mr Taylor had made him a bishop . . . Hsi got gentler and mellower as the years went by.

Through this experience, Dixon Hoste's wisdom and spirituality became deepened, and the rightness of his attitude and policy could not but be noted by those who watched him. John Stevenson and Hudson Taylor recognised in him another outstanding leader in the making. In his thinking he was in fact far ahead of the average missionary of his day. Two missionary generations were to pass before a determined attempt was made on a large scale in China to apply these principles (of establishing indigenous leadership), enunciated by the SPCK in the early eighteenth century; by Charles Gutzlaff in 1849–50; re-echoed by Henry Venn with qualifications in 1851; by William Burns; by the English Presbyterian George Smith before 1878, and by John Livingston Nevius in greater detail in 1864, 1880 and 1885–86; as well as by Hudson Taylor from 1870 onwards (see Note 14). By the twentieth century, when Roland Allen, Dr Thomas Cochrane and others through their publications brought the missionary world back to these first principles, the difficulty of extricating missions from the webs of alien methods and apparatus they had spun for themselves, and of freeing the Chinese Church from dependence on foreign funds and initiatives had become almost insuperable. The drastic surgery of Mao's revolution was needed to effect emancipation.

In August 1887 John Stevenson returned to Shanxi, to put before Pastor Hsi the suggestion that his opium refuges should be greatly increased in number, not only in Shanxi but in neighbouring provinces as well. Archibald Orr Ewing wished to provide the funds for renting premises if Hsi would choose the places, run the refuges, find and train the staffs, and supervise the evangelism. Coming at a time when opposition to him was at its height, Hsi was encouraged. Fan and his faction were a threat only in south Shanxi. Reassured by Stevenson, whom Hsi admired, he accepted the challenge. Orr Ewing's nickname among Shanxi Christians was 'Mr Glory-face', an affectionate play on his Chinese surname Yong (Glory) and the light in his eye.

They began together in the Pingyao plain, south of Taiyuan, and opened eight refuges. Opium smokers in Wenxi, a hundred miles south of Hongtong, pleaded with Hsi to open a refuge for them. Five refuges resulted, extending from Puzhou in the sharp angle of the Yellow River (Huang He) in the south-west, to Jincheng (then known as Tsechou) (map p 85), in the south-east of Shanxi. Across the great river in Henan five more were opened, and one at Nanho, over the Zhili border. But perhaps most gratifying were the two

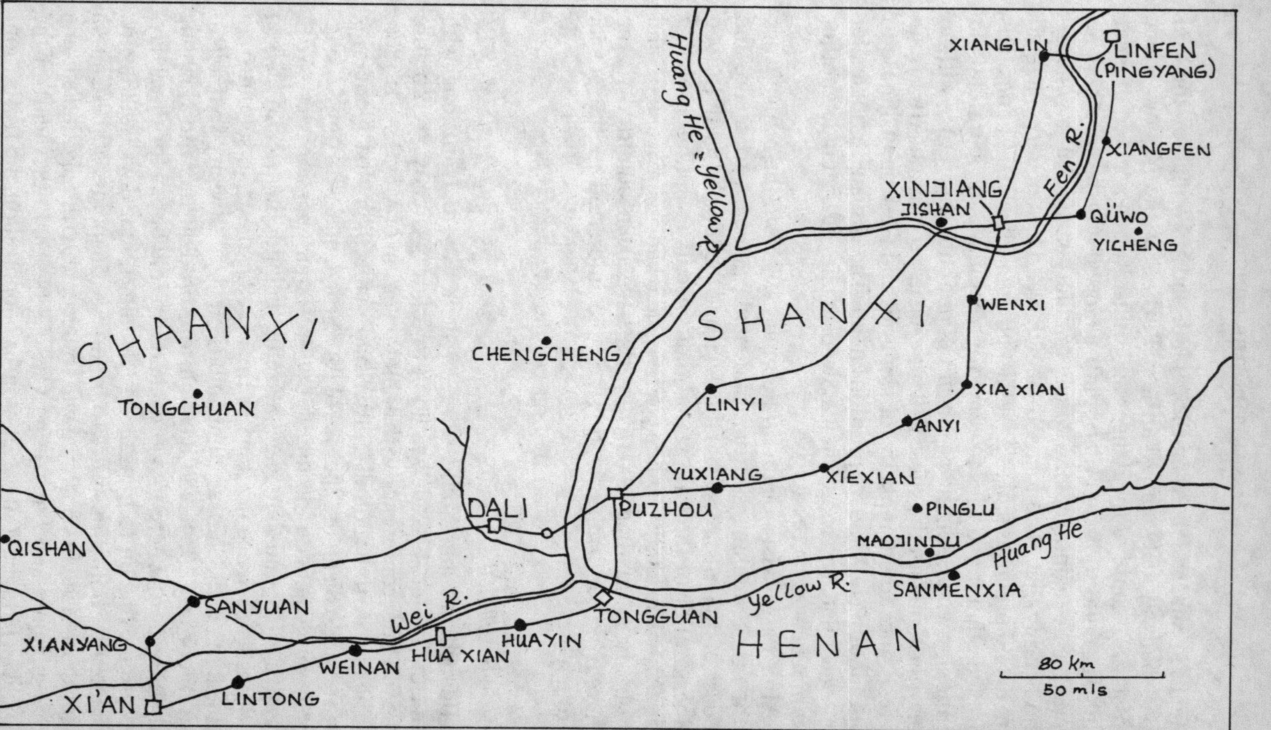

THE LINFEN-XI'AN CORRIDOR

refuges in Shaanxi, at Xi'an the capital, and at Weinan on the Wei River halfway between Xi'an and Puzhou at the Yellow River crossing. Because of the danger and difficulty he expected to meet with, Hsi undertook the Xi'an venture himself. On the way there he made the acquaintance of a Muslim military mandarin, a general, who hearing that Hsi practised medicine and opium cures, helped him to find premises and as an addict put himself in Hsi's hands. His cure led other mandarins to come for treatment, and a grateful old gentleman whose sons had been cured, presented the refuge with an honorific tablet for the guest-hall praising its promoters. After years of resistance to attempts by missionaries and Christian Chinese to gain a footing in Xi'an, opposition ended. The Hunanese ringleader was out-influenced, and when a Swedish missionary made another attempt he was successful.[15]

After Pastor Hsi's death on February 19, 1896, the refuge work went on, combining spiritual and medical means to secure the release of opium-slaves from the devil and the drug he used. In 1906 Albert Lutley of the CIM stated that since its inception 'probably not less' than 303,000 men and women had been treated, and 'probably more than 1000 converts have been admitted to the Church by baptism, who first became interested in the gospel through these refuges.'[16]

Sichuan 'claimed' *1886–87*

Beauchamp and Studd were on their way to Hanzhong with Hudson Taylor. Cassels was soon to follow. Already, well before 'the full tide' conference with John Stevenson of May 25–31, 1886, Cecil and Arthur Polhill-Turner had made their first pioneering journey into Sichuan, 'the size of three Englands' with only Chongqing and Chengdu occupied by Protestant missionaries. With months of sound language learning behind them, and eleven months' experience in China to their credit, they had set out from Hanzhong with Chinese companions on Cecil's twenty-sixth birthday, February 23. Seven days on foot brought them to Bazhong (then Pachou) where they preached and sold books for three days before moving on to Langzhong (Paoning), four days' walk away. Eventually, both cities were to become strongpoints of the Church in eastern Sichuan. Bazhong was to become Arthur Polhill's home for ten years, and Langzhong Cassel's base and the heart of the Anglican field, but only after months of opposition and frustration.

From Langzhong they tramped westwards for eight days to Chengdu and for two weeks saw how Samuel Clarke (unrelated to George) worked in and around 'this magnificent city'. The Clarkes had just lost their colleagues J H Riley and his wife Jane Kidd (pp 276, 420) in tragic circumstances. Returning to Langzhong with its mulberry orchards and hilltop pagoda above the Jialing River, the Polhill brothers put up in an inn and 'worked' the city for a month. Finally they tramped the 150 miles back to Hanzhong and the May Conference with John Stevenson, fully convinced that they were on the right course and should formally join the CIM. 'We had in God's name claimed Sichuan, and thrown down the gauntlet to Satan,' they declared with the zest of youth and inexperience. Time would show what defying Satan could cost.[17]

Eighteen years had passed since Griffith John and Alexander Wylie had prospected the province of Sichuan in 1868 by travelling from Hankou through Chongqing, Chengdu and Hanzhong (Book 5, pp 174, 380). And nine years since John McCarthy had crossed in 1877 from Wanxian to Nanchong (Shunking) and down to Chongqing. A house had been rented in that year, and using Chongqing as their base, Cameron, Nicoll, Easton, Parker, Riley, Samuel Clarke and Baller had made wide evangelistic journeys. Mollman of the Bible Society and the American Presbyterian Leaman had joined them from time to time. 1881 had seen the arrival of the American Methodist Episcopal missionaries at Chongqing, and the occupation of Chengdu by the CIM. By comparison, it was as if London and Glasgow had been 'occupied' in Britain, the rest of the British Isles remaining almost untouched. The Xichang region beyond the high mountain ranges in the far south-west, could be thought of as Devon and Cornwall. Two more Englands filling the North Sea beyond the east coast of Britain would then represent East Sichuan. Langzhong, halfway between Chongqing and Hanzhong, was strategically placed, from which to penetrate and develop the evangelisation of this great eastern half of Sichuan. 'Occupation' was so far only a foothold from which to begin.

Stevenson had gone north to the Shanxi conferences after writing to Hudson Taylor that Cecil Polhill had donated the rental of one or more premises at Langzhong and was preparing to return there. 'God has opened first this station (Hanzhong) to give us the means of opening northern and eastern Sichuan.' In Uganda at this very time thirty-two Christians were being burned alive on one great pyre but in China there was liberty of movement and careful progress was meeting only mild resistance.

On June 7 (as Hudson Taylor reached Dagutang on his Guangxin River journey), Edward Pearse, Mr Ho (the first Hanzhong believer), a teacher named Liang and Cecil Polhill set out from Hanzhong again for Langzhong. The city when they arrived was full of examination candidates with the usual high flash-point of emotions. After a week they judged it best to leave Ho and Liang to look for a place to rent while they themselves went on to Chongqing and back, preaching and selling portions of the Bible on the way. As they entered Chongqing on July 3, they saw the American Episcopal Mission's new building in a commanding position on a hilltop, in the process of being wrecked. And on their way to find the CIM they were told the house had been demolished, and were cautioned to hire sedan chairs in which to keep out of sight. The place was standing but ransacked, and the thirty foreigners in Chongqing were said to be under protection at the magistrate's *yamen*. Everyone had lost everything he possessed. The Catholic cathedral and other buildings had been razed to the

THE VILLAGE FERRY
a mere shadow of the Yellow River one

ground. Mr Bourne, the British Resident, had to be muffled up and hustled through the mob in the guise of a prisoner under arrest, and with all the Roman Catholics, was at the governor's *yamen*.

Pearse and Cecil Polhill were taken and held with the others in cramped quarters. There news reached them from Hudson Taylor of the seventy-two baptisms at Hongtong and Linfen. After two weeks the magistrate sent all but George Nicoll down the Yangzi at midnight, forbidding Pearse and Cecil Polhill to return to Langzhong. Nicoll had begged permission to stay, on the ground that he was responsible for the Mission's obligations to local Chinese. Lest the fugitives be attacked on the way, the magistrate personally escorted them through the streets to small, unpretentious boats.

All except Pearse and Polhill reached Yichang in safety. These two had made clandestine arrangements to have their own boat, and two ponies in another, so that after passing the major city of Wanxian they could pay the boatmen off and strike northwards across deep country to Hanzhong. J J Coulthard had once made this crossing by small roads with poor inns, and reported rough going. Five weeks after starting overland they were back again at Hanzhong feeling well initiated into the province. Hudson Taylor, Beauchamp, Studd and Herbert Taylor arrived from Shanxi a few days later, after an even more rigorous journey.

'The shock troops' of missions — *August–November 1886*

Montagu Beauchamp carried clear recollections for many years of the August journey he made with Hudson Taylor from Shanxi to Hanzhong.

> Mr Taylor, feeling the heat so intensely, gave up all hope of continuing that journey beyond Pingyang unless he could travel by night; but after a very small amount of (it) C T Studd and Lewis fell out [and followed by day], Herbert Taylor dragged on, but Mr Taylor on a mule and myself on foot pushed on by night and reached Hanchung some two days before the others, though Herbert Taylor was only a day behind us.[18]

Crossing the Yellow River, 'running high and very dangerous', they nearly came to grief. In an overloaded ferry boat with carts, mules and passengers closely packed together, they began to roll in the strong current as they were swept miles downstream. Three or four mules toppled overboard, which saved the situation, and they reached the other side.

> A remarkable thing about Mr Taylor was his power of endurance, and his ability to sleep in the daytime, at any time. . . . No matter what the surroundings (he) was always the same man with the same spirit – with food, without food, with rest, without it. . . . I would often carry him through the rivers which were all in flood [crossing strong streams waist-deep Beauchamp would have Hudson Taylor on his shoulders and a Chinese each side to steady them]. Still he would not be hindered – we would push on . . . With so much rain we often got soaked through. One thing Mr Taylor never left behind was his medicine chest.
>
> Night travelling is one of the hardest experiences I have ever had, because I could not sleep by day. When I did manage to sleep, I would find Mr Taylor looking after me, rigging up a mosquito net to keep the flies off. While walking at night I have been so sleepy . . . I have fallen right down. Mr Taylor rode but I preferred to walk. (He carried two pillows, one for the shoulder, the other for the thigh) and we each had a plaid . . . We often used to lie down on the roadside.

At other times when they spent a night in an inn and Beauchamp woke to feed the mules before daylight, he would see Hudson Taylor reading his Bible by candlelight. 'He used to sing as we went along.' In this way they covered 2,500 Chinese *li* (about 888 miles), to reach Hanzhong on September 7 – and the inevitable accumulation of letters. There he learned of the Chongqing riot and faced the choice between risking prolonged delay if he crossed Sichuan, or cutting his travels short. Reluctantly he accepted the inevitable, but first held a Shanxi-type conference with the Chinese and missionaries. 'I remember Mr Taylor saying,' Beauchamp wrote, 'we were not out in China just to settle down to girls' schools. The ladies must be up and out and amongst the women.'

Hudson Taylor's travel log noted that after a day of fasting and prayer for Sichuan on the 14th, Beauchamp and Cecil Polhill set off for Chengdu on the 17th, and Studd with Arthur Polhill on the 18th, for East Sichuan. 'The shock troops' of Protestant missions in China, the CIM, were living up to their growing reputation, with Hudson Taylor their 'general' firmly in the front line.[19] He stayed two days to help Dr William Wilson with some major operations before taking Edward Pearse's little daughter down the Han River rapids with him to Wuchang on October 14. 'But for (the Chongqing riots) I should have been on my way to Sichuan ere now,' he told Stevenson. Once again his greatly hoped for tour of the province had been thwarted. He could not afford to be immobilised as Pearse and Cecil Polhill had been for weeks on end. Instead he called the China Council of newly appointed provincial superintendents to meet at Anqing in November.[20]

John Stevenson had said that the Wilsons were all they should be as missionaries and colleagues. The Chinese of Hanzhong greatly admired the doctor's ability to make his own medicines from herbs and minerals bought in the city. But his electrical equipment, a 'galvanic battery', an electro-magnet, electric bell and telegraph, 'all made in this house by native workmen, to my direction', amazed them. When the chief mandarin's father had been given up by the best local doctors as beyond cure, he had recovered under Wilson's treatment. The mandarin arrived one day with an honorific signboard in black enamel with large gold characters extolling the virtues of the doctor's skills and hospital. When the formalities of the presentation were over, Wilson demonstrated his instruments and equipment until, with the ice broken and friendship established, the high dignitary was trying in vain to pick a copper coin out of a bowl of electrified water. Prejudice died hard, but responded to medicine and friendliness. Hanzhong was a success. After only seven years since the Kings (the first missionaries) had moved in, a thriving church of ninety communicants and many more under instruction had only one Christian worker, the teacher, paid by the Mission. All others were serving voluntarily while retaining their previous occupations or assisting the evangelists at ten outlying chapels.

After visiting Griffith John, David Hill and Consul Gardner at Hankou, Hudson Taylor pressed on to Shanghai, in time to meet the eighty-one-year-old George Müller on a brief visit to China. After consulate formalities at Zhenjiang he conducted Herbert's wedding at Yangzhou, the scene of their escape from the riot eighteen years before, and on November 11 was on his way up the Yangzi again, taking bride and groom, Maria and a group of other young women to Dagutang en route for the Guangxin River experiment. He then returned to Anqing in time to meet his China Council.

Two years in China packed with achievement and advance had also, from the moment of his arrival on March 3, 1885, been one of the most painful periods of his life;[21] but he had had no premonition of peril to the very existence of the Mission. News of illnesses and deaths inexorably added to the pain. That two of the Seventy should have died within a few weeks of each other in 1885 was distressing, but the sequence of sorrows following the birth of twins to the Rileys in Chengdu moved Hudson Taylor to the depths. On October 12 Jane (Kidd) died of puerperal fever, and their colleague Fanny Stroud (aged twenty-seven) took charge of the three children. But soon Riley himself became ill, with symptoms which made others fear he would not recover, seeing double and being unable to stand unsupported. He asked Fanny Stroud to bring the children and servants and travel with him down the Yangzi to Shanghai. Before they reached Yichang he was having convulsions, fit after fit in one day. The consul, Mr Gregory, gave up his own rooms in the consulate to them, but Riley 'needed nursing as only a wife could nurse, and so Miss Stroud and he concluded to be married at once'. The ceremony was performed at his bedside, and they went on to Shanghai. 'I never saw such a wreck as Mr Riley is,' Hudson Taylor said. Six weeks later, on April 19, 1886, Riley died in a convulsion, but on June 8 Hudson Taylor was still full of the pathos and nobility of the situation when he wrote to Jennie: '(Fanny Stroud's marriage) is about the noblest thing I have ever come across in my life. (Of his) recovery the doctor gave her no hope; just to nurse him to the grave and care as mother for the three children . . . is what few would have done . . . She had none of the joys but all the anxieties, toils and sorrows of a wife.'[22]

His own heartaches could be intense. Separation from Jennie often seemed intolerable. Before leaving home he had written an editorial for the *Millions* saying that costly sacrifice was God's chosen way, for 'though he was rich, yet for your sake he became poor', and 'He emptied Himself'.[23] 'It *is* crucifixion.' 'Sometimes I feel as if it was killing me, wearing me out.' 'Love to the dear Chicks. I feel as if my heart would break with longing. Let it break. And yours too, darling, if JESUS is glorified.'[24] But the end was in sight.

The 'Book of Arrangements' — *November 1886*

Saturday, November 13, 1886, was historic in the CIM as the day on which the General Director and the Deputy China Director and Superintendents whom he had appointed, met for the first time as the China Council, at Anqing. Only half the superintendents were present, McCarthy, Baller, Dorward and William Cooper. Meadows was not well enough to come. George Clarke and Benjamin Bagnall, James Cameron and George Easton were either on furlough or too far away to make the long journey on this occasion.[25] The meeting marked the climax of two years of thought and consultation, first with the London Council and by degrees with the individuals who agreed to be provincial superintendents. Their business was to achieve harmonious co-operation, by defining the practices which had been evolved by common consent over the years, and what are now called job descriptions of the various types of missionary. It was therefore to be largely administrative, much of it the dry mechanics of organisation; but clarification of the wording of the 'Principles and Practice', and a new proposition put forward by John Stevenson were to be considered. What follows may look tedious, but to the surprise of all who took part, within a few weeks it had become dynamite.

The Mission had grown to 187 missionary members, and the practical outworking of the 'P and P' needed to be down in black and white if all were to understand and apply it uniformly. Some leaflets already existed. A simple concise handbook was the obvious means to that end. It was to sum up all that the council agreed together. With it no one in any remote location need be in doubt about how to act, or lose time and energy consulting others about the commoner subjects, while the leaders would be left free to advise in unusual circumstances. Within the general framework the rank and file would be no less at liberty to show initiative. Most of it was obvious: instructive only to the uninitiated, and a restraint only on the individualist. To members of the London Council it would be a window on the obscure administrative domain of the directors in China. It was to be a little book of agreed 'arrangements' rather than rules and regulations. For supporters Hudson Taylor wrote an account of the council's meetings, in *China's Millions*. Neither he nor John Stevenson had any inkling of danger ahead. One hundred years later the Mission still works on the same pattern, with its periodically updated *Manual* and its graded language study requirements.[26]

'Several days' were first spent in prayer, with fasting on alternate days. For the tentacles of the Mission were stretching farther and farther into previously unworked regions, and more and more members were dependent upon each other's support in what was primarily a spiritual undertaking. Seventy-seven were experienced seniors, but no fewer than one hundred and ten were young and more vulnerable. When the council's agenda was tackled, the first subject to be dealt with was language study, their chief tool. John Stevenson had given this a great deal of thought and drafted a course in eight stages. Frederick Baller was formally charged with writing his *Mandarin Primer* and with establishing the Anqing Training Institute, with Robert Landale's help. The council itself was defined as existing 'to assist the Director and his Deputy with its counsel and co-operation in all such matters of gravity as the Director or his Deputy may feel it useful to lay before them'. That it was to be an advisory council and not executive was unquestioned, as the Minute read: 'That the said Council shall stand in the same relationship to the Director and his Deputy with reference to all the affairs of the Mission in China that the Home Council holds with reference to the affairs of the Mission at home.' Administration by directors and superintendents was not to be despotic but in Hudson Taylor's words, such as '*always leads the ruler to the Cross*, and saves the ruled at the expense of the ruler . . . Let us all drink into this spirit, then lording on the one hand and bondage on the other will alike be impossible.' He himself knew all too well the suffering entailed.

Clarification of the *P and P* began on the 17th and ended the next day. Some statements as they stood were open to misunderstanding and needed to be rephrased. And the reorganisation of the Mission needed to be incorporated. Instructions for all members in their different capacities, as beginners, women, secretaries, travellers, superintendents and so on, occupied them from November 19 to 23. On the 25th they agreed that large reinforcements should come to China soon, one hundred within one year, and that Hudson Taylor should return to Britain as soon as possible to promote this.[27] If this was the will of God, as they believed it was, the funds would be forthcoming.

Some difficult problems were discussed and solutions found. The fact that a body of such highly respected men agreed with Hudson Taylor in calling a halt to the actions of some individuals, made protests less likely to be strong. For example, friends, sisters, servants or governesses were not in future to be brought to China without prior correspondence and written approval by the China Director (that is, by Hudson Taylor or John Stevenson, whichever was currently in China). This ill-advised practice had become an embarrassment to colleagues, and the mobility or efficiency of a missionary could be severely limited by his ill-assorted household. A carefully worded paragraph about Chinese dress and customs, how to avoid offending the prejudices of the people, and about demanding supposed rights from the mandarins, all based on hard earned experience, led into a thornier subject which had to be firmly stated. The habitual use of CIM premises by travellers and members of very different societies had raised serious issues, even to the withholding of passports. High-handed treatment of the Chinese provoked resentment. Friends of missionaries could not be governed by CIM procedures, but neglect of these had led to violence, not always one-sided. In particular, the display of firearms directly contravened the Mission's principles.

> It is therefore to be understood that none of our missionaries resident in the interior are at liberty to invite their friends for residence or prolonged stay in the premises of the Mission without the written permission of the Superintendent . . . These remarks do not apply to hospitality to travellers passing through.

Recognising that considerable economies could be made in the course of time by using telegraphic code words to convey whole sentences, a system known as 'Unicode' was already in use by some business houses. Now a CIM equivalent was to be prepared. Its convenience and versatility, eventually using numerals, resulted in its being adopted not only by the CIM but by secular organisations as well.[28]

Within two weeks the council dispersed, Hudson Taylor and John Stevenson going to Dagutang to draft the 'Book of Arrangements'. They planned to distribute it in the form of a printer's page proof for comment by the London Council and absent superintendents, before eventually promulgating it. But the practical decisions it embodied were for immediate application. No thought occurred to them that this logical step in the Mission's development would provoke years of disharmony and be the reef on which the CIM could have come to grief.

The 'rich young ruler' *1886–87*

Going back to where we left them in September 1886 (p 418), Montagu Beauchamp and Cecil Polhill were heading for Chengdu, and Studd with Arthur Polhill for eastern Sichuan. With less than two years' experience in China they were still novices, but their directors had given them a free rein to show their mettle. In each case the journey shaped their lives. To pick up the threads: Arthur made Bazhou (Pachow) his sphere for ten years. Cecil found his niche in the Tibetan marches and embarked on romantic, dangerous adventures. C T Studd and a companion daringly went on down to Chongqing in November, and amazed the British Resident by appearing alive and unharmed at his beleaguered consulate (or quarters provided by the magistrate), despite continuing anti-foreign unrest. Mr Bourne invited Studd to stay with him, and they were together when Montagu Beauchamp arrived.[29] He was taken into the magistrate's *yamen* and protected as an unwilling guest until Bourne and Studd persuaded him for his own 'health' to leave by junk down the Yangzi. Between them they saw enough to be convinced that the mainly anti-Catholic rioting had the tacit approval of the viceroy.

So Beauchamp rejoined Hudson Taylor at Dagutang while he was working on the Book of Arrangements. When the time came for them to go on down to Shanghai, Beauchamp witnessed a typical example of Hudson Taylor's spirit. When carriers engaged to take his baggage to the ship arrived to collect it they demanded twice as much in payment as they had agreed on. Hudson Taylor would not yield, unpacked his luggage and wrote letters until after three hours the carriers came to terms. 'The battle was won for the benefit of all others though to (his own inconvenience).' He missed his steamer and did not get to Shanghai for Christmas, but the carriers would be less likely to take advantage of other travellers.

Rumour had it that the CIM had benefited immensely from the wealth of its rich young men. There was truth in it but by no means on the scale alleged not only in Britain. The *Millions* had to carry a formal denial that the Mission had large investments and sources to tap. The fact was that during C T Studd's two months in Chongqing (November–December 1886) official statements reached him of the fortune he had inherited on attaining the age of twenty-five on December 2 the previous year. He had given the matter prolonged thought and even before leaving London had consulted Hudson Taylor. There was no doubt in Hudson Taylor's mind that a life of sacrifice, poured out for Christ and China, made the words of Jesus 'Lay not up . . . treasures on earth' applicable to men like Studd.

'C T' had begun the process of self-denial even before associating himself with the CIM, and had gone further than the others in simplicity of living. He was ascetic to the point of choosing a bench rather than a seat with a back, 'a man who never spared himself, and took no care whatever of his health. Had he not married . . . it is doubtful whether he would have lived as long as he did,' the Polhill brothers wrote.[30] In Chongqing he was reading a 'harmony of the gospels' and came to Christ's words to the rich young ruler a few days before the letters arrived from his solicitor and banker. To him the will of God was stated in black and white. But the Resident refused to sign the papers 'C T' drew up granting power of attorney to his representatives in Britain. 'At the end of two weeks I took it back and he signed it and off the stuff went.' His inheritance was approximately £29,000 (at that time) and he decided to distribute £25,000 first. On January 13, 1887, he sent off four cheques of £5,000 each and five of £1,000 each, investing them in God's bank, he said, at 'a hundredfold', 10,000 per cent: £5,000 each to George Müller for his orphans and foreign missions; to D L Moody; to George Holland for God's poor in London; and to the Salvation Army in India – it paid for fifty new officers to be sent out. £1,000 each went to Annie Macpherson, General Booth, Archibald Brown and Dr Barnardo for their work in London's East End, and for similar use to Miss Ellen Smyly in Dublin.

Here we abandon chronological restraints to deal further with this subject of the CIM's 'rich young men'. Montagu Beauchamp kept his own secret for many years. He lived a peripatetic life in the hard school of doing what was required of him, first by assisting Hudson Taylor; then in making a long preaching colportage on foot through Henan to Shanxi and back to Sichuan; and another to Gansu; finally choosing to concentrate on Sichuan. Already more knowledgeable and widely experienced than the relatively static missionaries he found himself amongst, and at first unordained but in an Anglican field, he chafed under the ecclesiastical restrictions imposed upon him. He was known far and wide, speaking Chinese 'fluently and correctly', and often mistaken for a Chinese. Never at a loss how to act or to meet a difficult situation, he was also an attractive, able preacher, unflagging in his work and his praying. The consul at Wanxian paid him the tribute of saying that Beauchamp was so devoted to the Chinese people that he was 'at the beck and call of any coolie'.[31]

Many years later (May 10 but no year given) when the question was submitted to him, 'Has the reference to Montagu Beauchamp's having inherited and renounced a quarter of a million been verified?' he replied to Frank Houghton (later Bishop and the CIM's fourth General Director but at the time editor in London): 'Mr Taylor was the only living person who knew of my renunciation of my family estate of a quarter of a million; and he advised me to do so and to remain in China.' That was all. But he was never so well-heeled. The audited accounts of the CIM contain no record of a large gift, for he never had it to give. Sir Montagu's father, the 4th baronet, had died in 1874 and the eldest son, Sir Reginald, having no male heir would have bequeathed Langley Park and all that went with it to Montagu – on conditions that he returned home to administer it. For Christ's sake and for China he renounced this possibility. After twenty-five years Montagu was in England when the first world war broke out. He served in the Mediterranean Expeditionary Force as Principal Chaplain, and in North Russia. His second brother, Sir Horace, the 6th baronet, and Montagu's eldest son were both killed at Suvla Bay, Salonika, on August 12th, 1915, and Sir Montagu succeeded to the baronetcy without the fortune. Inheritance mattered little. The cost of discipleship involved greater things.

C T Studd's brother had been reading for the Bar, intent on being a barrister, but illness dogged him until his doctors recommended a voyage to Australia. When 'C T' invited George to visit him in China on the way home, 'G B' booked his passage to Shanghai and arrived in May, determined to make his visit brief and to avoid becoming embarrassed by the hot gospel atmosphere of the CIM. In fact, he was to confess, he was 'running away from God'. He had chosen to be the staid and sober kind of Christian, not Charlie's type. On arriving at Shanghai he booked his passage to Japan and created a sensation when he played Studd-quality cricket at the Club.[32] But at the CIM the contrast in atmosphere disturbed him. He envied the peacefulness and contentment of everyone, whatever the news or disturbances. He asked for an explanation. 'Capitulate to Jesus and trust Him for everything', he was told. Worse still, revival meetings were soon to begin. He determined to escape to Japan. But his craving for a heart and mind at peace decided him to acquire it at any price. 'I surrendered to the Lord Jesus, trusting that He would make my will His own.' At a public meeting with cricketers present from the club he described what had happened, cancelled his passage and stayed to face the music.

There was a girl from Northern Ireland at the Mission, Priscilla Stewart, so natural in speaking about Jesus that she was attracting people to him day after day. Charlie was smitten. She went on her way to Dagutang but he pursued her with letters and by October 3 they were engaged. When the final figures of his inheritance were known, he gave away what remained from his distribution, 'mainly to the CIM' but retaining £3,400. When he presented this to his bride before their marriage in January 1888, she said 'Charlie, what did the Lord tell the rich young man to do?' 'Sell all.' 'Well then, we will start clear with the Lord at our wedding.' They sold out and gave the £3,400 to the Salvation Army, before starting work together at Lungan in south Shanxi.

In July 1887 'G B', 'C T' and Archibald Orr Ewing travelled together to Shanxi – in time to play their part in an outbreak of typhus or typhoid (seldom clearly distinguished in those days). 'C T' went down with it first, nursed by 'G B' and Stanley Smith. Then 'C T' nursed Stanley Smith through it. A young missionary, J H Sturman, recovered from 'typhus' but died while convalescing at Chefoo. In January W L Elliston died of typhoid. After his years as a schoolmaster at Chefoo, he had undertaken to 'open' Huolu in Zhili. At Taiyuan smallpox had taken the life of Dr and Mrs Edwards' infant son, but both parents survived 'typhoid'. In caring for them Archibald Orr Ewing and Dr Stewart each caught it and were nursed by the BMS missionaries and Adamson of the Bible Society. But W E Terry of the CIM succumbed. Only the foundations of the Schofield Memorial Hospital had so far been laid. The cost of discipleship was not measured in monetary terms, as the growing list of widows testified.[33]

A hundred, or two — *November 1886*

How the idea arose, of calling for one hundred new missionaries before the end of 1887, is not known for certain. Hudson Taylor made no mention of it when he was in Shanxi, and when it was put to him he was at first reluctant to adopt it. But on September 16, 1886, John Stevenson wrote to Jennie Taylor from Taiyuan (following his triumphal visits to the churches of south Shanxi),

> We are fully expecting at least *100 fresh* labourers to arrive in China in 1887. I am happy to think that God is very likely to rebuke our small faith by sending many more than the (hundred) . . . The field is opening up most wonderfully.[34]

Manuscript sources are few, but thirty years later, when the Howard Taylors were writing the second volume of their father's biography, John Stevenson was still in harness as China Director and often consulted by them. Their account of the Hundred is still in print. He had been in the company of four of the Cambridge Seven since Hudson Taylor left Shanxi, and was himself euphoric after what he had seen at Hanzhong. 'Speaking subsequently of those days, he said: "I was just thinking and praying about it. We all had visions at that time, and Mr Taylor used to say I was going too fast."' 'We are fully expecting 100' suggests that the others shared his hopes.

John Stevenson reached Shanghai on Monday, October 25, two days after Hudson Taylor (and on the day the aged George Müller visited the CIM in their humble quarters). With such a thought so sharply present in Stevenson's mind it is unlikely that he would not have mentioned it. And with so much on Hudson Taylor's mind, 'going too fast' may have been his reaction, because one hundred was more than half the total strength of the CIM. But his mind was open. Then at Anqing when Stevenson raised the subject, the China Council prayed and fasted over it. If for no other reason a larger Mission would give wider scope for matching colleagues with each other – quite apart from matrimonial choices. On the last day but one, November 25, instead of himself writing to the Mission for the 'end of year day of prayer', Hudson Taylor deputed Stevenson to write. He noted that twenty-two new members had arrived in China during 1886 and went on:

> Our needs are, however, so great that this increase has appeared as nothing, and I would suggest that definite prayer for no less than one hundred new workers during 1887 be offered on our fast day, and also that it may be a subject of daily prayer afterwards.[35]

Writing to Jennie two days later, Hudson Taylor himself said 'We are praying for one hundred new missionaries in 1887. The Lord help in the selection and provide the means.' When they reached Dagutang and were working on the Book of Arrangements, the complexities of administration lay harshly before them. Already Hudson Taylor was carrying as heavy a burden as he thought he could bear, and from London evidence was mounting that the staff were no less hard pressed. For one hundred suitable men and women to be corresponded with, assessed, prepared and despatched within one year would increase the strain immeasurably. 'Yes,' John Stevenson contended, 'but with needs so great, how can we ask for less?' Deploying them would present no problem. Far more could be placed, with China so wide open. The expense was another matter, but if this was 'of God', the funds would come in.

Walking up and down as he dictated letters to Lewis his secretary, Hudson Taylor repeated what he had written to Jennie. 'A hundred new missionaries in 1887.' John Stevenson saw Lewis look up incredulously. So did Hudson Taylor, and a surge of certainty seemed to come over him.

> After that, he went beyond me altogether [Stevenson recalled]. Never shall I forget the conviction with which he said: If you showed me a photograph of the whole hundred taken in China, I could not be more sure than I am now.

This whole incident once more belies the claim sometimes heard, that Hudson Taylor was an autocrat. No *evidence* in the sources supports that epithet, even in the extreme circumstances he was approaching.

They cabled to London, 'Banded prayer next year hundred new workers send soon as possible,' and Hudson Taylor wrote to Jennie,

> We are ready for receiving fifty, say, of the hundred at once . . . The LORD did great things for us when He gave us Stanley Smith's party. He is able to do *more.* Let us honour Him with great expectations. [And to an inner circle] Some of us are hoping that His 'exceedingly abundantly' may mean fifty or sixty more missionaries besides the hundred for whom we are asking.[36]

It would cost fully £5,500 (equivalent to £200,000 today?) just to equip and send a hundred to China. If the bulk of this were to come in the usual small donations, the letters of thanks would alone need additional staff. The year 1886 was ending at a high point.

They wound up affairs at Dagutang and returned to Shanghai. On December 29, before two days instead of one of fasting and prayer, at last he could write, 'My darling, my own darling! I have wired tonight. Leaving on January 6th. I (am) almost wild with joy.' After he sailed, an enigmatic note from Stevenson followed him. 'Let me apologise for teasing you so much before you left.'[37]

In the two years, Hudson Taylor had travelled in nine provinces and covered as many miles in territory new to him as any member of the Mission. The scale of expansion which the China Inland Mission had entered upon was unprecedented among Protestant missions anywhere in the world and the prototype of the twentieth century international phenomenon. Many were to play their substantial part in the mobilising of the Hundred, but although others had initiated it, the task of publicising the appeal and arousing the Church to take it up, in the event fell to Hudson Taylor more than anyone. He was to work so hard that Jennie feared for his life and pleaded with him to slow down. Nothing, no one, could stop him. Once convinced, he believed he was doing the will of God.

There was ice on the decks when he sailed from Shanghai on January 6, 1887, with the companions he might have chosen had he been given the choice – Adam Dorward and William Cooper, escorting Mary Ann Nicoll.[38] Dorward had been nine years in China and owed it to his mother to visit her. But in September the Yellow River burst its banks and flooded parts of Henan. To them his duty was clear. Dorward left Britain again on October 6, returned to China and travelled a thousand miles, mostly on foot, taking relief to the devastated area.[39] Cooper was to marry in London a girl who had gone to China in 1881, the same year as he himself.

At Marseilles Hudson Taylor parted from the others to spend a few days with William Berger at Cannes. From there Hudson Taylor wired to Jennie, 'Leave Nice midnight meet Hudson Paris Wednesday midnight old hotel near Gare (du) Nord', their usual trysting place. So they reached London together.

POSTSCRIPT

Division of the period after 1875 into separate books is artificial. Dictated only by convenience in handling what proved to be too much for one last volume without mutilation, it ends Book Six, *Assault on the Nine*, in full flight on several themes.

The Nine provinces have yielded to the assault with the sole exception of Hunan. Even Taiwan, Manchuria and Mongolia have pioneers of other societies at work. Only Tibet and Turkestan remain, not untouched but unworked beyond the fringes.

'Occupation' as a first objective has been followed by 'consolidation' in the establishment of local churches, the nucleus of expansion. 'Reinforcement' of the pioneers with colleagues, and strengthening their lines of communication by the occupation of intervening cities have prepared the way for systematic evangelism of each area. The shock troops dig in.

Hudson Taylor's health at times has been failing. Satanic hostility, never absent, has taken new forms, 'deceiving if possible even the elect'. Portents of 'trouble ahead' suggest the withdrawal of the protecting hand of God. Disease has taken many. The dynasty is crumbling; violence is threatening. The saga, unbroken, is building up to its climax, and its thrilling sequel.

Book Seven's triumphant affirmation, '*It is not death to die! It's glorious!*' takes us through the massacres and Hudson Taylor's death to the Revolutions of 1911 and Mao Zedong, the end of the Open Century, and beyond.

APPENDIX 1

A KEY TO SOME CHINESE PLACE NAMES

Pinyin	*Wade-Giles*	*Postal, Press*
Adenzi	A-tun-tzu	Atuntsi
Anhui	An-hui	Anhwei
Anqing	An-ch'ing	Anking
Baoding	Pao-ting	Paoting
Baoji	Pao-chi	Paochi
Baoshan, Yongchang	Pao-shan	Paoshan
Baotou	Pao-t'ou	Paotow
Bazhong	Pa-chung	Pachung, Pachow
Bazhou	Pa-chou	Pachow
Beihai	Pei-hai	Pakhoi
Beijing	Pei-ching	Peking
Bose	Peh-seh	Pehseh
Changzhi, Lu'an	Ch'ang-chih	Changchih, Lungan
Chengdu	Ch'eng-tu	Chengtu
Chongqing	Ch'ung-ch'ing	Chungking
Dali	Ta-li	Tali
Datong, Tongling	Ta-t'ung	Tatong
Daxian	Ta-hsien	Tahsien
Dengzhou	Teng-chou	Tengchow
Dihua, Urumqi	Ti-hua	Tihwa
Dongchuan	Tung-ch'uan	Tungchuan
Duyün	Tu-yün	Tuyün
Ebian	O-pien	Opien
Emei	O-mei	Omei
Fujian	Fu-chien	Fukien
Fuzhou	Fu-chou	Fuchow
Gan Jiang	Kan-chiang	Kan Kiang
Gansu	Kan-su	Kansu
Guang'an	Kuang-an	Kwangan
Guangdong	Kuang-tung	Kwangtung
Guanghua (Laohekou)	Kuang-hua	Laohokou
Guangxi	Kuang-hsi	Kwangsi
Guangxin (Shangrao)	Kuang-hsin	Kwangsin
Guangyuan	Kuang-yüan	Kwangyuan
Guangzhou	Kuang-chou	Canton

Guan Xian	Kuan-hsien	Kwanhsien
Guide (Shangqiu)	Kwei-teh	Kweiteh
Guiding	Kuei-ting	Kweiting
Guihuacheng (Hohhot)	Kuei-hua-ch'eng	Kweihwacheng, Hohhot
Guilin	Kuei-lin	Kweilin
Guiyang	Kuei-yang	Kweiyang
Guizhou	Kuei-chou	Kweichow
Hangzhou	Hang-chou	Hangchow
Hankou	Han-k'ou	Hankow
Hanzhong	Han-chung	Hanchung
Hebei (Zhili)	Ho-pei (Chih-li)	Hopeh (-pei), Chili
Henan	Ho-nan	Honan
Hezuo	Ho-tso	Hochow
Hongjiang	Hung-kiang	Hungkiang
Hongkou	Hung-k'ou	Hongkew
Hubei	Hu-pei	Hupeh, Hupei
Huizhou	Hui-chou	Hweichow
Hunan	Hu-nan	Hunan
Huolu	Huo-lu	Hwailu
Huozhou	Huo-chou	Hochow
Jiading (Leshan)	Chia-ting	Kiating
Jiangsu	Chiang-su	Kiangsu
Jiangxi	Chiang-hsi	Kiangsi
Jiaxing	Chia-hsing	Kiahsing
Jilin	Chi-lin	Kirin
Jinan	Chi-nan	Tsinan
Jincheng, Zezhou	Chin-ch'eng, Tse-chou	Kincheng, Tsechow
Jinci	Chin-ts'u	Chintsi
Jinhua	Chin-hua	Kinhwa
Jinsha Jiang	Chin-sha-chiang	Kinsha Kiang
Jiujiang	Chiu-chiang	Kiukiang
Kangding	K'ang-ting	Kangting, Tatsienlu
Langzhong	Lang-chung	Langchung, Paoning
Lanxi	Lan-hsi	Lansi
Lanzhou	Lan-chou	Lanchow
Leibo	Lui-po	Luipo
Leshan, Jiading	Lo-shan, Chia-ting	Loshan, Kiating
Linfen, Pingyang	Lin-fen, Ping-yang	Linfen
Lishui (Qüzhou)	Ch'ü-chou	Chüchow
Lu'an, Changzhi	Lu-an, Lu-ngan	Lungan
Lüda, Dalian	Lü-ta, Ta-lien	Dairen, Port Arthur
Luoyang	Lo-yang (Ho-nan Fu)	Loyang
Luqü	Lu-ch'ü	Taochow
Mabian	Ma-pien	Mapien

Manyün	Man-yün	Manyün (Manwyne)
Nanchong	Nan-ch'ung	Nanchung, Shunking
Nanjiang	Nan-chiang	Nankiang
Nanjing	Nan-ching	Nanking
Ningbo	Ning-po	Ningpo
Ningxia	Ning-hsia	Ningsia
Puzhou	P'u-chou	Puchow
Qiantang	Ch'ien-t'ang	Tsientang
Qingdao	Ch'ing-tao	Tsingtao
Qinghai	Ch'ing-hai	Tsinghai
Qingjiangpu	Ch'ing-chiang-p'u	Tsingkiangpu
Queshan, Choshan	Ch'ueh-shan, Ch'o-shan	Choshan
Qü Xian	Ch'ü-hsien, Ch'ü-chou	Kiuchow
Qüzhou, Lishui	Ch'ü-chou	Chüchow
Runan	Ju-nan	Runing
Shaanxi	Shan-hsi	Shensi
Shandong	Shan-tung	Shantung
Shangqiu (Guide)	Kweiteh	Kweiteh
Shangrao (Guangxin)	Shang-rao	Shangrao (Kwangsin)
Shantou	Shan-t'ou	Swatow
Shanxi	Shan-hsi	Shansi
Shaoxing	Shao-hsing	Shaohsing
Sheng Xian	Sheng-hsien	Shenghsien
Shenyang	Shen-yang	Mukden
Sheqidian	She-chi-tien	Shekitien
Shijiazhuang	Shih-chia-chuang	Shikiachuang
Sichuan	Szu-ch'uan	Szechwan
Songjiang	Sung-chiang	Sungkiang
Suzhou	Su-chou	Suchow
Taibei	T'ai-peh (-pei)	Taipei
Taizhou, Linhai	T'ai-chou	Taichow
Tengyue	T'eng-yüeh	Tengyueh, Momein
Tianjin	T'ien-chin	Tientsin
Tianshui	T'ien-shui (Tsin-chou)	Tianshui, Tsinchow
Urumqi, Dihua	Ti-hua	Urumchi, Tihwa
Wanxian	Wan-hsien	Wanhsien
Wenzhou	Wen-chou	Wenchow
Wujiang	Wu-chiang	Wukiang
Wuxue	Wu-hsüeh	Wusueh
Xiamen	Hsia-men	Amoy
Xi'an	Hsi-an	Sian, Singan
Xiangfan	Hsiang-fan	Fancheng
Xichang	Hsi-ch'ang	Sichang, Ningyuan
Xinchang	Hsin-ch'ang	Sinchang
Xing'an, Ankang	Hsing-an	Hingan

Xining	Hsi-ning	Sining
Xizang	Hsi-tsang	Tibet
Yan'an	Yen-an	Yenan
Yangzhou	Yang-chou	Yangchow
Yangzi Jiang	Yang-tze Chiang	Yangtze (River)
Yantai	Yen-t'ai	Yentai, Chefoo
Yanzhou	Yen-chou	Yenchow
Yibin, Suifu	Yi-pin	Ipin, Suifu
Yichang	Yi-ch'ang	Yichang, Ichang
Yingkou	Ying-k'ou	Niuchwang
Yishan (Qingyuan)	I-shan (Ch'ing-yuan)	Ishan
Yongchang, Baoshan	Yung-ch'ang	Paoshan
Yüci	Yü-ts'u	Yütsi
Yuexi	Yueh-hsi	Yohsi
Yueyang	Yueh-yang, Yoyang	Yochow
Zhangjiakou	Chang-chia-k'ou	Kalgan
Zhaojue	Chao-chio	Chaokioh
Zhaotong	Chao-t'ung	Chaotung
Zhejiang	Che-chiang	Chekiang
Zhengzhou	Cheng-chou	Chengchow
Zhenjiang	Chen-chiang	Chinkiang
Zhenyuan	Chen-yuan	Chenyuan
Zhili (Hebei)	Chih-li, Ho-pei	Chili
Zhoujiakou, Zhoukouzhen	Chou-chia-k'ou	Chowkiakow
Zunyi	Tsun-yi	Tsunyi

APPENDIX 2

MEMBERS AND CHINESE COLLEAGUES OF THE CIM 1876

(Reduced facsimile from *China's Millions*)

134 *CHINA'S MILLIONS.*

"Brethren, pray for us, that the word of the Lord may have free course, and be glorified, even as it is with you."—*2 Thess. iii. 1.*

MISSIONARIES, NATIVE PASTORS, and other NATIVE HELPERS, in connection with the China Inland Mission:

MISSIONARIES. (36 and 16 wives of Missionaries: total, 52.)

• J. Hudson Taylor, Director,...	arrived in China	1854.
• James Meadows, ...	„	1862.
• George Crombie, ...	„	1865.
• George Stott, ...	„	1866.
• J. W. Stevenson, ...	„	1866.
• James Williamson, ...	„	1866.
• W. D. Rudland, ...	„	1866.
• J. A. Jackson,...	„	1866.
Miss Desgraz,...	„	1866.
• John McCarthy, ...	„	1867.
• J. E. Cardwell, ...	„	1868.
• C. H. Judd, ...	„	1868.
• Edward Fishe, ...	„	1868.
• T. P. Harvey, L.R.C.P., &c., Lond.	„	1869.
• C. T. Fishe, ...	„	1869.
Miss Turner, ...	„	1872.
• F. W. Baller, ...	„	1873.
M. Henry Taylor, ...	„	1873.
• A. W. Douthwaite, ...	arrived in China	1874.
Henry Soltau, ...	arrived in Burmah	1875.
Jos. S. Adams, ...	„	1875.
George King, ...	arrived in China	1875.
James Cameron, ...	„	1875.
George Nicoll, ...	„	1875.
G. W. Clarke, ...	„	1875.
J. F. Broumton, ...	„	1875.
G. F. Easton, ...	„	1875.
J. J. Turner, ...	„	1876.
Charles Budd, ...	„	1876.
Miss Knight, ...	„	1876.
Miss Goodman, ...	„	1876.
Miss Wilson, ...	„	1876.
Edward Pearse, ...	„	1876.
Francis James,...	„	1876.
George Parker, ...	sailed April 5,	1876.
Horace Randle, ...	„	1876.

The • indicates the Missionaries who are married.

NATIVE PASTORS. (7.)

Wông Læ-djün.
Chü Ying-tsiu.
Vaen Sin-sang
Tsiang Siao-vong.
Liu Sin-sang.
Tsiang Ah-liang.
Tsiang Soh-liang.

EVANGELISTS. (33.)

'O Ah-ho.
Tsiang Liang-yüong.
Kao Ziao-gyi.
Wông Teng-yüing.
Loh Ah-ts'ih.
Vong Sin-sang.
Sï Jün-kao.
Nyien Sin-sang.
Vaen Kwông-pao.
Nying Tsï-ky'ing.
Tsiu Uong-yiang.
Zi Sin-sang.
Dong Sin-sang.
Fông Neng-kwe.
Wông Kyüô-yiao.
Wông Sin-ch'ing.
Tsiang Ping-hwe.
Loh Kying-sih.
Kôh Yih-djün.
U Djün-yiao.
Tsiang Yüong-kao.
Ch'en Wen-loh.
Chang Sien-seng.
Ch'un Sien-seng.
Chu Sien-seng.
Hsü Sien-seng.
Wu Cheng-tsan.
Tæ Sin-sang.
Tsiu Fông-kying.
Han Sien-seng.
Yiao Sien-seng.
Lo Gan-fuh.
Chang Sien-seng.

COLPORTEURS. (27.)

Yiao Sï-vu.
Li Sin-sang.
Dzing Sï-vu.
Sing Sin-sang.
Moh Dziang-ling.
Lao Yiu-dzing.
Shih Da-tseng.
Liu Si-yüing.
Ling Hyin-djü.
Wông Yi-hying.
Ling Tsiao-sông.
Kying Tsing-saen.
Tsiu Din-ky'ing.
Seng Shü-nyün.
Lo Sï-fu.
P'un Sï-fu.
Ch'eng Sï-fu.
Wu Sï-fu.
King-shu.
Dzing Lao-yiao.
Tai Sï-fu.
T'ông Sin-sang.
Long-chong.
T'eng Sï-fu.
Ts'üen-ling.
P'en Sien-seng.
Yao Sï-fu.

BIBLE WOMEN. (6.)

Tsiu Sï-meo (senr.)
Tsiu Sï-meo (junr.)
Vaen Sï-meo.
Shih Sï-meo.
Yang Sï-meo.
Li Sï-meo.

NATIVE SCHOOLMASTERS. (2.)

Veng-ing.
Ing Sin-sang.

For the Stations of the Mission, see Table of Stations in Supplement to the number of "CHINA'S MILLIONS" for July, 1875. Price One Penny.

The Chinese names are in dialect, before standardisation.

APPENDIX 3

A PAGE FROM ADAM DORWARD'S LOG

(from *Pioneer Work in Hunan*)

Itinerary of land journey - Wu-chang to Hung-Kiang

Names of places	Names in Chinese	Distance from preceding place	Description of places
Wuchang	武昌		
Ci-fang-pu	紙坊舖	60 li	a small ~~cottage~~ hamlet
Shan-pŏ	山坡	60 "	a small village
Ho-sin-Kiao	河新礄	15 "	a village
Wu-hsing-Kiao	五興橋	35 "	a small town
Hsien-ling Hsien	咸甯縣	10 "	small & poor
Ting-si-Kiao	汀泗橋	30 "	a good town
Shih-an-tu	石岸渡	50 "	a small village
Fen-sha	分沙	15 "	do
Tsong-yang Hsien	崇陽縣	25 "	good city
Tong-ceng Hsien	通城縣	90 "	moderate
Ping-Kiang Hsien	平江縣	140 "	good city
Cang-tien-shi	張田市	40 "	a small village
Shae-Kang-shi	社港市	20 "	do
Hsie-Kia-cuang	謝家庄	40 "	a hamlet
Liu-yang Hsien	瀏陽縣	60 "	not very good
Tsen-chen		40 "	a village
Pu-tsih-shi	普積市	30 "	do
Li-ling Hsien	醴陵縣	90 "	good
Si-fen-pu	泗汾舖	30 "	a small town
Chuan-wang	船灣	30 "	a village
Sin-shi-pu	新市舖	70 "	a small village
Iu Hsien	攸縣	50 "	not very large
Chá-ling Chau	茶陵州	40 "	rather poor
Kiai-shi	界市	60 "	small market village
Shan-Kio-pu	山口舖	10 "	a hamlet
An-ren Hsien	安仁縣	20 "	small & poor

APPENDIX 4

A CHRONOLOGY 1875–88

(*See Appendix 5: Pioneer Journeys*)

1875	
	Zuo Zongtang halts at Hami to grow corn for troops
	D L Moody on first visit to London
January	Tong Zhi emperor dies; Guang Xü accedes; Ci Xi resumes regency
	CIM appeals for Eighteen pioneers for Nine provinces
Feb–April	Hudson Taylor recovering from paralysis
February 21	Augustus Margary murdered at Manyün
March 27–28	Emperor's widow Alude dies mysteriously
April–July	T F Wade in Shanghai
May	Japan asserts jurisdiction over Ryukyu Is.
May 14	Stevenson and Soltau arr. Burma; October 3, Bhamo
July	*China's Millions* Vol 1, No 1 published
August	T F Wade increases his demands; knighted in November
September	CIM *Plan of Operations* published in *China's Millions*
October	Theodore Howard becomes chairman of London Council
December	Plot to kill M Henry Taylor at Kaifeng
December 21	Eugene Stock becomes CMS editorial secretary
1876	
	Great Shandong-Shanxi famine begins
February	Chinese protest against Shanghai-Wusong railway
	Treaty agreed between Japan and Korea
April	First baptisms in Henan

May	CMS Uganda team in E Africa; Mackay arr. November 1878
	Nommensen to Lake Toba Bataks, Sumatra
May 26	10th anniversary of *Lammermuir* departure
August	M T Yates publishes his paper on Ancestor Worship
September 8	JHT dep. UK
September 13	Chefoo Convention signed; ratified May 6, 1886
October 22	JHT arr. Shanghai
October 1876–1880	'Like a bombshell scattering us' – 'the Eighteen' penetrate the Nine provinces
November	Zuo Zongtang ends Dungani Muslim rebellion, taking Manaas
December	Chonghou mission of apology, for Margary murder, arr. Britain
1877	
January	Yakub Beg defeated
	Samuel Dyer succeeds Alexander Wylie as BFBS Agent in China
January 21	Ambassador Guo Songdao arr. London
Feb–Nov 28	J J Turner and F James in Shanxi; famine severe
February 2	John McCarthy starts E–W walk to Burma with Yang Cunling
March 1–5	Yichang riot
April 2–26	Wuhan conference
May	Yakub Beg dies
May 10–24	2nd General Missionary conference Shanghai (1st, Hong Kong, 1843)
July	Gill and Mesny, Baber start explorations
Autumn	Zuo Zongtang takes Kashgar, Yarkand; rebellion ends Jan 2 with fall of Khotan
September 18	Edward Fishe dies at Guiyang
October 21	Wusong railway sold to Chinese; closed
November 9	JHT dep. Shanghai; December 20 arr. UK
November 30	T Richard arr. Taiyuan
December	*China's Millions* on shame of Britain's opium traffic
1877–78	Famine at its worst; relief committees at work
1878	
January	Hudson Taylor appeals for famine aid

January 30	J J Turner, D Hill, A Whiting to Shanxi famine relief
April 25	A Whiting dies of typhus
May 2	J E Taylor party dep. UK; March 5 arr. Shanghai
July	Powers force Russia to return Ili to China
October 22–25	General Missionary Conference, London
October 23	J E Taylor party arr. Taiyuan
October 28	First Chinese envoy to Washington
1879	
	China and Japan ask advice of Gen. Ulysses Grant on Ryukyu controversy
	Hsi Shengmo converted; D Hill leaves Shanxi
January 10	Consul W C Hillier on famine survey, to February
February 5	B Broomhall becomes General Secretary, CIM in UK, till 1895
February 10	Theodore Howard, Home Director
February 11	J E Taylor dep. Taiyuan; March 5 arr. Shanghai
February 24	JHT dep. UK; April 22 arr. Shanghai
May	CIM 'Chefoo', Yantai, health resort initiated
September 15	Chonghou signs treaty with Russia, unratified
December	JHT plans Chefoo School
December 9	JHT and J J Coulthard overland Yantai to Yangzhou; arr. January 2
1880	
	J L Nevius expounds his indigenous church principles (and 1885–86)
	First CIM doctors, Pruen and Schofield, arrive
	Dr J K Mackenzie saves life of Li Hongzhang's wife; builds hospital in Tianjin
February	JHT at Wuhan sends single women inland
March 3	Chonghou condemned to death, later reprieved
May 10	George King's wife dies at Hanzhong
July–August	C G Gordon advises Peking government
July 30	'Marquis' Zeng to Russia
November	Imperial decree sanctions telegraph lines
November 29	J W Stevenson and H Soltau start E–W, Bhamo–Wuhan journey
December 1	Chefoo School opens

1881	
	First 'year of testing'
	American Episcopal Church to Chongqing
February 24	Zeng signs new treaty on Sino-Russian border at Ili
April 9	Dowager Empress Ci An dies mysteriously
June	'Rocket of China' locomotive makes first journey
July	China recognises Japan's jurisdiction over Ryukyu Is.
July 2	Mrs James Taylor dies
August 13	Mrs Faulding dies
October 19	J E Taylor dep. Shanghai; December 1 arr. UK
November 23–30	Wuchang conference decides to pray for seventy new members
December 1	Shanghai–Tianjin telegraph opened
1882	
	Second 'year of testing'
	Colquhoun and Wahab cross South China, E–W
	D L Moody's wide influence in UK
	Jonathan Goforth applies to CIM
	Dr J K Mackenzie to UK
March 25	French occupy Hanoi
July 23	Anti-Japanese riot in Seoul, Korea
1883	
	Karl Marx dies
February 6	JHT dep. Yantai to UK
March	Alexander Hosie begins travels in SW China
March 27	JHT arr. London after 4 years, 15,000 miles travel in China
April 17	CIM London Council approve plans for reorganisation in China
July	D E Hoste makes first approach of 'Cambridge Seven' to CIM
August 1	Dr H Schofield dies
August 24	JHT writes to CIM re 'organisation for extension', Superintendents and China Council
	Sir Harry Parkes' treaty opens Korea to foreigners, Christians
September	Josef Holmgren, Sweden, meets JHT in London

Oct–Jan	A W Douthwaite's winter colportage through Korea
October 7	G W Clarke's wife dies at Dali
November	D L Moody's London campaign
December	S P Smith of Cambridge Seven applies to JHT
December 16	French take 'Sontay', Chinese garrison town
1884	
	Franco-Chinese war, 1884–85
	Imperial Edict of Religious Toleration
	American Presbyterians enter Korea; and Fujian Chinese missionaries for two years
April 8	Ci Xi degrades Prince Kong for fourth time
May	Quaker 'Friends' form a China Mission, the first Associate Mission of CIM
July 12	French ultimatum to China
August	Bible Christians form a China Mission; Associate Mission of CIM
August 23	French destroy Chinese fleet at Fuzhou
October	French blockade Taiwan
Nov–Feb 1885	'Cambridge Seven' nationwide meetings
December 4–5	Coup, riot and Sino-Japanese clash at Seoul
1885	
	A A Fulton occupies Guangxi; expelled
	Engels publishes *Das Kapital* Vol 2
	CIM occupy remote Xining and Ningxia
January 8	First farewells to JHT and 'Cambridge' men
January 20	JHT dep. UK to initiate organisation for expansion
January 26	C G Gordon killed at Khartoum
February 4	'Cambridge Seven' valedictory at Exeter Hall
February 5	'Cambridge Seven' dep. UK
March 3	JHT arr. Shanghai; the Seven arr. March 18
March 22	Sir Harry Parkes dies at Peking
April 18	Sino-Japanese convention on Korea signed
June	JHT decides on a Guangxin R. women's field
June 9	Sino-French treaty signed at Tianjin
June 10	Sir Robt. Hart gazetted Minister Plenipotentiary
July 18	Anglo-Chinese agreement on opium *likin* tax
August 15	Sir Robt. Hart resigns as Inspector General of Customs; Nov 5 resumes
September 5	Zuo Zongtang dies
Mid-October	Lord Shaftesbury dies

October 26	Jonathan Goforth applies again to CIM (1882 and in 1911)
October 29	Bishop Hannington and 46 companions massacred at Uganda border
December 23	JHT arr. Shanghai
	First American member, Dr J C Stewart, joins CIM
1886	
	Britain annexes Upper Burma; concludes Anglo-Chinese convention on Burma and Tibet
January	J F Broumton appointed Treasurer in China
March	J W Stevenson, Deputy Director in China
April	Imperial Edict of Toleration (1884) re-emphasised
	'Strong words' between CIM leaders
May–June	JHT to Jiangxi; inaugurates Guangxin R. Women's work
May 10	Henry Dick enters Changsha; evicted
May 26	20th anniversary of *Lammermuir* sailing
June 15	Contract signed for Wusong Road headquarters site
July–August	Taiyuan, Hongtong, Linfen conferences
October 18	T Richard leaves Shanxi
November	First meeting of China Council; appeal for 'the Hundred', and Book of Arrangements, agreed
1887	
	Francis Younghusband's *Heart of a Continent* journey
	Sustained attacks on Hsi by Fan
January 6	JHT dep. Shanghai to UK; February 18 arr. London
February	George Parker prepares to cross Xinjiang
February 7	Guang Xü emperor comes of age
March	United Conference of Foreign Missions, Leicester
April	H Lansdell plans Tibet venture
	CIM leadership crisis
April 14	Work starts on Wusong Road site
May	G B Studd visits Shanghai, Shanxi
July	Keswick Convention missionary emphasis begins

	Annie Royle Taylor on Tibetan border
July 3	Chongqing riots
July 19	Contract signed for Newington Green house and land
August	Hsi adopts a policy of expansion of his opium refuges
Sept 17, 15	Dr and Mrs E C Lord die of cholera
Nov–Dec	Henry W Frost applies and arr. UK, meets JHT
December	Josef Holmgren consults JHT on Swedish Mission in China
	The Hundred completed
	John N Forman tours UK (with JHT) for SVM; Robert P Wilder touring N. American colleges
1888	
	Dr J K Mackenzie dies
March 21	British and Tibetan troops clash in Sikkim
June 9–20	General Missionary Conference, London
	Anti-opium 'Christian Union' and *National Righteousness* launched
June 23	JHT dep. UK to North America; July 1 arr. New York
October 5	JHT party dep. Vancouver; October 30 arr. Shanghai

APPENDIX 5

TABLES OF THE MAIN PIONEER JOURNEYS 1875–78

	J Hudson Taylor	J McCarthy	C H Judd and J F Broumton	J W Stevenson	M Henry Taylor
1875	(arr. China 1854)	(arr. China Nov 1866)	(CHJ arr. 1867)	(arr. China Nov 1865)	(arr. China Oct 1873)
					April–May to HENAN (1) 56 days
				May 14 with H Soltau arr. RANGOON	
			June 10 Wuhan to Yueyang w. Yao, Zhang HUNAN (1) expelled		
				Sep 9 JWS/HS dep. Rangoon	
		July to UK		Oct 3 arr. BHAMO	
		Dec arr. China			
					Oct dep. Wuchang to HENAN (2) W Zhang 84 days
					Dec 10 to Kaifeng
1876			CHJ i/c Wuhan		Jan 15 Wuhan
					Mar 13 to HENAN (3) w G W Clarke 80 days
				May 15 T Harvey arr. Bhamo	May Wuhan
					Aug to HENAN (4) w G W Clarke and Zhang
	Sep 13: CHEFOO CONVENTION				Oct QUESHAN RIOT
	Oct 22 JHT arr. CHINA with R J Landale			Nov J Adams arr. Bhamo	Oct 25 to Wuhan
				JWS/HS to Kachins	
1877	Jan–Mar to Yangzi stations	Dec dep. Zhenjiang w Yang Cunling	Jan 2 J F Broumton dep. Wuhan via HUNAN (2)		Jan 27 Wuhan to HENAN (5)
	Zhenjiang-Wuhan				
	Mar 17–Apr 16 Zhenjiang	Feb 25 YICHANG	Feb 3 GUIZHOU (1)		
		Mar 1–5 YICHANG RIOT	Feb 19–29 GUIYANG (1)		
	April 23–26 WUHAN CONFERENCE	Mar 20 dep. to SICHUAN	Mar 2 CHJ dep.	April to UK	
		Apr 3 Wanxian	Mar 14 arr. CHONGQING (1) Sichuan		
	May 10–24 SHANGHAI CONFERENCE	May 1 CHONGQING			April 13 QUESHAN RIOT (2)
		May 10 to GUIZHOU	Mar 23 Yichang		May 12 Wuhan 'utterly sad'
	June 6–Oct 17 SOUTHERN TOUR	May 26–June 7 GUIYANG	Mar 29 Wuhan 2000 mls 3 months		
		July 2 YUNNAN KUNMING (1)	May w G Nicoll Yichang		
		July 12–Aug 26 to BHAMO	July CHJ occupies Yichang		to Qü Xian Zhejiang
		7 months' walk			
	Oct 6–16 NINGBO CONFERENCE	6 months in Bhamo			
		(April 28, 1879 Lecture at RGS on E–W journey)			
	Nov 9 dep. China				
	Dec 20 London				

	Geo. King	Geo. W Clarke	Jas. Cameron	Geo. Nicoll	G F Easton
1875	July arr. China	Sep arr. China Oct to Wuhan	Sep arr. China Oct to Jiujiang	Sep arr. China Oct to Wuhan	Dec arr. China
1876	Aug 9 dep. Anqing w F W Baller and Zhang Suoliang to SHAANXI (1) 2 months Nov 8 w C Budd, Yao and Zhang Suoliang Wuhan to SHAANXI (2) GANSU (1) Dec 20–24 at XI'AN w Yao & Zhang	Mar 13 w M H Taylor to HENAN 80 days May Wuhan Aug w M H Taylor to HENAN Oct QUESHAN RIOT Oct 25 Wuhan	Oct–Nov i/c Zhenjiang Dec 20 w G Nicoll to Yichang Dec–March travelling with Jiang Suo-liang	Aug 28 dep. Wuhan Sep 16 Yichang to Wuhan Dec 20 w Cameron and Jiang to Yichang	Nov 8 w G Parker Zhu & Zhang Wuhan to SHAANXI (2) Dec 20–24 XI'AN Dec 28/29 enter GANSU (1)
1877	Jan–March N E SHAANXI cities Mar 24 Wuhan May 12 w Easton to SHAANXI (3) (May 15 Budd & Chinese to YAN'AN, SHAANXI) June 20 XI'AN to GANSU	i/c Wuhan May 5 w E Fishe & R J Landale to HUNAN May 29 stoned at CHENXI June 27 arr. GUIYANG 53 days July 17 w E Fishe GUANGXI (1) Sep 6 Guiyang Sep 18 Edward Fishe dies Nov 7 arr. Wuhan 3000 miles in 9 provinces since Sep 1875 (ie arr. China)	Jan 1 first of CIM into SICHUAN (1) Mar 1–5 YICHANG RIOT Mar 20 w McCarthy to Wushan & back May w G Nicoll to CHONGQING June–July travelling together in SICHUAN Aug 14 w G Nicoll & C Leaman dep. Chongqing Sep 4–13 CHENGDU Sep 28 YA'AN Oct 5–10 Qingqi Oct 10–16 w one man and a mule to KANGDING Oct 23 LITANG Nov 1–5 BATANG Nov 14–Dec 3 fever at ADENZI Dec 23–28 DALI Dec 28 dep. to BHAMO	May w J Cameron CHONGQING Aug 14 w Cameron & C Leaman Sep 4–13 CHENGDU Sep 28 YA'AN Oct 5–10 Qingqi Oct 10–26 w Leaman to XICHANG to ZHAOTONG Yunnan Dec 9 to Chongqing	Jan 20 w G Parker arr. LANZHOU GANSU (2) April 6 Wuhan after 5 months' travel May 12 w G King to SHAANXI

	Geo. Parker	Joshua J Turner	Francis James	Augustus Margary E C Baber/Grosvenor	Wm Gill Gen Mesny
1875				Jan 17 Margary arr. Bhamo Feb 21 killed at Manyün Nov Grosvenor & Baber Wuhan to Chongqing	
1876		Dec arr. China		Mar 25 Grosvenor party dep. KUNMING May 21 T G Grosvenor & Baber arr. Bhamo	
	May 20 arr. China	Oct '76 to Jan '78 long treks to/in SHANXI		(May Mrs A Williamson Yantai, Shandong to JINAN)	
	Nov 8 w Easton Zhu & Zhang Wuhan to SHAANXI (2) Dec 20–24 XI'AN Dec 28/29 enter GANSU (1)	Oct 18 w F James Zhenjiang to SHANXI (1) 1700 miles 3 months	Oct 18 w Turner Zhenjiang to SHANXI (1)	Sep CHEFOO CONVENTION	
1877	Jan 20 w Easton arr. LANZHOU GANSU (2) April 6 Wuhan after 5 months' travel	Jan 8 Wuhan Feb 10 w F James to SHANXI (2) FAMINE April 24 TAIYUAN 2 months together 2½ months to Shanghai, Wenzhou to consult JHT about famine	Jan 8 Wuhan Feb 10 w Turner to SHANXI (2) (until Jan 22/78 arr. Wuhan) FAMINE April 24 TAIYUAN for 4½ months on Taiyuan plain	Jan 23 Baber/Gill dep. Shanghai Mar 5–9 Baber/Gill at Yichang after riot April 8–26 at CHONGQING	Feb 19 Mesny welcomes C H Judd & J F Broumton at GUIYANG Apr 8–26 Gill at CHONGQING May 9 CHENGDU June 4 SONGPAN June 20 CHENGDU joined by Mesny July 10–25 Gill & Mesny KANGDING
				July 8 Baber dep. Chongqing July 20 CHENGDU Aug 17 Fulin Baber XICHANG HUILI	Aug 17 Gill/Mesny at LITANG Aug 25–29 BATANG
		Sep–Nov YÜCI & TAIYUAN with typhoid Nov 28 dep. Taiyuan to WUHAN	Sep–Nov YÜCI & TAIYUAN with typhoid Nov 28 dep. Taiyuan carried to WUHAN Jan 22 arr. weak	Sep 10 crossed JINSHA JIANG (River of Gold) Oct 18 PINGSHAN Oct end arr. Chongqing	Sep 27 Gill/Mesny at DALI Yunnan Nov 1 arr. BHAMO
1878		Jan 22/78 arr. Jan 30 to Shanghai with D Hill A Whiting to SHANXI FAMINE RELIEF April 2 arr. Taiyuan			

WOMEN PIONEERS 1878–82

	E (Snow) King	F (Rossier) Clarke M A (Howland) Nicoll	E (McCarthy) Broumton J Kidd (m. Riley)	E Wilson A L Fausset	Shao Mianzi Parker Hannah Jones	J E (Jennie) Taylor
1878	Nov arr. China	FR arr. June '78 MAH arr. Feb '79	E McC arr. Mar '79 JK arr. Feb '79	Mar 16, 1876 arr. China	Mar 1881 arr. China	arr. Sep 30 1866
1879	Summer m G King Sep 18 dep. Wuhan up Han R Oct arr. HANZHONG	Sep 15 married at Shanghai Nov 3 dep. Wuhan up YANGZI gorges Dec 23 wrecked in SICHUAN Yangzi rapids			July Shao Mianzi engaged to George Parker	June 13, 1878 arr. Shanghai Sep 21/22 dep. to SHANXI Oct 23 arr. TAIYUAN (first deep into China) 1879 Feb 11 dep. Taiyuan Mar 5 Shanghai Aug 2 JHT to send WOMEN INLAND
1880		Jan 13 arr. CHONGQING Nicolls for 2 years Clarkes to GUIZHOU Feb 5 Clarkes arr. GUIYANG	Feb 19 dep. Wuhan c/o Baller, Broumton Feb 27 Yueyang (see Broumton & Trench) April 22 arr. GUIYANG	Feb 20 ALF w JET arr. Wuhan Mar 1 dep. to SHAANXI May 21 arr. HANZHONG Dec EW w Parkers dep. Hanzhong to TIANSHUI Gansu	Feb 25 Mianzi married to George Parker at Yantai May up Yangzi and Han R to HANZHONG Dec 2 E Wilson dep. Hanzhong	
1881	May E King died of typhoid Nov child died	May 16 dep. Guiyang June arr. DALI alone till June 1882 June '81 Geo Nicoll ill to YANTAI	Jan E McCarthy m J F Broumton Mar 26–June 21 nightmare journey via HUNAN with C Kerr, G Andrew, A Eason c/o Adam Dorward June 21 arr. GUIYANG Oct J Kidd w C Kerr ill to Chongqing, Shanghai J Kidd back to Chongqing m J H Riley	May EW with G F Easton to Hanzhong for E King typhoid	Jan TIANSHUI Gansu June Mianzi and EW working Tianshui	Oct 19 J Taylor to UK after 3 years away
1882				Feb w G King & Hannah Jones to GANSU Feb 17 arr. TIANSHUI Oct E Wilson to Hanzhong 17 days in rain	Feb H Jones w E Wilson & G King to GANSU TIANSHUI July 10 with Parkers to QINGHAI border Sep 18 Minzhou Sep 26 Tianshui 1000 mls 78 days	

MAIN PIONEER JOURNEYS: 1878–83

	JHT/JET	J W Stevenson H Soltau	Geo. King	G W Clarke	Jas. Cameron (T W Pigott)	Geo. Nicoll
1878	LONDON May 2 JET party dep. UK June 13 JET arr. Shanghai, to Wuhan, Nanjing Sep 22 w Baller to SHANXI Oct 23 TAIYUAN Oct 22–25 JHT Gen. Miss. Conf., London	Aug 6 dep. UK Oct BHAMO Br. Resident murdered Nov 3 BHAMO to Kachins	Jan to XI'AN Nov CHONGQING w Easton to GANSU Dec 12 TIANSHUI	April w H Taylor to HENAN May 13 rebuffed at KAIFENG	Jan 24 Cameron entered BHAMO to Rangoon to Hong Kong June 11 PAKHOI July 7 Bose GUANGXI Aug 17 KUNMING Sep GUIYANG to CHONGQING w R J Landale Back to Guiyang Nov 4 w Broumton to GUILIN, GUANGXI Dec 24 Pakhoi	Oct 15 joined at CHONGQING by J H Riley S R Clarke
1879	Feb 11 JET dep. TAIYUAN Feb 24 JHT dep. UK Mar 5 JET arr. SHANGHAI Apr 22 JHT arr. SHANGHAI July 30 dep. Yantai (typhoon) to WUHAN Sep 12 Yantai Dec 9–Jan '80 w J J Coulthard overland, Yantai to YANGZHOU	Nov 18 JWS Bhamo to BAOSHAN YUNNAN reconnaissance Dec Resident withdrawn	Summer: married Aug WUHAN Sep 18 up Han R w wife Emily (Snow) Oct HANZHONG	Feb 3 w Parrott dep. Wuhan to HENAN SHANXI May 21 expelled from JINCHENG (Tsechou) to LINFEN (Pingyang) Sep married F Rossier Nov 3 dep. WUHAN up Yangzi R w G Nicolls Dec 23 wrecked in Yangzi gorges	Jan–March ill at CANTON Mar 18–April 5 GUANGDONG Apr 11 JIANGXI Apr 28 FUJIAN May 6 JIANGXI May 13 ZHEJIANG to SHANGHAI Yantai Sep 4–13 w T W Pigott SHANDONG trial trek Sep 30 TIANJIN w Guang & Wu Oct 15 YINGKOU Manchuria Nov LIAODONG Dec 5–7 blizzard	Sept married Nov 3 dep. WUHAN up Yangzi R w G W Clarke Dec 23 wrecked in Yangzi gorges
1880	Jan 2 arr. YANGZHOU Feb 9–Mar 24 JHT at WUHAN July–Sept JHT GUANGXIN reconnaissance	July Bhamo fire Nov 29 JWS/HS dep. Bhamo Dec 12 Tengyue 16–20 BAOSHAN Dec 31–Jan 6 at DALI (1)	May 18 threats May 21 joined by E Wilson, A L Fausset Easton from Tianshui in 3 days to help	Jan 13 CHONGQING Jan 20 dep. Feb 5 GUIYANG	Jan 6 KOREAN 'Gate' Jan 23 SHENYANG (Mukden) Feb 16 JILIN (Kirin) Apr 12 dep. Manchuria to PEKING 4 wks May 20 dep. to North & N–W SHANXI 9 mos July 24 KALGAN Aug 17 to MONGOL border Sep–March SHANXI cities Oct 14 joined by A G [illegible]	2 years at CHONGQING

	G F Easton	Geo Parker	A C Dorward	S R Clarke J F Riley	J F Broumton F Trench	A G Parrott
1878	Mar 15–Apr 19 QINGHAI border ? dates CHONGQING to Langzhong smallpox so ret Chongqing Yichang Nov 15 w G King dep. Chongqing Dec 12 TIANSHUI alone famine relief	Jan w G King XI'AN expelled Worked Han R by boat w Budd July 16 YICHANG w Riley S R Clarke to Sichuan Engaged to Shao Mianzi Nov arr. CHONGQING w Riley, Clarke	June arr. China Aug alone w Chinese	June both arr. China Oct 15 both arr. CHONGQING w G Nicoll for Nosu	June Trench arr. China to ANQING Dec at NINGGUO Anhui	Dec arr. China
1879	6 mths alone in GANSU Travelling w/o companion June 3 Tianshui to XINING and Tibet border July 10 LANZHOU 26 back Tianshui Aug–Sep Oct to HANZHONG for famine relief clothing	Jan CHONGQING Sep w Easton to GANSU TIANSHUI ? date to WUHAN, Yantai	Aug–Sep in ANHUI (1) 6 weeks w Yang Cunling Dec ANHUI (2)	July 21 dep. to EMEI, EBIAN LESHAN Sep 25 Chongqing Oct 6 Clarke to CHENGDU Nov 25 Chongqing		Feb 3 dep. WUHAN w G W Clarke to HENAN Feb 8–12 QUESHAN to SHANXI (1) May 21 expelled from JINCHENG to LINFEN June 27 until Jan 1880 at LINFEN famine relief
1880	Feb 3 Tianshui famine relief May to Hanzhong in 3 days to help G King South GANSU journeys ending at Hanzhong ? date to Yantai (Chefoo)	Feb 25 married Shao Mianzi May 22 w Hunt Yantai to HANZHONG Left Hunt, Pruen at FANCHENG Sept dep. Fancheng Nov 23 HANZHONG 4 weeks Dec w E Wilson to GANSU TIANSHUI 6 months	DONGTING w Chinese Mar ANHUI (3) June 'young and alone' July overland to Yantai (G John visits HUNAN) Sep Dorward 'eager for Hunan' Oct 18 dep. Wuhan w Yang Cunling HUNAN (1) 5½ mos to Apr '81 Nov 16–Dec 9 at CHANGDE Dec 25 w Yao at HONGJIANG	Mar 8 both to PINGSHAN Apr 24 LEIBO May 8 YIBIN to Chongqing May Clarke to GUIYANG	Feb 9 w JHT arr. WUHAN Feb 19 F W Baller Broumton, Trench E McCarthy, Kidd dep. Wuhan Feb 27–Mar 31 in HUNAN Apr 14 Zhenyuan Apr 27 GUIYANG May 11 Trench & Broumton dep. to YUNNAN June 16 KUNMING July 30 JFB to GUIYANG Trench alone in Yunnan till December to Guiyang	Jan 16 SHANXI (2) 69 days 7 cities for B&FBS May 26 dep. w Zhang Yufa to SHAANXI (3) XI'AN July 3 arr. LINFEN Aug 9 SHANXI tour (4) Oct 8 LINFEN 14 dep.; met Cameron; to TAIYUAN Nov 1 dep. to SHANXI (5) Dec 1 arr. Taiyuan

	JHT / JET	J W Stevenson H Soltau	Geo. King	G W Clarke	Jas. Cameron (T W Pigott)	Geo. Nicoll
1881	'Year of testing' Feb 22 dep. Yantai to Shanghai WUHAN Apr ANQING to Yangzhou w Dorward Apr 23–26 NINGBO May 7 Shanghai 13 Yantai	Jan 6 dep. DALI Jan 21 KUNMING Feb 4 ZHAOTONG Feb 22 CHONGQING Mar 15 YICHANG Mar 25 WUHAN 1900 mls in 117 days	May 10 wife died of typhoid	May 16 child died dep. GUIYANG to YUNNAN June 7 KUNMING June 24 DALI till Dec 1883	Feb 8 dep. LINFEN w A G Parrott Feb 13–Mar 14 TAIYUAN Mar 14 to SHAANXI w Pigott Mar 28 GUIDE to ORDOS May 10 Yuling YAN'AN May 15 Pigott to Taiyuan JC via SANYUAN May 25 XI'AN	
	Oct JET dep. to UK Nov 9 JHT dep. Yantai Nov 16–21 ANQING Nov 23–30 at Wuhan, WUCHANG CONFERENCE (The Seventy) (Bk of Arrangements) Dec 3–9 Zhenjiang Conference	July JWS alone at Bhamo H Soltau dep. to UK	Nov 12 child died of dysentery	Nov 28 Clarkes rent own home to Dali	June 29 to HANZHONG arr. August Oct 8 XI'AN to TIANSHUI GANSU Nov 11 to G King HANZHONG to SICHUAN NANJIANG Dec end to WUHAN Shanghai Yantai	July 4 ill to YANTAI for 8 months
1882	Jan NINGBO Jan 22 HANGZHOU Shanghai Feb 4 WENZHOU 26 QÜ XIAN April Shanghai Yantai	JWS alone at BHAMO free to enter China	Jan w E Wilson & Hannah Jones to TIANSHUI GANSU while Ho, Zhang to XI'AN Feb 21 GK to XI'AN March rented April forced out to inns		Feb ANQING Mar Shanghai April Shanghai	Feb dep. Yantai
	June 24–July 1 ANQING CONFERENCE July NINGBO Yantai Nov 4 to TIANJIN PEKING BAODING Yantai Dec ANQING CONFERENCE		May 1000 RCs celebrate Easter July new rental retained Nov HANZHONG Dec: 1st believer at XI'AN	July Andrew & Eason visit DALI Clarkes to KUNMING	May Yantai June CHONGQING Aug to UK ending 7 years' travel Medical course in USA	May CHONGQING ill
1883	Jan Shanghai Jan 6 Yangzhou tempted to quit Feb 6 dep. Yantai to UK Mar 27 arr. UK 4 years away	July: first baptisms at BHAMO Nov Dr H Soltau & wife to Burma Kachin rebellion	Jan 9 GK rents larger house at XI'AN for Eastons Aug 4 Eastons expelled Aug 27 G King dep. XI'AN: returns	Oct Fanny Clarke died at DALI		

	G F Easton	Geo Parker	A C Dorward	S R Clarke J H Riley	J F Broumton F Trench	A G Parrott
1881	Feb 16 JINAN escorting Landale party to SHANXI May 10 TIANSHUI to HANZHONG w E Wilson for E King typhoid May 26 to HENAN RUNAN to help Hunt Aug at YANTAI m C Gardner Sep dep. Yantai to Shaanxi, Gansu w Hannah Jones Oct on HAN R to HANZHONG TIANSHUI	GANSU Jan arr. TIANSHUI Feb 22 son born June began extensive Gansu travels N–E GANSU NINGXIA	Frequent tours in HUNAN Jan 1 QIANYANG 6–10 YUANZHOU 14 dep. Hunan 29–Feb 7 GUIYANG 17–21 ZHENYUAN Mar 2 HONGJIANG Apr 1 WUHAN w JHT to ANQING May w Broumton party via HUNAN June 21 GUIYANG June 27 HONGJIANG July 26 CHANGDE WUHAN Dec 1 dep. Wuhan to S-E HUNAN SHAOYANG GUANGXI to HONGJIANG	May S R Clarke to GUIYANG freed G W Clarke for YUNNAN June 21 SRC to CHONGQING July consul attacked Oct J Kidd in Chongqing Nov viceroy's proclamation favoured SRC/JHR residence Dec 12 SRC rents in CHENGDU SICHUAN travels	Jan JFB m E McCarthy Trench ill to Shanghai Mar 26 Broumton party dep. WUHAN Apr 1 Trench dep. Wuhan to join Broumton party Apr Dorward joins Broumton party on nightmare journey May 31 FT arr. Guiyang June 21 Broumton arr. GUIYANG June FT travelling in GUIZHOU Sep FT ill to Chongqing, coast w Kidd & Kerr	Jan 1–25 in W SHANXI cities (6) May 24 Yantai June JHT's Corresponding Secretary Nov 9 Yantai to Shanghai w JHT
1882	at HANZHONG	Feb 21 dep. TIANSHUI on 5 mths travel in W GANSU Aug 9–17 on QINGHAI border w wife & H Jones GP at LABRANG Sep 18 MINZHOU Sep 26 TIANSHUI 1000 mls in 78 days	Jan 1 HONGJIANG Jan 20 rented at Hongjiang Feb to Shanghai consult JHT Apr 2 en route HUNAN May 4 SHASHI base for Hunan June 17 to CHANGDE HONGJIANG 3½ mths 'working quietly' Oct dep. Hongjiang Nov 14 Wuhan Dec 5–Feb 11 w/o Christian companion	Oct JHR married J Kidd; to CHONGQING SRC married A L Fausset; to CHENGDU	Jan 20 Andrew & Eason dep. Guiyang to KUNMING Mar FT SHAANXI Fancheng HENAN, Runan Sep FT Yantai Dec YICHANG	Mar 16 Shanghai Apr 4 A M Hayward arr. Shanghai Apr 'as good as engaged' June w JHT to ANQING CONF. (The Seventy) July Shanghai Dec 21 married A M Hayward
1883	July Hanzhong to XI'AN Aug 4 expelled		Jan 'rejoicing over progress' Jan 5 YONGTING 13 Longshan 25 CHANGDE Feb forced out of HONGJIANG Apr 3 mths circuit of HUNAN back to HONGJIANG 1300 mls July 29–Dec 20 5 mths residence G John & Archibald 'badly mobbed at DONGYANG' Dec 20 ACD dep. Hongjiang	Feb 6 Rileys to CHENGDU for SRC fever	Jan FT at Chongqing JFB Guiyang June FT arr. UK for medical course	Jan i/c YANGZHOU language school

APPENDIX 6

A Song of Sacrifice

HYMN BY PASTOR HSI

1

When Thou wouldst pour the living stream,
Then I would be the earthen cup,
Filled to the brim and sparkling clear.
The fountain Thou and living spring,
Flow Thou through me, the vessel weak,
That thirsty souls may taste Thy grace.

2

When Thou wouldst warn the people, Lord,
Then I would be the golden bell,
Swung high athwart the lofty tower,
Morning and evening sounding loud;
That young and old may wake from sleep,
Yea, e'en the deaf hear that strong sound.

3

When Thou wouldst slay the wolves, O Lord!
Then I would be the keen-edged sword,
Clean, free from rust, sharpened and sure,
The handle grasped, my God, by Thee—
To kill the cruel ravening foe
And save the sheep for whom Christ died.

4

When Thou wouldst light the darkness, Lord,
Then I would be the silver lamp,
Whose oil supply can never fail,
Placed high to shed the beams afar,
That darkness may be turned to light,
And men and women see Thy face.

5

When Thou dost sound the battle-call
Thy standard-bearer I would be.
With love for shield, and right for spear,
I'll sound Thy praise from East to West.
From Thy high throne speak forth the word,
And sin must yield before Thy praise.

6

When Thou wouldst write the records, Lord,
Then I would be the ready pen,
A medium subtle for Thy thought,
Desirous to write it true.
That when the Book of Life is read,
Therein those names be found inscribed,
Which hell nor death can e'er blot out.

REFRAIN

My body's Thine, yea, wholly Thine; My spirit owns Thee for its Lord.
Within Thy hand I lay my all, And only ask that I may be,
Whene'er Thou art in need of me, Alert and ready for Thy use.

Translation *by* MISS FRANCESCA FRENCH.

(From *PASTOR HSI: Confucian Scholar and Christian*)

NOTES

Page	*Note*	
Preface		
7	1	Broomhall, A J: *Hudson Taylor and China's Open Century* (HTCOC) Book 5 Ch 13
8	2	Octopus: *Chinese Recorder* 1905 p 382
Prologue		
25	1	March 27, 1875: Morse, Hosea Ballou: *International Relations of the Chinese Empire*, Vol 2 pp 279, 281, citing Bland and Backhouse: *China under the Empress Dowager*, p 129
25	2	HTCOC Book 5 pp 430–33; Gill, Capt Wm: *River of Golden Sand* the Narrative of a Journey through China and Tibet, Vol 1 p 69 comment on Margary's journals.
26	3	Parliamentary Papers, FO, China 1875; Morse, H B: *International Relations* 2.290–7
26	4	*Foreign Relations of the United States*: 1875 p 318
27	5	Morse H B: *International Relations*, 2.293; Cordier, Henri: *Histoire des Rélations de la Chine avec les Puissances Occidentales*; HTCOC Book 5 p 241. Chonghou said of Wade's changes of mood: 'now this, now that – today Yes, tomorrow No'; 'the rages, the sulks, and the outbursts in which he indulges leave us unaffected.' And on 24 Sep 1875 Wade himself wrote to Prince Kong, 'For my frequent loss of temper in argument, I put forward no excuse . . . The Chinese government leave me . . . little option'.
27	6	Morse, H B: *International Relations*, 2.299
28	7	Jackson-Wade: Latourette, Kenneth Scott: *History of Christian Missions in China*, p 353; Overseas Missionary Fellowship Archives (OMFA) 5117d, N9c pp 43, 59
29	8	Church: Latourette, K S: *Christian Missions*, pp 303–415; *Chinese Recorder* Jan 1875 pp 77, 80; Stock, Eugene: *History of the Church Missionary Society*, Vol 3 p 218
29	9	*China's Millions*, Magazine of the China Inland Mission, p 64; Broomhall, Marshall: *The Chinese Empire, General and Missionary Survey*, p 28
30	10	Veterans: *Chinese Recorder* 1875 p 340
31	11	Missions: *Chinese Recorder* 1875 p 136; Stock, E: *History of the CMS*, 3.35
31	12	Stock, E: *History of the CMS*, 3.244
32	13	Neill, Stephen C: *History of Christian Missions* p 240

33 14,15 Appeal: HTCOC Book 5 pp 383, 388, 433; Stock, E: *History of the CMS* 3.24–26, 73, 805; OMFA N9c 1875 pp 49–50; 5113k

34 16 OMFA H52.11, JHT's own claim in letter to CIM: OMFA H526 JET to E Turner

34 17 Broomhall, M: *John W. Stevenson, One of Christ's Stalwarts*, (Biography) p 36; OMFA 5113l

35 18 *China's Millions* July 1877 pp 94–5

35 19 Conferences: Stock, E *History of the CMS*: 3.29–33; OMFA 5115ci

36 20 Mark 11.22: not intended as translation: OMFA 8 Book 1, *After Thirty Years*; *China's Millions* 1875 pp 19, 55

Chapter 1

37 1 Consolidate: OMFA 5118, 5119; HTCOC Book 5 p 434

39 2 Plan: OMFA 8 Book 1 pp 8–9; *China's Millions* 1875 p 31

39,40 3,4 First of the Nine: HTCOC Book 5.433; 4.88, 130; Clarke: *China's Millions* 1875 p 36; OMFA N9c p 42; H537

40 5 Travel: in 1875 Thomas Weir, Shanghai, arranged with the Castle Line for members of the CIM to be charged only £50 between the UK and Shanghai. The French Mail cost £46 third class from Marseilles; Holt's Blue Funnel Line charged £84; and the P & O nearly £100. The Castle Line concession lasted into the 1880s. A saving of £4 per head or £20 for a party of five in 1875 may be thought of today as £800, well worth saving. Economy mattered; comfort was secondary. When a missionary spoke disparagingly of the French Mail after travelling with his wife by another line, Hudson Taylor wrote to Jennie, 'It makes me feel angry.'

40 6 OMFA 5114ai,ii

41 7 OMFA N9c p 49; 5114aii

42 8 Burma: OMFA H417; HTCOC Book 2 p 231; Book 3 pp 350, 356

42 9 Opium: Guinness, M Geraldine: *Story of the China Inland Mission*, Vol 2 p 130 citing S Wells Williams

43 10 *China's Millions* 1875 July suppl. pp 1, 7–8, 61; Broomhall, M: *John W. Stevenson* pp 35–45; OMFA 5118b, 5119, 52.10

46 11 Tsiang Siao-vong (? Zhang Xiaofeng): *China's Millions* 1875 p 2

47 12 OMFA H311, H53.12a; *China's Millions* 1965 (Centenary issue) pp 93–4

47 13 Benjamin Broomhall: HTCOC Book 2 pp 144, 353; Book 3 pp 233, 271; OMFA 5119, H515; 5115d

48 14 'Generous': HTCOC Book 5 pp 404–5; OMFA H417. The legacy from Jennie's uncle in Australia had come under her control. 'The whole is the Lord's (to be) used for Him and . . . not for private purposes,' she had said, and she had contributed £3500 (well over £100,000 today) already banked in Shanghai, for advance into the nine unoccupied provinces. To imagine that she encouraged him to shoulder the expense of the Pyrland Road property and Benjamin's help would be reasonable, though unsupported by specific evidence. Whatever the source, if God approved he would provide the means.

48 15 Pyrland Road property: factual evidence is scanty. On June 30, 1875, Hudson Taylor's father, James Taylor, resigned from the directorship of the Barnsley Permanent Building Society which he had founded,

and managed since 1855. He and his wife retired to the south coast. On December 30 he resigned all control. To share in the support of Amelia and her children, he invested capital in five newly built houses in Pyrland Road and assigned to her the income from their rental. (At her death, 1918, Nos 38, 40, 42, 46, 48.) On April 6, 1876, the CIM Council of Management minuted that it proposed to buy five homes in Pyrland Road, letting out two or three to tenants until they were needed, 'and thus securing on advantageous terms permanent possession for the Mission.' On April 27 another minute read that the two houses in use (Nos 4 and 5) would be secured for the rent of one. 'As the proprietor was willing to leave £500 out of £700 (the price of each house) on permanent mortgage, the total sum required to secure the five houses would be only £1000,' this 'wise' arrangement was adopted. By 1987 the value of each house, long since in other hands, was more than £100,000. Yet another minute noted that the landlord had donated a sum to the Mission, the property was in the hands of trustees, and the mortgage could be paid off at any time. Such unusual circumstances and the acceptance of this mortgage arrangement strongly suggest that an exceptional donor was involved. Nothing in the records hints that Jennie's legacy was used or that William Berger was the benefactor. Minutes of the London Council 1876, May, June 30, July 31. No 2 Pyrland Road was the home of Benjamin and Amelia for forty years.

48 16 OMFA 8513, Wm Sharp

49 17 The Eighteen: HTCOC Book 5 Ch 13; *China's Millions* 1965 (Centenary issue) pp 193–4, Easton reminiscences; OMFA H53.12a

50 18,19 Broumton: OMFA H539; JHT: OMFA 5112h, 1, n; Eighteen: OMFA H532b; *China's Millions* 1875 p 69; Broomhall, M: *The Jubilee Story of the China Inland Mission* p 103

50 20 Perspective: HTCOC Book 1 pp 141–2; Book 5 Ch 13

51 21 River of Gold: the highest reaches of the Yangzi River were (and are) known as the Jinsha Jiang (the River of Golden Sand); the northward-flowing reach of the great loop, as far as the junction with the Min River (map p 260) was the Jin He (the River of Gold).

51 22 Travellers: Gill, W: *The River of Golden Sand* Vol 1 p 61, Col H Yule's introduction re T T Cooper's route: Chengdu, Batang, Weixi and back to Ya'an.

52 23 J Cox: *Chinese Recorder* 1876 p 422; G John: pp 226–31; A Wylie, *Proceedings of the Royal Geographical Society* Vol xiv p 168; *Chinese Recorder* 1877 p 385; HTCOC Book 4 pp 218, 393; Broomhall, M: *The Chinese Empire* p 28; *Chinese Recorder* 1876 p 422

53 24 Objectives of the 'assault': Broomhall, M: *Jubilee Story* p 90, April 1873; Plan of Operations: OMFA 4513f; JHT's 1872 Bible flyleaf.

53 25 The Eighteen: Broomhall, M: *Jubilee Story* p 104. Already in China: J W Stevenson, J McCarthy, C H Judd, F W Baller, M Henry Taylor, Edward Fishe. New volunteers: Henry Soltau, George King, James Cameron, George Nicoll, George Clarke, J F Broumton, G F Easton, Joshua J Turner, Charles Budd, S Adams, Edward Pearse, Francis James, George Parker, Horace Randle, Robert J Landale. *See* Ch 2 Note 2

53	26	HTCOC Book 5 pp 433–4
53	27	Henan: 'He' means 'river'. From Zhoukouzhen (Chouchiakou) the Sha He flowing south-east into Anhui joined the Huai He, an unbroken waterway through the lakes and Grand Canal to the Yangzi at Zhenjiang. Southwards a fan of waterways, principally the Bai He and Tang He, feed into the Han River to join the Yangzi at Wuhan (Hankow) (map p 54). North of the Yellow River, the Wei He flows north-eastwards for 400 miles to Tianjin. Overland travel could be 20–40 times as expensive as by water on these navigable rivers. Only in 1905 was a railway begun between the chief cities of Kaifeng and Luoyang (Loyang), crossing the Peking–Hankou railway at Zhengzhou (Chengchou), soon to equal them in size and importance. The Yellow River was not bridged until June 1905, opening the 750-mile Peking–Hankou line at long last.
54	28	J McIntyre, United Presbyterian Church of Scotland, trying to reach Kaifeng from the north was turned back at the Yellow River in 1874. Henry Taylor's second journey, dep. Hankou Oct 24, 1875, returned Hankou Jan 15, 1876, via Runan, Zhoukouzhen, Chenzhou, Guide, Kaifeng (Dec 10).
55	29	*China's Millions* 1875 pp 2, 46, 60, 78; 1876 p 181; 1878 p 181
55	30	Broomhall, M: *Chinese Empire* pp 165–6. At one time six of the empire's seven viceroys were Hunanese. And General Zuo Zongtang's troops who quelled the Muslim rebellion in the north-west (Book 5 p 395) had a high proportion of Hunan men, many of whom settled in Gansu.

Chapter 2

56	1	Spurgeon: OMFA H539
57	2	*China's Millions* 1875 p 69; OMFA H532d. Francis James: Forsyth, Robert: *The China Martyrs of 1900* p 106. The Eighteen: several versions of the list of 'Eighteen' have been drawn up showing that this number was exceeded, as different factors have been taken into account, such as Robert Landale's private means delaying his formal membership of the Mission. He went to China in September 1876 and took part in strenuous pioneering. Of more than 60 applicants in 1875, 30–40 spent longer or shorter periods at Pyrland Road, to learn what would be involved and to be assessed for suitability.
57	3	Women: OMFA 5122b; the Misses Anna Crickmay, Celia Horne, Marie Huberty, Jessie Murray and Katherine Hughes.
58	4	*China's Millions* 1875 p 76; 1876 p 160
59	5	*China's Millions* 1876 p 158
59	6	CMS *Missionary Gleaner* Nov 1874
62	7,8	OMFA 5115a Sept 26
63	9,10	Yao Sifu: possibly Yao Shangda: Personalia. 'Sifu' means master-craftsman. *China's Millions* 1877 pp 10–11, 13–15, 30–1; 1875–76 p 225
63	11	*China's Millions* 1876 p 210; 1877 p 12
64,65	12,13	*China's Millions* 1882 p 94; 1877 pp 43, 76, 86–7; Guinness, M G: *The Story of the CIM*, Vol 2 p 100
65	14	M H Taylor: OMFA 5122e

65	15	Chefoo Convention: Morse, H B: *International Relations* 2.283–306; Parl Papers, FO, Murder of Mr Margary 1875–76; further corr. re Mr Margary 1876; Michie, Alexander: *Englishman in China* Vol 2 pp 273–81; Royal Geographical Society *Supplementary Papers* Vol 1 Part 1, pp 154–92; Parl Papers Report, China No 3, 1878; 1877 p 51, further corr. re Mr Margary; Parl Papers China No 3, 1876, Aug 5, 1876; Little, Alicia Bewicke: *Li Hung-chang* pp 99–109; Morse, H B: *International Relations* 2.203, 314
66	16	Gill, Wm: *River of Golden Sand* 1; Introduction by Col H Yule, pp 66–73
66	17	Zen Yüying: the man who had savagely ended the Yunnan Muslim rebellion.
66	18	Wen Xiang had died on May 26
67	19	Little, A B: *Li Hung-chang*, pp 1, 6. Detring became Li's adviser for 20 years and briefly succeeded Robert Hart as Inspector-General when Hart became British Minister at Peking.
69	20	Wade: In *The Englishman in China* Alexander Michie said that Wade had 'found himself cornered'. Certainly he 'was a chastened man' after all was over, and in H B Morse's words, 'the honours of the occasion were with Mr Hart.'
70	21	*China's Millions* 1875 p 77; Stock, E: *History of the CMS*, 3.225; Broomhall, M: *Pioneer Work in Hunan*, pp 3–4
71	22	Stock, E: *History of the CMS* 3.224–5
71	23	R J Landale: Minutes of CIM London Council, Aug 1876; OMFA H42.14
72	24	OMFA 5121 Oct 14; *Days of Blessing* p 80 (Conference Report)
72	25	OMFA 5121 Oct 25; 5122c Oct 11; 5126; 5122d
73	26	Duncan: HTCOC Book 5 p 157; OMFA 5121 Nov 8; *Chinese Recorder* 1876 p 74; *China's Millions* 1877 p 24
73	27	John Stronach: HTCOC Book 1 pp 277–8; *Chinese Recorder* 1879 p 150; cf Alexander Stronach, Feb 6, 1879; *China's Millions* 1878 pp 135–6
75	28	Bombshell: OMFA 5115p E Wilson; I 123, 'From 1876–80, Mr Taylor's advent, we used to say, was like a bombshell scattering us abroad.'
76	29	Stevenson: Broomhall, M: *John W Stevenson* p 46–9
77	30	Passports: OMFA 5123a,b
79	31	*China's Millions* 1877 pp 47, 57, 92, 104, 150
81	32	Gansu: *China's Millions* 1877 pp 58, 141
81	33	OMFA 5122g Jan 12
82	34	Henan: OMFA 5122e; 5124, 5127; I 123; *China's Millions* 1877 pp 64, 86–7
84, 86	35,36	Shanxi: OMFA 5115b; 5122g; 5124; 5127; *China's Millions* 1877 pp 56, 70–2; *Chinese Recorder* 1871 p 212
86	37	OMFA 5115p
86	38	Yangzi stations: Zhenjiang, Nanjing, Wuhu, Datong, Anqing, Jiujiang
87	39,40	OMFA 5122g; 5124 Jan 6, 1877; Feb 2, 16
88	41	*China's Millions* 1877 pp 154–6; 1878 pp 80–2
88,90	42,43	OMFA 5124.30; *China's Millions* 1878 p 69

Chapter 3

91 1 Han: HTCOC Book 1 p 32. 'Tribes' – not in the strict sense of having a dominant leader, but ethnic communities with distinct customs, dress and language, in three groups: 1. Mon Khmer including Akha, Miao, Yao; 2. Tibeto-Burman including Lisu, Moso, Nosu; 3. Shan, calling themselves Tai, and the Minjia. True independence of the 'tribes' ended with their subjugation by Kublai Khan in 1252, but the campaigns of a General Mang in AD 230–40 are remembered by a temple erected to his memory.

92 2 Guinness, M G: *Story of CIM* Vol 2 re 'General' Mesny: played a significant part in quelling the Miao rebellion. J F Broumton wrote of Mesny's concern for the Miao people. No evidence that he was one of Charles Gordon's officers in the Ever Victorious Army. Discretion led to his usually being referred to as 'Mr Mesny' but sometimes as 'General' or 'Major-General', the equivalent rank he eventually reached. The use of 'Chiang Chün', a very high rank, was probably inappropriate. In his *Middle Kingdom*, Vol 1, Samuel Wells Williams renders Chiang Chün as 'commander-in-chief, major-general' – as if taking 'major' to mean 'senior', in ignorance of Western military usage.

92 3 Latourette, K S: *Christian Missions* p 362; Broomhall, M: *Jubilee Story of the China Inland Mission* (1st Edn. 1915) p 111; *China's Millions* 1877 p 85

92 4 *China's Millions* 1877 pp 49, 93

93 5 *China's Millions* 1883 pp 2, 3; OMFA 5122g

94 6 Howell, George T: *Yang Ts'uen-ling*; *China's Millions* 1878 pp 57–63, J McCarthy to T T Cooper, Bhamo Resident.

95 7 Fengshui: *see* Glossary, p 14 and Book 4 Appendix 8

95 8 *China's Millions* 1877 pp 78–9; 1883 pp 2–3

97 9 Judd: OMFA 5124.28; *China's Millions* 1877 p 128

97 10 OMFA 5122g; *China's Millions* 1877 pp 64, 74, 84; *Chinese Recorder* 1877 pp 498–516 – fit for *Journal of the RGS*

99 11 *China's Millions* 1877 p 126; *Chinese Recorder* 1877 pp 498–516

100 12 Mesny: OMFA 5122g; *China's Millions* 1877 p 85

101 13 Hunan: *China's Millions* 1877 p 92 (anti-foreign literati)

101 14 Yangzi: *Chinese Recorder* 1877 pp 512–16

103 15 *China's Millions* 1883 p 3

103 16 Shaking of heads: Stock, E: *History of the CMS*, 3.225

104 17 *Shanghai Courier* Dec 12, 1876; *China's Millions* 1877 p 43

105 18 'Plan of Operations': *China's Millions* 1875 p 31

105,106 19,20 Conference: OMFA 5124.14.15; *Chinese Recorder* 1877 pp 98–9

106 21 Cross-loving men: OMFA 5124.17; 511

107 22 Resting, resting: OMFA 5115a

107 23 Wuchang conference: also present Horace Randle, E Wilson, Marie Huberty, Edward Pearse, Eliz. (Jane) Judd, Hudson Taylor; OMFA N 10b33

107 24 Judd wrote: 'Whenever there was a difficulty about opening a station Mr Taylor always called for a day of fasting and prayer, which rarely failed to remove the difficulty. . . . When difficulties arose and we could not get a footing, or were driven out, there was fasting and

prayer for a day. Of course the fasting was optional. Some would go without breakfast and dinner, but Mr Taylor always fasted the whole day till the evening. He would take food then. It was not asceticism. He simply felt it was the scriptural and right thing to do, when waiting on God for anything special.' (Recollections)

108 25 G John: *China's Millions* 1877 p 143

108 26 *Records of the General Conference of the Protestant Missionaries in China, Shanghai, May 10–24, 1877* (Shanghai 1878); *Chinese Recorder* 1877 pp 239–50; *China's Millions* 1877 pp 104–15, 119–25, 137–40, 147–8, 156–8: 1879 p 83; OMFA I 13.11; Latourette, K S: *Christian Missions* p 413; OMFA 4500 J L Nevius *et al.* Sept 1874 proposal.

108 27 Dyer: HTCOC Book 1, p 279

108 28 Attributed to A Koestler paraphrasing Goethe (Brit Med Journal)

109 29 Attendance: an accurate count impossible owing to irregular attendance and the presence of 15 associate members including some who had been missionaries previously or were otherwise involved (including Doctors McCartee and Macgowan, Charles Schmidt and merchants David Cranston and Thomas Weir). Fourteen members of CIM were present. Stock, E: *History of the CMS*, lists numbers.

110 30 Elected committees deliberated and reported on inter-mission comity; on Romanisation of Chinese sounds; on an appeal to the Churches of the West to send more missionaries; on the production of Christian literature, periodicals and school-books; on the term for 'God'; on opium; on a document summarising for the Chinese literati and officials the Protestant beliefs and practices; and on petitioning the Bible Societies of Europe and America to change their rules or constitutions to permit 'a short preface, captions and brief unsectarian notes' to make their publications more acceptable and intelligible in China.

110 31 Ancestor worship: Denunciation of ancestor worship and idolatry by the early missionaries had been discarded and discouraged by most, including Hudson Taylor. *See* summary by M T Yates at 1877 Shanghai Conference; *Chinese Recorder* 1877 pp 239–250, 489–98; *China's Millions* 1875–76 pp 171, 190, 204, 218, 230; OMFA N10b.51

111 32 Itineration: the terms itinerate, itinerant, itinerancy, itinerary (*Collins Dictionary*) were widely used in the world of missions, all relating to travel from place to place. *Chinese Recorder* 1875 pp 241–3. Early in the 19th century German missionaries of the CMS perplexed their bishop in Bengal, T F Middleton, whose restricted world of parish and parson offered no status to such people. 'I must either silence them or license them,' he wrote, but to what (non-existent) parish could they be licensed! Stock, E: *History of the CMS*, 1.187

112 33 Science: *China's Millions* 1877 p 109

112 34 Martin: Covell, R: *W A P Martin* pp 123, 249–50; Hubbard, G E, Director of Information, Royal Inst of International Affairs 1933–45 in *Chambers Encyclopedia* 3.451

112 35 Martin: Covell, R op. cit. p 123; *China's Millions* 1877 p 109

113 36 Compare Reginald Heber (1783–1826) Bishop of Calcutta, hymn-

writer, 'who soon after his arrival in India wrote affectionately to Carey and Marshman in favour of the union of the Churches, "If a reunion of our churches could be effected, the harvest of the heathen would ere long be reaped." The Baptist brethren were personally touched but theologically unmoved'. Neill, S C: *Christian Missions* p 268

113 37 Volunteers: Wilder, R: *The Great Commission* p 78; *The Christian* quoted in *China's Millions* 1877 p 121

115 38 Douglas: *Chinese Recorder* 1877 pp 432–6

115 39 No 7 Seward Road, with David Cranston as business manager.

116 40 V L Cameron: promoted Commander and CBE, 1875.

116 41 Livingstone Inland Mission: Neill, S C: *Christian Missions* pp 378–9, the Mission was 'eager and adventurous but without the needed staying power.' It was absorbed by the American Baptist Mission. True access to the interior, with a steamer on one thousand miles of navigable Congo and stations at one hundred mile intervals, fell to the English Baptists (BMS) in and after 1884.

116 42 Stock, E: *History of the CMS*, 2.94–104; Neill, S C: *Christian Missions* p 384

117 43 Mackay: Padwick, Constance E: *Mackay of the Great Lakes*, London 1917. He died of fever in early 1890.

117 44 Guizhou-Guangxi: *Chinese Recorder* 1878 pp 169–74; *China's Millions* 1877 pp 148–50; 1878 pp 7–8, 72

120 45 Canton: HTCOC Book 2.376–9; Book 3.110

121 46 E Fishe: *Chinese Recorder* 1878 p 179 by G W Clarke; *China's Millions* 1878 pp 14, 72; Guinness, M G: *Story of the CIM* 2.204, so different that it smacks of hazy recollections.

121 47 G W Clarke: *China's Millions* 1878 p 72 says dep. Guiyang Sept 21, arr. Hankou Nov 7; *Chinese Recorder* 1878 p 179 says dep. Guiyang Sept 24, arr. Wuchang Nov 1; this should probably read Yichang Nov 1, Wuchang Nov 7

Chapter 4

122 1 Baber: RGS *Supplementary Papers* Vol 1 Part 1 1882; Col H Yule, Introduction to Gill, W: *River of Golden Sand* Vol 1 p 72

122 2 Gill, W: op. cit. 1.3, 15, 23, 159

124 3 Gill, W: op. cit. 1.262

124 4 Gill, W: op. cit. 1.262, 277

125 5 McCarthy: OMFA I 128: *Proceedings of the RGS* August 1879, Vol 1 No 8 pp 489–509; paper read by J McCarthy on April 28, 1879; *China's Millions* 1877 pp 135–6, Diary; 1878 pp 3, 57–64, account for T T Cooper and Indian Government; *The Times* 1879 p 76; 1883 p 2

125 6 Teacher: i.e. a Christian capable of reading official documents, addressing mandarins correctly, advising the missionary on etiquette, and negotiating contracts with landlords or employees.

125 7 Cameron, not McCarthy or Judd had been the first of CIM to enter Sichuan. If Baber had not co-operated with Gill and Mesny in their private venture to court danger in Xinjiang and Tibet, J McCarthy might well have been thwarted.

128 8 Kunming: July 2 according to *China's Millions* 1878 p 57; also pp 3, 103–5; OMFA 5124, cf.I 128; 5123d (itinerary and dates); 5123e, f, g

129 9 Plague: Gill, W: *River of Golden Sand* 2.345

130 10 Distances: OMFA 5123d; *China's Millions* 1878 p 57

133 11 Bhamo: OMFA 5124

133 12 *China's Millions* 1877 pp 131–2: Harveys dep. Rangoon July 8, wrecked July 18, Rangoon 31–Aug 17; Calcutta steamer Aug 25 to UK Oct 10

133 13 McCarthy: OMFA 5123e,f; *China's Millions* 1878 pp 57–64

134 14,15 'Across China from Chinkiang to Bhamo,' Jan–Aug 1877 by J McCarthy, read at evening meeting of the RGS, April 28, 1879; OMFA I 128 *Proceedings of the RGS*, August 1879, Vol 1 No 8 pp 127, 489–509; map, p 544

137 16 Gill did not mention Minya Gongga. Was Nenda another name or another peak not mentioned by others because lower than Minya Gongga's 24,900 ft (7550 m)?

137 17 Mesny: played *micare digitis* (of old Rome; *morra* in Italy), possibly acquired by China from early contacts with the West. Yule, H in Gill, W: *River of Golden Sand* 2.203. 'With mounting excitement and ever louder voices the players thrust their hands in each other's direction with upheld fingers, calling out words and numbers fast and furiously until within half a minute one or other had lost and had to drain a cup of rice wine dry – except that Mesny would take nothing stronger than tea.'

139 18 Garnier: took an active part in the defence of Paris, 1871, and then returned to China hoping to reach Lhasa, but joined in the Indo-China war, where he fell.

139 19 Gill, W: *River of Golden Sand* 1.77–9. Yule cited Alexander Williamson's 'excellent work' in *Journeys in North China, Manchuria, etc*, London, 1870, and Alexander Wylie's lecture in the *Proceedings* of the RGS, Vol XIV p 168

139 20 Gill, W: *River of Golden Sand* 1.17, 77; H Yule Introduction; *Journal* of RGS Vol XLVIII p 57; *China's Millions* 1879 p 76 citing *The Times*; a fascinating description of the 'road over the high plateau'.

140 21 Baber: RGS *Supplementary Papers* Vol 1 Part 1 p 176

142 22 Nosu: I travelled twice by this route, and lived for nearly four years (1947–51) in the Daliangshan. Many Nosu were my height, 6 ft; a few were inches taller, but most between 5 and 6 feet – (Author).

142 23 Yule, H in Gill, W: *River of Golden Sand* Vol 1 Introduction p 74; Baber, Colborne: 'Travels and Researches', RGS *Supplementary Papers* Vol 1 Part 1 pp 118–24; RGS 1881 'Latest Edition' Vol XXIV, quoted at length in translation from the *Annales de la Propagation de la Foi*.

143 24 Daliangshan: means Great Cool Mts. The use of two different Chinese characters for the same sound *liang* in the same tone is due to the name Daliangshan being restricted in some maps to the highest region, using the character for 'ridge', and in others being applied to the whole range with the character for 'cool' or 'cold'. Cap of liberty: the conical cap given to a Roman slave on emancipation.

144 25 Sichuan: *China's Millions* 1883 pp 1–5; OMFA 5124.28. By July 2 Hudson Taylor had heard of this repossession of Yichang and the occupation of Sichuan.

144 26 Chongqing: *Chinese Recorder* 1878 p 89
146 27 Cameron: *China's Millions* 1878 pp 75–7; 1879 pp 65–73, 97–104, 109–116; 1880 pp 67–70; 1883 pp 1–5; OMFA 1221; Guinness, M G: *Story of the CIM* Vol 2 pp 225–8
148 28 *China's Millions* 1879 p 98
150 29 Adenzi: *China's Millions* 1879 pp 109–16
151 30 Nicoll: *Chinese Recorder* 1878 pp 85–100; *China's Millions* 1878 pp 75, 77; 1879 p 67; 1880 pp 67–70
152 31 Nosu (Lolo): *China's Millions* 1878 pp 75, 77
153 32 Director: based mostly on OMFA 5124.12, 17, 24–5, 27, 29, 33; 5127; 5115b
157 33 Shanghai: Mission Office moved to 351 North Soochow Road, Hongkew, from Seward Rd but still under David Cranston. *China's Millions* 1878 pp 15–27
157 34 Railway: little more than a tramway between Shanghai and Wusong, had been completed in 1876 after four years of haggling over *fengshui*. But before long a man was killed on it, and on October 21, 1877, it was handed over to the authorities to be torn up until public attitudes changed. HTCOC Book 5 p 310. OMFA 5122h; Phil 4.1
159 35 Crombie: 5124.36; 5127

Chapter 5
163 1 Giants: *China's Millions* 1875 pp 19, 55 ft.
163 2 Indigenous: HTCOC 4.356, architecture; *China's Millions* 1877 p 43
163,165 3,4 Opium: *China's Millions* 1876 pp 82, 168; 1877 pp 112, 147–8; 1888 ff. Mander, S S: *China's Millions* 1878 pp 31–2, 43, 65, 77, 129, 145, 153; Li Hongzhang, Guo Songdao: 1878 pp 35, 154
165 5 Millions: *Chinese Recorder* 1878 p 157
166 6 Famine: Morse, H B: *International Relations* 2.307–11; *China's Millions* 1879 pp 134–5
166 7 *Chinese Recorder* 1880 p 237; *China's Millions* 1878 p 116, F H Balfour; British Library 11102.6.20 *Illustrations by a Native Artist*.
167 8 Sit down: *Chinese Recorder* 1880 p 357; Latourette, K S, Tipple Lectures 2–5 *These Sought a Country*; Soothill, W E : *Timothy Richard of China* p 64; *China's Millions* 1877 pp 120, 71, 156, 69
167 9 OMFA 5127
168 10 Relief: OMFA 5125a,b; *China's Millions* 1878 p 30; OMFA 5124.36, 37
168,169 11,12 Roads: *China's Millions* 1879 pp 134–9; Morse, H B: *The Trade and Administration of China* p 323; Parl. Papers, China No 2, 1878, 'Report on the Famine' (R J Forrest)
170 13 Forrest report: *China's Millions* 1879 pp 135–6; *Shanghai Courier* June 25, 1878
170 14 Trafficking: Parl. Papers, China No 2, 1878 p 11; Morse, H B: *International Relations*, 2.309 note, May 24, 1877; *China's Millions* 1878 p 71; 1879 p 148; 1879 p 137
170 15 *Times: China's Millions* 1878 pp 114–16; *The Times* Jan 23, 1878; Feb 19, 1878
171 16 Appeals: *China's Millions* 1878 pp 56, 120. Inflation: 'Currency Equivalents in Nineteenth Century China', *see* HTCOC Book 1

Appendix 7; comparisons are misleading, values varying by factors of 50 to 200, very approximately. If £5000 is thought of as £250,000 to £500,000 the enormity of the opium outrage against China may be better realised.

172 17 Refusals: *China's Millions* 1878 pp 111, 117, 120, 130–4, 156, 178; 1879 p 138

172 18 OMFA 5124 Feb 1878, 5134; *China's Millions* 1878 p 72

172,173 19,20 OMFA 5132; 5222a. Fleeces: *China's Millions* 1878 p 98

174 21 Sharp: OMFA 5138b

174 22 Famine: *China's Millions* 1878 pp 72, 79, 111, 114–27, 133–9, 147–8

175 23 Cannibalism: *China's Millions* 1878 pp 115, 136

175 24,25 *China's Millions* 1879 pp 1, 48, 147–8; 1878 pp 69–71

176 26 Typhus: *China's Millions* 1879 pp 63, 148, 219, 224. Until a suitable burial place could be found, in December, his coffin lay in a ruined temple used as a government mortuary outside Taiyuan. Governor Zeng offered 400 taels to take his remains to the States, and on this being declined, refunded the price of the land eventually bought as a cemetery.

177 27 Deaths: *China's Millions* 1878 pp 122, 134; 1879 p 138; *London and China Telegraph*, July 13, 22, 1878; *Shanghai Courier*; *Chinese Recorder* 1878 pp 224, 232, 460; 1879 p 219

177 28 Li Hongzhang: reported by HBM Consul R J Forrest; *China's Millions* 1878 p 122

178 29 Distribution: *China's Millions* 1878 pp 116, 157; 1879 p 19; OMFA 5135 (JET)

178 30 Orphans: *China's Millions* 1878 p 157; 1879 p 19; OMFA 5135

178 31 *Chinese Recorder* 1878 p 389; *China's Millions* 1878 pp 165, 178

179 32,33 Tianjin: *Chinese Recorder* 1881 p 70 (JHT-AC); *China's Millions* 1879 pp 19,20

180 34 McIlvaine: *China's Millions* 1879 pp 12, 19–22, 40, 50, 137, 148

180 35 Orphans: *China's Millions* 1879 pp 138–9, 40; OMFA 5135

181 36 J E Taylor: OMFA I 131, 132; 513.10. In his reminiscences 30 years later, J J Coulthard, who travelled out with J H T, wrote of Jennie having dreamed that J H T was ill. She dep. Taiyuan Feb 3, arr. Shanghai March 5. From Baoding she wrote to him saying she would be better employed at Shanghai preparing to receive reinforcements than to stay at Taiyuan. She did not mention a dream, to him or to Amelia or Benjamin. J H T dep. London Feb 24, via Amsterdam and Cannes, and sailed from Marseilles, March 9; arr. Shanghai April 22, 1879.

182 37 Famine aid: Morse, H B: *International Relations* 2.309–10, 313; *China's Millions* 1879 p 137; *London and China Telegraph* July 26; *China's Millions* 1878 Preface, p 126; 1879 pp 79, 91–4

182 38 Respect: *China's Millions* 1878 pp 154–5

182 39 Forrest: British Library 112.6.20; *China's Millions* 1878 p 124

183 40 Steamships: Morse, H B: *International Relations* 2.313; Smith, A H: *The Uplift of China*, p 163

183 41 Macartney: Morse, H B: 2.315

183 42 Clarke: *China's Millions* 1881 pp 136–9

183 43 Hillier: later Sir Walter Caine Hillier, KCMG, CB; Order of the

Double Dragon; Adviser to the Chinese Foreign Office. *China's Millions* 1880 pp 4–8, 20–4; 1879 pp 133–9

186 44 Famine toll: *Chinese Recorder* 1879 p 139; 188. pp 237ff, 241. Chinese official estimate, 20 million dead. Population of China, 300 million. $500,000 received by Protestant and Roman Catholic agencies. $189,000 by RCs from their own appeals. More than forty RC distributors were listed, but reports of their work were apparently not made public. Latourette only noted Moir Duncan's allegation that land and property were acquired at this time, and stated that six priests died in Zhili alone, and orphanages were crowded with homeless children. *Annales de la Propagation de la Foi*, Vol 50 pp 385ff, 392

186 45 Easton: *China's Millions* 1880 pp 78, 106

186 46 Relief: *Chinese Recorder* 1880 p 237. In addition to fund raising by the CIM in UK and China, relief by J J Turner, Francis James, J E Taylor, A Crickmay, C Horne, F W Baller, M H Taylor, G W Clarke, A G Parrott, W L Elliston, S B Drake, J Markwick. *China's Millions* 1880 p 76.

187 47 Magistrate: transcribed in *Chinese Recorder* 1880 pp 260–9, 464

187 48 Woodcock, G: *The British in the Far East* p 106

189 49,50 Dangers: *China's Millions* 1878 pp 85–99; OMFA 5134 JHT to L Desgraz, Feb 22.

190 51 Stonemason: OMFA 10.321 (1880)

190 52 Miao: Minutes of London Council, May 21, 1878 (May, June, August)

190 53 Secretaries: Minutes, Feb 26, 1878.

191 54 'Organising': OMFA 5135 June 14

191 55 Switzerland: OMFA 5135, 5134, 5135. His nephew B C B spoke of borrowing JHT's ice axe.

192 56 B B, Gen. Sec.: London Council Minute, Feb 5, 1878

192 57 Theodore Howard: no statement found, but safe to assume that he had inherited his father's position as director of the family chemical manufacturing enterprise.

193 58 Members: Broomhall, M: *Heirs Together* p 97

193 59 Race course: *Chinese Recorder* 1879 pp 151ff; Stock, E: *History of the CMS* 2.227–9; OMFA 5139

194 60 Married T A P Clinton

194 61 JHT: OMFA N11a.95; 5138b; 5135

194 62 OMFA 5139; *China's Millions* 1879 p 52

195 63 *Sword and Trowel:* May 1879

195 64 JHT: OMFA I 127; Guinness, M G: *Story of CIM* 2.310

196 65 JET: OMFA 513.10

Chapter 6

199 1 Shanghai: Morse, H B: *Trade and Administration in China* p 247. Zongli Yamen: Morse, H B: *International Relations* Vol 2 p 231

199 2 Chonghou: Morse, H B: *International Relations* 2.331–9

200 3,4 Gordon: Boulger, D C: *Halliday Macartney* p 347

201 5 Modernisation: *China's Millions* 1881 pp 45–50

202 6 Chefoo: *Chinese Recorder* 1876 p 383; 1881 p 139

204 7 Typhoon: OMFA 5211

205 8 Anorexia nervosa: OMFA 5211, 5212, 5214

205 9 Passports: OMFA I 217, 5211, Nllb.41

205 10 Chefoo: Houghton, S: *Chefoo*, CIM/RTS 1931; *China's Millions* 1883 pp 88–9; 1880 p 76

206 11 Ascetic: OMFA I 319

208 12 Elliston: arr. China with A G Parrott and S B Drake, early December 1878; most of 1879 at Linfen (Pingyang), Shanxi, through the worst, final stages of famine. Arr. Yantai Nov 20, 1880, married Annie Groom, Oct 25, 1882.

208 13 Santorium: *Chinese Recorder* 1879 p 304; OMFA 5222b

211 14 Itineration: Broomhall, M: *Chinese Empire* p 27 quoting E Stock.

211 15 Coulthard: OMFA I 217

212 16 'Itinerate': Latourette, K S: *Christian Missions* p 374; *A History of the Expansion of Christianity*, Vol 6 p 323

212 17 G John: Latourette, K S: *Christian Missions* p 364; Thompson, R Wardlaw: *Griffith John, passim*

213 18 Qiantang: *Chinese Recorder* 1880 p 49; OMFA 5221a

213 19 Tears: OMFA I 22.14b

216 20 Bishops: Divided yet again after Russell's death in 1879, the name 'North China' was transferred to the SPG diocese of Yantai, Tianjin and Peking, nominally including Shaanxi, and George Moule's diocese of Shanghai and Zhejiang, extending theoretically to Sichuan, was called 'Mid-China'.

216 21 Burdon: Stock, E: *History of CMS* 3.318–20, 564, 774; *China's Millions* 1880 p 28; 1883 p 28; 1878 p 42, welcome CIM. Hudson Taylor helped by assessing and sending him potential diocesan assistants and ordinands, explaining that his own objective was not to extend the CIM but the knowledge of Christ. He had already met candidates of whom he had thought 'just the man for Bishop Burdon,' and two had joined the CMS. Burdon was holding out the prospect of ordination and recommendation to the CMS for those he trained, but Hudson Taylor advised caution, for 'secondary considerations may become primary almost unconsciously.' Let them come to help in his work for God, and if suitable would then be 'the more grateful if *you* are the one to first suggest CMS and ordination,' as a reward rather than a right mentioned in advance. Twenty-three years had passed since together they were manhandled on the island of Chongming. (HTCOC Book 2 pp 252–60)

216 22 Hainan: *China's Millions* 1883 pp 27–32, 41–44; where immigrants from Fujian were establishing a foothold against violent opposition by the aboriginal people.

217 23 Cameron: the merest sketch of his journeys can be given here, but his own summary of his journals well repays an interested reader. *China's Millions* 1879 pp 14, 31–4; 1880 pp 27–33; 1883 pp 1–5, 27–32, 41–4, 58–60, 126, 140–1, 147–9, 160–2; 1884 pp 39–40, 46–9, 58–63, 70–2

218 24 Spoor: cf. Job 13.27 NIV/NEB branded soles of feet.

218 25 Hosie, A: *Three Years in Western China* p 55

218 26 Creed: Latourette, K S: *Christian Missions* p 333 (331–7)

219	27	Baber: Feb–June 24, with 3 weeks at Kangding, April 23 to mid-May
219	28	Cameron: *China's Millions* 1883 p 32
220	29	Southern missions: CMS, LMS, Basel Mission, APM, American S. Bapt, Am. Episc. Church, English Presby. Mission, Berlin Mission, Rhenish Mission, Am. Board (ABCFM), Am. Reformed Mission; *Chinese Recorder* 1869 list for comparison.
220	30	Canton: probably A G Kerr MD of APM at Peter Parker's hospital; *China's Millions* 1880 pp 27–33
222	31	Cameron: OMFA 5211, 5214
222	32	North-east: *China's Millions* 1880 pp 38–43, 111–13, 130–1, 133–6, 146. Cameron and Pigott: 1881 pp 17–19, 127. Cameron: 1882 pp 24, 37, 108–10, 154. Cameron: 1883 (map of Cameron's journeys) pp 2–5, 27–32, 41–4, 58–60, 140–1, 147–9, 160–2; 1884 pp 39–40, 46–9, 58–63, 70–2
222	33	Manchuria: Latourette, K S: *Christian Missions* pp 259, 396
222	34	Pigott: *China's Millions* 1880 pp 38, 42–3; OMFA 5211
224	35	Blizzard: *China's Millions* 1880 p 41; 1883 pp 58–60, 140–1
224	36	Mukden: *China's Millions* 1880 pp 111–13, 130–1, 133–6; 1881 pp 17–19
226	37	Jilin: the boundary lay between Changchun and Jilin, but now between Changtu and Changchun.
226	38	RCs: *China's Millions* 1883 p 148
227	39	Colportage: *China's Millions* 1880 pp 111–13, 135 TWP; 1883 p 160 JC
227	40	North-west: OMFA 5224; *China's Millions* 1883 pp 160–2 (July 27, 1880, twenty cities. 'Kalgan' is 'Halag' in Mongolian, mangled by transliteration.
227,228	41,42	Guihuacheng: OMFA 5224 July 27, 1880; *Days of Blessing* p 3
228	43	Goodrich: OMFA 5221b Aug 23
228	44	Map: *China's Millions* 1884 pp 39–46, 58
230	45	Cameron: *China's Millions* 1884 pp 70–2
231	46	Mandarins: *China's Millions* 1883 p 126

Chapter 7

232	1	Ningbo: HTCOC Book 3; Hangzhou: HTCOC Book 4
232,233	2,3	OMFA I 214
233	4	Williamson: *China's Millions* 1876 pp 137–8
234	5	Marriage: OMFA 5224
234	6,7	Women: OMFA 10.321; I. 111 lists yearly totals *in* China, as against new arrivals; *China's Millions* 1879 p 15
235	8	Education: Stock, E: 3.232. Value of women to indigenous Church: The Society for Promoting Female Education in the East had in 1875 seconded a member to run a girls' school for the CMS in Fuzhou. As Eugene Stock recorded, it was not the policy of the CMS to send women, or on the whole to use unordained men. A separate Church of England Zenana Missionary Society (CEZMS) was formed to provide for India's women, and a few members found their way to China, the first in 1881. (Latourette, K S: *Christian Missions* p 369) Even F F Gough's daughter, fluent in Chinese and working as a missionary with her father and step-mother (Mary Jones) in Ningbo, after applying to the CMS was transferred to the CEZMS before

returning to China. (However, she married J C Hoare of Ningbo.) In 1882 Bishop Burdon strongly advocated 'Medical Missions and Women's Work', with little effect. (CM *Intelligencer*, Jan, Feb 1883) Miss Aldersey (HTCOC Books 1, 2) had been exceptional, going independently to Ningbo in 1843, after Malaysia and Hong Kong. The example of American Protestant Episcopal Church and the American Methodist Episcopal Church in 1859 had been followed by the Presbyterians and Baptists in 1866 in sending a few single women to China. Stock, E: *History of CMS* 3.227; *China's Millions* 1877 pp 119–21.

235 9 G John: Thompson, R Wardlaw: *Griffith John* pp 310–11; 314–5
236 10 King: Broomhall, M: *Chinese Empire* p 203
237 11 Clarke: 'A Daughter of Lausanne' (unpublished) OMFA 5211 Aug 16, 23; *China's Millions* 1881 p 35, Blakiston's sketch of gorges.
238 12 Policy: Latourette, K S: *Christian Missions* p 390
238 13 Clarke: *China's Millions* 1880 pp 76, 78
239 14 Nicoll: *China's Millions* 1880 p 78; Taylor, Howard: *Hudson Taylor* (Biog.) Vol. 2 p 340; Guinness, M G: *Story of the CIM* 2.325–8
239 15 Clarke: *China's Millions* 1880 pp 78, 138. Others also: *see* Taylor, Hudson: *After Thirty Years* pp 11–20; Guinness, M G: *Story of the CIM*, chapters 23, 24; *Letter from China passim*
239 16 Bombshell: OMFA 5115b; I 123; 5221b June 25; 5225
240 17,18 'Only God': *China's Millions* 1880 pp 125–6; 5223 March 6; 5225 March 20
240 19 Hunan: *China's Millions* 1880 pp 107–9, 118, 137–8, 151–2 (Baller); 1881 pp 125–6, 140 (Kidd and E McC); 1882 p 99
241 20 Broumton, Trench: OMFA 5221a,b
241 21 Women alone: *China's Millions* 1880 pp 74, 78, 91, 116; 1881 pp 2, 8, 32–3; OMFA 5222b; 5223 March 6; 5115b E Wilson
242 22 Han R travel: OMFA I 22, 12, A L Fausset remin
245,246 23,24 Parker, Easton: *China's Millions* 1878 pp 42, 111; King: *ibid* 1878 p 78; 1879 pp 35, 105, 143, 165; 1880 pp 14–19
246 25 Széchényi: *China's Millions* 1880 pp 13–15, 43–4, 57–60
247 26 Easton: OMFA 5232a; 5233b
248 27 Parker: OMFA 5138d July 5, 1878; 5215b
248 28 Shao: *Chinese Recorder* 1880 p 75; OMFA 5215b Feb 25, 1880. In 1987 78 Asian members from 10 countries.
249 29 E Wilson: *China's Millions* 1880 pp 25, 90, 147; 1881 pp 10, 33, 44; 1883 p 83
249 30 Qinghai: *China's Millions* 1883 pp 12, 78–9
250 31 OMFA 5314; *China's Millions* 1882 p 104.
251 32 Parker: 1931 p 200.

Chapter 8

252 1 'Daring and Success': Latourette, K S: *Christian Missions*, p 391
252 2 Yunnan: *China's Millions* 1881 pp 6–7
253 3 Trench: *China's Millions* 1881 pp 98–9
255 4 Consul: Parl. Papers, FO China No 3, 1880. (Conventionally only the consul's surname is given, but we excuse the anachronism by its use

in the *Chinese Recorder* and Mission papers.) *China's Millions* 1880 p 1.

254 5 Bhamo: *China's Millions* 1880 p 118; Broomhall, M: *J W Stevenson* (Biog.) *China's Millions* 1879 p 158; 1880 pp 26, 52, 92, 132; 1881 p 102; OMFA 5223

256 6 Széchényi: *China's Millions* 1881 p 103

256 7 West-east: *China's Millions* 1881 pp 101–6, 117–20, 140–1; Broomhall, M: *J W Stevenson* pp 52–3

258 8 Bhamo: *China's Millions* 1882 pp 27–8, 61, 141; 1883 pp 90, 137, 158, 172; *J W Stevenson* pp 53–6; *Proceedings of the RGS*, 1880–81: Soltau, H: 'Journey from the Irrawaddy to the Yangtze', Vol iii.493; 'Notes on Yunnan', Vol III.564, compiled by William Soltau from letters of H Soltau.

258 9 Franco–Chinese: Latourette, K S: *Christian Missions* pp 246–53

259 10 Chongqing: *China's Millions* 1881 pp 69–72, 140

261 11 Church: *China's Millions* 1880 pp 25, 34–6, 124; 1881 p 98

261 12 Nosu: *China's Millions* 1880 pp 124, 149; 1882 p 81

261 13 Blakiston: *China's Millions* 1880 pp 138–9

262 14 Clarke: *China's Millions* 1882 pp 61, 112; 1883 pp 38, 90

263 15,16 Dali: *China's Millions* 1881 pp 142, 145; 1882 pp 12, 22, 26, 28, 37, 53, 61; 1883 p 90; Colquhoun, Archibald R: *Across Chryse from Canton to Mandalay*, 1883, Vol 2 pp 183, 184–7, 247–63, 291; *China's Millions* 1883 p 12, Eason between June 24 and July 1; Hosie, Alexander: *Three Years in Western China*, 1890, p 55

265 17 Colquhoun: *Across Chryse* 2.356–8

265 18 Like '*Lolo*', 'Miao-tzu' was loosely used by Chinese for aboriginal people, including the Hmong or Miao. The translation occupies 30 pages of Colquhoun's book, *Across Chryse*, 2.364–94

265 19 Clarke: *China's Millions* 1883 p 12

266 20 Dorward: *Chinese Recorder* 1879 p 379ff; *China's Millions* 1878 p 74; 1880 pp 9–10, 122–3

266 21 'by my life': Broomhall, M: *Pioneer Work in Hunan*, p 12; OMFA 5221a, 5224 Sept 22, Oct 13, 1880

268 22 Broomhall, M: *Hunan* pp 12–14 and maps; *China's Millions* 1881 pp 106–11

268 23 Colportage: F W Baller said they were to deliver a consignment to Guiyang also. Oct 18 dep. Wuhan, Nov 16–29 Changde, Dec 25 Hongjiang. *China's Millions* 1881 p 10. Jan 14, 1881 dep. Hunan to Guiyang; Jan 17–21 and Feb 17–22 Chenyuan; March 2 Hongjiang again; April 1 Wuhan.

269 24 Good men: OMFA 5221a; *China's Millions* 1880 p 132; 1881 pp 6, 98–9, 129–35, 143–5

269 25 Long stride: OMFA 5233c Apr 2, 5233g Apr 8, I 22.10

270 26,27 Trench: *China's Millions* 1881 pp 122, 126 JHT: 1881 pp 121–2; OMFA I 228, 5231h

271 28 Wuhan: *China's Millions* 1881 p 122; OMFA 5231h,i,j,k,l; 5233f

273 29 Broumton: *China's Millions* 1881 pp 129–35, 143–5; Broomhall, M: *Pioneer Work in Hunan* p 14

275 30,31 Losiping: *China's Millions* 1882 pp 6, 23; 1881 pp 143, 145

276 32 Opium: *China's Millions* 1882 pp 23, 29, 33, 62, 80

276,277 33,34 Kunming, Dali: OMFA I 22.10; *China's Millions* 1882 p 80; 1883 pp 12, 38, 50, 72, 90

277 35 Dorward: *China's Millions* 1882 p 6; Broomhall, M: *Pioneer Work in Hunan* pp 18–19

278 36 Dorward: Broomhall, M: *Pioneer work in Hunan* p 24, 30; *China's Millions* 1882 p 141; 1883 pp 72–5, 93–4, 163–5

279 37 G John, J Archibald: Not reported in *Chinese Recorder* or G John biography. Thompson, R W: *G John* pp 339–346 describes mobbing at Xiangtan, 1880, but nothing about Longyang or mobbing in 1883. Broomhall, M: *Hunan* pp 26–7 incident not dated, nor references; *Chinese Recorder* 1905 G John jubilee: John Archibald tribute to 'numerous journeys made with Dr John, 'in perils oft'; *Chinese Recorder* 1912 p 541 G John obituary, no mention.

279 38 Dorward: Broomhall, M: *Hunan* pp 26–7

Chapter 9

283 1 Richard: *Chinese Recorder* 1880 pp 430–41

286 2 Ancestor: *Chinese Recorder* 1902 p 253, P F Price

287 3,4 *Chinese Recorder* 1903 p 199; 1904 pp 237–45; E O James, Prof. of History and Philosophy of Religion, London Univ., *Chambers Encyclopedia* 1.404; 3.443.

287 5 Sinologists (those versed in Chinese): *Chinese Recorder* 1881 p 154

288 6 Richard: Latourette, K S: *Christian Missions* pp 378–80; Tipple Lectures, *These Sought a Country*; HTCOC Book 5.314

289 7 Soothill, W E: *Timothy Richard of China*. Soothill appears to have hurried this biography into print without research into the facts. Anachronisms and mistakes of recollection impair it.

290 8 Soothill, W E: *Timothy Richard* pp 106, 111, 149

290 9 D Hill: *China's Millions* 1881 p 89; Barber, W T A: *David Hill, Missionary and Saint*, p 207

291 10 Mary Richard: Soothill, W E: *Timothy Richard* pp 111–12

291 11 F James: OMFA 5223, 5224, 5228; 513.10; I 22.14b; 4223 May 24, 1880; G Clarke: OMFA 5212 Aug 20

291 12 Richard: OMFA 5137, 5212 Aug 20, 5223, 5228, 5224 to Baynes, 5223 May 24, 1880

292 13 Taiyuan: OMFA 5231z; N12b.13

292,293 14,15 Soothill, W E: *Timothy Richard* pp 156–7; Neill, S C *et al*: *Concise Dictionary of the Christian World Mission* p 526

293 16 Dysentery: *China's Millions* 1878 p 99; 1880 p 1; 'dys-entery' from many causes struck all types of foreigners in China and killed many. To hazard a guess, Hudson Taylor's condition had a psychosomatic element: stresses were often linked directly with relapses; while his spirit rose to meet the situation his body protested. Infections accounted for most.

293 17 Jennie: OMFA 5232i, dep. UK May 2, 1878

294 18 Zhejiang: OMFA 5231A, 5241f; N13a.11

294 19 Hinderers: OMFA 5223

295 20 James Taylor: OMFA 5232l,m

295 21 Mary Landale: *China's Millions* 1880 p 70

295 22 Not death: *China's Millions* 1882 pp 35–6

296 23 Funds: *Chinese Recorder* 1881 p 394; OMFA 5134. The CMS income was £207,508; the BMS received 'the largest income yet'; and the WMMS suffered a deficit of £38,000
296 24,25 Funds: OMFA 511a, 5231A Shanghai Nov 14, 1881 to JET; 5226; *China's Millions* 1881 p 44; 1883 p 85
297 26 Marriage: OMFA 5223; 5231y
297 27 Life style: OMFA 5221b.1; I 226; 5231o,r; 5221b
298 28 OMFA 5224, 5223; N12a.27
299 29 Move: OMFA 5231A,C,D; N9c.61–2; 5124.1o; *China's Millions* 1882 p 26
299 30,31 Troubles: OMFA I 228; 5134, 5244a; *China's Millions* 1881 pp 84–6
300 32 'Mon centre cède, ma droite recule, situation excellente. J'attaque!' (Aston: *Biography of Foch*, 1923, ch 10)
300 33 Platforms: OMFA 513.60 March 18, 1879; I 231, 232
300 34 *China's Millions* 1881 p 143; Judges 5.23
301 35 Seventy: *China's Millions* 1888 p 111; I 232; 1883 p 53; 1885 p 4
302 36 Satan: OMFA I 233.14
302 37 Baptism: no reasons or discussion recorded. OMFA 5242a, 5241b
303 38 Appeal: OMFA 5242b; *China's Millions* 1885 pp 4–9
303 39,40 *China's Millions* 1882 pp 85–7, 90–1. Shaftesbury: 1882 pp 90–1
304 41 Radstock: *China's Millions* 1881 pp 77–96
304 42 Funds:*China's Millions* 1883 p 112
305 43 Funds: *China's Millions* 1878 pp 86, 89
305 44 Berger: OMFA 5233h
305 45 Pyrland Rd: OMFA 5231D, 5226, 5241C; *China's Millions* 1881 p 157
306 46 Funds: *China's Millions* 1883 pp 95–6
306 47 Hitches: OMFA 5241b,n,C,H,I,J,N,T,X
308 48 Latourette, K S: *Christian Missions* p 390; Taylor, Dr and Mrs Howard: *Hudson Taylor and the CIM* Vol 2 pp 360–70 (362)
309 49 Depression: OMFA 5241a,f,i,j,m,n,p,q,r,s,t,v
309 50 Anqing: OMFA 5241X, 5243c
310 51 Shanxi: OMFA 5241B,K,R-U
310 52 Tempted: OMFA 5241.1
311 53 Seal: *China's Millions* 1885 p 9
311 54 OMFA 5241.2, 3
311 55 Donor: *China's Millions* 1885 p 9; Broomhall, M: *Archibald Orr Ewing* (Biog.) p 50; *Jubilee Story of the CIM* pp 159–60; Taylor, Howard and MGG: *Hudson Taylor and the CIM* Vol 2 pp 369–70
312 56 Hostility: Latourette, K S: *Christian Missions* p 354; 311–2, 325, 354, 470; *Expansion of Christianity* p 251; Morse, H B: Vol 3 p 368
313 57 Stock, E: *History of the CMS* Vol 3 p 233
314 58 Japan: Stock, E: op. cit. 3.588
314 59 Schofield: OMFA 5314 A,B,C; 5221a; *China's Millions* 1880 pp 62, 132; *Chinese Recorder* 1881 p 139; OMFA 5226 Nov 6, 1879; July 14, 1880; Nov 14, 1880; Dec 23, 1881; *Memorials of the late Dr Harold Schofield by his Brother, Dr Alfred T S Schofield* (H & S)
314 60 Schofield: after winning a London matriculation bursary of £20 for two years (£1000 today?) he had gone to Owen's College, Manchester, where he won another £40 scholarship in Classics. From there he proceeded to London University, to graduate BA (1869)

aged 18, and BSc (1872). In October he went up to Lincoln College, Oxford, with a residential exhibition of £60 per an. for four years, taking first class honours in Natural Science and holding an appointment in the Museum of Comparative Anatomy. During this time he won a prize of £25 in New Testament Greek open to the whole university. He also won the Burdett Coutts award in geology, £80 per an. for two years, and an entrance scholarship of £100 to St Bartholomew's Hospital, London. There he added the Foster Scholarship in Anatomy, the Junior and Senior Scholarships of £20 and £30, the Brackenbury Medical Scholarship, £32, and the Lawrence Scholarship, £30, and gold medal. At about this time he was awarded a Radcliffe Travelling Fellowship in Natural Science at Oxford, worth £200 per an. for three years. (OMFA 5314A, a note in Geraldine Howard Taylor's hand adds MD Lond. and MRCP Lond. to the list of his qualifications, but his obituary in *The Lancet* did not include these, and the London University denies the MD (Registrar, personal letter).

315 61 Chinese dress: OMFA 5221a, 5223, 5224, 5226, 5227

316 62 Schofield: *Memorials* p 245; OMFA 5226 Dec 23, 1881; 5314B Aug 24, 1883; 5314C

316 63 Schofield: *Memorials* p 247; *China's Millions* 1882 pp 126–7; 112; 133–4; 1884 p 4

316 64 Schofield: *China's Millions* 1883 pp 134, 155, 174–6, 240, 249; 1884 p 13, *Lancet* obituary; OMFA I 316a–d; 5314B,C; *Memorials* p 244

317 65 Schofield: *Memorials* p 249

318 66 W Wilson: *China Medical Journal* 1884–95; Pruen: *The Provinces of Western China* pp 80ff

319 67 Mackenzie: *China's Millions* 1880 p 41; 1883 pp 58, 124

320 68 Douthwaite: OMFA 5225; *China's Millions* 1882 pp 40–3

320 69 Korea: *China's Millions* 1884 p 98; pp 25–6. Douthwaite 'circulated a considerable number of copies of the Word of God there.' Bishops Burdon, Moule and Scott proposed to the Archbishop of Canterbury an Anglican mission to Korea, which he referred to the CMS. In 1884 J R Wolfe visited Korea, and the Church in Fujian sent two Chinese preachers for two years.

320 70 Mackenzie: OMFA 5226 Nov 14

Chapter 10

321 1 Berger: OMFA 5322h Jan 22; July 16, 1883; 5313j

322 2 Radstock: OMFA 5313D,I

323 3 John 15.2 NIV

323 4,5 JHT: OMFA 5241X; Luce: OMFA I 315a,b

324 6 OMFA 5312, Lady Tankerville donated a two-storey Scandinavian chalet to the CIM, erected at Bidborough, Kent, and still in constant use.

325 7 Friends: OMFA 5313m; Salisbury: *China's Millions* 1883 p 144; OMFA I 32.10, 11; 5317

325 8 Rosa Minchin and Emily Whitchurch: OMFA I 313a; 5315b; Luce: I 315; Sharp-BB: 5313E; N13b.36

326 9 Sharp re JHT: *China's Millions* May 1932 Centenary Number, Vol LVII No 5

326 10 J E Howard: OMFA 5317

327 11 Seventy: OMFA 5313L; *China's Millions* 85 p 52. JHT reckoned 9+18+46=73; FHT reckoned 11+20+46=77. But Guinness, M G: *Story of the CIM* p 415: 76 in three years, but four more dep. UK Jan 16, 1885, i.e. ready before the end of 1884, making 80 at least without including those of the Cambridge Seven who would have gone in December. 10.321 lists 19+46; Broomhall, M, *Jubilee Story*, 9+18+46 in 1884 making 73. OMFA I 32.16

327 12 Stanley Smith: *Days of Blessing* p 60; Mott: OMFA I 32.14

328 13,14 Pollock, J C: *The Cambridge Seven*, on which I have drawn freely; pp 10, 124 (1985 Edn)

328 15 Gladstone: Pollock, J C: *Moody without Sankey* and *The Cambridge Seven* are essential reading; cf HTCOC Book 4 p 345

329 16 Blue: university athletic distinction, light blue for Cambridge, dark blue for Oxford.

330 17 Sir Thomas Beauchamp, Bt, died 1874

330 18 Studds: *see* N P Grubb *C T Studd*; J C Pollock: *Cambridge Seven*; Polhill-Turner brothers: 'Two Etonians in China' (unpublished, OMFA)

332 19 Studds: Stock, E: *History of CMS* 3.284 note

332 20 Dons: lecturers, tutors, professors

333 21 Polhill-Turner: the name Turner was assumed in satisfaction of a legacy and discarded later.

335 22 Hoste: when Queen Victoria bought Sandringham in 1861 the old house was demolished. Sir William Hoste, Baronet, GCB, KMT; at the head of four frigates defeated greatly superior combined French and Italian squadrons, March 13 1811, and was severely wounded; married 3rd daughter of 2nd Earl of Orford. Sir George Charles Hoste CB, married Mary, 3rd daughter of James Burkin Burroughes, Esq, of Burlingham Hall, Norfolk. OMFA I 317a

335 23 D E Hoste: OMFA I 317a,b; I 31.13 Reminiscences.

336 24 D E Hoste: OMFA I 317b; 1 Pet 4.11 AV, NIV; OMFA 5331a,b

338 25 *Days of Blessing* p 65; Broomhall, M: *W W Cassels* p 5

338 26 'Sporting hearties': Woodcock, G: *British in the Far East* p 107; Hoste: OMFA I 31.13; 5331c,d; 5423. D E Hoste signed P & P Sept 22, 1884

340 27 George Studd: Grubb, Norman P: *C T Studd* pp 32–41; Pollock, J C: *Cambridge Seven*, 1955, pp 66–76; *China's Millions* 1885 pp 36–7

341 28 McCarthy: HTCOC Book 4 pp 118–19

342 29 Beauchamp: OMFA I 315; I 317–19; 5135; *see* Pollock, J C: *Cambridge Seven* (1985), Manuscript Sources, Bibliography. *China's Millions* 1900 p 119

343 30 OMFA I 32.16

343 31 Orr Ewing: OMFA 5324a; Broomhall, M: *Archibald Orr Ewing* p 26

343 32 Belfast: Hogg and McMullen; OMFA 5323b. While at Belfast a friend wrote down for JHT the account of John Taylor's blow, 'Take that for Jesus Christ's sake.' HTCOC Book 1 p 282

344 33 Stock, E: *History of the CMS* 3.285; OMFA 5323c; N14a.9; I 32.18

344	34	OMFA I 32.18
344	35	Arthington: in 1886 sent £200 for use in Chinese Turkestan; no earlier donations listed.
345	36	Scotland: OMFA 5324c,e,g
346	37,38	OMFA I 319; 5322Gii; 5322H, 5334a,b; I 313a,b; *China's Millions* 1884 pp 154–7
347	39	JHT: OMFA 5325b, 5323f
347	40	Taiwan: OMFA 5322P
348	41	Stanley Smith: OMFA 5334a–f,m
349	42	Mothers: OMFA 5325b, 5333i; I 318a
349	43	Cheese: OMFA 5334j
349	44	Bible Christians: OMFA 5313K; I 32.15. Friends: OMFA 5313m
349	45	International: OMFA 5322A,B,Q; N14a.20,50
350	46	'Expanding circle': Padwick, Constance: *Henry Martyn* (IVP) 1953 edn. title of Chapter 15. C T Studd: *Daily Telegraph*, July 27, 1931, 'Death of great missionary'.
350	47	A printed card announcing Stanley Smith's Cambridge meetings named on the back as coming for the November meetings, Hudson Taylor; John McCarthy; R J Landale, MA, Exeter Coll, Oxford, seven years in China; W W Cassels BA, St John's Coll; S P Smith, Trinity Coll; and D E Hoste, late Royal Artillery, shortly to proceed to China. London Council Minutes, Nov 11, 1884; Miss A Maxwell, N14a.44
351	48	Stock, E: *History of CMS* 3.284; 3.184. OMFA 5334i
352	49	Radcliffe: OMFA 5334q,s; g,v; Broomhall, M: *J W Stevenson* p 60
353	50	A suggestion that JHT's departure before the Seven showed an 'anti-intellectual' bias is clearly groundless.
354	51	Stark: noted by Feb 10 minute of London Council. OMFA N14b.4,6; 5422
355	52	Radstock–JHT; *China's Millions* 1885 p 84; OMFA 5335a,c. At Liverpool the subject was to be 'The Evangelisation of the World', to us familiar but in 1885 it smacked of originality. Jan 9 L'pool; 10–12 Aberdeen; 13 Banff; 14 Huntley; 15 Montrose; 16 Perth; 17–19 Edinburgh; 20–23 Glasgow; 24–25 Newcastle. Hoping to add English towns including Sutherland, Leeds, L'pool or Manchester, Derby, Birmingham, Cardiff and Bristol.
355	53	Polhill: OMFA 5332a,b
358	54	Polhill: OMFA 5332d Studd: OMFA 5333j,l,m; 5411 Jan 22, 1885
359	55	Edinburgh: OMFA 5334g,x; *The Christian* Feb 19, 1885
359	56	Studd: Grubb, N P: *C T Studd* pp 46–7
359	57	Exeter Hall: OMFA 5336c; *China's Millions* 1885 p 28
359	58	Ship: note signed by Chas.Fishe stated £171 5s for five (before the P-Ts); OMFA 5336p; I 318c
360	59	Gordon: OMFA 5411; Neill, S C: *History of Christian Missions* p 388
361	60	Handley Moule: quoted in *China's Millions* 1885 p 28
362	61	Exeter Hall: OMFA 5336c; Pollock, J C: *Cambridge Seven* p 111; *China's Millions* 1885 pp 21–38
364	62	Amy Carmichael: Thompson, P: *D E Hoste* (biog.) p 36
364	63	*China's Millions* 1885 pp 72–75; OMFA I 318b, W W Cassels
365	64	F R Smith: OMFA I 318c; 5338b; *China's Millions* 1885 p 76

365 65 Mothers: OMFA 5336a, 5333e,f; N14b.13
366 66 Exeter Hall: OMFA 5336c,d; 5332d; 5336e,f
366 67 Cambridge Seven: OMFA 5332e; 5336e; Stock, E: *History of CMS* 3.275, 284–5

Chapter 11

367 1 Decree: Broomhall, M: *Chinese Empire* p 103
369 2 Hart: Morse, H B: *International Relations of the Chinese Empire*, Vol 2 pp 368–71
369 3 Martin: Covell, R: *W A P Martin* p 183
370 4 Mackay: Stock, E: *History of the CMS*, Vol 3 p 413
371 5 Soltau: *China's Millions* 1885 pp 48–9
372 6 Shanghai: *China's Millions* 1885 pp 81–2; OMFA N14b.21
372 7 JHT: OMFA 5338c, 5411, 5412i,v
373 8 Shanghai: *China's Millions* 1885 p 52; OMFA 5411, 6114
373,374 9,10 Cambridge Seven: Broomhall, M: *W W Cassels* pp 52–3. Divided on grounds of discretion, and influence on regions visited. In 1902 the Polhill-Turners by deed poll reverted to using Polhill alone; by then in common use, so a pardonable anachronism in this history. *Jubilee Story* p 206; *China's Millions* 1885 pp 81–2, 105, 122; OMFA 5338, 5412e
375 11 OMFA 5412k, 5422, 5412m,o,p
375 12 Richard: Latourette, K S: Tipple Lectures, *These Sought a Country*
376 13 Studd–Polhill: OMFA 5412s,u,N, 5423; *China's Millions* 1899.32
376 14 S P Smith: 'Two Etonians' p 21 OMFA (unpublished)
376 15 Hoste: OMFA 5423
377 16 *China's Millions* 1885 p 29; Stock, E: *History of CMS* 3.323
378 17 'Evangelisation': Broomhall, M: *Jubilee Story* p 166 and footnote
379 18 Benjamin Broomhall: Broomhall, M: *Heirs Together* pp 95 ff
380 19 OMFA 5412i,v; 7121g; I 241; Neill, S C *et al*: *Concise Dictionary of the Christian World Mission* p 230; Goforth, R: *Goforth of China*; McNab, J: *They Went Forth* pp 168–87
380 20 Goforth: OMFA 6113i
381 21 *China's Millions* 1888 p 137; OMFA 5242j; Howard Taylor: *Hudson Taylor and the China Inland Mission* Vol 2 p 293
381,382 22,23 Plans: 5316; Howard Taylor: *Hudson Taylor* 2.375
383 24 Leaders: OMFA 5139
383 25 Broumton: Howard Taylor: *Hudson Taylor* 2.395; OMFA J 132
384 26 Funds, credit: OMFA 5425; 5412P,x, V, iii
385 27 Stevenson: Broomhall, M: *J W Stevenson* pp 61–3; OMFA 5433 letters
386 28 Nevius: *Chinese Recorder* 1880 p 357 on Shandong Church, followed by 'Principles and Methods Applicable to Station Work', *Chinese Recorder* 1881 p 131; *China's Millions* 1886 pp 71, 118, 133, 142, and Nevius: *Methods of Mission Work* (CIM); OMFA N14b.49, 55
386 29 Shanxi: OMFA 14b.55; Bagnall took responsibility for S Shanxi later.
387 30 Broomhall, M: *J W Stevenson* p 66
387 31 *China's Millions* 1885 p 44; OMFA 5431a Feb 4; N14b.49b, 57–8
388 32 *China's Millions* 1887 pp 132–4, 147–8; OMFA 5431b
388 33 Selection: OMFA 5137

389 34 *China's Millions* 1886 pp 3, 62; OMFA 6211, 5431c, 5444
390 35 Henan: *China's Millions* 1886 p 81; Broomhall, M: *Chinese Empire* p 160
390 36 Conflict: *China's Millions* 1886 p 3; OMFA 5412iii
390 37 Shaanxi: Broomhall, M: *Chinese Empire* pp 198, 204–5
391 38 Broomhall, M: *Pioneer Work in Hunan* pp 50–54, 57–9; *China's Millions* 1886 p 157
391 39 Guangxi: *China's Millions* 1886 p 3
392 40 *China's Millions* 1885 p 135; OMFA 5412A,B,E,H,I,K
392 41 Nevius: *Chinese Recorder* 1880 p 357; 1881 p 131; *China's Millions* 1883 pp 170–1; *Missionary Methods in China* (reprint from *The Christian*); 1886 pp 71–2, 118–21, 133–6, 142–6; HTCOC Book 5 pp 315, 333
394 42 Tortured: OMFA5412 V.Y; *China's Millions* 1886 pp 41–4
394 43 Guangxin: *China's Millions* 1887 p 3, cf 1895 pp 154–6; OMFA 5431a, 5445a,b; 5431c, 5444, 5445a
395 44 OMFA 5445b, a
396 45 OMFA I 214; *China's Millions* 1876 p 193 (Jan 5, 6, 1876); 1880 pp 25, 98
399 46,47 Wusong: OMFA 5431b, 5421a; I 319.97
400 48 Newington Green: OMFA J 21.18; 8213; *China's Millions* 1888 p 94
400 49 OMFA 5431b, 5433

Chapter 12

401 1 Hsi: Taylor, Mrs H: *Pastor Hsi* (biography) *passim*; Thompson, P: *D E Hoste passim*; Broomhall, M: *Chinese Empire* pp 198, 204–5, 209–23; *China's Millions* 1881 pp 42, 48, 91; 1883 p 86; OMFA L21.12
402 2 Jewellery: Taylor, Mrs H: *Hsi* p 144
403 3 Hsi: Broomhall, M: *F W Baller* (biography) p 25
403 4 Cassels: Broomhall, M: *W W Cassels* pp 67–8; Zhang: Broomhall, M: *Chinese Empire* pp 213–15
405 5 Richard: dep. Taiyuan October 18, 1887, to Shandong; Soothill, W E: *Timothy Richard* p 155; *China's Millions* 1886 pp 81, 160–5; *Days of Blessing passim*; Grubb, N P: *C T Studd* p 61
405 6 Bagnall: OMFA 5431a Orr Ewing: Broomhall, M: *Archibald Orr Ewing* pp 40–1
406 7 Conferences: *China's Millions* 1887 pp 4–11; OMFA 5431b
407 8 Hsi: *China's Millions* 1886 p 138
408 9 *China's Millions* 1887 pp 1, 44–5
408 10 OMFA 5431b; Broomhall, M: *W W Cassels*; London Council Minutes, May 13, 1887; Jan 10, 1888; Jan 28, 1890
409 11 Baptisms: *China's Millions* 1887 pp 119, 122; 1892 p 89
410 12 Hsi: Thompson, P: *D E Hoste* pp 56, 58; Taylor, Mrs H: *Pastor Hsi* 197ff
411 13 Hsi-Hoste: OMFA 5423 Sept 12, 1886; 5446
411 14 Indigenous principles: SPCK: HTCOC Book 1 p 77; Gutzlaff: HTCOC 1 p 328; Venn: HTCOC 1 p 329; Stock, E: *History of CMS* vol 2 pp 411–7; Burns: HTCOC Book 2 p 320; Nevius: HTCOC Book 3 p 362; Book 6 p 412; Hudson Taylor: HTCOC Book 4 p 356; Book 5 pp 279, 334, 351, 373, (for example).

414	15	Xi'an: *China's Millions* 1884 p 89; OMFA J 425
414	16	Addicts: Broomhall, M: *Chinese Empire* p 213
415	17	OMFA 'Two Etonians' pp 36, 40–44; OMFA 5433; *China's Millions* 1886 pp 127–30
417	18	OMFA 5431b, 10.331
418	19	OMFA 5444, 5431b; Neill, S C: *Concise Dictionary* p 106
419	20	OMFA 5432; 10.331; *China's Millions* 1887 pp 17, 45
419	21	OMFA 5431b,c; 5442, 5444
420	22	Riley–Stroud: OMFA 5431a; *China's Millions* 1886 pp 17, 27, 103
420	23	Sacrifice: OMFA 5412i; *China's Millions* 1885 p 13; 5412H,J
420	24	OMFA 5431a
421	25	China Council: OMFA 5441c; 5442; 5444; J 132b,c; Broomhall, M: *Jubilee Story* pp 170–3; *China's Millions* 1887 p 42; Taylor, Howard: *Hudson Taylor* 2.735, 421
421	26	Council: *China's Millions* 1887 pp 42, 109, 111. Administration: Taylor, Howard: *Hudson Taylor* 2.421 (source uncertain)
422	27	Instructions: OMFA 5441
423	28	Code: OMFA 5433, 5432; chiefly concerned with matters of health, travel and business, it also provided for dealings with consuls, a fact misused to impugn the Mission as an agency of foreign governments. But the worst examples cited by critics were no more open to objection than 'Consul already requested Peking'; 'already obtained confidential intelligence'; 'according to intelligence received, state affairs indicated.' Perhaps ignorance of the fact that the word 'intelligence' was used in the nineteenth century as 'information' is now, accounts for the misunderstanding.
424	29	Beauchamp: OMFA 5445d Nov 26, 1886, Beauchamp from Ching Li Yamen, Chongqing. Another source says Bourne also in the *yamen*. Bourne and Studd were in good spirits; 'they seemed to be reconciled to their fate of always being disappointed at any suggestion of going out'. 'The authorities have no guarantee of the good behaviour of the people as there has not been a soul punished for all the rioting which really seems to have been very serious.'
425	30	Polhill: 'Two Etonians' p 30
425	31	Beauchamp: 'Two Etonians' p 46. Forty years later, 1939, when Sir Montagu returned to Sichuan, where he died, I (AJB) acted as his medical companion and driver by car and truck from Vietnam to Chongqing. An educated Chinese hearing him preach said to me, 'This is fascinating. He speaks the language of an old book.'
426	32	George Studd: *China's Millions* 1887 pp 125–6
427	33	Typhus: *China's Millions* 1888 pp 81, 115; 1892 p 90
427	34	Hundred: OMFA 5433; Guinness, M G: *Story of the CIM* Vol 2 pp 422–5; Broomhall, M: *Jubilee Story* pp 172, 175; *J W Stevenson* p 65
428	35	Hundred: Broomhall, M: *Jubilee Story* pp 172–3; *J W Stevenson* p 67; OMFA 5431c Nov 27, 1886
429	36	OMFA 5431c Dec 10; 5445m Dec 18
429	37	Tease: OMFA 6213a Jan 12
430	38	P&O £25 to Marseilles: OMFA 6221, 6231
430	39	Dorward: Broomhall, M: *Hunan* p 62; OMFA 6231

References to Bibliography

Atlas of China
Baber, E Colborne: *Travels and Researches in Western China*
Baber, E C: *Travels*
Barber W T A: *David Hill, Missionary and Saint*
Barber W T: *David Hill*
Bong Rin Ro (Editor): *Christian Alternatives to Ancestor Practice*
Broomhall, A J: *Hudson Taylor and China's Open Century* (HTCOC) + Book (3/4 etc)
Broomhall, A J: HTCOC Book
Broomhall, Benjamin: *Evangelisation of the World*
Broomhall B: *Evangelisation of the World*
Broomhall B: *National Righteousness* (Editor)
Broomhall B: *National Righteousness* (Editor)
Broomhall, Marshall: *Archibald Orr Ewing*
Broomhall M: *Archibald Orr Ewing*
Broomhall, Marshall: *Chinese Empire*
Broomhall Marshall: *Faith and Facts, as Illustrated in History of CIM*
Broomhall M: *Faith and Facts*
Broomhall, Marshall: *F W Baller, Master of the Pencil*
Broomhall, M: *F W Baller*
Broomhall, Marshall: *Heirs together of the Grace of Life:* Benjamin Broomhall and Amelia Hudson Broomhall
Broomhall, M: *Heirs Together*
Broomhall, Marshall: *Hudson Taylor's Legacy*
Broomhall, M: *Hudson Taylor's Legacy*
Broomhall, Marshall: *Islam in China*
Broomhall, M: *Islam in China*
Broomhall, Marshall: *Jubilee Story of the China Inland Mission*
Broomhall, M: *Jubilee Story*
Broomhall, Marshall: *John W Stevenson, One of Christ's Stalwarts*
Broomhall, M: *J W Stevenson*
Broomhall, Marshall: *Last Letters and Further Records*
Broomhall, M: *Last Letters*
Broomhall, Marshall: *Martyred Missionaries of the CIM*
Broomhall, M: *Martyred Missionaries*
Broomhall, Marshall: *Pioneer Work in Hunan by Dorward and Other Missionaries*
Broomhall, M: *Pioneer Work in Hunan (or) Hunan*
Broomhall, Marshall: *W W Cassels, First Bishop in Western China*
Broomhall, M: *W W Cassels*
Chefusian, Journal of the Chefoo Schools Association (+Vol)
Chefusian (omit Vol)
China Mail
China's Millions, Magazine of the China Inland Mission (Vol 1 p 2)
China's Millions (1.2)
Chinese Recorder and Missionary Journal
Chinese Recorder
Colquhoun, Archibald, R: *Across Chryse, from Canton to Mandalay*
Colquhoun, A R: *Across Chryse*

Colquhoun, A R in RGS *Journal* IV p 713
Cordier, Henri: *Life of Alexander Wylie*
Cordier, H: *Wylie*
Covell, Ralph R: *Confucius, the Buddha and Christ, a History of the Gospel in Chinese*
Days of Blessing in Inland China (compilation)
Days of Blessing
Fairbank, John King: *Trade and Diplomacy on the China Coast*
Fairbank, J K: *Trade and Diplomacy*
Foreign Office Library, Public Records Office: *Century of Diplomatic Blue Books*
F O *Blue Bk*
Forsyth, R C: *China Martyrs of 1900*
Gill, Capt Wm: *River of Golden Sand; The Narrative of a Journey through China and Tibet* to Burmah
Gill, Wm: *River of Golden Sand*
Goforth, Rosalind: *Goforth of China*
Goforth, R: *Goforth*
Grist, W A: *Samuel Pollard, Pioneer Missionary in China*
Grist, W A: *Pollard*
Grubb, Norman P: *C T Studd, Cricketer and Pioneer*
Grubb, N P: *C T Studd*
Guinness, Joy: *Mrs Howard Taylor: Her Web of Time*
Guinness, M Geraldine: *Story of the China Inland Mission*
Guinness, M G: *Story of CIM*
Haldane, Charlotte: *Last Great Empress of China*
Haldane, C: *Last Great Empress*
Hart, Sir Robert: *These from the Land of Sinim*
Hart, R: *Land of Sinim*
Hopkirk, Peter: *Foreign Devils on the Silk Road: the Search for the Lost Cities and Treasures of Chinese Central Asia*
Hopkirk, P: *Foreign Devils on the Silk Road*
Hosie, Alexander: *Three Years in Western China: a Narrative of Three Journeys*
Hosie, A: *Three Years in Western China*
Houghton, Stanley *et al*: *Chefoo*
Johnson Douglas: *Contending for the Faith; a History of the Evangelical Movement in Schools and Colleges*
Johnson D: *Contending for the Faith*
Latourette, Kenneth Scott: *History of Christian Missions in China*
Latourette, K S: *Christian Missions*
Little, Alicia Bewicke (Mrs Archibald): *Li Hung-Chang, His Life and Times*
Little, A B: *Li Hung-Chang*
Loane, Marcus: *Story of the China Inland Mission in Australia and New Zealand*
Loane, M: *Story of CIM in Australia and NZ*
London and China Telegraph
Lyall, L T: *Passion for the Impossible*
MacGillivray, Donald: *Century of Protestant Missions in China*
McCarthy, John: in *Proceedings of the RGS* Vol I 'Across China from Chinkiang to Bhamo'
McCarthy, J: 'Across China from Chinkiang to Bhamo'
Martin, W A P: *Cycle of Cathay*

Michie, Alexander: *Missionaries in China*
Michie, A: *Missionaries in China*
Michie, A: *The Englishman in China: as illustrated in the career of Sir Rutherford Alcock*
Morse, Hosea Ballou: *International Relations of the Chinese Empire*
Morse, H B: *International Relations*
Neil, Stephen C: *History of Christian Missions*
Neil, S C: *Christian Missions*
Neil, S C *et al*: *Concise Dictionary of Christian World Mission*
Neil, S C: *Concise Dictionary*
Nevius, Helen S C: *Life of John Livingston Nevius*
Nevius, H S C: *John Livingston Nevius*
North China Daily News
North China Herald
Overseas Missionary Fellowship Archives (OMFA)
OMFA
Padwick, E Constance: *Mackay of the Great Lakes*
Padwick, E C: *Mackay*
Parliamentary Papers
Parl. Papers
Peking Gazette
Pollock, John C: *Cambridge Seven. A Call to Christian Service*
Pollock, J C: *Cambridge Seven*
Pollock, John C: *Moody without Sankey. A New Biographical Portrait*
Pollock, J C: *Moody without Sankey*
Pruen *Provinces of Western China*
Royal Geographical Society: *Magazine*
RGS: *Proceedings*
RGS: *Journal*
RGS: *Supplementary Papers*
RGS: Supp. Papers
Shanghai Evening Courier
Smith, Arthur H: *The Uplift of China*
Smith, A H: *Uplift of China*
Soltau, Henry: 'Journey from Irrawaddy to Yangtze'
Soltau H: 'Journey'
Soothill, Wm E: *Timothy Richard of China*
Soothill, Wm E: *Timothy Richard*
Stock, Eugene: *History of the Church Missionary Society*
Stock, E: *History of the CMS*
Taylor, Dr & Mrs Howard: *Hudson Taylor in Early Years*
Taylor Howard and M G: *Hudson Taylor in Early Years*
Taylor Howard and M G: *Hudson Taylor's Spiritual Secret*
Taylor Howard and M G: *By Faith; Henry Frost and CIM*
Taylor Howard and M G: *Henry Frost*
Taylor, Mrs Howard (M Geraldine Guinness) (*see also* Guinness, M Geraldine): *Story of the China Inland Mission*
Taylor, M G G: *Story of CIM*
Taylor, Mrs Howard: *Behind the Ranges; J O Fraser*
Taylor, Mrs H: *J O Fraser*

Taylor, Mrs H: *Pastor Hsi: One of China's Scholars*
Taylor, Mrs H: *Pastor Hsi, Confucian Scholar*
Taylor, J Hudson: *China: Its Spiritual Need and Claims*
Taylor, J H: *China*
Taylor, J H: *Brief Account of Progress of CIM*
Taylor, J H: *Retrospect*
Taylor, J H: *After Thirty Years*
Taylor, J H: *Occasional Paper*
Taylor, J H: *Occ Paper*
Taylor, J H: *Summary of Operations of CIM*
Thompson, Phyllis: *D E Hoste, A Prince with God*
Thompson, P: *D E Hoste*
Thompson, R Wardlaw: *Griffith John*
Williams, S Wells: *Life and Letters*
Williams, Samuel Wells: *The Middle Kingdom*
Williams, S W: *Middle Kingdom*
Woodcock, George: *The British in the Far East*

PERSONALIA

Chinese, Manchu

ALUDE; Manchu; Tong Zhi emperor's choice as consort; niece of Chonghou (qv); granddaughter of Prince of Cheng; victim of Ci Xi's displeasure (qv); died in suspicious circumstances, 27 March 1875.

CHONGHOU; Manchu; 1870 Imperial Commissioner for Foreign Affairs, Tianjin; central figure at time of Tianjin massacre; 1879 envoy to Europe; saved from death sentence.

CHU: *see* Zhu

CI AN; Empress Dowager, co-regent with Ci Xi (qv); died in suspicious circumstances 1881.

CI XI (1835–1908); Yehonala (Yehe Nara), (Ts'u Hsi); Manchu concubine Yi, mother of Tong Zhi emperor (qv); Empress Dowager, co-regent with Ci An (qv); 1860–1908 supreme power in China.

GUANG; Bible Society colporteur, travelled June 1879–Dec 1882 with Jas. Cameron, Manchuria, Shanxi, Shaanxi.

GUANG XÜ (Kuang Hsü) emperor; 1875, four-year-old puppet of Ci Xi (qv); son of Prince Chun, 7th son of Dao Guang emperor; 1889 assumed power; 1898 imprisoned after *coup d'état* by Ci Xi; d. 14 Nov 1908, day before Ci Xi.

GUO SONGDAO; 1876 Chinese ambassador to France, Russia, Britain; arr. London 21 Jan 1877, succeeded by Marquis Zeng (qv); spoke out in UK against opium traffic.

HO Xianseng (i.e. 'Mr'); Sichuanese teacher at Hanzhong, Shaanxi; first Hanzhong Prot. Christian; pioneer evangelist to his home town, Tongjiang, with Jas. Cameron (qv); 1886 with Ed. Pearse and Cecil Polhill secured first foothold at Langzhong.

HSI SHENGMO (Xi Liaozhi) (1830–96); Shanxi classical scholar, opium addict, converted 1879 through David Hill (qv); 1886 ordained as leading pastor, south Shanxi; established scores of opium refuges, Shanxi, Shaanxi, Henan, Zhili; secured influential foothold in anti-Christian Xi'an, Shaanxi; had D E Hoste (qv) as colleague 1886–96.

HUANG KEZHONG; Christian with leprosy; key colleague of pioneers at Hanzhong, Shaanxi.

JIANG LIANGYONG; Hangzhou, Zhejiang, Christian; initiated Yühang church who provided his financial support.

JIANG SUOLIANG (*see* ZHANG)

JIANG XIAOFENG; evangelist at Shaoxing, Zhejiang; converted by seeing J W

Stevenson often on his knees. (In Ningbo dialect Tsiang Sia-Yong, *Pinyin* probably ZHANG)

KONG, Prince; son of Dao Guang emperor; brother of Xian Feng emperor and Prince Chun; survived Jehol plot; 1860 negotiated treaty with Allies at Peking; rank equivalent to Prime Minister; his own son rejected by Ci Xi and Prince Chun's made emperor; repeatedly degraded by Ci Xi; died 1898, 'a national calamity.'

LIANG Xianseng ('Mr'); Christian teacher at Hanzhong, Shaanxi; occupied Langzhong, Sichuan, with Ho (qv), Pearse and C Polhill.

LI HANZHANG (Li Hanchang); brother of Li Hongzhang; viceroy of Hubei, Hunan.

LI HONGZHANG (Li Hung-chang) (1823–1901); holder of the highest academic degrees, highest honours after defeat of Taiping rebels; enlightened liberal but failed in modernisation of China; 1895 forced to cede Taiwan to Japan; the Grand Old Man of China, leading statesman until death.

LO; Bible Society colporteur; 1880 crossed Hunan with Baller (qv), Evangelist Yao (qv), J McCarthy (qv) and Jane Kidd (qv), to Guiyang, Guizhou.

QÜ (Ch'ü); (1) scholar of Daning, Shanxi; became Christian with Zhang Zhiben (qv) through studying Mark's Gospel; three times publicly flogged; church leader.

QÜ (2) Wuchang evangelist; to Guiyang through hostile Hunan with Broumton (qv), Yao Shangda (qv) and Sen Sifu.

REN ZIQING (Pastor Ren); son-in-law of Wang Laedjün (qv); co-pastor with him at Hangzhou, Zhejiang; fully supported by church members.

SEN Sifu (i.e. master craftsman); Broumton's colleague at Guiyang, 1877

SHAO MIANZI; Yangzhou, Jiangsu, schoolgirl; 25 Feb 1880 married G Parker; pioneer in Gansu, Xinjiang, Henan; finally doyen of CIM after husband died 17 Aug 1931.

SUN YATSEN (Sun Zhongshan) (1866–1925); Chinese statesman; 1891 first medical graduate, Hong Kong; 1905 founded China Revolutionary League, in Europe, Japan; 1911–12 founder and first president Republic of China; m. descendant of Paul Xü, (SOONG QINGLING, dep. chairman Nat. People's Congress till d. 1981).

SU VONG, Dr V P; Chinese Christian scientist at Nanjing imperial arsenal with Dr Halliday Macartney (qv); delegate to 1877 General Missionary Conference, Shanghai.

TONG ZHI, emperor; only son of Ci Xi (qv); 1861 acceded to throne aged five; rejected Ci Xi's choice of consort, chose Alude (qv); died of smallpox 3 Jan 1875 having reinstated Ci An (qv) and Ci Xi as regents; Ci Xi believed guilty of ordering his infection.

WANG LAE-DJÜN (Wang Li-jün), Ningbo Mission convert; with JHT London, 1860–64; pastor, Hangzhou (Hangchow) until his death in 1900.

WEN XIANG; Manchu; Grand Secretary of the Imperial Council; used delaying tactics with T F Wade, British minister; died 26 May 1876.

WU, Colporteur; Bible Society; 1879 to Manchuria with James Cameron.

XI (*see* Hsi).

YAO SHANGDA, (possibly Yao Sifu); colporteur; 1877 crossed Hunan to Guiyang, Guizhou, with Judd (qv) and Broumton (qv); again with Judd Oct 1880; 1881 travelled with Adam Dorward.

YAO Sifu; (possibly Yao Shangda); Hunanese Christian converted in Jiangxi; accompanied missionaries; expelled from Yueyang, Hunan.

YAO Xianseng; Nanjing teacher; 1876 to Shanxi with J J Turner (qv), F James (qv).

YAO, Evangelist; 1880 crossed Hunan to Guizhou with Baller (qv), Trench (qv), Mrs Wm McCarthy (qv), J Kidd (qv).

YANG CUNLING; (Yang Ts'un-ling) ex-soldier; evangelist; 1877 with J McCarthy (qv) in Yichang riot; on foot Yichang to Bhamo and back.

YONG LU; Manchu imperial bannerman related to Ci Xi (qv); counsellor to Tong Zhi emperor; 1875 protected Ci Xi in her coup; loyal even when disgraced; became Viceroy of Zhili, Senior Guardian of the Throne.

YÜ, Captain; 1860 heard part gospel from Taipings; 1875 converted through Wang Lae-djün (qv); carried gospel to Yüshan, Jiangxi – beginning of Guangxin River churches.

YUAN BAOHENG; 1878 High Commissioner for Famine Relief, Taiyuan, Shanxi; well disposed towards Richard (qv), Hill (qv), Whiting (qv) who died; himself died of 'famine fever'.

ZEN YÜYING (Tsen); governor of Yunnan, savagely ended Muslim rebellion.

ZENG GUOCHUAN; brother of viceroy Zeng Guofan (qv); governor of Shanxi during Great Famine of 1878–79; welcomed relief teams.

ZENG, Marquis; son of viceroy Zeng Guofan (qv); 1879 ambassador to France, Russia, Britain; 1880 negotiated favourable treaty with Russia over Ili after Chonghou (qv) débâcle.

ZENG GUOFAN (Tseng Kuo-fan) (1811–72); scholar, provincial governor; 1854 defeated Taipings; viceroy of the 'Two Jiangs' (Jiangxi, Jiangsu and Anhui), then of Zhili (Chihli); 1870 after Ma Xinyi assassination returned Nanjing; d. 11 March, 1872.

ZHANG (Chang); colporteur with LMS; 1875 with M Henry Taylor to Henan; expelled from Queshan (Choshan); possibly the Zhang with Yao Shangda (qv), Judd (qv), Broumton (qv).

ZHANG SUOLIANG (also referred to as Jiang and Tsiang); pastor at Zhenjiang, Jiangsu; travelled with CIM pioneers.

ZHANG XIAOFENG (*see* JIANG).

ZHANG ZHIBEN (Chang Chihpen); 1885–86 leading Buddhist priest; converted with Qü (qv) through reading Mark's Gospel; beaten unconscious by magistrate; church leader, Daning, Shanxi.

ZHANG ZHITONG (Chang Chih-t'ung); literary chancellor of Sichuan; governor of Shanxi; viceroy of Hunan-Hubei; reformer, profound scholar, author.

ZHU (Chu); Christian who travelled with M Henry Taylor, expelled from Queshan (Choshan), Henan.

ZUO ZONGTANG (Tsuo Chung-t'ang); one of China's greatest generals; quelled Muslim north-western rebellion; 1875 sowed and reaped harvest for troops, Hami; reached Kashgar 1876; quelled Yakub Beg forces; viceroy of Gansu-Shaanxi; and later of Nanjing.

PERSONALIA

Non-Chinese

ADAMS, Joseph S; CIM, one of the Eighteen dep. UK Nov 1875 to Burma; joined CIM, Bhamo, later Zhejiang; resigned April 1884; joined Am. Bapt. Mission, Burma.

ALABASTER, Challoner; HBM consul, Yantai, Shantou, Hankou.

ALCOCK, Sir John Rutherford (1809–97); MRCS at 21; 1832–7, surgeon Marine Brigade and Spanish Legion, Peninsular Wars, Dep.-Director of Hospitals; 1835 partially paralysed; 1843 Diplomatic Service; 1846 HBM consul Fuzhou; Xiamen (Amoy), Shanghai; 1858 Consul-Gen. Japan; 20 June 1862 knighted, KCB; 1859–65 HBM minister, Japan; 1865–71 HBM minister, Peking; 1876 Pres. RGS.

ALDERSEY, Miss Mary Ann (*c*1800–64); 1824–5 learned Chinese from R Morrison; 1832 Malacca (Melaka); Batavia (Jakarta); 1842 Hong Kong; 1843–59 Ningbo.

ALLEN, Clement F R; HBM consul, Zhenjiang; member, Col. Browne's 1875 expedition, Burma-Yunnan.

ALLEN, Young J; Am. Meth. Episc. (South); 1860 Shanghai; edited reform publications read by Chinese from peasants to emperor; 1868–74 *Church News*, *Globe News*, *Review of the Times*; 1882 founded Anglo-Chinese College, Shanghai; 1887 Member, Socy. for the Diffusion of Christian and General Knowledge among the Chinese; consulted by reformers.

ANDREW, George; CIM, dep. UK 5 Jan 1881; Guizhou (Supt.), Yunnan; 17 Oct 1883 m. J Findlay.

ARCHIBALD, John; Bible Society agent, Hankou.

ARTHINGTON, Phoebe; sister of Robert; donor to CIM and Müller (qv).

ARTHINGTON, Robert (1823–1900); wealthy Quaker, lived frugally supporting missions; 'Arthington's millions' through Arthington Trust, half to BMS, two-fifths to LMS, £2000 to Free Church of Scotland Missionary Society, £100 to Müller's orphanage, sums to other institutions (incl. CIM) (ref. LMS archives).

BABER, Edward Colborne (1843–90); 1872 vice-consul, Taiwan; 1876 interpreter to Hon. W G Grosvenor expedition; 1877 Commercial Resident, Chongqing; explorer; consul; Chinese Secretary of Legation, Peking; 1883 Medal of RGS; 1885–86 Consul-General, Korea; Resident, Bhamo; 16 June 1890 died at Bhamo.

BABINGTON, Charles Cardale (1808–95); Prof. of Botany, Oxford Univ.; archaeologist.

BAGNALL, Benjamin; B&FBS, arr. China 1873; Baoding, Zhili; 1886 joined CIM; Supt. Shanxi, Zhili; China Council, resigned; 1900 killed by Boxers.

BALFOUR, Major-Gen. Sir George, CB; Capt 1840 opium war; 1843–46 first consul Shanghai; 1865 nominated JHT for FRGS; knighted after 1865.

BALLER, Fredk. William (1852–1922); linguist, Sinologue; b 21 Nov 1852; one of H Grattan Guinness' first Institute students; CIM, dep. UK 3 Sept 1873 with C H Judd, M Hy Taylor, M Bowyer (*see* HTCOC 4 Personalia); arr. Shanghai 5 Nov 1873; m. M Bowyer 17 Sept 1874; Supt. Anhui, Jiangsu; Hubei, Henan; pioneer traveller; famine relief; 1876 with G King to Shaanxi; 1878 with Mrs Hudson Taylor, Misses Horne, Crickmay to Shanxi; 1880 took party through Hunan to Guiyang; 1885 secretary, first China Council; 1887 began literary work, *Mandarin Primer* (used by consular service), 1900 *Analytical Chinese-English Dictionary*; translator, member Union Mandarin Bible Revision Committee, NT 1907, OT 1907–18 Peking; 1915 Life Governor of B&FBS; Vice-President Nat. B S of Scotland; Life Member Am. B S; author in Chinese of 18 books; pamphlets, millions in circulation; April 1922 Life of JHT in Chinese; widowed 1909; 23 Jan 1912 m. H B Fleming; 1919 first furlough, after 21 years; d. 12 Aug 1922.

BARCLAY, Florence; dtr of Robt Barclay, Reigate (Burke's LG); CIM dep. UK 13 Dec 1880; 24 May 1892 m. M Beauchamp (qv); d. 2 May 1955.

BARNARDO, Thomas John (4 July 1845–19 Sept. 1905); 1862 converted; 1866 met JHT in Dublin; April 1866 to London; 1866–69 CIM candidate; 1872 CIM Referee, while developing orphan work.

BEAUCHAMP, Rev. Sir Montagu Harry, Proctor-, Bart.; (Burke PB); (1860–1939); b. 19 April 1860, son of Sir Thomas (qv); Repton, Trinity Coll., Camb.; CIM dep. UK 5 Feb 1885, 'Camb. Seven'; pioneer, Shanxi, Sichuan; travelled extensively with JHT; 24 May 1892 m. F Barclay (qv); World War 1 Hon. Chaplain to Forces, Egypt, Greece, Murmansk; 1915 inherited baronetcy; 26 Oct 1939 d. at Langzhong, Sichuan.

BEAUCHAMP, Sir Thomas William Brograve Proctor-, 4th baronet, DL, High Sheriff of Norfolk 1869; Lieut. Royal Horse Guards; 1852 m. Caroline Waldegrave, yst dtr of 2nd Baron Radstock; sons: Reginald William, 5th bt; Granville Pelham, d. 1889; Horace George, 6th bt; Montagu Harry (qv) 7th bt, after Sir Horace and Montagu's eldest son killed in action, Suvla Bay, Gallipoli, 12 Aug 1915; friend, supporter JHT, CIM; d. 7 Oct 1874.

BENSON, Archbishop (1829–96); 1877 Bp. of Truro; 1882 Archbp. of Canterbury, after Tait.

BERGER, William, Thomas (*c* 1812–99); director Samuel Berger & Co., Patent Starch manufactuer, St Leonard St, Bromley-by-Bow; CES supporter; early donor to JHT; 1865 co-founder and UK director, CIM; generous life-time donor; home at Hackney village, then Saint Hill, East Grinstead, devoted to CIM; last years in Cannes.

BLAKISTON, Thomas Wright (1832–91) Captain; 1860 with Lt. Col. H A Sarel, Dr A Barton, S I J Schereschewsky dep. Hankou surveying Yangzi R; 25 May 1861 arr. Pingshan; author, standard work on Yangzi R; attempted India via Tibet, forced back.

BLODGET, Henry, DD (1825–1903); Am. Board; 'massive build and commanding presence', 'the soul of country and good breeding'; 1850–53 tutor, Yale; 1854 Shanghai with Aitchison (qv); 1860 to Tianjin with Br. forces, first Prot. to preach in streets; 1864 Peking 30 years; translator, Mandarin NT with Burdon (qv), Edkins (qv), W Martin (qv), Schereschewsky (qv), revised W H Medhurst's Southern Mandarin NT; 1870 Shanghai Vernacular NT with W J Boone, T McClatchie *et al*; 1889 'easy *wenli*' NT with Burdon (qv), Groves, J C Gibson, I

Genähr; 1890 Union Mandarin NT committee; 1890 with others submitted memorial to emperor 'setting forth the true nature of Christianity'; 1894 retired ill.

BOHANNAN, Annie; widowed sister of Mary Bell (*Lammermuir* party); in Yangzhou riot as Taylor children's nurse; 1868 m. Edward Fishe CIM (qv); 1875 returned to China; 1877 widowed, dep. to UK.

BONAR, Andrew (1810–92) Scottish Free Church divine; author; friend of Wm Burns (qv) and JHT.

BOONE, William Jones, Jr; Bishop, son of Bishop Wm Jones Boone, MD, DD; Prot. Episcopal Church; b. Shanghai 1846; 1870–84 fourth Am. Bp; d. Hankou 1891.

BRIDGMAN, Elijah Coleman, DD (1801–61); Am. Board (ABCFM); 1830 Canton; 1832 first editor *Chinese Repository* with R Morrison; 1843–44 US treaty interpreter-negotiator; 1845–52 translator, Chinese Bible, Delegates' Committee; 1847 Shanghai.

BOTHAM, Thomas Earlum S; CIM dep. UK 26 Aug 1885; pioneer in Shaanxi; Supt. Shaanxi, Gansu; China Council; 1889 m. Ella A Barclay; d. 22 Oct 1898.

BROOKE, Graham Wilmot; CMS 3 Dec 1889; pioneer leader in W Africa and Sudan; d. 5 March 1891

BROOMHALL, A Gertrude; eldest dtr of Benjamin (qv) and Amelia HT (qv); b. 18 June 1861; CIM dep. UK 24 Sept 1884; Shanxi; 7 Sept 1894 m. D E Hoste (qv); 3 sons; d. 12 April 1944.

BROOMHALL, Benjamin (1829–1911) b. 15 Aug 1829; m. 10 Feb 1859 Amelia Hudson Taylor (qv), 4 sons, 6 dtrs; Sec. Anti-Slavery Assn; 1875 CIM, Pyrland Rd; 1878–95 Gen. Sec. CIM, London; 1888 Sec. Christian Union for the Severance of the British Empire with the Opium Traffic; editor, *National Righteousness*; 3 sons, 2 dtrs in China; d. 29 May 1911.

BROOMHALL, Albert Hudson (1862–1934) eldest son of Benjamin (qv); b. 31 Aug 1862; CIM dep. UK 24 Sept 1884; Shanxi; m. 14 May 1890 Alice Amelia Miles; treasurer CIM, Shanghai; d. 18 Aug 1934.

BROOMHALL, Marshall, 2nd son of Benjamin (qv), MA Cantab.; author (*see* Bibliog.); CIM dep. UK Oct 1890; editor, Lond., d. 24 Oct 1937.

BROUMTON, James F; brother of Eliz. Judd; one of the Eighteen, dep. UK 21 Oct 1875; pioneer Guizhou; m. 1881 Mrs Wm McCarthy (qv); 1886–1905, treasurer CIM Shanghai; d.

BROWN, George Graham (1863); Company sec.; CIM dep. UK 21 April 1886; UK staff.

BROWNE, Col. Horace A; Indian Army, leader of Br. expedition, Burma-Yunnan 1875, when A Margary killed (qv).

BUDD, Charles; CIM, one of the Eighteen dep. UK Nov 1875; pioneer Henan, Shaanxi; resigned 1879.

BURDON, John Shaw (1826–1907); CMS 1853, Shanghai; pioneer evangelist; 1857 m. Burella Dyer, sister of Maria Taylor (qv); 1862 Peking; 1874 3rd Bishop of Victoria, Hong Kong; Bible translator (*see* Blodget); Jan 1897 resigned bishopric, to Pakhoi aged 71; dep. China 1907.

BURNS, William Chalmers (1815–68); first English Presby. to China; 1847 Hong Kong; Amoy; 1855 Shanghai; 1856 Swatow; 1863 Peking; 1867 Niuchuang (now Yingkou), d. Niuchuang; translated *Pilgrim's Progress*; close friend of JHT.

CABLE, A Mildred (1877–1952); CIM 1901, Huozhou, Shanxi, with E and F French (qv); 1923–36 Chinese Turkestan; author (*see* Bibliog).

CAMERON, James (1845–91) CIM, one of the Eighteen, dep. UK 4 Aug 1875;

pioneer traveller until end of 1881; 1882 Supt. Shandong, later W. Sichuan; 1884 MD (USA); m. Mrs Randall; 1886 China Council; d. 14 Aug 1891.

CAMERON, Verney Lovett, Lieut. RN; led search for D Livingstone (qv), March 1873; surveyed Lake Tanganyika, 1873–75; crossed Congo, W Coast Nov 1875; promoted Commander, CBE.

CARDWELL, J E; CIM, 1867 Hangzhou; 1868 Taizhou, Zheijiang; Dec 30, 1869 Jiujiang, pioneered Jiangxi; Shanghai business manager.

CAREY, William (1761–1834); Baptist Miss. Soc. founder; 1793 India, Serampore; 1800–30 Prof. of Oriental Languages, Calcutta.

CASSELS, William Wharton (1858–1925) b. 11 March 1858; Repton; 1877–80 St John's College, Cambridge; Ridley Hall; ordained 1882; 'Cambridge Seven', CIM dep. UK 5 Feb. 1885; 1885–86 Shanxi; 1886 Supt. China Council; Sichuan; 4 Oct 1887 m. M L Legge; 18 Oct 1895 consecrated Bishop in W China; d. 7 Nov 1925 (wife d. 14 Nov).

CAVAN, Fredk John Wm Lambart, 8th earl of (1815–87); Lt. Col. 7th Dragoon Guards; CES Gen. Committee; supporter of CIM, Mildmay Conf., D L Moody; Welbeck St Brethren.

CHALLICE, John; director of six companies, deacon, Bryanston Hall, Portman Square; 1872 member, first CIM council; hon. treasurer UK; d. 1887.

CHALMERS, James (1841–1901) LMS; 1866 S. Pacific; 1877 New Guinea; murdered by cannibals 2 Jan 1901.

CLARKE, George W; CIM, one of the Eighteen, dep. UK 4 Aug 1875; Dali, Yunnan; m. F Rossier 15 Sep 1879; (d. 7 Oct 1883); 1886 Guihuacheng; Supt. N Shanxi, Zhili; China Council; m. A Lancaster, April 1886 (d. 8 Aug 1892); m. R Gardiner 12 Oct 1893.

CLARKE, Samuel R; CIM dep. UK 2 May 1878; Chengdu, Sichuan; m. A L Fausset (qv); 1889 Guiyang; 1892 to Guizhou minority races.

COLQUHOUN, Archibald R; engineer, Indian govt.: 1881 travelled E–W, Canton to Burma, advised by J W Stevenson (qv) and J McCarthy (qv).

COOPER, T T; adventurer, Sichuan, Tibet; agent, Calcutta Chamber of Commerce; 1862 Rangoon; 1867 Shanghai; 4 Jan 1868 dep. Hankou; Kangding April 30; Tibet in Chinese clothes, forced back; 1871, author, *Travels of a Pioneer of Commerce*; proposed Yangzi-Bhamo (Irrawaddy) railway; Br. Resident, Bhamo; assassinated 24 April 1878.

COOPER, William; YMCA secretary, Gourock; CIM dep. UK 24 Nov 1880; Anqing Training Inst; Supt Anhui; China Council 1885; completed Maria (Dyer) Taylor's Romanised NT, published by BFBS 1888; m. 1887; Asst. China Director; Travelling Director; d. 1 July 1900.

COULTHARD, J J; CIM dep. UK 7 March 1879; personal secretary to JHT; Supt. Henan, 1888 m. Maria Hudson Taylor (qv).

COX, Josiah; 1852 Wesleyan MMS, Canton, joined G Piercy; 1860 invited by Taipings (by Hong Ren) to Suzhou, Nanjing, visited, disillusioned; 1862 invited by G John (qv) Hankou, began Hubei, Hunan Miss. of WMMS; 1863 first Prot. miss. to enter antagonistic Hunan; 1865 Jiujiang; 1875 invalided to UK, d. 1906.

CRANSTON, David; Shanghai merchant, Shanghai & Putong Foundry & Engineering Co.; Feb 1874 victim in Shanghai riot; friend of CIM; directed CIM HQ building developments.

CRICKMAY, Anna; CIM dep. UK Oct 1876; with Mrs JHT to Shanxi famine 1878, Taiyuan; 1 Feb 1881 m. J J Turner (qv).

DAVIES, Major H R; prospected proposed Burma–Yunnan railway; travelled widely, Dali, Batang etc.

DESGODINS, Abbé; Societé des Missions Étrangère de Paris; 1855–58 several attempts to reach W China through Tibet from Darjeeling; arr. Batang June 1860; driven from Bonga; host to Mesny (qv), Gill (qv), Jas. Cameron (qv).

DESGRAZ, Louise; Swiss governess to Wm Collingwood family, as a daughter; 1866 CIM, *Lammermuir*, Hangzhou; 1865 Yangzhou, riot; 1878 m. E Tomalin.

DETRING, Gustav; German in Imperial Maritime Customs under R Hart (qv); advised Li Hongzhang (qv), Chefoo Convention 1876; and for many years; 1885 briefly interim successor as Inspector General.

DICK, Henry; CIM dep. UK 29 Aug 1883; 1884 joined A C Dorward, Hunan pioneer.

DISRAELI, Benj (1804–81); 1st Earl of Beaconsfield; son of Isaac d'Israeli; statesman, social novelist; 1837 MP; 1868, 1874–80 Prime Minister, bought Suez Canal shares, friend of Queen Victoria, made her 'Empress of India'.

DOOLITTLE, Justus; Am. Board; 1850 Fuzhou; 1862 Tianjin, editor *Chinese Recorder*.

DORWARD, Adam C; Scottish manufacturer; Harley House under H Grattan Guinness, CIM dep. UK 2 May 1878; entered Hunan 18 Oct 1880; Supt. Hunan, Guangxi; China Council; d. 2 Oct 1888.

DOUGLAS, Carstairs, LLD (Glas.) (1830–77); English Presby. Mission; 1855 Amoy with W C Burns; Amoy vernacular dictionary; advocated occupying Taiwan; 1865 enlisted J L Maxwell (qv), with Maxwell began at Tainan; 1877 chairman General Miss. Conference, Shanghai; 1877 d. cholera.

DOUTHWAITE, Arthur Wm.; Harley House 1874; CIM dep. UK 26 Feb 1874; Zhejiang; 6 Feb 1875 m. E Doig; Qü Xian; 1882 Yantai; 1883–84 first Prot. missionary to tour Korea, distributed Scripture; 15 Oct 1890 m. Groves; 1894 Order of Double Dragon for service in Sino-Jap war; d. 5 Oct 1899. MD (USA).

DRAKE, S B; CIM dep. UK 29 Oct 1878; Shanxi famine relief; joined BMS.

DUNCAN, George; Banff, Scotland; high lander; CIM 1865; 1866, *Lammermuir*, Hangzhou; 1867 Lanxi, Nanjing, Qingjiangpu; 1868 Yangzhou; riot; 17 Sept 1868 m. Catherine Brown; 1872 UK; d. 1873; Catherine 1876 m. HBM Consul W G Stronach; d. 31 Oct 1877

DYER, Burella Hunter; b. 31 May 1835; elder daughter of Samuel Dyer Sr (qv); 1857 m. J S Burdon; d. 1858.

DYER, Samuel Sr (1804–43); Cambridge law student; 1827 LMS, m. Maria Tarn, daughter of LMS director; 1827 Penang; 1829–35 Malacca, 1835–43 Singapore; d. Macao.

DYER, Samuel Jr; b. 18 Jan. 1833, son of Samuel Sr.; brother of Maria Taylor (qv); 1877 agent of B&FBS, Shanghai, after Alex. Wylie (qv); d. 1898.

EASON, Arthur; CIM dep. UK 5 Jan 1881; 1882 pioneer, Guizhou, Yunnan; 1892 resigned to join Sal. Army.

EASTON, George F; printer; CIM, one of the Eighteen, dep. UK 21 Oct 1875; 29 Dec 1876–77 pioneer Xi'an, Shaanxi; Jan 1877 Lanzhou; with G Parker; Aug 1881 m. Caroline Gardner; 1885 Supt. Gansu, Shaanxi; China Council.

EDKINS, Joseph, (1832–1905); LMS evangelist, linguist, translator, philologist, expert in Chinese religions; 1860 visited Suzhou Taiping rulers; 1862 Nanjing; 1848–60 Shanghai; 1860–61 first to Shandong, Yantai; 1862 Tianjin, Peking; 57 years in China, 30 in Peking; 1880 retired from LMS, attached to Imperial Maritime Customs; author 1853 *Grammar Shanghai dialect*; 1857 *Mandarin*

Grammar; 1859 *The Religious Condition of the Chinese*; 1878 *Religion in China*; 1880 *Chinese Buddhism*; 1875 DD (Edin.); 1877 second wife died; *aet*. 80 survived typhoid; *aet*. 81 still writing, d. Easter Sunday.

EDWARDS, Dr Ebenezer Henry; CIM dep. UK 20 Aug 1882; Taiyuan, Shanxi; 1896 CIM Taiyuan work transferred to Shouyang Mission; 1910 Order of the Double Dragon.

ELIAS, Ney; explorer, studied new course of Yellow River; member of Col. Browne's 1874–75 Burma-Yunnan expedition; British Political Agent, Kashgar.

ELLISTON, W L; CIM dep. UK 29 Oct 1878 Shanxi; 1881 first headmaster Chefoo School; 27 Dec 1884 m. A Groom; Shanxi; d. 1887.

ELMSLIE, Dr W J; Scottish Presbyterian, CMS Kashmir dep. UK Sept 1864; May 1865 Srinigar; d. 18 Nov 1872. Biography led to H Schofield (qv) going to China.

FARTHING, John Cragg (1861–1947) Caius College undergraduate led delegation to 'Camb. Seven', Exeter Hall meeting 4 Feb 1885; bishop.

FAULDING, Joseph (William) F; father of Jane Elizabeth (Jennie) Taylor (qv) and 'Nellie' (C T) Fishe (qv).

FAUSSET, A L; CIM dep. UK 24 Jan 1878; pioneer with Eliz. Wilson (qv), Hanzhong, Shaanxi; m. S R Clarke (qv); pioneers of Guizhou aboriginal 'tribes'.

FISHE, Charles Thomas; son of Col. Fishe, Dublin; influenced by H G Guinness (qv), JHT; 1867 asst. to W T Berger (qv); 1868 CIM, Yangzhou; 1871 China Secy; m. Nellie Faulding; Financial Secretary CIM London; London Council; 1889 to China (in clipper *Lammermuir*); 17 years, administrator; China Council.

FISHE, Edward; elder son of Col. Fishe, Dublin; influenced by H G Guinness (qv), JHT; 1867 to China independently; 1868 m. A Bohannan (qv); Zhenjiang; 1877 pioneer journey to Guizhou, Guangxi; d. Guiyang 18 Sep. 1877.

FOCH, Ferdinand (1851–1929), Marshal of France; 1918 commander in chief of Allied armies, World War 1, Western front.

FORMAN, John N; Princeton Univ; Trav. Secy. Student Volunteer Movement, USA; 1887 to Britain, travelled with JHT, Scotland, Ireland, England.

FORREST, R J; 1860 HBM consular interpreter, later consul, Ningbo; Shanxi Famine Relief; consul Tianjin; chairman Famine Relief Committee; official report.

FOSTER, Arnold; LMS; 1871 Hankou; 1887–89 Secy. China Famine Relief Committee, London; d. 1919.

FOWLER, Sir Robert N, Bart. (1828–91); 1860 Treasurer Chinese Evang. Socy; 1871 MP, supported Anti-Slavery Socy; 1880 MP for City of London; 1883 Lord Mayor, re-elected 1885; July 1885 baronet; d. 22 May 1890.

FRENCH, Evangeline (1871–1961); CIM dep. UK 1 Sep 93; Huzhou, Shanxi; leader of 'the Trio' with Francesca French and Mildred Cable (qv); 1923 to Xinjiang till 1936; d. 1961 aged 90.

FRENCH, Francesca (1873–1961); CIM Shanxi (*see* Evangeline); d. 3 weeks after Eva.

FROST, Henry Weston; 1876–79 Princeton; civil engineer; 1885 read *China's Spiritual Need and Claims* and *A Cambridge Band*; influenced by J Goforth; 1887 London, met JHT; 1888 JHT to N. Am.; HWF secy., 1889 secy, treasurer, N. Am. Council; 1893 Home Director.

FULTON, A A and sister, M D; Am. Presby. Mission (North); 1885 pioneers in Guangxi; expelled from Guiping.

GARDNER, Christopher T; 1867 HBM consular interpreter, Ningbo; 1870 consul Zhenjiang; Yantai.

GARNIER, Lieut. Francis; 1868 French Yunnan expedition from Tongking; Jan 30 dep. Dongchuan via Huili to Dali; forced back; 1871 defence of Paris; killed in Franco-Chinese war, Tongking.

GILL, Lieut. Wm J Royal Engineers; 10 July 1877 dep. Chengdu; Batang Aug. 25; Dali Sep. 27; Bhamo Nov 1; author *River of Golden Sand*; R Geog. Soc. medal; promoted Captain.

GILMOUR, James (1843–91); LMS Mongolia; May 1870 arr. Peking; Kalgan; Kiahkta (Outer Mongolia); d. typhus, Tianjin.

GLADSTONE, Wm Ewart (1809–98); 1832 MP; Liberal PM 1868–74, 1880–85; 1892–94.

GOFORTH, Jonathan (1859–1936); Canadian Presby. Church; applied to join CIM 1885, 1888, 1911; advised to stay with own Church; 1888 arr. China; pioneer in Henan; Changde 1895; 1908 led great revival, Manchuria.

GOODRICH, Chauncey; American Board; Zhangjiakou (Kalgan); m. 30 May, 1878, widowed 3 Sep; Bible translator, Union Version with Mateer and Baller (qv); 1872 hymnbook with Blodget (qv).

GORDON, Maj. Gen. Charles George (1833–85); 1860 Tianjin, Peking campaign; 1862 Shanghai, commanding Ever-Victorious Army; 1864 Taiping Rebellion ended; emperor awarded Order of the Imperial Dragon, and Queen Victoria the CB; 1873 Gov. Equatorial Egypt; 1877–80 Gov. Sudan; 1880 Peking to advise govt.; 1884 Sudan, Mahdi rebellion, major-general; killed in Khartoum siege.

GOUGH, Frederick Foster, DD; CMS 1849–61 Ningbo; Mary, first wife, d. 1861; 1862–69 London, Ningbo vernacular romanised NT revision with JHT; 1866 m. Mary Jones (qv); 1869 Ningbo; founded Camb. Univ. Prayer Union; Bible translator-reviser; 34 years in CMS, Zhejiang.

GRAY, Jeanie Isabella, Newton Stewart, Scotland, b. 31 March 1863; CIM dep. UK 22 Oct 1884; one of the Seventy; Guangxin R. pioneer, Yüshan; 1 Nov. 1886 m. Herbert H Taylor (qv); Henan; d. 15 Jan 1937; grandmother of James Hudson Taylor III, CIM General Director, 1980– .

GRIERSON, Robert; dep. UK 4 Nov 1885; Jinhua, Wenzhou, Zhejiang.

GROSVENOR, Hon. T G; led expedition with E C Baber (qv), A Davenport after Margary (qv) murder; dep. Hankou 5 Nov 1875; via Zhaotong, Kunming 6 March 1876; Bhamo 21 May 1876.

GUINNESS, Dr Harry; eldest son of H Grattan Guinness (qv); principal, Harley College.

GUINNESS, Henry Grattan DD, FRAS (1835–1910); 1855 left New Coll. Lond. to become great evangelist of Evangelical Awakening; 1859 Ulster revival, drew thousands; 1865 offered to CIM, JHT advised continue UK; became JHT's friend; 1872 CIM Referee; 1873 founded East London Miss. Training Institute (Harley College); trained 1,330 for 40 societies of 30 denominations; 1877 Livingstone Inland Mission; 1888 Congo-Balolo Mission; 1898 initiated RBMU; NAM founded on his advice; greatly influenced Barnardo, John R Mott; author, astronomy, eschatology; 7 children, grandchildren in Christian ministry.

GUINNESS, Mary Geraldine (1862–1949) b. 25 Dec 1862; CIM dep. UK 26 Jan 1888; 24 April 1894 m. F Howard Taylor (qv); author (*see* Bibliog.); d. 6 June 1949; biography, *Her Web of Time* by Joy Guinness CIM 1949.

GULICK, John T; Am. Board; 1865 first missionary to Kalgan; evangelism with wife in Mongolia; ill, moved to Japan.

GULICK, H; Am Bible Society agent, 1876.

GUTZLAFF, Charles (Karl Friedrich Augustus) (1803–51); D D Groningen 1850;

1826–28 Netherlands Miss. Soc., Batavia (Jakarta), Java; 1828 independent, Bangkok; 1829 m. Miss Newell, Malacca, first single Prot. woman missionary to E. Asia d. 1831; 1831–35 voyages up China coast; 1834 m. Miss Warnstall d. 1849; 1839 interpreter to British; 1840, 1842 governor of Chusan Is.; 1842 interpreter-negotiator, Nanking Treaty; 1843–51 Chinese Sec. to British govt. Hong Kong; initiated Chinese Union, Chinese Associations and missions.

HAIG, Maj. Gen. F T; active Christian in Indian army; 1881 served in CMS Godavari Mission; CMS committee; Eastern surveys; friend of CIM.

HALL, William Nelthorpe; Methodist New Connexion; 1860 Shanghai; 1861 April Tianjin; 14 May 1878 d. famine fever.

HANNINGTON, Bishop James; Oxford; 1882 CMS dep. UK; 1884 first bishop, Eastern Equatorial Africa; 29 Oct 1885 murdered on Mwanga's orders; death roused 'the whole Church'; *Memoirs* inspired thousands; Hannington Hall, Oxford, counterpart of Henry Martin Hall, Cambridge.

HAPPER, Andrew P, DD; Am. Presby.; 1844–46 Macao (debarred from Canton); 1847 Canton; 1887 first president Canton Christian Coll.

HART, Sir Robert (1835–1911); b. 20 Feb 1835; 1854 consular interpreter, Ningbo; 1857 Canton; Nov. 1862 Inspector-General, Chinese Imperial Maritime Customs; 1865 Peking; 1864 3rd class mandarin; 1869 2nd class; 1881 1st class; 1885 Peacock's Feather; 1889 1st class of 1st Order for 3 generations; 1901 Junior Guardian of the Heir Apparent; 1911 posthumous Senior Guardian; CMG, 1882 KCMG, 1889 GCMG; 1st Baronet 1893; 1885 succeeded Sir Harry Parkes as Br. Minister, Peking; resigned to resume IG; 1900 40-year diary and house burned by Boxers; 1 May 1906 resigned, but Emeritus IG until death.

HARVEY, Thomas P; 1866 med. student with T J Barnardo, London Hospital; CIM dep. UK 14 July 1869; Nanjing; 1872 Lond. Hosp. graduated; 1876 Bhamo, Burma; shipwrecked; resigned.

HEDIN, Sven; Swedish archaeologist, explorer; studied under von Richtofen; 1894 Tashkent to Kashgar; 1895 crossed Taklamahan Desert; 1899–1902 explored Tarim Basin.

HILL, David (1840–96); 1865 WMMS, Hankou (independent means); 1878–80 with J J Turner (qv) CIM, to Shanxi famine relief; 1879 means of conversion of 'Pastor Hsi' (qv); Wusue; founded houses for aged, blind, orphans; fought opium trade; started a hospital; 1890 co-chairman with J L Nevius General Missionary Conference, Shanghai; d. 1896 aged 56, typhus from famine relief.

HILL, Richard Harris, FRIBA; civil engineer, evangelist; helped build Mildmay Miss. Hosp., CIM Newington Green; m. Agnes, daughter of Henry W Soltau (qv); 1872 Hon. Sec. London CIM.

HILLIER, Sir Walter Caine, KCMG, CB; 1910 Order of the Double Dragon; HBM Consul; China Famine Relief Committee, Tianjin; surveyed famine areas; adviser to Chinese Foreign Office.

HOGG, Charles F; CIM dep. UK 21 May 1884; pioneer in Shaanxi; 1887 expelled from Xi'an.

HOLMES, J L; Am. Southern Baptist; 1860 pioneer of Shandong, Yantai (Chefoo); Oct. 1861 killed with H M Parker (qv).

HOPKINS, Evan H (1837–1919) 1874 met American Pearsall Smith, 'Higher Christian Life' conference, Oxford; 1875 with Canon Battersby, G R Thornton, H W Webb-Peploe at Keswick for embryo Keswick Convention meetings: 1883 Cambridge convention on Keswick lines; 1884 published *Law of Liberty in the Spiritual Life*; 1886 joined by Handley Moule (qv).

HORNE, Celia; CIM dep. UK Oct 1876; 1878 Shanxi famine relief with J E Taylor (qv) one of the first women to go deep inland.

HOSTE, Dixon Edward (1861–1946) b. 23 July 1861, son of Major-Gen. D E Hoste, RA; Clifton College and Royal Military Academy, Woolwich; 1882 Lieut. R.A.; 1882, converted at D L Moody meetings; 23 July 1883, approached JHT; met Council Feb 1884, accepted 7 Oct 1884; 'Camb. Seven', dep. UK 5 Feb 1885; Shanxi 1885–96 colleague of Hsi Shengmo (qv); 1896 sick leave Australia; Supt. Henan; China Council; 1900 assistant to J W Stevenson; Jan 1901 Acting GD; Nov 1902 General Director; 7 Sep 1894 m. Amelia Gertrude Broomhall (qv); three sons; d. 11 May 1946.

HOSTE, William; brother of D E Hoste, Trinity Coll. and Ridley Hall, Cambridge; persuaded D E Hoste to hear Moody.

HOUGHTON, Frank; b. 4 April 1894, CIM dep. UK 10 Nov 1920; Sichuan; 1923 m. Dorothy Cassels, dtr of WWC; 1926–36 editorial secretary, London; 25 Jan 1937 consecrated bishop, East Sichuan; 21 Oct 1940 General Director; 1951–72 Consulting Director; d. 25 Jan 1972.

HOWARD, John Eliot (1807–83); quinologist, 1874 FRS, Fellow of Linnaean Soc.; manufacturing chemist; early leader of Brethren, Tottenham; member of B&FBS committee and CES Board; JHT's close friend and supporter; 1872 CIM Referee.

HOWARD, Mrs Robert; wife of J E H's brother, Tottenham; intimate friend and supporter of JHT, Maria and JET from first acquaintance.

HOWARD, Theodore; son of Robert, nephew of J E Howard (qv), 1872 CIM Lond. Council; Director, Howard Brothers, quinologists, manufacturing chemists; 1875 Council Chairman; 1879 first Home Director CIM UK.

HUBERTY, Marie S; Belgian, CIM dep. UK Oct. 1876; 1878 Shansi famine relief; Sep 1878 m. Francis James (qv) who adopted her name.

HUGHES, Katherine; CIM dep. UK Oct 1876; 1878 Shanxi famine relief; m. Dr W L Pruen; Chengdu, Sichuan; Guiyang, Guizhou.

JACKSON, Josiah A; CIM dep. UK 26 May 1866, *Lammermuir*; Zhejiang; 1873 m. (1) F Wilson d. 1878; (2) 20 Sep 1882, d. July 1883; dep. China; Aug 1884 left CIM; returned Shanghai, secular; d. 1906.

JAMES, Francis Huberty, b. June 1851; CIM, one of the Eighteen, dep. UK 1876; 1877–79 Shanxi famine relief; Sep 1878 m. Marie S Huberty, Belgian; 1881 to UK; 1883 BMS, Shandong, Qingzhou, Jinan; 1890 paper on Chinese secret sects, Shanghai General Conference; 1892 resigned from BMS; Europe and USA, 1895 Lowell lectureship, Boston, following Prof. Henry Drummond; 1897 Imperial Arsenal, Shanghai; 1898 Imperial Univ., Peking; 1900 with Dr Morrison rescued 2000 Chinese Christians, protected by Br. legation forces; 20 June 1900 reported beheaded on Yong Lu's (qv) orders.

JAMES, Thomas; CIM dep. UK 15 Jan 1885; April 1885 Hunan with Dorward (qv) and Dick (qv); Sichuan; m. F (Stroud) Riley (qv).

JOHN, Griffith (1831–1912); LMS; 1855 Shanghai; pioneer evangelist; 1861 Hankou; 1863 Wuchang; 1867 Hanyang; 1888 declined chairmanship, Congregational Union of Eng. and Wales; 1889 Hon. DD (Edin.); 24 Sep, 1905 jubilee in China; April 1906 retired ill. Author, many publications in Chinese. Translator, NT into 'Easy' and OT (part) into colloquial Mandarin, commissioned by B&FBS, NBSS.

JONES, Hannah; CIM dep. UK 16 Feb 1881; 1882 Gansu; 1885 m. W E Burnett.

JONES, John; CES; 1856–57 Ningbo; independent, 1857–63; early exponent of 'faith principle', influenced JHT; d. 1863.

JONES, Ann Maria (Mary); wife of John; 1863–66 with Hudson Taylors, London; 1866 m. F F Gough; 1869 Ningbo; 1869–71 fostered Chas Edw. Taylor; d. Nov 1877.

JUDD, Charles H Sr (1842–1919); 1867 CIM through influence of T J Barnardo; 1868 Yangzhou; 1869 Zhenjiang; 1872–73 UK; 1874 Wuchang, with JHT; 1875 with 'Yao' (qv) and 'Zhang' (qv) rented house at Yueyang (Yochow), Hunan, forced out; 1877 with J F Broumton via Hunan to Guiyang, Guizhou; Broumton settled, Judd via Chongqing to Wuchang; 1879 built at Yantai before school and sanatorium.

KENNAWAY, Sir John H, Bart.; son of first baronet; 1872 MP, anti-slave trade; 1887 President CMS; 1893 coined phrase 'Ask the Lord and tell His people'; 1897 Privy Council.

KERR, Charlotte, nurse; CIM dep. UK 15 April 1880; 1881 pioneer Guiyang; later Shanxi, Shouyang Mission.

KERR, Dr John G, MD; Am. Presby. Mission (North); 1854 Canton; trained 200 Chinese medical students; translated many medical books; performed 480,000 surgical operations; founded the Asylum for the Insane; d. Canton 1901

KIDD, Jane; CIM dep. UK 26 Dec 1878; 1880 first unmarried Western woman into far western provs. of China; Feb 19–April 20, journey to Guiyang; Oct 1882 m. J H Riley (qv); d. 12 Oct 1886.

KING, George; CIM dep. UK 15 May 1875, aged 18; one of the Eighteen, arr. Shanghai 14 July after shipwreck; pioneer, Shaanxi, Gansu, Henan; m. (1) E Snow (d. Hanzhong 10 May 1881); (2) Harriet Black; qualified physician.

KRAPF, Johann Ludwig (1810–81), German; linguist; 1836 CMS to Ethiopia; 1844 Mombasa; 1849 first Westerner to see Mt Kenya; 1853 broken health, Europe; author.

LANCASTER, Agnes; CIM dep. UK 14 Nov 1880; Shanxi famine relief; 1886 m. G W Clarke (qv); Guihuacheng, Mongolian border; d. 8 Aug 1892.

LANCHLAN, H N, barrister; CIM dep. UK 29 Nov 1888 aged 31; Guizhou, Yunnan, Chongqing; Principal, Anqing Training Inst. after Baller (qv); 29 Oct 1892 m. Katherine Mackintosh (qv); dtr H Evelyn m. D. de B Robertson, CIM architect; d. 18 April 1896.

LANDALE, Robert J; MA Oxford Univ.; dep. UK 1876, independent; joined CIM 1878; one of the Eighteen; pioneer in Hunan, Guizhou, Guangxi, Henan, Shanxi; associated with 'Camb. Seven'; 1881 m. Mary Jones, step-dtr of F F Gough (qv); 19 Jan 1882 widowed.

LANSDELL, Dr Henry, DD, FRGS, traveller in Bokhara, Samarkand; attempts on Tibet supported by Am. Bible Socy. and JHT, with G Parker (qv) foiled; may have reached Xinjiang, colportage with Parker.

LATOURETTE, Kenneth Scott; late Willis James and Sterling Prof. of Missions and Oriental History, Yale Univ.; author (*see* Bibliography).

LECHLER, Rudolf (1824–1908); Basel Mission pioneer; 1847 Hong Kong, Guangdong (Kwangtung) Hakkas, under Gutzlaff, with Hamberg (qv); 52 years in China, to 1899.

LEES, Jonathan; LMS; 1862 Tianjin, many years; 1869 pioneer visit to Shanxi; d 1902.

LEGGE, James, DD, LLD (1815–97); LMS; 1835 MA (Aberdeen), Congregational; 1839–43 Anglo-Chinese College, Malacca; 1843–70 Anglo-Chinese College, Hong Kong; 1861–86 translator, Chinese classics; 1875 Fellow, Corpus Christi, Oxford; 1877–97, first Prof. of Chinese, Oxford Univ.

LITTLE, Alicia Bewicke; author, *Li Hung-chang, His Life and Times*, 1903; wife of Archibald Little, British Legation official, Peking.

LIVINGSTONE, Dr David; (1813–73) Scotsman; Charing Cross Hospital 2 years; LMS Botswana; 1841–52 with Moffat, m. Mary Moffat; travelled through Bechuanaland, Kalahari Desert; 1849 found Lake Ngami; 1851 Zambesi R; 1852–56 major travels, Angola, W coast; W–E to mouth of Zambesi 20 May 1856; 1855 Victoria Falls; 1857 challenge at Cambridge; 1858–63 consul, led expedition Nyasaland; opened way for Church of Scotland and Universities' Mission; Tanganyika, Nyasaland (Malawi), Congo; 1859 Lake Malawi, 1866 search for source of Nile; 1871 met by H M Stanley (qv); 1871–73 Zambia; d. 1 May 1873; buried Westminster Abbey 18 April 1874. Exposed slave trade; awakened Church to Africa and world mission.

LOCKHART, William (1811–96); surgeon, FRCS; LMS; 1839 Macao; 1840 and 1843 Shanghai; 1840–41 Chusan with Gutzlaff, first British missionary Hong Kong; 1848 mobbed in 'Qingpu (Tsingpu) Outrage', Shanghai; 1861 first Prot. missionary in Peking; 1864 to UK; 1867 retired from LMS; surgeon, Blackheath.

LORD, Edward Clifford, DD (1817–87); ABMU; 1847 first Am. Baptist to Ningbo; 1853 NT Baptist version, with Dean and Goddard; 1863 independent Am. Bapt. Mission, Ningbo; 1887 still there; appointed US consul by Abraham Lincoln; JHT's friend; d. with wife, of cholera, 17 Sept 1887.

LYMAN, Henry; Am. Board, Sumatra; 1834 killed with Samuel Munson by cannibal Bataks, Lake Toba.

MACARTNEY, Sir Samuel Halliday, MD (1833–1906); related to Lord Macartney, ambassador to China 1792–93; in Ever-Victorious Army under Burgevine; appointed by Li Hongzhang (qv), director Imperial Arsenal, Nanjing, 1865–75; 1877 Secy. to Chinese Embassy, London, 30 years till Dec 1905, adviser to all Chinese ambassadors; 2nd degree mandarin, with Peacock's Feather; 1885 KCMG; m. a Chinese; son, consul-general Kashgar.

MACGOWAN, Dr D J, MD; Am. Bapt.; 1843 Ningbo.

MACKAY, George Leslie (1844–1901); first Canadian Presby. missionary to China; 1872 N Taiwan; 60 churches at his death; founded Taiwan Theol. Coll.: 1894 Moderator, Can. Presby. Church.

MACKENZIE, Dr John Kenneth; LMS 1875, Hankou, Tianjin; saved life of viceroy Li Hongzhang's wife; 1880 built hospital, trained doctors, sponsored by Li; 1882 to UK; d. 1888.

MACKINTOSH, Katherine B; CIM dep. UK 22 Oct 1884; one of the Seventy; Guangxin R pioneer, Yüshan; 29 Oct 1892 m. H N Lachlan (qv); mother of H B (Anuei) Lachlan who m. D de B Robertson, CIM architect.

MACPHERSON, Miss Annie; mid-19th-century schoolteacher, social reformer, evangelist; 'ragged schools'; organised emigration to Canada; firm friend of CIM.

MARGARY, Augustus Raymond; b. 1845; HBM consul Yantai; 1874 as interpreter to Col. Browne's Burma-Yunnan expedition, dep Shanghai 22 Aug 1874, via Hunan, arr. Bhamo 17 Jan 1875; murdered 21 Feb at Manyün.

MARKWICK, J; CIM dep. UK 7 March 1878; Shaanxi famine relief rejected, but 1880 eyesight failed from privations.

MARTIN, William Alexander Parsons, DD, LL D (1827–1916); Am. Presby. Mission; educationalist; 1850–60 Ningbo; 1858 with S Wells Williams (qv) interpreter, Am. treaty; 1862 Peking; 1869 president, Tongwen Imperial College; 57 years in China; book on Christian evidences had huge circulation, China, Japan.

MARTYN, Henry (1781–1812); Fellow of St John's Coll., Cambridge; inspired by

Chas. Simeon; ordained 1805; chaplain, East India Company, Calcutta, translated Urdu NT; worked on Persian, Arabic NTs; d. 10 October 1812 in Asia Minor.

MATEER, Calvin Wilson, DD (1836–1908) Am. Presby.; 1862 Dengzhou, later Yantai, Shandong; founded Shandong Christian Univ.; author *Mandarin Lessons*; opposed Nevius' methods; chairman, translation committee, Union Mandarin Version of Bible with Baller, Blodget, Nevius *et al*.

MATHESON, Donald; merchant partner, Jardine, Matheson; 1837 converted at Hong Kong; 1849 resigned over opium traffic; active in Presby. Missions; 1892 chairman, Soc. for the Suppression of the Opium Trade.

MATHIESON, James E; noted evangelist; director, Mildmay Conference Centre; with Grattan Guinness, Reginald Radcliffe promoted missions.

MAXWELL, James Laidlow, MD (b. 1836); English Presby. Mission; 1863 Amoy; 1865 Taiwan pioneer, Tainan, Dagao; 1871 invalided to UK, 8 years on his back; publ. vernacular NT; 1883 Taiwan again; 1885 founded Medical Missionary Association (London), Secy; 1888 co-founder with B Broomhall (qv), 'Christian Union for the Severance of the Connection of the British Empire with the Opium Traffic'.

McCARTEE, Divie Bethune, MD (1820–1900); Am. Presby.; 1844 Ningbo 28 years; 1845 organised first Prot. church on Chinese soil; 1851 extended work beyond treaty ports; 1853 m. Juana Knight, first single Presby. woman to China; adopted Yu Meiying, orphaned daughter of pastor as own daughter, first Chinese woman doctor educated abroad, returned as missionary to China; 1861 met Taiping leaders, Nanjing, negotiated protection Am. citizens, Chinese Christians; Dec 1861–April 1862 earliest Prot. miss. in Japan; McC's tract translated into Japanese was first Prot. lit. in Japan; 1862–5 Shandong, Yantai; 1864 Ningbo again; 1872 Japan with Chinese envoy negotiated release of coolie prisoners on *Maria Luz* (Macao-Peru), received gold medal; 1872–77 Prof. of law and natural science, Tokyo Univ; 1877 secy. foreign affairs to Chinese legation, Japan; 1880 USA; 1889 Presby. Miss. again, Tokyo; good scholar in Greek, Chinese, Japanese; 1899 invalided USA; d. 17 July, 1900 (*Chinese Recorder* 1902 Vol 33 p 497f).

McCARTHY, Frank, John's eldest; CIM dep. UK 31 Dec 1886; 1 March 1887 Chefoo School staff under H L Norris (qv), promoted morale, discipline; 20 Oct 1893 m. E Webb; March 1895–1930, Principal, 'did more than any for the schools.'

McCARTHY, John; Dublin, member H G Guinness (qv) training class; Feb 1866 influenced by JHT; 1866 CIM; 1867 Hangzhou; 1877 Jan–Aug Hankou to Bhamo, Burma on foot; 1886–91 Supt. Jiangxi, Jiangsu (Guangxin R and Yangzhou language school); influential speaker UK, USA.

McCARTHY, William; Dublin, John's brother; with wife dep. UK 7 March 1879; died heatstroke; widow married J F Broumton, Jan 1881.

McILVAINE, Jasper S; Am. Presby; 1868 arr. China; 1872 Jinan, Shandong; 1877 famine relief; 1878 Jincheng, Shanxi, famine relief.

McINTYRE, J; United Presby. Ch. of Scotland; 1874 forced back before reaching Kaifeng.

MEADOWS, James J (1835–1914); JHT's first recruit to Ningbo Mission, 1862, and CIM; wife Martha d. Ningbo 1863; 1866 m. Eliz. Rose (qv); 1868 began pioneering; 1869 Anqing; 1874 Shaoxing, 40 years; 1882 Supt. Zhejiang; China Council; 52 years' service.

MEDHURST, Sir Walter Henry, son of W H Medhurst DD (qv); HBM consul, and ambassador, Peking.

MEDHURST, Walter Henry, DD; (1796–1857); LMS printer; 1817–20 Malacca; 1820–21 Penang; 1822–43 Batavia, Java; 1826 toured Chinese settlements on Java coast; 1835 voyage of *Huron* up China coast; 1843 Shanghai, interpreter-adviser to Br. consul G Balfour (qv); 1845 inland journey in disguise; 1848 victim of 'Qingpu (Tsingpu) Outrage', Shanghai; translator, Delegates' Committee, 1852 Chinese Bible; doyen of Br. community.

MESNY, William (1842–1919) Jersey, Channel Is.; arr. China 1860; officer in Chinese army suppressed Miao rebellion; high rank in command Guiyang arsenal; with Gill (qv) travelled Chengdu, Batang, Dali, Bhamo; 1896 equiv. Brevet-Lt. Gen. under Zuo Zongtang in campaign to suppress Yakub Beg (qv), Kashgar.

MEYER, F B (1847–1929) Baptist minister York; Leicester; Regents Park Chapel, Lond.; Christ Church, Westminster; profilic writer; Keswick Council.

MOODY, Dwight Lyman (1837–99); 19th century's greatest evangelist; 1873–75 first Br. mission; 1882 Cambridge Univ. mission stimulated 'Cambridge Seven'; 1886 first Northfield student conference gave impetus to Student Volunteer Movement.

MOORE, C G; CIM dep. UK 24 Jan 1878; UK staff.

MORSE, Hosea Ballou; Imperial Chinese Customs, Taiwan; commissioner Hankou; historian, author (*see* Bibliog).

MOTT, John Raleigh (1865–1955); 1886 challenged by J E K Studd (qv); joined SVM; 1888 YMCA; chairman SVM.

MOULE, Arthur Evans; brother of G E and H C G Moule; CMS 1861, Ningbo; 1876 Hangzhou; archdeacon.

MOULE, George Evans (b. 1828); CMS 1858, Ningbo; 1864 Hangzhou; 1880 bishop in mid-China; 50 years' service.

MOULE, Handley Carr Glyn (1841–1920); 1880–99 Principal, Ridley Hall, Camb; Bishop of Durham 1901–20; author; Keswick Council.

MTESA, King of Uganda, visited by Speke, Grant, Stanley; invited CMS; sent envoys to Q. Victoria; d. 10 Oct 1884.

MUIRHEAD, William, DD (1822–1900); LMS; evangelist, renowned preacher, translator, like a son to W H Medhurst; 'a gigantic worker'; 1846–90 (53 years) at Shanghai; 1848 victim of 'Qingpu (Tsingpu) Outrage', Shanghai; 1877–79 organised famine relief funds; warm friend of JHT, CIM; 'passionately fond of children'. (*Chinese Recorder* 1900 Vol. 31 pp 384, 625; 1902 Vol. 32 pp 1, 42).

MÜLLER, George; (1805–98); German-born; converted aged 25 through LMS speaker; trained in London for mission to Jews; 1830 Teignmouth, pastor; m. sister of A N Groves; 1832 read biography of A H Francke; 1832 with Craik to Bristol; 1834 founded Scriptural Knowledge Institution for Home and Abroad; 1835 founded Orphan Homes, Bristol, on Francke's principle of trusting God to provide; 2000 children; 1872 CIM Referee, visited China; d. 10 March 1898.

MURRAY Sisters, Cecilia, Mariamne; CIM dep. UK 22 Oct 1884; in charge Yangzhou language school.

MURRAY, Jessie; CIM dep. UK Oct 1876; d. 22 Dec 1891.

MUNSON, Samuel; Am. Board; 1834 with H Lyman to Lake Toba Bataks, Sumatra; 1834 'killed and eaten'.

MWANGA, son of Mtesa; king, brutally persecuted Christians; had Bishop Hannington killed 29 Oct 1885.

NEILL, Stephen C; b. 31 Dec 1899; Dean Close; 1924 Fellow of Trinity College Cambridge, 1924 India; Bishop of Tinnevelly (120,000 Anglicans); member Joint

Committee, result Church of S. India; 1944 invalided Europe; author; 1962 Prof. of Missions and Ecumenical Theology, Univ. of Hamburg; Ridley Hall, Oxford; d.

NELSON, R, DD; Am. Prot. Episc. Church; arr. Shanghai 1851; 1870 translator, Shanghai colloquial NT; co-chairman Gen. Miss. Conf., Shanghai 1877.

NEVIUS, John Livingston (1832–93); Am. Presby. Mission; 1854 Ningbo; 1859 Hangzhou; 1860 Japan; 1861 Shandong (Shantung); 1864 UK, USA; 1867 DD; 1869 Shandong, Denglai; Bible translator, author; 1890 Moderator; co-chairman, Shanghai Miss. Conf.; 1886–87 exponent of 'indigenous church' policy, Korea 1890.

NICOLL, George; CIM, one of the Eighteen, dep. UK 4 Aug 1875; Dec 1876 Yichang riot; May 1877 Sichuan, circled Daliangshan; 1879 m. M A Howland; 1880–81 Chongqing; ill, Australia, N Zealand.

NOMMENSEN, Ludwig Ingwer (1834–1918); Schleswig-Holstein (Danish then); 1862 Rhenish Mission, Sumatra; 1876 L Toba; indigenous principles successful: by 1876, 2,000 Christians; 1914 nearly 1 million.

NORRIS, Herbert L; CIM dep. UK 28 Jan 1885; headmaster Chefoo School; d. rabies 27 Sept 1888.

ORR EWING, Archibald; b. 1 Aug 1857; 4th of 7 brothers, heirs to uncle's fortune, nearly £500,000; litigation settled by Law Lords July 1885; 1880–81 toured China coast; 1882 Moody Mission in Glasgow, dedication to Christ; invited J McCarthy; 6 April 1884 committed to China, 1885 with W B Sloan at Keswick commitment confirmed; CIM dep. UK 21 April 1886; 17 July 1886 officially joined CIM after Shanxi conference; 4 years Shanxi; walked 50 miles daily on trek; 6 May 1890 m. Mary Scott (of Morgan and Scott); 1891 Supt. Jiangxi 20 years.

PARKER, George; CIM, one of the Eighteen, dep. UK 5 April 1876; Nov 8 with Easton (qv) dep. Wuhan to Shaanxi, Gansu; Dec 20–24 Xi'an; 20 Jan 1877 Lanzhou; 1878 forced out of Xi'an; worked Han R by boat; 1879 Chongqing, engaged to Shao Mianzi (qv); Sept–Oct, Gansu with Easton; 25 Feb 1880 m. Shao Mianzi; to Hanzhong and Gansu; 1882 Tibet border; 1887–89 Xinjiang with Lansdell (qv); 1905 G Hunter of Urumqi reported evidence of Parker-Lansdell colportage found; d. 1931 doyen of CIM.

PARKER, Dr Peter, MD (1804–88); Am. Board (ABCFM); 1834 Canton; first medical missionary in China (not first Western physician); 1835 Ophthalmic Hospital after T R Colledge; 1838 formed 'Medical Missionary Soc. in China'; 1838, 1843–44, semi-skilled interpreter-negotiator for US treaty; 1850 General Hosp., Canton; several times US chargé d'affaires and minister.

PARKES, Sir Harry Smith (1828–85); cousin m. C Gutzlaff (qv); 1841 sister m. Wm. Lockhart (qv); 1841 Macao; 1842 asst. to J R Morrison (qv); 21 July 1842 with Sir H Pottinger at assault on Zhenjiang, *aet.* 14; present at signing of Treaty of Nanking; 1842–43 Zhoushan (Chusan) Is. with Gutzlaff; 1843 Canton consular asst.; 1845 Fuzhou, interpreter with R Alcock (qv); August 1846 Shanghai with Alcock; 1852–54 Canton; 1853 author Parl. Paper No. 263 on *Emigration* (Coolie Trade); concluded first Br. treaty with Siam for Sir John Bowring; 1856 vice-consul Canton; Oct, *Arrow* incident; 1858–60 Br. Commissioner, Canton; 1861 Hankou Feb–Apr with Adm. Sir Jas Hope; 20 May, 1862 KCB knighthood *aet.* 34; intimate friend of Col Gordon; strongly opposed by Li Hongzhang (qv); 1865 Br. minister, Japan, 'won the most signal victory Br. diplomacy ever gained in the Far East' (Dickens, F V: *Life of Parkes*, II.44); 1871 UK; 1872–79 Japan; 1879–82 UK received KCMG, to Japan; 1883 Br. minister Peking, after Sir Thos Wade; 1883 treaty with Korea opened ports; d. 22 March, 1885 'Peking fever'. (*Dicty. of Nat. Biog*. Vol XV; H B Morse).

PARROTT, A G; CIM dep. UK 29 Oct 1878; pioneered western hill cities of Shanxi; JHT's 'corresponding secretary'; Nov 1881 Wuchang Conference call for 'the Seventy'; 21 Dec 1882 m. Annie M Hayward.

PARRY, Dr Herbert, CIM dep. UK 24 Sept 1884; Chengdu, Sichuan.

PATON, John G (1824–1907) LMS; 1858–62 Tauna, New Hebrides, untenable; Aniwa, population turned Christian.

PATTESON, John Coleridge; 1861 1st bishop of Melanesia; 1871, killed.

PEARSE, Edward S; CIM, one of the Eighteen dep. UK 26 Jan 1876, m. 18 Dec 1877 L E Goodman; 1879 Anhui pioneer; ubiquitous, 1886–87 Shaanxi, Sichuan.

PIERSON, A T, DD; New York evangelist, Bible teacher; friend of JHT; 1886 with Moody held student conference for SVM (newly founded); 1888 at Centenary Conf. of Prot. Missions, Lond.; 1896 chief speaker, SVMU Liverpool Conference.

PIGOTT, Thomas W; CIM dep. UK 9 Mar 1789; Shanxi pioneer; m. Kemp 16 July 1883; resigned.

POLHILL-TURNER, Arthur Twistleton; 3rd son, Capt. F C Polhill, 6th Dragoon Guards; MP, JP, High Sheriff, Bedfordshire; 'Camb. Seven'; CIM dep. UK 5 Feb 1885; Hanzhong; Bazhong, Sichuan; ordained Anglican.

POLHILL-TURNER, Cecil Henry; 2nd son Capt. F C Polhill (see above); dep. UK 5 Feb 1885; Hanzhong; Xining, Gansu; Songpan, Sichuan; Darjeeling; Kangding, Sichuan.

POLO, Marco (1245–1324); son of Nicolo; 1275 Peking, served Kublai Khan; *aet*. 30 gov. of Yangzhou; official journeys of SW China, Burma, Indo-China, India; 1292 with Nicolo and Matteo escorted royal princess to Persia; to Venice; 1298 in war with Genoa, imprisoned, dictated travels.

POLWARTH, Baron Walter Hugh Hepburne Scott (1838–); friend of JHT and CIM.

PRUEN, Dr W L; LRCP, LRCS Edin.; CIM dep. UK 30 Nov 1879; Chefoo, Chongqing, Chengdu; Guiyang; m. K Hughes; Shanxi; author, *The Provinces of Western China*.

RADCLIFFE, Reginald; leading UK evangelist; 1860 initiated theatre services, Lond; the first in Victoria Theatre, Lambeth, denounced as travesty of religious worship, even illegal; 24 Feb 1860 defended in House of Lords 3-hour speech by Lord Shaftesbury describing the poor and common folk who flocked to hear Radcliffe; leading part in evangelical revival following 1858 US revival; devoted last active years to advocating worldwide evangelism, 'Consecration and the Evangelisation of the World ought to go together'; 1886–87 secured use of Keswick Convention tents for missionary use, JHT as speaker, 1887; travelled and preached in USA and Canada with JHT, 1888.

RADSTOCK, Lord; Hon Granville Augustus Wm Waldegrave (1833–1913); 3rd Baron; converted at Crimean War; raised, commanded W. Middlesex Rifles for 6 years; evangelical Anglican evangelist in aristocratic Russian, E. European society; closely associated with Brethren; friend of JHT and CIM; 1872 CIM Referee.

RANDLE, Horace A; CIM, one of the Eighteen dep. UK 5 April 1876, Jiangxi pioneer; qualified MD (USA).

RICHARD, Timothy (1845–1919); converted in Evang. Awakening 1859–60, Wales; offered services to JHT, referred to BMS; 1870 Shandong; 1875 sole survivor of twelve; 1876–79 Shandong, Shanxi famine relief; educationalist, views changed, left BMS, founded Univ. of Shanxi, Taiyuan (8 years), 1891 Soc. for

Diffusion of Chr. & Gen. Knowledge; 1906 Christian Literature Soc.; his policies to Christianise China akin to the techniques of Ricci (qv); adviser to emperor, Chinese govt. and Kong Yuwei; translated *History of the Nineteenth Century* (1 mill. copies); 1885 proposed a Christian college in every prov. capital; 1901 with Boxer indemnity funds founded Taiyuan Univ. College; received two of the highest honours of the empire.

RICHTOFEN, Baron Ferdinand von (1833–1905); geologist, geographer, explorer; 1860, first East Asian expedition; 1875 Prof. of Geology, Bonn; 1882 Leipsig; 1886 Berlin; author, *China*, 5 vols and atlas; 1872 dep. Chengdu to reach Dali, Kunming via Xichang (Ningyuan); forced back by troops on Da Xiang Ling; showed Jianchang valley to be Marco Polo's 'Caindu'.

RILEY, J H; dep. UK 2 May 1878; Sichuan pioneer, Chongqing, Chengdu; urged by G Nicoll to take gospel to Nosu, Daliangshan; Oct 1882 m. (1) J Kidd (qv) d. 1886; (2) F Stroud (qv) on own deathbed, d. 19 April 1886.

ROSSIER, Fanny; Swiss; CIM dep. UK 2 May 1878; 15 Sept 1879 m. G W Clarke; first woman to Yunnan, Dali; d. 7 Oct 1883.

RUDLAND, William D; Eversden, Cambridgeshire blacksmith/farm mechanic; 1856 CIM; 1866 *Lammermuir*, Hangzhou; 1867 m. Mary Bell (qv); 1868 printer, Yangzhou riot; 1869 Taizhou, Zhejiang many years; 1874 UK, wife died; translated (adapted) Taizhou vernacular romanised NT; 1878 m. Miss Brealey, d. cholera, 1878; later m. Miss Knight; d. 1913.

RUSSELL, William Armstrong; CMS; 1847 Ningbo; 1872–79 first bishop in N. China; d. 1879.

SAMBROOK, A W: CIM dep. UK 12 Dec 1878; Henan; 1884 secured permanent footing, Zhoujiakou, after 8 years' frustration of M H Taylor, G W Clarke, others; but driven out, resigned.

SCARBOROUGH, W; WMMS, 1865 Hankou with David Hill.

SCHERESCHEWSKY, Samuel Isaac Joseph (1831–1906) (pron. *Sher-e-sheff-skie*; called 'Sherry'); Russian Lithuanian rabbi, converted; 1854 USA Gen. Theol. Seminary, NY; 1859 ordained Am. Prot. Episc. Church by Bp Wm Boone Sr (Book 1, p 393); 1860 Shanghai; 1862–75 Peking, began Dicty. of Mongolian; alone translated OT into Mandarin while committee trans. NT; 1865 with J S Burdon (qv) trans. Anglican Book of Com. Prayer; 1875 nominated bishop, declined; 1876 consecrated; 1878 founded St John's College, Shanghai, and St Mary's Hall for girls; 1879 *wenli* Prayer Book, Wuchang; 1881 paralysed limbs, speech, to Europe; 1883 resigned episc. office; 1886 USA, began OT revision – impaired speech excluded Chinese help, typed with one finger, 8 hours daily – 1888–95 easy *wenli* OT, NT romanised; 1895–7 Shanghai, romanised into Ch. character; 1897 Japan, to supervise printing; 1902 OT revision publ.; sole object 'to make plain the Word of God to the Chinese'; d. Tokyo, 15 Sep, 1906, *aet.* 75 in working chair. (*Chinese Recorder* 1906 Vol 37 p 615f).

SCHMIDT, Charles; 1864 officer in Ever-Victorious Army; converted through Jas. Meadows (qv); missionary in Suzhou 1867; friend of JHT, CIM.

SCHOFIELD, Robert Harold Ainsworth; b. 18 Jan 1851; 1869 grad. London Univ; 1870 Oxford; 1877 MA, BM Oxon.; May 1878 FRCS Eng.; dep. UK 7 April; 1880 with wife; Taiyuan, Shanxi; d. typhus 1 Aug 1881.

SCOTT, Charles Perry; SPG; 1874 dep. UK with Albert Capel; Yantai; 1878–79 Shanxi famine relief; 1880 Bishop North China, Shandong, Zhili, taking over CMS (J S Burdon) work in Peking.

SHAFTESBURY, 7th Earl of; Anthony Ashley-Cooper (1801–85); evangelical philanthropist legislated to relieve ill effects of industrial revolution; friend of CIM, chaired annual meetings.

SHARP, William; solicitor; 1883 CIM London Council, active member; patron, secretary, Tibetan Pioneer Mission.

SLADEN, Col. E B; 1868 (Major) led Brit. expedition, Burma-Yunnan; resisted by Col. Li Zhenguo; promoted colonel; 1874–75 Li Zhenguo hospitable to Margary, warned Ney Elias (qv); 1875 a member of Sladen expedition visited CIM Lond. requesting missionaries.

SLOAN, Walter B; company secretary, Keswick Convention speaker; CIM dep. UK Sep 1891; became Gen. Secy. CIM UK after B. Broomhall.

SMITH, Pearsall; American exponent of the 'higher Christian life'; influenced originators of Keswick Movement.

SMITH, Lieut George Shergold; son of naval officer on anti-slave trade patrol who 1822 rescued Adji (Samuel Crowther), future bishop of the Niger; 1876 Shergold Smith led first CMS Uganda party including Alexander Mackay; 13 Dec 1876 massacred.

SMITH, Stanley Peregrine; b. 19 March 1861; youngest son of Henry Smith, FRCS; Repton and Trinity Coll., Cambridge; 1882 BA; influenced by Granville Waldegrave (qv); capt. of Trinity boats, stroke of Camb. Univ. eight 1881; 'about the end of 1883' in touch with JHT; 1 April 1884 accepted by CIM Council; 5 Feb 1885 'Camb. Seven' dep. UK; 1885 Shanxi; 1889 opened Lu'an, Lucheng; 1902 Jincheng (Tsechou); m. (1) Sophie Reuter (Norwegian) who d. 7 Mar 1891; (2) Feb 1893 Anna M Lang.

SOLTAU, George; son of Henry W (qv); Lamb and Flag Mission and schools, London; 1872 on first CIM London Council; Tasmania; Australian Council.

SOLTAU, Henrietta E; daughter of H W Soltau (qv); 1873 London, asst. to Emily Blatchley; Tottenham home for children of missionaries; later, CIM Women's Training Home and Ladies' Council.

SOLTAU, Henry, Jr; son of H W Soltau (qv); Aug 1872 Hon. Sec. CIM, London with R H Hill (qv); 1875 to Bhamo, Burma with J W Stevenson (qv); 1880 with Stevenson first Westerners to cross China W. to E., Burma, Chongqing, Wuchang, Shanghai; qualified as doctor of medicine, to India.

SOLTAU, Henry W; Chancery barrister, Plymouth and Exeter Brethren; sons George, Henry, daughters Henrietta, Agnes (m. Richard Hill qv), all in CIM.

SOLTAU, Lucy; daughter of H W Soltau (qv), d. young, 1873.

SOLTAU, William; son of H W Soltau (qv); 1875 Asst. Secy. CIM, London, with R H Hill, B Broomhall.

SOOTHILL, Prof. W E; United Meth. Free Church; 1888 translated Gospels, Acts into Wenzhou dialect, publ. 1894; 1901 NT completed, printed by CIM press; educator, author, biographer of T Richard; Analects of Confucius in English; elected President, projected Wuhan Christian University; Prof. of Chinese, Oxford Univ. following Legge (qv) 1897.

SPEER, Robert E (1867–1947); son of lawyer, member of Congress; 1889 graduated, Princeton; Student Volunteer Movement; 1886 travelling secy; Board of Foreign Missions, Presby. Church of USA, senior Secy till 1937; Moderator; author.

SPURGEON, Charles Haddon (1834–92); renowned Baptist preacher, Metropolitan Tabernacle; lifelong friend of JHT.

STACEY, Miss; one-time Quaker, member of Brook Street chapel, Tottenham; CES Ladies' Assn.; long a friend of JHT, CIM and T J Barnardo; d. 1876.

STANLEY, H M (1841–1904); Welshman; fought for Confederates in Am. Civil War; 1867 correspondent of *N Y Herald*, sent to find Livingstone; 1871 found at Ujiji; with him explored northern end of Lake Tanganyika; founded Congo Free State (under Belgians); author; knighted, GCB.

STEIN, Sir Aurel (1862–1943); b. Budapest; Brit. archaeologist, central Asia.

STEVEN, F A; CIM dep. UK 1 Mar 1883; Yunnan, Dali, Tengyue; crossed to Bhamo second attempt; CIM N. Am. and UK staff.

STEVENSON, John Whiteford (1844–1918); son of laird of Thriepwood, Renfrewshire; m. Anne Jolly; with G Stott (qv) first of CIM after Crombie; Oct. 1865 dep. UK; 1866–74 Ningbo, Shaoxing; 1875–80 Burma; 1880 with H Soltau, Jr. (qv) crossed China W. to E., Bhamo–Chongqing–Wuchang then Shanghai; 1,900 miles, 86 days; 1885–1916 deputy director, CIM.

STEWART, Dr J C; 1885 med. grad. Philadelphia, USA; to UK Council; CIM dep. UK 21 April 1886 with Orr Ewing, Graham Browne; Shanxi, Guihuacheng.

STOCK, Eugene (1836–1928); CMS UK staff; editor 21 Dec, 1875–11 Dec, 1906; historian, author *The History of the Church Miss. Soc.*, Vols I–III; warm friend of CIM; d. 7 Sep 1928 aged 92.

STOTT, George; Aberdeenshire schoolmaster, one leg; Oct 1865 dep. UK; 1866 Ningbo; 1869–89 Wenzhou (Wenchow); 1870 m. G Ciggie (qv); d. 1889.

STRONACH, Alexander; LMS; 1838–39 Singapore; 1839–44 Penang; 1844–46 Singapore; 1846 Amoy.

STRONACH, John; LMS, 1838–76, 30 years without furlough; 1838–44 Singapore; 1846 Amoy; Bible translator, Delegates' Committee, 1852; S Dyer Sr's friend.

STRONACH, W G; HBM consul; son of John Stronach (qv); m. Catherine Duncan (née Brown), widow of George Duncan (qv); she died 31 Oct 1877 leaving a daughter whom JHT adopted at her dying request.

STROUD, Fanny; CIM dep. UK 25 Oct 1882; Chengdu, Sichuan, pioneer; cared for Jane Riley (née Kidd) (qv) children when she died; then nursed J H Riley (qv), married him on his deathbed; April 1886; later m. Thos. James, CIM 1885.

STUDD, Charles Thomas; 3rd son of Edward Studd, Tedworth House, Andover; b. 2 Dec 1860; Eton and Trinity Coll., Cambridge; 1884 BA; cricket 'blue' 4 years, captain 1883; CIM dep. UK 5 Feb 1885; Hanzhong, Shaanxi; Shanxi; Jan 1888 m. Priscilla Livingstone Stewart (arr. Shanghai 1887); Lu'an, Shanxi; sick leave, resigned; 1900–06, India; founded Heart of Africa Mission; d. 16 July 1931.

STUDD, George; 2nd son, Eton and Cambridge, cricketer, captain 1882; Nov 1883 seriously ill; 1887 visited Shanghai, Shanxi; pastor, Los Angeles, USA.

STUDD, Sir John Edward Kynaston, Bart.; eldest son; Eton and Cambridge cricketer, captain 1884; 1885 m. Hilda Beauchamp; twice Lord Mayor of London, 1st baronet.

SZÉCHÉNYI, Count Béla; Central Asian explorer; 1882 met Easton (qv) at Xining, Stevenson, Soltau at Bhamo.

TALMAGE, John van Nest, DD; American Board; Amoy 1847 (Dutch Reformed Church of America).

TANKERVILLE, Earl of (1810–) Chillingham Castle, Northumberland; friend of JHT and CIM.

TAYLOR, Annie Royle; dtr of well-to-do Cheshire businessman; aged 28 sold valuables, took basic medical course as lady probationer, London Hospital; CIM dep. UK 24 Sept 1884 aiming for Tibet; Taozhou, Gansu–Qinghai border nr. Kumbum; 2 Sept 1892 dep. Taozhou; 3 Jan 1893 100 miles from Lhasa; expelled; 1893 to Darjeeling, India–Tibet border.

TAYLOR, Ernest Hamilton 6th son of JHT, by JET, b. 7 Jan 1875; accountant, m. E Gauntlett; dep. UK after 1900 Boxer rising, volunteered (with C H Judd) for Shanxi; 9 July 1901 arr. Taiyuan with D E Hoste, A Orr Ewing (first anniversary of massacres).

TAYLOR, Frederick Howard (1862–1946); b. 25 Nov 1862, 2nd son of JHT, by M J Dyer; present at Yangzhou riot; qualified MB, BS, 1888 MD Lond; 1889 MRCP; FRCS Edin.; initiated Student Foreign Missionary Union; (later combined with SVMU); 1888 toured US, Canada with JHT; 23 Jan 1890 dep. UK Henan, peripatetic medical; 24 April 1894 m. M Geraldine Guinness; Supt. Henan; travelled frequently with JHT; JHT's biographers; d. 15 Aug 1946.

TAYLOR, Herbert Hudson; eldest son of JHT and Maria; b. London 3 April 1861; CIM dep. UK Jan 1881; 24 Nov 1886 m. Jeanie Gray (CIM 1884); Jiangxi, Henan; 1886 travelled with JHT, Shanxi and Shaanxi; father of James Hudson Taylor II; d. 6 June 1950; grandfather of James Hudson Taylor III, General Director 1980– .

TAYLOR, James (1807–81); father of JHT; chemist; founded, managed Barnsley Permanent Building Society 1855–75; retired Dec 1875.

TAYLOR, James Hudson (21 May 1832–3 June 1905); 1853 dep. UK; 1 Mar 1854 arr. Shanghai; 20 Jan 1858 m. Maria Jane Dyer; 1857 with J Jones (qv) began Ningbo Mission; June 1865 founded China Inland Mission; 28 Nov 1871 m. Jane E Faulding; 3 June 1905 d. Changsha, Hunan.

TAYLOR, Jane (Jennie) Elizabeth (née Faulding) b. 7 Oct 1843; 1865 assistant to JHT and Maria, London; 1866 CIM; *Lammermuir*; Hangzhou; m. JHT 28 Nov 1871; 1877–78 took Anna Crickmay (qv) and Celia Horne (qv) to Shanxi famine relief, Taiyuan; first women deep into interior; d. 30 July 1904.

TAYLOR, Maria Jane, née Dyer (1837–70); daughter of Samuel Dyer (qv); wife of JHT; mother of Grace, Herbert Hudson, Frederick Howard, Samuel, Jane, Maria, Charles, Noel; d. Zhenjiang, 23 July, 1870.

TAYLOR, Maria Hudson, daughter of JHT and Maria; b. Hangzhou, 3 Feb, 1867; 1884 CIM to China *aet.* 17; m. J J Coulthard (qv) d. 28 Sept, 1897.

TAYLOR, M Henry; CIM dep. UK 3 Sept 1873; first CIM pioneer Henan; met strong opposition, heartbroken; to Zhejiang; 1878 Henan famine relief rejected by mandarins; resigned.

TOMALIN, E; CIM dep. UK 12 Dec 1878; 1882 m. Louise Desgraz (qv), Shandong.

TRENCH, Frank; independent, dep. UK 19 May 1878 with CIM; pioneer, Hunan, Guizhou, Yunnan; June 1884 medical course, Edin.; retired.

TURNER, Joshua J; CIM, one of the Eighteen, dep. UK Nov 1875; Oct 1876 to Jan 1877 Shanxi; famine relief, typhoid, Taiyuan; 1 Feb 1881 m. A Crickmay.

VENN, Henry (1796–1873); son of John Venn, a founder and first chairman CMS; 1841–73 Hon. Sec. CMS; sent 498 clergy overseas.

WADE, Sir Thomas Francis (1818–95); 1860 consular interpreter, negotiated release of Harry Parkes; 1861 Peking legation; 1869–71 plenipotentiary; 1875 knighted, KCB; minister; 1876 Chefoo Convention; 1883 retired; 1888 Prof. of Chinese, Oxford; 1887 GCMG; d. 31 July 1895.

WALDEGRAVE, Hon. Miss; sister of 3rd Baron Radstock (qv), and of Lady Beauchamp (qv); friend of JHT and CIM; aunt of Montagu Beauchamp.

WALDEGRAVE, Hon. Granville; eldest son of Lord Radstock (qv); active Christian, Repton and Trinity Coll., Cambridge; since childhood knew JHT well, introduced him to Earl of Tankerville.

WEIR, Thomas; Shanghai merchant, 1865 influenced by JHT Glasgow; long a friend; negotiated reduced fares by Castle Line, UK–China, effective many years.

WHITEHOUSE, S F; CIM dep. UK 5 Oct 1888; personal secretary to JHT.

WHITING, Albert; Am. Presby. Mission, Nanjing; joined David Hill, dep. Shanghai (March 1878) to Shanxi famine relief; d. 25 April, famine fever (typhus).

WILDER, Robert Parmelee (1863–1938); son of India missionary; 1886 grad. Princeton; initiated SVM; 1886 promoted SVM at Moody's student conference; 1888 travelled for SVM to colleges, univs; 1889 to UK univs, after J N Forman (qv); Gen. Sec. SVM; 1891–92 UK, SVMU; 1902 India, students; thereafter evangelist to students in UK, Europe. (1891–92 at Med. Miss. Ass. c/o Dr J L Maxwell, negotiated union of (FHT's) Students' Foreign Miss. Union with SVM, completed 2–9 April, 1892, with A T Polhill as trav. sec.)

WILLIAMS, E O; Trinity Coll Oxford; vicar, St Stephen's, Leeds; CIM dep. UK 13 Dec 1888; East Sichuan; d. July 1899, typhoid.

WILLIAMS, Sir George (1821–95) of Hitchcock, Williams & Co, London; 1844 founded YMCA for employees; friend of CIM, of Lord Shaftesbury (first YMCA President); chairman, CIM meetings; 1894 YMCA Jubilee, knighted.

WILLIAMS, Samuel Wells DD (1812–84); Am. Board, printer, scholar; 1833 Canton; 1847 author *The Middle Kingdom*; 1851 succeeded E C Bridgman (qv) as editor, *Chinese Repository*; 1856 interpreter and Secy. to US minister, Peking; 9 times chargé d'affaires to 1876; 1884 *Syllabic Dicty. of Chinese Language*, 12,527 characters; prof. of Chinese, Yale Univ. 8 years.

WILLIAMSON, Alexander, LL D (1829–90); Falkirk, Scotland, b. 5 Dec, 1829, eldest of seven sons; Glasgow Univ.; 1858–63 LMS invalided UK; 1863 National Bible Soc. of Scotland, Shandong, Yantai; 1864–69 travelled extensively distributing Scripture, Peking, Mongolia, Manchuria; Aug 1869 brother, James Williamson, LMS, murdered near Tianjin; 1869 UK; 1871 LL D Glasgow, 1871–80, 1881–83 Yantai, NBSS and United Presby. Soc. of Scotland; 1883–85 Scotland ill, founded Book & Tract Socy. for China, later (1887) Socy. for Diffusion of Christian and General Knowledge among the Chinese (Christian Lit. Soc.); 1886 Shanghai, wife d.; 1890 d. Yantai. Author, *Natural Theology*, and others. 'Very tall, striking in appearance; intellectually also among the giants.'

WILLIAMSON, James; Arbroath, Aberdeen; CIM dep. UK 26 May 1866 *Lammermuir*; Hangzhou, JHT's assistant pioneer; 1869 Anqing riot; Fenghua, Zhejiang.

WILSON, Eliz; Kendal; b. 1830, niece of Miss Stacey (qv); CIM dep. UK 26 Jan 1876 (aged 46); 1880 pioneer, Hanzhong, Shaanxi; Tianshui, Gansu.

WILSON, Dr Wm; Oxford; nephew of Eliz. Wilson (qv); CIM dep. UK 20 Aug 1882; pioneer, rejected at Xi'an, welcomed at Hanzhong, Shaanxi, m. Caroline Sarah Goodman.

WINDSOR, Thomas; CIM dep UK 27 Feb 1884; Guiyang, Anshun.

WOLFE, John R; 1862 CMS, Fuzhou; 'missionary par excellence of Fukien'; 1864 began indigenous expansion of church by deploying catechists and visiting them; 1873–75 alone, missionary colleagues all ill or dead; church members, adherents, doubled 800 to 1656 under persecution; 4450 in 1882; 1884 and 1886 visited Korea; 1884 Fujian Christians to Korea learned language, withdrew after two years; 1899 JRW still active in Fujian.

WYLIE, Alexander (1815–87); LMS; 1847 Shanghai, printer, Delegates' version of Bible; 1863 Bible Soc. (B&FBS); one of the greatest Sinologues; completed distribution of the million NTs provided 1855 by Bible Soc. special fund; 1877 retired with failing eyesight; succeeded by Maria Taylor's brother Samuel Dyer, Jr (qv).

YAKUB BEG; Muslim conqueror, 1864 captured Kashgar, Yarkand; appointed ruler by Emir of Bokhara; added Urumqi, Turfan to his kingdom; 1872 independence recognised by Russia, GB, Turkey; honoured with title only used by caliphs of Baghdad; great Muslim revival predicted, with conquest of China; but 1876 Urumqi fell to Zuo Zongtang (Tso Tsung-t'ang) (qv); May 1877 Yakub Beg died suddenly; Dec 1877 Kashgar taken, kingdom ended.

YATES, Matthew T (1819–88); Am. S. Baptist; 1847 Shanghai; Sinologue, learned contributor to *Chinese Recorder*; Am. vice-consul; translator, Shanghai vernacular NT; leading proponent of orthodox views on Ancestor Worship at Gen. Miss. Conf., May 1877.

YOUNGHUSBAND, Lt. Col. Sir Francis Edward; 1887 (Lieut.) across China and Turkestan by Mongolian route; 1889 wished to attempt Lhasa, politically untimely; 1902 Russian intentions re Tibet prompted Brit. armed expedition, 1000 troops, 10,000 coolies, 7000 mules entered Tibet 12 Dec 1903; 1904 led troops into Lhasa; 23 Sept 1904 dep. Lhasa; 1919–22 Pres. R G Soc.; 1936 founded World Congress of Faiths.

YULE, Col. Sir Henry, CB, RE; geographer, historian, author *Marco Polo*; Dec 1879 introduction (95 pp) to Gill (qv): *River of Golden Sand*.

SELECTED BIBLIOGRAPHY

AITKEN, J T, Fuller, H W C, and Johnson, D, *The Influence of Christians in Medicine*, Christian Medical Fellowship, London 1984

ATLAS of China, *Zhonghua Renmin Gongheguo Fen Sheng Dituji*, Ditu Chubanshe, Beijing (Chinese People's Republic Provincial Atlas)

BABER, E Colborne, *Supplementary Papers of the Royal Geographical Society*, 'Travels and Researches in Western China'; John Murray, London, 1882; *Journal of the RGS*, 1884, Vol. XLIX, pp 421 *seq*

BARBER, W T A, *David Hill, Missionary and Saint*, Charles H Kelley, London 1903

BROOMHALL, Benjamin, *The Evangelisation of the World; A Missionary Band; A Record of Consecration and an Appeal*, China Inland Mission, 1886–'87–'89

National Righteousness (Editor); periodical of The Christian Union for the Severance of the Connection of the British Empire from the Opium Traffic, 1888–1911

BROOMHALL, Marshall, *Archibald Orr Ewing, That Faithful and Wise Steward*, China Inland Mission, 1930

The Chinese Empire, A General and Missionary Survey, Marshall, Morgan & Scott, and China Inland Mission 1907 BL 4767.eeee.4

Faith and Facts, as Illustrated in the History of the China Inland Mission, China Inland Mission 1909

F W Baller, A Master of the Pencil, CIM 1923

Heirs Together of the Grace of Life; Benjamin Broomhall and Amelia Hudson Broomhall, Morgan & Scott, and CIM 1918

Hudson Taylor's Legacy, Hodder & Stoughton 1931 BL 10823.a.16

Islam in China, Marshall, Morgan & Scott, and CIM 1910

The Jubilee Story of the China Inland Mission, Morgan & Scott, and CIM, 1915 BL 4763.g.4

John W Stevenson, One of Christ's Stalwarts, Morgan & Scott, and CIM, 1919 BL 4956.aa.33

Last Letters and Further Records of Martyred Missionaries of the China Inland Mission, Morgan & Scott, and CIM 1901

Martyred Missionaries of the China Inland Mission, with a Record of the Perils and Sufferings of Some who Escaped, Morgan & Scott, and CIM 1901

Pioneer Work in Hunan by Adam Dorward and Other Missionaries of the China Inland Mission, Morgan & Scott, and CIM 1906

W W Cassels, First Bishop in Western China, CIM 1926

BONG RIN RO (Editor); *Christian Alternatives to Ancestor Practice*, Asian Theological Association 1985

CHEFUSIAN, THE, Journal of the Chefoo Schools Association, Vol 79, No 2, December 1986

CHINA'S MILLIONS, Magazine of the China Inland Mission 1875–1951

CHINESE RECORDER AND MISSIONARY JOURNAL: Vols 1–3, 5–12 May 1868–May 71, editor Justus Doolittle; Vol. 5 bi-monthly Jan–Dec 1874 (after 2-year interlude) – Vol. 12, 1881

COLQUHOUN, Archibald R, *Across Chryse, from Canton to Mandalay*, 2 vols, Sampson Low, Marston, Searle & Rivington, London 1883; *RGS Journal* IV p 713

CORDIER, Henri, *The Life of Alexander Wylie*, 1887 BL 10803.cc.4/6

COVELL, Ralph R, *Confucius, The Buddha and Christ, a History of the Gospel in Chinese*, Orbis Books 1986 (USA)

W A P Martin, Pioneer of Progress in China, Wm B Eerdmans Publishing Company 1978

DAYS OF BLESSING in Inland China, being an Account of Meetings held in the Province of Shansi (compiled), Morgan & Scott 1887

FAIRBANK, John King, *Trade and Diplomacy on the China Coast*, 2 vols 1953 Edn. Cambridge, Massachusetts BL Ac.2692.10

FOREIGN OFFICE LIBRARY, Public Records Office, *A Century of Diplomatic Blue Books*, China FO/17

FORSYTH, R C; *The China Martyrs of 1900*, Religious Tract Society 1904

GILL, Capt Wm, *The River of Golden Sand; The Narrative of a Journey through China and Eastern Tibet to Burmah; with an Introductory Essay by Col Henry Yule, CB, RE,* 2 vols, John Murray 1880; *Journal of the Royal Geographical Society*, Vol xlviii, pp 57 *seq*

GOFORTH, Rosalind, *Goforth of China*, Marshall, Morgan & Scott 1937

GRIST, W A, *Samuel Pollard, Pioneer Missionary in China*, Cassell & Co., Ltd (undated)

GRUBB, Norman P, *C T Studd, Cricketer and Pioneer*, Religious Tract Society 1933

GUINNESS, Joy, *Mrs Howard Taylor: Her Web of Time*, CIM 1949

GUINNESS, M Geraldine, *The Story of the China Inland Mission,* 2 vols, Morgan & Scott, London 1893

HALDANE, Charlotte, *The Last Great Empress of China*, Constable 1965

HART, Sir Robert, *These from the Land of Sinim* BL 8022.cc.48/01 and 0817.d.10

HOPKIRK, Peter, *Foreign Devils on the Silk Road; the Search for the Lost Cities and Treasures of Chinese Central Asia*, Oxford University Press 1984

Trespassers on the Roof of the World; the Race for Lhasa, John Murray 1982

HOSIE, Alexander, *Three Years in Western China; A Narrative of Three Journeys*, George Philip & Son, London 1890

HOUGHTON, Stanley *et al*, *Chefoo*, CIM 1931

JOHNSON, Douglas, *Contending for the Faith; a History of the Evangelical Movement in the Universities and Colleges*, Inter-Varsity Press 1979

LATOURETTE, Kenneth Scott, *A History of Christian Missions in China*, SPCK 1929 BL 4763.g.4

A History of the Expansion of Christianity 1800–1914, Eyre and Spottiswoode BL 4533.ff.22

These Sought a Country: Tipple Lectures, 1950 edn, Harper & Brothers BL 4807.e.25

LITTLE, Mrs Archibald (Alicia Bewicke) *Li Hung-chang, His Life and Times*, Cassell & Co. Ltd 1903

LOANE, Marcus, *The Story of the China Inland Mission in Australia and New Zealand*, CIM Overseas Missionary Fellowship 1965

LYALL, L T, *A Passion for the Impossible*, Hodder & Stoughton 1965; OMF Books 1976

MacGILLIVRAY, Donald, *A Century of Protestant Missions in China* (Centennial Conference Historical Volume) Shanghai 1907 BL 4764.ff.11

McCARTHY, John, 'Across China from Chinkiang to Bhamo', *Proceedings of the Royal Geographical Society*, Vol. 1 Aug 1879, No. 8, pp 127, 489 *seq*

MARTIN, W A P, *A Cycle of Cathay*, 1896 BL 010056.g.7

MICHIE, Alexander, *Missionaries in China*, Edward Stanford Ldn. 1891; 2nd edn Tientsin Press 1893 BL 4767.ccc.10

The Englishman in China: as illustrated in the Career of Sir Rutherford Alcock, Wm Blackwood & Sons, Edin. 1900 2 vols BL 09057.d.3

MORSE, Hosea Ballou, *The International Relations of the Chinese Empire* vols 1–3, 1910 BL 2386.c.17

NEILL, Stephen C, *A History of Christian Missions* (Pelican History of the Church) Penguin Books 1964;

Colonialism and Christian Missions, Lutterworth Press: Foundations of Christian Mission 1966

NEILL, S C *et al*, *Concise Dictionary of Christian World Mission*, United Society for Christian Literature, London 1971

NEVIUS, Helen S C, *The Life of John Livingston Nevius*, Revell 1895 BL 4985.eee.5

NORTH CHINA DAILY NEWS (newspaper) British Library, Colindale

NORTH CHINA HERALD (newspaper) British Library, Colindale

OVERSEAS Missionary Fellowship Archives (OMFA)

PARLIAMENTARY PAPERS: Foreign Office Blue Books, Official Publications Office

POLLOCK, John C, *The Cambridge Seven, A Call to Christian Service*, Inter-Varsity Fellowship 1955; Centenary Edition, Marshalls 1985

Moody without Sankey, A New Biographical Portrait, Hodder & Stoughton 1963

POLO, Marco, *The Book of Ser Marco Polo, the Venetian, 1298*. First printed edition 1477 (*see* YULE)

POTT, F L Hawks, *A Short History of Shanghai*, Kelly & Walsh 1928 010056.aaa.46

RATTENBURY, Harold B, *David Hill, Friend of China*, Epworth Press 1949

REAVELY, Wm, *Reminiscences of the late Adam C. Dorward, Missionary to China* (publ. 1904)

ROYAL GEOGRAPHICAL SOCIETY, *Journal* IV, p 713 'The South China Borderlands', Colquhoun; Vol XLIX, pp 421 *seq*, Baber; Vol XLVIII pp 57 *seq*, Gill; *Magazine* iii pp 493, 564; *Proceedings* X.485 'A Journey across Central Asia', Younghusband; *Supplementary Papers* Vol I, Part I, Baber: 'Travels and Researches in Western China'

SMITH, Arthur H, *The Uplift of China*, The Young People's Missionary Movement of America 1909

SOLTAU, Henry: 'A Journey from the Irrawaddy to the Yangtze', compiled by Wm Soltau from letters; RGS Magazine iii pp 493, 564

SOOTHILL, Wm E, *Timothy Richard of China*, Seeley, Service & Co., Ltd, London 1924

STOCK, Eugene, *The History of the Church Missionary Society*, Vols I–III 1899–1916 BL 4765.cc.28

TAYLOR, Dr & Mrs Howard, *Hudson Taylor in Early Years: The Growth of a Soul*, CIM and RTS, 1911

Hudson Taylor and the China Inland Mission: The Growth of a Work of God, CIM and RTS, 1918

Hudson Taylor's Spiritual Secret, CIM, 1932

By Faith; Henry W Frost and the China Inland Mission, CIM 1938

TAYLOR, Mrs Howard (M Geraldine Guinness), *The Story of the China Inland Mission*, 2 vols, 1892, Morgan & Scott

Behind the Ranges: A Biography of J O Fraser, CIM

Pastor Hsi: One of China's Scholars (2 vols), CIM

Pastor Hsi, Confucian Scholar and Christian, CIM 1900

TAYLOR, J Hudson, *China: Its Spiritual Need and Claims*, 1st–6th edns 1865 et seq, CIM

China's Spiritual Need and Claims, 7th edn. 1887, CIM 8th edn. 1890, CIM

Brief Account of the Progress of the China Inland Mission, May 1866 to May 1868, J Nisbet & Co. 1868

A Retrospect, 1875, CIM
After Thirty Years, 1895, Morgan & Scott and CIM
Occasional Paper Vols 1–6, Jas Nisbet & Co.
Summary of the Operations of the China Inland Mission, 1865–1872, J Nisbet & Co. 1872

THOMPSON, Phyllis: *D E Hoste, 'A Prince with God'*, CIM 1947

THOMPSON, R Wardlaw: *Griffith John, The Story of Fifty Years in China*, Religious Tract Society 1907

WILLIAMS, Fredk Wells, *The Life and Letters of Samuel Wells Williams, LLD, Missionary, Diplomatist, Sinologue*, G P Putman & Sons, New York and London 1889

WILLIAMS, Samuel Wells, *The Middle Kingdom*, 1847

WOODCOCK, George, *The British in the Far East*, Weidenfeld & Nicolson 1969 (A Social History of the British Overseas)

YOUNGHUSBAND, Capt Francis, *The Heart of a Continent*, abridged as *Among the Celestials*, John Murray, London 1898; *Proceedings of the RGS*, X.485 'Journey Across Central Asia'

YULE, Sir Henry, *The Book of Ser Marco Polo the Venetian*, 1878, 2 vols
Introductory essay to Gill, Wm, *River of Golden Sand*, 95 pp.

INDEX